NY RESTAURANT
ACCESS®

Orientation	4
Lower Manhattan	8
Chinatown/Lower East Side/Little Italy	16
SoHo/TriBeCa	32
Greenwich Village	54
East Village	76
Union Square/Gramercy Park/Murray Hill	90
Chelsea	104
Theater District	112
Midtown	130
East Side	154
Upper East Side	168
West Side	186
Upper West Side/Harlem/Heights	194
E...	208
In...	222

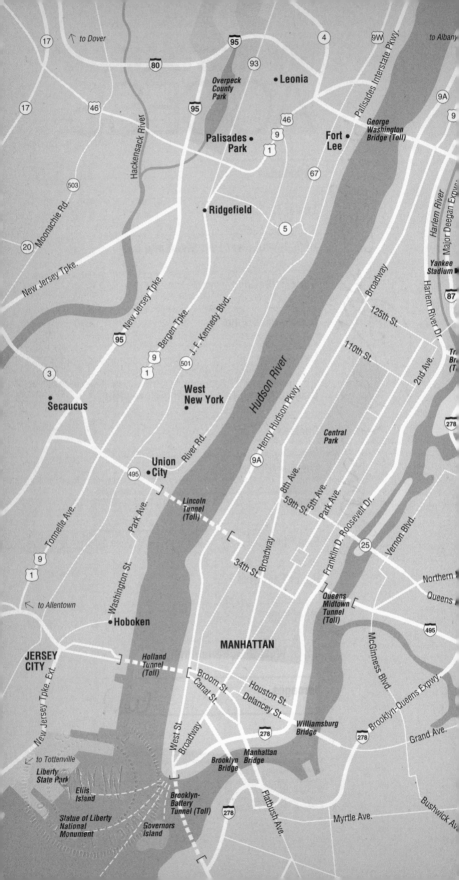

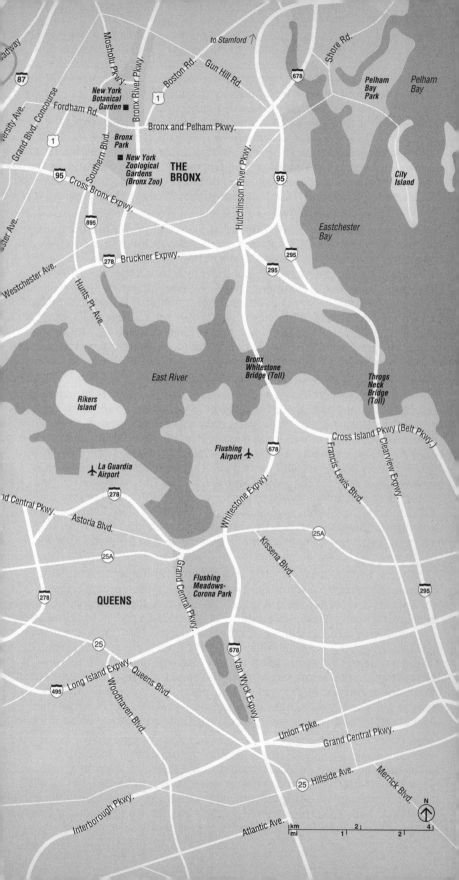

Orientation

Dining is among the few obsessions shared by most New Yorkers, running a close third after real estate and personal safety. Eavesdrop on random conversations (elsewhere it's rude—here it's unavoidable), and you're likely to overhear discussions about where friends went for dinner the night before or a debate about which restaurant has the best dim sum, sushi, pasta, pastrami, cheesecake, or crème brûlée. For a table at one of the more popular restaurants, New Yorkers—notorious for their impatience—are suddenly willing to wait for hours. The person who can score reservations fastest at such coveted hot spots as the **Monkey Bar**, **Gramercy Tavern**, **Restaurant Daniel**, or **Bouley** is bound to provoke envy, if not respect, among friends. As people seem to work harder and take fewer vacations, eating well has become, for many, a sustaining pleasure.

Visitors too reap the benefits of this passion, and at press time, the number of places open to serve both locals and tourists was approximately 16,000—and counting. Some months it seems that a high-profile place is opening every other day. But more impressive than sheer numbers is the staggering variety: Burmese, Cajun/Creole, Chinese, French, Greek, Hungarian, Indian, Italian, Japanese, Malaysian, Mexican, Russian, Southwestern US, Spanish, Sri Lankan, Thai, Tibetan, Turkish, and many others. For many creative chefs, however, preparing a single cuisine isn't enough; the latest buzzword is "fusion," and new combinations of flavors—French and Italian, Asian and French, Asian and Southwestern US, among others—are the result.

New Yorkers reverently accept the word of food critics, especially those who write for *The New York Times,* and a blessing from that paper immediately results in jammed phone lines and solidly booked reservation lists. Talented and lucky chefs who have made such star turns often appear in gossip columns, becoming as well known as their restaurants. But for every restaurant that creates a star, there's another started by a celebrity. Actors, sports figures, rock stars, and models alike are getting into the restaurant business, not only for the profit potential, but for the excitement of being part of the scene. Recent additions to the ranks of celebrity restaurateurs include Rob Morrow, Tom Berenger, Lee Mazzilli, Claudia Schiffer, Elle Macpherson, and Naomi Campbell. Robert DeNiro is so entrenched in the TriBeCa restaurant scene, with more than one popular spot to his name, that the neighborhood is now being referred to as Bob Row.

Mere fame and the flash associated with it is not enough to guarantee a restaurant's success, of course, particularly its long-term prestige. Even restaurants that seem to be doing well—good press, location, and food—may be laboring under heavy real estate costs and on the verge of buckling under economic pressure. Restaurants that are considered "hot" may remain so for a few months, then cool when the peripatetic foodies move on to the next place of the moment. Unless you know for sure that a dining spot is still open, it always pays to call before setting out. And even if the restaurant is physically there, the menu you expect may not be; offerings may change with the season, the week, or the chef—musical kitchens is the rule here, not the exception. In fact, change is the only thing that can be counted on where New York eateries are concerned.

The prevailing changes of late are very much to the diner's advantage. Following the expansive 1980s when nothing seemed too extravagant, a shakedown of sorts occurred as diners' purse strings tightened. In response, restaurants began to concentrate on value rather than drama. So while it's still possible to blow the gross national product of a developing nation on dinner in one of New York's finest restaurants, a good meal can be had for considerably less. In fact, many of the very best places are attracting new customers by offering reasonable prix-fixe lunches and dinners. For lunch, it is a common practice to charge the dollar amount that corresponds to the year, and at New York's more expensive venues, a $19.95 prix-fixe meal is not a bad deal. Call ahead to find out if the restaurant in question offers this special.

With even a bare minimum of planning, you're likely to have a memorable experience when dining out in New York. From formal French dining rooms in Upper East Side town houses to old-fashioned steak houses in Brooklyn, from sprawling spaces serving fusion cuisine to cozy diners that have been around for decades, this city has it all. After all, even the most sophisticated diners agree that New York is among the greatest restaurant cities in the world.

How To Read This Guide

NEW YORK RESTAURANT ACCESS® is arranged so you can see at a glance where you are and what is around you. The numbers next to the entries in the following chapters correspond to the numbers on the maps.

The restaurant star ratings system takes into account the quality, service, atmosphere, and uniqueness of the restaurant. An expensive restaurant doesn't necessarily ensure an enjoyable evening; while a small, relatively unknown spot could have good food, professional service, and a lovely atmosphere. Therefore, on a purely subjective basis, stars are used to judge the overall dining value (see the star ratings below). Keep in mind that chefs and owners often change, which sometimes drastically affects the quality of a restaurant. The ratings in this guidebook are based on information available at press time.

The restaurant price ratings, as categorized below, describe general price-range relationships among other restaurants and are based on the average cost of an entrée for one person, excluding tax and tip.

Rating the Restaurants

★	Good
★★	Very Good
★★★	Excellent
★★★★	An Extraordinary Experience
$	The Price Is Right (less than $15)
$$	Reasonable ($15–$20)
$$$	Expensive ($20–$30)
$$$$	Big Bucks ($30 and up)

Wheelchair Accessibility

Wheelchair accessibility is noted by a ♿ at the end of the entry. An establishment (except a restaurant) is considered wheelchair accessible when a person in a wheelchair can easily enter a building (i.e., no steps, a ramp, a wide-enough door) without assistance. A restaurant is deemed wheelchair accessible *only* if the above applies, *and* if the rest rooms are on the same floor as the dining area and their entrances and stalls are wide enough to accommodate a wheelchair.

Symbols

For everything from soup to nuts, the following symbols indicate where you can stop or shop:

baked goods

coffee/tea

cooking supplies/ cookbooks

markets/food shops

tableware

wine/liquor

Map Key

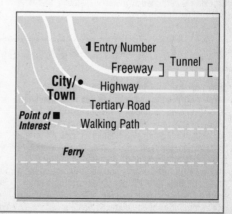

1 Entry Number

Freeway] Tunnel [

City/● Highway
Town

Tertiary Road

Point of ■
Interest Walking Path

Ferry

FYI

Area code 212 unless otherwise noted.

Drinking
The legal drinking age is 21, and many bars, restaurants, and clubs require an ID. Bar hours vary (all are closed before noon on Sunday), but the legal limit for closing is 4AM. On Sunday, restaurants may not serve alcohol until noon, and liquor stores are closed. Beer, however, which is sold in grocery stores, may be purchased after noon.

Hours
It's a good idea to call ahead to find out if a particular restaurant or shop will be open the day and time you plan to visit. Generally shops are open 9AM to 6PM Monday through Saturday, but keep in mind that this information may change with the seasons, the economy, or even the whim of the owner.

Reservations
Calling in advance to see if you need a reservation is always a good idea, especially if the restaurant is popular. Monday nights are generally the slowest, and getting a table is somewhat easier. Thursday through the weekend is considered prime time and is usually heavily booked, especially around 8PM—the preferred dinner hour. If your schedule is flexible, you will have an easier time getting a table earlier (at around 6PM) or later (after 9:30PM). Always call as far ahead as possible, but if you are shut out of the day and time you want, try again around 5PM that day. By then, the staff will know which reservations were confirmed and which were canceled, and they'll be more than happy to fill any last-minute vacancies. Some places might also require or recommend reservations for brunch and lunch.

Smoking
A city law enacted in April 1995 prohibits smoking in the dining area of all restaurants with a capacity of more than 35 people; in these places, smoking is restricted to the bar area or enclosed lounges. Smoking is permitted anywhere in establishments that seat fewer than 35 persons.

Tipping
A 15-20 percent gratuity to wait staff is standard in most dining spots. Most people simply double the sales tax (at press time it was 8.25 percent). Restaurant staffs often pool tip money and give a percentage of it to bartenders, busers, and maître d's. If you choose to tip the maître d' separately, $20 or five percent of the check is usually appreciated. A tip is a reward for service; if you don't get it, you're not obligated to pay for it.

Food Tours
The culinary treats to be explored in New York's rich ethnic neighborhoods are legion. To help you sort out the best from the rest, a variety of walking tours can literally show you the way. The undisputed "king of noshing," **Louis Singer** (718/875.9084), conducts tours of the "twin cities"—Manhattan and Brooklyn, with a special emphasis on the food stores of the Lower East Side. **Big Onion Walking Tours** (439.1090) offers a "From Naples to Bialystok to Beijing" tour that covers the Lower East Side, Little Italy, and Chinatown. **Harold Goldberg** of **Adventures on a Shoestring** (265.2663) leads several ethnic rambles: the Greek enclave in Astoria, Queens; "Little Odessa" in Brighton Beach, the Polish neighborhood of Greenpoint, and the Middle Eastern portion of Atlantic Avenue in Brooklyn; the Italian section of Arthur Avenue in the Bronx; and the Ukrainian stronghold in the East Village and the new Little India on the lower part of Lexington Avenue, in Manhattan. **Pat Olmstead** of **Urban Explorations** (718/721.5254) specializes in cultural tours, but will personalize a food tour in Manhattan, Brooklyn, or Queens.

Food Phone
(777.FOOD) This is a free service sponsored by *Food and Wine* magazine that conveniently organizes over 3,000 restaurants by cuisine (50 different types), neighborhood, and price range. The instructions are clear, and selections are registered by pushing touch-tone buttons on a telephone. Your call can then be transferred (at no extra charge) to the restaurant of your choice, ? you can make reservations or place a delivery order.

Fabulous Food Festivals

New York's ethnic riches are regularly put on display during the myriad street festivals that seem to be everywhere, once the weather turns warm. Some fiestas have not only culinary interest, but national or religious significance as well. All tend to be crowded, noisy, fragrant, and colorful affairs, brimming with local pride. In addition, many loosely structured events pop up under the guise of "block parties," and it's possible to stumble upon such a celebration unexpectedly. The following are some regularly scheduled festivities:

February

19 Chinese New Year celebrates the lunar new year with color and noise, turning the streets of **Chinatown** by turns into a parade ground and a small war zone of firecracker explosions. Because of the cold weather, eating goes on inside—it's customary to celebrate with a multicourse banquet at one of the neighborhood's many restaurants.
♦ Between the Manhattan Bridge and Lafayette St, Canal St, and City Hall

May

9-21 The Ukrainian Festival marks the coming of Christianity to the Ukraine. Feast on pierogi, stuffed cabbage, and borscht while dancing the night away or shopping for crafts. ♦ Seventh St (between Second and Third Aves). 674.1615

9-21 Ninth Avenue Food Festival features the wares of local international food shops and restaurants along a 20-block stretch of the avenue. ♦ Ninth Ave (between W 37th and W 57th Sts). 757.6173

June

?-13 Feast of St. Anthony commemorates San Antonio of Italy and features carnival test-your-aim games, along with vendors grilling sausages and frying *zeppole*. ♦ Sullivan St (at W Houston St). 777.2755

?0 St. Anthony's Day Festival celebrates the saint's life Hungarian-style, with strudel, goulash, chicken paprikash, and more. ♦ E 82nd St (between York and First Aves). 861.8500

?0-11 Philippine Independence Street Fair observes the archipelago's independence from the United States with dancing, singing, and a display of typical Philippine dishes. ♦ 45th St (between Madison and Sixth Aves). 764.1330

July

Mid-month Our Lady of Mt. Carmel Feast memorializes the bravery of a bishop from Nola, Italy who offered himself as a hostage in exchange for the return of children captured by Turkish invaders in AD 400. Such Italian fare as sausage and peppers is offered. ♦ East 187th St (between Cambreleng and Arthur Aves), Bronx. 718/295.3770

?0-23 Fiesta de Santiago Apóstol is a celebration of Spain's patron saint, St. James the Apostle; the culture and food of various Latin American nations are represented. ♦ W 14th St (between Seventh and Ninth Aves). 243.5317

August

?9-20 Harlem Week features food displays—barbecued ribs, fried chicken, ham hocks, and the works—at numerous celebration sites. ♦ 427.7200

?7 Brighton Beach Street Fair is an international fiesta offering rides for children, shopping stalls, and food from all over the world—Greece, Italy, Russia, and Asia—as well as knishes from nearby **Mrs. Stahl's** and the all-American hot dog. ♦ Brighton Beach Ave (between Coney Island Ave and Corbin Pl), Brighton Beach, Brooklyn. 718/891.0800

September

?0 Lower East Side Jewish Festival spotlights the foods of Israel. ♦ E Broadway (between Clinton and Essex Sts). 463.8588

14-24 Festa di San Gennaro is a larger version of the **Feast of St. Anthony** (see above), and a traffic nightmare for locals because of the suburbanites who attend in droves. ♦ Mulberry St (between Worth and E Houston Sts). 226.9546

16 St. Stephen's Day memorializes the Eastern Orthodox church's Hungarian patron saint as a remembrance of the role the church played in welcoming new immigrants to this country. The street celebration features such dishes as chicken paprikash and an array of cakes. ♦ E 82nd St (between York and First Aves). 861.8500

October

1 Atlantic Antic turns the busy Brooklyn avenue into a giant sidewalk sale. With all the Middle Eastern shops and restaurants showing off their stuff, the food is always top-notch. ♦ Atlantic Ave (between Flatbush Ave and the East River), Brooklyn. 718/875.8993

Bests

Pat Olmstead
Owner, Urban Explorations

Golden Unicorn: They're really good with groups—serving them banquet style and bringing out an array of interesting dishes.

Nha Trang: Delicious, inexpensive; the only problem is that it's so popular that the service can be incredibly slow.

The Adoré: It's so quaint and the food is delicious. Also great coffee, and the building has all the original beams.

Sylvia's: I still think it's a really good restaurant. It's a little pricey but you're paying for the atmosphere too, and you're always treated so well.

Eileen Yin-Fei Lo
Cookbook Author; Writer; Teacher, China Institute in America

Café des Artistes, New York's most romantic restaurant, with wonderful pâté.

Golden Unicorn, whose dim sum reminds me of Hong Kong.

Chinatown on a sunny spring morning, for the marvelous sidewalk food displays.

Alleva in **Little Italy,** when I want true cheese of Italy.

Aureole and **Le Cirque,** two restaurants that are quintessentially New York.

Ronasi on First Avenue, a small Sicilian restaurant that shines when you ask Filippo to cook for you.

Gourmet Garage in SoHo, after noon, when it becomes one of the city's best groceries.

La Réserve, Jean-Louis Missud's restaurant for the joys of classical French cooking.

Proving that the colonists really knew how to live, a dinner party given by a Duer in New York in 1787 listed no less than 15 different wines.

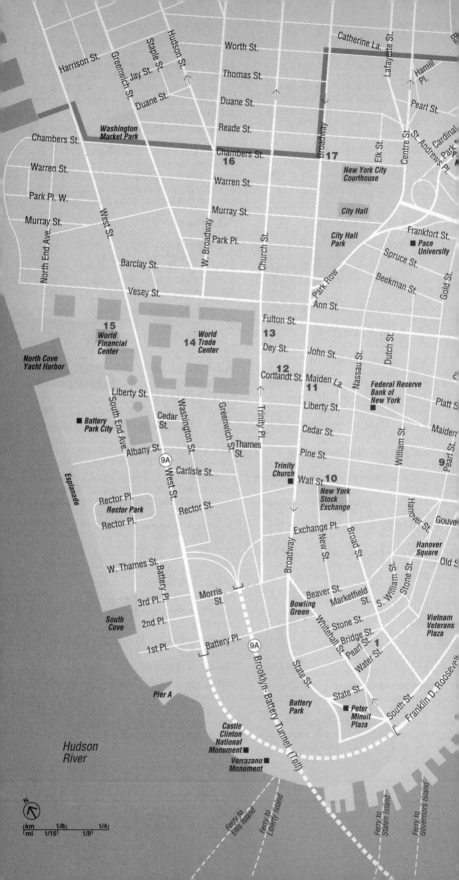

Lower Manhattan

Looking at the towering skyscrapers in today's **Financial District**, it may be hard to imagine that this stretch of land bordered by **Chambers Street** and the **East** and **Hudson Rivers** at the south end of Manhattan island is where New York City humbly began in 1624. First settled by the Dutch, who called it Nieuw Amsterdam, the town was renamed New York by English colonialists in 1664. Today very little remains from those early days. Still, if you walk the narrow, winding streets and alleys—some with evocative names like **Maiden Lane** and **Coetis Slip**—you'll get a sense of the early layout of the place. And there are also a few buildings, such as the 18th-century landmark **Fraunces Tavern Restaurant**, that lend a historical feeling.

The focal point of culinary Lower Manhattan is undoubtedly the **Fulton Fish Market** on **South Street** at the East River. The market dates back to 1821, when New York's existence revolved around its commercial ports. That part of the city's history is celebrated in the nearby **South Street Seaport**—partly new, partly restored, with a few museums and many shops. Restaurants abound here as well, and not surprisingly, those with the best views charge very high prices for unexceptional food.

Across town from the **Seaport** are two megaprojects—the world-renowned **World Trade Center (WTC)**, and the lesser-known **World Financial Center (WFC)**, enjoyed mostly by city-weary locals. **The World Trade Center** includes the famous **Twin Towers**, and the complex is a veritable city-within-a-city, with concourses lined with shops, food stalls, and restaurants—including the sky-high **Windows on the World**. All business at this giant maze came to a temporary halt in 1993, when a massive bomb in an underground parking garage exploded, killing six people, injuring many more, and causing millions of dollars of damage. At press time, it was expected that all of the affected establishments would reopen before the end of 1995, and some even earlier.

On the other side of **West Street**, the **WFC** is the more aesthetically pleasing of these two bustling hubs: The **Winter Garden**—an imposing glass-enclosed atrium—treats denizens of the temperate zone to towering palm trees, and outdoor cafes overlook the **North Cove Yacht Harbor.** On sunny summer days, the **WFC** waterfront is alive with in-line skaters, families eating ice cream, and stressed urbanites ogling the yachts moored in the harbor.

It's easy to feel removed from the hustle and bustle in this pocket of tranquillity. The piers bedecked with ferries and dinner cruise ships, the cobblestone streets in the shadow of the majestic **Brooklyn Bridge**, the time-worn taverns, all take residents and visitors alike away from the frenzied pace of New York City.

1 Fraunces Tavern Restaurant ★$$$ Samuel Fraunces, George Washington's steward, opened a tavern in this 1719 Georgian brick building in 1763. Twenty years later, Washington made the place famous by bidding farewell to his officers here. Now, Wall Streeters congregate for such dependable American fare as steaks, chops, and seafood, surrounded by Colonial-era decor and wood-burning fireplaces. ♦ American ♦ M-F breakfast, lunch, and dinner. Reservations recommended. 54 Pearl St (at Broad St). 269.0144

1 Zigolini's Cafe ★$ A friendly, casual spot, this cafe is an oasis in an area dominated by serious expense-account restaurants or the ubiquitous coffee shops. Such pasta dishes as rigatoni with sun-dried tomatoes and artichokes and focaccia sandwiches with a variety of fillings are the order of the day. If they call ahead, customers are also welcome to design their own sandwich concoctions, a few of which have become part of the menu; the popular "Roger" is grilled chicken breast with pesto, St. Andre cheese, and sun-dried tomato. Sandwiches also come on baguettes, *panini* (minibaguettes), and sourdough bread. ♦ Italian/American ♦ M-F breakfast and lunch. 66 Pearl St (between Broad St and Coetis Slip). 425.7171

2 St. Maggie's Cafe ★$$ With its carved plaster, brown-and-cream walls, and antique chandeliers, the opulent decor of this eatery would be oppressive were it not for the huge windows that let in sunlight and views of the East River. Young Wall Streeters come here for such light fare as the Mulberry Street grilled chicken salad, and for seafood dishes, including Maryland crab cakes with tequila-chili mayonnaise or angel-hair pasta with sea scallops, shrimp, and crab in sherry-lobster sauce. ♦ American ♦ M-F lunch and dinner. Reservations recommended. 120 Wall St (at South St). 943.9050

3 La Barca ★$$$ Tucked away on a side street, this seafood restaurant with an Italian accent offers creative preparations by chef Rosario Degrezia, who composes each day's menu based on what looks good at the market. Dishes to sample are snapper in tomato-basil sauce and fresh spinach ravioli. The antipasto is always good, but head elsewhere for dessert. This place is quite lively at noon, while at dinnertime you could be the only customer. ♦ Italian/Seafood ♦ M-F lunch and dinner. Reservations recommended at lunch. 40 Fletcher St (between South and Front Sts). 514.9704

Sloppy Louie's

4 Sloppy Louie's ★$$$ Before the renaissance of **South Street Seaport** forced Louie to clean up his act and raise his prices, this was a no-nonsense restaurant that catered to the people who worked in the area' markets. The bouillabaisse and shrimp scampi, among other dishes, are still good enough for the most demanding fishmonger; but now the ambience is more genteel.

◆ Seafood ◆ Daily lunch and early dinner. Reservations recommended for six or more. 92 South St (between John and Fulton Sts). 509.9694

⑤ Fulton Fish Market Established in 1821, this venerable institution has been at this location since 1907. It was given the name **Tin Building** by old salts who still remembered the wooden structure it replaced. The market was located here to conveniently receive the daily haul from local fishing boats, but today the catch from cleaner waters arrives via refrigerated truck. Daytime visitors find the market a quiet place, but it is positively frantic between midnight and 8AM. Early risers can watch the activity wind down by taking guided tours at 6AM on the first and third Thursday of each month from May through October; reservations are required. ◆ Daily. South St (at Fulton St). Tour information 669.9416

6 Pier 17 Modeled after the recreation piers of the last century, this development was built directly over the water. In good weather, it's packed with people enjoying the pleasures of the waterfront. Such shops and food stalls as **Cindy's Cinnamon Rolls, Minter's Ice Cream Kitchen, Bain's Deli,** and the Chinese fast-food **Wok N'Roll** fill the inside. During the summer, the pier becomes a venue for concerts and other special activities. There are many busy restaurants here as well, offering spectacular scenery at spectacular prices, although the food is generally no better than average. ◆ Daily. On the East River (between Fulton and Beekman Sts). 732.8257 ♿ Within Pier 17:

SEQUOIA

Sequoia $$ The maritime motif of this spacious dining room overlooking the water practically hits customers over the head—a collection of canoes is suspended from the ceiling. The requisite fish is given a sophisticated spin here in such dishes as pecan-crusted rainbow trout and mahimahi with pineapple salsa. ◆ Seafood ◆ M-F lunch and dinner; Sa-Su brunch and dinner. Ground and second floors. 732.9090 ♿

Harbour Lights $$$ This restaurant has an extensive menu of fish specialties, such as grilled salmon and broiled scallops with Oriental greens. But the draw here is not the food, it's the view—a picture-postcard vista of the **Brooklyn Bridge.** At night, when the bridge is lit, it would be difficult to conjure a more romantic spot. ◆ Seafood ◆ M-F lunch and dinner; Sa-Su brunch and dinner. Third floor. 227.2800 ♿

Sgarlato's Cafe $$$ Across from **Harbour Lights,** this restaurant offers pasta, seafood,

sandwiches, burgers, and dreamy upriver views of three bridges. ◆ Italian/Seafood ◆ M-F lunch and dinner; Sa-Su brunch and dinner. Third floor. 619.5226 ♿

Liberty Cafe $$ This spot boasts sensational panoramic views of the harbor, the Financial District, and the masts of the tall ships—**Peking, Ambrose,** and **Waverley**—moored nearby. The food ranges from oysters on the half shell and pepper-seared mahimahi to pizza baked in a wood-burning oven. ◆ American/Seafood ◆ M-Sa lunch and dinner; Su brunch and dinner. Third floor. 406.1111 ♿

⑦ South Street Seaport Back when sailing ships ruled the seas, New York's most active ports were along this stretch of the East River. With the coming of steamships, the deeper piers on the Hudson River attracted most of the seafaring traffic, and the East River piers fell into decline. In 1967, a group of preservation-minded citizens banded together to buy the rundown waterfront buildings and a collection of historic ships. Twelve years later, commercial interests moved in and provided funds to restore the old buildings and add some new ones. The result, thanks to the ingenuity of architects **Ben** and **Jane Thompson,** is a lively historic site that has revitalized a derelict neighborhood, transforming it into one of New York's most fascinating enclaves. Especially active after 5PM, the place is a magnet for young Wall Streeters, who drift by for an after-work drink in surroundings dramatically different from their high-tech offices. Contributing to the historical air are the cobblestone streets paved with Belgian blocks. ◆ Daily. East River to Water St (between Fletcher and Dover Sts). 669.9400

Within South Street Seaport:

7 Cafe Fledermaus $ Perfect for people watching, this unpretentious spot for coffee, pastries, salads, and sandwiches has tables on the Fulton Street promenade. ♦ Cafe ♦ Daily. 1 Seaport Plaza (at Water St). 269.5890 &

7 Gianni's ★$$ This casual outdoor cafe and sophisticated indoor restaurant are right in the middle of the Fulton Street promenade. Although it doesn't have a view of the water, it's a great place on weekend days to take in the colorful crowds and the street performers who play to them. At dinnertime, stick to the basics—chilled shellfish plate, grilled swordfish, and whichever risotto is being served that day. ♦ Italian ♦ Daily lunch and dinner. Reservations recommended. 15 Fulton St (at Front St). 608.7300 & at the outdoor cafe

7 Fulton Market The 1882 building on this spot used to house a fresh produce and meat market. It was filled with merchandise brought from Long Island farms on the now-defunct *Fulton Ferry,* which connected Fulton Street in Manhattan with Fulton Street in Brooklyn. The reconstructed building (pictured above) now houses shops, restaurants, and, in the spirit of the old market, stalls selling fresh food. Outlets in the market include **Zaro's Bread Basket,** the **Fulton Market Retail Fish Market, Rocky Mountain Chocolate Factory,** and **Ferrara** (for Italian pastries). ♦ Daily. 11 Fulton St (between South and Front Sts). 732.8257

Within Fulton Market:

7 Fulton Street Cafe $$ As one would expect from a cafe in the **Fulton Market** building, seafood in all varieties and preparations is offered on the menu. Hearty eaters should try the Fulton Street Clambake (with steamers, corn, and boiled lobsters). The outdoor tables are generally packed in good weather. ♦ Seafood ♦ Daily lunch and dinner. Ground level. 227.2288 &

The first ice cream made commercially in the US was manufactured in 1786 in New York by a Mr. Hall at 76 Chatham Street (now Park Row).

Stomachs were obviously stronger a century ago. If you had breakfast at Delmonico's in 1893 you were offered, among other choices, truffled pigs' feet, codfish tongues with chopped sauce, rum omelette, guinea fowl with sauerkraut, and baked small green turtles.

BRIDGE CAFE

8 Bridge Cafe ★★$$ The walk to this aptly named cafe situated under the **Brooklyn Bridge** can take you down some streets that look a bit rough and deserted. But don't be put off—the food, including dishes like pecan and cornbread trout and duck with red wine and green peppercorn sauce, is probably the best in the **Seaport** area. The whitewashed room with a tin ceiling, brick walls, red-and-white tablecloths, and old-time New York posters is quite cozy. ♦ International ♦ M-F lunch and dinner; Su brunch and dinner. Reservations recommended. 279 Water St (at Dover St). 227.3344 &

9 The Captain's Ketch ★$$$ The green vinyl banquettes and wood paneling may tempt you to nickname this place "The Captain's Kitsch," but cooking is taken seriously at the neighborhood's oldest and most traditional seafood restaurant. Try the seafood *fra diavolo* (lobster, clams, scallops, shrimp, and mussels in a spicy marinara sauce over linguine) or the lighter grilled swordfish on a bed of steamed spinach. ♦ Seafood ♦ M-F breakfast, lunch, and dinner. Reservations recommended. 70 Pine St (between Pearl and William Sts; entrance on Pearl St). 422.1965

10 La Tour D'Or ★$$$ This staid restaurant on the 31st floor of the Bankers Trust Building was once J.P. Morgan's pied-à-terre. Its views extend in every direction, but the best is from the comfortable bar that overlooks the harbor and the **Statue of Liberty.** The menu, featuring such classic dishes as duck *à l'orange,* seems not to have changed in decades, which is exactly as the regulars like it. ♦ French ♦ M-F lunch; dinner if arranged in advance. Reservations recommended. 14 Wall St (between Broad St and Broadway). 233.2780 &

11 McDonald's $ Believe it or not, this is the home of the golden arches, despite the tuxedo-clad doorman, glass-and-wood dining room, and classical pianist serenading diners. With the exception of espresso and cappuccino served from silver trays and the pastries from Dumas (an Upper East Side bakery), the food is standard Ronald McDonald fare. Serious investors will appreciate the Dow Jones ticker tape, informing them of market fluctuations as they munch their Big Macs. ♦ Fast food ♦ Daily breakfast, lunch, and dinner. 160 Broadway (near Maiden La). 385.2063 &

12 Century 21 A larger version of the Brooklyn discount department store, this place has three bustling floors of top-quality housewares and appliances, in addition to clothing, toys, and electronics. Even high-rolling Wall Streeters love a bargain. ♦ M-Sa. 22 Cortlandt St (between Broadway and Church St). 227.9092. Also at: 472 86th St (between Fourth and Fifth Aves), Brooklyn. 718/748.3266

13 Taliesin ★$$$ Located within **The Millenium Hilton** hotel, this formal, pretty room with wood paneling and etched glass is the setting for ambitious food, some of which succeeds. Try the clam and corn chowder lightly scented with thyme, tuna carpaccio with vegetable relish and black-olive croutons, and grilled swordfish with shrimp, clams, and mussels in a shellfish broth. ♦ American ♦ Daily breakfast, lunch, and dinner. 55 Church St (between Dey and Fulton Sts). 312.2000 &

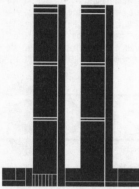

14 World Trade Center (WTC) Seven buildings, including the **Vista Hotel** and the two landmark towers, make up this massive complex set on a semicircle around a five-acre plaza. Designed by **Minoru Yamasaki & Associates** and **Emery Roth & Sons, WTC** was begun in 1962 and finished in 1977. At 110 stories, the monolithic twin towers are the tallest in the city. All the structures are connected underground by the concourse—a vast pedestrian mall filled with shops, banks, public spaces, and restaurants, including branches of **Au Bon Pain** and **Ben and Jerry's.** Beneath it all are parking garages, where on 26 February 1993, a terrorist bomb went off in **One World Trade Center,** killing six people, injuring many more, and causing millions of dollars of damage. At press time, the dining spots listed below in **One World Trade Center** were undergoing renovation; the doors at all three restaurants were scheduled to reopen in early 1996. Call 435.4170 for updated information. ♦ Church St (between Liberty and Vesey Sts). 435.4170

Within the World Trade Center:

●**The Restaurant at Windows on the World** For years it's been one of the most spectacular restaurants in New York, although, frankly, it was about due for a face-lift. When the restaurant closed after the bombing, the

Joseph Baum and Michael Whiteman Company (the original designers) got busy. When they're through, they promise that the place will be even more stunning than before, featuring once again those breathtaking panoramic views. There's no reason to believe that this hiatus will cause the kitchen's standards to do anything but rise, and the wine list, heretofore boasting over 600 selections, should be just as extensive. ♦ International ♦ Reservations required; jacket and tie required. 1 World Trade Center. No phone at press time

●**The Hors d'Oeuvrerie at Windows on the World** No doubt this place will still be a great spot to sip a cocktail and marvel at the views to the south and west when it reopens. The revamped bar area will feature a light menu and a dance floor. ♦ International ♦ Cover. Jacket required. 1 World Trade Center. No phone at press time

●**Cellar in the Sky** Previously, this small 40-seat dining room within **Windows on the World** was located in a windowless wine cellar, but no longer. When it reopens, it will have moved to an area with floor-to-ceiling windows that have "The View." ♦ Continental ♦ Reservations required; jacket and tie required. 1 World Trade Center. No phone at press time

Rooms with a View

At one time, if a restaurant offered a great view of either the water or city lights, the food was invariably undistinguished. In many cases that's still true, especially in the <u>South Street Seaport</u> area, where we say let the tourist beware. But these days, competition for customers is fierce, and a growing number of places are doubling their chances of survival, cashing in with spectacular settings and sumptuous food.

To see lights twinkle as you dine, some choices tower above the rest: **The <u>Rainbow Room</u>** (30 Rockefeller Plaza, between E 49th and E 50th Sts, 65th floor, 632.5100); **The Terrace** (400 W 119th St, at Morningside Dr, 666.9490); and **Win<u>dows on the World</u>** (1 World Trade Center; at press time the restaurant was scheduled to reopen; no phone). For river views, try **River Cafe** (1 Water St, at the East River, Brooklyn Heights, Brooklyn, 718/522.5200); **Hudson River Club** (4 World Financial Center, Upper level, enter at 225 Liberty St, 786.1500); **Le Pactole** (4 World Financial Center, Second level, enter at 225 Liberty St, 945.9444); and **Wa<u>ter Club</u>** (E 30th St, at the East River, access from E 34th St, 683.3333). For a bucolic view, head to **Central Park**'s **Boathouse Cafe** (E 74th St, at East Dr, 517.2233).

Greenhouse Cafe ★$$ This gardenlike, sun-drenched cafe within the **Vista Hotel** has a skylight roof that gives an unusual view of the **Twin Towers** soaring above. Executive chef Walter Plendner has put together an eclectic menu, featuring such dishes as glazed duck breast and andouille sausage over greens with pumpkin dressing. There are also daily curries and a buffet, featuring roasted meats and a daily-changing antipasto that is likely to include mozzarella and sun-dried tomatoes, various smoked fish, and a variety of salads. ◆ American ◆ Daily breakfast, lunch, and dinner. 3 World Trade Center, Plaza level. 938.9100

Tall Ships Bar & Grill ★$$ As befits the name, the decor is strictly nautical, with canvas sails draped overhead, polished mast-worthy woods, and stripes on the walls. The food here is simple—blackened or broiled swordfish steak with grilled vegetables, barbecued chicken medaillons with spring onions and corn sticks, and freshly baked pies for dessert. ◆ American ◆ M-F lunch and dinner; Sa-Su dinner. 3 World Trade Center, Lobby level. 938.9100

15 World Financial Center (WFC) Built in 1981 on a landfill produced by the construction of the **World Trade Center,** this six-building complex designed by **Cesar Pelli & Associates** includes a four-acre plaza, and a glass **Winter Garden** containing 16 giant palm trees—45 feet high. Tenants include **Caswell-Massey, Godiva Chocolatier,** and **Rizzoli International Bookstore.** The **World Financial Center Plaza** is a stellar example of public space design: Its **Courtyard,** a two-level outdoor piazza, houses four international restaurants and cafes, and beyond that are 3.5 beautifully landscaped acres of parkland with twin soft reflecting pools on the Hudson River. In this lovely setting, concerts, performances, and art installations are presented. ◆ Daily. West St (between Liberty and Vesey Sts)

Within the World Financial Center:

HUDSON RIVER CLUB

Hudson River Club ★★★★$$$$
Esteemed chef Waldy Malouf's seasonal menu specializes in food from New York State's Hudson River Valley, prepared with techniques he picked up at **The Four Seasons** and **La Côte Basque.** Don't miss the pumpkin-apple soup, house-smoked quail and warm Coach Farm goat cheese, fillet of salmon in woven potatoes, T-bone of Millbrook venison, and roast free-range

chicken with red-beet risotto. But save room for dessert; pastry chef Martin Howard creates whimsical confections that are a chocoholic's idea of heaven. Try the Statue of Liberty (a plateful of chocolate desserts—its centerpiece fashioned like the Harbor Lady's crown), the Tower of Chocolate (a construction of brownie, mousse, and meringue), or the Chocolate Planet (a dense Saturnian—and saturnalian—ball of chocolate and caramel mousse with a white chocolate ring). Have the tasting plate if your senses overload trying to decide among them. The extensive wine list gives special attention to affordable New York State wines. The country-chic room—apricot-colored walls, blond wood, and numerous plants—has a breathtaking view of **North Cove Harbor Marina** and the **Statue of Liberty.** ◆ American ◆ M-F lunch and dinner; Sa dinner; Su brunch. Reservations required; jacket required. 4 World Financial Center, Upper level (enter at 225 Liberty St). 786.1500 ♿

15 Le Pactole ★★$$$ This 10,000-square-foot restaurant with giant windows overlooking the Hudson features the estimable talents of French chef André Laurent. In the dignified, rose-colored dining room, expect such classic French dishes as terrine of duck with pistachio nuts and tournedos of beef with black truffle sauce, as well as newer creations that include grilled tuna steak with a ginger and cucumber *coulis* (a thick pureed sauce). There's also a lounge area where food from the bar menu is served, and separate banquet facilities, with such amenities as telex and fax machines, and audio and video facilities. Next door is the gourmet shop, **Le Pac to Go** (945.9387), which delivers to offices and homes in the area. ◆ French ◆ M-F lunch and dinner; Su brunch. Reservations recommended. 4 World Financial Center, Second level (enter at 225 Liberty St). 945.9444 ♿

15 Pipeline ★$$ Designed by Sam Lopata to look like an oil refinery, this vast space has indoor seating and tables set up outside in warm weather. The interior features brightly colored pipes, catwalks, ladders, and a great video/jukebox system. Try chef Gonzalo Figueroa's corn chowder followed by penne with tuna and white-bean salad; for dessert, the chocolate mousse cake and chocolate-chip cheesecake are musts. On Saturday and Sunday nights there's in-house baby-sitting, a boon for harried parents. The restaurant also offers Battery Park Picnic Baskets for special lunches and dinners to go. ♦ American ♦ M-F lunch and dinner; Sa-Su brunch and dinner. Reservations recommended. 2 World Financial Center, Ground floor. 945.2755 ♿

15 Au Mandarin ★$$ The authentic Mandarin menu served here—particularly the tangy, spicy chicken; diced chicken marinated with minced garlic, ginger, and peppercorns; and Peking duck—is popular at lunchtime. ♦ Mandarin ♦ Daily lunch and dinner. 2 World Financial Center, Courtyard. 385.0313 ♿

15 Donald Sacks ★★$$ Neighborhood regulars remember when this place, now located in an elegant mahogany and marble room that opens onto the pedestrian mall, was just a take-out shop known for its high-quality sandwiches, potpies, and salads. A full-fledged restaurant since chef Kurt Sippel expanded the menu, it still offers 12 freshly made salads, including the signature curried chicken salad. Heartier fare includes such dishes as duck-confit quesadilla and grilled rack of lamb served with roasted-garlic mashed potatoes and port wine sauce. Children especially like the 10-ounce grilled burgers. Regular customer and famous clothing designer Geoffrey Beene is a big fan of their wonderful gumbo; at his request, it's offered every Friday night. ♦ American ♦ Daily lunch and dinner. 2 World Financial Center, Courtyard. 619.4600 ♿

15 Sfuzzi ★$$ This downtown version of the popular **Lincoln Center** eatery has stylish surroundings, featuring a "sidewalk cafe " on the marble floor of the WFC's **Winter Garden.** The menu is the same as the uptown venue, featuring pizzas with a variety of ingredients, including barbecued chicken and spicy sausage and peppers, and such pastas as smoked-chicken ravioli and linguine with rock shrimp and scallops in a spicy marinara. ♦ Italian ♦ Daily lunch and dinner. 2 World Financial Center, Winter Garden Atrium. 385.8080 ♿. Also at: 58 W 65th St (between Central Park West and Broadway). 873.3700

15 Johnney's Fish Grill ★★$$ The dark-green walls mounted with stuffed fish and black-and-white photos of fishermen plying their nets make you feel as if you were in a New England seafood house. The very fresh fish offered here does nothing to disturb this impression, and the rich New England clam chowder could ward off any chill or soothe any spirit. Standouts are clams on the half shell, poached lobster, and grilled swordfish. The sushi may well rate among the freshest, most artistically designed you've ever tasted, perhaps because several

of the owners are Japanese. ♦ Seafood ♦ M-F lunch and dinner. 4 World Financial Center. 385.0333 ♿

16 Ecco $$$ This restaurant has none of the downtown funkiness you'd expect of its nearby Tribeca neighbors. Carved mahogany, beveled mirrors, and a two-story-high tin ceiling provide a clubby, 19th-century atmosphere. The waiters bustle through the crowd: equal parts Wall Streeters and art dealers. Stick with pasta and dessert. ♦ Italian ♦ M-F lunch and dinner; Sa dinner. Reservations required. 124 Chambers St (between Church St and W Broadway). 227.7074

17 Ellen's Cafe and Bake Shop ★$ Ellen Hart Sturm, a former Miss Subway beauty queen, runs this bustling upscale cafe and bakery across from **City Hall,** where the walls are lined with photos of former Miss Subways (Ellen sponsors yearly reunions). Try the "Mayor's Special" (toasted Thomas' English Muffin halves layered with tuna salad and tomato slices and topped with melted cheese). Be sure to save room for Ellen's pecan pie. For more of the same, try **Ellen's Stardust Diner,** 1377 Sixth Avenue (307.7575). ♦ American ♦ M-Sa breakfast, lunch, and early dinner. 270 Broadway (at Chambers St). 962.1257 ♿

Bests

Sylvia Carter
Restaurant Critic, *New York Newsday*

My favorite old-fashioned coffeehouses (not those new coffee bars) are **Veniero's Pasticceria** and **Caffè Dante.** One newish place I do favor is **Les Deux Gamins** for big bowls of true café au lait, French style.

For blueberry pancakes and fried pork chops, no place beats the **Pink Teacup.** (All the pink tea cups broke a long time ago.) For gnocchi, I go to **Tanti Baci.** For Charlotte Bero's all-American fruit pies and incomparable banana cream, I go to **Anglers & Writers;** only a few years ago, Bero was baking her pies on a wood stove back home in Wisconsin.

For rustic Italian cooking that's deceptively simple, letting the flavors of wondrous ingredients shine, I cross the East River to **Manducatis** in Long Island City. Chef Ida Cerbone jars all the tomatoes she uses in the restaurant all year, working late at night in season, and her husband Vincenzo tends to a fine wine cellar and is a gracious host.

Chinatown/Lower East Side/Little Italy

Perhaps because it is a city of immigrants, New York may well be the world's most flavorful "melting pot." This is especially true of the areas in and around the Lower East Side, the traditional first stop of many arriving groups. Here, an abundance of exotic colors and aromas attracts adventure-seeking gourmets, as well as those homesick for a taste of the old country. Just north of City Hall, Chinatown is the largest Chinese enclave outside Asia, occupying 40 blocks and still growing. The community has been steadily increasing since immigrants began flooding into the area in the 1870s. In addition to the Chinese, there is also a growing population of Southeast Asians. Today, a trip to Chinatown is made not only for shrimp in black-bean sauce or barbecued duck, but for some of the best and most reasonably priced Thai, Vietnamese, and Indonesian food anywhere this side of the international date line. A seemingly endless number of restaurants—some little more than storefronts outfitted with Formica-top tables and fluorescent lights, others gargantuan, garish affairs—line the streets. But don't make your selection solely on looks: All too often the best food is found in the most unlikely surroundings. Around lunchtime or at weekend brunch, look in almost anywhere and you'll catch a glimpse of the ubiquitous rolling carts of steaming bamboo baskets filled with dim sum (an assortment of filled dumplings and buns).

Chinatown is not only a great place to eat, it's a wonderful spot to shop for seemingly exotic food. Open produce markets are stacked with bok choy, snow peas, various kinds of mushrooms, and oranges—all at substantially lower prices than uptown. Ice-filled stalls peddle a wide variety of seafood: crabs, clams, sea bass, salmon, lobsters, and carp swimming in barrels. Meat markets sell hand-stuffed dumplings, red sausage, and even salty Smithfield ham. Grocery stores offer dried seafood, spices, ginseng, and rice. Vendors and stores alike provide intricately designed soup bowls, plates, and chopsticks at very reasonable prices.

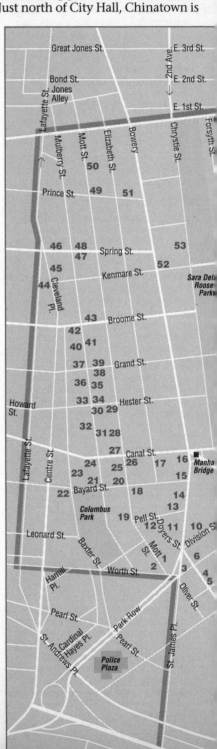

Busy shops line **Canal Street**, the major thoroughfare that used to form the border between Chinatown and its neighbor to the north, Little Italy. In recent years, however, with the Asian community bursting at its seams, Chinatown has been insinuating itself between Italian *caffès* on **Mulberry, Mott,** and **Elizabeth Streets;** more character-covered signs advertising new businesses appear all the time. But if Little Italy's physical presence seems to be diminishing, its popularity does not, especially during boisterous feast-day celebrations. The food is the main attraction here, and those who crave a

Southern Italian meal will be treated to such specialties as clams *oreganata* and veal *sorrentino,* rounded out by a cappuccino and cannoli. Since the social clubs of reputed mobsters, such as alleged godfather John Gotti, are also located down here, there is also the added attraction of the chance to spot local "goodfellas."

East of Little Italy is the Lower East Side, once a haven for some 1.5 million Jewish immigrants who began fleeing en masse from relentless European pogroms in 1881. Although many people visit the Lower East Side primarily for the wholesale clothing and linen outlets clustered along **Orchard** and **Grand Streets,** those enamored of Jewish "soul" food make the pilgrimage for sour pickles, knishes, smoked Nova Scotia salmon, and pickled herring—or for a perfect pastrami sandwich from **Katz's.** Sharing the neighborhood with these *Yiddishe* culinary meccas are bodegas, grocery stores opened by Latinos, a more recent group that includes immigrants from various Spanish-speaking countries. Eateries serving Hispanic favorites, such as fried *platanos* (green bananas) and the ever-popular rice and beans, have also sprung up.

The same low rents that make this neighborhood a revolving door for immigrants have attracted, for almost as long, a healthy supply of artists and bohemians, who add their coffeehouses and cabarets to the mix of delis and dim sum parlors, pasta palaces, and south-of-the-border standbys. In its charming, motley way, this part of town keeps a fascinating record of New York's cultural past, while keeping pace with its future.

1 Mott Street General Store A tiny, dark, dusty store filled floor to ceiling with ceramics from China and Taiwan, this establishment has delicate teapots and teacups, platters, plates, serving utensils, and even an abacus or two in its stock. The staff may be a bit inattentive, even surly, but they will show you items if asked. ♦ Daily. 32 Mott St (between Park Row and Pell St). 962.6280

1 Peking Duck House ★★$ As the name suggests, this is the place to come for Peking Duck. The thoroughly crisped delicacy is carved tableside in what is called home style (with the flesh clinging to the skin), rather than the usual banquet style (skin only), and is served with the traditional accompaniments: thin pancakes in which to roll the duck, slivered cucumbers, and a scallion brush to swab the duck with *hoisin* sauce. Also great as an appetizer, one order serves six hearty diners. Otherwise, get some steamed pork dumplings to munch on while you wait.
♦ Beijing/Szechuan ♦ Daily lunch and dinner. 22 Mott St (between Park Row and Pell St). 227.1810

The corner of East Broadway and Rutgers Street, now occupied by the Chinese restaurant Wing Shoon, was once a hotbed of political revolution. Years ago it housed The Garden Cafeteria, a 24-hour diner, where such radicals as Trotsky and Castro gathered at various times to discuss overthrowing their respective governments and eat some very cheap food.

20 Mott Street ★★$ This is as close to the Hong Kong dining experience as you'll find in New York. Specialties include baked conch stuffed in its own shell, fried squab, and salt-baked shrimp. The dim sum is among the best in the neighborhood; order a combination plate as an appetizer at dinner. ♦ Cantonese ♦ Daily breakfast, lunch, and dinner. 20 Mott St (between Park Row and Pell St. 964.0380

2 Kam Kuo Food Corp. This is the Chinatown equivalent of an upscale food bazaar like **Zabar's** on the Upper West Side. The downstairs aisles at this place are packed with delicacies: Preserved duck eggs; assorted condiments, vegetables, and meats; jars of ginseng; and exotic herbs line the shelves. Upstairs on the housewares mezzanine are rice cookers, tea sets, woks, plates, and pots, all at reasonable prices. ♦ Daily. 7 Mott St (between Park Row and Pell St). 233.5387

2 Hunan Garden ★★$ This friendly restaurant has a large and interesting menu featuring spicy Hunan specialties and Cantonese favorites, among them Peking duck, spicy lobster in Hunan sauce, and sautéed chicken and shrimp in a bird's nest. Gather several friends together for the specia

Chinese banquet—but call a day ahead. ♦ Hunan/Cantonese ♦ Daily lunch and dinner. 1 Mott St (at Worth St). 732.7270 ♿

3 Pho Bâng Restaurant ★$ Come here for authentic Vietnamese cooking, especially the excellent whole shrimp summer rolls. A plate of exotic lettuces and an array of sauces accompany the meal. ♦ Vietnamese ♦ Daily lunch and dinner. 6 Chatham Sq (at the corner of Mott St and Bowery). 587.0870. Also at: 117 Mott St (between Canal and Hester Sts). 966.3797; 3 Pike St (at Allen St). 233.3947

4 Family Noodle Restaurant ★$ This tiny restaurant has enticing roast duck and pig

displayed in the window, but many customers come back for the soul-satisfying Chinese "chicken" soup—a hearty broth containing octopus, wontons, and pork bones. ♦ Cantonese ♦ Daily breakfast, lunch, and dinner. 19 Henry St (at Catherine St). 571.2440

5 Catherine St Meat Market Dumpling fanciers who want to serve dim sum at home can load up on the handmade pork-stuffed delicacies here; they're displayed in pans in the window so it's hard to miss them. Inside, you can pick up minced beef or Smithfield ham. ♦ Daily. 21 Catherine St (between Henry St and E Broadway). 693.0494 ♿

The Goods on Greenmarkets

Given New Yorkers' general lack of contact with nature, there's something especially satisfying about buying fruits and vegetables directly from the farmers who grow them. (Shopping at greenmarkets is also generally less expensive.) In addition to the cornucopia of fresh produce, the larger markets also feature flowers and potted plants, baked goods, organic meat and dairy products, jams and preserves, "homegrown" honey, and, in December, fresh wreaths and trees. Greenmarkets are scattered around town, and new ones are starting all the time. Most take place one or two days a week. Schedules tend to change, so for up-to-the-minute information, call 477.3220. Otherwise, here's where and when to find them:

Bowling Green Greenmarket
Th Aug-Oct
Broadway and Battery Pl

World Trade Center Greenmarket
Tu Jun-Nov; Th year-round
Church and Fulton Sts

Washington Market Park Greenmarket
Sa year-round
Greenwich and Reade Sts

City Hall Greenmarket
Tu, F year-round
Chambers and Centre Sts

Federal Plaza Greenmarket
 year-round
Broadway and Thomas St

Smith Barney Greenmarket
W year-round
Greenwich and N Moore Sts

St. Mark's Church Greenmarket
Tu Jun-Dec
10th St and Second Ave

Abingdon Square Greenmarket
Sa May-Dec
Eighth Ave and W 12th St

Union Square Greenmarket
M, W, F-Sa year-round
17th St and Broadway

West 57th Street Greenmarket
W, Sa year-round
Ninth Ave

Columbus Circle Greenmarket
Th mid-May–mid-Nov
58th Street and Eighth Ave

West 70th Street Greenmarket
Sa May-Nov
Amsterdam Ave

West 77th Street Greenmarket
Su year-round
Columbus Ave

West 97th Street Greenmarket
F Jun-Dec
Amsterdam Ave

West 175th Street Greenmarket
Th Jun-Dec
Broadway

Lincoln Hospital Greenmarket
Tu, F Jul-Nov
149th St and Park Ave, Bronx

Poe Park Greenmarket
Tu Jul-Nov
Grand Concourse and 192nd St, Bronx

Borough Hall Greenmarket
Tu, Sa year-round
Montague and Court Sts, Brooklyn

Albee Square Greenmarket
W Jul-Oct
Fulton St and DeKalb Ave, Brooklyn

Grand Army Plaza Greenmarket
W May-Nov; Sa year-round
Prospect Park's north entrance, at Flatbush Ave and Union St, Brooklyn

St. George Greenmarket
Sa Jul-Nov
Ferry Terminal, Borough Hall parking lot, Staten Island

6 Golden Unicorn ★★★$$ Larger and more elegant than the typical Chinatown storefront restaurant, this place is decorated in sleek black and peach with lots of mirrors and even a napkin folded in your glass. It is popular with families who come to sample the amazing variety of dim sum, so be sure to arrive early. Dinner is equally good, and interestingly enough, the nonspicy dishes are better than the hot ones. Start with tasty fried dumplings, then move on to *egg foo yong*, salt-baked shrimp, and chicken with black-pepper sauce. ♦ Cantonese ♦ Daily breakfast, lunch, and dinner. 18 E Broadway (at Catherine St), Second floor. 941.0911 &

6 W.S.W. Market One of many markets selling glisteningly fresh fish, fruits, and vegetables in this part of Chinatown, this establishment boasts baskets of squirming crabs, red snapper on ice, ripe melons, bok choy, baby eggplant, and much more. It's a good place to one-stop shop for dinner. ♦ Daily. 7-10 E Broadway (at Catherine St). 227.4065 &

7 Nice Restaurant ★★★$ One of Chinatown's better Cantonese restaurants, this place serves excellent barbecued duck and minced squab wrapped in lettuce leaves. The dim sum here is also very good. For dessert, try the cold melon and tapioca. ♦ Cantonese ♦ Daily breakfast, lunch, and dinner. 35 E Broadway (between Catherine and Market Sts). 406.9510

7 Long Shine Restaurant ★★$ To most diners the decor may seem as jarringly unfamiliar—posters of the Alps and Hawaii, shiny metallic chairs, and a karaoke setup for sing-alongs—as the food. The cuisine here is Fujianese, a recent import from one of China's southern provinces, and well worth trying. Don't miss the soups, particularly the savory fish *mein* soup, with shredded pork, shrimp, and Chinese cabbage. And for intricate flavors, try the *lee chi* pork (chunks of pork braised in red soy sauce and rice wine). For those who want more traditional fare, there's also an extensive Cantonese menu. ♦ Fujianese/Cantonese ♦ Daily breakfast, lunch, and dinner. No credit cards accepted. 53 E Broadway (between Catherine and Market Sts). 346.9888 &

8 Triple 8 Palace Restaurant ★$$ It helps to be Chinese in this large, garish restaurant—the staff can be surly to outsiders. If you can get your waiter's attention, try the steamed dumplings, fresh oyster pancakes, moist and tender soy chicken and abalone, and vegetable soups. Hordes of workers stop by at lunch, and it's crowded on weekends as well. ♦ Hong Kong ♦ Daily breakfast, lunch, and dinner. 88 E Broadway, top floor (under the Manhattan Bridge). 941.8886

8 East Corner Wonton ★$ There's nothing fancy about this place, it's just a cramped spot for a quick fix of ginger-and-scallion noodles, salt-baked chicken, or *congee* (a popular porridgelike Asian breakfast). If the glistening roast duck and roast pork in the window don't draw you in, nothing will. ♦ Cantonese ♦ Daily breakfast, lunch, and dinner. No credit cards accepted. 70 E Broadway (at Market St). 343.9896 &

9 Canton ★★$$ Have the owner, Eileen, order for you at this sophisticated restaurant that attracts uptowners, including architect I.M. Pei. Special dishes on the fairly small menu include squab wrapped in lettuce. ♦ Cantonese ♦ W-Su lunch and dinner. No credit cards accepted. 45 Division St (at the Manhattan Bridge). 226.4441

9 Sunrise Kitchen Supplies Piled high with every type of utensil for cooking meals Asian and otherwise, this shop has stockpots, knives, baking pans, bowls, bamboo steamers, and myriad other items on sale here all at very low prices. The porcelain cats, however, are just for decoration. ♦ Daily. 41 Division St (between the Manhattan Bridge and Bowery). 941.8961 &

10 Great Shanghai ★★$ This restaurant has been here forever—though you wouldn't guess it from the modern pink, gray, and neon decor—and the food remains pure Chinatown. Recommended are the steamed vegetable dumplings and the prawns in ginger sauce with carrots and scallions. ♦ Shanghai ♦ Daily lunch and dinner. 27 Division St (between the Manhattan Bridge and Bowery). 966.7663

10 New Hong Kong City ★★$ Occupying the space formerly inhabited by the restaurant Kwong and Wong, this small eatery is popular for its sophisticated Hong Kong cuisine. Standouts are the clams with black beans and scallions and the scallops baked on the half shell. ♦ Hong Kong ♦ Daily lunch and dinner. 11 Division St (between the Manhattan Bridge and Bowery). 431.1040 &

11 Malaysia & Indonesia ★★$ One of the non-Chinese newcomers in the area, this dimly lit, tiny restaurant features dishes from the countries that make up its name. The *sot ayam* (broth filled with shredded chicken, egg, and rice) and *keow teow* (a noodle dish with pork, shrimp, egg, and bean sprouts) are both popular. ♦ Malaysian/Indonesian ♦ Daily breakfast, lunch, and dinner. No credit cards accepted. 18 Doyers St (between Bowery and Pell St). 267.0088

A century ago, Jewish housewives sold bagels made from recipes they brought with them from Eastern Europe. The women carried these homemade wares around in baskets through the streets of the Lower East Side and sold them for a penny.

12 Nam Wah Tea Parlor ★$ After 75 years, this is the oldest and most colorful—if a bit seedy—Hong Kong dim sum parlor in the area. The funky atmosphere is the lure here rather than the food, which is not as good as at other restaurants in Chinatown. ♦ Dim sum ♦ Daily breakfast, lunch, and early dinner. No credit cards accepted. 13 Doyers St (between Bowery and Pell St). 962.6047

12 Vietnam ★★★$ The patience it takes to find this place will be amply rewarded. Enter at the flashing sign, descend the steep staircase, and you'll be treated to some of the best and most authentic Vietnamese food in the city. What this restaurant has saved on the decor, it has invested in the food—the menu lists about a hundred items. Start with the perfectly done Vietnamese spring rolls—filled with shrimp, pork, lemongrass, and cilantro, all wrapped in rice noodles and served with a delicious fish dipping sauce. Follow with the chicken with lemongrass. Wash it all down with Hue beer from Hue City, the ancient capital of Vietnam. ♦ Vietnamese ♦ Daily lunch and dinner. 11 Doyers St (between Bowery and Pell St). 693.0725

13 10 Pell Street ★★★$ A real find, this restaurant with a friendly staff serves excellent Szechuan and Cantonese fare from an extensive menu. Try the vegetable dumplings or cold noodles with sesame sauce to start, followed by the tofu home-style (lightly fried with vegetables in a spicy sauce) and one of the savory chicken dishes. It's filled mostly with Chinese people, which is probably a good sign that the food is authentic. ♦ Szechuan/Cantonese ♦ Daily lunch and dinner. 10 Pell Street (between Bowery and Doyers St). 766.2132

14 N.Y. Noodletown ★$ Ever since *The New York Times* rhapsodized about the salt-baked crabs here, it's been virtually impossible to get a seat in this place—which is not to imply that it was easy to get one before. The noodles with beef are deservedly popular, as are the various crisp roast meats—such as the pig—and the softshell crabs in season. ♦ Cantonese ♦ Daily breakfast, lunch, dinner, and late-night meals. No credit cards accepted. 28 Bowery (at Pell St). 349.0923

15 First Taste ★★★$$ Probably the best Hong Kong cuisine in Chinatown is served in this charming restaurant where the staff speaks English and is more than willing to explain each dish. Start with broiled eel shish kebab or cold jellyfish topped with baby squid, or chicken or beef consommé. Less adventurous types should try the soft, silky bean curd steamed with fresh scallops or the crisp salt-baked chicken with spicy ginger sauce. Hot red-bean soup or lotus seeds in a cool broth with rock sugar are great for dessert. ♦ Hong Kong ♦ Daily lunch and dinner. 53 Bayard St (between Bowery and Elizabeth St). 962.1818 ⑤

16 Silver Palace ★★$$ This bustling dining room is best for dim sum. Regulars get preference when the line grows long, which it usually does on Sundays. Point to what you want off the carts rolling by, and enjoy. Bills are totaled by the number of empty plates on your table. ♦ Dim sum ♦ Daily breakfast, lunch, and dinner. 50 Bowery (between Bayard and Canal Sts). 964.1204

16 Hee Seung Fung (HSF) ★$$ Long lines are common because these folks are especially welcoming to Westerners. It's easier than usual to order dim sum here, as the restaurant offers a photographic guide to the 75 available varieties. The *ha gow* (steamed shrimp dumpling) is always a winner. A full menu is offered at dinner but isn't especially recommended. ♦ Dim sum ♦ Daily breakfast, lunch, and dinner. 46 Bowery (between Bayard and Canal Sts). 374.1319

17 Oriental Garden Seafood ★★$$ Don't be surprised; the staff often seat strangers together at one table to accommodate the crowds here, which seem to be ever present. But the seafood, particularly the golden walnut prawns, is good enough to make diners forget the feeling of being packed in like sardines. ♦ Cantonese/Seafood ♦ Daily breakfast, lunch, and dinner. 14 Elizabeth St (between Bayard and Canal Sts). 619.0085 ⑤

17 Lin's Sister Associates Corp. In Chinatown, foods not only satisfy the palate but heal the body too. Herbs, vitamins, and various traditional medicines are carried in this drugstore. If you're feeling poorly, stop in for a detailed consultation and prescription from an herbalist, who might recommend a tea, capsules, or a poultice. ♦ Daily. 18A Elizabeth St (between Bayard and Canal Sts). 962.5417

17 Jing Fong ★★$$ Recently renovated, this place is a combination of every Chinese restaurant you've ever been to, replete with lanterns, lions on pedestals, fan-shaped windows, and dragons. It's also gigantic, with a capacity of 892 diners. Despite the large scale, everything here is done with care, right down to the table settings. The food is excellent and beautifully presented. Try the baked chicken with garlic, the paper-thin beef with Mongolian hot pot, and the baked pork chops with black beans. ♦ Cantonese ♦ Daily

Dim Sum and Then Some

Small tea pastries, dim sum originated in Hong Kong and have become a delicious **Chinatown** institution. Although dim sum is usually eaten for brunch, some restaurants will also serve it as an appetizer before dinner. The food is rolled over to your table on carts, and you simply point at whatever looks good. This eliminates the language barrier and encourages experimentation—two big pluses. When you're finished, the small plates you've accumulated are counted and the bill is drawn up accordingly. The most popular dim sum dishes include *cha siu bow* (steamed buns filled with barbecued pork), *ha gow* (delicate little dumplings stuffed with shrimp), and *siu mai* (steamed pork dumplings). And for dessert, try one of the little custard tarts.

Jow Nn Hueng Gai
Chicken lollipops

Jow Ha Gok
Shrimp turnovers

Four-color Shui Mai
Meat-and-vegetable-filled dumplings

Pot Sticker (Kou Teh)
Meat-filled dumplings

Gee Yoke Go
Savory pork triangles

Floweret Siu Mai
Meat-filled dumplings

Pot Sticker Triangles
Meat-filled wonton skins

Cha Siu Bow
Steamed barbecued pork buns

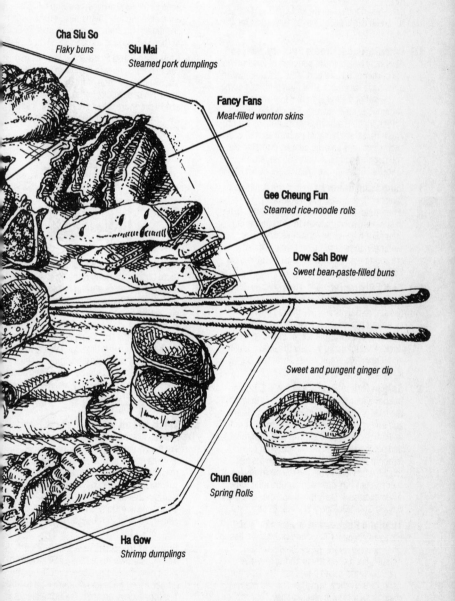

Cha Siu So
Flaky buns

Siu Mai
Steamed pork dumplings

Fancy Fans
Meat-filled wonton skins

Gee Cheung Fun
Steamed rice-noodle rolls

Dow Sah Bow
Sweet bean-paste-filled buns

Sweet and pungent ginger dip

Chun Guen
Spring Rolls

Ha Gow
Shrimp dumplings

breakfast, lunch, and dinner. 20 Elizabeth St (at Canal St). 964.5256 &

18 Sun Lin Garden ★$ The kitchen of this greasy-spoon restaurant has a tendency to swamp every dish in oyster sauce, but the place remains popular because of the low, low prices, generally good-humored staff, and heaping plates of delicious *chow fun* (wide noodles). Also try the big, batter-dipped fried fantail shrimp. Expect long lines but a fast turnover on weekends. ♦ Cantonese ♦ Daily breakfast, lunch, dinner, and late-night meals. No credit cards accepted. 69 Bayard St (at Mott St). 227.1173

18 Chinatown Ice Cream Factory Haagen Dazs may have a more convenient location on the corner of Bayard and Mott, but diners who must have ice cream after dinner should come a little out of their way to this tiny store for authentic Eastern flavors. Specialties include ginger, litchi, red bean, and mango ice cream. Western tastes are satisfied here as well with such selections as oreo cookie, pumpkin pie, and coconut fudge. ♦ Daily. 65 Bayard St (between Elizabeth and Mott Sts). 608.4170

19 Lung Fong Bakery Most of the beautiful sweets offered here, like black-bean doughnuts, are acquired tastes, and this is the best bakery in Chinatown to start garnering them. For the less adventurous, the huge, meltingly good almond and walnut cookies are a sure bet. ♦ Daily. 41 Mott St (at Pell St). 233.7447 &

20 Bo Ky Restaurant ★$ The specialty of this popular restaurant, owned by Chiu Chow people from Vietnam, are the big bowls of steaming hot rice noodles topped with shrimp, fish, shrimp balls, or sliced roast duck. ♦ Vietnamese ♦ Daily breakfast, lunch, and dinner. No credit cards accepted. 80 Bayard St (at Mott St). 406.2292

21 Saigon House Restaurant ★★$ Some interior decoration couldn't hurt this place, but the food is authentic Vietnamese. Appetizers and soups are best: crisp spring rolls, shrimp with sugar cane, cold shrimp and pork roll, and seafood and chicken soups with lemongrass. A favorite among lawyers and judges who work at the nearby courthouses, it tends to get very crowded around lunchtime. ♦ Vietnamese ♦ Daily lunch and dinner. 89-91 Bayard St (at Mulberry St). 732.8988

22 Thailand Restaurant ★★$$ Some of the best and cheapest Thai food Chinatown has to offer is served here. All of the dishes are reliable, but a specialty is *koong kratiam* (garlicky shrimp and peppers). Try also the *kang karee* (yellow curry) or the *pra raam* (peanut sauce) with chicken, beef, shrimp, or pork. Vegetarian dishes are also available. ♦ Thai ♦ Daily lunch and dinner. 106 Bayard St (at Baxter St). 349.3132 &

23 Nha Trang ★★$ The menu—with more than 100 choices—may seem daunting, but don't worry. It's hard to go wrong at this Vietnamese restaurant, as all the dishes are fresh and vibrantly flavored. Try the spring rolls, steamed ravioli, barbecued shrimp on sugar cane, barbecued pork chops, chicken with lemongrass, marinated grilled beef topped with peanuts, or anything else that captures your fancy. The setting is spare—stark lights, linoleum floors, and glass-topped tables, but as soon as the food arrives, you won't give it another thought. ♦ Vietnamese ♦ Daily lunch and dinner. No credit cards accepted. 87 Baxter St (between Bayard and Canal Sts). 233.5948

24 Kam Man Food Products, Inc. Even if you're not planning to buy, drop in to see the astonishing selection of fresh vegetables, dried fish of all kinds, herbs, teas, noodles, and kitchenware. The barbecued duck and chicken available for takeout are delicious. ♦ Daily. 200 Canal St (at Mulberry St). 571.0330

25 Mandarin Court ★★$ Sisters Kitty and Carol Chan from Hong Kong offer such well-prepared dishes as shrimp baked with spicy salt, clams with black-bean sauce and pork chops Hong Kong–style. The dim sum is also especially good and served without the bustle of larger nearby dim sum palaces. The decor is a bit more stylish than one usually finds at these prices, with recessed lighting, shiny black vases, plum-colored chairs, and a teal floor. ♦ Hong Kong ♦ Daily breakfast, lunch, and dinner. 61 Mott St (between Bayard and Canal Sts). 608.3838

26 Tai Hong Lau ★$ This is a great place for inexpensive, authentic Cantonese cooking. Try the Winter Melon Treasure, a curved piece of white melon atop a mixture of mushrooms, roast duck, chicken, pork, and shrimp, surrounded by broccoli florets. The baby clams with lettuce taco is good too. ♦ Cantonese ♦ Daily breakfast, lunch, and dinner. 70 Mott St (between Bayard and Canal Sts). 219.1431

26 House of Vegetarian ★$ More stylish than most Chinatown restaurants, this place looks like it belongs on the Upper East Side, with hunter-green walls and modern light fixtures. The food is very creative, featuring dishes for herbivores such as shredded "pork" with garlic sauce, orange "beef," and sautéed roast "pig," in which soybean flour, tofu, and tofu skin all convincingly take the place of the above-mentioned meats. ♦ Chinese vegetarian ♦ Daily lunch and dinner. No credit cards accepted. 68 Mott St (between Bayard and Canal Sts). 226.6572

26 **Wonton Garden** ★$ This is a fine place for the many varieties of Cantonese noodle dishes, especially wonton noodles in chicken broth with roast pork and various Chinese vegetables. ♦ Cantonese ♦ Daily breakfast, lunch, and dinner. No credit cards accepted. 52-56 Mott St (at Bayard St). 966.4886

27 **Oriental Pearl** ★$ Suggested items on the extensive menu at this large, dull-looking restaurant are Peking spare ribs, steamed flounder, or shrimp with walnuts. Also recommended is Peking-style chicken in a bird's nest. ♦ Cantonese ♦ Daily breakfast, lunch, and dinner. 103 Mott St (at Canal St). 219.8388 &

28 **New Chao Chow** ★$ This place serves up what is perhaps the best *lo soi* duck in New York. The bird is cooked in a rich sauce flavored with cinnamon, eight-star anise, and nutmeg. ♦ Northern Chinese ♦ Daily breakfast, lunch, and dinner. No credit cards accepted. 111 Mott St (between Canal and Hester Sts). 226.2590

28 **Wong Kee** ★$ The good, fresh food offered at ridiculously low prices makes one wonder how they stay in business. Try the wonton-cabbage soup, any of the wide rice noodles, boiled skinless chicken breast, roast duck, or scrambled eggs with glazed pork. Skip the chef's suggestions. ♦ Cantonese ♦ Daily lunch and dinner. No credit cards accepted. 113 Mott St (between Canal and Hester Sts). 226.9018

29 **Vincent's Clam Bar** ★$ Choose the fresh seafood with a choice of hot, medium, or mild tomato sauce at this venerable neighborhood institution. Hot is for serious masochists, of which there appear to be many. An expanded menu offers a variety of meat entrées, chicken, salads, coffee, and dessert. ♦ Seafood ♦ Daily lunch, dinner, and late-night meals. 119 Mott St (at Hester St). 226.8133 &

30 **Forzano Italian Imports Inc.** Here is the place to buy a souvenir of Little Italy. Italian music is piped onto the street to lure customers inside, where they'll find a large selection of all things Italian, including records and tapes; espresso makers in every shape, size, and price; a variety of meat grinders; T-shirts celebrating Italian heritage; and devil horns to keep bad luck away. ♦ Daily. 128 Mulberry St (at Hester St). 925.2525

31 **Luna** ★$$ A century old, this restaurant feels more like an oversized kitchen than the requisite tourist stop it is. The hallway that leads to the dining room gives you a full view of the bustling kitchen. Despite, or perhaps because of, the haphazard mix of tables and booths, propped-up photographs, and occasionally gruff service, the experience feels authentic. The food is predictably filling. ♦ Southern Italian ♦ Daily lunch, dinner, and late-night meals. No credit cards accepted. 112 Mulberry St (between Canal and Hester Sts). 226.8657

32 **Il Cortile** ★$$$ The lines to get in may be too long, the rooms too noisy, and the waiters too harried, but the fresh food at this dining spot is well prepared and the room beautifully decorated. ♦ Northern Italian ♦ Daily lunch and dinner; F-Sa late-night meals. 125 Mulberry St (between Canal and Hester Sts). 226.6060

33 **Umberto's Clam House** $$ This standby is a popular landmark because famed underworld figure Joey Gallo was assassinated here, but the seafood is probably better at **Vincent's**. ♦ Seafood ♦ Daily lunch, dinner, and late-night meals. 129 Mulberry St (at Hester St). 431.7545

33 **Sal Anthony's S.P.Q.R.** $$ Though the multilevel room is grand and gorgeous, what comes out of the kitchen usually isn't. Stick to such simple items as chicken with olive oil and garlic. ♦ Neapolitan ♦ Daily lunch and dinner. 133 Mulberry St (at Hester St). 925.3120

34 **Caffè Napoli** ★$ It feels like a sidewalk cafe even inside this *pasticceria*. Take a cue from the locals, who have dessert here rather than at the more famous **Ferrara**. The cannoli is a definite star among the many marvelous-looking pastries. ♦ Cafe ♦ Daily. No credit cards accepted. 191 Hester St (at Mulberry St). 226.8705

PUGLIA Restaurant

34 **Puglia Restaurant** $ Come here for generous portions of rigatoni in vodka sauce or veal parmigiana—just two of the many dishes served at this rambling restaurant. The mostly young crowd sits at communal tables and sings along with the waiters to the live music, which adds to the festive *ambiente*. ♦ Southern Italian ♦ Tu-Su lunch, dinner, and late-night meals. No credit cards accepted. 189 Hester St (between Mott and Mulberry Sts). 966.6006

The redbrick building located at 354 Elizabeth Street on the corner of Broome Street played a part in the creation of the mobster term "iced." In the early part of this century this building was the site of the Knickerbocker Ice House. Gangsters stored the bodies of their murdered victims here until they could find a permanent gravesite for them.

Pick of the Pasta

Oodles of noodles, some of the best in the world, are served in New York, where thriving Italian communities have existed since the turn of the century. Although Italian restaurants and cafes can be found all over town, the greatest numbers are concentrated in **Greenwich Village,** the **Upper East Side,** and of course, **Little Italy.** If spaghetti is the only noodle you know by name, here's a primer to help you pick a pasta.

Agnolotti

Manicotti

Bucattini

Orzo

Capellini d'angelo

Pappardelle

Conchiglie

Penne

Farfalle

Ravioli

Fettuccine

Rigatoni

Fusilli

Rotelli

Lasagna

Tagliatelle

Linguine

Tortellini

35 Angelo's of Mulberry Street ★$$ An old Little Italy standby that is a little on the touristy side, this restaurant can be counted on to churn out consistently decent meals of veal *valdostana* (stuffed with cheese and ham) and veal parmigiana. ♦ Southern Italian ♦ Daily lunch and dinner. 146 Mulberry St (between Hester and Grand Sts). 966.1277

36 Ristorante Taormina ★$$ With its blond wood and peach furnishings, exposed brick walls, large windows, and graceful tall plants, this is not the typical Little Italy restaurant. The stuffed artichokes are excellent, and the veal entrées are also quite good, as are most items on the Neapolitan menu. Those who know something about Italian geography shouldn't be fooled by the restaurant's name, which is a town in Sicily. ♦ Neapolitan ♦ Daily lunch and dinner. 147 Mulberry St (between Hester and Grand Sts). 219.1007 ♿

37 Italian Food Center The De Mattia family has run this one-stop shopping emporium—filled with domestic and imported Italian foodstuffs—for over 20 years, to the great delight of Italophiles. More than a dozen kinds of breads are baked on the premises daily, and the vast array of Italian cold cuts is mouthwatering. Try the New York Special hero sandwich, a fresh pizza, focaccia, *bruschetta* (toast seasoned with garlic and oil), or one of the temptingly displayed spinach or sausage rolls. If you can't wait until you get home to enjoy the delicious takeout, stop at the park bench outside and dig in. ♦ Daily. 186 Grand St (at Mulberry St). 925.2954 ♿

38 Ferrara $ A slick emporium, this cafe includes an extensive take-out department, featuring a wide variety of Italian pastries, cookies, and candies. The espresso bar is one of the city's more popular places for cappuccino and the like. In nice weather, the bar extends out onto the sidewalk, where a counter dispenses Italian gelati. ♦ Bakery/Cafe ♦ Daily. 195 Grand St (between Mott and Mulberry Sts). 226.6150

38 E. Rossi & Co. This old-fashioned, crowded, family-run store sells boccie balls, pasta machines, cookbooks in both Italian and English, and a variety of kitchen gadgets, such as cheese graters. ♦ Daily. 191 Grand St (at Mulberry St). 966.6640

39 Alleva Dairy This old-fashioned cheese store has been run by the same family for over a century. Not a day goes by without a proud Alleva on hand to tend to the regular customers who come from all over the city for the mozzarella (fresh and smoked) made daily. There's also a small selection of noncheese items, including dried pasta, an excellent fresh tomato sauce packaged to go, and several types of smoked and cured meats. ♦ Daily. 188 Grand St (at Mulberry St). 226.7990

39 Piemonte Ravioli Company Since 1920, the same family has been churning out freshly made pasta from old family recipes in this modest-looking store that is, in fact, one of America's major suppliers. The refrigerator and counter are always stocked with pasta of all types, colors, shapes, and fillings. The filled pastas, such as ravioli and cannelloni, are favorites. Try the plump ravioli stuffed with cheese, spinach, or porcini mushrooms. ♦ Tu-Sa; Su until 3PM. 190 Grand St (between Mott and Mulberry Sts). 226.0475

39 DiPalo Dairy Step into this shop and be greeted by the intoxicating aromas of salami, mortadella, and a full line of cheeses, including fresh mozzarella, aged parmigiano reggiano, and large wheels of fresh pecorino flown in from Rome. There's also a wide variety of homemade pasta, such as tortellini with sun-dried tomatoes. In business for seven decades, this store, like others on the block, has a fiercely loyal clientele. ♦ M-Sa; Su until 3PM. 206 Grand St (at Mott St). 226.1033

40 Benito I and Benito II ★$ The original owners of this pair of small trattorie sold out and moved to Los Angeles. The restaurants are no longer related, except by name, but either one is a good choice for a hearty low-cost meal. ♦ Neapolitan ♦ Daily lunch and dinner. No credit cards accepted. Benito I: 174 Mulberry St. 226.9171. Benito II: 163 Mulberry St. 226.9012

DA NICO

40 Da Nico ★$ The decor is more stylish—terra-cotta floors, hanging copper pots, brick walls lined with shelves of olive oil and wine bottles, a marble bar with antipasto platters—and the atmosphere less raucous here than at surrounding neighborhood joints. This is an excellent place for coal-fired–brick-oven pizzas, both plain and Wolfgang Puck–inspired (with mixed seafood, for example), Nico Rolls (chicken in fresh dough with tomatoes and onions), pastas, and roast pig, which is cooked fresh daily and in full view. ♦ Neapolitan ♦ Daily lunch and dinner. 164 Mulberry St (between Grand and Broome Sts). 343.1212 ♿

Label Vishinsky, inventor of an early automatic bagel maker, claimed that the first New York bagel emerged from 15 Clinton Street exactly in 1896.

41 La Mela ★$ This small, bright, yellow cafe is decorated with curling posters and the kind of seaside paintings you generally find tucked away in the attic. Among the wall hangings are many signed photographs of celebrities, such as Kathie Lee Gifford, who are also satisfied customers. Don't wait for the menu—there isn't one—and despite what customers may order, the waiter basically serves what he wants, often antipasti and an assortment of pasta. But the owners must be doing something right—on weekends, the waiters also have to practice crowd control.
♦ Neapolitan ♦ Daily lunch and dinner. 167 Mulberry St (between Grand and Broome Sts). 431.9493

42 Caffè Roma ★★$ Knowledgeable New Yorkers favor this lovely old-world bakery over all others. No redecorating was ever necessary to make this place look authentic—it just is. The cannoli, whether plain or dipped in chocolate, are perfect. ♦ Bakery/Cafe ♦ Daily. No credit cards accepted. 385 Broome St (at Mulberry St). 226.8413

42 Grotta Azzurra ★$$ The kitsch of dining in an ersatz blue cave may appeal to some, even though the food is nothing extraordinary. Chicken cacciatore is a safe bet, but avoid the seafood. Still, the portions are ample, you don't need a reservation, and it's fun.
♦ Neapolitan ♦ Daily lunch and dinner. No credit cards accepted. 387 Broome St (at Mulberry St). 226.9283

43 Road to Mandalay ★★$$ In typical New York fashion, you'll find this cozy Asian restaurant right in the heart of Little Italy. All the food is good, but the noodle dishes are special. Don't miss the ruby rolls (prawns and vermicelli in triangular pastry) and the grilled tiger prawns in lemongrass sauce.
♦ Thai/Burmese ♦ M-F dinner; Sa-Su lunch and dinner. 380 Broome St (between Mott and Mulberry Sts). 226.4218

44 Cascabel ★★★$$$ Geraldine Ferraro's son, John Zaccaro Jr., opened this stylishly decorated restaurant—a red-and-black color scheme with mirrors and metallic sculptures—as an outgrowth of his **Ravioli Store.** At first, it was a modest success, but the place became a runaway hit when he brought in star chef Tom Valenti who had just left Soho's **Alison on Dominick.** Valenti's food isn't subtle: it's hearty, robust Mediterranean and extremely delicious. Two superb offerings are the chicken-and-foie-gras-stuffed *agnolotti* (half-moon-shaped ravioli) with chickpeas and leeks, and his signature dish—braised lamb shanks served with white-bean puree. End the meal with a maple crème brûlée. For sheer perfection, enjoy the repast at one of the corner fabric-draped banquettes, which look like something out of Picasso's Cubist period and afford a sweeping view of the room. ♦ Mediterranean ♦ M-Sa dinner. Reservations recommended. 218 Lafayette St (between Broome and Spring Sts). 431.7300

45 Kwanzaa ★★$$ Injecting a bit of variety into the neighborhood is this newcomer, which bills itself as the home of international soul food. The decor is strictly African, with Egyptian figures on the apricot-colored walls, teak sculptures, and West African masks, but the food lives up to its globe-trotting promise, including Maryland crab cakes; jerk chicken wings; curried chicken with potatoes, apples, and raisins; and spicy collard greens. All are deeply satisfying, but try to save room for dessert, particularly the sweet potato cheesecake prepared by **Eileen's** next door (see below). ♦ Soul food ♦ Daily lunch and dinner. Reservations recommended. 19 Cleveland Pl (between Kenmare and Spring Sts). 941.6095

A New York invention, the egg cream is generally credited to Louis Auster, a Jewish immigrant, who owned a candy store at Stanton and Cannon Streets during the early part of the century. Mostly to amuse himself, he started mixing carbonated water, sugar, and cocoa together until he got a drink he liked. It was such a hit that Schrafft's reportedly offered him $20,000 for the recipe. Auster wouldn't sell and secretly continued making his own syrup in the back room of his store. When he died his recipe died with him. Some years later, Herman Fox created another chocolate syrup, which he called U-Bet—Fox's brand is regarded as the definitive egg cream syrup to this day.

oven in a nearby basement. Those who know go for the heavenly prosciutto loaf studded with strips of meat, or one of the other breads with cheese, olives, herbs, or drizzled with olive oil. ♦ Daily until 2PM. 45 Spring St (between Mott and Mulberry Sts). 226.6688

45 Eileen's Special Cheesecake Eileen Pezzino started baking her rich, cream-cheesy cheesecakes in Queens nearly twenty years ago. When she moved to this location 17 years ago, it was still a warehouse district with no fashionable restaurants nearby. Yet, cheesecake fans made their way here, and still do, for the perfect plain cheesecakes and the 19 other varieties, including butter pecan, Amaretto, maple walnut, chocolate cappuccino, and candy (Nestle's Crunch or Snickers). To make it harder to resist, Pezzino sells them in various sizes: a whole cake, a half cake, or an individually sized cake. Other treats tempt as well, notably the chocolate velvet cake—its hard chocolate frosting coats a scrumptious chocolate mousse. ♦ Daily. 17 Cleveland Pl (at Kenmare St). 966.5585

46 Ceci-Cela A tiny patisserie with a stand-up bar for on-the-spot coffee and pastry consumption, this place feels like a slice of Paris—from the French-speaking owners to the authentic baked goods. The shiny brioche bread is practically a work of art—beautifully shaped, rich, and eggy. The fruit and lemon tarts, *palmiers* (a sweet and flaky pastry), opera cakes, and éclairs couldn't be more delicious. ♦ M-Sa. 55 Spring St (between Mulberry and Lafayette Sts). 274.9179

47 Lombardi's ★★$ Opened in 1905, this pizzeria with plain wooden booths and brick walls feels like it's been here forever (even though it closed for a while before reopening a few years later down the block from the original). In fact, it was a Lombardi who introduced pizza to this country. (See "Pizza—What's Old is What's New" on page 38.) And in his 75-year-old brick oven in the back room, Gennaro Lombardi makes pizza the way his grandfather, also named Gennaro, did—the crust is crisp, the tomato sauce homemade, and the toppings high quality. ♦ Pizza ♦ Daily lunch and dinner. 32 Spring St (between Mott and Mulberry Sts). 941.7994

48 D & G Bakery For more than three decades this bakery has been a Little Italy landmark. Come early for the breads, which are baked fresh daily in a 100-year-old, coal-fired brick

49 Kitchen Club ★★$$ This cozy 32-seat restaurant is the domain of former Dutch performance artist and caterer Marja Samsom, who is responsible for the construction of the room, its decoration (peach-colored walls, heavy turquoise drapes, and a mixture of antique settees and chairs), as well as the preparation of the cuisine, a combination of European and Japanese influences. A job well done, especially where the food is concerned; each course is artistically designed, delicious, and health conscious. The menu, which bears some relation to the seasons, may include an appetizer called Japanese delicacies (a mélange of fish wrapped creatively around mushrooms, cucumber, and radishes), an entrée of stuffed quail with spinach and shiitake mushrooms, and ginger ice cream for dessert. The wine list is excellent, and the house variety is reliable. The restaurant's intriguing name comes from the once-a-week meal Marja cooked in her Greenwich Village apartment for friends before she turned restaurateur in 1990. The open-kitchen design and loving attention to detail encourages all customers to feel a part of that special club—and lucky to be. ♦ European/Japanese ♦ Tu-F lunch and dinner; Sa-Su dinner. Reservations recommended. No credit cards accepted. 30 Prince St (at Mott St). 274.0025

50 Cafe Gitane ★$ Named after a brand of French cigarettes, this would seem to be a haven for smokers, increasingly shunned everywhere else. It does tend to get smoky, mainly because this small, red-and-green cafe doesn't have separate smoking and no-smoking sections. But the staff insists that the name derives from the design on the Gitane package—and is not an endorsement of the brand or the habit. In any case, smokers and nonsmokers alike come for the creative salads, which throw together noodles, shiitake mushrooms, mango, marinated tuna, and sesame-chili dressing, and sandwiches of roasted chicken with avocado, ginger, and dill mayonnaise on toasted focaccia. ♦ Cafe ♦ Daily breakfast, lunch, and dinner. No credit cards accepted. 242 Mott St (between Prince and Houston Sts). 334.9552

51 Connecticut Muffin Co. A friendly staff offers fresh-baked goods at this small shop; there are even a few tables for those wanting immediate gratification. Try a banana-nut muffin or cheddar-cheese scone. ◆ Daily until 4PM. 10 Prince St (between Bowery and Elizabeth St). 925.9773

51 Le Poème Restaurant Tea Room and Bakery ★★$ Tunisia-born, Corsica-raised Martine Abitbol presides over this casual room with brick walls and primary-color portraits. Poetry readings are held here every Saturday and there are music performances from time to time. The main feature is Martine's food, a combination of cuisines from her two former homes. Specialties include muffins made from chestnut flour, thin-crusted fruit tarts, anise and orange cookies, and Corsican chicken with sage, garlic, and lemon. ◆ Corsican/Tunisian ◆ Daily breakfast, lunch, and dinner. No credit cards accepted. 14 Prince St (at Elizabeth St). 941.1106

52 Mazer Store Equipment Co. Craig Claiborne, Mimi Sheraton, Lauren Bacall, and Stockard Channing come here to buy their restaurant-quality Garland stoves, which come with porcelain-coated oven walls, back, and roof. But you don't have to be a celebrity to enjoy the discount prices and expert installations that include a burner adjustment. Service is what distinguishes this store from others of its kind. ◆ M-F. 207 Bowery (at Kenmare St). 674.3450

53 Sammy's Famous Roumanian Jewish Steakhouse ★★$$$ This is the best Jewish restaurant in the city, but it's not kosher. The room is low-down and tacky, and the so-called entertainment—an electric piano and a comic who thinks he's Henny Youngman—is so bad it's good. If you're unfamiliar with the cuisine, order whatever the waitress tells you to, but only half of the recommended quantity. Among the goodies are chopped liver with "the works": chicken cracklings (rendered fat) with shredded black radishes and onion; and *kishke* (herb stuffing in an intestinal casing)—and those are just the appetizers. For a main course, a rib steak, a fried breaded veal chop, or boiled beef with mushroom-barley gravy will do just fine. Mashed potatoes with fried onions, and *kasha varnishkes* (buckwheat groats with bowtie macaroni) are great on the side. Portions are large and the food is authentically heavy (even without liberal pourings from the pitcher of chicken fat on the

table). To wash it down, try an egg cream, the classic New York *digestif*. Management supplies a self-mixing kit that includes a container of milk, a bottle of Fox's U-Bet chocolate syrup, and seltzer. ◆ Eastern European/Jewish ◆ Daily dinner; entertainment nightly. Reservations required. 157 Chrystie St (between Delancey and Rivington Sts). 673.0330

54 Wolsk's Around since 1938, this candy emporium sells home-roasted nuts, dried fruit and a range of chocolates from domestic brands to Perugina Baci. M-F, Su. 81 Ludlow S (between Broome and Delancey Sts). 475.070

55 The Sweet Life Fantasyland for those with sweet tooth, this small shop is crammed with every temptation, from boxes of Swiss Lindt chocolate to chocolate-covered marshmallow sold by the piece. There are also glass jars of dried fruits and nuts, and for lovers of halvah, varieties from all over the world. ◆ M-F, Su. 6 Hester St (at Ludlow St). 598.0092

55 Gertel's Bake Shop The baked goods sold at this veteran shop are the basics: rye bread, *babka* (Russian coffee cake), marble cake, jelly doughnuts, and apple strudel. They may not satisfy a demanding gourmet, but for anyone raised on them, they're tremendously comforting. ◆ M-F, Su. 53 Hester Street (between Essex and Ludlow Sts). 982.3250

55 Kadouri Import Corp. The plump dried apricots, pears, and other fruit displayed in the window are just a small sampling of what's for sale inside: an all-around spread of international products, from coffee beans to condiments to Israeli candy. ◆ M-F, Su. 51 Hester St (at Essex St). 677.5441 &

56 Essex Street Pickles This purveyor of pickles is the best place in New York to get a kosher dill sour enough to make your face pucker. The sauerkraut and the pickled peppers and tomatoes are terrific as well. Fin the merchandise displayed in the shop and o the sidewalk in brine-filled barrels. You may recognize the place from one of the scenes in the movie *Crossing Delancey,* where Peter Reigert, Amy Irving's soon-to-be husband, worked. ◆ M-F, Su. 35 Essex St (between Grand and Hester Sts). 254.4477 &

57 Kossar's Bialystoker Cousins of the better known bagel, bialys are humbler and flatter, and some New Yorkers prefer their taste. Thos who do come here for the bialy that is considered the best in town: chewy, flavorful, and studded with garlic or onion. Bagels are also sold but are offered almost as an afterthought. ◆ Daily 24 hours. 367 Grand St (between Essex and Norfolk Sts). 473.4810 &

58 Ratner's ★$$ Its glory days far behind, this New York institution is now more of a cultural, rather than a gustatory, destination. All the standard Jewish dairy dishes are listed, but fe are worth the inevitable heartburn. It's best to soak in the *Yiddishkeit* over a bowl of soup, a plate of panfried blintzes (with a pot-cheese or potato filling), or the deep-fried pierogis. ♦ Eastern European/Jewish ♦ M-Th breakfast, lunch, and dinner; F breakfast and dinner; Sa dinner; Su breakfast and lunch. 138 Delancey St (between Suffolk and Norfolk Sts). 677.5588

59 Streit's Matzoth Company This is the only Manhattan producer of the unleavened bread used during Passover. Watch the huge sheets of matzos as they pass by the windows on conveyor belts and buy some samples on your way out. ♦ M-F, Su. 150 Rivington St (at Suffolk St). 475.7000

60 Schapiro's House of Kosher and Sacramental Wines Take a tour of the only winery still operating in the city. Wines are also available for purchase here. ♦ Weekdays by appointment only; Su 11AM-4PM. Nominal fee. 126 Rivington St (between Norfolk and Essex Sts). 674.4404

61 Economy Candy Company People with a longing for old-fashioned penny candy will find it in this store, which has been selling candy of all kinds, as well as dried fruits, nuts, coffees, teas, and other delicacies, since 1937. Though the prices are good, a penny just doesn't go as far as it used to. Ask for the mail-order catalog. ♦ Daily. 108 Rivington St (between Essex and Ludlow Sts). 254.1832 ♿

62 The Hat/El Sombrero $ You won't find the best Mexican food here, but this popular neighborhood eatery has its defenders. Try the *nachos tradicionales* (topped with beef, beans, cheese, and salsa), wash it down with a margarita, and soak in the local color. ♦ Mexican ♦ Daily breakfast, lunch, and dinner. No credit cards accepted. 108 Stanton St (at Ludlow St). 254.4188

63 The Ludlow Street Cafe ★$ This dark, bohemian cafe used to be known as a live-music hangout, not a dining spot. Since a new chef came along in 1993 and changed the menu to Cajun, the food has begun to draw as many fans as the bands. Particular favorites include blackened salmon, pickled shrimp, gumbo, and crawfish étouffée. ♦ Cajun ♦ W-Sa dinner; Su brunch and dinner. 165 Ludlow St (between Stanton and E Houston Sts). 353.0536

64 Pink Pony Cafe $ There's attitude aplenty in this Day-Glo playroom, where would-be poets while away the day on the comfy, 1950s-era couches. Even if you're not waxing philosophical about anything, it's a stylish place for a sandwich, salad, or piece of cake. ♦ Snacks ♦ Daily. 176 Ludlow St (between Stanton and E Houston Sts). No phone

65 Katz's Delicatessen ★$ A well-known old delicatessen, this place was made even more famous by the memorable deli scene shot here for the 1989 movie *When Harry Met Sally*. Sit at a table and enjoy the whole experience, only if you're not in a hurry. For counter service, take a ticket when you come in, and while you wait, take in the atmosphere: the sign that says, "Send a salami to your boy in the Army" is a World War II relic. Sausages or warm brisket on rye are good. ♦ Deli ♦ Daily breakfast, lunch, and dinner. No credit cards accepted. 205 E Houston St (at Ludlow St). 254.2246 ♿

66 Ben's Cheese Shop This inconspicuous shop (so unassuming that there's no sign) takes the idea of specialization very seriously. Come for fresh-tasting homemade natural cream cheese, sold in plain, scallion, or garlic and herb flavors. Farmer cheese and sweet butter in bulk are sold here as well. ♦ M-F, Su. 181 E Houston St (between Orchard and Allen Sts). 254.8290

66 Russ & Daughters A shopping mecca for serious connoisseurs of bagels and lox with a schmear of cream cheese, this establishment is also not bad for golden smoked whitefish, unctuous sable carp, tart/crisp herring, salads, dried fruits, nuts, and other items that belong to a category of food some native New Yorkers call "appetizing." ♦ Daily. 179 E Houston St (between Orchard and Allen Sts). 475.4880 ♿

67 Yonah Schimmel ★$ Jewish specialties, including legendary knishes, clabbered milk (yogurt), and borscht, have been dished up in this dumpy old storefront since the turn of the century. ♦ Eastern European/Jewish ♦ M-F, Su. breakfast, lunch, and early dinner. 137 E Houston St (at Forsyth St). 477.2858

Bests

Seth Kamil
Director, Big Onion Walking Tours

Vietnam: Great, great Vietnamese food.

Primorski in **Brighton Beach:** Really well prepared Russian food.

Elk Candy Company: For great candy and marzipan.

Katz's Delicatessen: For the atmosphere as well as the food.

Boca Chica: Also for the food and for Brazilian dancing that starts at midnight on the weekends.

Caffè Roma: For the best Italian pastries in town.

When people think of pickles and New York, the Jewish area of the Lower East Side comes to mind. But pickle making goes back to colonial times. The first pickles made in America were produced by Dutch farmers in Nieuw Amsterdam.

New York's rich oyster beds were famous in the mid-18th century, and oyster cellars and stands lined Canal Street. For a mere six cents, you could eat all the oysters you wanted until the proprietors decided you'd had enough and slipped you a bad oyster to make you stop. Qualifying as New York's premier gourmand, Diamond Jim Brady generally consumed 1,000 oysters a week.

SoHo/TriBeCa

No two neighborhoods personify downtown chic as much as SoHo and TriBeCa. Even their names, with their unusual upper- and lower-case letter combinations, are more interesting than other area designations. The term SoHo was coined to describe the district **S**outh of **Ho**uston Street; TriBeCa was also named for its location: **Tri**angle **Be**low **Ca**nal Street. Together, they comprise the territory bounded by **Chambers, Houston,** and **Lafayette Streets** and the **Hudson River.**

SoHo first gained notice as the home of many of the city's resident painters and sculptors. During the mid-1960s, artists moved en masse into the cheap loft spaces of SoHo's many abandoned industrial buildings. Galleries followed the artists, and later fashionable shops and restaurants began to open, catering to well-heeled art buyers. Real estate prices escalated and today only successful artists can afford to live and work here.

The new affluence has also given a jolt to the restaurant scene; new, chic restaurants line **West Broadway** and all of its side streets. On weekend afternoons, New Yorkers, suburbanites, and visitors stroll the streets window shopping and looking for a place to have brunch; at night, models, wannabe celebrities, and their escorts crowd the tables at **Diva,** the **Cub Room,** and **Match.** At such places, velvet ropes and all-powerful doorkeepers have been known to keep the late-night crowd selectively hip. SoHo and its high style are running at high speed.

South of **Canal Street** in TriBeCa, the picture is somewhat different. While no one disputes that it is now definitely upmarket and fashionable, TriBeCa doesn't attract as much tourist traffic as its northern neighbor. The expensive lofts are hidden in cast-iron buildings on semideserted, mostly commercial streets, and there are no expensive boutiques to draw weekend browsers. But some of the best restaurants in the city, such as **Bouley, Chanterelle, Montrachet,** and the immediately standing-room-only newcomer **Nobu,** are located here. These gems are often stashed in out-of-the-way, unobtrusive storefronts surrounded by warehouses and much lower-profile businesses. TriBeCa still feels a little rough, a little uncharted. And residents like it that way. They don't want their neighborhood to go the way of SoHo.

Despite their differences, however, the two neighborhoods share a certain sensibility—cutting edge but upscale, places where a charcuterie or a showplace restaurant spotlighting New American cuisine will find a receptive audience. Downtowners definitely like to eat well.

1 Salaam Bombay ★★$ This handsome room with mauve walls, violet tapestry banquettes, and gold-edged Indian fabrics suspended from the ceiling is the scene for a culinary tour around India, including dishes from such regions as Goa and Gujrat—areas not often featured on New York menus. Don't miss the *kachori* (crisp fried balls stuffed with vegetables), *murg xaccuti* (chicken cooked with roasted coconuts and aromatic spices), and *achaar gosht* (lamb cooked with spices in a sealed pot). There's also an extensive, high-quality, but very reasonably priced, lunch buffet. ◆ Indian ◆ Daily lunch and dinner. 317-319 Greenwich St (between Reade and Duane Sts). 226.9400

1 Gigino ★$$ When the sizzle behind Positano in the Flatiron District began to cool after nine years, owners Bob Giraldi and Phil Suarez and chef Luigi Celentano reconceptualized and decided to open a casual, rustic trattoria here. The dishes reflect the pasta and fish specialties of Celentano's native Positano but include some delicious preparations you won't see anywhere else; for example, try *spaghetti del padrino* (with beets, escarole, garlic, olive oil, and anchovies). Avoid the unappetizing sounding (and tasting) spaghetti with jellyfish. The chocolate-covered eggplant dessert mystifies. Within weeks of opening, this place was a neighborhood favorite. ◆ Italian ◆ M-F breakfast, lunch, and dinner; Sa-Su brunch and dinner. Reservations recommended. 323 Greenwich St (between Reade and Duane Sts). 431.1112

Grove St.
Barrow St.
Commerce St.
7th Ave.
Cornelia St.
Bleecker St.
W. 3rd St.
New York University (NYU)
E. 4th St.
E. 3rd St.
Morton St.
Bedford St.
Carmine St.
Bleecker St.
Avenue of the Americas (6th Ave.)
MacDougal St.
Bleecker St.
La Guardia Pl.
Leroy St.
Walker Park
Clarkson St.
Downing St.
E. Houston St.
Lafayette St.

86 85   80 79 78
87   77   76   75   71
84   74
W. Houston St.
Varick St.
90   89 88   83   72 70
Hudson St.   73 69
Greenwich St.   82   68 67
King St.   Prince St.
Charlton St.   81
Sullivan St.
Thompson St.
54   56
53
Vandam St.   52   63 64
48   51   59 60 61 65
50   55   58 62
Mercer St.
Spring St.   57
Spring St.
66
Dominick St.   49   W. Broadway
43
Wooster St.
Greene St.
Broadway
38
Crosby St.
rsey   46   45   44 42
ty   47   Avenue of the Americas
Renwick St.   Broome St.   40   39
Watts St.   41   Broome St.
Holland Tunnel   31 32   36 37
Canal St.   29 30   33   35
Grand St.
Watts St.
27   34   Howard St.
Washington St.
Desbrosses St.   28   Canal St.
Vestry St.   Varick St.   (6th Ave.)   Lispenard St.
Laight St.
Collister St.   25
Hubert St.   26   Church St.
Beach St.   Ericson Pl.   Walker St.
24
Broadway
23   White St.
22   Cortlandt Alley
West St.   19 20 21   Franklin St.
N. Moore St.   17 18   Lafayette St.
15 16   Leonard St.
14   13   Catherine La.
Franklin St.   11 12   Centre St.
9   Worth St.
Harrison St.   10
8   Jay St.   Staple St.   Hudson St.
Greenwich St.   7   Thomas St.
Independence Plaza   2   3   6   Duane St.
Duane St.   4   5
1   Reade St.
River Terr.   Chambers St.
Washington Market Park
New York City Courthouse
North End Ave.
Park Pl. W.   W. Broadway   Warren St.   Church St.   Broadway
Chambers St.
Murray St.   Murray St.
Park Pl.
City Hall
km 1/8 1/4
mi 1/16 1/8

②Bouley ★★★★$$$$ According to one competing restaurateur, David Bouley used to be a chef, now he's a god. Those in the know say a table here is the best in Manhattan. His masterful French menu changes daily, but dishes not to miss include eggplant terrine; Maine halibut with toasted sesame seeds in tomato water; rack of lamb; medaillons of venison; and roasted Maine lobster served in its own consommé with crisp asparagus, winter mint, and fresh black truffles. Any dessert will induce euphoria, but crowd pleasers include the Valrhona chocolate soufflé with hot chocolate sauce, maple ice cream, and the banana tart. For diners who are utterly overwhelmed and don't know which dishes to try, prix-fixe lunch and dinner menus provide the perfect answer. And Bouley thrills to the challenge of special diets. The extensive American and French wine list will delight oenophiles. The handsome Provençal interior with hand-carved wooden doors and baskets of flowers was designed by Bouley and architect **Kevin White.** Two caveats: The formal staff can sometimes be snooty, and even with a reservation, which often must be procured weeks in advance, you may have to wait for a table. ◆ French ◆ M-F lunch and dinner; Sa dinner. Reservations required; jacket and tie required. 165 Duane St (between Hudson and Greenwich Sts). 608.3852

3 Duane Park Cafe ★★$$$ This comfortable place offers something not often available in a New York restaurant—elbow room and relative quiet. In the pretty room with cherrywood accents, diners are offered a creative mix from the menus of the now-defunct **K-Paul's** and **Hubert's** (chef/owner Seiji Maeda logged time at both). Maeda's former partner, Kenji Asano, studied with Marcella Hazan (the Italian chef and cookbook author), and some of her specialities also make an appearance. Standouts include braised lamb shank with lime-coconut rice, pan-blackened scallops, and a gorgeous pear-hazelnut tart. ◆ Continental ◆ M-F lunch and dinner; Sa dinner. Reservations required. 157 Duane St (between W Broadway and Hudson St). 732.5555

4 Washington Market ★$ Local businesspeople mix with stroller-wielding mothers at this friendly neighborhood cafe/take-out shop. Try the roast turkey with sun-dried tomatoes and arugula sandwich, soy-honey chicken salad, penne with broccoli and pine nuts, and homemade bundt cake. High-quality preserves, chocolates, breads, teas, and other essentials to take home are for sale. ◆ Cafe ◆ M-Sa. 162 Duane St (at Hudson St). 571.4500

Bouley is known for its long dinners, but the lengthiest meal on record lasted six hours, when nine courses and nine different wines were consumed.

5 Basset Coffee & Tea Co. ★$ Dog lovers will appreciate the company's logo as well as the oil paintings in this former industrial space now filled with barrels of coffee beans, racks of tea, and a counter showcasing sandwiches and pastries. Try the hound-dog salad of fennel, sun-dried tomato, radicchio, red-leaf lettuce, goat cheese, and fresh herbs or the ham sandwich with sweet onion and creole honey mustard on black bread. The lemon bars are divine. ◆ Cafe ◆ Daily breakfast, lunch, and early dinner. 123 W Broadway (at Duane St). 349.1662

ROSEMARIE'S

6 Rosemarie's ★★$$$ With an attractive display of Italian plates decorating the bare brick walls, the warm and romantic ambience of this restaurant adds to the pleasures of the *nuova cucina* cooking. The ravioli filled with spinach and ricotta (available as an appetizer or main course) is exceptional, and the choice of healthy and delicious salads is extensive. The excellent menu includes shrimp and white-bean salad, osso buco, and roasted striped bass with white beans and tomatoes, but the roasted cod with lightly fried onion rings and roasted chicken with mashed potatoes are wonderful and shouldn't be missed. Popular desserts include tiramisù and a crème napolean. Another plus: The service is outstanding. ◆ Northern Italian ◆ M-F lunch and dinner; Sa dinner. Reservations recommended. 145 Duane St (between Church St and W Broadway). 285.2610

6 Zut! ★ $$$ It's hard to keep from smiling when you take a look at this fanciful room with its Mad Hatter light fixtures, wallpaper adorned with dancing rabbits and card-playing penguins, and other animal figures on the ceiling and over the bar. But you'll pay a price for whimsy here—the noise level is so high that normal-volume converstions are almost impossible. The good bistro fare includes roasted beet salad with white truffle oil; escargots with garlic, watercress, and leeks; coq au vin rouge with chickpea spaetzle; and steak *frites* (with french fries). End the meal with warm chocolate cake with melted center. The extensive and reasonably priced wine list includes nightly specials.

♦ French ♦ M-W dinner. Reservations recommended. 139 Duane St (between W Broadway and Church Sts). 513.0505

7 The Odeon ★$$ A good place to sit and schmooze over a late-night drink, this neon-lit room was the hottest spot downtown with the art crowd when it first opened in 1980. In the restaurant game, places that opened just a year ago may be considered ancient history, but this one has managed to remain on the map and stargazers still have a chance to sight the occasional celebrity. The food is generally good, but the pretentions of the kitchen and sometimes uppity staff turn off serious diners. Try the *pappardelle* (broad noodles) with chicken and chanterelle mushrooms and grilled lamb shank with arugula and roasted peppers. Recommended on the lower-priced brasserie menu are the crab fritters or steak *frites*. ♦ American/French ♦ M-Sa lunch, dinner, and late-night meals; Su brunch, dinner, and late-night meals. Reservations recommended. 145 W Broadway (at Thomas St). 233.0507 &

8 A.L. Bazzini Company The city's largest dried-fruit and nut supplier, this place has been in business for more than a century. Delicious smells from nuts being dried or honey roasted fill the shop and even waft into the street. A full array of gourmet treats, including breads, vinegars, preserves, pesto sauces, great coffee beans, and exotic condiments and spices are all here for the buying. There are also a few tables at which to enjoy such homemade prepared foods as overstuffed peanut butter and jelly sandwiches (among others), along with pastries, cookies, cakes, and muffins. ♦ Daily. 339 Greenwich St (at Jay St). 334.1280

9 Spartina ★$$ This open, brick-colored dining room is a great place for splitting a thin-crusted pizza with a friend. The menu, which darts all over the map for inspiration—Morocco, Spain, Italy—is hit-and-miss; best bets are the pizzas, and such simple dishes as monkfish *basquaise* (in a stew of sautéed peppers), roasted chicken, lamb shanks with onions and bosc pears, and beet-and-onion salad. There's an extensive, well-priced wine list, but go elsewhere for dessert. ♦ Eclectic ♦ M-F lunch and dinner; Sa dinner. Reservations recommended. 355 Greenwich St (at Harrison St). 274.9310 &

10 Yaffa Tea Room ★$ Decorated with wrought-iron lawn chairs, marble tables, and elaborate floral displays, this eccentric, romantic room is a perfect place for an espresso and pear tart or piece of chocolate truffle cake. More substantial food is offered too. There is a couscous special on Thursday, bouillabaisse on Tuesday, and a regular menu that includes Moroccan chicken and fettuccine with shrimp in pesto cream sauce. The daily high tea is worthy of an English country inn, and the brunch—featuring scrambled eggs in puffed pastry with a red-pepper *coulis* (puree)—is very good. ♦ Eclectic ♦ M-F breakfast, lunch, high tea, and dinner; Sa-Su brunch, high tea, and dinner. 19 Harrison St (at Greenwich St). 966.0577

11 Chanterelle ★★★★$$$$ Young chef David Waltuck, acclaimed as a fresh, unspoiled genius, and his wife, Karen, have moved the dining room they established on Grand Street to this pretty space designed by Bill Katz, which fittingly (for SoHo) is decked with original prints, drawings, and lithographs as well as stunning floral arrangements. The menu features an artist of the month; Louise Nevelson and Robert Motherwell have been two of the more prominent names. The food—original, artfully presented, and always delicious–continues to lure a natty crowd, including one-time US attorney general nominee Kimba Wood and fashion designer Isaac Mizrahi. The seafood sausages are justifiably renowned, as are such dishes as pepper-crusted venison with onion compote, and saddle of lamb stuffed with *merguez* (spicy lamb sausage) and topped with olive *jus*. Game and fish entrées are particularly felicitous—don't miss the pheasant in red-wine sauce or the roasted monkfish. The house treats its guests to after-coffee cookies and chocolate. Otherwise, for dessert try the warm and crispy chocolate soufflé cake, pepper-pear *tarte tatin* with pear-infused caramel sauce, or one of the famous homemade ice creams and sorbets. The sommelier here is one of the best in town, and the wine list, composed of French and Californian selections, is reasonably priced. This place is unusual among high-priced restaurants in that it employs women as servers and hosts, and the service is especially deft. The prix-fixe luncheon is a bargain. ♦ French ♦ M dinner; Tu-F lunch and dinner; Sa dinner. Reservations required. 2 Harrison St (at Hudson St). 966.6960 &

12 Aux Delices des Bois Amy and Thierry Farge import mushrooms from all over the world and sell them out of this long, narrow shop. Stop in for a supply of the same mushrooms that the chefs at **China Grill** and **21** use, be it shiitake, cremini, portobello, enoki, chanterelle, or lobster. ♦ M-F. 4 Leonard St (between W Broadway and Hudson St). 334.1230

13 The Sporting Club $$ Up to nine different events can be beamed in by satellite at one time onto screens in every corner of this room straight out of a sports fanatic's dream. The main event is shown on three 10x10-foot screens above the bar. A glance at the patented electronic scoreboard will tell you the status of every pro and college game being played that day. The menu is made up of aptly named dishes, such as the George Steinbrenner (a burger with a choice of two toppings) and the San Diego Chicken (with lettuce, tomato, and mayonnaise on sourdough bread). ◆ American ◆ M-Sa lunch, dinner, and late-night meals; Su brunch, dinner, and late-night meals. Reservations required for major sporting events. 99 Hudson St (between Leonard and Franklin Sts). 219.0900

14 Tribeca Grill ★★$$$ In 1990, Drew Nieporent (owner of **Montrachet**) teamed up with several celebrity partners, including actor Robert DeNiro, to open this loftlike restaurant in the former Martinson Coffee Building, and it's still going strong. Sketches and paintings by DeNiro's late father, Robert Sr., adorn the walls. The menu features first-rate bistro fare, including rare seared tuna with sesame noodles, arugula salad with *bocconcini* (mozzarella balls) and basil oil, fried oysters with anchovy aioli, and pan-seared snapper with warm vinaigrette. Desserts are a must, especially the chocolate cake and banana tart. Wine lovers take note: The list is carefully chosen and well priced. ◆ American ◆ M-F lunch and dinner; Sa dinner; Su brunch and dinner. Reservations required. 375 Greenwich St (at Franklin St). 941.3900 ⅃

riverrun
RESTAURANT & BAR

15 Riverrun Cafe ★$$ Opened in 1979, this is one of TriBeCa's pioneer restaurants and remains a neighborhood staple for chicken potpie and Mom's meat loaf. It's also a comfortable place to sit, eat, and talk without feeling hassled. ◆ Continental ◆ M-F lunch and dinner; Sa-Su brunch and dinner. 176 Franklin St (between Hudson and Greenwich Sts). 966.3894

16 Nobu ★★★$$$$ One of the splashiest restaurant openings of 1994 was Drew Nieporent's and Robert DeNiro's latest venture, a wonderland for out-of-this-world sushi, featuring Los Angeles's star sushi chef, Nobu Matsuhisa. The million-dollar fairy-tale forest setting features a copper-leaf ceiling, wood floor with stenciled cherry blossoms, birch trees, and a wall of 50,000 black river pebbles. If you think a lot of creative energy has been poured into the decor, wait until you try chef Matsuhisa's inventive cooking. The sashimi is dressed with a sweet sesame sauce and served atop salad greens; squid "pasta" is actually strips of the seafood made to look like pasta and served with mushrooms and asparagus in a garlicky red-pepper oil. Even simple-sounding dishes, such as black cod marinated in miso and grilled, are prepared with unusual vibrance, as are the mussels with salsa and soft-shell crab rolls. Desserts include a chocolate-orange torte, ginger crème brûlée, chestnut cake, and assorted ice creams and sorbets. It's no surprise that the clientele list is studded with stars like Madonna, Sting, and many a familiar face from *Vogue*. ◆ New Japanese ◆ M-Sa dinner. Reservations required. 105 Hudson St (at Franklin St). 219.0500 ⅃

17 Commodities A natural foods supermarket, this place carries a large stock of organic and otherwise healthy comestibles, as well as bodycare products, cookbooks, and health food for pets. There's an extensive variety of flour, rice, cereal, beans, and pasta sold in bulk. ◆ Daily. 117 Hudson St (at N Moore St) 334.8330

18 Bubby's ★$ Across the street from **Nobu**, but inhabiting a completely different universe, is this homey place decorated with kitschy kitchen tins and toys from the 1950s. Come here for rosemary chicken, homemade soup, spinach salad niçoise, and fresh roasted turkey sandwiches. Salads come in large and small sizes, and sandwiches may be ordered in whole or half portions. Save room for dessert— homemade fruit pies, triple-layer chocolate cake—because the portions come in only one size: massive. ◆ American ◆ M-F breakfast, lunch, and dinner; Sa-Su brunch and dinner. 120 Hudson St (at N Moore St). 219.0666

19 Walkers $ Run by the people who own **The Ear Inn** (see below), this is a good place to have a drink with off-duty police officers from the First Precinct or to chat with other friendly folk over free Happy Hour munchies. For more substantial fare, try a sandwich or burger. ♦ American ♦ Daily lunch, dinner, and late-night meals. 16 N Moore St (at Varick St). 941.0142

20 Franklin Station ★$ The owners are French and Malaysian and so is the menu at this light airy space that also doubles as an art gallery. The paintings on display were done by the proprietors, who are artists as well as restaurateurs. As for the food, it's vibrant and as nicely displayed as the paintings; try the chicken satay with a gutsy peanut sauce; shrimp soup with noodles, lemongrass, and chilies; a tender, flavorful smoked-salmon sandwich; and the pear tart for dessert. Bring your own beer or wine. ♦ French/Malaysian ♦ Daily breakfast, lunch, and dinner. 222 W Broadway (at Franklin St). 274.8525

TWO ELEVEN
RESTAURANT & BAR

21 Two Eleven ★$$ This light and airy restaurant serves a little of everything—try the linguine with radicchio, arugula, and grilled shrimp in a citrus vinaigrette; or duck confit with baby greens. In warm weather, umbrella-shaded tables are set out on a deck overlooking West Broadway; in any season, sit inside among the plants and ceiling fans and you'll feel as if you're outdoors. ♦ Eclectic ♦ M-F lunch and dinner; Sa brunch and dinner; Su brunch and supper. Reservations recommended Thursday-Saturday. 211 W Broadway (at Franklin St). 925.7202

21 El Teddy's ★$$ Inside this three-story building topped with a life-size replica of the **Statue of Liberty**'s crown are old-fashioned booths, vintage 1940s wallpaper, and a neon fish tank, among other varied and unusual touches. The cuisine is creative Mexican fare—goat-cheese quesadillas, etc., and the margaritas are reputed to be among the best in town. ♦ Mexican ♦ M-Th lunch and dinner; F lunch, dinner, and late-night meals; Sa dinner and late-night meals; Su dinner. 219 W Broadway (between Franklin and White Sts). 941.7070

21 The Cleaver Company This tiny store, owned by longtime caterer Mary Cleaver, does a huge catering business. During the week, it's also open as a retail takeout. Locals pile in on weekday mornings for freshly baked apricot, apple-cinnamon, or lemon-pecan scones, doughnuts (a lower-fat version that's baked, not fried), or brioches. The rest of the day, the store offers an array of prepared foods, such as mixed green salad with wild rice, and dried fruits and nuts, herb-roasted chicken, chicken potpie, vegetarian chili empanadas, and pasta with roasted vegetables *provençale*. If you need a special cake for a birthday or other occasion—the bakers created a Chanel-bag cake for *Vogue* editor Anna Wintour–just call in advance. ♦ M-F. 229 W Broadway (at White St). 431.3688

22 Montrachet ★★★$$$ The low-key setting created by **Spanier & Dennis** is very stylish and the food very good in this very French establishment. Former sous-chef Chris Gesualdi officially took over the kitchen in 1994 following the departure of Debra Ponzek, with a transition so seamless that even most regulars didn't notice. The popular salmon with a truffle crust, moist roast chicken, and spiced, seared tuna continue to be as sensational as ever. The extensive wine list is well chosen and the wine service knowledgeable. ♦ French ♦ M-Th dinner; F lunch and dinner; Sa dinner. Reservations recommended. 239 W Broadway (at White St). 219.2777

23 Arqua ★★$$$ The poor acoustics in this pretty, peach-colored dining room with white, flying saucer–shaped light fixtures make conversation difficult. Concentrate instead on the food, especially the *pappardelle* with duck-and-mushroom sauce, gnocchi with tomatoes, and rabbit braised in white wine and herbs. ♦ Italian ♦ M-F lunch and dinner; Sa-Su dinner. Reservations recommended. 281 Church St (at White St). 334.1888

24 Barocco ★★$$$ No one seems to mind that they are practically sitting on the laps of their neighbors in this sparse but lively trattoria. Try the spinach ravioli filled with ricotta and Swiss chard and topped with a basil-tomato sauce; or rigatoni with pureed eggplant, peppers, and tomato. During the week, these and other meals are available to take out from the shop next door. ♦ Italian ♦ M-F lunch and dinner; Sa-Su dinner. Reservations recommended. 301 Church St (at Walker St). 431.1445

25 American Renaissance ★★$$$ Not a place for a casual night out, this dramatic dining room—with an indoor waterfall, 23-foot ceilings, Ionic columns, and intricately carved plaster painted aqua and gold—could be a room in an Austrian palace or a concert set from *Amadeus*. But this grand showcase is the perfect setting in which to enjoy former **Colors**' chef Erik Blauberg's opulent food. Try the foie gras with caramelized pears; roasted Atlantic salmon glazed in vintage port with shaved asparagus and tahini-lime dressing; seared Arctic char (a delicate white fish) with shrimp and wild-herb and mushroom ravioli; and for dessert, the hot chocolate soufflé with a melted center and homemade ice cream. Make sure to take a peek at the rest rooms: The women's room is a marble and mirror extravaganza with a red lizard ceiling; the men's is cream, black, and gold marble, with TV sets positioned above the urinals at eye level. ◆ American ◆ M-F lunch and dinner; Sa dinner. Reservations recommended. 260 W Broadway (at Ericson Pl). 343.0049

Downstairs at American Renaissance:

25 The Vodka Bar and Cafe ★$ If the surroundings and prices upstairs at **American Renaissance** are too lavish, consider this casual cousin. Some fans come just to sit at the bar and try the assortment of flavored vodkas, others indulge in the varied fare served at the few tables and simple gray banquettes. The short menu features raw oyster selections; a good combination platter of smoked salmon, oysters, trout, shrimp, and mussels; burgers with "name your own toppings"; and pizzas or focaccia with "name your own ingredients"—among them sautéed shiitake mushrooms and roasted duck. Be sure to leave room for dessert because the same irresistible choices served upstairs are also available here. Don't miss the hot chocolate soufflé with a melted center and comice-pear *tarte tatin*. ◆ International ◆ M-Su dinner and late-night meals. 343.0049

Pizza—What's Old is What's New

When Gennaro Lombardi was growing up in New York City, he worked in his grandfather's pizzeria after school making dough and carrying cartons. "It was the family business, it's what we did," he says. And this is a family that knows pizza: his grandfather, an immigrant from Naples and also named Gennaro Lombardi, opened the first pizzeria in America in 1905.

In Italy, the Lombardis—like all original pizza makers—were bread makers. "That's how pizza was invented," says Lombardi. "While the baker was waiting for the bread to bake, he'd plop some tomato on bread that was ready, throw on some cheese, and throw it back in the oven. Then he'd eat it waiting for the next bread to finish. The original pizza was in the shape of a loaf of Italian bread; it only became round when they began to bake large round loaves of bread."

Baked in coal-fired brick ovens, Lombardi pizza was a staple on Spring Street in **SoHo** until 1987, when the restaurant closed. In 1994, grandson Gennaro, joined by pizza maker Andrew Bellucci and childhood friend John Brescio, reopened **Lombardi's** in a new location down the street at 32 Spring (between Mott and Mulberry Sts, 941.7994). "I got tired of getting bad pizza," he reasons. "What people are making now is getting everyone sick."

Lombardi and his partners adhere strictly to grandpa Gennaro's methods. First the dough must be aged for 24 hours, stretched to release the moisture, and brought to room temperature before it's baked. "It swells up in your stomach if it's cold," explains Lombardi. Instead of the processed cheese used on so many pizzas, the mozzarella they use is custom made at **Alleva Dairy** in **Little Italy;** the tomato sauce is homemade, its acidity siphoned off the top (in a manner similar to skimming fat) before it's used. Most places don't take this last step. "That's what gives people heartburn," he says. "No one gets heartburn here and they can taste everything—the sauce, the toppings, the cheese."

When asked about the ideal pie, Lombardi waxes lyrical: "The crust is thin, but not paper thin, baked in the brick oven, and cooked six to seven minutes, while being moved around so it doesn't burn and develop black spots. The crust should be crisp but still soft, you should be able to fold the pizza without it cracking. The sauce should be spread evenly but thin enough so that you can see spots of dough, like looking through clouds. Then you place the cheese in slices extending like the hours on a clock face, with two more [slices] split in half in the middle. Then you put on extra virgin olive oil. And when you eat it, it feels light. I've had a lot of people be surprised that they could eat the whole pie."

As a pizza expert, Lombardi generously gives his stamp of approval to the best of the rest. Nearby, the ever-popular and ever-crowded **John's Pizza** (278 Bleecker St, between Morton St and Seventh Ave S, 243.1680) also offers some very fine coal-fired, brick-oven pizza. Although there are other locations around town, the original **John's** is still the best. When in Brooklyn, stop in at **Patsy's Pizza** (19 Old Fulton St, between Water and Front Sts, Brooklyn Heights, 718/858.4300); the sauce and dough are homemade and the coal-fired, brick-oven–baked crust is crisp and delicious. Although this place is pretty new on the pizza parade, owner Patsy Grimaldi earned his stripes from his late uncle, who started the acclaimed **Patsy's** in **East Harlem.** Also in Brooklyn is **Totonno's** (1524 Neptune Ave, between W 15th and W 16th Sts, Coney Island, 718/372.8606), where the recipe for the sauce goes back a hundred years. The pizzeria itself has been around since 1924. And don't even think about asking for toppings here—these babies are strictly for purists.

26 Thai House Cafe ★$ The background Muzak is the only serious drawback at this small, unassuming, and generic-looking place. The authentic Thai food includes lemongrass soup, spicy half-duck in coconut curry, and a dish called Thai Boat (steamed seafood with Thai herbs served in a foil basket). Another plus is the friendly, helpful service. ♦ Thai ♦ M-Sa lunch and dinner. No credit cards accepted. 151 Hudson St (at Hubert St). 334.1085

Capsouto Frères

27 Capsouto Frères ★★$$$ The *frères* (brothers) who own this place—one of TriBeCa's original trendsetters—are almost always on hand to make their guests feel welcome. Drop in at the bar for a midafternoon cup of espresso, or linger over a long dinner. The menu reflects French and American styles, and there are always some specials worth sampling, as well as good desserts. Try the shrimp and scallops on a bed of pasta, duck with ginger and cassis, cassoulet, or poached salmon with vinaigrette. Be sure to save room for one of the luscious desserts, including chocolate, raspberry, and praline soufflés (not served during brunch), *tarte tatin* (upside-down apple tart), ice-cream terrine, and profiteroles. ♦ French ♦ M dinner; Tu-F lunch and dinner; Sa-Su brunch and dinner. Reservations recommended. 451 Washington St (at Watts St). 966.4900

28 Nosmo King ★★$$$ Take a second look at the name and you'll understand why smokers have always had to huddle outside the front door for a nicotine fix. The smoke-free dining room is charming, with fish lights over the bar, towers of jade-glass coffee cups, huge crystal chandeliers, and roomy banquettes. There's a commitment here to organic and free-range ingredients creatively and deliciously prepared. Try the calamari-and-octopus salad with mesclun, red-pepper strips, and *tapenade* (a thick paste of capers, anchovies, olives, olive oil, and lemon juice); warm skate salad; grilled rainbow trout; or seared tuna with white beans, served with lime-marjoram vinaigrette. Some desserts feature little or no dairy products; others, such as basmati-rice pudding with orange-rum sauce, are just too good to resist. ♦ American ♦ M-F lunch and dinner; Sa-Su dinner. 54 Varick St (at Canal St). 966.1239

What's in a name? Made with milk, seltzer, and chocolate syrup (no eggs, no cream), the egg cream—the quintessential New York beverage—has been a favorite since the turn of the century.

29 Triplet's Roumanian Restaurant ★$$$ As the name suggests, this place is owned and run by identical triplets, brothers who were separated at birth and reunited at age 19. Once inside, don't be misled by the decidedly un-Roumanian decor; the food is as authentic as it gets this far from the Danube. Stuffed cabbage and good professional egg creams made at your table are among the highlights. ♦ Eastern European/Jewish ♦ Tu-W lunch; Th-F lunch and dinner; Sa-Su dinner. Reservations required. 11-17 Grand St (at Sixth Ave). 925.9303

THE Moondance DINER

30 Moondance Diner ★$ A refurbished diner with gussied-up diner fare, this spot jibes with the creative atmosphere of the neighborhood. Soups, burgers, and sandwiches are the best bets. Barbecued chicken is moist, tender, and wonderfully sloppy. The coffee, tinged with cinnamon, is served as it should be—in a pitcher. Wine prices are good and breakfasts are great. ♦ American ♦ Daily breakfast, lunch, and dinner; Th-Sa 24 hours. No credit cards accepted. 80 Sixth Ave (at Grand St). 226.1191

31 Felix ★$$$ Another player in the see-and-be-seen intersection of Grand Street and West Broadway, this place, like **Lucky Strike, La Jumelle,** and **Jour et Nuit** (see below), attracts a cross section of models, downtown hipsters, and trendy professionals who dine on such simple bistro fare as roast chicken and steak *frites.* The outdoor cafe is a good place to people watch. ♦ French ♦ Daily lunch and dinner. 340 W Broadway (at Grand St). 431.0021

32 Jour et Nuit ★★$$$ The constant parade of beautiful people here may be distracting, but the food is too good to be treated merely as a prop. The chic, tightly packed upstairs dining room, where black-and-white abstract paintings hang on the wall and banquettes are covered in Native American blanket prints, offers a French menu that includes foie gras sautéed in raspberry sauce, tuna *tartare,* lobster cannelloni, roast duck with cider sauce, steak with shallot sauce, mocha *dacquoise*, and lemon tart. Downstairs, in what used to be referred to as "Siberia" (i.e., where no self-respecting scenester would want to sit), a sushi bar has been installed, earning this French bistro an "A" for originality. The wine list is small and contains some nice choices, generally in the higher price ranges. ♦ French/Japanese ♦ M-F dinner; Sa brunch and dinner; Su brunch. Reservations required. 337 W Broadway (at Grand St). 925.5971

32 Diva ★$ On weekends the action spills out onto the street, and this place is fashion models' central. It's calmer during the week and is a good place for basic pasta dishes, especially *rigatoni Divinita* (with *prosciutto di parma,* asparagus, peas, wild mushrooms, and a touch of cream). ♦ Italian ♦ M-F lunch, dinner, and late-night meals; Sa-Su brunch, dinner, and late-night meals. 341 W Broadway (between Grand and Broome Sts). 941.9024 ♿

33 La Jumelle ★$ This place must have been separated at birth from its twin (the name in French) **Lucky Strike,** just two doors down (see below). Although owned by different people, both are charmingly frumpy bars-cum-restaurants with bistro menus written on blackboards. The clientele at both is made up of the young and the trendy. Try the duck with olives or chicken with mustard sauce. ♦ French ♦ Daily dinner and late-night meals. Reservations recommended. 55 Grand St (between Wooster St and W Broadway). 941.9651

33 Lucky Strike $$ At this very popular late-night hangout, the food is the least of the attractions. This is a place people come to sit, talk, and smoke, and to be seen sitting, talking, and smoking. If you must eat, try the vegetable tart or steak *frites*. ♦ French ♦ M-F lunch, dinner, and late-night meals; Sa-Su brunch, dinner, and late-night meals. 59 Grand St (between Wooster St and W Broadway). 941.0479

34 Chez Bernard ★$ This charcuterie/cafe features Bernard Eloy's exceptional homemade pâtés, home-cured hams, house-smoked salmon, and other warm food, including beef stew and veal- or pork-stuffed cabbage (all are also available for takeout). Pieces of beef and homemade sausages can be purchased at the butcher counter, and delicious pastries, including an estimable *tarte*

tatin, are sold in the bakery section. If you're not in a hurry, pull up a chair and dig in. ♦ French cafe ♦ Daily breakfast, lunch, and dinner. No credit cards accepted. 323 W Broadway (between Canal and Grand Sts). 343.2583

34 Le Streghe ★$$ "Witches" (as the name translates from Italian) are the theme at this trattoria, where the ocher walls are covered with metal moon sculptures. If vivacious co-proprietors, Teresa Rovito or Maria Pezzella, are on the premises, either or both may well stop by your table. This place really picks up steam after 10PM on weekends, when it becomes a raucous social scene. Until then, it's a stylish spot for imaginative Italian food, some of which works well. Don't miss the poached shrimps and calamari on eggplant puree or green gnocchi with saffron cream. ♦ Italian ♦ M-F lunch and dinner; Sa-Su brunch and dinner. Reservations recommended. 331 W Broadway (at Grand St). 343.2080 ♿

35 L'Ecole ★★$$ This place is run by students of the **French Culinary Institute.** Alain Sailhac (formerly the chef at **Le Cirque** and **Le Cygne**) is the Dean of Culinary Studies here and Jacques Pepin (cookbook author) is the Dean of Special Events. Dishes are selected for their teaching value, so a fair number of classics usually appear on the menu. Offerings may include fish soup and rack of lamb with Provençal herbs, along with various pâtés and terrines. The quality can vary from day to day, but the food is generally well prepared and well priced. Diners also get a chance to play food critic by filling out the report card that comes with the check. ♦ French ♦ M-F lunch and dinner; Sa dinner. 462 Broadway (at Grand St). 219.3300

36 Pure Mädderlake This is an eclectic, spirited store with three identities: a florist specializing in fresh flowers that grow in English gardens; a home-furnishings boutique stocked with antique furniture; and a gift shop full of tabletop items, including an exclusive line of Viennese crystal that's expensive but exquisite. ♦ M-Sa. 478 Broadway (between Grand and Broome Sts). 941.7770

An early precedent of the currently popular prix-fixe dinners was an eight-course set meal offered by the fashionable Cafe Martin in 1899. Among the courses were lobster, beef, and a roast; the price was $1.25.

37 ñ ★$ Owner David Selig, with help from his sister Narea and architect **Chris Sullivan,** turned this long, narrow space on a lesser-traveled block into a casually elegant spot for tapas and drinks. The subtly colored and lit room contains several striking details, such as welded-penny lamp shades, copper-topped bars, bar-stool booths, and a mosaic-encrusted sink at the back of the room. The sausage dishes are bold and satisfying, and the *calamares* (squid) in a tomato and green-pepper sauce flavored with cloves, cinnamon, and laurel, and *ensaladilla de pulpo* (baby octopus in vinaigrette) are unusually delicate and tender. The well-chosen and affordable wine list, featuring excellent Spanish sherries, recently received an award from *Wine Spectator* magazine and in 1994 was rated among the top five wine lists in town by the *Daily News*. ♦ Spanish ♦ Daily dinner and late-night meals. No credit cards accepted. 33 Crosby St (between Grand and Broome Sts). 219.8856

38 Broadway Panhandler If the cookware item you're looking for isn't here, chances are it doesn't exist. This barnlike place has it all—sets of pots and pans, gadgets, high-quality knives, espresso machines, finely crafted copper pots, and much, much more. The prices are generally lower than at other such stores around town and the service is especially helpful. ♦ Daily. 520 Broadway (between Broome and Spring Sts). 966.3434

39 Gourmet Garage This produce emporium offers a wide variety of goods at decent prices. The fruits and vegetables, cheeses, and other shelf items aren't as artfully displayed as in nearby **Dean & DeLuca** (see below), but you pay a lot less. Whether you're looking for a supply of crusty breads, blood oranges, portobello mushrooms, sun-dried tomatoes, calamata olives, parmigiano reggiano, English farmhouse cheddar, or one of several chutneys, this store probably has it. ♦ Daily. 453 Broome St (at Mercer St). 941.5850

40 The Cupping Room Cafe ★$$ Waffles with berries, giant muffins, bagels with fixings, and a choice of terrific coffees and teas draw a fiercely loyal crowd at this cozy cafe. Be prepared to wait at brunchtime. ♦ Continental ♦ M breakfast, lunch, and dinner; Tu-F breakfast, lunch, dinner, and late-night meals; Sa brunch, dinner, and late-night meals; Su brunch and dinner. Reservations recommended for dinner. 359 W Broadway (at Broome St). 925.2898

40 Kenn's Broome Street Bar $ Frozen in time, this dark room looks exactly as it did 20 years ago, and the menu hasn't changed a bit either. The burgers served on pita bread, soups, and such basic sandwiches as tuna are all good. ♦ American ♦ M-F lunch, dinner, and late-night meals; Sa-Su brunch, dinner, and late-night meals. 363 W Broadway (at Broome St). 925.2086

41 Mika ★★$$ The restaurant's name comes from a misspelling of owner Mica Sharon's nickname, which occurred back when she worked at **Tribeca Grill.** Born in Germany and raised in Israel, this cosmopolitan SoHo resident noticed that her neighborhood was lacking a comfortable, relaxing place for good sushi. She decided to marshall her restaurant experience and open one. The long, narrow dining room with navy touches and circular gold fixtures on the wall is both pretty and comfortable. Chef Kenji Asano prepares unusual and sometimes spectacular sushi. Try the whimsically named Tootsi Roll (with crab meat, avocado, flying fish roe, and cucumber), house roll (a mixture of fluke, oba, shrimp, avocado, and flying fish roe), and Mika roll (with smoked salmon and papaya). Cooked dishes include grilled salmon with vegetable stir-fry; skewers of beef, chicken, squid, or scallops wrapped in bacon; and a succulent, rare seared tuna with scallion pesto and somen noodles. ♦ Japanese bistro ♦ Daily lunch and dinner. 349 W Broadway (between Grand and Broome Sts). 941.9537

42 Manhattan Brewing Co. $$ Once a Con Edison power station, this massive building is now a microbrewery and restaurant. At any given time four or five ales are brewed on the premises, ranging from the very pale to the more full-bodied, including a seasonal choice: Honey Winter Beer, Wheat Beer (in summer), and an Ocktoberfest brew. The accompanying fare is better-than-usual bar food—wild-mushroom strudel, shepherd's pie, and roast chicken. For dessert, there's a stout ice cream.

♦ International ♦ M-Th, Su lunch and dinner; F-Sa lunch, dinner, and late-night meals. Reservations recommended for dinner Friday and Saturday. 42 Thompson St (at Broome St). 925.1515 ⅃

43 Country Cafe ★★$ SoHo doesn't lack for cozy French bistros, but there's an intimacy and friendliness about this place—owned by Alain Castel of Gramercy Park's **Pigalle**—that puts it above the others. The rustic decor starts with the rooster sign outside and continues inside with pale yellow walls dotted with illustrations of farm animals, wood pumpkins on shelves, and dried flowers scattered artfully about. The delicious food is also earthy—try the wild-mushroom casserole, onion tart, cornish hen with tarragon juice, hanger steak with shallot sauce, and the rich *tarte tatin*. There's also a good, inexpensive wine list. Sounds of Edith Piaf fill the room, adding to the Gallic ambience. The only negative is the sometimes long wait on weekends. ♦ French ♦ M dinner; Tu-F lunch and dinner; Sa-Su brunch and dinner. No credit cards accepted. 69 Thompson St (between Broome and Spring Sts). No phone

44 Tasca Porto ★★$ The below–ground-level dark room of this restaurant, decorated with wooden tables and wrought-iron chandeliers that look like fishing lights, resembles a bar on a Portuguese fishing dock. That was the intention of owners Jose de Meirelles and Philippe Lajaunie (also the proprietors of **Les Halles** in Murray Hill)—to create an easygoing, slightly rough-hewn spot in which to enjoy Portuguese tapas. There are 70 choices, many vividly spiced and utterly delicious, including sardines *escabèche* (in a spicy marinade), codfish pancakes, spicy tiger shrimp, grilled calamari, and lamb tenderloin with cumin. There's also an extensive list of Portuguese wines by the glass. ♦ Tapas ♦ M-F dinner and late-night meals; Sa-Su brunch, dinner, and late-night meals. No credit cards accepted. 525 Broome St (between Sixth Ave and Thompson St). 343.2321

45 Alison on Dominick Street ★★★$$$ It took owner Alison Becker Hurt several months to replace chef Tom Valenti after he decamped for **Cascabel** near Little Italy, but her eventual choice, Daniel Silverman, has settled in nicely and is turning out solid versions of the restaurant's signature hearty French food. Try the oyster stew with leeks and potatoes, sliced duck breast over lentils and cabbage with a sherry and cider-vinegar sauce, braised beef shin in red-wine sauce, roasted quail with currant couscous, seared tuna with fricasee of artichokes, plum tart, and pear cake with caramel sauce. The wine list is well chosen and not outrageously priced. The candlelit, whitewashed room, decorated with black-and-white photos, has been long considered one of the most romantic spots in town. ♦ French

country ♦ Daily dinner. Reservations recommended. 38 Dominick St (between Varick and Hudson Sts). 727.1188

46 Bell Caffè $ The neighborhood artists who hang out here want to keep this place a secret, lest the crowds that choke the streets east of Sixth Avenue begin to encroach. The food is decent (homemade breads, soups, and vegetable pies), but the scene is more the point. The decor is eclectic and fun: an assemblage of stuff saved from the garbage dump by co-owner Kurt, obviously a skillful scavenger. Check out the bathrooms, where the decor reaches its zany apex. There's live music every night and never a cover. ♦ Cafe ♦ Daily lunch, dinner, and late-night meals. 310 Spring St (between Hudson and Greenwich Sts). 334.2355

47 The Ear Inn $ The building that houses this dark and dusty bar/restaurant built in 1817 has been designated a landmark. Back then, the shoreline was only five feet away from the entrance, and the joint was full of seafaring rowdies. Today, it serves a landlubbing crowd decent pub food, including burgers and sandwiches. This place is on SoHo's outskirts, but worth the detour for its weekend poetry readings and what some maintain is the best jukebox in town. ♦ American ♦ M-Sa lunch, dinner, and late-night meals; Su brunch, dinner, and late-night meals. 326 Spring St (between Greenwich and Washington Sts). 226.9060

48 Let Them Eat Cake ★$ Don't come to this bakery/cafe unless you're willing to surrender to dessert; one look at the pecan pie, chocolate-chip fudge cake, or carrot cake, and the strictest dieter's resolve will turn to jelly. Those who don't live by cake alone could try one of the homemade soups, a bowl of chili, or a sandwich. ♦ Bakery/Cafe ♦ M-F breakfast and lunch. 287 Hudson St (at Spring St). 989.4970

49 Sullivan Street Bakery Joe Allen, proprietor of **Joe Allen's** and **Orso** in the Theater District, is also part owner of this bakery. The bread made here can be found at his and many other restaurants in the neighborhood, among them **Jean Claude** and the **Cub Room** (see below). The dense, crusty, and delicious breads include *genzanese* (a peasant sourdough), semolina, and rosemary focaccia. A nice touch: The staff will let you sample before buying. Daily. 73 Sullivan St (between Spring and Broome Sts). 334.9435 ⅃

49 The Ravioli Store John Zaccaro Jr.'s original venture before opening **Cascabel** was this pasta emporium. Here ravioli are made with dough and fillings that go way beyond the usual beef, spinach, or cheese. Try black beans and peppered monterey jack in blue-corn ravioli, lobster and scallop mousse in egg dough, and wild-mushroom and white-truffle saffron ravioli. There are also varieties of freshly cut flavored pastas, including lemon parsley, carrot, and tomato coriander; some must be ordered in advance. M-Sa. 75 Sullivan St (between Broome and Spring Sts). 925.1737

50 3 Degrees North $$ Richard Picasso, grandson of the famed artist, previously operated the smoky **European Cafe** in this space. Together with Malaysian Princess Zerafina Idris, he now presides over this bustling overnight success. The Malaysian cuisine is hit-and-miss, with a tendency toward overcooked meats and oily sauces. Stick to the simple dishes, such as green beans with *belacan* (dried-shrimp sauce) and *ching yue* (steamed whole red snapper with scallions). ♦ Malaysian ♦ Tu-F dinner and late-night meals; Sa-Su brunch, dinner, and late-night meals. Reservations recommended. 210 Spring St (at Sixth Ave). 274.0505

51 Nick & Eddie ★★$$ This dependable restaurant is a local favorite—the bar starts filling up in late afternoon. The menu is solid American fare—smoked trout salad with a garlicky dressing, grilled salmon, catfish, and tilapia (a moist, flaky fillet resembling snapper). Another good choice is shellfish and vegetables with curry, coriander, and pepper cooked in a clay pot. Go elsewhere, however, for dessert. ♦ American ♦ M-F lunch and dinner; Sa-Su brunch and dinner. Reservations recommended. 203 Spring St (at Sullivan St). 219.9090

52 Mezzogiorno ★★$$$ Designed by architect and interior designer **Roberto Magris,** this airy restaurant opens out onto the sidewalk during the warmer months. Highlights include wood-burning–oven pizzas (served at lunchtime and after 9PM) and beef carpaccio offered a variety of ways, although you can't go wrong with such pasta dishes as rigatoni with eggplant and ricotta or black linguine in a spicy tomato sauce. ♦ Italian ♦ Daily lunch, dinner, and late-night meals. No credit cards accepted. 195 Spring St (between Sullivan and Thompson Sts). 334.2112

If money is no object when selecting a bottle of wine, try a 1961 Château LaTour à Pomerol at Montrachet or a 1915 Clos de Roi at Box Tree. Each costs about $2,500.

52 Baluchi's ★★$ This oddly named Indian restaurant—owner Rakesh Aggarwal liked the sound of it—is a handsome, romantic place with apricot-sponged walls. The tableware and serving dishes are copper, adding to the elegant feel. Try the vegetable fritters, leg of lamb, and chicken *tikka masala* (cooked with tomato and cream). ♦ Indian ♦ Daily lunch and dinner. Reservations recommended for dinner. 193 Spring St (between Thompson and Sullivan Sts). 226.2828

53 Blue Ribbon ★★$$$ The kitchen of this bustling spot is open until very late, which is one reason it's a favorite stop for chefs who arrive after their own shifts end. The other incentive is the eclectic menu, featuring such dishes as duck breast with orange sauce, paella *basquez* (with seafood and chicken), and shrimp *provençale*. The wine list is small but well chosen, and desserts, such as the banana split, will transport you back to your childhood. ♦ Eclectic ♦ Tu-Su dinner and late-night meals. 97 Sullivan St (between Prince and Spring Sts). 274.0404

53 Melampo Imported Foods All sandwich shops should be like this place. Owner Alessandro Gualandi has elevated sandwich making to an art form: High-quality Italian ingredients sit atop a buttery focaccia. The sandwich names reflect Gualandi's personal associations—his friends' children, for example. Among the many good choices are Allison (prosciutto, smoked mozzarella, and sweet peppers) and Geppetto (*sopressata*—a mild sausage), eggplant caponata (cooked with onions, tomatoes, anchovies, olives, pine nuts, capers, and vinegar), bel paese cheese, and arugula). Be sure to scan the window on your way in or out: You'll find selected stories from *The New York Times* or movie box office receipts from *Daily Variety*. ♦ M-Sa. 105 Sullivan (between Spring and Prince Sts). 334.9530

54 Omen ★★$$ Quiet and attractive, this restaurant with exposed-brick walls, light fixtures wrapped in filmy white fabric, and gleaming dark tables has cultivated a loyal following. The namesake dish, *omen* (Japanese noodles served with a variety of toppings and flavorings), is a perfect introduction to the extensive menu, which includes a tuna steak with ginger, oysters-in-miso casserole, raw tuna with mountain yam and quail egg, yellowtail and string bean teriyaki sautéed with sake, and seafood tempura. Dig in and start tasting, but keep in mind that the delicious small-portion servings can add up to a mighty bill. ♦ Japanese ♦ Daily dinner. Reservations recommended. 113 Thompson St (between Spring and Prince Sts). 925.8923

55 Berrys ★$$ A convivial bistro, and one of SoHo's earliest culinary attractions, this dark, cozy place maintains its popularity with solid brunches and simple continental dinners, such as filet mignon in a cracked peppercorn glaze and duck confit. The menu changes every couple of months with the seasons. ♦ Continental ♦ M-F lunch and dinner; Sa-Su brunch and dinner. Reservations recommended; reservations required for

Sunday brunch. 180 Spring St (at Thompson St). 226.4394

56 Vucciria ★★$ Named for a food market in Palermo, Sicily, this cozy restaurant even looks like a market, with paintings of arcades, awnings, a cloud ceiling, and faux-marble columns. The cooking is correspondingly earthy and very satisfying. Try the penne with ricotta and eggplant, angel-hair pasta with seafood, and chicken paillard. The reasonably priced wine list, which is especially strong when it comes to reds, is composed of Italian and California varieties. ♦ Italian ♦ M-F lunch and dinner; Sa-Su brunch and dinner. Reservations recommended. 422 W Broadway (between Spring and Prince Sts). 941.5811

The Brunch Bunch

Nothing beats the luxury of being served breakfast in bed, but for those without room or butler service, the next best thing is rolling out of bed late on a Sunday morning and going to where the coffee's already made and the griddle is hot. This lazy late-morning/early-afternoon Sunday meal is a New York tradition, so popular that many places offer it on Saturdays too. The following is a sampling of New York's finest:

Cozy Corners

For dependably good food in a relaxed environment, **Sarabeth's Kitchen** (1295 Madison Ave, between E 92nd and E 93rd Sts, 410.7335; 423 Amsterdam Ave, between W 80th and W 81st Sts, 496.6280; and at the Whitney Museum, 945 Madison Ave, at E 75th St, 570.3670) is so popular that you may become faint with hunger while waiting for a table. Regulars maintain that the cornmeal waffles with apple butter and sour cream, apple-cinnamon French toast with bananas, and farmer's omelette with leeks, bacon, gruyère, and chunks of potato are easily worth the wait. Reminiscent of a grand Midwestern hotel dining room, **Mackinac Grill** (384 Columbus Ave, between W 78th and W 79th Sts, 799.1750) serves creative brunch dishes, including omelettes with Smithfield ham or salmon caviar, macadamia nut and coconut pancakes, and Eggs Benedict with Smithfield ham and spinach on a toasted brioche, and covered with chervil hollandaise. **Danal** (90 E 10th St, between Third and Fourth Aves, 982.6930) is a charming spot that looks as if it were decorated by a flea-market addict. One of the best brunch offerings here is a luscious French toast made from croissants, topped with cinnamon apples. Funkier still is **Yaffa Tea Room** (19 Harrison St, at Greenwich St, 274.9403), an idiosyncratic but comfortable room decorated with tapestries, sculptures made from plumbing fixtures, and wrought-iron furniture. The food is savory: scrambled eggs in puff pastry and fluffy waffles served with sautéed apples. **Paris Commune** (411 Bleecker St, between W 11th and Bank Sts, 929.0509) is a bohemian-looking **West Village** bistro with a roaring fireplace and a tin ceiling. It offers good omelettes and French toast, but it's been discovered, so be prepared to wait. For an attack of nostalgia, try

T (142 Mercer St, at Prince St, 925.3700) below the **SoHo** branch of the **Guggenheim Museum.** This quaint tea salon and shop has a variety of savory selections, ranging from a delicious smoked fish platter to tea waffles with apple chutney. In Brooklyn, stop by **Aunt Sonia's** (1123 Eighth Ave, at 12th St, Park Slope, 718/965.9526) for an eclectic menu that includes a smoked salmon platter, potato latkes, Eggs Benedict with salmon, and quesadillas.

Creative Kitchens

When making the scene in SoHo, try **Zoë** (90 Prince St, between Broadway and Mercer St, 966.6722), a handsome place that changes its brunch menu weekly. A typical sampling includes such delectables as banana-stuffed almond French toast, scrambled eggs with scallions and ham, and wood-oven pizzas. **Verbena** (54 Irving Pl, at E 17th St, 260.5454) offers such elegant selections as cinnamon toast with duck rillettes and red plum compote, herbed omelette with mushrooms and chorizo, and scrambled eggs with Osetra caviar, all served in a tastefully subdued room. Looking for Mr. Goodbrunch? At **Ferrier** (29 E 65th St, between Park and Madison Aves, 772.9000) the bar scene starts hopping as early as brunchtime, and the food—scrambled eggs with ham, mushrooms, and red wine in puff pastry, and challah French toast—is good too. At **Matthew's** (1030 Third Ave, at E 61st St, 838.4343) the kitchen's creativity sounds a wake-up call: lemon pancakes with blackberries, plums, and cinnamon honey; wild mushroom omelette with crisp pancetta and venison pepper steak and eggs.

Haute Hotcakes, Exceptional Eggs

Café des Artistes (1 W 67th St, between Central Park W and Columbus Ave, 877.3500), an elegant spot for any meal, is a positively charming place to brunch. Among the excellent choices are scrambled eggs and brioche with dill-marinated gravlax, a caviar omelette, and scallop salmon cakes with tomato basil sauce. The **River Café** (1 Water St, at the East River, Brooklyn Heights, 718/522.5200), with the New York skyline across the **East River** as a backdrop that somehow makes the food taste better ffers such brunch dishes as French toast made with marbled brioche and poached eggs with red flannel ash. For a vista of another river, try the **Hudson River Club** (4 World Financial Center, enter at 225 berty St, 786.1500) in a grand room overlooking e **Statue of Liberty**. Delicacies here include herbed otato pancakes with clabbered cream and caviar, nd omelettes with lobster, potato, and onion.

erhaps the most elegant buffet spread in town is at e formal **Le Regence** (37 E 64th St, between Park nd Madison Aves, 606.4647). Indulge in pâté, roast nderloin, poached salmon, iced crab claws and hrimp, a variety of vegetable salads, hot dishes— ouillabaisse, pasta with curried seafood, and hicken with Cabernet and truffle sauce—and a tunning array of desserts. Another opulent (but wer-priced) buffet of vegetable salads, pâtés, moked fish, oysters, roasted meats, and a huge ble of desserts is offered at **Le Pactole** (4 World nancial Center, enter at 225 Liberty St, 945.9444), here views of the **Hudson River** and the **Statue of iberty** complete the experience. If you can't imagine aving eggs without smoked salmon or caviar, **etrossian** (182 W 58th St, at Seventh Ave, 45.2214) is the obvious choice. Eggs Benedict at **avern on the Green** (W 67th St, at Central Park W, 73.3200) might be the same as you would find sewhere, but you can't beat the experience of eling as if you're eating them inside a crystal handelier.

Spectrum of Spices

ne very popular alternative to the traditional early unday meal is the gospel brunch, which celebrates the Lord's day with lip-smacking food and toe-tapping hymns. The downtown favorite, **Lola** (30 W 22nd St, between Fifth and Sixth Aves, 675.6700), tempts with such dishes as corn salsa omelettes, baby-back ribs Asian, and fried chicken. The original home of the gospel brunch and **Harlem**'s most famous nightclub, **The Cotton Club** (656 W 125th St, between Broadway and Riverside Dr, 663.7980), offers hearty food—fried chicken, grits, greens and apple tarts—and even heartier singing. But perhaps the most popular is **Sylvia's** (328 Lenox Ave, between 126th and 127th Sts, 996.0660), also in Harlem, which features top-notch, Southern-style cooking that attracts patrons from all over the city.

If gospel's not your style, go south of the border to **Mi Cocina** (57 Jane St, at Hudson, 627.8273), where the kitchen shines at brunch with poached eggs in roasted-tomato sauce with poblano chili strips and cheese, and scrambled eggs with Mexican sausage and *pico de gallo*. The sunny, brightly painted **Negril Island Spice** (362 W 23rd St, between Eighth and Ninth Aves, 807.6411) offers infectious Caribbean rhythms from a live band and the scent of island specialties—roti chicken, codfish fritters with avocado salsa, banana pancakes, and ginger-glazed ham and eggs. The tiny **Cafe Andrusha** (1742 Second Ave, between E 90th and E 91st Sts, 360.1128) has a blini-based menu with such toppings as salmon caviar and other Russian favorites, including herring and borscht, served with glasses of tea sweetened with cherry preserves. Sunday dim sum at the **Golden Unicorn** (18 E Broadway, at Catherine St, Second floor, 951.0911) provides an Asian alternative, and a very authentic version at that.

57 Barolo ★★$$$ During inclement weather, the dining room provides a sophisticated setting for excellent pasta and broiled fish dishes, but once the weather warms up, the scene moves to the back garden decorated with cherry trees. Try the tuna *tartare, cappelletti* with calamari and broccoli, grilled scallops with white beans, or steamed red snapper with clams and fennel. ♦ Italian ♦ M-Th, Su lunch and dinner; F-Sa lunch, dinner, and late-night meals. Reservations recommended. 398 W Broadway (between Broome and Spring Sts). 226.1102 ⚬

58 Boom ★$$$ Innovative creations at this popular SoHo spot for "world cuisine" range from Senegalese *mafta* (a peanut-based vegetarian dish) to avocado blinis with lobster, Ossetra caviar, and crème fraîche. The candlelit setting is eclectic yet romantic. ♦ Eclectic ♦ M-W lunch and dinner; Th-F lunch, dinner, and late-night meals; Sa brunch, dinner and late-night meals; Su brunch and dinner. 152 Spring St (between Wooster St and W Broadway). 431.3663

59 Kin Khao ★$$ The trendiest place around for Thai fare (the scene seems to overwhelm the food at times), this dark, cavelike spot offers decent versions of such dishes as *pla gung* (a hot-and-sour prawn salad with onions, chili, lemongrass, and basil) and *kwaytio ki mow* (sautéed spicy rice noodles with basil and tomatoes). For refreshment, try a Cosmopolitan (fresh lime juice, cranberry juice, Absolut Citron, and Grand Marnier), which arrives in a chilled martini glass. ♦ Thai ♦ Daily dinner. 171 Spring St (at W Broadway). 966.3939

60 Tennessee Mountain ★$$ The smells wafting down Spring Street will whet your appetite for the food: ribs, fried chicken, and vegetarian chili—but the aromas are usually better than the actual food. The frozen margaritas are sure to elevate your mood. ♦ American ♦ M-F lunch and dinner; Sa-Su brunch and dinner. Reservations recommended. 143 Spring St (at Wooster St). 431.3993

61 Manhattan Bistro ★$ In the front, the marble-topped tables and bar are great for a glass of wine and bowl of fish soup, or a cappuccino and dark-and-white chocolate mousse dessert. Farther back is a simple yet elegant dining room. Here, the best choices are homey French specialties: slow-cooked stews, such as coq au vin and *boeuf bourguignon,* and small steaks that come with delicious skinny fries. Those great potatoes show up again during brunch. ♦ French ♦ M-F breakfast, lunch, dinner, and late-night meals; Sa-Su brunch, dinner, and late-night meals. Reservations recommended for dinner. 129 Spring St (between Greene and Wooster Sts). 966.3459

62 Platypus 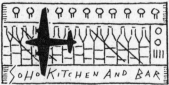 All sorts of upscale housewares are available here, from designer kettles and flatware by Alessi, Michael Graves, and Aldo Rossi to 18th- and 19th-century pine armoires, cupboards, and cribs. Godiva chocolates are sold as well. ♦ Daily. 126 Spring St (at Greene St). 219.3919

63 SoHo Kitchen and Bar ★$ Pizzas, grilled fish, and such basic pasta dishes as fettuccine with sun-dried tomatoes are the menu's mainstays. But the food takes second place to the theatrical interior designed by owner Tony Goldman–dramatic lighting, immense canvases, a black ceiling, and suspended airplanes. It also boasts Manhattan's longest wine list: 96 wines and 14 brands of champagne. Oenophiles shouldn't miss the "flights of wines," a heady experience, during which anywhere from four to eight wines within a specific category are sampled in two-and-a-half-ounce portions. ♦ American ♦ M-Th, Su lunch and dinner; F-Sa lunch, dinner, and late-night meals. 103 Greene St (between Spring and Prince Sts). 925.1866

64 Wolfman-Gold & Good Company The contents of this boutique make a strong argument for table setting as mode of self-expression, if not an art form. Fine china, linens, flatware, and glassware are offered here, among other home accessories, and the shop's open-stock selection of restaurant china means you can mix and match to your heart's content, especially if money is no object. ♦ Daily. 116 Greene St (between Spring and Prince Sts). 431.1888

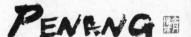

65 Penang ★★$$ This artfully designed restaurant (a fancier version of its sister in Flushing, Queens) looks a little like Walt Disney's idea of Malaysia, with a slanting straw roof suspended over the dining room, strings of white lights, and waitresses wrapped in sarongs. Try the beef *rendang* (strips cooked until tender with ground onions, chili peppers, coconut, and lemongrass) and the noodle, vegetable, and shrimp soup. ♦ Malaysian ♦ Daily lunch, dinner, and late-night meals. Reservations recommended. 109 Spring St (between Mercer and Greene Sts). 274.8883. Also at: 38-04 Prince St (near 37th Ave and Main St), Flushing. 321.2078

66 Spring Street Natural ★$ The healthy menu is mostly vegetarian, although even the nonconverted should be able to find something satisfying to eat in this airy place filled with greenery. The vegetable or seafood stir-fry and the roasted chicken with honey-mustard glaze are among the best choices. ♦ American ♦ M-Th lunch and dinner; F lunch, dinner, and late-night meals; Sa brunch, dinner, and late-night meals; Su brunch and dinner. 62 Spring St (at Lafayette St). 966.0290

67 Savoy ★★$$$ Run by chef Peter Hoffman and his wife, pastry chef Suzan Rosenfeld, this small, cozy place with a working fireplace features an eclectic menu that follows the seasons. During the winter months the menu offers such dishes as red Maine shrimp seviche with fennel, served with a salad of rice, beans, and green olives; and the signature dish, salt-crusted baked duck with walnut-pomegranate sauce. Desserts also change, but the chocolate-hazelnut ganache (iced) torte is an often repeated standout. The carefully chosen wine list offers some good values, especially at the higher end, and features the products of "artisan" vintners. ♦ Continental ♦ M-Sa lunch and dinner; Su dinner. Reservations recommended. 70 Prince St (at Crosby St). 219.8570

68 Dean & DeLuca The ultimate and original high-tech gourmet grocery is housed here in a blocklong, 9,700-square-foot space. Wonderful kitchenware, cookbooks, and samplings from the world's gastronomic centers are displayed with extraordinary panache. Added bonuses: a coffee/espresso bar, butcher, fish counter, and a full range of prepared take-out dishes. This place is a must for anyone passionate about food. ♦ Daily. 560 Broadway (at Prince St). 431.8350 &

69 Zoë ★★$$$ The cuisine keeps getting better and better at this stylish restaurant where the crowd is a fairly even mix of uptown and downtown types. Don't pass up the salmon *tartare* with chili potato chips and wasabi crème fraîche, grilled loin of lamb with horseradish mashed potatoes, or grilled salmon with Moroccan spices. Brunch offerings include banana-stuffed French toast with vanilla-maple syrup and raspberries and a sandwich of grilled portobello mushrooms and smoked onions on a semolina roll. The marble-top bar is a lovely place to sit and sip one of the many wines available by the glass. ♦ Contemporary American ♦ M-F lunch and dinner; Sa brunch and dinner; Su brunch. Reservations recommended. 90 Prince St (between Broadway and Mercer Sts). 966.6722 &

70 T ★$$ A very elegant salon and emporium below the Soho branch of the **Guggenheim Museum,** this is the perfect setting for downtown ladies and gentlemen who lunch. The airy space is whimsically decorated with chandeliers made of bronze teapots and cups, a long marble bar festooned with platters of apples, marbleized pillars, and in the emporium section, tables of unusual teapots and colorful canisters of tea. Most items on the menu have tea as an ingredient, although some stretch the point. The most successful dishes are crispy tea-roasted duck with peaches and Granny Smith tea waffles with apple chutney and maple ice cream. ♦ American ♦ M-Sa lunch and dinner; Su brunch and dinner. Reservations recommended. 142 Mercer St (at Prince St). 925.3700

71 Match ★$$ Late in the evening, the velvet rope comes out and a discriminating door person begins selecting which souls are hip enough to enter the crowded, hopping bar. But even during dinner hour, this place is a scene: The close-together tables are jammed, and if you come in without a reservation, expect some attitude and a long wait. The decor is serious SoHo—wood walls, green banquettes, blown-glass light fixtures, smashed-metal sculptures—and the food is a fusion of Asian and Southwest cuisines. There's a good, fairly extensive sushi list, including the elegantly wrapped Match roll (shrimp, cucumber, and eel). Other popular picks include spicy beef salad with mint, basil, and peanuts, and wok-seared bluefin tuna with sautéed butter greens. The sampler dessert has everything from chocolate cake to lemon tart. There's a well-chosen, fairly priced wine list. ♦ Fusion ♦ M-F lunch, dinner, and late-night meals; Sa-Su brunch, dinner, and late-night meals. Reservations required. 160 Mercer St (between Prince and Houston Sts). 343.0020. Also at: 33 E 60th St (between Park and Madison Aves). 906.9173

HONMURA AN

71 Honmura An ★★★$$$ This elegantly
spartan Japanese restaurant, with exposed
brick walls and wooden banquettes,
specializes in homemade soba noodles in
broth, filled with poultry, prawns, or
vegetables. There are also other exquisite,
flavorful dishes, such as prawn tempura (with
giant prawns flown in from Tokyo's Tsukiji
fish market), *momiji tataki* (Japanese rare
roast beef), and salmon *oroshi* (salmon caviar
and strips of smoked salmon mixed with
freshly grated daikon radish). ♦ Japanese ♦
Tu dinner; W-Sa lunch and dinner; Su dinner.
Reservations recommended. 170 Mercer St
(between Houston and Prince Sts). 334.5253

72 Jerry's ★$$ This is a bustling lunch spot for
SoHo's working population, especially the
gallery crowd (Jerry used to own the frame
shop down the street). Fresh salads,
sandwiches, and daily soups are served. The
dinnertime tempo is considerably slower, but
brunch can be madness. ♦ American ♦ M-F
breakfast, lunch, and dinner; Sa brunch and
dinner; Su brunch. 101 Prince St (between
Mercer and Greene Sts). 966.9464. Also at:
302 Columbus Ave (between W 74th and W
75th Sts). 501.7500

73 Fanelli Cafe $ A holdover from the days
when this was a neighborhood of factories,
this cafe has a gritty, tavernlike atmosphere.
The ambience is a greater draw than the
generally adequate food—except for the
terrific hamburgers and fries. ♦ American ♦
Daily lunch, dinner, and late-night meals. No
credit cards accepted. 94 Prince St (at Mercer
St). 226.9412

74 Prince Street Bar & Restaurant ★$ The
faithful clientele come as much for the lively
bar scene as for the fairly standard burgers,
salads, and sandwiches. On a more
interesting note, there are also Indonesian
specialties, including *gado gado* salad (with
peanut sauce and shrimp chips), spicy shrimp
jakarta (jumbo shrimp with brown rice and
broccoli), and beef *rendang*. ♦ Eclectic ♦ M-
Sa lunch and dinner; Su brunch and dinner.
125 Prince St (at Wooster St). 228.8130

74 Dean & DeLuca Cafe ★$ An airy, white-
brick space provides a refreshing backdrop
for a peaceful breakfast, lunch, or snack. Run
by the same people who manage the gourmet
food emporium of the same name (see
above), it's a good place to come on Sunday
morning to read the paper—thoughtfully
provided—sip a cappuccino, and munch
pastry. The salads are good too. ♦ Cafe ♦

Daily breakfast, lunch, and early dinner. 121
Prince St (between Wooster and Greene Sts)
254.8776. Also at: 75 University Pl (at 11th
St). 473.1908 &; 9 Rockefeller Plaza (at 49th
St). 664.1363 &

74 Whole Foods A full selection of everything
you need for a sound body and soul is
available here: vitamins, grains, fresh fish,
organic vegetables, kosher chicken and
turkeys, cosmetics, and an impressive
assortment of books to explain what you
should be doing with all these things. ♦ Daily
117 Prince St (between Greene and Wooster
Sts). 982.1000. Also at: 2421 Broadway (at
89th St). 982-1000 &

75 Kelley and Ping ★★$ The atmosphere is
pure Southeast Asian noodle shop, with bare
hanging light bulbs, floor-to-ceiling wooden
cases filled with Thai herbs and ingredients,
and an open kitchen that allows a full view of
the chef at work. Owned by **Kin Khao**'s (see
above) Brad Kelley and Lee Ping, this informal
place has been a neighborhood favorite since
it opened. Try *yam woosen* (clear noodles
with chicken, shrimp, scallions, and red
onion), Malaysian curried noodles, and
lemongrass chicken. Serious cooks and
kitchen dabblers may want to buy the
ingredients in the surrounding cases on sale
at the restaurant. ♦ Asian ♦ Daily lunch and
dinner. 127 Greene St (between Prince and
Houston Sts). 228.1212

76 Casa La Femme ★$$ SoHo's version of
the Casbah, this romantic place resembles a
Moroccan desert oasis at night, right down
to the white tents around the banquettes for
privacy. There's a decent menu including
harira (tomato, chickpea, and lentil soup);
grilled octopus; lamb salad with dates,
oranges, pine nuts, and *frisée* (curly endive);
Moroccan vegetable *tajine* (a stew of fruits
and vegetables with pistachio couscous);
grilled salmon with roasted beets; and
seared tuna with coriander. ♦ Eclectic ♦
Daily dinner. Reservations recommended.
150 Wooster St (between Prince and
Houston Sts). 505.0005 &

Tennessee Mountain is one of the smaller
barbecue places in town, but it still goes through
a lot of food: Customers consume 1,000 pounds
of chicken per week and 300 pounds of ribs.

77 SoHo Wine & Spirits Welcome to what may very well be the most civilized, not to mention the best-stocked, small wine store in town. You won't encounter any wine snobbery in this well-organized, well-designed outlet, which also carries the city's most extensive choice of single-malt Scotch whiskeys. ◆ M-Sa. 461 W Broadway (between Prince and W Houston Sts). 777.4332

77 I Tre Merli ★$$$ The exposed brick walls and high ceiling give this Italian restaurant and wine bar a quiet charm. Though the service can be inattentive, the food—especially the raw artichoke salad and the pasta—is quite good. During the summer, the tables spill out onto West Broadway. ◆ Italian ◆ M-F lunch, dinner, and late-night meals; Sa-Su brunch, dinner, and late-night meals. Reservations recommended. 463 W Broadway (between Prince and W Houston Sts). 254.8699

78 Amici Miei ★$$$ Another SoHo venue to eat and be seen, this place features a wood-burning oven that turns out good pizza, focaccia, and grilled shrimp. The pastas are popular, particularly the gnocchi, spaghetti with Manila clams, and homemade black squid-ink pasta with spicy tomato sauce. ◆ Northern Italian ◆ M-F lunch and dinner; Sa-Su brunch and dinner. 475 W Broadway (at W Houston St). 533.1933

For Lovers Only

For dinner with that special someone, New Yorkers and visitors alike look for a quiet room, subtle lighting, and maximum privacy. Candles and fresh flowers are de rigueur, but fireplaces, gardens, and fantastic views are definite pluses. And they demand that the food be top-notch. Fortunately, there are a number of places that warm the heart:

Café Nicholson (323 E 58th St, between First and Second Aves, 355.6769) Low lighting, antique furniture, and a small American/French menu featuring soufflés conspire to play Cupid here, but be sure to call ahead as this place keeps capricious hours.

Casa La Femme (150 Wooster St, between Prince and Houston Sts, 505.0005) Like characters out of an *Arabian Nights* tale, you and your sweetheart can pull a gauzy tent closed around your table as you feast on Moroccan cuisine in this dimly lit, exotic place.

March (405 E 58th St, between Sutton Pl and First Ave, 754.6272) This cozy town house is the perfect setting for intimate conversations over chef Wayne Nish's unique, multicultural menu.

Eros (1076 First Ave, between E 58th and E 59th Sts, 223.2322) As its name suggests, this place is a sultry spot for Greek fare. Owned by the same team as **Casa La Femme,** it has dim lights, very private tables, and banquettes for two. Even the women's room is candlelit.

La Colombe d'Or (134 E 26th St, between Third and Lexington Aves, 689.0666) Intended to resemble a bistro in the south of France, this place with its brick walls, Provençal fabrics, and intimate lighting succeeds charmingly.

Marys (42 Bedford St, between Leroy St and Seventh Ave S, 741.3387) A slanting 1820 town house is the setting for seasonal eclectic American fare. The roaring fireplaces and federal-style drapes make this a very popular place for amorous gay men.

La Metairie (189 W 10th St, at W Fourth St, 989.0343) This cozy French outpost is rustic in feeling and very romantically lit.

New City Cafe (246 DeKalb Ave, at Vanderbilt Ave, Fort Greene, Brooklyn, 718/622.5607) Creative American cuisine is served in a small, brick-walled dining room with a fireplace, guaranteed to warm things up when it's cold outside. In nice weather, sit in a garden-bower setting, and watch *amour* bloom.

One If By Land, Two If By Sea (17 Barrow St, between W Fourth St and Seventh Ave S, 228.0822) Within Aaron Burr's former town house is *ne plus ultra* romance complete with a pianist, a roaring fireplace, candlelight, and decadently rich continental fare.

The Rainbow Room (30 Rockefeller Plaza, between E 49th and E 50th Sts, 632.5100) You can pretend you're Fred and Ginger whirling around the revolving dance floor with the lights of New York twinkling around you. The continental fare here is elegant and showy.

River Café (1 Water St, at the East River, Brooklyn Heights, Brooklyn, 718/522.5200) In addition to fine American cuisine, the picture-postcard view of the Manhattan skyline makes this one of the most sensual spots along any waterfront.

Rubyfruit Bar & Grill (531 Hudson St, between Charles and W 10th Sts, 929.3343) Set in a Greenwich Village town house, this restaurant catering primarily to lesbians serves a gourmet turn on American home-style cooking. It has exposed-brick walls, private booths in the back, low lighting, and candles.

The Terrace (400 W 119th St, at Morningside Dr, 666.9490) The classic French dishes are an accompaniment to the shimmering candles and the views that seem to go on for miles.

79 Can ★$$ Stylish presentations of French-Vietnamese fare are served at this attractive restaurant, designed by Japanese architect **Stomu Miyacaki** to resemble an art gallery. There are two levels–downstairs is the bar area, and upstairs a skylit dining room—and an interesting series of "water paintings," which are also the work of the architect. Try the Vietnamese pâté, barbecued beef in vine leaves, lemongrass duck, grilled stuffed squid with pork, and Vietnamese curried chicken. ◆ French/Vietnamese ◆ Daily lunch and dinner. Reservations recommended for dinner. 482 W Broadway (at W Houston St). 533.6333

80 Arturo's Pizzeria ★$ Some say the crowd here is an overflow from **John's Pizzeria** a few blocks away, while others argue that this place is better. Although the quintessential-pizza-experience debate rages endlessly on, it's safe to say that both places turn out some of the city's best brick-oven, thin-crust pies. However, if you want live jazz, come here any night after 8PM. ◆ Pizza ◆ Daily lunch, dinner, and late-night meals. 106 W Houston St (at Thompson St). 677.3820 ♿

81 Milady ★$ This neighborhood bar is frequented by locals who come here for a beer and conversation. The simple entrées include great burgers and salads. ◆ American ◆ Daily lunch and dinner. 162 Prince St (at Thompson St). 226.9340

81 Vesuvio's Bakery A SoHo landmark, this charming storefront has been selling chewy loaves of bread, breadsticks, and immediately addictive pepper biscuits since 1928. If you want to catch up on neighborhood goings-on, speak to owner Anthony Dapolito, one of SoHo's genuinely concerned citizens. ◆ M-Sa. 160 Prince St (between W Broadway and Thompson St). 925.8248

82 Raoul's ★★$$$ The fare at this reliable, consistently popular spot is as French as it gets in SoHo, which may be as French as it gets anywhere in the US. This lovely old-fashioned bistro has wood floors, an Art Deco bar, leather booths, and an old stove in the middle of the room. In pleasant weather, diners can sit in the garden room in back of the kitchen. Try the pan-seared foie gras, steak au poivre, and rare breast of duck with figs. The extensive wine list (120 selections) includes French, Italian, Spanish, American, and Australian wines. For some spirited entertainment, a tarot-card reader is on hand Sunday through Wednesday from 7PM until midnight. ◆ French ◆ M-Th, Su dinner; F-Sa dinner and late-night meals. Reservations recommended. 180 Prince St (between Thompson and Sullivan Sts). 966.3518

83 Cub Cafe ★$ Around the corner from the more upscale **Cub Room** (see below) is this more casual cafe serving simpler food: lamb stew, grilled chicken, sandwiches, and fruit crumble. ◆ Cafe ◆ M-F breakfast, lunch, and dinner; Sa-Su brunch and dinner. 183 Prince St (between Thompson and Sullivan Sts). 777.0030 ♿

83 Daniel's Market This sparkling white-tile butcher shop has a French spin, selling homemade sausages including *boudin noir* (blood sausage) and *boudin blanc* (a veal, cream, and egg sausage), pâtés, quiches, roast chickens. There are the usual cuts of meat, pork, and chicken, as well. Also offered are such morning essentials as *pain au chocolat* (a chocolate-filled croissant). ◆ Daily. 179 Prince St (between Thompson and Sullivan Sts). 674.0708

84 Cub Room ★$$$ The bar scene is primeval, especially on weekends, but entirely another world exists in the handsome wood-and-brick dining room in the back—sophisticated and suave, but friendly. Chef Henry Meer, formerly sous-chef at **Lutèce,** wanted to create high-level cuisine without the snootiness inherent to gastronomic temples, and he's succeeded for the most part. Some dishes that work include lobster salad with mango, duck confit, baby beets, and grilled onion; roasted quail with French lentils; fillet of black bass with onion confit, mushrooms, and *pommes Anna* (potato chips layered and pressed into a scallop-shaped garnish); and the mission-fig *tarte tatin*. ◆ American ◆ M-F dinner; Sa-Su lunch and dinner. Reservations required. 131 Sullivan St (between Prince and W Houston Sts). 677.4100 ♿

85 Jean Claude ★$ A picture of this brightly lit, tiny, smoky, bustling room decorated with shafts of wheat and wine bottles should be in the dictionary under "bistro," so thoroughly does it look the part. The food, however, sometimes takes a back seat to the convivial atmosphere. Appetizers are uneven; stick to the mesclun salad with goat-cheese croutons and olive dressing. The entrées are more successful; good choices include roast pork loin with Pommery mustard and roast game hen with herb risotto. ◆ French ◆ Daily dinner. Reservations recommended. No credit cards accepted. 137 Sullivan St (between Prince and W Houston Sts). 475.9232

85 Once Upon a Tart ★$ This is the kind of easygoing place every neighborhood could use—salads, sandwiches, soups, and baked goods can be taken out or ordered from one of the marble-topped tables, where diners are treated to the sounds of 1930s jazz. The sandwiches and salads change daily, but the menu usually includes a roasted chicken sandwich with oven-baked tomatoes and tarragon vinaigrette; a goat-cheese sandwich with artichokes, baby greens, and black-olive vinaigrette; and fresh vegetable slaw. Don't miss the rich, smooth onion soup. The high-quality, flaky tarts filled with vegetables, pumpkin, pecans, and apples are scrumptious; and the banana-poppyseed muffins are great to take home for tomorrow's breakfast. ♦ Cafe ♦ Daily breakfast, lunch, and dinner. No credit cards accepted. 135 Sullivan St (between Prince and W Houston Sts). 387.8869

86 Joe's Dairy Today, only about three storefronts remain of the old Italian-American enclave along Thompson and Sullivan Streets. This store, with its checkered tile floor and sweating glass cases, is one of them. Parmigiano reggiano is hewn from fragrant wheels, and sweet ricotta is drawn from moist, cool places. A few times a week intense acrid smoke pours from its basement door when mozzarella *afumicato* (smoked) is being made. ♦ Tu-Sa; call ahead for weekend hours. 156 Sullivan St (between Prince and W Houston Sts). 677.8780

Be Our Guest

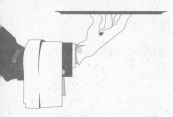

ity dwellers generally have fairly sophisticated palates, but most are cursed with woefully small kitchens. For those without the space or time to host a party themselves, having someone else do it is a viable alternative. Caterers can whip together wonderful food and provide the perfect ambience for any occasion. Although there are many culinary guardian angels to choose from, some are real standouts.

The Cleaver Company (229 W Broadway, at White St, 431.3688) Mary Cleaver, the owner, is a former food stylist, as well as a chef and cookbook writer. She makes "handmade" food her first priority, emphasizing pretty presentations. Cleaver is also known for her custom cakes.

Creative Edge Parties (410 E 13th St, between Ave C and First Ave, 473.2700) Whatever your needs—from private dinner parties to large corporate functions–this professional operation can organize the whole event from start to finish.

Feast and Fetes Catering (20 E 76th St, between Madison and Fifth Aves, 737.2224) The kitchen of this full-service company adjoins restaurant Daniel's, and both share chefs and recipes. It offers international cuisine to both private and corporate clients and can arrange sit-down dinners for up to 500 guests.

Flavors (8 W 18th St, at Fifth Ave, 647.1234) Chef Pamela Morgan owns this catering service and retail shop, and all food is prepared in her kitchen. Her cocktail/buffet for Martha Stewart's *Living Magazine* included herb topiaries.

Fletcher Morgan (432 W 19th St, between Ninth and Tenth Aves, 989.0724) World-famous chef—and co-owner—Hervé Rossano (formerly of Maxime's and Jour et Nuit) specializes in "Azure" cuisine, a blend of Asian and European flavors.

Food in Motion (309 W 17th St, between Eighth and Ninth Aves, 807.8935) Lloyd Zimet and Michelle Lovelace offer creative and sophisticated (yet unpretentious) cocktail parties and sit-down dinners featuring New American cuisine that borrows from French, Italian, and Asian fare.

Great Performances (287 Spring St, between Varick and Hudson Sts, 727.2424) One of the largest caterers in Manhattan, this company features a wide range of cuisines—from French to Pacific Rim, Southwestern to Tuscan—at dinners and cocktail receptions.

Herban Kitchen (290 Hudson St, between Spring and Dominick Sts, 627.2257) Specializing in eclectic American cuisine "in harmony with nature," this may be the only caterer that uses exclusively organic ingredients.

Manna Catering (24 Harrison St, at Greenwich, 966.3449) Owner/chef Dan Lenchner puts a personal stamp on his eclectic American kosher cuisine—a mélange of Asian, French, Italian, and Mediterranean flavors in unexpected combinations.

Moveable Feast (284 Prospect Park W, between 16th and 17th Sts, Brooklyn, 718/965.2900) Offering complete party planning, this company can provide for parties from 25 to 2,000 people. The creative cuisine is best categorized as contemporary international. An added plus: all cakes, desserts, and breads are homemade.

Spoonbread (333 E 75th St, at First Ave, 734.3204) This may well be the only catering company to actually star Off Broadway. A production of *Spoonbread and Strawberry Wine,* (which at press time was still on stage at the **American Place Theatre**) tells the story of Norma Jean Darden's family history through food–from slavery to the present time—and audiences are served a full meal during the performance. Otherwise, the seven chefs on staff cater assorted parties and galas, featuring a variety of cuisines, including African, Chinese, Southern, Continental, and Asian.

Taste (113 Horatio St, between Washington and West Sts, 255.8571) Exquisitely presented quality foods in season—carved vegetables with unusual garnishes served on black lacquered trays—are what distinguish Jon Gilman's eclectic and spirited cuisine.

87 Cafe Le Gamin ★$ A transplanted Parisian cafe (note the map of the Paris **Metro** on the wall), this is a perfect place for a morning wake-up jolt of café au lait, *croque monsieur* (grilled ham and cheese sandwich), or ham-and-cheese crepe. The menu is simple and the environment pleasing, although it can get a little much when what seems like the entire neighborhood piles in for lunch. ♦ Bistro ♦ Daily breakfast, lunch, and dinner. No credit cards accepted. 50 MacDougal St (between Houston and Prince Sts). 254.4678. Also at: 170 Waverly Pl (at Grove St). 807.7047

PROVENCE

87 Provence ★★★$$ From its rustic slate-blue painted wooden front to its charming garden in back, Michel and Patricia Jean's Provençal bistro has a lot to recommend it. The dining room is a simple but warm haven with ocher walls, wood accents, columns, and dried flower arrangements—*très romantique*. The food is decidedly vibrant. Start with the creamy and potent fish soup or *pissaladière* (a heady onion tart), and follow it with roasted chicken in garlic, roasted curried monkfish with saffron, or pan-roasted lamb with ratatouille. End this delicious dinner on a sweet note with a fruit tart du jour, chocolate marquise (a chocolate terrine with coffee *crème anglaise*), or a perfectly charred crème brûlée. The wine list includes some interesting choices; it spotlights, naturally, selections from Provence. ♦ French ♦ Daily lunch and dinner. Reservations required. 38 MacDougal St (at Prince St). 475.7500

88 Umaxatta ★$ This hole-in-the-wall fills a real need in the neighborhood: fresh, well-prepared, and reasonably priced Japanese food that can be eaten at one of the small tables or taken out. There's a daily *obento* box that includes such selections as a salad of bean thread noodles and chicken with sesame dressing, fish and vegetable sushi, and soba dishes. ♦ Japanese ♦ M-F lunch and dinner; Sa dinner. No credit cards accepted. 201 Prince St (between Sullivan and MacDougal Sts). 353.3099

FRONTIÈRE

88 Frontiere ★★$$$ The name of this romantic SoHo place refers to the French and Italian border—the regional influence of this cuisine. Old-fashioned stone walls, a fireplace, and intimate lighting add up to an inviting experience. The food is sophisticated but earthy; try the terrine of duck made with foie gras, prunes, and Armagnac; bowtie pasta with fresh seafood in garlic and saffron broth; and grilled *poussin* (young chicken) with lemon, mustard, and rosemary. ♦ Southern French/Northern Italian ♦ M-Sa lunch and dinner. Reservations recommended. 199 Prince St (between Sullivan and MacDougal Sts). 387.0898

89 Souen Downtown ★$ This pretty, airy Japanese-style room serves scrupulously healthy food that includes soba-noodle dishes and many delicious fish and vegetarian specialties. ♦ Macrobiotic ♦ M-F lunch and dinner; Sa-Su brunch and dinner. 210 Sixth Ave (at Prince St). 807.7421. Also at: 28 E 13th St (between University Pl and Fifth Ave). 627.7150

90 Le Pescadou ★$$$ Simply decorated and glass-enclosed, this charming cafe once specialized in seafood exclusively, but the menu now caters to meat eaters as well. The fish dishes, however, still shine: Try the snapper in parchment with herbs, grilled tuna with tomato *concassee* (crushed) and *pistou* (crushed basil, garlic, and olive oil), bouillabaisse, and herb-crusted rack of lamb. ♦ French ♦ M-F lunch and dinner; Sa-Su brunch and dinner. Reservations recommended. 18 King St (at Sixth Ave). 924.3434

Bests

Adrian Bryan-Brown
Broadway Press Agent, Boneau/Bryan-Brown

John's Pizzeria on Bleecker Street: Has the best pie crust in the world. The pizza is even better now that they have pepperoni. As the sign on the door clearly states: no slices! Tip: The lines can be long (no reservations). If there is a line, go next door to **John's Too** where they serve the same pizza. There's a **John's** on the **East Side** and one near **Lincoln Center,** but I pretend these aren't as good!

Union Square Greenmarket: A great seasonal market for vegetables, salads, flowers, plants, fish from Montauk, Amish dairy products, etc. Free samples of Pennsylvania pretzels and clam fritters! Best selection of apples and root vegetables in the city in the fall/winter months. Bargain lettuce, arugula, beets, herbs, etc. in the summer.

Faicco's: This neighborhood meat and cold cuts store makes an unbelievable *soppressata* sausage (take the hot over the sweet). Get a quarter-pound sliced and enjoy on a loaf of bread from **Zito's Bakery** across the street (go in the morning because the bread sells out), with a smear of "ready to use" brie from **Murray's Cheese Store**, which is next door.

Bubby's: A TriBeCa breakfast institution absorbing the overflow from the nearby DeNiroville restaurants t night: The **Tribeca Grill** (the appetizers and esserts are much better than the entrées) and **Nobu** he sakes served in bamboo logs remind me of mily outings to Benihana as a kid and are verpriced.) The food is very good, mixing traditional apanese/American with some nouvelle-ish style ixes. If you can't get a reservation, go around 10:20 M just before the kitchen closes and beg a place at e bar or an empty table. My favorite sandwich at ubby's is the fresh mozzarella and sun-dried mato.

hristopher Idone
od Consultant and Cookbook Author

ureole: Two lovely, airy flower-filled rooms serving e classiest and best American-style food in the ty—if not the country. Tea-smoked and fruit-moked fish and duck, salmon *tartare* that sparkles, nd scallops that shimmer between layers of thin aky potato. Desserts are outlandish.

ceana: The decor suggests a luxury yacht in the iddle of **Midtown.** Ruffled gravlax with sweet onion elish and golden crusted crab cakes with chipotle auce are a must.

arocco: Hip, downtown crowd that still dresses in lack. Fried calamari and lasagnette in a creamy heasant or rabbit sauce are outstanding.

Jo: Foie gras any time of the year and Pavlova for essert and the Valrhona chocolate cake oozes eaven.

afe Luxembourg: Still the best bistro in the city.

affè Lure: Mostly fish—little miracles served from a alley-sized kitchen—includes spinach with a sweet-otato puree that nestles warm lobster tossed in a azed Port wine–lemon sauce and pan-seared onkfish with potatoes pureed with pungent niçoise ives. There's a wood-burning pizza oven too.

an Domenico: Classic and elegant Northern alian dishes, *raviolo* encases a poached egg nothered in truffle butter, cuttlefish pasta and ame are spectacular. The cellar is a history of alian wines that will thrill the wine lover with deep ockets.

ar Six: Lots of long legs and bare midriffs—cluding the snappy help. The bar is packed from PM on. And the kitchen offers briny oysters, steak ites, and such well-prepared Moroccan specialties s *tajines* and *bastila*. Chic and easy downtown owd.

dochine: Tony Vietnamese clubhouse where odels, photographers, and designers ogle one nother and munch on Nos. 8, 16 and 12—fried ring rolls, steamed Vietnamese ravioli, and spicy eef salad.

obu: It's NOH theater 1990s—Sushi samurai repare the best, and dining can be the finest Asian xperience in the city.

ama Bar: Late-night hangout for smart and quirky ung things. Oyster bar and drinks.

Joe's Dairy: Mozzarella—plain, smoked, and wrapped in prosciutto—is made in the back-room kitchen and is still warm when you buy it. Quality and prices for *grana,* parmesan, and olives that can't be beat.

Sahadi: Best buy on quality olives, olive oil, dry pasta, coffee, pine nuts, dried fruits, herbs, and spices.

William Gillen and Patricia MacKenzie
Publishers, The *NY Food Letter*

Knowing you can buy the best bread. Our favorites include the Za'atar bread from **Damascus Bakery** on Atlantic Avenue in **Brooklyn,** and the bagels, still warm from the oven, at **H & H Bagels.**

Lunch or dinner anytime at **C.T.** with friends. We love to watch chef Claude Troisgros perform his French-Brazilian magic through the open kitchen.

Emerging from the subway at Canal Street in **Chinatown** and feeling like we've just arrived in a foreign land. When we watch women ferociously bargaining with fishmongers on the street, we understand what makes this New York neighborhood so special.

Wandering through **Dean & DeLuca** to see what's new and exciting.

Celebrating our wedding anniversary at **Restaurant Daniel.**

Shopping at **Sahadi** in Brooklyn, where we get a sense for the Middle East, combined with a nostalgic general store feeling.

Buying a fresh-killed bird at one of the more than 25 live poultry markets in New York City.

Knowing a pie is enough, but ordering the calzone too, at **John's Pizzeria.**

Biting into a custard-filled plum pastry from **Marquet Patisserie** in **Greenwich Village.**

Talking fruits and vegetables with the produce men at **Balducci's.**

Splurging on a wonderful and elaborate lunch at **Lespinasse** in the **St. Regis** hotel.

Spending an entire Saturday morning food shopping along Arthur Avenue in **the Bronx.** And finishing off with lunch at **Dominick's.**

Sinking our teeth into perfect porterhouse steaks at **Peter Luger's.**

Wandering through the aisles at **Lamalle Kitchenware** in the **Flatiron District.**

Sitting at a red-checkered covered table and ordering the burgers and home fries at **P.J. Clarke's.**

Li-Lac Chocolates, in Greenwich Village, for an old-fashioned valentine heart.

Running in to pick up a cupcake and a mug of coffee at the **Cupcake Cafe.**

Having a **Nathan's** hot dog and french fries only at the **Coney Island** original.

Greenwich Village

When it was first settled in the late 1700s, Greenwich Village—bordered by **Broadway** and the **Hudson River**, and **Houston** and **Fourteenth Streets**—was a pastoral refuge from the epidemics of smallpox, yellow fever, and cholera ravaging Manhattan's Wall Street area. A hundred years later, the area had become a retreat of another sort—a place where artists and other independent thinkers were regarded with tolerance and where rents were cheap. One house in particular, 75 Bedford Street (the narrowest house in the city—at just nine and one-half feet wide!), might be considered the cradle of American letters, having sheltered, at various times, Edgar Allan Poe, Horace Greeley, Walt Whitman, Mark Twain, and Edna St. Vincent Millay.

Since the beginning of the 20th century, the Village (as locals call it) has also been home to such famous artists and art movements as the Hudson River School, Edward Hopper and the Ashcan School, and Willem De Kooning and

he Abstract Expressionists. Political activists lived here too, among them ohn Reed and Upton Sinclair. But the neighborhood's bohemian reputation vas sealed as first the Beat generation, and after that the hippies, settled into he smoky cafes lining **Bleecker** and **MacDougal Streets**, and the jazz clubs on **Seventh Avenue South** and **West Third Street**.

The same air of tolerance that lured artists, Beats, and hippies to the Village also attracted the gay and lesbian communities. The gay rights movement began here in 1969 when a spontaneous protest against police brutality took place at a bar called, appropriately enough, **The Stonewall**. Today, the Universal Grill, **Orbit**, and **Rubyfruit** are also popular local hangouts.

Corresponding to its adventurous and very social image, the Village has traditionally been a mecca for restaurants, particularly small, idiosyncratic cafes of varying ethnicities which tend to stay open very late. On weekends, scads of visitors crowd the streets around **Sixth Avenue**, Bleecker Street, **Washington Square**, and **Sheridan Square** checking out posted menus and deciding where to dine.

Although the area is famous as a haven for alternative lifestyles and a generally fun place to be, there is another side to the Village. In the mid-1800s, prominent, wealthy families built beautiful town houses around **Washington Square** on what came to be called the "Gold Coast." These mansions are still home to the neighborhood's more affluent residents. Catering to Gold Coast denizens are elegant restaurants including the estimable **Gotham Bar and Grill** and **The Markham**, and such food emporia as the haute **Jefferson Market** for superb meat and fish or **Balducci's** *tavola calda* for sublime prepared foods.

Farther south, the neighborhood takes on a more down-to-earth, Italian cast, resulting from the Italian immigration wave at the turn of the century. Walking down Bleecker Street between Sixth and Seventh Avenues you'll see women going from store to store with string bags, buying pasta in one place, bread in another, fish in one shop, pork in another, as they have for generations.

In the small, eccentrically laid out streets of Greenwich Village, the radical and the traditional, the gay and the straight, the bourgeois and the bohemian, all live side by side. The Village welcomes everyone.

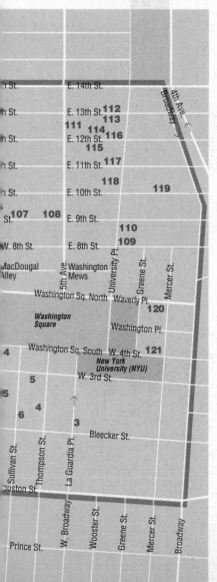

1 Toukie's ★$ This exuberant, very red place (particularly the banquettes and the theatrical velvet curtain at the dining room's entrance) is very much the reflection of extroverted hostess Toukie Smith, sister of the late clothing designer Willi Smith and former girlfriend of actor Robert DeNiro. But here Toukie takes center stage: Her likeness graces the menu and appears again in the diva mural alongside Lena Horne, Elizabeth Taylor, and Marilyn Monroe. She's also the hostess, and even unknowns get a kiss. The uneven menu is based on her recipes. Good bets are the smoky short ribs or fried chicken in cornmeal batter. Be sure to share the huge portion of the delicious peach cobbler with a dining companion. ♦ Southern ♦ Reservations recommended. M-F lunch and dinner; Sa dinner; Su brunch. 220 W Houston St (between Sixth Ave and Varick St). 255.1411 &

1 Brother's Bar-B-Q ★$ A funky dive loved for its down-home Southern grub, this place runs a close second to Harlem's well-known, more expensive, and somewhat more authentic **Sylvia's.** Come for heaping portions of tangy ribs, barbecued chicken smoked over hickory wood for 10 hours, and hefty side orders of mashed potatoes, collard greens, and corn bread. Monday is All-You-Can-Eat BBQ Night. ♦ Barbecue ♦ M-Th, Su lunch and dinner; F-Sa lunch, dinner, and late-night meals. 228 W Houston St (between Sixth Ave and Varick St). 727.2775

2 Aggie's ★$ It looks like an LA diner, but the attitude is pure New York, and you'll find the home-style cooking hearty no matter where you're from. This place has been here forever and has a loyal local following, especially at breakfast time. Aggie's friendly cats roam amid the tables to most customers' delight. ♦ American ♦ M-Sa breakfast, lunch, and dinner; Su lunch. No credit cards accepted. 146 W Houston St (at MacDougal St). 673.8994

2 Raffetto's Fresh pasta is made daily (witness the alchemy next door) and cut into a variety of widths before your eyes. Stuffed versions—including ravioli and tortellini—are also for sale, as are imported Italian products that will help you create first-rate dishes. ♦ Tu-Sa. 144 W Houston St (between Sullivan and MacDougal Sts). 777.1261 &

3 Ennio & Michael ★★$$$ Welcome to a well-run, cheerfully bustling trattoria. The large, airy dining room features photographs taken by New York radio personality Cousin Brucie, as well as paintings by local artists. The hearty food is first-rate and includes stuffed artichokes, *spaghetti puttanesca* (with tomatoes, capers, and olives), and salmon *cartoccio* (oven-cooked in a bag with white wine, butter, and vegetables). End the meal with possibly the best cannoli in New York. ♦ Italian ♦ Daily lunch and dinner. 539 La Guardia Pl (at Bleecker St). 677.8577

4 Grand Ticino ★★$$ A neighborhood fixture since 1919, this dark little Italian restaurant will satisfy the most romantic notions of an evening out in Greenwich Village—forest-green walls and burnished wood, muted wall sconces and linen tablecloths. The cuisine—homemade ravioli stuffed with goat cheese and arugula and osso buco with risotto—won't disappoint, either. For a dramatic dessert, order the hot zabaglione to be flambéed at your table. The restaurant scene with Olympia Dukakis from the movie *Moonstruck* was filmed here. ♦ Northern Italian ♦ Daily lunch and dinner. 228 Thompson St (between Bleecker and W Third Sts). 777.5922

4 El Rincon de España ★$$ The Spanish fare is good—if you stick to the seafood. The paella is the best bet. ♦ Spanish ♦ Daily lunch and dinner. 226 Thompson St (between Bleecker and W Third Sts). 260.4950

4 Il Ponte Vecchio ★$$ This bustling white dining room decorated with posters is one of the old reliable Italian places in the neighborhood, and it offers a large, traditional menu. Try the calamari with marinara sauce; asparagus topped with parmesan; spaghetti *amatriciana;* rigatoni with sausage and cream; fettuccine with sun-dried tomatoes and arugula; chicken with white wine, artichokes, mushrooms, and peppers; veal parmigiana; and old-fashioned cheesecake. Request *agnolotti* (half-moon–shaped ravioli stuffed with either meat or cheese) if it's not on the menu. ♦ Italian ♦ Daily lunch and dinner. Reservations recommended. 206 Thompson St (between Bleecker and W Third Sts). 228.7701

5 Il Mulino ★★★$$$ Behind this most unassuming facade is one of the best Italian restaurants in the Village. Only the wait at the crowded bar for a table—even with a reservation—brings it down a notch. Once seated in the cozy dining room with exposed-brick walls, begin with something from the antipasto table—carpaccio, clams casino, or the crispy fried zucchini. Move on to any of the pastas, including spaghetti *bolognese* or carbonara. Follow with one of the delicious entrées: chicken braised in wine and artichokes; fillet of beef in caper sauce; rolled veal with wine, cream, and wild mushrooms; o salmon with porcini mushrooms. For dessert indulge in the sinfully good chocolate mousse (this wicked concoction is made fresh daily), or if that's too rich, try a poached pear topped with fresh cream. Choose a wine from the extensive list or opt for the decent house red. ◆ Italian ◆ M-F lunch and dinner; Sa dinner. Reservations required. 86 W Third St (between Thompson and Sullivan Sts). 673.3783

6 Caffè Lure ★★$ Jean Claude Iacovelli, owner of the authentic Parisian-style bistro **Jean Claude** in SoHo, has created another raffish place for bistro specialties and Gauloise-smoke–laden conversation. The name refers to fishing lures, which are used for decoration all around the blue and ocher room. Not surprisingly, the fish is good here, as are the pastas, brick-oven pizzas, and confit of duck, among other French specialties. ◆ Bistro ◆ Daily breakfast, lunch, and dinner. No credit cards accepted. 169 Sullivan St (between Houston and Bleecker Sts). 473.2642

7 Caffè Borgia ★$ This old-world coffeehouse is authentic right down to the smoke-dulled mural. It's a perfect place to spend an afternoon sipping cappuccino and reading a good book. Since the cafe stays open very late, it's also a good place to wind up a bar crawl. ◆ Cafe ◆ M-F until 2AM; Sa-Sun until 4AM. 185 Bleecker St (at MacDougal St). 674.9589. Also at: 161 Prince St (between Thompson St and W Broadway). 677.1850

8 Le Figaro Café $ In the old days, this place was a Beat hangout, with underground shows downstairs. But that, as they say, is history. Today, this high-volume beanery caters to the weekend blitz of young tourists on Bleecker Street. ◆ Bistro/Cafe ◆ M-F until 2AM; Sa-Su until 4AM. No credit cards accepted. 184 Bleecker St (at MacDougal St). 677.1100

9 Chez Jacqueline ★★$$ This popular bistro owned and run by lively Jacqueline Zini specializes in dishes from her native Provence, including one of the best fish soups in town and a delicious beef stew niçoise. The garlic-laden *brandade* (warm salt-cod puree) is a good starter. ◆ French ◆ Daily lunch and dinner. Reservations required. 72 MacDougal St (at W Houston St). 505.0727 &

10 Au Bon Coin ★$ Parisian Franck Bismuth had dreamed of coming to New York for 20 years, and when he finally arrived in 1994, he immediately set about re-creating a Parisian-style cafe, full of reminders of his native city: posters, photographs, and Edith Piaf

recordings. Best bets are the crepes, sandwiches, onion soup, salads, and whatever entrée is on special that night. He also does an estimable *tarte tatin* (upside-down apple tart) and chocolate cake. ◆ French ◆ Tu-F lunch and dinner; Sa-Su brunch and dinner. 85 MacDougal St (between W Houston and Bleecker Sts). 673.8184 &

10 Caffè Dante ★$ Although Italian is spoken here, it's the strong coffee and the let-them-sit-as-long-as-they-want attitude that really makes this place authentic. Treat yourself to the cheesecake. ◆ Cafe ◆ M-F until 2AM; Sa-Sun until 4AM. No credit cards accepted. 79 MacDougal St (between W Houston and Bleecker Sts). 982.5275

11 Porto Rico Opened in 1907, this old-time coffee store isn't even one of the Village's oldest, but the long lines of caffeine-oholics on Saturday mornings is evidence that it's the uncontested favorite. Two reasons: the quality of the beans and the price. ◆ Daily. 201 Bleecker St (between MacDougal St and Sixth Ave). 477.5421

11 Pravinie Gourmet Ice Cream East meets West at this ice-cream parlor. Such rich, familiar flavors as butterscotch and chocolate chocolate chip are available, along with popular Asian varieties, including green tea, mango, and the exotic fruit durian, which some consider to be an acquired taste. ◆ Daily. 193 Bleecker St (between MacDougal St and Sixth Ave). 475.1968

12 Minetta Tavern ★$$ The caricatures and murals behind the old oak bar and elsewhere around this Italian restaurant will take you back to the Village of the 1930s. The menu offers standard Italian fare, which is nicely prepared, if not very exciting. ◆ Italian ◆ Daily lunch and dinner. 113 MacDougal St (at Minetta La). 475.3850

13 Caffè Reggio ★$ The first cafe in America, this fabulously dingy and dark place was built around 1785. It's a great spot for deep conversation or journal writing. Sip your coffee outside in nice weather. This landmark cafe appeared in the movies, *The Godfather II* and *Serpico*. ◆ Cafe ◆ M-F until 3AM; Sa-Su until 4AM. No credit cards accepted. 119 MacDougal St (at W Third St). 475.9557

VP2

14 Vegetarian Paradise 2 ★$ Vegetarian versions of iron steak and Peking duck are made out of bean curd, taro root, and other vegetable products. There's not a speck of meat in this restaurant, and only real die-hard carnivores will miss it. ◆ Chinese vegetarian ◆ Daily lunch and dinner. 144 W Fourth St (between MacDougal St and Sixth

Ave). 260.7130. Also at: 33-35 Mott St (between Bayard and Worth Sts). 460.6988

LA BOHÊME

15 La Bohème ★$$ With its open kitchen, floral arrangements, and dim lighting, this bistro is a cozy spot to enjoy specialties from Provence—confit of duck with orange and pear sauce and herb-crusted grilled chicken served with mashed potatoes and caramelized garlic. In warmer months, the room opens onto Minetta Lane, a charming, quiet street—something of a rarity in noisy Manhattan. The wood-oven pizza is another favored item, and owner Pari Dulac is one of the warmest hostesses in town. Desserts include lemon tart, *marquise du chocolat* (a light chocolate mousse cake) served with orange sauce, and cold lemon soufflé topped with ice cream and raspberry sauce. ♦ French ♦ M-Sa dinner; Su brunch and dinner. 24 Minetta La (at Sixth Ave). 473.6447

16 Da Silvano ★$$ An uneven, but quite interesting menu features central Italian fare. Start with chicken-liver *crostini* (croutons), followed by *rigatoni focaccia* (in a sauce of butter, cream, garlic, sage, rosemary, tomato, and double-smoked bacon), or one of the game dishes that include quail in a Barolo wine sauce with radicchio. The elegantly rustic rooms bring in a handsome, affluent clientele. The service is correct, and the wine list well-chosen. ♦ Italian ♦ Daily lunch and dinner. Reservations recommended. 260 Sixth Ave (between W Houston and Bleecker Sts). 982.0090 &

bar pitti

16 Bar Pitti ★$ Less expensive than **Da Silvano** (see above), this place–owned by Silvano's partner Giovanni—thrives when the weather is warm. Diners sit for hours at the outdoor tables lingering over bowls of competently made pasta and bottles of wine. ♦ Italian ♦ Daily lunch and dinner. No credit cards accepted. 268 Sixth Ave (between W Houston and Bleecker Sts). 982.3300 &

17 Trattoria Spaghetto ★$ For years this corner restaurant was the **Bleecker Luncheonette,** known for its green-pea–based minestrone and erratic opening hours. Now, under a new name and management, it's a bustling cafe serving decent, hearty pastas. In deference to old-time customers, the hearty minestrone is still on the menu. ♦ Italian ♦ Daily lunch and dinner. No credit cards accepted. 228 Bleecker St (at Carmine St). 255.6752

17 Caffè Lucca $ Visitors and a sprinkling of locals flock to this dark, dowdy cafe, decorated with fading posters of Lucca, for cappuccino and very good cakes. (Skip the pasta.) It's a smokers' paradise: The place is often filled with Italian tourists who, horrified at the city's no smoking rules, cluster here to puff away at will. ♦ Cafe ♦ Daily breakfast, lunch, and dinner. 228 Bleecker St (at Carmine St). 675.7331

18 Cent' Anni ★$$$ The food can be inconsistent, but when the kitchen is performing well you can get a very good meal in this casual, friendly, Tuscan-style trattoria. The menu features an extraordinary minestrone; a few outstanding pasta dishes—try penne with sun-dried tomatoes and fettuccine with rabbit; snapper roasted in garlic and oil; and a huge porterhouse steak. ♦ Italian ♦ M-F lunch and dinner; Sa-Su dinner. Reservations recommended. 50 Carmine St (between Bedford and Bleecker Sts). 989.9494 &

18 Tutta Pasta Ristorante ★$ An outgrowth of the store next door (see below), this cafe serves its freshly made pasta and sauces with above-average results. Linguine with white clam sauce, gnocchi with pesto, and meat-filled tortellini in a *bolognese* sauce are especially recommended. Meat, chicken, and fish dishes are also available, but it's best to stick with the pasta and the thin-crust, brick-oven pizzas. ♦ Italian ♦ Daily lunch and dinner. 26 Carmine St (between Bleecker and Bedford Sts). 463.9653. Also at: 504 La Guardia Pl (between Bleecker and Houston Sts). 420.0652; 160 Seventh Ave (between Garfield and First Sts, Brooklyn). 718/788.9500; 8901 Third Ave (between 89th and 90th Sts, Brooklyn). 718/238.6066; 108-22 Queens Blvd (between 71st and 72nd Sts, Queens). 261.8713

18 Bianca Pasta Neapolitan immigrants Fortunato and Tania DiNatale chose this location for their pasta store nearly 20 years ago because of its unique view: When the doors of **Our Lady of Pompeii Church** across the street were open, Tania could see clear through to the altar. In those days, they had one pasta machine churning out uniquely flavored pastas—artichoke, tomato, lemon, and mushroom among them. Today their factory makes about 40 kinds, including an exotic variety with saffron, black squid ink, corn, and fennel. Also offered are pasta sauces, barbecued pizza, a very tender homemade mozzarella, and various prepared foods, including stuffed artichokes and baked ziti. ♦ Daily. 24 Carmine St (between Bedford and Bleecker Sts). 242.4871

19 Trompe l'Oeil ★$$ Love is in the air in this open, pretty brick-walled room with murals and statues of lovers and white fabric draped romantically across the ceiling. Fans of Art Nouveau and Deco will appreciate the carved-wood bar with painted marquetry that was previously on a steamship. Like the decor, the food manages to be both sophisticated and homey; try pan-roasted salmon with garlic mashed potatoes or grilled shrimp in a citrus peppercorn sauce. ♦ American ♦ M-F lunch and dinner; Sa dinner; Su brunch. 55 Carmine St (at Bedford St). 647.1840 &

19 Cafe Español $$ Spanish cuisine—chicken or lobster with garlic sauce, and paella—is served in an authentic Catalan atmosphere dominated by a mural of Spanish villages. Dining options include a skylit room in back and outdoor tables on a small patio in warmer weather. ♦ Spanish ♦ Daily lunch and dinner. 63 Carmine St (at Seventh Ave S). 675.3312. Also at: 172 Bleecker St (between Sullivan and MacDougal Sts). 505.0657

20 Dama ★$ The third enterprise in hip downtown entrepreneur Jean Claude Iacovelli's empire (the others are the nearby **Caffè Lure** and SoHo's **Jean Claude**) is this dark, candlelit late-night oyster bar that feels like a desert outpost in Morocco. Stop in after midnight if you have a hankering for fresh Belon, Fisher Maine Point, or Blue Point oysters, smoked salmon over greens, or such light sandwiches as truffle cream, tomato, and basil on *bruschetta*. ♦ Oyster bar ♦ Daily dinner and late-night meals. 9 Seventh Ave S (between Carmine and Leroy Sts). 675.2638

Marys
RESTAURANT

21 Marys ★$ A slanting 1820 town house is the setting for this restaurant that underwent big changes in 1994 when longtime owner Giovanni Celenza sold the place to Todd Merrill and Jack Miller, proprietors of the **Universal Grill** (see below). The new owners kept the name but completely revamped the old Italian menu into one featuring such seasonal eclectic American fare as sautéed, curried shrimp with blackened fennel and corn salsa, and grilled pork medaillons with yucca-apple mash and roasted beet and onion *jus.* The roaring fireplaces and federal-style drapes are, however, still in place. An intimate room for private dinner parties is available. Called the **Angie Room,** it's decorated with pictures of actress Angie Dickinson. ♦ American ♦ M-F lunch and dinner; Sa dinner; Su brunch and dinner; no lunch in summer months. 42 Bedford St (between Leroy St and Seventh Ave S). 741.3387

21 Universal Grill ★$ Having dinner here is like being at a continuous party, so joyous and noisy are the nightly celebrations. The mostly gay clientele is no doubt put into the spirit by the loud 1960s music, kitschy Elvis mementos, and bright plastic tablecloths. The down-home fare includes pork chops, roast chicken, and ice-cream sundaes, but it's the overall experience that draws patrons in. ♦ American ♦ M-F lunch and dinner; Sa-Su brunch and dinner. 44 Bedford St (at Leroy St). 989.5621

21 Orbit ★$ This rustic room with a beautiful, ornate wood bar and the seemingly ubiquitous combination of ocher walls and dried flowers draws a gay crowd. The good, earthy food served here includes slow-roasted pork loin with black-bean salsa, pan-seared brook trout, and an interesting variety of pizzas. For those who want to have an intimate conversation over dinner, it's best to sit outside in nice weather—the music indoors can be loud. ♦ American ♦ M-F dinner; Sa-Su brunch and dinner. 46 Bedford St (at Leroy St). 463.8717

22 Rocco Pastry Shop & Cafe ★$ Rocco Generoso started this *pasticceria* over 20 years ago to showcase the specialties of Sicily and Calabria. The shop, which also has a few tables, refuses to grow old gracefully—its silvery decor is punctuated with pink and green neon. But the cookies and *sfogliatelle* (pastry stuffed with semolina, ricotta, and fruit), thankfully, haven't changed a bit. ♦ Cafe ♦ Daily. 243 Bleecker St (between Carmine and Leroy Sts). 242.6031

22 Bleecker Street Pastry Shop ★$ The desserts of Northern Italy are represented in this pastry shop and cafe, among them: cheesecake, panettone (cylindrical sweet breadlike cake with raisins), and rum pastries. The chef betrays a whimsical sense of humor with such creations as mushroom cake, decorated with bits of cake shaped and colored like mushrooms and filled with chestnut cream. There's also homemade gelato. ♦ Cafe ♦ Daily. 245 Bleecker St (between Carmine and Leroy Sts). 242.4959

23 Faicco's The floor-to-ceiling shelves are stocked with such Italian staples as olive oil, dried pasta, San Marzano canned tomatoes, but regulars come here for the pork—tender chops, loins, ground sausage, and ribs. Other specialties include homemade mozzarella wrapped around prosciutto, *pizza rustica* (an Italian quiche with chunks of ham, salami, and prosciutto), and roast pork. ♦ Tu-Sa; Su until 2PM. 260 Bleecker St (between Leroy and Cornelia Sts). 243.1974

23 Trattoria Pesce Pasta ★★$$ Beginning with the bright red entrance and the windows displaying the catch of the day and an array of antipasti, this is one of the neighborhood's more welcoming places. Inside, the decor is simple–wood tables, painted wood breakfronts, paintings of fish on the walls—and so is the food in a hearty, soul-satisfying way. Start with a selection of antipasti—marinated peppers, grilled fennel, marinated white beans, mozzarella—or *pasta e fagioli* (a broth rich with beans, vegetables, and macaroni), and then move on to any of the pastas, particularly the flavorful linguine with white clam sauce. The fish specialties change according to what was available at the market that day, but keep an eye out for the excellent *zuppa di pesce* (an Italian bouillabaisse) and the mixed seafood grill. Feel free to ask the waiters what's good that day; they're friendly, accommodating, and very honest. ♦ Italian ♦ Daily lunch, dinner, and late-night meals. 262 Bleecker St (at Cornelia St). 645.2993. Also at: 1079 First Ave (at E 59th St). 888.7884

23 Aphrodisia Whether seeking remedies or flavors, scoop your choice from among the 800 herbs and spices into a small paper bag and label it with the appropriate name and price. Those ready to turn over a new leaf could consult the wide selection of books for healthy living. ♦ Daily. 264 Bleecker St (between Sixth Ave and Seventh Ave S). 989.6440 &

24 Murray's Cheese Store The competitive prices, a large assortment of cheeses (90 percent are imported), and superior service keeps customers coming back. Grocery items, salads, meats, and delicacies are also offered at this self-styled "mini-**Balducci's**." ♦ Daily. 257 Bleecker St (at Cornelia St). 243.3289. Also at: 198 Eighth Ave (at 20th St). 691.3948

24 A. Zito & Sons Bakery The bread's crunchy crust and delicate inside texture lures its share of devoted customers like Frank Sinatra, who is pictured in a photo on the wall admiring a loaf. These breads, fresh from the oven, are easy to love; the whole wheat is especially delicious. ♦ M-Sa; Su until 1PM. 259 Bleecker St (between Cornelia and Jones Sts). 929.6139

25 Home ★★$$ In a cozy spot best described as an urban farmhouse, this neighborhood restaurant offers classic and nostalgic American cooking with a contemporary flair. Heartwarming entrées such as peppered Newport steak and cumin-crusted pork chops are as memorable as the signature homemade ketchup, onion rings, and must-have chocolate pudding. Who says you can't go home again? ♦ American ♦ M-F breakfast and dinner; Sa-Su brunch and dinner. 20 Cornelia St (between Bleecker and W Fourth Sts). 243.9579

25 Andalousia ★$ The dining room of this tiny restaurant resembles a North African bazaar: brass candleholders, figurines, bowls crammed into every available space, deep-green carpets, and heavy mirrors. The food is well prepared, particularly the *tajines* (stews) and couscous. Especially good is the chicken *tajine* (with prunes, toasted almonds, and sesame seeds) and the royal couscous with chicken, lamb, and *merguez* (spicy lamb sausage). ♦ Moroccan ♦ Daily dinner. 28 Cornelia St (between Bleecker and W Fourth Sts). 929.3693

"29" yrs.
#91
Pó
July 25, 1997
wer

26 Po ★★★$ Chef Mario Batali and partner Steve Crane change the menu seasonally, but whenever you visit this tiny, romantic place, you can count on such inventive, flavorful dishes as tomato ravioli filled with white beans in balsamic vinegar or marinated brown-butter quail with a beet reduction on a salad of *frisée* (curly endive). If you're having trouble making up your mind about which Tuscan-inspired dish to select, a tasting menu is the way to go. One choice offers six courses, including an appetizer, two pastas, an entrée, cheese, and dessert; the other, five courses (without the entrée). While deciding, munch on the delicious *bruschetta* (toasted bread seasoned with garlic and oil and topped with rosemary-flavored white-bean salad). The wine list is full of wonderful and reasonably priced Italian wines, and the desserts, rarely the high point of an Italian meal, are especially good here, particularly the terrine of dark chocolate, *amaretti* (macaroons), and *vin santo* (dessert wine), all drizzled over with espresso caramel. ♦ Northern Italian ♦ Tu dinner; W-Su lunch and dinner. Reservations required. 31 Cornelia St (between Bleecker and W Fourth Sts). 645.2189

26 The Cornelia Street Café ★$ Started by
artists nearly 20 years ago, this cafe has
always been charming, with whitewashed
brick walls and glass-panel doors that open
onto the quiet street of the same name. The
food has improved significantly, though, since
Leslie Harris, formerly of **Chanterelle** and **Le
Bernardin,** took over the kitchen in 1994. The
menu changes seasonally, but there's always
a good roasted free-range chicken and
interesting pastas, such as this fall favorite:
pumpkin ravioli with chestnut-cream sauce.
Save room for some of the homemade
desserts—the smooth-as-silk maple custard,
for example. ♦ Bistro/Cafe ♦ M-F lunch and
dinner; Sa-Su brunch and dinner. 29 Cornelia
St (between Bleecker and W Fourth Sts).
989.9318 &

27 The Bagel ★$ The Village Breakfast—
strawberry pancakes—is the big draw at this
tiny restaurant and deli. It's also known for
such standard deli fare as pastrami and
corned beef sandwiches. ♦ American/Deli
♦ Daily breakfast, lunch, and dinner. No credit
cards accepted. 170 W Fourth St (at Cornelia
St). 255.0106

28 Patisserie Claude Very good French pastry
(particularly the fruit tarts and croissants) is
for sale at this tiny storefront. There are also a
couple of tables for those who want to eat
their purchases right away. ♦ Daily. 187 W
Fourth St (between Jones and Barrow Sts).
255.5911 &

29 Boxers $ The bar here probably sees as
much action as any in the Village and offers its
customers a fairly unusual bar snack: hard-
boiled eggs. It's the scene that counts; the
food is just so-so. If hunger strikes, order the
decent hamburger or grilled chicken salad.
♦ American ♦ M-F lunch, dinner, and late-
night meals; Sa-Su brunch, dinner, and late-
night meals. 186 W Fourth St (at Barrow St).
633.2275 &

30 One If By Land, Two If By Sea ★★$$$$
The onetime home of Aaron Burr, this
charming restaurant doesn't have a sign,
which can make it a little tricky to find. Well
worth the hunt, it has a large bar and working
fireplace just inside the door, and the two-
level interior is romantically candlelit. The
food, traditionally very rich, features such
dishes as beef Wellington and roasted squab
with foie gras, wild mushrooms, and roasted
chestnuts. ♦ Continental ♦ Daily dinner.
Reservations required. 17 Barrow St (between
W Fourth St and Seventh Ave S). 228.0822

31 Jekyll and Hyde $ The atmosphere is dark
and reminiscent of a 19th-century pub,
littered with mad-scientist paraphernalia and
such assorted grotesquerie as a roaring
dinosaur head. The menu includes the
standard range of pastas, salads, and burgers,
but the bar offers an amazing selection of
beers—over 250 varieties—served in
authentic English yard glasses and traditional
pints. ♦ American ♦ Daily lunch, dinner, and
late-night meals. 91 Seventh Ave S (between
Barrow and Grove Sts). 255.5388. Also at:
1409 Sixth Ave (between 57th and 58th Sts).
541.9517 &

32 9 Jones Street ★★$$ Chef Marcey Bassoff
was Wayne Nish's *chef de cuisine* at **March** in
Midtown. The influence of her mentor shows
on the seasonal menus, which are full of
various and intriguing influences—especially
Indian and Asian. Don't miss the tender
roasted quail with Silk Road spices—
cinnamon, ginger, coriander, and sage. The
buttery hickory-smoked salmon and grilled
pork chops with sweet potatoes and prunes
are also highly recommended. For dessert,
get the 9 Jones ice-cream sandwich: praline
cookies and ice cream covered with
chocolate-and-caramel sauce. Chef Bassoff's
habit of meeting and greeting her customers
adds to the homey, intimate quality of this
cozy, beige-toned place. ♦ American/Fusion
♦ M-Sa dinner; Su brunch and dinner.
Reservations recommended. 9 Jones St
(between Bleecker and W Fourth Sts).
989.1220 &

FLORENCE
PRIME MEAT MARKET

32 Florence Meat Market Tony Pellegrino
and company carve meat by hand in this tiny,
old-fashioned shop, where opera is often
heard playing in the background. There's a
bench for waiting, a good thing as the line can
get long and the staff doesn't rush. Regular
customers use the opportunity to catch up on
neighborhood gossip. Try Tony's trademark
Newport steaks: They're affordable and
tender, if a bit mysterious—he keeps the cut
a secret—but they're extremely popular
nonetheless. ♦ Tu-Sa. 5 Jones St (between
Bleecker and W Fourth Sts). 242.6531

33 Caffè Vivaldi ★$ This Old World Village favorite always pleases with its relaxed and cozy atmosphere—it offers Manhattan a taste of turn-of-the-century Vienna, with dramatic arias playing in the background, the smell and sound of the espresso machine, and a crackling fire in the fireplace. Come here on a cold winter's day with your significant other for a light lunch or sweets. ◆ Cafe ◆ Daily. 32 Jones St (between Bleecker and W Fourth Sts). 929.9384

34 Cucina Stagionale $ The best thing that can be said about this place is that the prices are low. The food is marginal, but the menu gives a twist to basic Italian fare (try the eggplant manicotti). Don't arrive hungry; there's almost always a line of people waiting for a table, bottles of wine in hand (there's no liquor license). ◆ Italian ◆ Daily lunch and dinner. No credit cards accepted. 275 Bleecker St (between Jones St and Seventh Ave S). 924.2707

34 Ottomanelli's Meat Market For years, the window display of stuffed rabbits and game birds here gave pause to even the least repentant of carnivores. Fortunately, this shop's reputation for very fresh game is such that there is no longer a need to advertise quite so explicitly. All the meat is cut to order and fans of the veal roast stuffed with prosciutto are legion. ◆ M-Sa. 285 Bleecker St (between Jones St and Seventh Ave S). 675.4217

35 John's Pizzeria ★★$ Arguing about the best pizza in New York is something of a local sport, and this place is always on everyone's lips. The thin-crust pies are made in a coal oven—one reason it's so good. Another is the delicious toppings—fresh mushrooms, spicy sausage, or whatever you like. The inevitable wait prolongs the anticipation, but the end result always satisfies. ◆ Italian ◆ Daily lunch and dinner. 278 Bleecker St (between Morton St and Seventh Ave S). 243.1680 ₺. Also at: 48 W 65th St (between Central Park West and Columbus Ave). 721.7001; 408 E 64th St (between York and First Aves). 935.2895

35 Cafe Mona Lisa ★$ Leonardo's subject with her enigmatic smile is everywhere in this charming cafe, from the mural on the wall to the figurines all around. The comfy chairs in a variety of tapestry fabrics were obtained in a flea market sweep; antique chandeliers and gold-framed mirrors add to a feeling of slightly dissolute grandeur. Although the menu offers salads and sandwiches, they are merely so-so; stick to coffee and dessert–namely the triple-mousse cake and key lime pie. ◆ Cafe ◆ Daily lunch and dinner. No credit cards accepted. 282 Bleecker St (between Jones St and Seventh Ave S). 929.1262

36 Anglers & Writers ★$ Literary Paris of the 1930s is recaptured in this cozy, unpretentious cafe/tearoom owned by mother-and-son team Charlotte and Craig Bero. It's filled with charmingly mismatched English and Austrian china, turn-of-the-century American country furniture, and shelf after shelf of books–with an emphasis on Hemingway, Fitzgerald, and fly-fishing guides. The atmosphere is ideal for reading (or writing) a novel, reminiscing with friends, or gazing out the large picture windows, which overlook **James J. Walker Park** and the Hudson River. The food is hearty and all-American—old-fashioned lamb stew, open-face roast turkey sandwiches, and an assortment of sensational pies. ◆ American ◆ Daily breakfast, lunch, and dinner. 420 Hudson St (at St. Luke's Pl). 675.0810

36 Bespeckled Trout Owned by the same team as **Anglers & Writers** (see above), this vintage country general store sells many of the same things that make the restaurant so charming—porcelain teacups, penny candy, fishing lures and flies, fish postcards, and baked goods. Stop in, if only for the feeling of being suddenly transported to Maine. ◆ Daily. 422 Hudson St (between St. Luke's Pl and Morton St). 255.1421

37 Village Atelier ★$$$ The farmhouse setting is an appropriate backdrop for the well-prepared American food served here. Try the roast stuffed boneless quail with montmorency cherry and brandy sauce or fruitwood grilled tuna with spicy salsa. ◆ American ◆ M-F lunch and dinner; Sa dinner. Reservations required. 436 Hudson St (at Morton St). 989.1363 ₺

38 The Grange Hall ★$ This raucous, Generation X scene (site of the former **Blue Mill Tavern**) is popular for farm-fresh food at reasonable prices. Grazers can choose from a large variety of vegetable and grain dishes, such as warm gingered beets with raisins, available in appetizer sizes. Main courses include herb-crusted organic chicken breast with honey-glazed carrots, grilled lambsteak with rosemary red cabbage, and a platter of oven-roasted seasonal farm vegetables. The farm theme is carried through to the decor: A large mural of farmers graces the wall. ◆ American ◆ M-F lunch and dinner; Sa-Su brunch and dinner. 50 Commerce St (between Bedford and Barrow Sts). 924.5246

39 Moustache ★$ Stop by this tiny hole-in-the-wall for delicious fresh-tasting Middle Eastern dishes. The best are the pitzas—pizzas baked on pita bread—topped with a variety of ingredients including lemon-marinated chicken with garlic and peppers. ◆ Middle Eastern ◆ Tu-Su lunch and dinner.

90 Bedford St (between Barrow and Grove Sts). 229.2220. Also at: 405 Atlantic Ave (at Bond St, Brooklyn). 718/852.5555

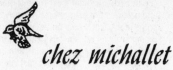

39 Chez Michallet ★$$$ Charming and intimate, this French-style bistro is always packed with a neighborhood crowd. The food here is classic French cooking that's been given a slight spin. Dinners include rack of lamb with rosemary red-wine sauce and monkfish in fresh vinaigrette. The steak *frites* (with french fries) is especially good too. ♦ French ♦ Daily dinner. Reservations recommended. 90 Bedford St (at Grove St). 242.8309 &

40 Chumleys $$ A speakeasy during the 1920s, this anonymous, signless building has a convenient back door on Barrow Street still used by insiders. Cozy and convivial, with working fireplaces and wooden benches deeply carved with customers' initials, the place has atmosphere aplenty, but the food isn't terrific. Nevertheless, it's a great place to stop for a drink, especially if you like ghost stories. According to local legend, the long-departed Mrs. Chumley comes back and rearranges the furniture in the middle of the night. ♦ American ♦ Daily dinner. 86 Bedford St (between Barrow and Grove Sts). 675.4449

41 Pink Teacup ★$ Even the walls are pink in this longtime Village soul-food hangout, and displayed on them are photos of famous admirers—from Oprah Winfrey to Brooke Shields. The prices have steadily crept up over the years, but for big eaters, a complete dinner of smothered pork chops or ribs, with soup, cabbage salad drenched in French dressing, black-eyed peas, collard greens, cornbread, and bread pudding is a satisfying value indeed. ♦ Southern ♦ Daily breakfast, lunch, dinner, and late-night meals. No credit cards accepted. 42 Grove St (between Bedford and Bleecker Sts). 807.6755

Grove
Restaurant & Garden

42 Grove ★★$ Whether you choose the pale yellow dining room—with wood floors and softly lit oil paintings—or the 70-seat garden in back, this is a quiet, civilized place to dine. The food is hearty and well prepared, with some unusual touches. Highlights include fried calamari appetizer with chipotle mayonnaise, chicken *ortolana* (a breaded chicken paillard with chopped arugula and tomatoes), and grilled pork chop with garlicky greens and sautéed apples. ♦ American ♦ M-F lunch and dinner; Sa-Su brunch and dinner. Reservations recommended. 314 Bleecker St (at Grove St). 675.9463

43 Grove Street Cafe ★$$ This quaint dining room is stylish and bohemian, with exposed-brick walls and recessed lighting. Its nouvelle cuisine is mostly very good. Featured dishes include chicken rolled with prosciutto, mozzarella, and sun-dried tomatoes, and covered with a cognac cream sauce. Convenient to all the Village theaters, it also boasts a well-balanced, affordable wine list and attentive service. ♦ Continental ♦ M-Tu, Th-F lunch and dinner; W dinner; Sa-Su brunch and dinner. Reservations recommended. 53 Grove St (between Seventh Ave S and Bleecker St). 924.8299

44 Les Deux Gamins ★$ From the copper pots on the walls to the café au lait and *tartines* (toasted baguettes with butter and jam), this cozy cafe imparts a little bit of Paris to New York. It's a relaxing place to read one of the newspapers or magazines provided, while trying out classic bistro dishes, such as an *assiette* (assortment) of charcuterie, steak *frites,* or roast duck with tomatoes, olives, and mushrooms. ♦ French ♦ Daily breakfast, lunch, and dinner. Reservations recommended. No credit cards accepted. 170 Waverly Pl (at Grove St). 807.7047. Also at: 50 MacDougal St (between Houston and Prince Sts). 254.4678

45 Gus' Place ★$$ Casual and gracious, this place specializes in Mediterranean—predominantly Greek—cuisine. The *mezedes* (a platter of assorted appetizers) is enough to send you away satisfied and mighty happy, but if you stopped there you'd miss Gus's specialty—lamb shank—and that would be a shame. ♦ Greek/Mediterranean ♦ M-Sa lunch and dinner; Su brunch and dinner. 149 Waverly Pl (near Gay St). 645.8511 &

46 Rumbul's Pastry Shop ★$ This small, dark-wood cafe makes a pretense of offering food, but everyone really comes here for the cake—big old-fashioned slices of chocolate mousse cake, layer cake, banana cream pie, carrot cake, and a list of other baked goods too numerous to mention. If you lack for company, cozy up to the stuffed gorilla; his regular table is at the front near the window. ♦ Bakery/Cafe ♦ Daily. 20 Christopher St (between Gay St and Waverly Pl). 924.8900. Also at: 559 Hudson St (between Perry and 11th Sts). 929.8783; 128 E 7th St (between 1st Ave and Ave A). 473.8696

47 Lion's Head ★$$ Local journalists, writers, and community politicians have been known to congregate here. The bar is the main thing, but the food—ever since Richard Glavin, formerly of the **Box Tree,** took over—has taken a turn for the better. Now, along with the stalwart burgers or bangers and mash, you can order such upscale dishes as confit of duck salad. ♦ American ♦ Daily lunch, dinner, and late-night meals. 59 Christopher St (at Seventh Ave S). 929.0670

48 Riviera Cafe $$ The people watching here is better than anything on the casual menu, which includes burgers and salads. Sip some wine and watch the ongoing parade that is Greenwich Village pass by your table. In nice weather, choose between indoor and outdoor dining, or just belly up to the sports bar year-round. ♦ American ♦ Daily lunch, dinner, and late-night meals. 225 W Fourth St (between Christopher St and Seventh Ave S). 929.3250

49 Pot Belly Stove Cafe $ In the wee hours, this place is better than most when it comes to satisfying an uncontrollable urge for a hamburger with any conceivable topping, an omelette, or a salad. ♦ American ♦ Daily 24 hours. 94 Christopher St (between Bleecker and Bedford Sts). 242.8036

49 Li-Lac Chocolates This place has been making top-quality chocolate truffles, chocolate-covered caramels, and all kinds of filled and plain chocolate since 1923. Satisfy a serious sweet tooth with a chocolate Empire State Building. The chocolate computer keyboard and diploma are perfect gifts. ♦ Daily. 120 Christopher St (between Bleecker and Bedford Sts). 242.7374

50 McNulty's Tea and Coffee Company In business since 1895, this place has been quietly selling exotic coffees (from China, Sumatra, and Indonesia) long before the trend for specialty coffees. There are also more than 250 varieties of tea. ♦ Daily. 109 Christopher St (between Bleecker and Bedford Sts). 242.5351

51 Cowgirl Hall of Fame ★$ A rousing spot with twangy country-western recordings being played at maximum volume, this place is part barbeque joint, part cowgirl museum, and part western gear shop (fringed vests, spurs, etc.). Good bets on the menu are the tender smoked brisket, fried catfish, and fried chicken. Hungry cowhands should check out the all-you-can-eat specials on Wednesday nights. It's a popular spot among young people, and a framed letter from then-candidate Bill Clinton thanks the place for hosting a luncheon for his daughter Chelsea. ♦ Southern ♦ Daily lunch and dinner. 519 Hudson St (at W 10th St). 633.1133

51 Taylor's The prodigious success of this snug gourmet take-out shop started by Cindi Taylor and her brother Spartan spurred the opening of two other locations. The lines at lunchtime for such salads as chicken with bacon and tomato, or Moroccan chicken with sun-dried tomatoes, may be daunting, but the food is worth the wait. It requires a great deal of willpower to leave without snapping up a sample of Cindi's supremely tempting baked goods. The selection of sweets changes daily but is likely to include triple-fudge brownies, chocolate soufflé cake, and Key lime bars. ♦ Daily. 523 Hudson St (between W 10th and Charles Sts). 645.8200. Also at: 228 W 18th St (between Seventh and Eighth Aves). 366.9081; 175 Second Ave (between 11th and 12th Sts). 674.9501

51 Rubyfruit Bar & Grill ★$ The down-home cooking at this intimate dining spot frequented by lesbians is creative and offered in abundant portions. Try not to fill up on the basket of warm bread—the star is a delicious focaccia—served with a sun-dried tomato spread. Start the meal with crab cakes and spicy mayonnaise dressing, and follow with either the blackened pork chop or roast free-range chicken (both are accompanied by terrific mashed potatoes). Top the meal off with New York cheesecake, Key lime pie, or homemade pecan pie. At the upstairs lounge, light eaters can munch on appetizers either at the bar or at a table in one of the cozy seating areas. ♦ American ♦ M-Sa dinner; Su brunch and dinner. 531 Hudson St (between W 10th and Charles Sts). 929.3343

51 Sazerac House ★★$$ It's worth a visit to this 30-year-old restaurant for the building alone. Part of an 18th-century farm purchased from the Earl of Abingdon, this place was fixed up in 1826 by a local carpenter who made it his home. A knowing crowd, homesick New Orleanians among them, have always come here for gumbo, jambalaya, and the perennially popular crab cakes. Lately, such brunch favorites as eggs Sazerac (scrambled eggs with ham, cream cheese, and hollandaise sauce) and *pain perdu* (French toast) are attracting a following of their own. The early prix-fixe dinner (4:30-6:30PM) is a real bargain. ♦ Cajun/Creole ♦ M-F lunch and dinner; Sa-Su brunch and dinner. Reservations recommended. 533 Hudson St (at Charles St). 989.0313

52 Chez Ma Tante Cafe ★$$ In an attempt to appeal to budget-minded customers, this stylish French cafe introduced a low-priced pasta menu, which is decent. But regulars still come for such reliably prepared French food as grilled salmon with rosemary-dijon sauce and chicken breast filled with sweet pepper and spinach. ♦ French ♦ M-F dinner; Sa-Su brunch and dinner. Reservations recommended. 189 W 10th St (between Bleecker and W Fourth Sts). 620.0223 &

"Cawffee" Breaks

The espresso craze that began in Seattle worked its way slowly across the country before infecting New York. But once it finally hit, New York rallied with typical Gotham gusto—sprouting coffee bars like alien pods on every corner. Now practically anywhere you go in the city, a **Starbucks, Cooper's, New World, Dalton's, Timothy's,** or **Seattle Coffee Roasters** is probably within striking distance.

As a result, the coffeehouses that have been around the city for years have been inspired to offer variations of the standard espresso and cappuccino and are an alternative for starting or breaking up the day. With so many places offering a good caffeine blast these days, the discriminating java drinker can seek one of the unique surroundings detailed below.

Since the days of the Beat poets, New Yorkers have always had their favorite coffeehouses, especially those that have been here forever and ooze Old World charm. **Greenwich Village** has an embarrassment of these treasures, all of which are perfect for soaking up atmosphere as well as delicious brew. They include the oldest cafe in America, **Caffè Reggio** (119 MacDougal St, at W Third, 475.9557); the authentic, Italian-is-spoken-here **Caffè Dante** (79 MacDougal St, between W Houston and Bleecker Sts, 982.5275); the smoke-darkened **Caffè Borgia** (185 Bleecker St, at MacDougal St, 674.9589); and the cozy and relaxed **Caffè Vivaldi** (32 Jones St, between Bleeker and W Fourth Sts, 929.9384).

For a sleeker environment, there's **Espresso Madison** (33 E 68th St, between Park and Madison Aves, no phone), an Italian-style stand-up espresso bar, with high-voltage, delicious coffee; the handsomely minimalist **News Bar** (2 W 19th St, at Fifth Ave, 255.3996; 366 W Broadway, at Broome St, 343.0053; 969 Third Ave, at 57th St, 319.0830), with no less than 400 periodicals for sale, as well as sublime espresso and perfectly steamed milk; or a branch of **Dean & DeLuca Cafe** (121 Prince St, between Wooster and Greene Sts, 254.8776; 75 University Place, at E 11th St, 473.1908; 9 Rockefeller Plaza, at W 49th St, 644.1363), all of which are attractive and dependably good.

Hip and arty places to sip "joe" are also legion. **Big Cup** (228 Eighth Ave, between W 21st and W 22nd Sts, 206.0059) is as comfortable as a living room, with couches to lounge on; **Cafe Mona Lisa** (282 Bleecker St, between Jones St and Seventh Ave S, 929.1262), a new-style Greenwich Village coffeehouse with antique chandeliers and tapestry-covered chairs, has depictions of the woman with the mysterious smile; **Limbo** (47 Ave A, between E Third and E Fourth Sts, 477.5271) is a sunny yellow room furnished with 1950s-style dinette sets—perfect for journal or poetry writing; the **Pink Pony Cafe** (176 Ludlow St, between Stanton and E Houston Sts, no phone) is a Day-Glo–painted playroom for more would-be poets to while away the afternoon drinking coffee; and **La Linea** (15 First Ave, at E First St, 777.1571) is a handsome electric-blue and yellow cafe, with a relaxing living room in the back.

Those in search of cafe society won't have any trouble finding it, but they may have trouble choosing between the many comely spots to fashionably sit and sip. Enjoy your coffee in the gracious surroundings of **Caffe Med** (1268 Second Ave, between E 66th and E 67th Sts, 744.5370), a striking room decorated with a deep-blue mural; **Edgar's Cafe** (255 W 84th Street, between Broadway and West End Ave, 496.6126), named for the writer of uncanny stories and reminiscent of a ruined palazzo; and **Cafe Mozart** (154 W 70th Street, between Columbus Ave and Broadway, 595.9797), a replica of a grand faded Viennese coffeehouse—replete with ornate crystal chandeliers, portraits of the composer, and scattered violins.

You also can enjoy a caffeine buzz al fresco. **Café La Fortuna** (69 W 71st St, between Central Park W and Columbus Ave, 724.5846) has a garden in the back, ideal for sipping an unparalleled iced cappuccino laced with homemade chocolate or coffee ice. **Cafe Fledermaus** (1 Seaport Plaza, at Water St, 269.5890) has tables on the **Fulton Street** promenade that are perfect for people watching. **Pasqua** (55 E 53rd Street, between Park and Madison Aves, 750.7140) is not exactly outdoors but is within the atrium of the **Park Avenue Plaza;** with its gently rushing waterfall, this may be the closest thing to nature in **Midtown.**

65

52 La Metairie ★★$$$ The Village is known for its romantic restaurants, and this rustic and candlelit place, with a white picket fence and hand-painted duck sign, is one good reason why. The menu is chef John DiLeo's take on Provençal cooking—duck with orange and balsamic-vinegar sauce, and sautéed salmon with a garlic-mustard crust—with the addition of lobster risotto, or some equally unexpected dish. ♦ French ♦ Daily dinner. Reservations required. 189 W 10th (at W Fourth St). 989.0343 ♿

53 Cafe Picasso ★$ Owner Michael Colonna learned how to make pizza in Florence, and his brick-oven pizza is among the best in the neighborhood. There are also tempting sandwiches on focaccia, fresh salads, and any type of coffee you could ever want. In warm weather, there's a pleasant garden in the back. ♦ Cafe ♦ Daily lunch and dinner. No credit cards accepted. 359 Bleecker St (between W 10th and Charles Sts). 929.6232

54 Little Cafe $ For years this was known as the **Little Mushroom Cafe,** a name most of its neighbors found curious. The menu offers a combination of Thai and Italian food. Neither cuisine is entirely authentic, but the food is decent. It's best to skip the satays, and stick to simple noodle dishes. ♦ International ♦ M-Sa lunch and dinner. Su brunch and dinner. 183 W 10th St (at W Fourth). 242.1058

55 Dix et Sept ★$$ When this cafe opened, its reviews all raved about the abundance of Gallic charm, which no longer seems very much in evidence. But the food—steamed mussels in white wine with shallots, grilled salmon with basil oil, and braised lamb shank in red wine—still appeals to most who climb down the stairs to this subterranean dining room. ♦ French ♦ Daily dinner. Reservations recommended. 181 W 10th St (at Seventh Ave S). 645.8023

56 Tanti Baci Caffè ★★$ Owner Paola Tottani says she was forced to open this restaurant in 1993 because her house was constantly jammed with dinner guests. Judging by the way she treats her customers—warm welcome at the door, friendly discussions about what they should eat—it's no wonder. Everything on the simple menu of pastas and sauces is cooked fresh daily and according to old family recipes. The *bolognese* sauce tastes as if it were made in Emilia-Romagna. From Friday through Sunday there are fresh seafood specials, as well. ♦ Italian ♦ Daily breakfast, lunch, and dinner. 163 W 10th St (between Seventh Ave S and Waverly Pl). 647.9651

57 Woody's ★$ The menu is very large and not everything on it is successful, but the linguine with mixed seafood, grilled chicken with pineapple salsa, and chicken fajitas with black beans and fresh guacamole are all impressive. The burgers and sandwiches are made with very fresh ingredients and good breads, and the brunch is a cut above average with excellent omelettes, variations of French toast, and pancakes. ♦ Eclectic ♦ M-Sa lunch and dinner; Su brunch and dinner. 140 Seventh Av S (between W 10th and Charles Sts). 242.120◆

58 Sevilla ★$$ Garlic lovers will find it impossible to resist this place; the aromas wafting from the kitchen through the vents onto Charles Street act like a siren's song, drawing diners in their door. Once inside, have some sangria and share a paella; it's one of the best around. ♦ Spanish ♦ Daily lunch and dinner. Reservations recommended. 62 Charles St (at W Fourth St). 929.3189 ♿

59 Cucina Della Fontana $ This place has been mobbed since it opened. Part of the reason is the funky decor. Upstairs it sports a semiformal, peach-colored dining room, but downstairs, with cloud-painted walls, fountains, and a skylight, it's like a fantasy garden. The huge portions and low prices for such Italian standards as linguine with clam sauce and chicken parmigiana also contribute to its popularity. However, the kitchen's execution is uneven and indigestion is an ever-present possibility. ♦ Italian ♦ M-Sa lunch and dinner; Su brunch and dinner. Reservations recommended. No credit cards accepted. 368 Bleecker St (at Charles St). 242.0636

60 Rafaella Restaurant ★$$ The green-and-white mural of trees is left over from the days when this long narrow room housed a florist shop. With the addition of ornate wrought-iron chandeliers and lamplights on the exposed-brick walls, it is now an attractive dining room reminiscent of old New Orleans. The menu is strictly Italian, however, with good pasta, seafood, and veal dishes. Specialties include homemade ravioli (fillings change daily) and veal with artichokes and sun-dried tomatoes. ♦ Italian ♦ Daily dinner. 381 Bleecker St (between Charles and Perry Sts) 229.9885

61 Caffé Cefalú ★$ Provincial and traditional Italian specialties are served in this cozy, brick-walled room decorated with Roman masks and lace curtains. Pastas—black-pepper fettuccine with gorgonzola or *capellini* (thin spaghetti) with vegetables in garlic olive oil—are especially good. ♦ Italian ♦ Daily dinner. 259 W Fourth St (between Charles and Perry Sts). 989.7131

Patisserie J. Lanciani

62 Patisserie J. Lanciani ★$ Magnificent cakes, tarts, brownies, and croissants are offered in this pretty storefront cafe. In the mornings, it's a breakfast club of locals leisurely reviewing the newspaper over coffee. ♦ Cafe ♦ Daily. 271 W Fourth St (between Perry and W 11th Sts). 929.0739 &

63 Fishs Eddy This shop collects and sells odd and interesting bits of glassware and porcelain. Expect to find dishes and other treasures from old railroad cars, hotels, and extinct social clubs. ♦ Daily. 551 Hudson St (between Perry and W 11th Sts). 627.3956. Also at: 889 Broadway (at 19th St). 420.9020; 2176 Broadway (at 77th St). 873.8819

63 White Horse Tavern $; Come here for the sense of history, not for the barely edible food—with the exception of good burgers and okay fries. The poet Dylan Thomas drank himself to death in the corner of the bar, and the apocryphal story still circulating is that his last words were: "I've had 19 straight whiskeys. I believe that's the record." ♦ American ♦ M-F lunch, dinner, and late-night meals; Sa-Su brunch, dinner, and late-night meals. 567 Hudson St (at W 11th St). 243.9260

64 Caribe ★$ Although this place is not exactly original—there are a number of similar island-motif restaurant/bars like this joint offering Jamaican food and music in a junglelike setting—the food here is pretty good (try the jerk chicken or pork), and the atmosphere (West Indies meets West Village) is funky and fun. ♦ West Indian ♦ Daily lunch and dinner. 117 Perry St (at Greenwich St). 255.9191

65 The Black Sheep ★★$$$ This place is the archetype of the ultimate Village restaurant—brick walls, original paintings, comfortable, and dark. The six-course dinner with limited choices is a good value; otherwise, try the crispy confit of duck leg. The wine list is excellent, and homemade desserts irresistible; don't miss the banana cake with praline-butterscotch frosting. ♦ French ♦ M-Sa dinner and late-night meals; Su brunch, dinner, and late-night meals. Reservations recommended. No credit cards accepted at brunch. 342 W 11th St (at Washington St). 242.1010

66 Burgundy Wine Company The finest wines of Burgundy and the Rhône are this shop's specialty. Be sure to ask for the mail-order catalog: It's an informative brochure filled with vignettes about wine merchant Al Hotchkin's travels through the vineyards plus his thoughts on the wines he discovered. ♦ Tu-Sa. 323 W 11th St (between Greenwich and Washington Sts). 691.9092

67 Cottonwood Cafe $$ This noisy low-down Texan joint serves basic chicken-fried steak, fried chicken livers, and hefty barbecued beef ribs (mesquite-smoked Texas-style) with sides of lumpy skin-flecked mashed potatoes, cornmeal-dipped fried okra, and the obligatory cream gravy. After 10PM the place transforms into a roadhouse with "original Texas" music—country-western with an overlay of Village artiness—performed at a volume loud enough to preclude anything but listening and downing great margaritas or Lone Star beer. ♦ Southern ♦ Daily lunch and dinner. 415 Bleecker St (between W 11th and Bank Sts). 924.6271

THE PARIS COMMUNE

67 Paris Commune ★$$ An especially cozy Village restaurant, this place offers a roaring fireplace and a country-French and American menu. The quality of the food can vary, but usually reliable dishes include grilled spiced pork chops with apple chutney and pan-seared chicken Basque style (with prosciutto, hot and sweet peppers, and tomatoes). Brunch—especially the French toast with fruit—is very popular, so be prepared to wait. ♦ Bistro ♦ M-F lunch and dinner; Sa-Su brunch and dinner. Reservations recommended for dinner. 411 Bleecker St (between W 11th and Bank Sts). 929.0509

68 Tartine ★★$ Not for claustrophobics, this minuscule bakery/restaurant has a loyal neighborhood clientele that packs its close-together indoor tables and few outdoor tables for exquisite fruit tarts and beautifully composed salads. Also on the menu are such Provençal specialties as grilled tuna with tomatoes and olives, and sautéed chicken with lemon and sage. There's also takeout. ♦ Bakery/Bistro ♦ Tu-F lunch and dinner; Sa-Su brunch and dinner. 253 W 11th St (at W Fourth St). 229.2611

69 Greenwich Cafe ★$ The owners of **Ye Waverly Inn** (see below) opened this stylish round-the-clock cafe with sponged-beige and exposed-brick walls, an oxidized copper ceiling, gilt-edged mirrors, chandeliers, and curved banquettes. The atmosphere is sub-dued, except for the background music, which is played slightly too loud. The food has a Mediterranean slant. Try the antipasto with prosciutto, shrimp, and calamari; clams with olive oil, tomato, cilantro, and leeks; bouillabaisse; pork chop with honey and caraway seeds; or chicken saltimbocca with prosciutto, sage, and Marsala. Save room for the dense chocolate Viennese or lemon tart. ♦ Mediterranean ♦ Daily 24 hours. 75 Greenwich Ave (between Seventh Ave S and Bank St). 255.5450 ᛦ

69 Chez Brigitte ★$ Come to this counter-only eatery for inexpensive French food. A friendly Frenchwoman named Rose, who has worked here for 25 years, has taken over the kitchen from the late Brigitte and continues to cook such homey, simple dishes as *boeuf bourguignon* and veal stew. ♦ French ♦ Daily lunch and dinner. No credit cards accepted. 77 Greenwich Ave (at W 11th St). 929.6736

70 Artepasta ★$ On weekends be prepared for long lines at this better-than-average pasta emporium boasting a charming mural depicting local artists and low prices. Try the carpaccio, *penne puttanesca,* or homemade fettuccine with grilled chicken and shiitake mushrooms in a light cream sauce. There's a very reasonable prix-fixe dinner weekdays from 4 to 6PM. ♦ Italian ♦ M-F lunch and dinner; Sa-Su brunch and dinner. No credit cards accepted. 81 Greenwich Ave (at Bank St). 229.0234

71 Taquería de México ★$ Billing itself as a "Mexico City Style Taquería," this bright place serves very good south-of-the-border fare at very reasonable prices. The same owners as **Mi Cocina** (see below) offer authentic Mexican tacos, enchiladas, tamales, and burritos that are far more interesting than what you'll usually find in New York. Try the *burritos de hongo con elote* (with shiitake mushrooms, onions, and corn) or *tacos de puerco en mole verde* (pork in pumpkin-seed sauce). Those with a sweet tooth will like the caramel bread pudding. ♦ Mexican fast food ♦ Daily lunch and dinner. No credit cards accepted. 93 Greenwich Ave (between Bank St and Waverly Pl). 255-5212

72 Ye Waverly Inn $$ Longtime Village residents don't seem to care that the quality of the food here—chicken potpie, Southern fried chicken, and peasant meat loaf (wrapped in homemade dough)—has declined somewhat over the years. They continue to flock to this dining spot for authentic Early American charm—irregularly shaped rooms, low ceilings, rustic print wallpaper, and in winter, roaring fireplaces. Traditional Thanksgiving and Christmas dinners are served. ♦ American ♦ M-F lunch

and dinner; Sa-Su brunch and dinner. 16 Bank St (at Waverly Pl). 929.4377

72 Cafe Risque $$ Owned by the same peopl as **Artepasta** (see above), this place resembles a high-tech brothel: there are raspberry and gold-flecked walls covered with peacock designs, shimmering taffeta curtains suspended over brick walls, and TV sets playing rock videos with the sound off. The food is uneven; stick to such simple dishes as meat loaf or linguine with olive oil garlic, and baby clams. Diners are treated to one nice bonus: When music is played downstairs, it wafts upward to be enjoyed gratis. Performances are sporadic; call or check listings for schedule and cover charges. ♦ American ♦ M-F lunch and dinner; Sa-Su brunch and dinner. 2 Bank St (between Greenwich Ave and Waverly Pl). 675.7710

73 La Focaccia ★$$ This simple dining room is decorated with tiles and metal trays on th walls that take on a certain charm by candlelight. You could easily make a meal o the bread, but be sure to save room for such Italian Riviera specialties as herb ravioli wit creamy walnut sauce and brick-oven grilled sirloin with rosemary. ♦ Italian ♦ Daily dinner. 51 Bank St (at W Fourth St). 675.3754

74 L'Auberge du Midi ★★$$ With its garder paintings, lace curtains, and jars of preserves lined up on the wall, this tiny, charming cafe feels like a country inn in France. The countryside is also brought to mind with such dishes as grilled Provençal sea bass stuffed with vegetables and herbs; and roast breast of duck with garlic, olives, and fresh rosemary. ♦ French ♦ Tu-Su dinner. Reservations recommended. 310 W Fourth St (between Bank and W 12th Sts). 242.4705

75 Casa di Pré ★$$ The honest, home-style food at this place that has been a fixture in the neighborhood for quite some time is cooked with a sure, light hand. Try veal *sorrentino* (cooked in a marsala sauce with prosciutto and mozzarella) or sole *francese* (dipped in a flour and egg batter and sautéed in lemon butter). ♦ Italian ♦ Daily lunch and dinner. Reservations recommended for three or more. 283 W 12th St (at W Fourth St). 243.7073 ᛦ

76 Corner Bistro $ If strolling around the Village has whet your appetite for a fat, juicy burger, this neighborhood standby is the place to go. You'll have plenty of time to chec out the locals in this dark, cozy pub because the indifferent staff provides extremely slow service. ♦ American ♦ Daily lunch, dinner, an late-night meals. No credit cards accepted. 331 W Fourth St (between W 12th and Jane Sts). 242.9502

77 Mappamondo Restaurant ★$ Globes are the only decorative touch at this simple, lively cafe, but the crowds that pack it daily don't come for the decor. They're drawn by the well-prepared and affordable pasta, pizza, and fish dishes. Try the penne primavera, grilled radicchio and artichoke pizza, and baked striped bass with mussels and clams. ♦ Italian ♦ Daily lunch and dinner. No credit cards accepted. 11 Abingdon Sq (Eighth Ave near W 12th St). 675.3100. Mappamondo Due at: 581 Hudson St (at Bank St). 675.7474

78 La Ripaille ★★$$ The setting, much like a French farmhouse, makes this one of the most romantic dining spots in a neighborhood full of romantic dining spots. Its Provençal-style dishes, such as breast of duck with seasonal fruit, shell steak in green peppercorn sauce, and Norwegian salmon in a light champagne velouté (sauce) are always good—sometimes quite good. ♦ French ♦ M-Sa dinner. Reservations recommended. 605 Hudson St (between Bethune and W 12th Sts). 255.4406

79 Nadine's ★$$ The dark walls and bright-red lamps draped with filmy fabric make this place seem a little like a haunted bordello. But that's part of the fun. The menu seeks to please just about everyone and in many cases succeeds. Try the Cajun meat loaf, sautéed salmon in a potato crust with cilantro-mustard vinaigrette, or seafood paella. ♦ Eclectic ♦ M-F lunch and dinner; Sa-Su brunch and dinner. 99 Bank St (at Greenwich St). 924.3165

80 Tortilla Flats $ This popular West Village dive is known for its wild times and cheap Tex-Mex eats—chicken, shrimp, or steak fajitas, *enchiladas verde* (in a green-chile salsa), and chimichangas (deep-fried chicken and refried-bean burritos)—made from natural ingredients. Monday and Tuesday are big-prize bingo nights; don't bring your mild-mannered grandma. ♦ Tex-Mex ♦ Daily lunch, dinner, and late-night meals. 767 Washington St (at W 12th St). 243.1053 &

81 Piccolo Angolo ★$ With its brick walls and open kitchen, this casual cafe is a good place for a relaxed dinner with friends. The kitchen serves solid renditions of traditional Italian dishes, on the order of chicken parmigiana. Come here for comfort food; lobster ravioli is about as experimental as it gets. ♦ Italian ♦ Tu-Su dinner. 621 Hudson St (at Jane St). 229.9177

82 Mi Cocina ★★$ For fans of authentic Mexican cuisine—the real thing, not fast-food tacos and burritos—this small cafe with its nubby salmon-pink walls and bright tiles is a neighborhood favorite. Recommended are the calamari seviche or shrimp cooked with toasted tomato, chipotle peppers, white wine, and spinach. To shake up the same old Sunday brunch, come here for Mexican-style fare. ♦ Mexican ♦ M-F lunch and dinner; Sa dinner; Su brunch. Reservations recommended. 57 Jane St (at Hudson St). 627.8273

83 Jane Street Seafood Cafe ★$$ Fresh seafood dishes—from the good and simple to the surprisingly well-executed and complex—include sole *portuguesse* (sautéed in seasoned butter with fresh tomatoes and a dash of sherry over brown rice), monkfish *mahnket* (cooked in brown butter with onions, broccoli, tabasco sauce, and lime juice, and then flambéed), and a marinated seafood kebab of shrimp, scallops, swordfish, and tuna. One caveat: The service tends to be nonchalant. ♦ Seafood ♦ Daily dinner. Reservations recommended. 31 Eighth Ave (at Jane St). 242.0003

84 Bonsignour This tiny take-out shop used to be **Priscilla's,** to which the neighborhood was devoted, but Philippe Bonsignour has kept the regulars coming. A native New Yorker raised in France, he offers a tempting array of pâtés, cheeses, muffins, salads, and prepared fixings, including roast chicken and crab cakes. ♦ M-Sa; Sunday until 4 PM. 35 Jane St (at Eighth Ave). 229.9700

85 Myers of Keswick Anglophiles should enjoy perusing this English grocery and its selection of Oxo, Bovril, Marmite, Lucozade, Smarties, fresh pork pies, and bangers. It also stocks Kensington teapots, mugs, and circular tea bags. ♦ Daily. 634 Hudson St (between Jane and Horatio Sts). 691.4194

86 El Faro ★$$ A dark, minimally decorated den of a restaurant, this place has been around forever serving good-quality, full-flavored Spanish food. You can't go wrong with the rich and fragrant paella, seafood stew, or other fish dishes, including grilled shrimp with wine sauce. There's also a moderately priced wine list that spotlights Spanish wines. ♦ Spanish ♦ Daily lunch and dinner. 823 Greenwich St (at Horatio St). 929.8210

87 Restaurant Florent ★★$$ A diner-turned-hip-bistro, this is a welcome late-night spot for those seeking a complete meal. Given the number of meatpacking plants in the neighborhood, meat entrées are, of course, specialties of the house. The *boudin noir* (blood sausage) appetizer and the steak *frites* are both popular. Any of the fish dishes are also worth trying. After midnight there's an all-night breakfast menu. Part of the attraction of this establishment is its stylish look: Tibor Kalman's M & Co. is responsible for the design, and to some extent the layout, of the restaurant itself. ◆ Continental ◆ Daily 24 hours. No credit cards accepted. 69 Gansevoort St (between Greenwich and Washington Sts). 989.5779 ⌖

88 Gansevoort Market The action at this wholesale meat market—housed in a collection of old brick buildings—intensifies in the early morning hours before the sun comes up, when people from restaurants all over New York converge to find the best meat to serve for dinner. Some of the stores here also sell to the public (in mass quantities only). ◆ Gansevoort and W 14th Sts (between Ninth Ave and the Hudson River). 924.2211

89 Barocco Food to Go An uptown outpost of the TriBeCa restaurant, this take-out shop has extremely well prepared pasta and chicken salads, sandwiches, chicken potpies, a juice bar, and delectable baked goods. There are also a couple of tables if you want to dig in right away. ◆ Daily. 121 Greenwich Ave (at Horatio St). 366.6110 ⌖

90 Day-O $ The gold and bronze walls at this popular spot are decorated with African masks. The music is deafening, but the young crowd that comes here for exotic tropical drinks, jerk chicken, blackened catfish, or Dixie fried chicken likes it like that. There's also a Caribbean brunch buffet on weekends. ◆ Caribbean/Southern ◆ M-F dinner; Sa-Su brunch and dinner. 103 Greenwich Ave (at W 12th St). 924.3160 ⌖

90 Benny's Burritos ★$ After sipping one of Benny's high-octane margaritas, you'll understand why it gets so rowdy here. Any one of the 12-inch-long burritos with a tempting choice of fillings at bargain prices is worth trying. This is the Village's *numero uno* cheap tortilla joint, so expect a line. ◆ Tex-Mex ◆ M-F lunch, dinner, and late-night meals; Sa-Su brunch, dinner, and late-night meals. No credit cards accepted. 113 Greenwich Ave (at Jane St). 727.0584. Also at: 93 Ave A (at Sixth St). 254.3286

91 Tea and Sympathy ★$ Homesick Brits and Anglophiles line up in the street for the afternoon tea at this cozy spot decorated with portraits of the royal family and unusual teapots. Those enamored of bangers and mash, shepherd's pie, and other English specialties flock here too. For traditionalists, there's a Sunday dinner of roast beef and Yorkshire pudding. ◆ English ◆ M-F lunch and dinner; Sa-Su brunch and dinner. 108 Greenwich Ave (between Jane and W 13th Sts). 807.8329

91 Cafe de Bruxelles ★$$ A sophisticated bar scene is the real attraction at this lovely spot, which has also made a name for itself as the only Belgian restaurant in the downtown area. Don't miss the rich *waterzooi* (Belgian bouillabaisse). ◆ French/Belgian ◆ Tu-Sa lunch and dinner; Su brunch and dinner. Reservations recommended. 118 Greenwich Ave (at W 13th St). 206.1830

92 Integral Yoga Foods Right next to the Integral Yoga Institute, this food store sells all types of organic and macrobiotic foods, including vegetables, grains, and beans. A body care department carries a selection of natural cosmetics. The **Integral Yoga Natural Apothecary** (234 W 13th St, 645.3051) across the street sells vitamins and homeopathic remedies. ◆ M-Sa. 229 W 13th St (between Seventh and Eighth Aves). 243.2642

93 Cafe Loup ★★$$ Cozy and comfortable, this French bistro serves solid fare, including grilled escargots; smoked brook trout; Colorado lamb chops in a Cabernet sauce; grilled skirt steak in shallot sauce; and grilled salmon over greens, corn salad, marinated tomato *concasse* (reduction), and *brunoise* of beets (shredded and sautéed). The emphasis on fresh, local organic produce is clearly evident in such dishes as tuna carpaccio over sunflower sprouts. Desserts—rice pudding with Tahitian vanilla sauce, Valrhona double chocolate pudding, wedges of intense chocolate fudge, and lemon crepes—are luscious. The eclectic and well-priced wine list includes good specials served by the glass. Be sure to check out the photos on the walls: There is a near-museum quality collection of 20th-century masters, including Brassai and Cartier-Bresson. ◆ French ◆ M-F lunch and dinner; Sa dinner; Su lunch and dinner. Reservations recommended. 105 W 13th St (between Sixth and Seventh Aves). 255.4746 ও

94 Salam ★$ Syrian-born Bassam Omary creates upscale Manhattan versions of the food of his youth, all made with top-quality ingredients from the **Jefferson Market** (see below). A self-taught cook, he has managed to win a very loyal clientele who followed him to this new, spiffier location in this restaurant-saturated neighborhood. The mixed kebabs, marinated in oil and garlic, are especially good, as are curried chicken, and chicken or shrimp in coriander sauce. There is no liquor license, so bring your own beer or wine. ◆ Middle Eastern ◆ M-F dinner; Sa-Su brunch and dinner. 104 W 13th St (between Sixth and Seventh Aves). 741.0277

95 Bar Six ★★$ With its aged ocher walls and mirrors, this bistro looks like it's been here forever, but is actually a relative newcomer on the scene. Models love this place; neighborhood celebrities Tim Robbins and Susan Sarandon have been known to stop in too. The combination French, American, and Moroccan food is given less attention than the scene, but it's perfectly good. Best bets are the grilled spicy shrimp with warm lentil salad, grilled lamb kebabs with lemon couscous, and chicken *tajine*. ◆ Bistro ◆ M-F lunch and dinner; Sa-Su brunch and dinner. 502 Sixth Ave (between W 12th and W 13th Sts). 645.2439

96 Zinno ★$$ Occupying the ground floor of a town house, this sleek bar and restaurant offers chamber jazz and some good food. Stick to the pastas; a good choice is homemade linguine with pancetta (Italian bacon), porcini mushrooms, and tomatoes. ◆ Italian ◆ M-Sa lunch and dinner. 126 W 13th St (between Sixth and Seventh Aves). 924.5182

97 Cuisine de Saigon ★$ A long, narrow restaurant, this is a Village favorite for fresh, authentic Vietnamese food. Try the crispy spring rolls; pork roll (pork, lettuce, and mint leaves wrapped in rice paper); squid stuffed with minced pork, dried mushrooms, and vermicelli; lemongrass chicken; crispy noodles with vegetables; and barbecued beef skewers. ◆ Vietnamese ◆ Daily lunch and dinner. 154 W 13th St (between Sixth and Seventh Aves). 255.6003

The original Original Ray's (despite claims by dozens of Ray's pizzerias around town) is on Sixth Avenue at West 11th Street.

THE JAMES BEARD FOUNDATION

98 James Beard House ★★★★$$$$ At the urging of fellow food titan Julia Child, this brownstone of the late cooking teacher and cookbook author was converted into a center for the celebration and education in the ways of fine cuisine. Major chefs from New York and around the country do special dinners almost nightly here, which are open to members and the public. Although it's pricey, considering the five or six courses that are served with almost as many wines, diners get their money's worth and more. Practically every dinner is a special event worth attending, but as each is presided over by a different guest chef, the menus are as entirely unpredictable as they are fabulous. Call ahead for a schedule and membership information. ◆ Eclectic ◆ Single seating at 7PM. Reservations required. 167 W 12th St (between Sixth and Seventh Aves). 675.4984

99 Famous Ray's Pizza $ Though a number of imposters have tried to claim title to the name "Famous Ray the Pizza King," this Village institution is the only real heir to the throne, serving more than 2,000 loyal customers a day. Expect a line for pizza that's hardly as good as it used to be but is, at least, still fresh out of the oven. Ray's "Famous Slice" has *all* the toppings, but purists opt for the traditional "Red, White, and Green" (tomato sauce, mozzarella, basil, and parsley). ◆ Pizza ◆ Daily lunch, dinner, and late-night meals. No credit cards accepted. 465 Sixth Ave (at W 11th St). 243.2253

100 French Roast ★$ Don't come here if you're looking for quiet ambience or attentive service, but if you want pot-au-feu (meat and vegetables cooked in their own broth), steak *frites*, or a good cappuccino at 4AM, this very French cafe is a reliable spot. ◆ Bistro ◆ Daily 24 hours. 458 Sixth Ave (at W 11th St). 533.2233 ও

101 Jefferson Market Devoted customers of this old-fashioned market were shocked to learn that there were plans to move the store, but happy that the new location was right across the street. This space is bigger, more modern, and has wider aisles. The quality of the fresh produce, meats, cheeses, and other grocery items is as high as ever, and the longtime staff (familiar with regular customers' names) are all there. So are the famous rotisseried chickens; on Sunday nights in the summer, there is always a long line of customers at the prepared foods counter doing battle for these birds—they were a big seller even before the rotisserie craze began. ♦ Daily. 450 Sixth Avenue (at W 10th St). 533.3377 &

101 Melanie's Natural ★$ Melanie hasn't owned it for years, but this tiny cafe bearing her name is still popular with the collegiate crowd who come here for such fresh salads as the curried chicken with raisins, homemade soups, and frozen-yogurt sundaes. ♦ American ♦ Daily breakfast, lunch, and dinner. No credit cards accepted. 445 Sixth Ave (at W 10th St). 463.7744 &

102 Peacock Caffè $ This dark, veteran coffeehouse evokes the spirit of Florence with its large oil portraits of Renaissance-era figures, ornate gold-leaf columns, and opera playing in the background. The menu includes such pasta dishes as fettuccine with meat sauce, prosciutto and provolone sandwiches, and tomato and mozzarella salad, but most people come here for cappuccino and dessert. Try the Florentine apple torte, chocolate truffle cake, or homemade tiramisù. ♦ Cafe ♦ Daily lunch, dinner, and late-night meals. 24 Greenwich Ave (between W 10th and Charles Sts). 242.9395 &

103 Gran Caffè Degli Artisti ★$ Ask for a table in the back, where it's dark, cozy, candlelit, and filled with funky antique furnishings. Don't bother with the Italian entrées; go directly to the iced mochaccino and one of the more decadent pastries or cakes. ♦ Cafe ♦ Daily lunch, dinner, and late-night meals. 46 Greenwich Ave (between Perry and Charles Sts). 645.4431

103 Reality Bake Shop This hole-in-the-wall bakery sells delicious crusty country breads, rosemary focaccia, onion bread, and bagels. Also featured are such simple, hearty cakes as cinnamon coffee cake and banana bread. ♦ Daily. 50 Greenwich Ave (between Charles and Perry Sts). 229.2035

104 El Charro Español ★$$ A favorite local spot for earthy, garlicky Spanish food, this casual white stucco dining room offers *mariscada* (Spanish bouillabaisse); chicken

with garlic and white wine; veal with onions, peppers, garlic, and sausages; shrimp grilled in the shell with lemon, garlic, and parsley; and several varieties of paella—*valenciana* (with chicken, sausage, and seafood), marinara (all seafood), and *hortelana* (vegetarian). Wash it all down with a potent margarita. ♦ Spanish ♦ Daily lunch and dinner. Reservations recommended Friday-Sunday. 4 Charles St (at Greenwich Ave). 924.5915. Also at: 58 E 34th St (between Park and Madison Aves). 689.1019

105 C3 ★★$ Attached to the moderately priced **Washington Square Hotel,** this restaurant looks a lot like a coffee shop. However, there's some serious cooking going on inside. Chef Charles Simmons turns out earthy, satisfying food with a sophisticated twist: try jalapeño-cilantro linguine with sautéed shrimp, grilled leg of lamb with white-bean salad and herbed red-pepper polenta, or Mom's meat loaf accompanied by the rich and delicious herb-and-parmesan mashed potatoes. ♦ American ♦ M lunch; Tu-Sa lunch and dinner; Su brunch. 103 Waverly Pl (at MacDougal St). 254.1200

106 Balducci's This is the grocer ne plus ultra in Greenwich Village. It began humbly many years ago as a produce stand across the street from the present site, and today this family-run store is one of the grandest and best-stocked specialty shops in New York City. Not only is the produce still top-notch, but the cheese selection is first-rate too, as are the fish, meat, cold cuts, and prepared take-out dishes (try Mama's pasta—a rich, delicious sun-dried tomato sauce over spaghetti created by the late, beloved Mama Balducci) and everything from the bakery department. The shelves hold packaged products from all over the world, but specialize in delicacies from Italy and France. Despite constant reorganization and expansion, the store is always crowded no matter the time of day. ♦ Daily. 424 Sixth Ave (at W Ninth St). 673.2600 &

Greenwich Village tearooms in the 1920s used a variety of gimmicks to attract customers. Romany Marie's Rumanian Den tried to recreate the atmosphere of the old country; The Pirates Den was rigged out like a pirate's ship; the decor at Toby's Tavern included a coffin bearing a flickering candle; and in the spirit of Lewis Carroll, The Mad Hatter had the words "Down the Rabbit Hole" written backwards over its basement entrance.

Marylou's

07 Marylou's ★★$$$ Skip the appetizers and soups here and go directly to the generous main courses, particularly the perfectly broiled fresh fish, of which there are usually at least a half-dozen choices. And given the graceful, traditional appointments in several dining rooms—pleasant wood-framed paintings, fireplaces, library walls—and the friendly service, this could be considered the best seafood restaurant in the Village. It can also be a good place for celebrity spotting; Jack Nicholson always stops in when he's in town—the owner is his pal Tommy Baratta, who designed a special weight-loss diet for the star. ♦ Seafood ♦ Daily dinner and late-night meals. Reservations recommended. 21 W Ninth St (between Fifth and Sixth Aves). 533.0012

T H E   R O S E
C A F E   &   B A R

08 Rose Cafe ★★$$ The glassed-in sidewalk cafe is the most popular spot to sit at this restaurant—understandable, as the windows are a moving tableau of passersby strolling down Fifth Avenue to **Washington Square Park.** But the sophisticated dining room, with beige walls accented with mirrors and whimsical yellow, white, and green striped lighting fixtures, is also a good place to enjoy rosemary-roasted chicken salad, an assortment of gourmet sandwiches, and pizzas with ingredients that include grilled chicken and smoked salmon. More elaborate dishes include butternut squash ravioli in mushroom-herb sauce, grilled chicken paillard with ratatouille, and pepper-crusted loin of pork with cider sauce. For dessert, try the Granny Smith apple tart. ♦ American bistro ♦ M-F lunch and dinner; Sa-Su brunch and dinner. Reservations recommended. 24 Fifth Ave (at W Ninth St). 260.4118

09 Dallas BBQ $ Popular with **New York University (NYU)** students for the inexpensive, early-bird barbecued chicken dinners, this basic, bustling place serves decent chicken and ribs, onion rings, and cole slaw. ♦ Barbecue ♦ Daily lunch and dinner. 21 University Pl (at E Eighth St). 674.4450. Also at: 1265 Third Ave (at E 73rd St). 772.9393; 27 W 72nd St (between

Central Park W and Columbus Ave). 873.2004; 132 Second Ave (at St. Mark's Pl). 777.5574

110 Knickerbocker Bar & Grill ★$$ Fascinating 19th-century artifacts and posters fill this casual yet classy bar and restaurant. Chef Peter Fiori, formerly of **Bouley,** has given the menu—featuring good steak-house fare, as well as grilled fish and pasta—a lift. T-bone steak, pork chops, and pan-roasted chicken are among the more popular dishes. But the subdued atmosphere and live jazz (Wednesday through Sunday starting at 9:45PM)—often featuring name performers—are the main draws. There's a cover charge and minimum during music shows. ♦ American ♦ M-F lunch and dinner; Sa dinner; Su brunch and dinner. Reservations recommended. 33 University Pl (at E Ninth St). 228.8490 &

the M A R K H A M

111 The Markham ★★★$$$ The name comes from two sources: the 19th-century poet Edwin Markham and a type of peach. Such understated cool fits right in with the similarly understated decor of the upstairs dining room of this 19th-century town house—only crystal chandeliers and mirrors give it a touch of elegance. Turned out by Chef Mark Spangenthal, formerly of **Gotham Bar & Grill** and **Alison on Dominick Street,** the food is both refined and assertive. Try the panfried artichokes, pan-roasted quail with stewed tomatoes in a basil vinaigrette, cedar-plank–roasted salmon on braised greens, and pan-roasted pork loin in a Jack Daniels sauce. For dessert, don't miss the moist, spicy gingerbread served with preserved plums. The wine list is well chosen and nicely priced. ♦ American ♦ M-F lunch and dinner; Sa-Su brunch and dinner. Reservations recommended. 59 Fifth Ave (at W 13th St). 647.9391

Downstairs at the Markham:

The Markham Cafe ★★$ This casual, cafeteria-style cafe shares the same high standards as the upstairs restaurant, and many of the same items. There are several salads, among them black bean with scallion-cilantro vinaigrette, beet and walnut, a pasta variety, and chicken salad; sandwiches include roasted chicken on rosemary bread; and avocado, smoked mozzarella, and tomato on health bread. Save room for the luscious desserts: the same gingerbread as upstairs, cheesecake brownies, chocolate layer cake, and blueberry buckle. ♦ American ♦ Daily breakfast, lunch, and dinner. 807.1715

112 The Adoré ★★$ A small menu of sandwiches, salads, and homemade croissants is offered at this tiny, charming upstairs cafe that feels like a room in a country inn. Especially good are the sandwiches, particularly smoked duck with tomatoes, onions, and arugula with mustard sauce; and crabmeat and avocado. There is also a good selection of pastries and teas. ♦ Cafe ♦ M-Sa breakfast, lunch, and afternoon tea. No credit cards accepted. 17 E 13th St (between Fifth Ave and University Pl). 243.8742

113 The Cake Bar & Cafe ★★$ Upstairs is a smart dining spot with interesting design ideas (hammered cake pans constitute the metallic ceiling); downstairs is a take-out shop. TV personality Maury Povich's daughter Susan turns out the sumptuous Mediterranean-influenced pastas, sandwiches, and salads that include a vinaigrette-drizzled portobello and moz-zarella sandwich, low-fat turkey sandwich with carrot-soy dressing, and a salad of roast vegetables. Her partner Jude Quintiere makes such cakes as banana rum mixed with chocolate mousse and a chocolate pyramid filled with passion-fruit mousse that is nigh impossible to resist, as are the cookies. ♦ Bakery/Cafe ♦ M-Sa breakfast, lunch, and dinner. 22 E 13th St (between University Pl and Fifth Ave). 807.1313

114 Asti $$$ Enjoy the singing waiters and professional opera singers while you eat routine Southern Italian standards. Go for the fun, which begins nightly at 6:30PM, not for the food. ♦ Italian ♦ Tu-Su lunch and dinner. 13 E 12th St (between University Pl and Fifth Ave). 741.9105

114 Marquet Patisserie ★$ The baguettes here are every bit as good as they are in France, as are the croissants and tempting pastries. For those who do not live by cake alone, there are a few salads and sandwiches to have first at tables in the back. ♦ Bakery/Cafe ♦ M-Sa breakfast and lunch. No credit cards accepted. 15 E 12th St (between University Pl and Fifth Ave). 229.9313 &

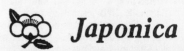

115 Gotham Bar and Grill ★★★$$$$ It's hard to overestimate the magnitude of chef Alfred Portale's influence on the New York culinary scene. So many notable chefs, including **Aja**'s Gary Robins and **Verbena**'s Diane Forley, ascended under Portale's tutelage. In this impressive, multilevel loft space—accented with massive overhead lights draped in white fabric, mustard-colored columns, and a statue of Lady Liberty—the master still appears to be in top form. This is the home of tall food, dishes that qualify as architectural wonders as well as palate pleasers. Try the sautéed skate wings with eggplant caviar; butternut squash risotto; seared yellowfin tuna with *pappardelle* (broad noodles) and caponata (a relish of eggplant, onions, tomatoes, anchovies, olives, pine nuts, capers, and vinegar cooked in olive oil); saddle of rabbit with white beans; squab and grilled foie gras with apple cider sauce; and rack of lamb with Swiss chard. Be sure to save room for one of the devastating desserts: warm Gotham chocolate cake; vanilla and crème fraîche cheesecake with Michigan blueberries and blueberry ice cream; warm apple financier with ginger ice cream; a caramelized banana tart; and maple crème brûlée. The wine list is well chosen, international in scope, and expensive. ♦ American ♦ M-F lunch and dinner; Sa-Su dinner. Reservations required. 12 E 12th St (between University Pl and Fifth Ave). 620.4020

115 The Big Enchilada ★$ There are numerous Tex-Mex joints around town but this basic place serves generous, tasty versions of the old familiar burritos and enchiladas fare. Try the signature Big Enchilada, which is stuffed with rice, beans, lettuce, tomatoes, a choice of vegetables, beef, or stewed chicken, and topped with jack cheese and guacamole. ♦ Tex-Mex ♦ Daily lunch and dinner. 28 E 12th St (between University Pl and Fifth Ave). 627.7940. Also at: 160 E 28th St (between Third and Lexington Aves). 447.7940

116 Japonica ★★★$$ Friendly service, spectacular specialty rolls, and an unusual assortment of sushi—baby yellowtail, giant clam, spicy smelt caviar, and baby octopus, all rolled with white or brown rice—draw diners from all over the city to this very small place. Those who are feeling experimental (and have some money to play with) should let the chef put a sushi assortment together–the artistry is extraordinary. The hot food is sublime as well— try broiled eel, Royal Japonica (half-broiled, half-steamed salmon on slices of orange, topped with salmon caviar and mint leaves), grilled bluefin tuna, or sizzling vegetables. Those who dislike raw fish can have their sushi cooked. There's even a complimentary glass of plum wine served after dinner. The only complaint is there are long waits for a table. ◆ Japanese ◆ Daily lunch and dinner. 100 University Pl (at E 12th St). 243.7752

17 Cedar Tavern $ This barnlike restaurant and beautiful dark bar with decent hamburgers has long been a hangout for artists. ◆ American ◆ Daily lunch, dinner, and late-night meals. 82 University Pl (between E 11th and E 12th Sts). 929.9089

18 Bradley's ★$$ Some of the most famous musicians in contemporary jazz show up to play a set in this Village hangout (the music starts at 10PM). Simple but good food is also served here—pasta, steak, lamb chops, catch of the day, and great burgers. Cover; minimum. ◆ American ◆ Daily lunch, dinner, and late-night meals. 70 University Pl (between E 10th and E 11th Sts). 228.6440

19 Il Cantinori ★★$$$ Country antiques from Italy set the stage for an authentic Tuscan meal here. For a starter, try the assortment of grilled vegetables, then move on to *tonno al pesto* (grilled tuna steak sliced and served with pesto vinaigrette and diced tomatoes). For dessert, good luck trying to choose among the apple tart, various gelati, tiramisù, and double-layer chocolate cake. ◆ Italian ◆ Daily lunch and dinner. 32 E 10th St (between Broadway and University Pl). 673.6044

120 Caffè Pane e Cioccolato ★$ After working up an appetite strolling around the Village, come here for light fare that's perfect for a nosh. The pastas and salads are surprisingly good, and the cappuccino is downright excellent. ◆ Cafe ◆ Daily lunch, dinner, and late-night meals. 10 Waverly Pl (at Mercer St). 473.3944

121 Dojo West ★$ Like its East Village twin, this cheap, healthy place seems to be a lifeline for **NYU** students. The chicken sukiyaki salad and the incredibly inexpensive soy burger with tahini sauce are popular picks. The natural wood tables are packed together and often full. ◆ Japanese/Health food ◆ Daily breakfast, lunch, and dinner. No credit cards accepted. 14 W Fourth St (at Mercer St). 505.8934. Also at: 24 St. Mark's Pl (between Second and Third Aves). 674.9821

Bests

Peter Kump
President, The James Beard Foundation

Foodies' mecca: Conceived by Julia Child, the **James Beard House** is the former home of America's father of gastronomy, now used as a showcase for chefs from all over the country. Some call it the best restaurant in town—a different chef cooks each night. You can visit Beard's kitchen, see art exhibits related to food, visit the gift shop, or come for a meal.

Special places for meals and entertaining: For brunch during spring and summer weekends nothing could be more picturesque than a table in the gardens at **Tavern on the Green** in **Central Park.** When the weather is cold or bleak, try **Lola's** for a rousing gospel-singing brunch that you won't forget. For cocktails, don't miss **The Rainbow Room** at sunset.

Favorite bistros: **Park Bistro** (French); **Mi Cocina** (Mexican); **Becco** (Italian); **Vince & Eddie's** (American).

Equipment: The **Bowery** on the **Lower East Side** has unparalleled shops for eager foodies, each generally specializing in such things as glassware and tableware, restaurant equipment, etc. Take a taxi to the 200 block. Low, low prices but closed Saturdays. Further uptown try **Lamalle Kitchenware.**

Food emporiums: The hustle and bustle at **Zabar's** can be overwhelming but it is still almost everyone's favorite on the **Upper West Side. Balducci's** in **Greenwich Village** is just as much fun, and **Dean & DeLuca** is the store that set the standards for upscale shops and the whole gourmet take-out business. Hidden away on the **Upper East Side** is Eli Zabar's **Vinegar Factory,** which, in spite of its name, is a gourmet's food oasis that may be the pleasantest in the city.

Books for cooks: **Kitchen Arts & Letters** is the nation's best cookbook store, and the **Strand Bookstore** with literally miles of used books offers review copies of cookbooks at great prices.

East Village

Manhattan's last bastion of bohemia, the East Village—bordered by the **East River**, **Broadway**, **Houston Street**, and **14th Street**—was once the city's most fashionable part of town. During the mid-to-late 1660s, the area was the site of the estate of the last Dutch Governor General, Peter Stuyvesant; it ranged from the East River to present-day **Fourth Avenue** and from **Fifth** to **17th Streets**. During the 1830s, houses belonging to the Astors, Vanderbilts, and Delanos lined **Lafayette Street** from **Great Jones Street** to **Astor Place**. Almost nothing remains of those glory days, except the **Old Merchants' House** on **Fourth Street** and **Colonnade Row** (also known as **LaGrange Terrace**) on Lafayette Street, where the likes of John Jacob Astor and Warren Delano, Franklin Delano Roosevelt's grandfather, once lived.

Today, the most prominent denizens of the neighborhood are likely to be clad in leather and sporting green- or raspberry-colored hair. But they are no Johnny-come-latelys; the counterculture's history here goes back at least 30

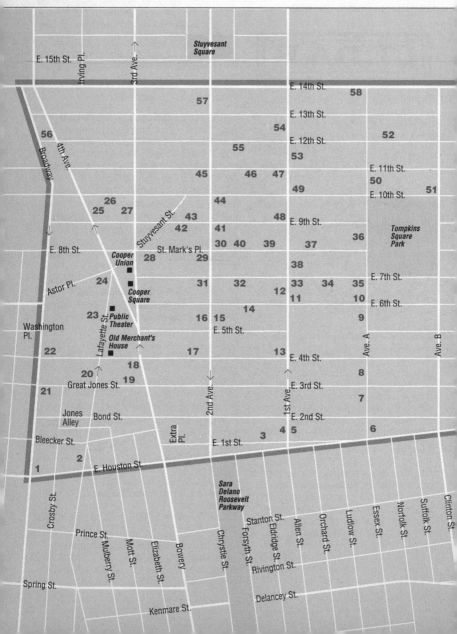

years. It began during the 1960s, when hippies crowded into Dayglo-painted crash pads on and around **St. Mark's Place** and attended the **Fillmore East** or all-night Grateful Dead concerts or went to the **Electric Circus** to dance to songs by Iron Butterfly. Something of a spillover phenomenon from its western neighbor, Greenwich Village, the unconventional community of today's East Village is younger, less manicured, and more cutting-edge. During the past 20 years, the area has made a name for itself as the locus of trend-setting art, music, and fashion; now it's also becoming known for its vibrant, thriving restaurant scene.

Here coexist small, dark, zebra-stripe-wallpapered cafes offering poetry readings, sushi bars with shiny black walls, fine French bistros, Italian trattorie, and cozy soul food parlors. Even the streets of so-called **Alphabet City (Avenues A, B, C, and D)**, once known for their seediness and drug activity, are now filled with restaurants—one more interesting than the next.

Trendy restaurants, however, are only part of the food scene in the area. The East Village is an ethnic melting pot—like its neighbor the Lower East Side—and its waves of immigration (past and present) influence the local restaurants and shops. **Little India**, the stretch of **Sixth Street** between **First** and **Second Avenues**, contains at least 20 East Indian restaurants, with another half-dozen spilling around the avenue corners. Little India got its start in 1968, when five brothers arrived from India and found that they liked everything about New York except the dearth of good Indian cooking. One brother took matters into his own hands by opening a restaurant, and before long his brothers also entered the food business; others soon followed, and the rest is history. **Little Ukraine**, near Astor Place at **Cooper Square** (**Third Avenue** and **Seventh Street**), is characterized by Byzantine churches with onion-shaped domes, shops stocking Slavic music and painted eggs, and such restaurants as **Kiev** and **Ukrainian** that serve piroshki and stuffed cabbage in much the same surroundings as they have for decades. Lining First Avenue are shops selling pierogi and Polish sausage for those who want to serve those meals at home.

What the Indian and Ukrainian residents of the East Village think of their more flamboyant neighbors, one can only imagine. But the various groups do live peacefully and offer one of the most stunning arrays of dining options around.

East River

E. 15th St.

E. 13th St.

Franklin D. Roosevelt Dr.

Szold Pl.

E. 10th St.

East River Park

E. 9th St.

E. 8th St.

E. 7th St.

E. 6th St.

E. 5th St.

Ave. C

E. 4th St.

Ave. D

E. 3rd St.

E. Houston St.

Hamilton Fish Park

Columbia St.

Ridge St.

Pitt St.

Delancey St.

Williamsburg Bridge

N

km
mi   1/8   1/4   1/4   1/2

1 Louisiana Community Bar and Grill ★$$ The chefs at this Cajun restaurant—formerly **K-Paul's**—were all trained by Paul Prudhomme. Come for the food: blackened tuna, blackened prime rib, étouffée, jambalaya; and the music: blues, jazz, and zydeco. New Orleans natives swear by the crawfish. ◆ Cajun ◆ Daily dinner. Reservations recommended. 622 Broadway (at E Houston St). 460.9633

THE NOHO ★ STAR

2 Noho Star ★$ This soaring space with colorful marbleized columns is the setting for a freewheeling array of food that takes the scenic route from Southeast Asia to Southwest US. Try the Aztec corn soup, the bamboo-steamed vegetables with steamed whole fish, the British burger with stilton cheese, and the rich, sweet Indian pudding. The salads, sandwiches, and egg dishes are also good. ◆ Eclectic ◆ M-F lunch and dinner; Sa-Su brunch and dinner. Reservations recommended. 330 Lafayette St (at Bleecker St). 925.0070 ♿

3 Casani's ★$$ The food served in this tiny dining room, with bulbous lamps, humorous figurines from liquor companies, and mirrored beige walls is uneven but the best dishes, particularly the fish soup with saffron, the garlicky roast chicken, and the sweet *tarte tatin* (upside-down apple tart), practically wing your taste buds across the Atlantic. In the warmer weather, tables are available in a cobbled courtyard outside. ◆ French ◆ M-F dinner; Sa-Su brunch and dinner. 54 E First St (between First and Second Aves). 777.1589

3 One on One Need a tasty energy boost? This little orange shack offers your favorite freshly squeezed juice blend (try strawberry and banana) on the spot, even in winter. ◆ Daily. No credit cards accepted. 72 E First St (at First Ave). No phone ♿

4 Boca Chica ★$ Spicy Latin music on weekends makes this funky East Village spot a must for night owls. Other days of the week aren't exactly bland either, with rivers of exotic Brazilian drinks to keep customers in jovial spirits and staples from the South American menu, such as garlicky chicken and shredded beef, which can get as hot as the music. ◆ South American ◆ M-Sa dinner; Su brunch and dinner. 13 First Ave (at E First St). 473.0108

4 La Linea ★$ A handsome electric-blue and yellow cafe, this is a great place for a sandwich or a pastry and cappuccino. There's a living room in the back with easy chairs perfect for all-day slouching. ◆ Cafe ◆ Daily breakfast, lunch, and dinner. 15 First Ave (at E First St). 777.1571

5 Baby Jake's ★$ Jake is the baby son of the owner, a reference that sets the tone for this friendly, homey place. The decor feels thrown together, and combined with the very open kitchen, gives the impression that you're dining at a friend's apartment—but that's part of the charm. Other pluses are the accommodating policy of serving breakfast at whatever hour of the day you desire and offering great burgers, fried catfish, salmon fajitas, and sweet-potato fries until late at night. ◆ American/Cajun ◆ Daily lunch, dinner, and late-night meals. 14 First Ave (between First and Second Sts). 254.2229

5 Lucky Cheng's ★$ At this trendy Asian spot, the waitresses in their tight silk dresses are not what they seem—it's sort of a lighthearted version of *M. Butterfly*. The whole experience is meant to be exotic: dim lighting tones of turquoise, lacquered red, and gold, and a fish pond downstairs that was constructed from a bath leftover from the days when this was a Lower East Side bathhouse. The food is as dramatic as the decor—miso salmon on stir-fried Chinese greens, Shanghai noodles with mixed vegetables in sesame-citrus sauce, and stir-fried noodles with scallops, mussels, and calamari in lobster sauce. The place is so popular that on a given night it's entirely possible to be waiting in line next to Prince Albert of Monaco or Barbra Streisand (who couldn't get a table one evening because of the crush). ◆ Asian ◆ Daily dinner. 24 First Ave (between First and Second Sts). 473.0516

6 Mekka ★★$ This low-key downtown sibling of the Upper West Side's **Shark Bar** serves spicy soul food in very cool surroundings—the dark dining room has a metallic wall and banquettes of brick red and royal blue. Try the blackened catfish, the baby-back ribs, or the smothered pork chop with collard greens and yams. Be sure to save room for the sweet-potato pie and the buttery apple crunch. ◆ Southern ◆ Daily dinner and late-night meals. 14 Avenue A (at Houston and First Sts). 475.8500 ♿

7 Two Boots ★$ An East Village original, this place serves Louisiana cuisine with an Italian twist—the boots refer to the shape of both state and country. Try the pecan-crusted catfish with cilantro aioli or the barbequed-shrimp pizza. The decor is part of the experience—there's the memorabilia-embedded, see-through plastic bar to admire or the Cajun-flavored jukebox to play—but if it's home delivery you want, **Two Boots to Go** (505.5450) is right across the street. ♦ Cajun/Italian ♦ M-F lunch and dinner; Sa-Su brunch and dinner. 37 Ave A (between E Second and E Third Sts). 505.2276 ৬. Also at: 74 Bleecker St (at Broadway). 777.1033; 75 Greenwich Ave (at Seventh Ave S). 633.9096; 514 Second St (between Seventh and Eighth Aves, Brooklyn). 718/499.3253

8 **Limbo** ★$ This sunny, yellow dining room, furnished with dinette sets from the 1950s, is a good place to spend a couple of hours writing tortured prose while munching on a delicious sandwich or piece of cake. Commune with fellow belle lettrists at readings every Tuesday at 7PM. ♦ Cafe ♦ Daily breakfast, lunch, dinner, and late-night meals. 47 Ave A (between E Third and E Fourth Sts). 477.5271 ৬

9 **Ci Vediamo** ★$ The kitschy murals of gondolas and the crooning strains of *Moon River* almost make you forget this is the East Village. The pastas range from good to excellent—even better when you consider what you'd be paying uptown. Try the lusty tomato-based *fettuccine alla siciliana* (with eggplant and mozzarella), but save room for the classic Italian ricotta cheesecake. The restaurant's name means "see you later," and considering the food and the prices, they're probably right. ♦ Italian ♦ Daily dinner and late-night meals. No credit cards accepted. 85 Ave A (between E Fifth and E Sixth Sts). 995.5300

9 **Takahachi** ★★$ The room is drab and too brightly lit for comfort, but the superlative sushi—the freshest in the area—more than makes up for the third-rate surroundings. ♦ Japanese ♦ Daily dinner. 85 Ave A (between E Fifth and E Sixth Sts). 505.6524

10 **Pisces** ★★$$ As the name might suggest, this handsome place with wood beams and exposed brick walls is known for very fresh, well-prepared fish, much of it smoked in house. Try the tuna and smoked-onion pie with red mole sauce, the sautéed skate with *colcannon* (mashed potatoes with finely chopped onions and greens) and fried artichokes, and the hickory-roasted whole trout with potato-and-carrot purée. ♦ Seafood ♦ M-F dinner; Sa-Su brunch and dinner. Reservations recommended. 95 Ave A (at E Sixth St). 260.6660

11 **Caravan of Dreams** ★$ Welcome back to the 1960s: wood tables and chairs, plants, posters, and a notice on the menu advertising massages. Backrubs aside, neighbors flock here for such creative, imaginative vegetarian dishes as polenta with winter squash sauce, vegetable burgers with tahini, and ginger-curried stir-fry with pasta, vegetables, and a sweet-and-sour sauce. ♦ Vegetarian ♦ M dinner; Tu-F lunch and dinner; Sa-Su brunch and dinner. 405 E Sixth St (between Ave A and First Ave). 254.1613

12 **Teresa's** ★$ A very plain luncheonette with often uncommunicative servers, this place offers basic Polish food. But if you're in the market for pierogi, blintzes, stuffed cabbage, or other exports from the old country, you'd be hard-pressed to find a restaurant that serves better quality dishes than this one. ♦ Polish ♦ Daily lunch and dinner. No credit cards accepted. 103 First Ave (between E 6th and E 7th Sts). 228.0604

13 **Three of Cups** ★$ This cozy cafe's name is taken from a tarot card that represents success and abundance—an appropriate nomenclature indeed. The food, most of which comes out of the prominently displayed wood-burning oven, is simple, well-prepared, and plentiful. Particularly popular are the thin-crust pizzas, such as the *puttanesca* (with olives, anchovies, and capers). Also popular is chicken marinated in olive oil, rosemary, and coarse salt. ♦ Italian ♦ M-F dinner and late-night meals; Sa-Su brunch and dinner. 83 First Ave (at E Fifth St). 388.0059

13 **First** ★★$$ A model of understated elegance downtown style, the dining room at this trendy eatery has a long brick wall, hammered metal tables, low lighting, and circular gray banquettes. But that's not why uptowners make the pilgrimage; they come for Samuel DeMarco's cooking, which is complex but not fussy, inventive, and, considering the effort that goes into it, reasonably priced. Try the *brandade* (a creamy salt-cod puree) cake with salad niçoise, olive paste, and oven-dried–tomato vinaigrette; the spicy beer-braised short ribs with jicama slaw; the soy-honey marinated duck; the roast pig (a Sunday night special); and the warm chocolate-pudding cake. ♦ Eclectic

♦ Daily dinner and late-night meals. Reservations recommended. 87 First Ave (between Fifth and Sixth Sts). 674.3823

14 Passage to India ★$ With more than 20 Indian restaurants in the area, competition is heavy, but this small spot is among the better ones. The freshly baked breads and tandoori specials are highlights. ♦ Indian ♦ Daily lunch, dinner, and late-night meals. 308 E Sixth St (between First and Second Aves). 529.5770

14 Mitali ★★$$ The running gag about the Indian restaurants on and around Sixth Street is that one central kitchen supplies them all. The cooking at this dark—even dingy—place, however, has always stood out. Try the *murgha tikka muslam* (chicken barbecued over charcoal and then cooked in a sauce of cream and almonds), *chana shaag* (chickpeas and spinach with a spicy sauce), *alu mottor gobi* (a stew of potatoes, peas, and cauliflower), or any of the tandoori meats. ♦ Indian ♦ Daily lunch and dinner. Reservations recommended. 334 E Sixth St (between First and Second Aves). 533.2508. Also at: 296 Bleecker St (at Seventh Ave). 989.1367

15 Haveli ★$ The ambience at this bilevel Indian restaurant is more tranquil and the food more refined than at most of the places around the corner on Sixth Street. Try the banana fritters, the tandoori mixed grill, or any of the numerous vegetarian specialties. ♦ Indian ♦ Daily lunch and dinner. 100 Second Ave (between E Fifth and E Sixth Sts). 982.0533

16 Global 33 ★$ After a long run with a Caribbean motif, the owners of the former tenant of this space—**Sugar Reef**—decided to transform it into a futuristic showcase for food and drink from all over the world. The lighting is subdued, courtesy of beams filtering through holes in ceiling panels, and the 1960s' samba sound track. Among the international fare is couscous with fennel, orange, mint, and onion; fried zucchini polenta with roasted-pepper cream sauce; grilled pork kebabs with Moorish seasoning; and sautéed trout with wasabi crème fraîche. Global drinks include Brazilian *caipirinhas,* Jamaican dark and stormys, and British Pimms. ♦ International ♦ Daily dinner and late-night meals. 93 Second Ave (between E Fifth and E Sixth Sts). 477.8427

17 Cucina di Pesce ★$ A more reasonably priced good Italian seafood restaurant would be hard to find in Manhattan. Try the spinach penne with asparagus and sun-dried tomatoes in cream sauce or the tuna steak grilled with sautéed sweet peppers, capers, olives, and onions. To accommodate the crowds, the same management opened **Frutti di Mare,** an annex across the street (84 E Fourth St, 979.2034) that serves both lunch and dinner;

both are conveniently located on the same block as the **La Mama** theater complex. ♦ Italian ♦ Daily dinner. No credit cards accepted. 87 E Fourth St (between Second Ave and Bowery). 260.6800

18 Marion's Continental Restaurant and Lounge ★$$ This was the place to be in the 1960s, when senators, presidents, and movie stars were all regulars here. It closed in the early 1970s but Marion's son and a business partner reopened the landmark in 1990 with much of its signature decor intact: the corner banquette (once reserved for John and Jackie Kennedy); tropical fish tank; tile bar; and walls adorned with clown paintings, Utrillo reproductions, and signed photographs of Clark Gable and Frank Sinatra. The food is not uniformly dependable, although the Caesar salad and steak au poivre are both good. Come for the inexpensive Vodka Gibsons, old fashioneds, and Manhattans. ♦ Continental ♦ Daily dinner. 354 Bowery (between Great Jones and E Fourth Sts). 475.7621

BOWERY BAR

18 Bowery Bar ★$$ The hot spot of the moment, this place was so well hyped that it was booked solid before it even opened. A former gas station, the dining room flaunts its roots with a haute garage motif—from photos of car engines to displayed truck parts. Food is secondary here—getting the chance to furtively gawk at such celebrities as Cindy Crawford and Donna Karan is more the point. However, you can get a perfectly acceptable pan-seared salmon, roasted free-range chicken, grilled lemon-ginger tuna, and for dessert, a hot fudge sundae or gingerbread ice-cream sandwich with caramel sauce. As reservations can be hard to come by, dropping in for a drink at the bar is the quicker way to check out the scene for yourself. Sit on the patio in warm weather, set off from the Bowery behind a high wall. ♦ American ♦ M-F lunch and dinner; Sa-Su brunch and dinner. Reservations required. 358 Bowery (at E Fourth St). 475.2220

19 Great Jones Cafe $ Blackened fish, sweet-potato fries, gumbo, and other decent, reasonably priced eats are served in a loud and lively roadside bar atmosphere. The Blue Plate special, usually meat loaf or pork chops, is probably a lot like your Mom used to make. The jukebox is full of rare soul and classic country cuts, and the spicy Cajun Bloody Marys are potent enough to clear away even the most serious cobwebs. ♦ Cajun/American ♦ M-F dinner; Sa-Su brunch and dinner. No credit cards accepted. 54 Great Jones St (between Bowery and Lafayette St). 674.9304

20 **Time Cafe** ★$$ Trendy crowds populate this spot from breakfast until late at night. They come not only to talk on their cellular phones and be seen, but to dine on deliciously healthy dishes that include charred yellowfin tuna salad and free-range chicken tortillas with cilantro pesto. Within the cafe is a bilevel Moroccan club called **Fez**, which offers jazz, poetry readings, and cushy couches at night; there's a cover charge. ♦ American ♦ Daily breakfast, lunch, dinner, and late-night meals. Reservations recommended. 380 Lafayette St (at Great Jones St). 533.7000

21 **Acme Bar & Grill** ★$$ If you're looking for food that will stick to your ribs, you've come to the right place. The selection includes Cajun-style chicken, jambalaya, and gumbo. Don't miss the wonderful mashed potatoes with cream gravy. A ledge along one entire wall is lined with samples of every conceivable kind of hot sauce—experiment at your own risk. After dinner, head downstairs for live music; there's a cover charge. ♦ Southern ♦ M-F lunch and dinner; Sa-Su brunch and dinner. 9 Great Jones St (between Lafayette St and Broadway). 420.1934 ♿

22 **Bayamo** ★$$ This is one of the better eateries on the lower Broadway strip; the menu seems a little gimmicky, but the food is consistently good. The inventive appetizers include fried or grilled chicken wings and fried wontons. Happy Hours and late nights tend to get a little crowded; the mob at the bar clamoring for frozen margaritas can be six-people deep. If that's not your speed, maybe lunch or an early evening dinner on the balcony is best. Note painter Nadia Rodin's wonderful party scene on the wall just as you enter. ♦ Cuban/Chinese ♦ Daily lunch and dinner; F-Sa late-night meals. 704 Broadway (between E Fourth St and Washington Pl). 475.5151

23 **Toast** ★★$$ The decor of this restaurant is decidedly vibrant, particularly the red-and-yellow lacquered walls, but the flavors you'll find here are subtle, complex, and exotic. Try the wontons with curried lamb and mango chutney, duck breast over greens and chive vinaigrette, marinated prawns with orzo and tamarind, and a perfect crème brûlée flavored with mango and Madagascan vanilla. This place, like neighboring **Indochine** and **L'Udo** (see below), has the advantage of being close to the **Astor Place Theater** and across the street from **The Public Theater.** ♦ Fusion ♦ Tu-Su dinner. Reservations recommended. 428 Lafayette St (between E Fourth St and Astor Pl). 473.1698

23 **Indochine** ★★$$ This trendy spot boasts consistently good French/Vietnamese food, which is served in a softly lit tropical-themed room that's filled with an attractive and well-dressed crowd. Try the spring rolls, the crispy duck with ginger, and the whole sea bass with lemongrass. The beautiful old apartment building above the restaurant is **Colonnade Row** (also known as **LaGrange Terrace**), where the likes of John Jacob Astor and Warren Delano, Franklin Delano Roosevelt's grandfather, once lived. ♦ French/Vietnamese ♦ Daily dinner. Reservations recommended. 430 Lafayette St (between E Fourth St and Astor Pl). 505.5111

23 **L'Udo** ★$$ The name comes from the Latin word for fresco, and this two-tiered restaurant designed to look like the ruins of a Tuscan villa is covered with dreamy, fantasy-laden frescoes full of mystical characters. The decor and the location—it's across the street from the **Public Theater**—are the big draws here. The menu, which features southern French fare with a few pasta dishes tossed in, is hit-and-miss. Among the more successful choices are the white-bean salad with fresh tomatoes and shaved parmesan, hanger steak with shallot and red-wine sauce, and roasted rack of lamb. Skip the desserts. ♦ French/Italian ♦ M-F lunch and dinner; Sa-Su brunch and dinner. Reservations recommended. 432 Lafayette St (between E Fourth St and Astor Pl). 388.0978

24 **Astor Wines and Spirits** A large selection and generally good prices are the draws of this spacious wine shop, but sometimes the staff is less than thoroughly knowledgeable. ♦ M-Sa. 12 Astor Pl (at Lafayette St). 674.7500

25 **Briscola** ★★$$$ In Italy, *briscola* is a popular card game played by young and old alike. At this neighborhood find, the tables are too small to hold a full deck, but who cares about playing cards when you can feast on such authentic Sicilian specialties as artichokes with mint; tagliatelle with sausage, peas, and cream; *bucatini* (macaroni) with sardines; and swordfish carpaccio. ♦ Sicilian ♦ M-F lunch and dinner; Sa dinner. 65 Fourth Ave (between E Ninth and E 10th Sts). 254.1940

Horn and Hardart opened its first automated cafeteria at Broadway and East 13th Street in 1902. Branches of this popular institution sprang up all over the city until they numbered several dozen. Their popularity waned, and the last automat—on East 42nd Street and Third Avenue—closed in 1991.

25 Macmed Spuntino ★$ An offshoot of neighboring Briscola (see above), this informal cafe is a pleasant place to stop for light snacks. Try any of the *panini* (sandwiches), such as the mozzarella special with sun-dried tomatoes, a pizza, or simply a pastry and cappuccino. There's also sensational homemade gelato. ◆ Cafe ◆ M-Sa breakfast, lunch, and dinner. 65 Fourth Ave (between E Ninth and E 10th Sts). 979.5725

26 Danal ★★$ This cozy, below-ground cafe looks like a room assembled from yard-sale finds—wooden farmhouse tables with mismatched chairs, hanging baskets with dried flowers, lamps, birdcages, the odd rug—but the overall effect works. Along with the charming country feeling comes hearty American food, which might include (the menu changes daily) grilled pork chops with onion confit, chicken pot pie, or stuffed roast chicken. Brunch is so popular—featuring such dishes as French-toasted croissants with cinnamon apples—that a crowd is likely to gather on the benches outside waiting to get in; afternoon tea may be slightly more relaxed. ◆ American ◆ W-Th breakfast, lunch, and dinner; F breakfast, lunch, afternoon tea, and dinner; Sa brunch, afternoon tea, and dinner; Su brunch and dinner. Reservations recommended. 90 E 10th St (between Third and Fourth Aves). 982.6930

Meals on Reels: Take One

New Yorkers see so many location trucks around town that they've grown blasé. Unless the filming blocks traffic or prevents them from getting into their favorite restaurant, locals just blithely ask, "Which movie is this?" and go about their business.

If the location happens to be the **Rainbow Room**, the movie in question could have been any of these: *The Prince of Tides* (1991), when Nick Nolte and Barbra Streisand dance the night away; *Sleepless in Seattle* (1993), when Meg Ryan breaks up with fiancé Bill Pullman at **The Rainbow Promenade Lounge;** and *Six Degrees of Separation* (1993), when Will Smith and his male companion are thrown out after a rowdy turn on the dance floor. Here are some other films that feature New York eateries:

Arthur (1981) Dudley Moore begins his tour de farce by stumbling out of his limo and reeling into the **Plaza Hotel**'s **Palm Court Room.**

Broadway Danny Rose (1984) Comedians gather to talk about agent Woody Allen at the **Carnegie Deli**—one of New York's most revered institutions.

Crossing Delancey (1988) **Essex Street Pickles** was the place Amy Irving's soon-to-be husband, Peter Reigert, worked.

Ghostbusters (1984) Rick Moranis, after being chased by a demonic monster through **Central Park,** ends up pounding desperately on the window of **Tavern on the Green**'s **Crystal Room,** only to be politely ignored by the very patrician clientele.

Jungle Fever (1991) In Spike Lee's dramatic meditation on interracial dating, Wesley Snipes and Annabella Sciorra encounter Queen Latifah, a disapproving waitress at **Sylvia's**—the **Harlem** dining institution.

Manhattan (1979) Woody Allen and Mariel Hemingway go shopping at **SoHo**'s premiere gourmet market, **Dean & DeLuca.**

Moscow on the Hudson (1984) **Brighton Beach**'s **National Restaurant** was where Soviet defector Robin Williams sang and danced with his compatriots.

Night and the City (1992) The bar at **Boxers** in **Greenwich Village** is the scene of some heavy-duty flirting between Jessica Lange and Robert DeNiro.

The Paper (1994) Marisa Tomei has dinner with her in-laws at **Gus' Place** in Greenwich Village while waiting for husband Michael Keaton to show.

Reversal of Fortune (1990) Fans of the **Nam Wah Tea Parlor** in **Chinatown** recognized their favorite spot when Jeremy Irons meets with his lawyer.

State of Grace (1990) Sean Penn as an undercover cop joins tough **West Side** gang leader Ed Harris and member Gary Oldman to shake down an old chum—the bartender/owner at **Old Towne Bar and Grill**—who resists, much to his own peril.

Tootsie (1982) Dustin Hoffman works as a waiter at **Jim McMullen** on the **Upper East Side** and then meets with his agent at the **Russian Tea Room** in **Midtown.**

When Harry Met Sally (1989) Meg Ryan's famous orgasm-faking scene was filmed at **Katz's Deli** on the **Lower East Side.**

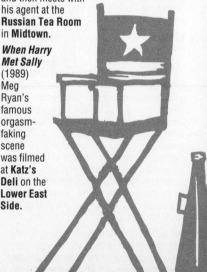

27 East Village Cheese Store As you stand in this tiny store with what seems like the entire population of the East Village, take comfort in the fact that the original store, around the corner on Ninth Street, was even smaller. The draw is a large assortment of international cheeses at very good prices; be sure to check out the specials listed outside on the door. For those who do not live by cheese alone, other offerings include breads, preserves, olives, olive oils, and coffee. ♦ Daily. 34 Third Ave (between E 9th and E 10th Sts). 477.2601

28 Dojo ★$ Students of nearby **New York University** seem to depend on the food served here for their very existence. Try the chicken sukiyaki salad or the incredibly inexpensive soy burger with tahini sauce. In nice weather you can dine on the outdoor porch, which is great for people watching, but be prepared for panhandlers and exhaust fumes. ♦ Japanese/ Health food ♦ Daily lunch, dinner, and late-night meals. No credit cards accepted. 24 St. Mark's Pl (between Second and Third Aves). 674.9821. Also at: 14 W Fourth St (at Mercer St). 505.8934

28 Khyber Pass ★$ A former judge of the Supreme Court in Afghanistan runs this authentic Afghan restaurant. Knowing you're in good hands, just sit back on a throw pillow and get ready to enjoy stuffed ravioli with lamb; tender, moist lamb kebabs; fresh salads with yogurt dressing; and for dessert, rice pudding topped with pistachios. ♦ Afghan ♦ Daily lunch, dinner, and late-night meals. 34 St. Mark's Pl (between Second and Third Aves). 473.0989

29 Gem Spa Smoke Shop Although the long counter has been replaced by racks of international magazines and newspapers and the owners are East Indian, this veteran shop still serves a good egg cream, the quintessential New York drink. Ask for it when you walk in; the egg cream station is a small counter at the very front. ♦ Daily 24 hours. 131 Second Ave (at St. Mark's Pl). No phone

29 B & H Dairy and Vegetarian Cuisine Restaurant ★$ Once upon a time the initials "B & H" stood for owners Bergson and Heller, and the clientele comprised the cast and crew of the Yiddish theater productions along Second Avenue. The restaurant (and its menu) has been refurbished several times since then—the vegetarian offerings are recent—but thank goodness the challah recipe is still the same. The French toast is heavenly. ♦ Vegetarian ♦ Daily breakfast, lunch, and dinner. 127 Second Ave (between E Seventh St and St. Mark's Pl). 505.8065

30 Dallas BBQ $ Cheap barbecued chicken and ribs are served with corn bread and coleslaw in this bargain-hunter's paradise. Come for the early-bird special, from 11AM until 6:30PM, and beat the dinner crowd. ♦ American ♦ Daily lunch, dinner, and late-night meals. 132 Second Ave (at St. Mark's Pl). 777.5574. Also at: 27 W 72nd St (between Central Park W and Columbus Ave). 873.2004; 1265 Third Ave (at E 73rd St). 772.9393; 21 University Pl (at E Eighth St). 674.4450

31 Kiev ★$ A better buy, not to mention better borscht, would be hard to find in New York. This is one of the best of the Eastern European joints around. The constant traffic sometimes makes it difficult to get a table, but the food and prices are wonderful. The cheese blintzes, pierogi (filled with cheese or potato), fried veal cutlets, and all of the soups are very satisfying. ♦ Russian ♦ Daily 24 hours. No credit cards accepted. 117 Second Ave (at E Seventh St). 674.4040 &

32 Caffè della Pace ★$ This warm and unpretentious little cafe, a few steps up from the street, has good cappuccino and a very rich tiramisù. ♦ Cafe ♦ Daily. No credit cards accepted. 48 E Seventh St (between First and Second Aves). 529.8024

33 Miracle Grill ★★$$ Grilled chicken on skewers with papaya-tomatillo salsa, New York steak with chipotle (smoked jalapeño pepper) butter, and vanilla-bean flan are just a few of the inventive specialties served at this tiny and casual restaurant. Dine alfresco in the garden when the weather is fine. ♦ Southwestern ♦ M-F dinner; Sa-Su brunch and dinner. 112 First Ave (between E Sixth and E Seventh Sts). 254.2353 &

34 Roettele A.G. ★$$ This quaint, pretty restaurant looks like a country inn in the Alps, complete with wooden beams, red-and-white tableclothes and an Alpine mural covering one wall. The German-Swiss fare is hearty and includes roast goose with chestnut stuffing, sauerbraten with spaetzle and red cabbage, and dandelion salad with warm bacon. Cold weather brings a craving for this food, but don't neglect this place in warmer weather: There's also a very pleasant garden in the back. On Thursday nights, diners are treated to live Swiss music. ♦ German/Swiss ♦ M-F lunch and dinner; Sa brunch and dinner. 126 E Seventh St (between Ave A and First Ave). 674.4140

35 7A $ The menu of this cozy cafe, with peach-colored and exposed-brick walls, has a little bit of everything for everybody at all hours of the day. And since the crowd ranges from senior citizens to bikers, the place is often packed. The burgers, including the veggie variation, are good, as is the fusilli with smoked chicken. The yummy waffles with rum butter are served all day. ♦ American ♦ Daily 24 hours. 109 Ave A (at E Seventh St). 673.6583

36 Zitella ★$ With gray banquettes and pastel shades over the lights, this refined dining room seems more like an uptown trattoria than an East Village eatery. That sophistication spills over into the food as well: Try the grilled portobello mushroom with fontina, followed by any of the pastas, particularly the goat cheese ravioli with sage butter. ♦ Italian ♦ M-F lunch and dinner; Sa-Su brunch and dinner. No credit cards accepted. 131 Ave A (between St. Mark's Pl and E Ninth St). 777.5642 ♿

37 Yaffa Cafe ★$ If out-of-town visitors want to see a typical East Village cafe, bring them here. The intense decor features lights in primary colors with leopard-print lampshades, and the scene is buzzing 24 hours a day. There are such Middle Eastern appetizers as hummus and tahini, salads, grilled sandwiches, crepes, vegetarian dishes, stir-fried chicken dishes, and pasta—in short, something for everybody. ♦ Eclectic ♦ Daily 24 hours. 97 St. Mark's Pl (between Ave A and First Ave). 677.9001

37 Cafe Mogador ★$$ Moroccan cuisine is prepared here without fanfare. Lamb, beef, and *merguez* (sausage) kebabs, and several varieties of couscous follow a selection of appetizers brought to your table on an enormous tray. Go all the way and top off your meal with Turkish coffee—as delicious as it is muddy. ♦ Middle Eastern/Moroccan ♦ Daily lunch, dinner, and late-night meals. No credit cards accepted. 101 St. Mark's Pl (between Ave A and First Ave). 677.2226

38 Kurowycky This old-fashioned Ukrainian butcher shop has all the basic cuts of chicken, pork, and beef, but it's known best for ham

and sausages—especially the homemade kielbasa. And the prices can't be beat. ♦ M-Sa 124 First Ave (between E Seventh St and St. Mark's Pl). 477.0344

38 Pierogi and Deli Polish specialties, including—of course—pierogi, are the draw here, but good cheese blintzes, rice-and-meat stuffed cabbage, and a very satisfying cabbage soup make this place well worth a stop. ♦ M-Sa. 130 First Ave (between E Seventh St and St. Mark's Pl). 420.9690

39 Jules ★★$$ With its red banquettes, mirrored walls, beaded curtains, and wooden bar, this bistro feels like a slice of Paris. The menu offers traditional fare: homemade country pâté, a solid pot-au-feu, duck with apricot sauce, and escargots, along with such reinvented dishes as green-vegetable terrine, goat-cheese flan, and vegetarian couscous. Don't forget your Ray Bans and Gauloises. ♦ French ♦ M-F lunch and dinner; Sa-Su brunch and dinner. No credit cards accepted. 65 St. Mark's Pl (between First and Second Aves). 477.5560

39 Passport ★$ This softly lit restaurant is your ticket to another world. From the balcony bar, look down on what appears to be an outdoor cafe—with painted-tile tables and a terra-cotta floor—in a Mexican square. It's even flanked on one side by a frieze of a massive pink stone church. Complete the illusion by ordering some seviche, guacamole, or gazpacho, followed by shrimp with chili sauce, scallops with cilantro aioli, chicken with avocado and tomatillo sauce, or any of the burritos, tacos, or enchiladas. ♦ Mexican ♦ M-F dinner; Sa-Su brunch and dinner. 79 St. Mark's Pl (between First and Second Aves). 979.2680

39 Rangoon Cafe ★$ Burmese food is much less well known than other Asian cuisines, and this tiny inexpensive cafe is a perfect place to try it out. Have the zingy chicken satay; Rangoon noodles with duck; spicy rub chicken with carrots, peppers, scallions, and zucchini; and the special vegetarian platter with small portions of six tempting dishes, including Burmese ginger salad and sesame string-bean salad with peanuts. ♦ Burmese ♦ Daily lunch and dinner. 81 St. Mark's Pl (between First and Second Aves). 228.2199. Also at: 137 First Ave (between St. Mark's Pl and E Ninth St). 777.5141

40 Cafe Orlin $ Neighborhood regulars congregate here for good coffee and desserts, homemade soup, and such dishes as grilled chicken with Indian-spiced red lentils. During the warmer months, choose an outside table and watch the people parade by on St. Mark's Place. ♦ Cafe ♦ Daily breakfast, lunch, dinner, and late-night meals. 41 St. Mark's Pl (between First and Second Aves). 777.1447

41 Veselka ★$ An amazing array of Eastern European fare—pierogi, kielbasa, blintzes, and stuffed cabbage—is turned out at bargain-basement prices in this unadorned yet cozy establishment. ♦ Ukrainian ♦ Daily 24 hours. 144 Second Ave (at E Ninth St). 228.9682

41 Ukrainian ★$ Located within the **Ukrainian National Home** community center, this place serves such wonderful Eastern European specialties as pierogi, blintzes, and stuffed cabbage. The combination platter gives a sampling of all three. ♦ Ukrainian ♦ Daily lunch and dinner. No credit cards accepted. 140 Second Ave (between St. Mark's Pl and E Ninth St). 529.5024

42 Cloisters Cafe $ At this most delightful spot in the neighborhood for escaping the city, the inside is dark and encrusted with stained glass, while the outside is a beautiful grapevine-canopied bower. Gigantic salads, good challah French toast, and fresh fish entrées are featured. In hot weather, the yogurt ambrosia (with fresh fruits and nuts) and a glass of iced mint tea is the next best thing to air-conditioning. ♦ American ♦ M-F lunch, dinner, and late-night meals; Sa-Su brunch, dinner, and late-night meals. No credit cards accepted. 238 E Ninth St (between Second and Third Aves). 777.9128

42 Cafe-Tabac ★$$ This dining spot is a hangout for celebrities, including Madonna, Keith Richards, Naomi Campbell, and Calvin Klein, as well as their wannabes. Consequently, food takes a back seat here to people watching. Since its inception, the menu has evolved from bistro to continental-influenced American cuisine and features roasted chicken with creamy polenta, pan-roasted red snapper, and shredded duck served with wild-mushroom pancakes and white beans. Be forewarned: The upstairs is unofficially reserved for regulars and big names, and the downstairs dining room and bar are generally noisy and crowded. ♦ American ♦ Daily dinner and late-night meals. 232 E Ninth St (between Second and Third Aves). 674.7072

43 In Padella ★$ The yellow walls decorated with copper pots and Italian pottery make this a homey spot for affordable, decent pasta. The low prices will help you overlook the sometimes overburdened wait staff and tables that are wedged closely together. It's a good place for a quick meal of comforting *pasta e fagioli* (with beans), *tagliolini puttanesca* (thin noodles in a tomato-based sauce with olives, anchovies, and capers), or *pappardelle* (broad noodles) with tomato and bacon—don't expect to linger over your espresso. ♦ Italian ♦ Daily lunch and dinner. No credit cards accepted. 145 Second Ave (at E Ninth St). 598.9800

43 Col Legno ★★$ The aromas emanating from this rustic trattoria and its very open kitchen are sufficient to draw customers in from the street. Maybe it's one of the sauces or maybe the rosemary used during grilling, but why waste time wondering? Just sit down and order the tagliatelle with wild-mushroom sauce flavored with mint, the spaghetti served with onion, tomato, pancetta, and *peperoncini* (hot peppers), or the whole baby chicken grilled over rosemary. You won't be sorry. The wine list is reasonably priced, and the house red is good. ♦ Italian ♦ Tu dinner; W-F lunch and dinner; Sa-Su dinner. Reservations recommended. 231 E Ninth St (between Second and Third Aves). 777.4650

The Raw Deal

During the boomtime of the 1980s, sushi bars were the fast-food joints of the fashionable set, and to this day, New Yorkers love to wrap their chopsticks around succulent bits of raw fish on rice. Although many fans are content to order the assortment plates concocted by the chef, true aficionados prefer to select by the piece. To tailor your next sushi meal to your own specific tastes, here's what you need to know to "have it your way."

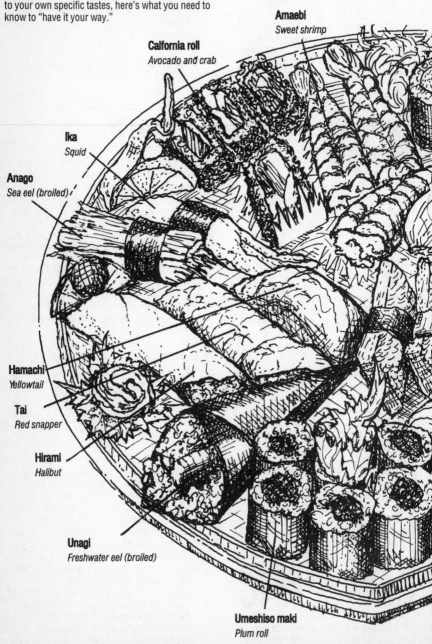

Amaebi
Sweet shrimp

Calfornia roll
Avocado and crab

Ika
Squid

Anago
Sea eel (broiled)

Hamachi
Yellowtail

Tai
Red snapper

Hirami
Halibut

Unagi
Freshwater eel (broiled)

Umeshiso maki
Plum roll

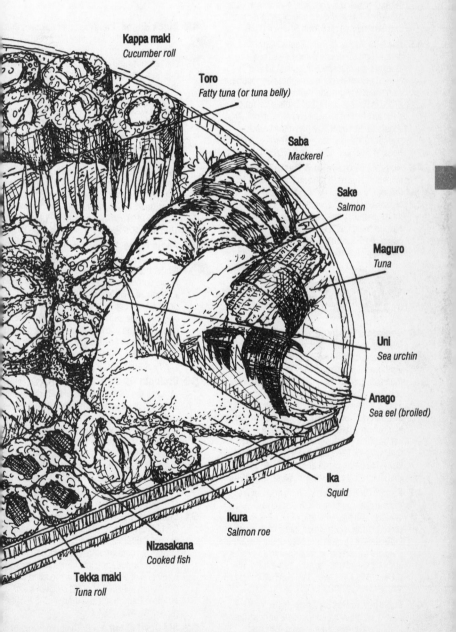

Kappa maki
Cucumber roll

Toro
Fatty tuna (or tuna belly)

Saba
Mackerel

Sake
Salmon

Maguro
Tuna

Uni
Sea urchin

Anago
Sea eel (broiled)

Ika
Squid

Ikura
Salmon roe

Nizasakana
Cooked fish

Tekka maki
Tuna roll

44 2nd Avenue Deli ★$$ Ask to be seated in the **Molly Picon Room** in this very famous and popular deli where the wealth of Yiddish theater memorabilia will certainly enhance the dining experience. As for the food, certain Jewish specialties are very good. Try the superb chopped liver (passed out on bits of rye bread to placate the hungry crowds when lines get long on weekends), stuffed breast of veal, Romanian tenderloin steak, boiled beef, stuffed derma, or *kasha varnishkes*. ◆ Jewish ◆ Daily breakfast, lunch, dinner, and late-night meals. 156 Second Ave (at E 10th St). 677.0606

45 Iso ★$$ At this favorite East Village destination for creative Japanese food, quarters are cramped, but the staff and customers make do in an upbeat atmosphere with fresh flowers and Keith Haring artwork. Sushi is the specialty, but cooked selections, such as chicken teriyaki and shrimp or vegetable tempura, are given the same attention. ◆ Japanese ◆ M-Sa dinner. 175 Second Ave (at E 11th St). 777.0361 ♿

46 Russo's Mozzarella & Pasta Corp. This tiny shop stocks all the staples required for an Italian-style picnic: good homemade mozzarella (made several times a day), crusty Italian bread, salami, and olives. You can also pick up fresh pastas and sauces to serve at home. ◆ M-Sa; Su until 3:30PM. 344 E 11th St (between First and Second Aves). 254.7452 ♿

46 Veniero's Pasticceria & Cafe ★$ Mirrors and chandeliers decorate this century-old bakery/cafe. But customers generally don't notice the decor; they're hypnotized by the biscotti (cookies), the creamy pastries, and the golden cheesecakes. Many of New York's Italian cafes serve the baked goods made here. There's also a seating area which is often crowded with tourists, where cappuccino goes well with a *sfogliatelle* (a flaky cheese-filled pastry). ◆ Bakery/Cafe ◆ Daily. No credit cards accepted. 342 E 11th St (between First and Second Aves). 674.7264

47 Ferruci's Gourmet With its array of fresh mozzarella, salamis, barrels of olives, cheeses, shelves of virgin olive oil, and fresh produce, this store would be right at home in Little Italy. But what most residents line up for here are the prepared foods, such as pastas and chicken dishes, to take home for dinner. ◆ Daily. 171 First Ave (between E 10th and E 11th Sts). 529.7903 ♿

47 DeRobertis Pastry Shop If you can get past the display counters filled with traffic-stopping cheesecakes, pies, cakes, and biscotti, you'll find a wonderfully tiled coffeehouse that hasn't changed a bit since it

began serving frothy cappuccino here back in 1904. ◆ Bakery/Cafe ◆ Tu-Sa. 176 First Ave (between E 10th and E 11th Sts). 674.7137

48 Black Hound There are other bakeries that make wonderful cakes, chocolate truffles, and pies, but rarely do their wares approach the sheer beauty and sumptuousness displayed in this little gem of a shop. For a knockout gift, try the chocolate-berry basket (a woven basket of Belgian chocolate filled with almond cake, raspberry sauce, pastry, whipped cream, and fresh berries) or a chocolate basket filled with various handmade truffles and other chocolate confections. There are also such individual pastries as triple-chocolate mousse cake; 23 types of cakes, including hazelnut mocha and lemon mousse; and perfect little cookies, such as palmiers, ginger-lemon buttons, and coffee shortbread, which you can buy by the piece. ◆ Daily. 149 First Ave (between E Ninth and E 10th Sts). 979.9505

49 Pasta Place The shelves are filled with olive oil, salamis, and barrels of olives, but the tender homemade pasta is what keeps the locals coming back for more. Try the ravioli with any of a variety of fillings: lobster, broccoli and garlic, and porcini and garlic; or the fettuccine and spaghetti flavored with most anything you can think of—the garden fettuccine with beets and spinach is a real treat. ◆ M-Sa. 247 E 10th St (between Ave A and First Ave). 460.8326

50 Orologio ★$ The name means clock, which explains the display of timepieces scattered around this rustic trattoria, with wood tables and mustard-colored walls. You can get a crusty pizza or a well-prepared, inexpensive plate of pasta here, such as the *farfalle* (butterfly-shaped) with smoked salmon. Don't overlook their inexpensive but well-chosen Italian wine list. ◆ Italian ◆ Daily dinner. No credit cards accepted. 162 Ave A (between E 10th and E 11th Sts). 228.6900

51 Life Cafe ★$ This quintessential dark, artsy East Village cafe specializes in well-prepared natural California/Mexican and vegetarian food. It's a comfortable, easy place to hang out undisturbed for a few hours accompanied by a book of poetry and a burrito filled with vegetarian chili or a charred chicken salad. ◆ Cafe ◆ Daily lunch and dinner. 343 E 10th St (at Ave B). 477.8791

52 Old Devil Moon ★★$ The primary-color walls, paper Chinese lanterns, and Charles Addams cartoons on the tables may well bring a smile to your face even before the food arrives. Once it does, you'll grin even more. This is hearty stuff with lots of personality—spice-crust chicken, Thai steak salad in a tangy sauce, and noodles with vegetables in a spicy peanut sauce. The weekend brunch comes straight out of a South Carolina diner; don't miss the sticky buns, the roasted-corn hot cakes, the farmer's omelette with country ham, and their spin on a fast-food favorite—the Egg Mik Moon, with cheese and ham (or sausage) piled on an English muffin. ◆ American ◆ Tu-F dinner; Sa-Su brunch and dinner. 511 E 12th St (between Aves A and B). 475.4357 &

53 Sahara East ★$ When a Middle Eastern restaurant is recommended by Jihan Sadat, the widow of Egyptian president Anwar Sadat, you have to take the praise for this tiny place seriously. Come in for the *baba ganooj, kafta kebabs* (ground lamb seasoned with onions and parsley), and vegetarian couscous. ◆ Middle Eastern ◆ Daily lunch and dinner. No credit cards accepted. 184 First Ave (between E 11th and E 12th Sts). 353.9000

53 Brunetta's ★★$ This tiny place doesn't look like much with its plain walls and Formica tables, but locals treasure it for its simple, well-prepared dishes. Try the grilled portobello mushrooms with arugula and radicchio followed by the roasted half chicken with rosemary, marjoram, and balsamic vinegar. ◆ Italian ◆ M dinner; Tu-F lunch and dinner; Sa-Su brunch and dinner. No credit cards accepted. 190 First Ave (between E 11th and E 12th Sts). 228.4030

54 Palermo Bakery Nothing fancy here, just top-quality crusty Italian breads, pans of rich fruit cobblers, flaky apple crumb turnovers, and cookies dipped in chocolate. Even the humble chocolate chip cookie is perfectly executed. ◆ Daily. 213 First Ave (between E 12th and E 13th Sts). 254.4139 &

55 Angelica Kitchen ★$ Named after an herb believed to bring good luck, a place like this could only exist in the East Village. The seasonal vegetarian macrobiotic menu (no dairy products or sugar) changes with the solstice and equinox. The vegetarian fare, including the lentil/walnut pâté, is made with organically grown ingredients and is, for the most part, delicious. A Zenlike setting complements the mood and provides a tranquil backdrop; the eclectic clientele provides plenty of color. ◆ Organic vegetarian ◆ Daily lunch and dinner. 300 E 12th St (between First and Second Aves). 228.2909

55 John's of Twelfth Street ★$$ This place could have been the model for every little Italian restaurant that was ever lit by candles stuck in wine bottles. It's one of the city's oldest and was once a favorite of Arturo Toscanini. The menu is red-sauce traditional, the special salad, outstanding. ◆ Italian ◆ Daily dinner. Reservations recommended. No credit cards accepted. 302 E 12th St (between First and Second Aves). 475.9531

56 Strand Bookstore "Miles and miles of books" is the trademark description of this epic store, and its vast collection includes about 3,000 cookbooks. Many of these are current editions, sold at a discounted price if new, and half-price if used. There's also a large selection of rare and out-of-print books. Find such unusual items as a 1920s guide for "household managers" or an 1824 British cookbook, in addition to a world of recipe books for every conceivable type of cuisine. ◆ Daily. 828 Broadway (at E 12th St). 473.1452. Also at: 159 John St (at Front St). 809.0875

57 Flamingo East ★$$ Cool and dark, this place looks like a sophisticated cocktail lounge from the 1950s; you half expect to hear Mel Torme crooning at the piano. The menu continues the high-toned retro effect, featuring such dishes as truffle ravioli, calamari in lime vinaigrette, and steak *frites*. ◆ International ◆ Daily dinner. 219 Second Ave (between E 13th and E 14th Sts). 533.2860

flamingo east

58 Pedro Paramo ★★$ The authentic food at peso-friendly prices might fool you into thinking that you're south of the border. If you're still not convinced, just wait until the Mexican beers and excellent margaritas start flowing. Start off a traditional meal with some of the city's best guacamole, and take it from there; you can't go wrong. ◆ Mexican ◆ Daily lunch and dinner. 430 E 14th St (between Ave A and First Ave). 475.4581

Bests

Howard Goldberg
President, Adventure on a Shoestring

Mocca Hungarian.

The **Dallas BBQ** restaurants.

2nd Avenue Deli, the best mushroom-barley soup and pastrami in New York.

Sapporo, a Japanese restaurant in the Theater District.

Parnell's on the East Side, great for Irish breakfast.

Union Square/ Gramercy Park/ Murray Hill

The neighborhoods of Union Square and Gramercy Park, nicknamed in recent years the **Flatiron District** after an unusual building (literally shaped like a flatiron), are the new sure-bet locations for New York City restaurant dining. The district, bounded by **Third** and **Sixth Avenues** and **14th** and **23rd Streets**, began its culinary ascent slowly during the 1980s, and increasingly in the 1990s with high-profile restaurants sprouting up, on, and around the stretch of **Park Avenue South** between **17th** and **22nd Streets**. Today, streets that used to be deserted after dark are now teeming with people looking for the latest gastronomic experience.

The area surrounding **Union Square** has experienced a significant demographic shift during the past 20 years. The industrial spaces that once housed printing plants and manufacturing concerns are now home to advertising agencies, publishers, architectural firms, and upscale loft dwellers. The professionals who have taken over the neighborhood—bringing their

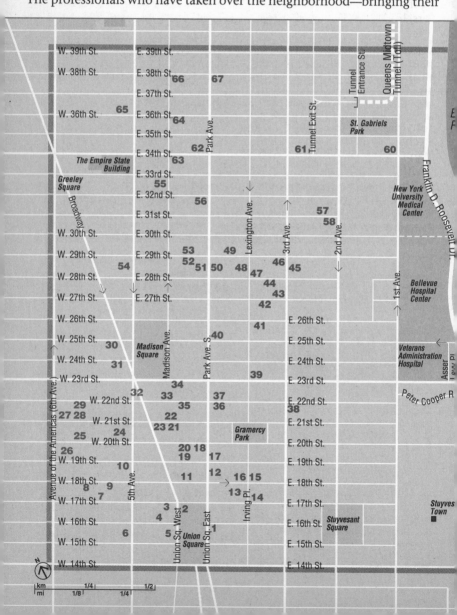

xpense accounts with them—are primarily responsible for this restaurant boom, a phenomenon that shows no signs of slowing down.

Notable changes have also occurred in the district around **Gramercy Park**. Always a quiet, upscale neighborhood, it's suddenly become a high-profile host with many new dining options. **Gramercy Park** itself—a private, London-style fenced plaza—was once part of an estate owned by Peter Stuyvesant, and was developed during the 1830s by lawyer and landowner Samuel Ruggles. This square block of greenery remains a slice of urban paradise that still entices would-be tenants to the surrounding buildings with the promise of their very own park key.

A different scenario has unfolded in and around Murray Hill (from **Third** to **Sixth Avenues**, and between **23rd** and **39th Streets**). The well-heeled residential enclaves that once included elegant mansions are now crowded with high rises. But many worthwhile dining experiences still await those who venture north of the restaurant-laden Flatiron District.

During the early 1980s, chef Larry Forgione was among the area's culinary pioneers, locating his innovative restaurant **An American Place** in a large, airy space on **East 32nd Street.** Several years later, Danny Meyer opened his still-popular **Union Square Cafe** in what was a large storefront on **East 16th Street.** Around the same time, commercial and rock video director Bob Giraldi and his partner Phil Suarez opened the stylish **Positano** in a soaring space on Park Avenue South. The era of fine-but-fun dining had begun.

Drawn by large spaces, lower-than-Midtown rents, and an energetic zeitgeist, innovative restaurateurs continue to try their luck here. Second-generation French chef Claude Troisgros makes his New York debut at **C.T.**, and Miamian Douglas Rodriguez redefines Latin cuisine in **Positano**'s former home with **Patria. Mesa Grill**'s Bobby Flay puts his own spin on Spanish food at **Bolo**, his second restaurant in the neighborhood, and Danny Meyer throws his hat in the ring again with **Gramercy Tavern**, which initially appears to be laboring under the weight of its own hype. But far from saturating the district, the growing number of hot new places has served only to draw in more and more patrons—the public appetite for what these talented young chefs will do next certainly is hearty.

---

1 Zen Palate ★★★$$ The sponged-yellow walls; rosewood, bamboo, and copper accents; and chanting sound track at this wonderful, multilevel restaurant inspire a serenity befitting a temple. Those seeking enlightenment of the Asian culinary sort should begin their journey with the basil rolls (herb-filled dumplings) or mushroom-filled sushi autumn rolls. Continue with any entrée that features mushrooms, such as West Lake (a delightful pile of shiitake mushrooms with a ginger-scallion and sherry sauce) or Mushroom Forest (an exotic combination of fungi, pine nuts, and vegetables on a bed of Boston lettuce). Those who desire beverages other than fruit drinks can bring their own refreshments. The tranquil decor, attentive wait staff, and fine fare contribute to a unique dining experience. ♦ Asian vegetarian ♦ M-Sa lunch and dinner; Su dinner. Reservations recommended. 34 Union Sq E (at E 16th St). 614.9345 &. Also at: 663 Ninth Ave (at 46th St). 582.1669 &

2 Union Square Greenmarket In 1976, New York City's Council on the Environment attempted to open a greenmarket in what was then a parking lot. It got off to a slow start because of the community's skepticism—a result of previously unsuccessful attempts to clean up the longtime illicit activities within the park. The effort gained momentum in 1984 after the city refurbished the park and rebuilt the public space just north of it. Today this location is the largest and arguably the most interesting of the city's greenmarkets. In addition to a huge variety of fresh (a regulation stipulates that all perishables must be sold within 24 hours of harvesting) seasonal fruits and vegetables sold here, fish, cheese, eggs, baked goods, honey, and plants are offered. Some locals make a beeline for the fresh flowers, and at Christmastime, the freshest trees, wreaths, and garlands can be found here. M, W, F-Sa. E 17th St and Broadway. 788.7900 &

THE CITY BAKERY

3 The City Bakery ★★$ Fresh ingredients from the **Union Square Greenmarket** just a half-block away are turned into tasty dishes at this bakery/cafe. Such hearty soups as lentil or potato with cumin, served with warm focaccia, are made on the premises each morning, as is the heavenly range of sweets for which the bakery is well known. The tart-as-art follows the fruits of the season. ♦ American ♦ M-Sa breakfast, lunch, and early dinner. 22 E 17th St (between Broadway and Fifth Ave). 366.1414 ♿. Also at: Sony Plaza, 550 Madison Ave (between E 55th and E 56th Sts). 833.8020 ♿

Union Square Cafe

4 Union Square Cafe ★★★★$$$ Owner Danny Meyer is one of the brightest and most innovative among the new generation of restaurateurs. Food festivals, featuring produce from the **Union Square Greenmarket,** add to the liveliness of this popular dining spot. The very light, airy, modern space has rich cherry-wood floors and beige walls, wainscotted with hunter green and dotted with small brightly colored paintings. Chef Michael Romano's inventive dishes include pumpkin risotto with arugula, mozzarella, and parmesan and gazpacho risotto with shrimp, cucumber, tomatoes and peppers, as well as seared salmon with a peppery orange marmalade; roasted lemon-pepper duck with couscous and fig-ginger compote; and grilled marinated filet mignon of tuna with wild greens and eggplant. An excellent lunchtime offering is the tuna burger, served with grilled onions and a creamy cabbage slaw. Be sure to save room for one of the delectable desserts, including the banana tart and the pumpkin flan. The wine list isn't extremely extensive, but it is "user friendly." Those looking for a romantic culinary adventure should ask to sit in the balcony that overlooks a mural called *The Women of USC* (Union Square Cafe) by Judy Rifka. A full menu is offered at the long, dark wood bar, which is a pleasant place to sit when dining alone. The young staff is cordial and professional. ♦ American ♦ M-Sa lunch and dinner; Su dinner. Reservations required. 21 E 16th St (between Union Sq W and Fifth Ave). 243.4020

4 Steak Frites ★$$ Steak and fries are the meat and potatoes at this spot off Union Square, but there are also good soups, sandwiches, and pasta specials. It's dimly lit and romantic, but service could be improved. ♦ Bistro ♦ Daily lunch and dinner. Reservations required. 9 E 16th St (between Union Sq W and Fifth Ave). 463.7101 ♿

5 Coffee Shop ★$ Trendy "club kids" spill in pleasant weather into the sidewalk cafe of this slick diner with a Brazilian flair. The food includes the Sonia Braga chicken salad sandwich (rolled with papaya and cashews in a flour tortilla), and a traditional Brazilian *feijoada* (pork and bean stew) served on Saturdays. For nouvelle "world" cuisine, try the menu in the **World Room,** offering brick-oven cooking that ranges from the casual (pizza) to the not-so-causal (wood-roast rack of lamb). At night, the bar gets very crowded with those wanting to be "seen." The cozy back room, with its fish tank and TV, is a fun hideaway. ♦ Eclectic ♦ Daily breakfast, lunch, dinner, and late-night meals. 29 Union Sq W (at E 16th St). 243.7969

5 Union Square Wines & Spirits This large new liquor store has a wide variety of French, Italian, California, and South American wines all at very competitive prices. Wine tastings and seminars are also offered here. M-Sa. 33 Union Sq W (at E 16th St). 675.8100

6 Mesa Grill ★★$$$ Despite the spacious setting and high ceilings, the high noise level here eliminates any chance of intimate chitchat. Still, this upscale, hip Southwestern restaurant draws a crowd for chef/owner Bobby Flay's cooking. The menu includes such innovative dishes as red snapper wrapped in a blue-corn tortilla with fire-roasted *poblano*-chili vinaigrette as well as shellfish and green-chili pan roast. ♦ Southwestern ♦ M-F lunch and dinner; Sa-Su brunch and dinner. 102 Fifth Ave (between W 15th and W 16th Sts). 807.7400 ♿

7 Flowers ★★$$$ The decor is haute farmhouse with rough-hewn beams, artistic-looking lanterns suspended from the walls, and hanging baskets of dried flowers. The flower motif continues on the menu: Appetizers are listed under the heading "early bloomers," entrées under "blossoms," and side dishes under "buds." Flowery language aside, chef Marc Salonsky creates strongly flavored, savory food. Try the tuna *tartare* timbale with vine-ripened tomatoes and avocado salsa; spicy grilled quail with cilantro, cumin, cardamom, and ginger; and roast bab lamb chops with Moroccan spices. Be forewarned: The mammoth bar scene and loud music may be off-putting to some diners. ♦ Eclectic ♦ M-F lunch and dinner; Sa dinner. Reservations recommended for dinner. 21 W 17th St (between Fifth and Sixth Aves). 691.8888 ♿

Book-Friends Café

8 Book-Friends Cafe $ Books from the Victorian, Edwardian, and Modern eras, among other belle epoques, line this old-fashioned salon. Stop in for a sandwich, afternoon tea, or one of the "Conversations," on such subjects as Kiki's Paris, New York Literary Neighborhoods, or Sylvia Beach and the Expatriates. ♦ American ♦ M-F lunch, afternoon tea, and dinner; Sa-Su brunch, afternoon tea, and dinner. 16 W 18th St (between Fifth and Sixth Aves). 255.7407 ♿

9 Flavors Caterer Pamela Morgan converted a former industrial space into a rustic take-out shop that's been popular since day one. The long marble counter is filled with such irresistible baked goods as lemon bars and ginger-spice cookies. Salads and sandwiches offered here include herbed carrot salad with ginger dressing, Tuscan bean and herb salad, grilled chicken and fennel Caesar salad, and mozzarella and roasted peppers on focaccia. A few tables in front accommodate those who want to consume their purchases on the spot. ♦ M-Sa. 8 W 18th St (between Fifth and Sixth Aves). 647.1234 ♿

news BAR

10 News Bar ★$ A magnet for the artistic crowd from nearby ad agencies, architectural firms, and photography studios, this sleek espresso bar/newsstand was designed in a handsome minimalist style by architect **Wayne Turett.** The fresh pastries and sandwiches are great, but the espressos, cappuccinos, and steamed milks are superlative. Pull up a chair at the counter and immerse yourself in your favorite periodical, which is probably among the selection of 400 newspapers and magazines available here. ♦ Cafe ♦ Daily. 2 W 19th St (at Fifth Ave). 255.3996. Also at 366 W Broadway (at Broome St). 343.0053; 969 Third Ave (at 57th St). 319.0830 ♿

11 Old Town Bar ★$ The popularity of this century-old tavern may be sufficient to keep it in business for another hundred years. Sit in the time-worn wooden booths and enjoy the famous chicken wings, an excellent burger (served with fried onions on an English muffin), a mountainous portion of crisp fries, and an icy mug of draft beer. ♦ American ♦ Daily lunch, dinner, and late-night meals. 45 E 18th St (between Park Ave South and Broadway). 529.6732

PARK AVALON

12 Park Avalon ★$ This stylish, cream-colored, hangar-sized place is owned in part by fashion designer Nicole Miller, but the kitchen is presided over by chef Jim Botsacos, the former sous-chef at **21.** Given the restaurant's popularity and pedigree, the food is surprisingly uneven. Even the better dishes, among them grilled portobello mushrooms and grilled chicken with garlic crust and string beans *provençal,* look better than they taste. The pizzas are merely fair. Still, in this increasingly pricey neighborhood, this is one of the few places where you can dine in stylish surroundings for a reasonable price. ♦ American ♦ M-Sa lunch and dinner; Su brunch and dinner. Reservations required. 225 Park Ave S (between E 18th and E 19th Sts). 533.2500 ♿

SAL ANTHONY'S

13 Sal Anthony's $$ The menu is basic but reliable at this casual restaurant; a huge bay window in front adds cheer to the place. Try the chicken in olive oil and garlic or the linguine with white clam sauce. During the summer, tables are set out on the sidewalk for alfresco dining. ♦ Italian ♦ Daily lunch and dinner. Reservations required. 55 Irving Pl (between E 17th and E 18th Sts). 982.9030

Although you'll encounter about 70,000 other people shopping at the Union Square Greenmarket on a typical Saturday, there are rewards: In the summer, you can choose among 20 different types of lettuce; in the fall, among 40 varieties of apples.

☾erbena

14 Verbena ★★★$$$ At a time when most restaurants try to double as designer showrooms, this small, plain dining room of understated beige and khaki is a welcome change. Here all the necessary drama is supplied by Diane Forley's intense, soul-satisfying food from her seasonal menu. Although it won't be easy, try not to fill up on the freshly baked bread in order to save room for the autumn mushrooms with angel-hair pasta in truffled mushroom broth; butternut-squash ravioli flavored with roasted oranges and sage; seared venison chop with twice-baked sweet potatoes, chestnuts, and pomegranate seeds; or succulent beer-braised ribs of beef with root vegetables and horseradish dumplings. Desserts are uniformly excellent—especially the rum-soaked savarin filled with warm bittersweet chocolate, chocolate soufflé and chocolate-chip ice cream, black plum tart, fig profiteroles, and crème brûlée with lemon verbena. Sunday brunch is equally exciting. There's also a very well-chosen wine list, and in summer, a beautiful garden in back. ♦ American ♦ Tu-Sa lunch and dinner; Su brunch and dinner. Reservations required. 54 Irving Pl (at E 17th St). 260.5454

15 Pete's Tavern ★$$ One of several saloons that claim to be the oldest in town, this place also claims that O. Henry did some of his writing in a corner booth. If the bar was as busy then as it is now, his powers of concentration must have been incredible. The food, which runs from standard Italian specialties to hamburgers, isn't exceptional, but the atmosphere is great, and the sidewalk cafe sits on one of the city's more pleasant streets. ♦ Italian/American ♦ Daily lunch and dinner. 129 E 18th St (at Irving Pl). 473.7676

16 Friend of a Farmer ★$$ The country cooking and on-the-premises baking might well take you back to your grandma's kitchen. The Long Island duckling and Cajun-style chicken are always good. ♦ American ♦ Daily breakfast, lunch, and dinner. 77 Irving Pl (between E 18th and E 19th Sts). 477.2188

16 Choshi ★★$$ The fresh and well-prepared sushi and sashimi here are great buys at lunch. Prix-fixe dinner menus are a terrific deal. Choose between indoor and outdoor dining. ♦ Japanese ♦ Daily lunch and dinner. 77 Irving Pl (at E 19th St). 420.1419

CITY CRAB
AND SEAFOOD COMPANY

17 City Crab ★$$ Previously the home of Cafe Iguana, this large, wood-appointed space was redesigned to resemble a Maryland crab house. In the tradition of its predecessor, a larger-than-life version of its namesake is suspended above the entrance. Under the watchful gaze of this giant crab diners can count on good steamed crabs, crab soup, and other simple but well-prepared fish dishes. Don't miss the clam chowder, grilled tuna, lobster roll, or the clambake special, which includes a steamed lobster, mussels, clams, new potatoes, and corn-on-the-cob (available daily after 5PM). ♦ Seafood ♦ M-Sa lunch and dinner; Su brunch and dinner. 235 Park Ave (at E 19th St). 529.3800

18 Patria ★★$$$ This handsome bilevel room decorated with golden columns and earthy paintings of avocados was formerly Positano. The same fashionable crowd, emphasis on *crowd,* still shows up, but now they come for the pan-Hispanic food of Miamian chef Douglas Rodriguez. The menu is inconsistent; among the hits are: the Honduran seviche (a vibrant combination of tuna marinated in chilies, ginger, and coconut milk), crispy red snapper with coconut-conch rice, or the seafood *chupe* (a spicy stew of lobster, clam, shrimp, calamari, and scallops). Vegetarians delight in *caramiñola* (Colombian-style yucca stuffed with cheese in a mushroom broth, served with spinach). A chocolate cigar with spun-sugar matches is a whimsical and tasty conclusion to a delicious meal. Specialty drinks, such as *mojito* (rum, sugarcane juice, lime juice, and mint), *manguini* (champagne and fresh mango juice), and the Patria colada (a variation of the piña, with passion fruit and shaved coconut) receive the same attention as the food. Everything at this place–right down to the pulsating salsa music—is part of the fun. ♦ New Spanish ♦ M-F lunch and dinner; Sa dinner. Reservations required. 250 Park Ave S (at E 20th St). 777.6211

19 Cafe Beulah ★★$$ Owner Alexander Smalls named this restaurant for his aunt— the handsome black-and-white dining room gets a homey touch from the scattering of family portraits. The Southern cooking presented here is a little more upscale and healthier than is generally found down home—but no less delicious. Try free-range duck in barbecue-wine sauce; baked ham in bourbon-praline sauce; or the massive gumbo plate with duck, shrimp, and crabmeat in a spicy creole sauce. Such side dishes as lemon-candied yams or an unusual salad of cabbage and apricots deserve attention too. ♦ Southern ♦ M-F lunch and dinner; Sa dinner; Su brunch and dinner. Reservations recommended. 39 E 19th St (between Park Ave S and Broadway). 777.9700 ♿

20 Gramercy Tavern ★★$$$ In a *New York Magazine* cover story that preceded the restaurant's opening, owner Danny Meyer (of **Union Square Cafe** fame) stated his "modest" ambition: to reinvent the four-star restaurant. That Meyer and his chef, Tom Colicchio, haven't yet achieved this goal could be due to the overwhelming stampede of diners who have jammed the place and tied up the phone lines from the moment the doors opened. For those who do gain entry, the menu can be hit-and-miss, with presentations coming off more successfully than flavors. But the tuna *tartare;* eggplant Napoleon (layered with assorted vegetables and parmesan cheese); and sirloin of beef with barley, mushrooms, and horse-radish are all superb and can be topped off successfully by the cheese selection, *tarte tatin* (upside-down apple tart), or chocolate mousse cake with caramel sauce. The carefully chosen, reasonably priced, wine list adds to the enjoyment. Those with neither the patience nor connections to get a table in the country-inn style dining room can try the small menu at the ever-crowded bar and be surrounded by *Cornucopia,* Robert Kushner's 91-foot wraparound mural of vividly colored fruits and vegetables. ♦ American ♦ M-F lunch and dinner; Sa dinner. Reservations required. 42 E 20th St (between Park Ave S and Broadway). 477.0393 ♿

20 Chutney Mary ★★$$ This restaurant's name refers to the style of cooking practiced here: Traditional Indian food is given a modern slant, with lighter preparations and organic ingredients. The resulting cuisine is the best of both worlds. Tandoori meats are charred and flavorful but still tender and juicy—a rarity—and the intense flavor of chicken *sagwala* (free-range chicken sautéed with organic spinach and onions) is preserved, minus the usual abundance of oil. The breads, such as the house special *poori,* are puffy and light, and there are a number of delicious vegetarian dishes to choose from.

♦ Organic Indian ♦ M-F lunch and dinner; Sa-Su dinner. 40 E 20th St (between Park Ave S and Broadway). 473.8181 ♿

21 Campagna ★★$$$ Chef Mark Strausman's legion of fans followed him here when he left **Coco Pazzo** to start his own restaurant—a faux-Tuscan trattoria decorated with white walls, country Italian antiques, and abstract paintings. Start with a selection from the dazzling display of fresh vegetables antipasto, bowtie pasta with cèpes, six-layer lasagna, or fried calamari. Then move on to grilled tuna with warm beets, osso buco, and Florentine ribsteak. Desserts are more opulent here than at most Italian restaurants, especially the plum tart and the three-layer torte with chocolate cake, mascarpone, and chocolate-mascarpone mousse. The wine list features a nice selection of California and Italian wines at every price level. ♦ Italian ♦ M-F lunch and dinner; Sa-Su dinner. 24 E 21st St (between Park Ave S and Broadway). 460.0900 ♿

22 La Boulangère ★$ With the rise of upscale restaurants in the neighborhood, there are very few casual places left. But luckily this bakery/cafe is among the survivors. Stop in for good croissants, fruit tarts, pizzas, pasta salads, and sandwiches. ♦ Bakery/Cafe ♦ Daily. No credit cards accepted. 49 E 21st St (between Park Ave S and Broadway). 475.8582

23 Mayrose ★$ The noise level at this modern-style diner tends to reach a fevered pitch with everyone screaming to be heard. But the din doesn't seem to deter the crowds. Brunch is a major scene here—such dishes as puffy cinnamon-raisin French toast are good, and for this neighborhood, inexpensive. It's also crowded at lunch and dinner hours when locals pile in for decent basic American food, including meat loaf and grilled chicken. ♦ Diner ♦ M-Sa breakfast, lunch, and dinner; Su brunch and dinner. 920 Broadway (at 21st St). 533.3663 ♿

English muffins really were first made by an Englishman. In 1880 Samuel Bath Thomas produced the muffins using his mother's recipe at a bakery on East 20th Street. The company he founded to market them is Thomas' English Muffins.

24 Caffe Bondì ★★$$$ What began as a small neighborhood cafe and *pasticceria* has grown into a full-blown restaurant, complete with an outdoor patio. The bright, tiled decor, friendly and efficient staff, and delicious food make this a lovely setting for a meal or snack. Try any of the simple yet delicious pastas, which include *taglierini* (thin noodles) with tomatoes, mushrooms, and rosemary cream, or one of the Sicilian specialties, such as caponata (a stew of seasonal vegetables). ♦ Italian ♦ Daily breakfast, lunch, and dinner. 7 W 20th St (between Fifth and Sixth Aves). 691.8136

25 Periyali ★★$$$ The friendly staff at this comfortable taverna is unabashedly proud of its traditional but upscale Greek menu, and judging from the crowds that fill this off-the-beaten-path place, their pride is completely justified. Giant white beans with garlic sauce, charcoal-grilled octopus or shrimp, lamb chops with rosemary, anything in phyllo pastry, and fresh whole fish are all good picks. For dessert there's baklava, of course, and the wonderful *diples* (thin strips of deep-fried dough dipped in honey). The extensive wine list includes a good selection of Greek wines. The white stucco walls, wooden floor, and soft Greek music complete the experience. ♦ Greek ♦ M-F lunch and dinner; Sa dinner. Reservations recommended. 35 W 20th St (between Fifth and Sixth Aves). 463.7890

26 L'Acajou ★$$$ The modern whitewashed room dotted with colorful Picasso-esque paintings is popular for its Alsatian menu, featuring such dishes as sautéed baby chicken with apples and Calvados, poached salmon with sorrel sauce, and roast breast of duck with honey and spices. There's also an extensive, well-chosen wine list, including a number of good offerings by the glass. The bar is a popular local hangout—ask for the lacy homemade potato chips. ♦ Alsatian ♦ M-F lunch and dinner; Sa-Su dinner. 53 W 19th St (at Sixth Aves). 645.1706 ♿

27 Lox Around the Clock $ Few are the places that can satisfy a burning desire for a good pastrami sandwich at 3AM. During the wee hours, the place caters to a young crowd (hungry from dancing at the nearby **Limelight** club, formerly a church), offering a full-scale deli menu with decent lox and television monitors playing music videos full blast. ♦ Deli ♦ M-W, Su until midnight; Th-Sa until 4AM. 676 Sixth Ave (at W 21st St). 691.3535

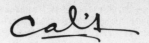

28 Cal's ★★$$ The dining room here is reminiscent of a Parisian grand cafe with soaring ceilings, a large carved-wood bar, and massive columns. The menu is varied and well executed, featuring such dishes as oven-roasted beet and endive salad, saffron risotto primavera, roast stuffed quail with dates and onions, house-cured salmon with grapefruit zest and star anise, whole roasted baby chicken with wild mushroom sauce, and honey- and herb-glazed duck. Desserts too good to miss include bananas in a chocolate cookie crust, and brownie ice-cream sandwich, which made the cover of *Chocolatier Magazine*. The well-chosen, affordable wine list offers a choice of over 100 bottles from France, America, and Italy. ♦ American ♦ M-F lunch and dinner; Sa-Su dinner. Reservations recommended. 55 W 21st St (between Fifth and Sixth Aves). 929.0740 ♿

29 The N.Y. Cake & Baking Distributor If you are seriously into dessert making, you will want to know about this place, which was formerly **The Chocolate Gallery**. It carries every implement, no matter how small, a pastry chef or candy maker could ever need, including the complete Wilton line. This is where the professionals shop. Classes in chocolate making, cake baking, and cake decorating are offered (see "New York Cooking Schools" on page 220). ♦ M-Sa. 56 W 22nd St (between Fifth and Sixth Aves). 675.2253

29 Lola ★$$$ Simply and attractively decorated, this restaurant serves authentical spiced and curried foods from the Caribbean along with some familiar Italian fare. Try Lola's fried chicken or grilled snapper, and don't forget the onion rings. During weekday lunches, the private dining room becomes the less-expensive **Lola Bowla**, serving all entrées—mainly pastas and salads—in bowls. If you're a frozen margarita fan, allow yourself to be seduced by the "Lolita," an intoxicating frozen drink of brandy, triple sec and lemon juice. ♦ Caribbean/Italian ♦ M-F lunch and dinner; Sa dinner; Su brunch and dinner. Reservations required. 30 W 22nd St (between Fifth and Sixth Aves). 675.6700

A "schmear" means one thing only—the spreading of cream cheese on top of a bagel; the lox (slices of smoked salmon) is optional.

30 Lamalle Kitchenware Founded by Charles Lamalle in 1927, this treasure trove of kitchen supplies was originally geared toward French chefs—as the dozens of decades-old soufflé dishes attest. Since 1994, when food entrepreneur Chip Fisher (of **Fisher and Levy** catering and **Mr. Chips** ice-cream parlor) took over, it's been moving away from the charming-but-rarefied stock of yore to the more practical items used by today's cooks. Alongside wooden mustard spoons, work-of-art copper pots, and *mazagrans* (tall ceramic glasses used to serve frothed hot chocolate), there are now stainless-steel pots and baking pans in all sizes. Gadgets also abound, from the device that forms a design on an orange skin to the contraption that lops the top off a hard-boiled egg. ◆ M-Sa. 36 W 25th St (between Broadway and Sixth Aves). 242.0750 &

31 Follonico ★★$$$ Veteran chef Alan Tardi, formerly of **Le Madri,** is the chef and owner of this charming trattoria with Tuscan yellow walls, exposed brick, and wood paneling. The open kitchen and prominently positioned wood-burning oven add to the feeling of traditional, Old World warmth. Try calamari roasted with garlic; ravioli filled with rabbit, veal, and pork in a butter and sage sauce; scallops in shellfish broth; smoked goose breast with white beans and pomegranate seeds; osso buco; roast chicken; and baked salt-crusted red snapper. Top the meal off with a sliced-apple tart baked in the wood-burning oven. The wine list is filled with unusual Italian selections that are affordably priced. ◆ Italian ◆ M-F lunch and dinner; Sa-Su dinner. Reservations recommended. 6 W 24th St (between Fifth and Sixth Aves). 691.6359

32 Aja ★★★$$$ **Gotham Bar and Grill** graduate Gary Robins recently opened this cavernous, highly stylized place and woke up the taste buds of those who figured they'd tried it all. Robins proves his mastery in designing structural wonders on the plate by avoiding the all-too-common trap of subordinating flavor to appearance. The major influences are Asian, the undercurrents European, and the overall flavors, entirely unique. To start your culinary adventure, try grilled foie gras with pears in red wine with apple celeriac puree, five-spice grilled squab with caramelized mango, or electrifying spicy tuna *tartare*. Continue with roasted grouper with lobster summer rolls and chili-garlic dipping sauce; giant prawns and clams in a green curry, cumin, and caraway broth; or honey-roasted chicken with butternut-squash dumplings. For a cooling finish, the home-made mango ice cream and lemongrass sorbet are just right. The wine list is small but interesting, with good affordable choices from France, Italy, California, and South Africa. ◆ Fusion ◆ M-F lunch and dinner; Sa dinner. Reservations recommended. 937 Broadway (at E 22nd St). 473.8388 &

33 Bolo ★★$$$ The decor is a manifestation of the vibrant energy at work here: vivid greens, reds, and golds, as well as collaged graphic images. This is the place where Bobby Flay, who reconceptualized Southwest cuisine at his **Mesa Grill** a few blocks away, takes on Spanish food and makes it hum. Try the warm octopus and chickpea salad with grilled tomatoes and garlic-parsley vinaigrette; baby clams steamed in green-onion broth; roasted pork loin in sherry-vinegar sauce served with pan-seared, apricot-almond relish; and curried shellfish and chicken paella. ◆ New Spanish ◆ M-F lunch and dinner; Sa dinner; Su brunch and dinner. Reservations recommended. 23 E 22nd St (between Park Ave S and Broadway). 228.2200 &

34 Live Bait $$ An extremely popular after-work destination, the bar is packed, sardine style, with a crowd downing oysters from shot glasses and sipping Rolling Rocks straight from the bottle. The decor is pure fishing shack, and although a cheeky sign above the bar says, "If you want home cooking, stay home," the cuisine is Carolina home-style. The menu includes chili, smothered pork chops, fried chicken, and a gumbo of andouille sausage, shrimp, and chicken, served over creole rice. ◆ Southeastern ◆ Daily lunch, dinner, and late-night meals. Reservations recommended. 14 E 23rd St (at Madison Ave). 353.2400

35 Alva ★★$$$ Gone are the white walls and large mural from this small, narrow restaurant which was formerly the **Chefs' Cuisiniers Club.** Today the black walls are mirrored, adorned with photos of Thomas Edison (Alva was his middle name), and illuminated by light bulbs. Clearly, owner Charlie Palmer, also of **Aureole** and the **Lenox Room,** is hoping to capture the spirit of genius, or at least invention. The earthy and flavorful fare includes grilled skinless duck breast in a star-anise sauce served with a poached pear stuffed with duck confit, and double-garlic roast chicken. Cigar smokers take note: cigar smoking is allowed after 10PM, and special cigar prix-fixe dinners are offered on Mondays. ♦ American ♦ M-F lunch and dinner; Sa-Su dinner. Reservations recommended. 36 E 22nd St (between Park Ave S and Broadway). 228.4399 &

36 Novità ★★$$ Designed by co-owners (and sisters) Elizabeth Yoshida Fregonese and Gina Yoshida, this handsome (though sometimes noisy) place is decorated with Tuscan yellow walls, Murano glass sconces, Etro paisley fabric banquettes, and vases collected from all over Italy. Presiding over the kitchen is the third partner in this venture, chef Marco Fregonese, formerly of **Mezzaluna** and **Mezzogiorno.** Blending influences from Northern and Southern Italy are such dishes as tuna carpaccio with Liparian red-pepper mayonnaise, capers, and scallions; warm calamari salad of arugula, cannellini beans, and tomato with avocado dressing; pasta roses of crabmeat and artichoke with tomato *coulis* and fava beans; roasted red snapper with red-pepper crust and shrimp stuffing; and roasted duck with Barola sauce, pomegranate, and pine nuts. Save room for the *crema tostata* (crème brûlée with toasted almonds, sautéed pears, and amaretti-cookie crust). The wine list features carefully selected, medium-priced Italian choices. ♦ Italian ♦ M-F lunch and dinner; Sa dinner. Reservations required. 102 E 22nd St (between Lexington Ave and Park Ave S). 677.2222

37 C.T. ★★★★$$$ After spending 15 years in Brazil, Claude Troisgros (the son of Pierre Troisgros, of the three-star Troisgros restaurant in Roanne, France) has come up with the perfect blend of French classical technique and South American spice. Try the jumbo ravioli with taro-root mousseline, white truffle oil, and mushrooms; black-and-blue tuna in a sesame-seed crust with ginger vinaigrette; sautéed duck foie gras with jicama, cinnamon, and star-anise sauce; herb-encrusted beef tenderloin in brown coriander sauce; and *Daurade Acacia* (red snapper with scales; see exclusive recipe on page 99). Cap the meal off with the *caipirinha* (a crisp napoleon filled with cream in a lime and sugarcane sauce that's as potent as the Brazilian drink of the same name) or with the *poire, poires, poivre* (slices of Asian pears layered between pear sorbet with pear syrup and white and black pepper). The sunny decor in the dining room is also a happy mix: it's at once elegant and relaxed. ♦ Brazilian/French ♦ M-F lunch and dinner; Sa dinner. Reservations required. 111

E 22nd St (between Lexington Ave and Park Ave S). 995.8500 &

38 Rolf's Restaurant ★$$ New York was once famous for its German restaurants, and this is one of the very few still operating. The walls and ceilings are covered with lots of art, stained glass, and carved wood. Try the veal shank, shell steak, and excellent potato pancakes. ♦ German ♦ Daily lunch and dinner. 281 Third Ave (at E 22nd St). 473.8718

39 Fresco Tortilla Grill ★$ Run by Rose and Deshi Zheng, this remarkable little storefront offers incontrovertible proof that tacos, quesadillas, and fajitas don't have to taste heavy, greasy, and mass-produced. The ingredients are zesty and fresh; once you've eaten here, your Mexican fast-food standards will be much higher. ♦ Mexican ♦ Daily lunch and dinner. No credit cards accepted. 36 Lexington Ave (between E 23rd and E 24th Sts). 475.7380

40 Benny's $ In addition to the fare available at the uptown location—lemon chicken with snow peas, ricotta chicken, sautéed spinach with lemon and garlic, cauliflower with carrot and tahini sauce, tabbouleh, couscous with vegetables, and spinach pie—the downtown location also offers such sandwiches as grilled marinated chicken and grilled marinated vegetables served rolled in thin Lebanese shepherd's bread (it's like a soft flour tortilla). There's also a sit-down area. ♦ Lebanese/Takeout ♦ Daily lunch and dinner. No credit cards accepted. 102 E 25th St (at Park Ave S). 674.4337. Also at: 321 Amsterdam Ave (between W 75th and W 76th Sts). 874.3032

41 La Colombe d'Or ★★★$$$ This romantic bistro was one of the first to open back in the mid-1970s, when the area was still considered uncharted territory. But by the time former employees Wayne Nish and Joseph Scalice of **March** returned as owners in 1994, the one-time pioneer had grown a little stale. Nish gave the menu a much-needed shot in the arm with Mediterranean influences that woke up the overall flavors without changing the restaurant's identity. Don't miss the thick *minestra* (a hearty vegetable, bean, and pasta soup with pecorino cheese), the intense fish soup, cassoulet, duck confit, bouillabaisse, and grilled rib steak with shallot and balsamic-vinegar sauce. There's also a very carefully chosen wine list featuring wines of the Rhône Valley and nationally produced Rhône varietals. ♦ Provençal ♦ M-F lunch and dinner; Sa-Su dinner. Reservations recommended. 134 E 26th St (between Third and Lexington Aves). 689.0666

A C.T. Secret Recipe

Claude Troisgros, the owner/chef of the very hot restaurant **C.T.**, literally grew up in the kitchen of the celebrated Troisgros restaurant in Roanne, France, which was founded by his father Pierre and uncle Jean. But it wasn't until he moved to Rio de Janeiro that he began to incorporate native Brazilian ingredients into the classic French recipes—and voilà, his unique hybrid of French and Brazilian cuisine was born.

In one of the most exciting restaurant openings of 1994, he brought his talents to appreciative New Yorkers. Now you can try one of his signature dishes in your own kitchen with this exclusive recipe for *Daurade Acacia* (Red Snapper with Scales).

INGREDIENTS:

For the stock:
- cup Xeres sherry vinegar
- 1/2 cup of honey
- white peppercorns
- sprig thyme
- bay leaf
- sprig rosemary
- teaspoon ground ginger
- salt and pepper to taste

For the eggplant:
- medium eggplants
- cups olive oil (for frying throughout recipe)

For the sauce:
- tomatoes
- 1/2 onion
- cloves garlic
- salt and pepper to taste

For the snapper:
- red snapper fillets
- salt and pepper to taste
- bay leaves
- sprigs fresh thyme
- sprigs fresh rosemary

DIRECTIONS:

To prepare the stock:
1. Combine all of the stock ingredients in a saucepan and bring the mixture to a boil; simmer for five minutes.
2. Remove the mixture from heat and strain, retaining the liquid.

To prepare the eggplant:
1. Cut the eggplant into 1/4-inch-thick slices. In a skillet, heat enough olive oil for sautéing; when very hot, fry the eggplant slices until golden on each side; season well with salt and pepper.
2. Drain the olive oil from the pan and add 3/4 of the stock. Bring the mixture to a boil for five minutes; remove from heat and let it steep for several hours.

To prepare the sauce:
1. Peel, seed, and coarsely chop the tomatoes; chop the onion and mince the garlic.
2. In a skillet, heat the olive oil and gently sauté the onion and garlic; add the tomatoes and simmer the mixture for five minutes.
3. Stir in the reserved stock; return the mixture to a boil and remove from heat. Puree the mixture in a blender and check the seasonings.

To prepare the snapper:
1. Season the red snapper fillets with salt and pepper.
2. Heat a nonstick frying pan with olive oil. When the oil is very hot, fry the red snapper fillets with their scale side down for approximately 10 minutes.
3. When fillets are cooked through, turn over in the pan briefly to finish; scales should be golden and crispy. Remove from heat.

To assemble the dish:
1. Spoon some of the tomato sauce in the center of each plate; top with several eggplant slices.
2. Place a red snapper fillet, with the scale side up, on top of the eggplant.
3. Drizzle each plate with olive oil and garnish the fish with sprigs of thyme, bay leaf, and rosemary. Serves 4.

i Trulli

42 I Trulli ★★★$$$ Nicola Marzovilla (owner of the nearby **Tempo**) tried to recreate his childhood memory of the many trattorie he visited in his native Puglia in Southern Italy when he opened this warm, simple place. The dining room is dominated by a glassed-in fireplace and a whitewashed wood-burning oven which mirrors the distinctive beehive shape of *trulli*—ancient Pugliese houses. The result is a selection of wonderfully earthy dishes, such as the clay casserole of potatoes, portobello mushrooms, and herbs; baked oysters with pancetta; ricotta dumplings with tomato sauce; spicy chicken with vinegar and garlic; grilled free-range chicken; and stewed baby octopus. For dessert, try the fruit poached in wine. There's also an extensive wine list with good choices at all price levels. In nice weather, sit in the garden out back. ♦ Italian ♦ M-F lunch and dinner; Sa dinner. Reservations recommended. 122 E 27th St (between Lexington Ave and Park Ave S). 481.7372

42 Per Bacco ★$ An extensive menu of such Northern Italian standards as saltimbocca and veal milanese is offered at this well-established neighborhood restaurant. Friendly service and a relaxing setting also make coming here a pleasurable experience. ♦ Northern Italian ♦ M-F lunch and dinner; Sa dinner. 140 E 27th St (between Third and Lexington Aves). 532.8699

43 Silk ★★$$ So much attention is lavished on the restaurants around Park Avenue South that this elegant, creative place off the beaten track on Third Avenue is often overlooked. It shouldn't be. Owner Henry Tao has created a calm, beautiful environment with subdued lighting and beige-striped satin banquettes— complete with pillow rolls. Behind the scenes, chef Kimiaki Kageyama blends Osaka with Paris more seamlessly than most who try the same. Specialties include the odd-sounding— but delicious—coffee-smoked rare beef and grilled tuna steak with a lush balsamic-teriyaki sauce nicely complemented by horseradish mashed potatoes. ♦ Fusion ♦ M-F lunch and dinner; Sa-Su dinner. 378 Third Ave (between E 27th and E 28th Sts). 532.4500

44 The Big Enchilada ★$ Like its sister branch in Greenwich Village, this casual spot offers tasty Tex-Mex fare. All the portions are generous, but the signature Big Enchilada, stuffed with rice, beans, lettuce, tomatoes, a choice of vegetables, beef or stewed chicken, and topped with jack cheese and guacamole, is seriously hefty. ♦ Tex-Mex ♦ Daily lunch and dinner. 160 E 28th St (between Third and Lexington Aves). 447.7940. Also at: 28 E 12th St (between University Pl and Fifth Ave). 627.7940

45 Jaiya Thai Oriental Restaurant ★★$$ The food here can be incendiary—pay close attention to the spiciness ratings on the menu, but whatever you choose from the extensive menu, you know it will be delicious. Try the excellent spicy chicken and coconut soup, spicy shredded jellyfish, chicken and beef satays, pork with very hot chili peppers and onions, pad thai, naked shrimp (rare shrimp with lime, lemongrass, and chili), roast duck curry, whole crabs in black bean or ginger sauce, and pork with string beans, red chili, and basil. The small casual room has a very nice touch: fresh orchids on the table. ♦ Thai ♦ Daily lunch and dinner. Reservations recommended for Friday and Saturday dinner. 396 Third Ave (at E 28th St). 889.1330. Also at: 81-11 Broadway (between 81st and 82nd Sts), Elmhurst. 718/651.1330

46 Tammany Hall ★★$$ The name is Old New York (there's a lineup of black-and-white photos of the city's mayors on the walls), but the decor is modern and sleek at this fashionable tavern. Ocher walls, green-leather circular booths, and redwood panels are the backdrop for a rustic Italian menu that La Guardia himself would have loved. To start, try the huge *terra mista* (a selection of vividly flavored salads and appetizers), steamed clams and mussels, or bruschetta of the day. Follow with salmon trout baked in grape leaves and prosciutto or osso buco, and be sure to save room for the silky, luscious lemon mascarpone cheesecake. ♦ Italian ♦ Daily lunch and dinner. Reservations recommended. 393 Third Ave (at E 28th St). 696.2001

46 Sam's Noodle Shop ★$ Decorated with colorful rose and blue tiles, this large restaurant has an extensive menu—about 15 dishes long—including good chicken *chow fun,* General Tso's Chicken, mixed dumplings, roast pork buns, and some 20 vegetable dishes. Furthermore, the noodle soups and dishes, which also figure prominently, can be custom-made—you pick the type of noodle, meats, vegetables, and sauce—making it nigh impossible not to get exactly what you want here. ♦ Chinese ♦ Daily lunch and dinner. 411 Third Ave (at E 29th St). 213.2288

47 Kalustyan's All the ingredients needed to cook Indian food are available at this emporium located on a stretch of Lexington Avenue that's rapidly becoming—after Sixth Street in the East Village—a second Little India. Inside is a swirl of enticing spicy aromas and colorful sights: bags of different colored lentils, jars of dried fruit, canisters of tea and deeply hued curry powder, jasmine, basmati and wild rice, and much, much more. ♦ Daily. 123 Lexington Ave (between E 28th and E 29th Sts). 685.3451 ♿

48 Sonia Rose ★★$$$ When looking for this place, don't look for a sign; look instead for a large window holding a table set for two. Inside the cozy brownstone dining room (there are only 11 tables), the decor features antiques, an authentic Art Deco bar, and on the cream-colored walls a series of oil paintings by Virginia Deutch and a group of photographs by Daniel Geist. The menu includes breast of free-range hen with sun-dried tomato and tarragon sauce, pan-fried oysters in cornmeal, and asparagus in puff pastry with beurre blanc. The food is just as good as it sounds, and considering the quantities served at the prix-fixe–only lunches and dinners, it could be considered something of a deal. ♦ French ♦ M dinner; Tu-F lunch and dinner; Sa-Su dinner. Reservations recommended. 132 Lexington Ave (between E 28th and E 29th Sts). 545.1777

49 Manhattan Fruitier Owner Jehv Gold puts together stupendous baskets filled with exotic seasonal fruits from all over the world. He can supply the appropriate arrangement, according to your needs, and will deliver throughout Manhattan. In addition to the beautiful fruit baskets, other exquisite food gifts include jars of fruit in maple syrup, chocolate truffles in beautiful boxes, European cookies, and New Hampshire honey. ♦ M-F. 105 E 29th St (between Lexington Ave and Park Ave S). 686.0404

49 Pigalle ★★$$ In 1991, former **Park Bistro** sous-chef Eric Lagrange moved around the corner to open his own very Parisian-style bistro. The mirrored walls and other authentic appointments might recall the City of Light only too well for the waiters who have a tendency to speak in French and become somewhat impatient when their customers fail to understand. However, the words, *"C'est magnifique,"* veritably trip off the tongue in response to the simple but juicy herb-crusted grilled chicken salad or the more ambitious saffron ravioli stuffed with pheasant. ♦ French ♦ M-F lunch and dinner; Sa dinner; Su lunch and dinner. 111 E 29th St (between Lexington Ave and Park Ave S). 779.7830

50 Les Halles ★★$$ A recreation of the nameless hangouts that once surrounded the great wholesale food market in Paris, this place has been a success since it opened in 1991. Some people patronize the butcher shop in front; others go to the often noisy dining room in back for onion soup, garlicky sausage, steak with *pommes frites* (french fries), or cassoulet. The crowds that line up to wait for a table are mostly advertising and publishing executives who work nearby. ♦ French ♦ M-F lunch and dinner; Sa-Su brunch and dinner. Reservations recommended. 411 Park Ave S (between E 28th and E 29th Sts). 679.4111 ♿

51 Park Bistro ★★$$$ Black-and-white photos of Paris in the 1950s line the walls at this friendly bistro. Chef Jean-Michel Diot's specialties include a warm potato salad topped with goat cheese and served with a small green salad; duck rillettes with celeriac and smoked duck breast; wild-mushroom ravioli in port sauce; sautéed skate in a red-wine vinegar sauce with white beans; fresh codfish with onion sauce and fried leeks; and onglet, known here as hanger steak (the prime section of beef that French butchers usually keep for themselves) served with green-peppercorn sauce. For dessert, try the warm chocolate torte or the thin apple tart with Armagnac. There's a good selection of mostly French wines. ♦ French ♦ M-F lunch and dinner; Sa-Su dinner. 414 Park Ave S (at E 29th St). 689.1360

MAVALLI PALACE

52 Mavalli Palace ★$ While all Indian restaurants have some vegetarian specialties, this place offers nothing but meatless creations. All the dishes are unusual and delicious—even to avowed carnivores. For a taste of everything, try the combination platter, featuring *dosais* (crepes of assorted vegetables and potatoes), which are served with coconut chutney and lentils, curries, and *iddlies* (steamed lentil-and-rice cakes). ♦ Indian vegetarian ♦ Daily lunch and dinner. 46 E 29th St (between Park Ave S and Madison Ave). 679.5535

52 Tempo ★★$$$ A capacity crowd of diners packs this dull brown dining room at lunchtime. The lure is Southern Italian food from owner Nicola Marzovilla's home region of Puglia. If you need help deciding what to have, Marzovilla is always on hand to offer suggestions. Good picks include clams in tomato pesto; stuffed squid; *orecchiette* (ear-shaped pasta) with fresh tomato, arugula, and fennel; tricolored *raviolini*; swordfish; or breaded veal chop. Don't miss the ethereal pasta made by his mother Dora. ♦ Southern Italian ♦ M-F lunch and dinner; Sa dinner. Reservations recommended. 30 E 29th St (between Park Ave S and Madison Ave). 532.8125

53 Cafe Journal ★$ If the charming green-and-yellow front of this cafe, owned by the proprietors of **Park Bistro** (see above) isn't enough to attract business, the heady aromas emanating from the pizza du jour, Val d'Aoste sandwich (prosciutto, mozzarella, and tomato), and buttery almond croissants should do the trick. This is a good place to linger for hours over a grilled chicken sandwich on baguette, pasta salad, or a slice of perfect Opera cake—rich chocolate ganache (frosting), layered with mocha cream and almond sponge cake with espresso syrup. As the name implies, newspapers are thoughtfully supplied. ♦ Bakery/Cafe ♦ M-F breakfast and lunch. 47 E 29th St (between Park Ave S and Madison Ave). 447.1822 &

54 Abby Restaurant and Bar ★$$ Chef Michel Abaza is Egyptian but his culinary upbringing included a stint in Italy, which explains the numerous influences from the other side of the Mediterranean. Don't miss the porcini risotto or seared yellowfin tuna with black pasta and *tapenade* (a thick paste flavored with capers, anchovies, olives, and lemon juice). The paintings displayed on the walls are varying exhibitions by local and international artists and are for sale. ♦ International ♦ Daily lunch and dinner. Reservations recommended. 254 Fifth Ave (between 28th and 29th Sts). 725.2922

55 D. Sokolin This shop boasts a highly touted selection of wines and spirits from all over the world, but has a special concentration in the wines of Bordeaux. The service is knowledgeable and unpretentious. ♦ M-Sa. 178 Madison Ave (at E 33rd St). 532.5893

56 An American Place ★★$$$ Larry Forgione, wunderkind of new American cooking, isn't as involved here as he used to be, but his influence survives in this cheery bistro. Try the barbecued-duck salad over greens with a roasted-corn salsa; the roasted quail with foie gras and apple ravioli in a ham, sweet onion, and cabbage broth; or grilled duck breast with a black-pepper and molasses glaze and ginger-smashed sweet potatoes. ♦ New American ♦ M-F lunch and dinner; Sa dinner. Reservations recommended. 2 Park Ave (at E 32nd St). 684.2122

57 Marchi's ★$$$ Not much has changed since this restaurant opened in 1930. The fixed menu has been the same for nearly that long: an antipasto platter, homemade lasagna, deep-fried whiting with cold string beans and beets in vinaigrette, roast veal and roast chicken with mushrooms and tossed greens, and dessert. The five generally well prepared courses come in a relentless procession, defying even the most indomitable diner to stagger through to the final stage of fruit, cookies, and coffee. ♦ Northern Italian ♦ M-Sa dinner. Reservations recommended; jacket required. 251 E 31st St (between Second and Third Aves). 679.2494

58 Todaro Brothers A typical Little Italy grocery store that moved uptown and expanded, this emporium has been providing top-quality food in this neighborhood for over 70 years. Come here for an excellent variety of smoked fish, olives, baked goods, fresh pastas, and sauces. There are meat and sandwich counters too, and a selection of Italian cheeses—including the store's own mozzarella, which isn't as good as you can get downtown but would certainly do in a pinch. ♦ Daily. 555 Second Ave (between E 30th and E 31st Sts). 532.0633

59 The Water Club ★★★$$$ Fluttering triangular flags give the entrance of this restaurant the look of a fancy yacht club. Inside the glass-enclosed, skylit former barge anchored at the river's edge, landlubbers are treated to views that are among the best in town—the cocktail lounge area opens into a terraced dining room with a panorama of the **East River.** Naturally seafood is the best choice here, and the many varieties of oysters and clams are dependably spectacular. Although the service can be harried and the noise level a bit high for intimate conversation, this place with its vacation atmosphere is well worth a visit. It's also a great venue for weddings and other festive occasions. ♦ American ♦ Daily lunch and dinner. Reservations required. E 30th St and the East River (access from E 34th St). 683.3333

60 El Parador ★★$$$ Opened long before the current craze for Mexican food, this spot remains popular among Mexican food aficionados as well as those looking for a good time. The inevitable wait at the bar gives diners a chance to unwind with margaritas potent enough to make them forget their hunger pangs. After being seated by a host who has a knack for making each person feel important, you'll be served a meal well worth the wait. Among many estimable selections are the chicken *parador* (marinated and steamed), grilled-sirloin fajitas, and *chilaquiles* (stewed chicken with sour cream and green-tomatillo sauce). ♦ Mexican ♦ Daily lunch and dinner. Reservations recommended. 325 E 34th St (between First and Second Aves). 679.6812

61 Nicola Paone ★$$$ Decorated with stone designs to resemble an Italian marketplace, this place has a serious Northern Italian menu that is enlivened by such imaginative offerings as artichokes stuffed with breadcrumbs and anchovies, shrimp with basil, smoked salmon and white wine, the whimsically named Nightgown (sliced veal and eggplant topped with mozzarella), *baci baci* (boneless chicken breast, spinach, and prosciutto covered in white-wine sauce with mushrooms), and shrimp *tritone* (with smoked salmon and basil in a white-wine sauce). Good desserts include a banana and strawberry shortcake. Service is courtly and helpful, and the wine list boasts a 400-bottle selection. ◆ Italian ◆ M-F lunch and dinner; Sa dinner. Reservations recommended. 207 E 34th St (between Second and Third Aves). 889.3239

62 Dolci On Park Caffè ★$$ You can get a satisfying meal here of linguine with sausage, penne with four cheeses, tortellini with ham, fettuccine with smoked salmon, chicken marsala, or salmon with mushrooms and cream sauce. But far and away, the best part of a meal here is dessert. Indulge in a cannoli, chocolate eclair, mocha sponge cake, fruit tart, cheese cake, or tiramisù with a cup of espresso or cappuccino. In fair weather, sit at one of the sidewalk tables. ◆ Italian ◆ M-Sa breakfast, lunch, and dinner. 12 Park Ave (between E 34th and E 35th Sts). 686.4331 &

63 El Charro Español ★$$ With the same menu as the Greenwich Village spot, this place offers delicious *mariscada* (Spanish bouillabaisse); chicken with garlic and white wine; veal with onions, peppers, garlic, and sausages; shrimp grilled in the shell with lemon, garlic, and parsley; and several varieties of paella—*valenciana* (with chicken, sausage, and seafood), *marinara* (all seafood), and *hortelana* (vegetarian). Here, as there, you can wash it all down with a potent margarita. ◆ Spanish ◆ Daily lunch and dinner. Reservations recommended Friday-Sunday. 58 E 34th St (between Park and Madison Aves). 689.1019. Also at: 4 Charles St (at Greenwich Ave). 924.5915

64 Morgan Cafe ★$ A refined place indeed for the true lady (or perfect gentleman) who lunches, this elegant skylit cafe at the **Pierpont Morgan Library** is near the bookshop. Sandwiches, salads, and afternoon tea are among the appropriately light and delicate offerings. ◆ Cafe ◆ Tu-Su breakfast, lunch, and afternoon tea. 29 E 36th St (at Madison Ave). 685.0008

65 Woo Chon ★$$ Near the **Empire State Building**, this brightly lit and plainly decorated room serves good Korean food around-the-clock. The menu makes ordering a breeze—there's a picture of each dish next to its listing. The beef barbecue is a good bet, as are the scallion pancakes, kimchi (preserved cabbage), and a stir-fry of cellophane noodles, onions, carrots, strips of beef, and scallions. ◆ Korean ◆ Daily 24 hours. 8-10 W 36th St (between Fifth and Sixth Aves). 695.0676

66 Chez Laurence Patisserie ★$ On a stretch of Madison Avenue overrun with coffee shops, this little place is an oasis. Stop in for a plate of pâté or a breast of chicken sandwich on toasted brioche, topped off by an espresso and *pain au chocolat* (chocolate-filled croissant) or fruit tart. There are also croissants and baguettes to take home. ◆ Bakery/Cafe ◆ M-Sa breakfast, lunch, and dinner. 245 Madison Ave (at E 38th St). 683.0284

67 Rossini's $$$ The Hot Antipasto Rossini in champagne sauce—clams *oreganata,* shrimp scampi, and mozzarella *in carrozza* (wrapped in bread and fried)—is a specialty of this casual, friendly restaurant, where entrées include chicken *romano* (stuffed with spinach and roast veal). A strolling guitarist serenades diners Monday through Thursday; a pianist performs on Friday; and an opera trio entertains on Saturday. ◆ Italian ◆ M-F lunch and dinner; Sa-Su dinner. Reservations recommended. 108 E 38th St (between Lexington and Park Aves). 683.0135

Bests

Lisa Simon

Supervising Producer/Director, "Sesame Street"

Union Square Greenmarket: A great neighborhood activity. At the end of summer into fall, the abundance and variety of produce, flowers, and products is at its best. A visual treat and great energy and good will from the vendors. A little bit of the country in the city.

Fairway: It's what New York is about. Diversity, crowds, bargains, and great prepared foods—if you don't want to cook.

Union Square Cafe: Room is lovely, the service good, food is always good. Great bar. It is a consistently good restaurant—always a pleasure to share with old friends or new friends.

Aggie's: Good casual neighborhood restaurant. Food like mom used to make—comforting and great when wandering through the Village or SoHo.

Periyali: It's like being in Greece but the food is better.

Chelsea

Bounded by **West 14th Street**, **West 34th Street**, **Sixth Avenue,** and the **Hudson River,** Chelsea has gone through many ups and downs over the years. In 1830, it was a well-heeled subdivision of the family property inherited by Clement Clarke Moore—author of the poem *A Visit from St. Nicholas.* A mere 21 years later, this changed when the **Hudson River Railroad** opened on **11th Avenue,** breweries and slaughterhouses moved in, and shanties and tenements sprang up to house the workers who flooded in. The neighborhood continued its slide downhill during the 1870s, when a number of town houses built by Moore's affluent contemporaries were sacrificed to make way for the city's first elevated railroad on Ninth Avenue.

The area enjoyed an upturn during the 1870s when New York's fashion retailing district was located here, and Sixth Avenue south of **West 23rd**

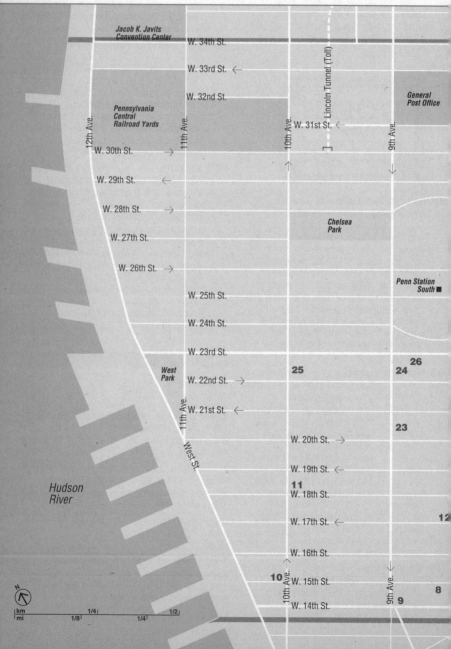

treet became known as "Ladies Mile" because of its numerous shops. But by he turn of the century the new uptown department stores had effectively ured shoppers away. In the 1880s, during the area's demise as a shopping enter, the neighborhood became the city's theater district. Yet in the next lecade the theaters also moved uptown. In the early 1900s, the filmmaking ndustry was briefly headquartered here, before moving to Queens and then vest to California. For years thereafter, Chelsea remained a place of shabby enements and neglected town houses.

'hings improved during the middle of this century when the city began a rogram of urban renewal, and Chelsea was discovered again. Some enements were leveled, while others were cleaned up and renovated. With he restoration of rundown town houses, wealthier residents began to return. s they did, upscale businesses followed, a pattern that continues today.

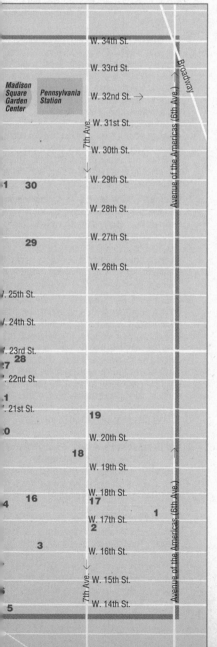

The ongoing transformation of this neighborhood can be seen by taking a culinary tour up **Eighth Avenue**, starting at West 14th Street. Older establishments—inexpensive, funky Cuban-Chinese greasy spoons and Spanish bodegas (grocery stores)—remain, but now they share the spotlight with chicly designed bistros and top-quality food stores. The neighborhood also boasts a colorful mosaic of international cuisines—including Caribbean, Austrian, Thai, and Japanese. Those who crave American home-style cooking can choose between refurbished diners and old-fashioned steak houses, while fans of American new wave and fusion cooking can find their more adventurous tastes catered to as well.

The food and retailing scene is humming—a sign that Chelsea's star is again on the rise. And for the lucky diner, a fine time can be had for something more than a song but considerably less than an arm and a leg.

1 **Da Umberto** ★★$$$ This casual and restful trattoria specializes in Tuscan dishes, especially wild game (hare, pheasant, and venison, for example). The veal chop with cognac sauce is a favorite here, and the antipasti selections are worth a try. ♦ Italian ♦ M-Sa lunch and dinner. Reservations required. 107 W 17th St (between Sixth and Seventh Aves). 989.0303

2 **Le Cafe** ★$$ If shopping at **Barney's** has left you tuckered out and hungry, this cafe on the store's lower level will restore you. The service is cafeteria-style, but with better-than-usual offerings—pasta salads, green salads, freshly grilled tuna salad, grilled salmon, chocolate cake, and plum tarts. The

cappuccino is good too. ♦ Cafe ♦ Daily breakfast, lunch, and afternoon tea. Seventh Ave (at W 17th St). 929.9000 ♿

3 Cafe Riazor ★$ Located on a side street, several steps down, this place is not very easy to find. But for a good basic Spanish meal in a decidedly untrendy milieu—old-fashioned stucco ceiling, dim lighting, heavy wood tables—it's worth seeking out. Try the marinated octopus salad, *mariscada* (seafood stew of clams, mussels, shrimp, and lobster in a red sauce), or broiled chicken. ♦ Spanish ♦ Daily lunch, dinner, and late-night meals. 245 W 16th St (between Seventh and Eighth Aves). 727.2132

4 Cajun ★$$ The honky-tonk atmosphere and live Dixieland music (nightly at 8PM) are fun, and the creole-Cajun food, which comes in hearty portions, doesn't disappoint. ♦ Creole/Cajun ♦ M-F lunch and dinner; Sa dinner; Su brunch and dinner. Reservations recommended for five or more. 129 Eighth Ave (at W 16th St). 691.6174

4 Kaffeehaus ★$ The desserts at this nouvelle Austrian restaurant/coffeehouse aren't authentically Viennese; neither, in the strictest sense, is the food—it's lighter and more inventive than is usually found in the old country. Don't miss the risotto with whole grains and autumn vegetables in a parmesan-vegetable broth. The caraway-and-garlic-crusted loin of pork in a caramelized onion-beer sauce is very good as well. There's also an interesting wine list, mixing well-chosen and fairly priced bottles from California, Italy, France, and of course, Austria. The simply decorated brown-toned room draws a diverse crowd for lively conversation over the strains of Billie Holiday and other jazz divas. ♦ Nouvelle Austrian/Contemporary American ♦ M-F lunch and dinner; Sa-Su brunch and dinner. Reservations recommended. 131 Eighth Ave (between W 16th and W 17th Sts). 229.9702 ♿

5 One City Cafe ★$ This not-for-profit cafe has a special mission: to employ people who were formerly homeless and to offer well-prepared meals for minimal cost (meals paid for with food stamps—restaurant-approved ID card necessary—are half price). The brainchild of Ellyn Rosenthal, executive director of Food & Hunger Hotline, this restaurant offers a more dignified alternative to charity kitchens and pantries. Formerly **Quatorze,** the pale modern dining room— white walls, blond wood floors—is punctuated with vibrant paintings that were done by homeless women. The food, given a Latin/Southern spin, is colorful as well. Try the grilled chicken with jerk sauce, vegetable lasagna, catfish po'boy, and for dessert, banana bread budding. Because part of the restaurant's purpose is to train new employees, the service may be more well-intentioned than professional, but nobody minds. At press time, the restaurant was open Thursday to Sunday, and plans were afoot to expand its hours; call for more information. ♦ Eclectic ♦ Th-F lunch and dinner; Sa-Su brunch and dinner. 240 W 14th St (between Seventh and Eighth Aves). 807.1738

6 La Taza de Oro ★$ Of the few remaining restaurants specializing in Latin food on this stretch of Eighth Avenue, this is one of the best. The decor isn't much—a few Formica tables and basic luncheonette stools at the counter—but the dishes, such as roast pork and shredded beef, are satisfying and flavorful. Some regulars just come in for the *cafe con leche* (coffee light, and unless you say "no sugar," sweet). ♦ Latin ♦ M-Sa breakfast, lunch, and dinner. No credit cards accepted. 96 Eighth Ave (between W 14th and W 15th Sts). 243.9946

7 Chelsea Trattoria ★$$ This pretty trattoria with peach walls and exposed brick is a reliable place for standard Italian fare. The osso buco and the fettuccine with artichokes, mushrooms, and tomatoes are especially recommended. ♦ Italian ♦ M-F lunch and dinner; Sa dinner. 108 Eighth Ave (between W 15th and W 16th Sts). 924.7786

8 El Cid ★★$ Small and cheerful, this tapas bar with blue tablecloths and mirrored walls is an informal, fun place to come with a group to try out a range of different small plates. Don't miss the white asparagus in vinaigrette, grilled shrimp, marinated pork, or chicken in garlic sauce. And the paella should satisfy the most hungry diners. The wine list showcases good, inexpensive Spanish wines. ♦ Spanish ♦ Tu-F lunch and dinner; Sa-Su dinner. 322 W 15th St (between Eighth and Ninth Aves). 929.9332

9 Old Homestead ★★$$$$; Established in 1868, this is the oldest steak house in Manhattan, and huge steaks and prime ribs are served here the way they always have been. One nod to newer tastes, and clients, is the inclusion on the menu of Japanese *Kobe* beef (more correctly known as *wagyu*), for which diners are asked to pay dearly—$100 a steak. Those who prefer to do their own broiling or grilling can buy fresh cuts of beef (including one-inch-thick steaks) at the **Old Homestead Gourmet** shop (807.0707) next door, where various sauces and a variety of gourmet items, including the *crème de la* *crème* of chocolates, the French Valrhona and the Belgian D'Orsay. ◆ American ◆ Daily lunch and dinner. Shop: M-Sa. Reservations recommended. 56 Ninth Ave (at W 14th St). 242.9040 ⌖

10 Frank's ★★$$$ This place has been a meat district fixture since 1912, serving some of the best steaks around to the guys who work in the business and know what's good. After a fire gutted the ground floor in 1994, the restaurant moved temporarily upstairs to its banquet room and then relocated right around the corner from the old 14th Street location. It's still serving extraordinary beef—dry aged shell steak, loin lamb chops, and a piece of filet mignon that weighs nearly a pound. Also on the menu are such homemade pasta as fettuccine *bolognese* as well as basic, good-quality desserts, including giant slabs of cheesecake. ◆ American ◆ M-F lunch and dinner; Sa dinner. Reservations recommended. 85 10th Ave (at 15th St). 243.1349

la Lunchonette

11 La Lunchonette ★$$ The homey bar and open kitchen in this bistro-style restaurant seem familiar enough, but the free-range chicken with mustard, lamb sausage with sautéed apples, and panfried whole trout with wild mushrooms add interesting variations to a time-honored cuisine. ◆ French ◆ M-F lunch and dinner; Sa dinner; Su brunch and dinner. Reservations recommended. 130 10th Ave (at W 18th St). 675.0342

Alley's End

12 Alley's End ★★$ Hidden at the back of an alley off West 17th Street, this restaurant sports a flashing neon fork and knife to help customers find their way. Inside this funky hideaway is a bar that looks like the lounge of a bowling alley, a handsome dining room with white brick walls, a reproduction of the painting *The Rape of the Sabine Women* done by the owners' neighbor, and a glass wall overlooking the ultimate urban garden, which includes a sputtering waterfall. Standouts among the creative dishes are the rock shrimp with white beans and baby artichokes served with a tomato and arugula salad; juicy, flavorful thyme-grilled boneless breast of chicken; and oven-roasted salmon with whole-grain mustard sauce accompanied by sweet butternut squash and caramelized onions. For dessert, there's a remarkably light

brioche bread pudding. ◆ American ◆ Daily dinner. Reservations recommended. 311 W 17th St (between Eighth and Ninth Aves). 627.8899

FOOD BAR

13 Food Bar ★$ The decor—plain wood walls with silver geometric light fixtures—is much more understated than the boisterous customers. The fare is a little of everything—nicely composed salads, steaks, pastas (such as angel hair with artichokes), and olive *tapenade* (a thick paste flavored with capers, anchovies, olives, and lemon juice). But as good as the food here is, it definitely takes a back seat to the thriving social scene. ◆ Eclectic ◆ M-F lunch and dinner; Sa-Su brunch and dinner. 149 Eighth Ave (between W 17th and W 18th Sts). 243.2020 ⌖

EIGHTEENTH & EIGHTH

13 Eighteenth and Eighth ★$ The cozy—some would say cramped—dining room is decorated with dried leaves, eccentric teapots, and drawings of the male anatomy. Served here are large portions of such creative comfort food as roast loin of pork stuffed with herbs; grilled leg of lamb with sun-dried tomatoes and black olives; roast chicken with lemon, garlic, and rosemary; and a very satisfying meat loaf. There are good sandwiches and salads as well as terrific breakfast dishes, including French toast made with brioche. ◆ American ◆ Daily breakfast, lunch, and dinner. 159 Eighth Ave (at W 18th St). 242.5000

14 Cola's ★★$ Here you'll find a casual mix of Northern and Southern Italian cuisine. Hand-painted, antiqued walls lend a gentle ambience to the small room, where a lively downtown crowd comes to sample such pasta dishes as penne with goat cheese and eggplant and heartier fare like pork chops in balsamic vinegar. The wine list offers many fine selections. ◆ Italian ◆ Daily dinner. 148 Eighth Ave (between W 17th and W 18th Sts). 633.8020

14 Gascogne ★★$$ Chef Pascal Condomine recreates the rich, hearty foods from the southwest region of France, including a superb fish soup, foie gras, roast duck, and an excellent cassoulet; also featured are wines from the same region. The cozy, charming room makes you feel as if you've escaped to the country. ♦ French ♦ M-F lunch and dinner; Sa dinner; Su brunch and dinner. Reservations required. 158 Eighth Ave (between W 17th and W 18th Sts). 675.6564

14 The Viceroy ★$$ The dining room here,

with a silver tin ceiling, ceiling fans, plants, and metallic blinds, is perpetually abuzz with what seems to be the entire gay male population of Chelsea, who turn out nightly to table-hop and be served hearty food by young muscle-bound waiters in black T-shirts. Owned by brothers Nick and John Accardi, who also own the Italian-theme **Cola's** (see above) down the street, this venture is more of a bustling American bistro. Offerings include barbecued quail salad with black-eyed peas and *frisée* (curly endive), seared peppered tuna with stir-fried Asian greens, roast chicken, and steak *frites* (french fries). For dessert, don't miss the chocolate mousse cake. Be sure to come early—by 7:30PM the place is mobbed. ♦ American ♦ M-F lunch, dinner, and late-night meals; Sa-Su brunch, dinner, and late-night meals. 160 Eighth Ave (at W 18th St). 633.8484

15 Man Ray ★$$ Sleek and minimalist, this Art Deco–inspired cafe serves such creative international food as black-pepper linguine with seafood, tomato, lemon, garlic, and olive oil; grilled breast of duck with arugula and watercress in a raspberry vinaigrette; and roasted leg of lamb with ratatouille. It's conveniently located right next to the **Joyce Theater.** ♦ International ♦ M-F lunch and dinner; Sa-Su brunch and dinner. 169 Eighth Ave (between W 18th and W 19th Sts). 627.4220

16 Taylor's This branch of Cindi Taylor's popular Village bakery and take-out store has good chicken and pasta salads and excellent baked goods, including breads (some homemade), brownies, and Key lime bars. ♦ Daily. 228 W 18th St (between Seventh and Eighth Aves). 366.9081. Also at: 523 Hudson St (between W 10th and Charles Sts). 645.8200; 175 Second Ave (between 11th and 12th Sts). 674.9501

17 Le Madri ★★★$$$ Pino Luongo's stylish restaurant turns out Tuscan-style specialties for the illustrious crowds that flock here. Order roasted vegetables for the whole table and any of chef Gianni Scappin's homemade pastas, which include the delicious *agnolotti* (half-moon ravioli) filled with spinach and ricotta and served with mixed mushrooms. Osso buco and whole roasted fish are also treats. On summer weekends the restaurant hosts an "al fresco" film series; Italian movies are shown on a screen in the parking lot next door, while the crowd munches on salads, pizzas, and pastas. ♦ Italian ♦ M-Sa lunch and dinner; Su dinner. Reservations required. 168 W 18th St (at Seventh Ave). 727.8022

18 Claire ★$$ Although the atmosphere is often marred by its high-volume din, this seafood restaurant is reliable and reasonably priced. Set designer Robin Wagner (*Dream Girls*, *A Chorus Line*) is responsible for the inventive decor, which brings a little bit of Florida's Key West to New York; and like the Florida Keys, this restaurant has a predominantly gay clientele. The food, rife with sometimes fierce and often intricate flavors, has been devised by the restaurant's Thai chef; popular dishes include blackened bluefish, seared tuna steak with creole mustard sauce, and crawfish patties with cayenne-and-cilantro sauce. ♦ Seafood ♦ M-Th, Su lunch and dinner; F-Sa lunch, dinner, and late-night meals. Reservations recommended. 156 Seventh Ave (between W 19th and W 20th Sts). 255.1955

19 Meriken ★$$ New wave Japanese food is served to the trendy crowd that frequents this popular spot, which is decorated in an interesting Art Deco style featuring the color celadon. ♦ Japanese ♦ M-F lunch and dinner; Sa-Su dinner. Reservations recommended. 189 Seventh Ave (at W 21st St). 620.9684

20 Murray's Cheese Store Larger than the original shop in Greenwich Village, this branch offers such prepared foods as lasagna, pasta sauces, and smoked fish, in addition to coffee, breads, and approximately 300 types of cheeses. Also featured are the sensational country pâtés produced by Simone Roskam, a Frenchwoman who owned **Walter's Meat Market** in the Village for many years and made slavish devotees of her customers. ♦ Daily. 198 Eighth Ave (at W 20th St). 691.3948. Also at: 257 Bleecker St (at Cornelia St). 243.3289.

21 Bright Food Shop ★★$ This minimally decorated room with black Formica tables and gray folding chairs is one of the most creative outposts of fusion cuisine in the city. Here that means Mexican and Asian, or as the restaurant describes it, "Where the Southwest meets the Far East." The more successful dishes include Moo Shu Mex (tortilla-wrapped rolls of shiitake mushrooms, black beans, and bok choy in a peanut-coconut-ginger sauce), the Bright noodle salad (a mix of chilled soba noodles with chili peppers, carrots, and jicama in a sesame vinaigrette), and Gulf-shrimp wontons. There's no liquor license—bring your own bottle to make this place an even bigger bargain. ♦ Asian/Mexican ♦ Tu-Sa lunch and dinner; Su lunch. No credit cards accepted. 216 Eighth Ave (at W 21st St). 243.4433

21 Kitchen Market The shelves of this food shop are stocked with chilies, salsa, spices, rices, different varieties of beans, and jars of mole sauce—everything you need to make the perfect Mexican meal. There are also quality take-out dishes, such as Yucatán pork stew, stewed chicken, tortilla pie, and burritos. ♦ Daily. 218 Eighth Ave (between W 21st and W 22nd Sts). 243.4433

21 Big Cup $ This brightly painted hangout—one wall is purple, another chartreuse—is convenient to the local movie theater. Movie selections and times are listed on a blackboard for those stopping here for a pre-theater bite. The mostly young crowd consumes sandwiches, muffins, cakes, and coffee while sitting on big overstuffed couches. ♦ Cafe ♦ Daily breakfast, lunch, dinner, and late-night meals. No credit cards accepted. 228 Eighth Ave (between W 21st and W 22nd Sts). 206.0059

BENDIX DINER

22 Bendix Diner ★$ A retro-style Chelsea diner, this place is popular with the locals because it has a little of everything—old fashioned meat loaf, great pancakes, and even Thai and Chinese dishes, including stir-fried honey chicken. The decor is also a mélange: The walls are vibrantly painted with flowers and vegetables, while the faux-marble columns are wound with strings of neon. The look appeals to the eclectic crowd of artists, would-be artists, and young families. ♦ Diner ♦ Daily breakfast, lunch, and dinner. No credit cards accepted. 219 Eighth Ave (at W 21st St). 366.0560

23 La Madama Cafe and Bakery ★$ The Caribbean specialities offered at this tiny cafe are prepared in a Brooklyn kitchen. Recommended dishes include the curried chicken or goat, fried silverfish with rice and peas, and curried crab and dumplings (served Saturdays only). ♦ Caribbean ♦ M-Sa breakfast, lunch, and early dinner. No credit cards accepted. 170 Ninth Ave (between W 20th and W 21st Sts). 255.0779

24 Luma ★★★$$$ This small, subdued dining spot has recently undergone a radical change. With Scott Bryan now in the kitchen, this formerly upscale health-food restaurant highlights beef, cream sauces, and very rich desserts. Bryan has obviously heard the siren song of fusion cuisine: There are Asian influences in the wonderfully spicy Thai seafood salad with shrimp, scallops, calamari, and bean sprouts in a ginger lemongrass vinaigrette, and spotted prawn dumplings in a cilantro-parsley sauce. But there's classical French technique in the superlatively tender and flavorful pan roast filet mignon with shallot-Cabernet reduction, and a hint of Morocco in the hearty basil roasted chicken with preserved lemons and black olives. For dessert, don't miss the Valrhona chocolate soufflé and the rich lemon tart. There are 250 good wines to choose from (including a reserve list); *Wine Spectator* names the selection as one of the best in town. ♦ International ♦ Daily dinner. Reservations recommended. 200 Ninth Ave (between W 22nd and W 23rd Sts). 633.8033

24 Joe Babbington's Joint ★$ A reliable neighborhood hangout, this is where locals come for large portions of good basic food, such as grilled ribsteak and baked trout stuffed with spinach. Especially popular are the ribs, which come in a couple of varieties—baby-back, honey glazed, or smoked Tennessee in plum, barbecue, or hot-and-spicy sauce. ♦ American ♦ M-F lunch and dinner; Sa-Su brunch and dinner. 202 Ninth Ave (between W 22nd and W 23rd Sts). 741.2148

EMPIRE

25 Empire Diner ★$ Refurbished in 1976 by designer Carl Laanes, this 1930s-style diner has retained the trappings of the original establishment—the Art Deco aluminum-winged clock near the entrance, the baked-enamel finish outside, and the signs—everything except, of course, the grease stains and the prices. It may be the only diner in America where late-night customers arrive in stretch limousines. Open round-the-clock, it has a bar and is a favorite among late-night/early-morning patrons who come here to enjoy the best diner breakfast in town; try the omelettes with salsa or smoked mozzarella. The rest of the menu is a mixed bag, featuring chicken fajitas; a roast turkey platter; linguine with smoked salmon, watercress, and garlic; and lentil burgers. Don't miss the Cajun bread pudding with bourbon sauce for dessert. In the summer-time, sit at one of the sidewalk tables for front-row viewing of the local action. ◆ American ◆ Daily 24 hours. 210 10th Ave (between W 22nd and W 23rd Sts). 243.2736

N E G R I L
ISLAND SPICE

26 Negril Island Spice ★★$ This place is a downtown branch of **Island Spice** in the Theater District, with a decor that tries its best to whisk you away to the island of Jamaica, with paintings of the sea inset in the sunny yellow walls. If that doesn't quite get you there, the food definitely will. Try the codfish fritters with avocado salsa; the ginger-lime chicken; the fried whole red snapper with onions, peppers, scallions, tomatoes, and thyme; the callaloo (Jamaican greens with onions and tomatoes), or any of the rotis. For dessert, the bread pudding in a caramelized raisin sauce is hard to resist and harder to forget. A live band plays pop reggae nightly, and there's a calypso brunch on Sundays. ◆ Jamaican ◆ M-Sa lunch and dinner; Su brunch and dinner. 362 W 23rd St (between Eighth and Ninth Aves). 807.6411 も. Also at: 402 W 44th St (between Ninth and 10th Aves). 765.1737 も

26 Chelsea Bistro and Bar ★★$$ The dinosaur heads and Lascaux cave paintings that were the decor of **T-Rex**—this bistro's predecessor—are gone, and in their place are a carved wood bar, floral borders and Impressionist prints on white walls, and an exposed brick fireplace. In other words, it's much more tasteful—and so is the food. Chef Philippe Roussel, formerly of **La Metairie** and **L'Udo**, produces such satisfying dishes as salmon *tartare,* escargots Provençal, house-smoked salmon with horseradish sauce, hanger steak with red-wine sauce and confit of shallots, and roasted free-range chicken with thyme rosemary *jus.* A rich *tarte tatin* (upside-down apple tart) and a glass of prune Armagnac are the perfect endings to a meal. There's an extensive, reasonably priced wine list with good choices from California and France. ◆ French ◆ Daily dinner. Reservations recommended. 358 W 23rd St (between Eighth and Ninth Aves). 727.2026

27 Royal Siam ★★$ The subdued beige dining room, decorated with postcards and paintings, resembles any number of Thai restaurants, but this relative newcomer serves some of the most vibrant food in the area. Don't miss the *tom yum koong* (seafood broth with shrimp and mushrooms), *tod mun pla* (fish cakes), *nuuryunk namtok* (spicy beef salad), *yum pla muk* (squid salad), chicken and beef satays, Royal Siam roast duck (with coconut milk and panang sauce), and the familiar noodle dish pad thai. ◆ Thai ◆ M-Sa lunch and dinner; Su dinner. 240 Eighth Ave (between W 22nd and W 23rd Sts). 741.1732

Blu

28 Blu ★★$$ The room upstairs is a twilight fantasy, with dark-green and blue walls affixed with gold stars and leaves. It becomes even more romantic at night when the candles are lit. Downstairs, the warm and cozy cafe dispenses with the drama and some of the expense. On both levels, however, the food is inventive and satisfying. Dishes include black pepper fettuccine with Peconic Bay scallops, sugar-snap peas, and brown garlic; wild-mushroom dumplings with white-truffle oil; and pan-seared quail with pickled peppers, mango, and hot curry vinaigrette. The desserts, especially the chocolate truffle cake with whipped cream and caramel sauce, are spellbinding. ◆ Fusion ◆ M-Sa lunch and dinner; Su brunch and dinner. Reservations recommended. 254 W 23rd St (between Seventh and Eighth Aves). 989.6300

CHELSEA CAFE

29 Chelsea Cafe ★★$ This stylish room with peach walls and faux-marble columns is popular with **Fashion Institute of Technology (F.I.T.)** students for the sophisticated yet affordable Italian fare offered here. Try the antipasto, grilled salmon *provençale,* and *rigatoni siciliano* (with grilled eggplant, plum tomatoes, and mozzarella). ◆ Italian ◆ M-F lunch and dinner; Sa dinner. Reservations recommended. 250 W 27th St (between Seventh and Eighth Aves). 989.3804 も

30 Vernon's Jerk Paradise ★$ The dining room here doesn't have any of the garish colors and kitsch usually associated with Caribbean restaurants; the decor—peach-colored walls, subdued lighting, and handsome paintings of tropical foliage—is quietly tasteful. But the food is as vibrantly authentic as can be found in these parts. Try the Jamaican beef patties, the spicy jerk chicken or pork, or ackee and saltfish (a Jamaican root vegetable with salted codfish). ◆ Jamaican ◆ M-F lunch and dinner; Sa dinner. 252 W 29th St (between Seventh and Eighth Aves). 268.7020 ♿

30 Biricchino ★★$$ Such straightforward offerings as bowtie *pasta primavera* or any dish featuring the sausages made at nearby **Salumeria Biellese** (see below) are the best bets at this simple trattoria. The charcuterie platter and the *pappardelle* (broad noodles) with chicken sausage and wild mushrooms are both outstanding as well. ◆ Italian ◆ M-F lunch and dinner; Sa dinner. Reservations recommended. 260 W 29th St (between Seventh and Eighth Aves). 695.6690

31 Salumeria Biellese Such star chefs as Gray Kunz of **Lespinasse,** Daniel Boulud of **Restaurant Daniel,** and Larry Forgione of **An American Place** depend on this humble pork store for its unique varieties of sausage. Unusual offerings include lamb, rosemary, and red wine; and chicken and apple. Leftovers from these special orders are sold to the public. ◆ M-Sa. 376 Eighth Ave (at W 29th St). 736.7376

24-Hour New York

The city that never sleeps is full of restaurants that stay open all night. Catering to nightclubbers, insomniacs, and those working the late shift are a variety of eateries that offer a greater range of choices—French, Korean barbecue, Polish-Ukrainian—at 4AM than most medium-sized towns can supply during the dinner hour:

Brasserie (100 E 53rd St, between Lexington and Park Aves, 751.4840) has been *the* place in **Midtown** since 1959 for an omelette at 5AM.

Empire Diner (210 10th Ave, between W 22nd and W 23rd Sts, 243.2736), a sleek Art Deco diner, is a popular post-nightclub breakfast destination.

French Roast (456 Sixth Ave, at W 11th St, 533.2233) features a classic French bistro menu in the heart of the **West Village.**

Greenwich Cafe (75 Greenwich Ave, between Seventh Ave S and Bank St, 255.5450) is a stylish bistro offering Mediterranean-style fare.

Restaurant Florent (69 Gansevoort St, between Washington and Greenwich Sts, 989.5779), an atmospheric French diner, is unexpectedly located in the middle of the meatpacking district.

7A (109 Ave A, at E Seventh St, 673.6583) features a wide-ranging menu in a cozy East Village cafe setting.

Veselka (144 Second Ave, at E 9th St, 228.9682) offers fairly heavy Polish-Ukrainian food and slightly harsh lighting—but its many fans keep coming back for more.

Woo Chon (8-10 W 36th St, between Fifth and Sixth Aves, 695.0676) is a great place for Korean barbecue anytime, and maybe the only place to get it in the middle of the night.

Yaffa Cafe (97 St. Mark's Pl, between Ave A and First Ave, 677.9001) offers an extensive menu and affordable prices at a bohemian **East Village** hangout.

Theater District

Even the savviest New Yorkers used to panic when forced to pick a place for dinner west of Midtown, in the neighborhood bounded by **Sixth Avenue** (officially, **Avenue of the Americas**) and the **Hudson River**, and **West 34th** and **West 59th Streets**. For many years, the better restaurants in this area had a well-deserved reputation for being overpriced and generally mediocre, thanks to a never-ending supply of tourists and pre-theater diners. But that was then.

Today, the alternatives in and around the Theater District have increased tremendously—and the dining trail also makes a few detours into the **Garment Center**, home of New York's clothing manufacturers. With this rash of new restaurant openings (and consequently more traffic from hungry theatergoers and nearby residents of the **Manhattan Plaza** artists' complex),

ave come many improvements in cuisine, price, and ambience. A number of mospheric, old-fashioned French bistros in the fifties between **Eighth** and **inth Avenues** now provide affordable prix-fixe dinners for the pre-theater owd. New, reasonably priced cafes have popped up around **Broadway** too. urthermore, on the area's western edge—around **Ninth Avenue**—the food ene is virtually exploding.

he range of cuisines includes Caribbean, Mexican, Greek, Italian, French, d Southwestern US. Some of these new places are sophisticated, others, stic. Ninth Avenue is now a lesser known, but more diversified, version of estaurant Row (officially **West 46th Street** between Eighth and Ninth venues).

ach May, the Ninth Avenue International Food Festival, extending from Vest 37th to **West 57th Streets**, showcases an increasingly impressive spread f multiethnic gourmet offerings. But you don't need a festival to be dazzled y the cornucopia of wonderful food for sale on this stretch. Walk north from Vest 36th Street and you'll pass meat markets selling everything from lambs' eads to filet mignon; fresh fish markets with prices roughly half of what ou'd pay elsewhere; cheese stores with selections that may even surprise nnoisseurs; and many other shops offering a wide array of exotic egetables, prepared foods, exceptional baked goods, coffees, teas, and spices. me of these places have been around for years; others are newcomers.

iven this new burst of energy, the Theater District is hardly the wasteland at many have come to expect. Search a place out or walk a few blocks west find it; there are ample options that are a joy to explore.

---

1 The Cellar Many years ago, **Macy's Herald Square** converted its basement into this fashionable emporium. All types of cookware, gadgets, china, and serving utensils are lined up on one side; the other side of the floor is stacked with food—cheeses of all nations, smoked fish, fresh pasta, prepared foods, gourmet condiments, freshly baked cinnamon rolls, and many other tempting items. The department store also regularly sponsors cooking demonstrations featuring chefs from the city's major restaurants. ♦ Daily. 151 W 34th Street (between Broadway and Seventh Ave). 695.4400 ♿

Within The Cellar:

Cellar Grill $ If the array of foods in the **Cellar** causes you to become overwhelmed with hunger, drop in here for a burger, steak, or plate of grilled chicken. ♦ Cafe/Grill ♦ Daily lunch and dinner. 695.4400 ext 2699 ♿

1 Patio Restaurant $ When you need a quick respite from shopping at **Macy's,** this old-fashioned lunch counter is the place. Enjoy a trip down memory lane with such dishes as onion soup, roast beef, or tuna sandwiches. And as long as you're revisiting days gone by, why not treat yourself to an ice-cream sundae for dessert? ♦ American ♦ Daily breakfast and lunch. 151 W 34th St (between Broadway and Seventh Ave), 8th floor. 695.4400 ext 2920 ♿

1 Cafe L'Etoile $ This replica of a French cafe in "the world's largest department store" has such purportedly Gallic items as a mediocre salad niçoise on its menu. A better bet is the credible afternoon tea on weekdays. ♦ Cafe ♦ M-F lunch and afternoon tea; Sa-Su lunch. 151 W 34th Street (between Broadway and Seventh Ave), 34th St balcony. 967.6034 ♿

2 Trio French Bakery The primary purchasers of the crusty rolls and baguettes offered at this long-established bakery are various restaurants around town, but anyone can indulge in their savory stock. ♦ M-Sa. 476 Ninth Ave (between W 36th and W 37th Sts). 695.4296

3 DiLuca Dairy and Deli Before you even taste the delectable delicacies at this old-fashioned Italian grocery, you'll be bowled over by the heavenly smells. Freshly made mozzarella, sweet *soppressata* (a mild sausage), crusty breads, sausage sandwiches, and succulent olives in varieties of green and black are only some of the goods offered here. ♦ M-Sa. 484 Ninth Ave (between W 37th and W 38th Sts). 563.2774 ♿

3 Manganaro Foods This century-old grocery store with molded tin ceilings and antique scales looks as if it hasn't changed at all since opening day. The food on the antique shelves, however, has kept pace with the times and includes such ultramodern offerings as truffle tortellini and herb-infused olive oils. The stock hasn't left behind high-quality traditional provisions, such as smoked mozzarella, pignoli, and prosciutto, either. There are also a few tables in the back for immediate consumption of these goodies. ♦ Daily. 488 Ninth Ave (between W 37th and W 38th Sts). 563.5331

3 Hero Boy ★$ According to the Manganaro family, who established this enterprise as a satellite of their grocery store next door, the sandwich term "hero" (variously known in other parts of the country as "grinder," "po'boy," or "submarine") was coined at this stand. *New York Herald-Tribune* food writer Clementine Paddleford wrote in 1940 that a person would have to be a hero to finish the sandwich because of its prodigious size—not its lack of appeal. The Manganaros also claim to be the first to sell these by the foot. The hot meals—lasagna, baked ziti—are good too. ♦ Italian ♦ M-Sa breakfast, lunch, and dinner; Su lunch and dinner. 492 Ninth Ave (between W 37th and W 38th Sts). 947.7325 &

3 Giovanni Esposito & Sons Meat Shop This onetime pork store still offers terrific homemade sausages; varieties include garlic, cheese and parsley, Cajun, and sweet sausage with fennel. Today it also stocks filet mignon, quail, squab, and pheasant, as well as pork knuckles and goat shanks. ♦ M-Sa. 500 Ninth Ave (at W 38th St). 279.3298 &

4 Chantale's Cajun Kitchen ★$ Chantale Bayard-Fabri worked in the Garment Center as a model and designer for 20 years before opening this restaurant in 1994. Now, lovers of New Orleans's spicy stew make a beeline for her gumbos—seafood, vegetable, chicken, chicken and sausage, or Chantale's specialty with shrimp, sausage, scallops, fish, and chicken. ♦ Cajun ♦ M-Sa lunch and dinner. No credit cards accepted. 510 Ninth Ave (between W 38th and W 39th Sts). 967.2623

4 Michael's and Sons Meat Market Some may find the contents of this meat store extremely exotic, where such items as lambs' heads, oxtails, pork knuckles, and pigs' feet are offered. Chicken breasts can be found as well. ♦ M, Tu, Th-Su. 516 Ninth Ave (between W 38th and W 39th Sts). 279.2324

4 Cupcake Cafe Loyal customers consider Ann and Michael Warren's cakes to be works of art. Not coincidentally, the Warrens and their team of assistants are all artists in other media—painting, sculpture, photography— who transfer those talents to a baked and frosted canvas. Wedding and birthday cakes are specialties; Madonna, Caroline Kennedy, and Calvin Klein are among the clients. Even if

you don't need a fanciful cake, stop by for a great muffin (especially corn), a doughnut, fruit pie, or cup of soup du jour. The shop ha a few tables where you can sit and munch a slice of pizza, a sandwich, or of course, the namesake cupcake. ♦ Daily. 522 Ninth Ave (at W 39th St). 465.1530

5 Guido's ★$$ In the rear of the **Supreme Macaroni Co.**—a store that leads you back to a time before the words "gourmet" or "nouvelle cuisine" were ever uttered—is a restaurant serving the best macaroni this sid of Naples. The prices are moderate and the service straightforward. ♦ Italian ♦ M-Sa lun and dinner. Reservations recommended. No credit cards accepted. 511 Ninth Ave (betwee W 38th and W 39th Sts). 564.8074 &

6 Vegetarian's World Although such commonplace items as oranges and potatoes are offered at this vegetable marke it's best known for its Caribbean bounty. Here you can find dried codfish, callaloo, *batatas* (a tubular root vegetable), and chayotes, and various West Indian, African, and Spanish groceries. ♦ 523 Ninth Avenue (at W 39th St). 268.6935 &

6 Ninth Avenue Cheese Market The owners of this emporium are Greek, so Heller, table cheeses are displayed prominently here. But with approximately 300 varieties of chees you'll find every other kind here too, from the better known to the obscure, imported from Austria, Britain, France, Italy, Norway, Switzerland, and even Bulgaria. There is also a large selection of fresh herbs, coffee beans, grains, dried fruit, salamis, and canned fish— including sardines from the Black Sea. ♦ M-Sa 525 Ninth Ave (at W 39th St). 564.7127. Also at: 615 Ninth Ave (between W 44th and W 45t Sts). 397.4700 &

6 Central Fish The air inside this 60-year-ol fish market smells so briny you could easily imagine yourself on a fishing boat off the coast of Maine. The shop sells 50 varieties of top-quality fish and seafood, such as salmon red snapper, scallops, tuna, and Florida shrimp—all at about half the price of uptown stores. ♦ M-Sa. 527 Ninth Ave (at W 39th St). 279.2317

6 International Groceries & Meat Market Walking into this store is like stepping into a Middle Eastern bazaar. The a is filled with competing aromas emanating from bins holding deeply colored, fragrant spices—Greek oregano, cumin, and coriander—among the sacks of assorted grains and flours. There is also every type of nut imaginable, as well as dried fruits, feta cheese, Greek olives, and olive oils. In short, this place has an impressive array of products that, despite the name, doesn't include meat—it hasn't been sold here for years. A sister store, **International Food**, a few doors north (543 Ninth Ave, at W 40th St, 279.1000 ᕒ), sells hummus, *baba ganooj,* and freshly made yogurt. ♦ M-Sa. 529 Ninth Ave (between W 39th and W 40th Sts). 279.5514 ᕒ

6 Sea Breeze Fish Market This top-quality market is roughly equivalent to **Central Fish** (see above) a few doors away, so patronize whichever shop has the fish you want in stock—or has the shorter line. One appealing aspect here is the lobster tank near the door. ♦ M-Sa. 541 Ninth Ave (at W 40th St). 563.7537

7 World Yacht Cruises ★$$$$ This five-yacht fleet cruises New York harbor year-round. All excursions include music, but dinner cruises also feature dancing and the romance of the port lights. Either way, the food (a four-course dinner usually featuring a salmon or beef entrée) is okay; the scenery, better. A unique venue for weddings, it offers the chance to exchange vows with the "Lady of the Harbor" (the **Statue of Liberty**) as your witness. ♦ Continental ♦ Apr-Nov: M-Sa dinner, Su brunch and dinner; Dec-Mar: F-Sa dinner, Su brunch and dinner. Reservations required; jacket required for dinner. Pier 81 (W 41st St and 12th Ave). 630.8100

8 Stiles Farmers Market Once called **Stiles Big Top,** this extensive fruit and vegetable market still sports its large trademark blue-and-yellow tent, despite the name change. A real boon to the neighborhood, it sells very fresh produce, coffee by the pound, nuts, and candy at remarkably low prices. ♦ M-Sa. 569 Ninth Ave (at W 41st St). 695.6213 ᕒ

8 Big Apple Meat Market If you have an army to feed, this is the place to save money on large quantities of meat. The wide selection—filet mignon, lamb chops, hams, and chicken breasts—is kept in a chilly meat locker, so bring your gloves. If you can't find what you need prepackaged, the staff will cut your meat of choice to order. ♦ Daily. 575 Ninth Ave (between W 41st and W 42nd Sts). 563.2555 ᕒ

9 Chez Josephine ★★$$$ In 1986, the ebullient Jean Claude Baker launched this unique restaurant as a tribute to his late adoptive mother, cabaret legend Josephine Baker. Fittingly, the place has become a great hit with critics and the public alike. The special decor, an homage to the intimate Parisian nightclubs of the Roaring 20s, adds to the enjoyment of what many consider the best *boudin noir* (blood sausage) in town, served with red cabbage. Also featured is lobster bisque, goat-cheese ravioli, and roasted duckling with tart red cherries. Bluesy pianists and a French tap dancer add to the heady atmosphere. ♦ French ♦ M-Sa dinner. Reservations recommended. 414 W 42nd St (at Ninth Ave). 594.1925

WEST BANK CAFE

10 West Bank Cafe ★$$ The tables at the upstairs dining room of this place are covered with butcher paper, which can be graced with an assortment of pasta dishes, such seafood specials as seared tuna steak with coriander pepper, various salads, and burgers. After dinner (or before), head downstairs to the cabaret and enjoy a musical comedy or a group of short plays. ♦ American ♦ Restaurant: M-F lunch and dinner, Sa-Su dinner; Cabaret: Tu-Sa 8PM, 10:30PM. Reservations recommended. 407 W 42nd St (at Ninth Ave). 695.6909

11 Empire Coffee and Tea When it comes to coffee, if this almost-a-century-old store doesn't sell it, chances are the bean doesn't exist. In stock are 90 kinds of coffee beans, from Tanzanian Peaberry to three types of Colombian. The shop also carries 75 varieties of teas, from China black to mango. ♦ Daily. 592 Ninth Ave (between W 42nd and W 43rd Sts). 596.1717 ᕒ

Where's the Beef?

New Yorkers love exotic cuisines, but sometimes nothing satisfies like a nice, juicy steak. For a while, red meat had fallen out of favor, as a health-conscious public sought white meats—chicken, pork, veal—in droves. Lately people seem more willing to throw caution to the wind, and a citywide craving for prime cuts is reaching epidemic proportions. Luckily, New York has more than enough steak houses to handle the growing demand, and they range from the traditional clubhouse to some that are stylishly refined.

For an old-fashioned New York steak experience that has been practically untouched by time, try **Old Homestead** (56 Ninth Ave, at W 14th St, 242.9040), established in 1868; **Peter Luger's** (178 Broadway, at Driggs Ave, Williamsburg, Brooklyn, 718/387.7400), opened in 1887; **Frank's** (85 Tenth Ave, at W 15th St, 243.1349), a meat-district favorite since 1912; **Frankie and Johnnie's** (269 W 45th St, between Broadway and Eighth Ave, 997.9494), which began life in 1926 as a speakeasy; **Palm** (837 Second Ave, between E 44th and E 45th Sts, 687.2953), which opened the same year; or **Gallagher's** (228 W 52nd St, between Broadway and Eighth Ave, 245.5336), established a year later.

If your hankering for beef coincides with a desire for fancy dining, New York offers a few spots that fit this bill: **Cité** (120 W 51st St, between Sixth and Seventh Aves, 956.7100); **The Post House** (28 E 63rd St, between Park and Madison Aves, 935.2888); and the **West 63rd Street Steakhouse** (44 W 63rd St, at Broadway, 246.6363).

12 Zuni ★★$ The block where this restaurant is located may look rough-and-tumble, but the cuisine here is definitely upscale. Try *empanaditas* (here a puree of roasted chicken and black beans rolled in a sheet of spinach pasta, lightly fried and served with a fricassee of wild mushrooms and fresh corn), sesame-dusted salmon fillet served with frizzled leeks and black-bean-and-lime sauce, or grilled duck-breast fajitas with cilantro rice. The requisite burritos and enchiladas are on the menu too. ◆ Mexican ◆ M-F lunch and dinner; Sa-Su brunch and dinner. 598 Ninth Ave (at W 43rd St). 765.7626

12 Rachel's ★★$ The cozy dining room with lace curtains, dried flower arrangements, and subdued lighting is the perfect setting for such hearty yet creative dishes as grilled portobello mushroom salad, sautéed escargots with tomato and mozzarella, lobster ravioli, chicken coated with pecans in a honey-mustard sauce, braised lamb shank, duck breast on braised lentils, and snapper grilled in pesto oil. Irresistible desserts include chocolate peanut butter pie, cherries jubilee cheesecake, and chocolate mascarpone. The wine list is brief but represents Chilean, California, and French vintages. ◆ American ◆ M-F lunch and dinner; Sa-Su brunch and dinner. Reservations recommended. 608 Ninth Ave (between W 43rd and W 44th Sts). 957.9050

13 Revolution ★$ This is the place to show off a black wardrobe and a serious attitude. Actor/model/whatevers hang out on the couches around the TV monitor–framed bar, but even those who aspire to anonymity can get a good meal in the back. Salmon served with lemon risotto and mushroom ravioli with porcini and truffle oil are among the best picks. ◆ Eclectic ◆ M-F lunch and dinner; Sa-Su brunch and dinner. Reservations recommended. 611 Ninth Ave (between W 43rd and W 44th Sts). 489.8451 ও

13 44 Southwest $ Don't be misled by the name, which refers to the address, *not* the type of cuisine. This sunny, simple trattoria is a reliable place for basic Italian specialties. Good standards include eggplant *rollatini* (baked eggplant with ricotta, prosciutto, and mozzarella), and *penne siciliano* (with eggplant, tomatoes, and melted mozzarella). ◆ Italian ◆ M-F lunch and dinner; Sa-Su brunch and dinner. 621 Ninth Ave (at W 44th St). 315.4582

A Manhattan Special is not an express bus from Brooklyn, and it has nothing to do with the subways. But it's been part of New York City since 1885. Described as "the world's most delicious coffee soda," the Manhattan Special is a hand-brewed concoction of freshly roasted coffee beans and 100 percent granulated sugar (practically unheard of in the beverage industry today). The result is a lusty coffee soda (it also comes sugar- and caffeine-free, too).

14 Le Madeleine ★$$$ This casual bistro features salads, pastas, fish, and such light meat dishes as grilled chicken breast with a Pommery mustard sauce. There's also a separate skylit garden room that is always booked up for brunch. ◆ French ◆ M-F lunch and dinner; Sa-Su brunch and dinner. Reservations recommended. 403 W 43rd St (between Ninth and 10th Aves). 246.2993

15 Good & Plenty to Go At this gourmet catering service and take-out joint (designed by Milton Glaser, Inc.), you'll find fresh breads, including sourdough onion rolls; soups; salads; hot and cold pastas; sandwiches; pizza; and such down-home favorites as bourbon-baked ham, jambalaya, crab cakes, and vegetarian chili. There are a few small tables outside in fair weather for those who want instant gratification. ◆ Daily. 410 W 43rd St (between Ninth and 10th Aves). 268.4385 ও

15 Little Pie Company The aromas here are glorious and the all-natural pies are just like Mom used to make—if you were lucky. This small, bright shop offers a selection of 10 pies: Fresh fruit pies predominate in summer, sour cream–apple and pumpkin pies are highlights in fall. Pies come in regular and five-inch sizes, but at the very least, treat yourself to a slice of heaven right there at the counter. ◆ Daily. 424 W 43rd St (between Ninth and 10th Aves). 736.4780 ও

16 Negril Island Spice ★★$ The cheerful dining room with bright-green walls and tropical plants is like a Jamaican oasis in the middle of the urban jungle. Owner Marva Layne serves spicy, vibrant versions of the foods from her native island, including beef patties, jerk chicken or pork, ginger-lime chicken, and curried goat. For vegetarians, there's a bean and vegetable stew or callaloo (stew with onions, tomatoes, peppers, and spices). Save room for the wickedly rich bread pudding with rum-raisin sauce. ◆ Jamaican ◆ Daily lunch and dinner. 402 W 44th St (between Ninth and 10th Aves). 765.1737 ও. Also at: 362 W 23rd St (between Eighth and Ninth Aves). 807.6411 ও

17 Poseidon Greek Bakery The Fable family has been turning out paper-thin phyllo-dough pastries in this tiny shop for nearly 75 years. Try the rich, sweet baklava, spinach pies, and tempting cinnamon-and-sugar almond cookies. For those who want to make their own delicacies, the phyllo dough is for sale. ◆ Tu-Su. 629 Ninth Ave (between W 44th and W 45th Sts). 757.6173 ও

17 Turkish Cuisine ★★$ The rug-and-hookah decor may not win any design awards, but the food is fresh and delicious. To begin, try *tarama* (a puree of fish roe, potato, olive oil, and lemon) or *baba ganooj*. Of the entrées, the lamb shish kebab is the most successful. If you like, finish with an authentically sludgy

Turkish coffee. ◆ Turkish ◆ Daily lunch and dinner. 631 Ninth Ave (between W 44th and W 45th Sts). 397.9650

17 Film Center Cafe ★$ This Art Deco–style upscale diner is a theater hangout for Broadway cast members: Alec Baldwin and Jessica Lange had many a lunch here when they were in *A Streetcar Named Desire,* and Madonna was a regular when she was in *Speed the Plow.* JFK Jr. also comes here for his favorite dish, meat loaf, which he eats at the bar. A young and lively crowd of "extras" pack the place to indulge in good, gently priced food, including chicken satay (the chefs are Thai), Cajun chicken with Dijon sauce, and of course, meat loaf. ◆ American ◆ M-F lunch and dinner; Sa dinner; Su brunch and dinner. 635 Ninth Ave (between W 44th and W 45th Sts). 262.2525

18 Jezebel ★★$$$ The nondescript exterior doesn't prepare you for the dramatic interior, which suggests nothing so much as a New Orleans bordello. Unexpected delights include two-story-high tropical trees, lawn swings, mirrored columns, Egyptian rugs on the walls, and crystal chandeliers. The lavish setting provides the perfect counterpoint to owner Alberta Wright's earth food—she-crab soup, smothered chicken, oxtail stew, garlic shrimp, broiled seafood platter (lobster tails, scallops, and shrimp), and shrimp creole. And don't forget the corn bread. Finish with pecan or sweet potato pie. The extensive wine list concentrates on French varieties. ◆ Soul food ◆ M-Sa dinner. Reservations required. 630 Ninth Ave (at W 45th St). 582.1045

19 Monck's Corner For good down-home Southern food to go, come to this tiny shop run by Don and Robert Wright, the sons of Alberta Wright—owner of **Jezebel** down the street (see above). Among the tempting specialties are fried chicken, smothered chicken, collard greens, black-eyed peas, and sweet potato pie. ◆ M-Sa. 644 Ninth Ave (between W 45th and W 46th Sts). 397.1117

20 Bali Burma ★$; Rare are the restaurants that specialize in Balinese and Burmese cuisine. The prices are reasonable, but the food is hit-and-miss. Try the *soto ayam* (spicy chicken broth with bean sprouts, glass noodles, and chicken). ◆ Balinese/Burmese ◆ Daily lunch and dinner. 651 Ninth Ave (between W 45th and W 46th Sts). 265.9868

20 Bruno The King of Ravioli This retail shop sells a vast selection of fresh pastas and sauces, including ravioli, manicotti, cannelloni, lasagna, stuffed shells, and gnocchi, all made in a nearby factory since 1888. ◆ M-Sa. 653 Ninth Ave (between W 45th and W 46th Sts). 246.8456. Also at: 249 Eighth Avenue (between 22nd and 23rd Sts). 627.0767; 2204 Broadway (at W 78th St). 580.8150

20 Zen Palate ★★★$$ A vegetarian oasis, this place serves excellent cuisine in an upscale, minimalist setting (some of the chairs, however, are the comfortable caned models found in Paris bistros). It's a bit pricey, but worth the culinary and cultural adventure of such dishes as basil *moo shu* rolls (with nuts and vegetables), zen retreat (a squash shell stuffed with vegetables, beans, and tofu), dreamland (panfried spinach noodles with shiitake mushrooms and ginger), and mushroom forest (an exotic combination of fungi, pine nuts, and vegetables on a bed of Boston lettuce). Alcoholic beverages are not served, but you can bring your own. ◆ Asian vegetarian ◆ M-Sa lunch and dinner; Su dinner. Reservations recommended. 663 Ninth Ave (at W 46th St). 582.1669. ♿ Also at: 34 Union Sq E (at E 16th St). 614.9345 ♿

21 Mike's American Bar and Grill ★$ If you brave the unquestionably sleazy parade down this stretch of 10th Avenue, you'll find a cheerful, intentionally down-at-the-heels joint. Go for the grilled specials, though some faithfuls claim that Mike has the best enchiladas in Manhattan. Other good picks are spinach fettuccine with spicy shrimp or chicken stewed with prunes, onions, thyme, garlic, and tomatoes. ◆ American/Mexican ◆ M-F lunch and dinner; Sa-Su dinner. Reservations recommended. 650 10th Ave (between W 45th and W 46th Sts). 246.4115

22 Landmark Tavern ★$$ An old waterfront tavern, this once rowdy place now offers modern-day diners a cleaner and more refined version of its 19th-century rooms, where food is still served from genuine antique sideboards. Although some of the dishes could be better—and the better ones more consistently so—the Irish soda bread, baked every hour, is a gem. The fish-and-chips, shepherd's pie, prime rib, and hamburgers are good too. ◆ American ◆ Daily lunch and dinner. Reservations recommended. 626 11th

Ave (between W 45th and W 46th Sts). 757.8595 &

23 Amy's Bread This pretty little store looks looks like it belongs on the Upper East Side. With a devotion to good, earthy flavors, however, it fits right into the neighborhood. Try the black-olive, rosemary, or parmesan bread twists; country sourdough loaves; or semolina bread with golden raisins and fennel. ♦ M-Sa. 672 Ninth Ave (between W 46th and W 47th Sts). 977.3856

24 Barbetta ★★$$$ This romantic old-timer boasts a beautiful garden and wonderful truffles, sniffed out by dogs in Tuscany. The menu changes seasonally but may include such dishes as beef braised in red wine with polenta, charcoal-grilled squab with cranberry beans and red beet olive oil, and scallopini with porcini. The service can be a bit snooty at times. ♦ Northern Italian ♦ M-Sa lunch and dinner. Reservations recommended. 321 W 46th St (between Eighth and Ninth Aves). 246.9171

24 Les Sans Culottes West ★$$$ Like its Midtown sibling, this rustic bistro features old-fashioned French food. Start with the basket of vegetables, sausages, and pâtés, and then move on to baby rack of lamb, *boeuf bourguignon,* roast duck with cherry sauce, or grilled salmon with basil sauce. Desserts are traditional as well—try apricot mousse or crème brûlée. The prix-fixe lunch and dinner are reasonably priced. ♦ French ♦ Daily lunch and dinner. Reservations recommended. 347 W 46th St (between Eighth and Ninth Aves). 247.4284. Also at: 1085 Second Ave (between E 57th and E 58th Sts). 838.6660

24 Becco ★$$ The Bastianich family, who own the felicitous **Felidia** restaurant on the East Side, are also the proprietors of this informal spot on Restaurant Row. A wide variety of flavorful Italian dishes, such as wild-mushroom risotto and roast suckling pig, are featured. The prix-fixe lunch and daily menus are both good values. ♦ Italian ♦ M-Sa lunch and dinner; Su dinner. 355 W 46th St (between Eighth and Ninth Aves). 397.7597

24 Lattanzi ★$$$ Enjoy a taste of the Roman Jewish Quarter in a casual atmosphere. Baby artichokes sautéed in olive oil, homemade pastas, and grilled fish are all made to order. ♦ Italian ♦ M-F lunch and dinner; Sa dinner. Reservations recommended. 361 W 46th St (between Eighth and Ninth Aves). 315.0980

24 Hour Glass Tavern $ Like it or not, the hourglass above the table gives customers exactly 60 minutes to savor the reasonably priced, three-course prix-fixe dinner, featuring such entrées as grilled spicy blackened shrimp and homemade lamb sausage. Young Broadway hopefuls are well represented among the clientele. ♦ American ♦ M-F lunch and dinner; Sa-Su dinner. No credit cards accepted. 373 W 46th St (between Eighth ar Ninth Aves). 265.2060 &

25 Orso ★$$$ It's easy to relax at this Norther Italian bistro serving pasta, seafood, veal, a wonderful pizzas—try the pie topped with roasted peppers, sun-dried vegetables, provolone, and sage. The handsome marble bar is an inviting place to unwind either befc or after the theater. ♦ Italian ♦ Daily lunch a dinner. Reservations recommended. 322 W 46th St (between Eighth and Ninth Aves). 489.7212

25 Joe Allen $$ Here is an opportunity to ga upon posters of failed Broadway shows, handsome waiters, a stagestruck clientele, and occasionally, the stars themselves. A blackboard menu lists the simple fare, but food is not really the point at this place. If you must have nourishment, try a salad, hamburger, bowl of chili, or grilled fish. ♦ American ♦ Daily lunch and dinner. 326 W 46th St (between Eighth and Ninth Aves). 581.6464

25 Marlowe ★$$ The pleasant beige dining room with subdued lighting and a working stone fireplace is a relaxing place to be amid the hubbub of the Theater District. The menu is a very pleasant blend of Asian and Mediterranean cuisine, prepared by Japanese chef Kunio Takeuchi, who has been aflame with creativity now that he is n longer processing food in mass quantities the **Saloon** across from **Lincoln Center.** However, some dishes succeed better than others; try the pan-roasted oyster and smoked-corn chowder; angel-hair pasta with julienne vegetables and New Orleans prawns; and spiced, seared yellowfin tuna with a wasabi beurre blanc on black-rice risotto. ♦ Fusion ♦ Daily lunch and dinner. Reservations required for pre-theater dinners. 328 W 46th St (between Eighth and Ninth Aves). 765.3815

25 Lotfi's Moroccan ★$ This simple Moroccan cafe recently relocated from its former spot a block away. In the process the decor has become more upscale, with tapestries and Art Deco mirrors. Luckily, the food, so much admired, remains the same. Try the couscous, kebabs, or any of the *taji* (stews). ♦ Moroccan ♦ Tu-Sa lunch and dinner; Su dinner. 358 W 46th St (between Eighth and Ninth Aves). 582.5850

CARMINE'S

26 Carmine's $$ Like the Upper West Side outpost, this place serves huge family-size portions that can be shared with one other person, at the very least. Simple Southern Italian fare—chicken parmigiana, rigatoni with broccoli, and linguine with calamari—is served. So, *mangia*. ♦ Italian ♦ Dinner. 200 W 44th St (between Broadway and Eighth Ave). 221.3800. Also at: 2450 Broadway (between W 90th and W 91st Sts). 362.2200

26 Sardi's ★$$$ Practically synonymous with Theater District dining, this three-quarters-of-a-century mainstay went through a troubled couple of years before the return in 1990 of Vincent Sardi Jr, son of the founder. He brought back some old hands, and in 1994 added a new one, French chef Patrick Pinon, who spiced up the moribund menu with dishes that include a good roasted free-range chicken with garlic. Sentimental favorites, however, such as cannelloni, were retained. Once in a while, you can still spot a celebrity; otherwise, stargazers can content themselves with identifying famous customers who are immortalized in the numerous caricatures gracing the walls. ♦ Continental ♦ M-Sa lunch, dinner, and late-night meals. Reservations recommended; jacket required. 234 W 44th St (between Broadway and Eighth Ave). 221.8440

27 Osteria al Doge ★★$$ This rustic trattoria has wooden farmhouse tables and dark metal chandeliers straight out of a Venetian magistrate's palace. Delectable pasta and seafood are served to a lively crowd that comes here even when not going to the theater. Originally the kitchen was Venetian, but the current chef, Pietro Luca Marcato, is Milanese. As a result, the menu shows influences from both locales. Try the marinated mixed-seafood antipasto; fresh, tender grilled Peconic Bay scallops; gnocchi with gorgonzola; seafood risotto; or tagliatelle with porcini. There are also rich, delicious desserts, such as flourless

chocolate cake and an apple tart with cinnamon gelato. The primarily Italian wines are well chosen and affordable. ♦ Italian ♦ M-Sa lunch and dinner; Su dinner. Reservations recommended. 142 W 44th St (between Sixth and Seventh Aves). 944.3643

27 Virgil's ★$$ The place mats at this mammoth barbecue restaurant detail the search for perfect versions of each dish—Texas for sliced brisket, North Carolina for pulled pork. The walls are a source of more information—a history of barbecue in articles and pictures. Although authenticity, by its very definition, can't be copied, this place does a pretty good job—especially when it comes to ribs, pulled pork, mashed potatoes, and greens. The portions are huge, including such desserts as butterscotch and lemon chess pies. Despite the name, there is no Virgil; the owners here are the same ones responsible for the other huge ethnic feed stations, **Carmine's** (nearby and on the Upper West Side) and **Ollie's Noodle Shop** (one right down the block and two more on the Upper West Side). ♦ Barbecue ♦ Daily lunch and dinner. 152 W 44th St (between Sixth and Seventh Aves). 921.9494

28 The Manhattan Chili Company ★$ When you're in the mood for a good bowl of chili, go no farther. This place (a refugee from Greenwich Village) aims to please, offering all kinds of chili—including vegetarian and turkey—with a wide range of spiciness. There are plenty of other fixings to keep you happy, such as drunken peanut chicken and chicken in a roasted-peanut and chipotle sauce that's spiked with tequila and dark ale. Fortunately, the Dos Equis beer is inexpensive because you may need more than one for items classified as "hot hot"–the Texas Chain Gang Chili, for example. There's also a kids' menu. ♦ Tex-Mex ♦ Daily lunch, dinner, and late-night meals. 1500 Broadway (entrance on W 43rd St). 730.8666

28 Le Max ★$$ Designed in the style of the grand Paris cafes—mirror-covered walls, crystal chandeliers, and painted columns—this is a handy place to know about for well-prepared worldly cuisine. There's a little French, a little Italian, and a little somewhere else. Chef/owner Chai Wattana, formerly of **Cafe Un Deux Trois,** is Thai, which explains the satays on the menu. Try the salmon in whatever sauce he has made that day or boneless chicken breast with mustard sauce. For dessert, don't miss the rich *gâteau au chocolat* (chocolate cake with a layer of chocolate mousse). There's also an extremely reasonable prix-fixe dinner. ◆ Eclectic ◆ M-F lunch and dinner; Sa dinner; Su brunch and dinner. Reservations recommended. 147 W 43rd St (between Sixth Ave and Broadway). 764.3705 ᶀ

29 Century Cafe ★★$$ The sophisticated dining room, decorated with light wood, white columns, and individual spotlights, creates a very stylish setting indeed for the theater crowd, including cast members of nearby shows. The food is as refined as the decor, featuring such outstanding dishes as seared yellowfin tuna with crushed coriander, grilled muscovy duck with roasted figs, and grilled salmon with Moroccan spices. On Saturday afternoons, there is a special under-$10 matinee menu with such upscale items as panfried backfin crab-cake sandwiches. The wine list is extensive, well-chosen, and prices reflect only a fraction of the restaurant markup usually encountered. ◆ International ◆ M-Sa lunch and dinner. Reservations recommended. 132 W 43rd St (between Sixth and Seventh Aves). 398.1988 ᶀ

30 Cafe Un Deux Trois ★$$ Crayons for doodling on the paper-covered tables provide a charming bit of bohemia for those who never venture downtown. The gimmick isn't really necessary, however, as the place delivers satisfaction with such simple but good food as scallops *provençale* and steak *frites* (with french fries). ◆ French ◆ Daily lunch and dinner. Reservations recommended. 123 W 44th St (between Sixth and Seventh Aves). 354.4148

31 Cabana Carioca ★★$$ The narrow, exuberantly painted staircase leads to several different floors, but wherever you decide to sit, you can count on seriously large servings of Brazilian food. Don't miss the suckling pig, steak dishes, and *feijoada,* a traditional Brazilian Sunday afternoon dish of black beans and pork, served here every day. If you really want to get into the spirit, try a potent *caipirinha* (a drink made from a sugarcane-derived spirit, crushed lemon, ice, and sugar). ◆ Brazilian ◆ Daily lunch and dinner. 123 W

45th St (between Sixth and Seventh Aves). 581.8088

31 Hamburger Harry's ★$ In addition to the 16 varieties of major-league burgers served at this casual grill, the mesquite-grilled seafood and steaks lure connoisseurs of the rare and well done. A Mexican accent adds color to the menu—the Ha-Ha Burger comes freighted with chilies, guacamole, *salsa verde,* and cheddar cheese. ◆ American ◆ Daily lunch and dinner. 145 W 45th St (between Sixth and Seventh Aves). 840.2756. Also at: 157 Chambers St (between Greenwich and Hudson Sts). 267.4446

32 Frankie and Johnnie's ★$$$ A former speakeasy and onetime celebrity hangout for the likes of Al Jolson and Babe Ruth, this joint is still popular—some would say too much so, as it tends to get hectic and noisy. But the crowds get more than nostalgia for their money—this old Broadway chophouse can still turn out a good steak. ◆ Steak house ◆ M-Sa dinner. Reservations required. 269 W 45th St (between Broadway and Eighth Ave). 997.9494

32 Sam's ★$ A popular hangout for theater people, this place has exposed-brick walls and very reasonable prix-fixe dinners, featuring ribs, shell steak, and grilled Cajun chicken. Although stars sup here occasionally, its most devoted fans are the "gypsies," members of the chorus lines. To ensure that cast members and ticketholders leave on time, maître d' Craig Dawson plays a Broadway overture at 7:30PM as a reminder. Around midnight several times a week, he and the staff treat late-night diners to a Broadway melody. ◆ American ◆ M-Sa lunch, dinner, and late-night meals; Su lunch and dinner. Reservations recommended. 263 W 45th St (between Broadway and Eighth Ave). 719.5416

33 The Mezzanine ★$$$ Enter the lobby of the futuristic **Paramount Hotel,** designed by Philippe Starck, and ascend the dramatic gray staircase leading upstairs to this mezzanine-level dining room. Though you'll be able to watch the comings and goings of people down in the lobby from this perch, the food will make a bid for your attention too. The varied menu ranges from light grilled-chicken and wild-mushroom salad to the more substantial mustard-glazed salmon fillet and roast loin of lamb in a red-wine sauce. It's also a good place to come for dessert—the banana splits and ice-cream sodas are great. ◆ American ◆ Daily breakfast, lunch, and dinner. 235 W 46th St (between Broadway and Eighth Ave). 764.5500

34 Pierre au Tunnel ★★$$$ A good Theater District standby, this place serves excellent bistro fare, especially such Old World specialties as *tripes à la mode de Caen* (calf intestines in a consommé with white wine, apple brandy, potatoes, carrots, and white turnips) and *tête de veau vinaigrette* (calf brains, tongue, and cheek in a thick mustard vinaigrette with capers). The salmon and veal dishes are wonderful too. The solicitous staff will make sure you're out in time to make the curtain. ♦ French ♦ M-Sa lunch and dinner. Reservations required. 250 W 47th St (between Broadway and Eighth Ave). 575.1220

35 Dish of Salt $$$ This Chinese restaurant offers two levels of bamboo-decorated sophistication—at a price. The Cantonese specialties include Seafood King (an edible yam basket filled with lobster, scallops, shrimp, vegetables, and chicken) and Peking duck (available daily). Tasteful piano music is played in the cocktail lounge. ♦ Cantonese ♦ M-F lunch and dinner; Sa dinner. Reservations recommended. 133 W 47th St (between Sixth and Seventh Aves). 921.4242

Child's Play

It's a rite of passage experienced by many an adult restaurant goer: one day the bottles of wine, flowers, and candlelight disappear, replaced by plastic-topped tables and food wrapped in waxed paper. Suddenly a family includes a younger member and dining out becomes a different experience. But there's no need to worry—New York has many child-friendly places that an adult can also enjoy:

Each has its own theme—mausoleum, laboratory, grand salon, observatory, and library—and is full of things to scare you. Monsters are everywhere, ceilings lower and threaten to crush you, skeletons sing, and mad doctors gad about, of course. The food is perfunctory—burgers, pasta, and not really the point.

1 Barking Dog Luncheonette This upscale luncheonette is friendly, casual, and open to visits by dogs or children, not necessarily in that order.

2 Cowgirl Hall of Fame Despite the high noise level in the dining room, this place is fun (kids of all ages will be intrigued by the Wild West merchandise in the general store attached to the restaurant), and the chargrilled burgers, barbecued brisket, and barbecued chicken are tasty too.

3 Hard Rock Cafe The first of the "theme park" restaurants, it still attracts scores of teenagers, who come to gaze upon such "holy" relics as Eric Clapton's guitar, among many others. The hamburgers are edible and the music level high.

4 Harley Davidson Cafe The gimmick here is motorcycles of the rich and famous, which are on display everywhere. Way cool, sort of, but the burgers, pasta, and barbecued pork probably wouldn't survive on their own.

5 The Jekyll and Hyde Club As if New York weren't scary enough, this **Midtown** haunted house/restaurant has five floors of horror.

6 Main Street Basic American food is served in huge family-style portions; crayons for the paper-topped tables provide entertainment, and everyone is pretty easygoing.

7 Planet Hollywood Co-owners Sly Stallone, Arnold Schwarzenegger, and Bruce Willis have constructed a temple of movie memorabilia. The food is minimal but the artifacts are interesting for children of all ages.

8 Serendipity The ultimate **East Side** ice-cream parlor, this place serves foot-long hot dogs and famous frozen hot chocolate, among lots of other treats.

9 Two Boots The vivid colors are fun look at it, as are the lights strung along the bar. The pizza (with toppings galore) is good, and the portions generous. The jukebox blares the lastest music, which should appeal to older children, and there are coloring books for their younger siblings.

10 Virgil's BBQ Located in the **Theater District,** this barnlike restaurant, featuring barbecue styles from all over the South, will keep kids amused and everyone well fed. It's a good place to go before or after a matinee outing.

36 Acropolis $ A very plain taverna, this place is good to know about if you're in the market for affordable but authentic Greek food—souvlaki, moussaka, stuffed grape leaves, and spinach pie. ♦ Greek ♦ Tu-Su lunch and dinner. 767 Eighth Ave (at W 47th St). 581.2733

36 B. Smith's ★$$$ With its sleek, contemporary decor, this dining spot is one of the more popular restaurants in the Theater District. The entrées are creatively presented and include shrimp scampi and filet mignon; sweet potato—pecan pie and profiteroles are favorite desserts. A variety of small plates—potato-leek pancake with roasted tomatoes; smoked salmon, caviar, and crème fraîche; and warmed cheeses with roasted peppers, plum tomatoes, and basil vinaigrette on *focaccia fritti*—are available for the after-theater crowd. ♦ International ♦ Daily lunch and dinner. Reservations recommended. 771 Eighth Ave (at W 47th St). 247.2222

37 Koyote Kate's $$ If you've got a hankering for honky-tonking, this is the place. The Tex-Mex menu here includes a good 10-ounce burger and jalapeño shrimp (the peppers are stuffed with whole shrimp, breaded, and deep fried). Dip these in sour cream to put out the fire, or better yet, order a frozen margarita or two and go hog wild. Live country-western music is performed every night except Wednesday, when the blues reign supreme. ♦ Tex-Mex ♦ M-F lunch and dinner; Sa-Su dinner and late-night meals. 307 W 47th St (between Eighth and Ninth Aves). 956.1091

38 Avanti ★★$$$ Subdued and sophisticated, with beige walls, wood trim, and recessed lighting, this trattoria is popular for its large portions of creative, well-prepared dishes. Try the roasted elephant garlic soup; grilled shiitake mushroom Napoleon (with grilled asparagus in white truffle sauce with lemon truffle oil); grilled smoked duck breast salad over field greens with champagne-tangerine vinaigrette; bowtie pasta with fresh grilled yellowfin tuna, capers, roasted red peppers, garlic, and sweet onion; pan-roasted snapper with grilled-balsamic red onions; and roast pork loin with sun-dried cherries. Desserts include new twists on familar favorites, such as toasted-hazelnut chocolate tiramisù. ♦ Italian ♦ Daily lunch and dinner. Reservations recommended. 700 Ninth Ave (at W 48th St). 586.7410

39 Pong Sri ★$$ Manhattan has become nearly saturated with Thai restaurants, but this one has long received high marks for being among the most authentic (although some Thai food fanatics complain that the usual fiery spices have been toned down to accommodate the American palate). Dishes include lobster stir-fry with basil leaf and chili paste, whole deep-fried red snapper with a hot and spicy sauce, and assorted vegetables with bean curd in red curry and coconut milk. Carnivores take note: The menu doesn't offer much in the way of meat. ♦ Thai ♦ Daily lunch and dinner. 244 W 48th St (between Broadway and Eighth Ave). 582.3392. Also at: 106 Bayard St (between Baxter and Canal Sts). 349.3132

40 Broadway Grill ★$$$ This sleek, peach-colored restaurant in the **Holiday Inn Crowne Plaza** hotel has an open kitchen that keeps the room from feeling overly formal. Owner David Liederman, of **David's Cookies** fortune and fame, was a classically trained chef before becoming a cookie czar, and his kitchen turns out some serious work. Try David's pizza (mushrooms, onions, black olives, garlic, sun-dried tomatoes, and parmesan on a thin, crispy crust), rack of baby lamb chops in a garlic-rosemary sauce, or herb-roasted chicken. ♦ American ♦ M-F lunch and dinner; Sa dinner. 1605 Broadway (between W 48th and W 49th Sts). 977.4000

41 Sapporo ★$ It's not much to look at, and the bright lights can make you feel as if you're under interrogation, but at this Theater District standby the service is quick and the prices unbelievably low. The tasty Japanese fare includes teriyaki, sukiyaki, and *donburi* (bowls of rice with eggs and your choice of meats). If you're in a big hurry, grab a seat at the counter, where the service is even quicker. However, sitting near the open kitchen has one disadvantage: The steam wafting out of the pots drifts in your general direction. ♦ Japanese ♦ Daily lunch and dinner. No credit cards accepted. 152 West 49th St (between Sixth and Seventh Aves). 869.8972

42 New World Grill ★$ During nice weather, diners at this tiny cafe can sit at tables outside on **Worldwide Plaza,** a relatively quiet spot (for New York) and a good place to enjoy the sunny flavors featured on the menu. Not unlike many other New York chefs, Katy Keck specializes in fusing dissimilar cuisines; in this case, her influences are predominantly Asian and Southwestern. Some of the combinations work very well. Try the Asian marinated pork tenderloin with chili lentils and citrus salsa; crispy Cajun chicken with creole salsa; and grilled pears with field greens, stilton cheese, and crunchy walnuts. ♦ Fusion ♦ M-F lunch and dinner; Sa dinner. Reservations recommended. 329 W 49th St (between Eighth and Ninth Aves). 957.4745 ₺

43 Peruvian Restaurant ★$ Ignore the fluorescent lighting and Formica tables; instead concentrate on what is probably the best and most authentic Peruvian cuisine in New York: terrific baked fish with tomatoes and coriander, hearty stews, and delicious *papas asadas* (potatoes boiled in broth). The pleasant service is another plus. ♦ Peruvian ♦ Daily lunch and dinner. No credit cards accepted. 688 10th Ave (between W 48th and W 49th Sts). 581.5814

44 Uncle Nick's ★$ The food at this informal Greek cafe isn't very consistent; some items are great one night, not so great on others. But the appetizers are generally tops, particularly the *taramasalata* (fish roe paste); and lamb souvlaki and swordfish kebab are usually excellent. ♦ Greek ♦ Daily lunch and dinner. 747 Ninth Ave (between W 50th and W 51st Sts). 315.1726

45 Rice and Beans ★$ This tiny, friendly Brazilian cafe is just the place when you want a tasty *feijoada* or Brazilian beef stew. There are a few lighter items on the menu too, such as chicken Ipanema (grilled chicken with tomatoes in an herb sauce). ♦ Brazilian ♦ M-Sa lunch and dinner. No credit cards accepted. 744 Ninth Ave (between W 50th and W 51st Sts). 265-4444

46 Chez Napoléon ★★$$$ Tucked away at the edge of the Theater District is this casual bistro where the decor pays homage to Napoléon—posters and statuettes bear his likeness. The menu features such classic French dishes as onion soup, escargots, steak au poivre, *choucroute garni* (sauerkraut garnished with potatoes and pork), and chocolate mousse, and the kitchen does them all justice. A hearty bouillabaisse is offered on Friday and Saturday nights. ♦ French ♦ M-F lunch and dinner; Sa dinner. Reservations required. 365 W 50th St (between Eighth and Ninth Aves). 265.6980

47 Café Des Sports ★$ Although regular customers would no doubt prefer that this dining spot remain one of New York's better-kept secrets, the staff ensures that all newcomers are warmly welcomed. The menu features such traditional French dishes as roast breast of chicken and grilled steak. ♦ French ♦ M-F lunch and dinner; Sa-Su dinner. 329 W 51st St (between Eighth and Ninth Aves). 974.9052

47 René Pujol ★★$$ A truly old-fashioned bistro, this town-house dining room is filled with French country atmosphere and decor, including exposed-brick wall and pottery on display. Try the lobster bisque, roast breast of duck, grilled steak, or rack of lamb. The crème brûlée and any of the soufflés are highly recommended, as is the good, reasonably priced wine list. ♦ French ♦ M-F lunch and dinner; Sa dinner. Reservations recommended. 321 W 51st St (between Eighth and Ninth Aves). 246.3023

47 Tout Va Bien ★$$ From the atmosphere to the menu, this very cozy brick-walled bistro, decorated with posters of France, is a trip back in time. Come here for such hearty, old-fashioned dishes as coq au vin and *boeuf bourguignon.* ♦ French ♦ Daily lunch and dinner. Reservations recommended. 311 W 51st St (between Eighth and Ninth Aves). 265.0190

48 Les Pyrénées ★$$$ The working fireplace at this casual country restaurant makes it a cozy spot, especially in winter. It's also about a block closer to the theaters than the other traditional French places nearby. Recommended dishes include rack of lamb, escargots, cassoulet, grilled Dover sole, thin apple tart, and chocolate mousse. ♦ French ♦ M-Sa lunch and dinner; Su dinner. Reservations recommended. 251 W 51st St (between Broadway and Eighth Ave). 246.0044

49 Le Bernardin ★★★★$$$$ The death of owner Gilbert Le Coze stunned the food world in 1994, but this esteemed seafood dining spot—which he opened in 1986—continues apace under the supervision of his sister Maguy. The elegant wood-paneled room with a collection of maritime art is a gracious setting in which to appreciate the fine cooking of Le Coze protégé Eric Ripert. Start with marinated black bass seviche with cilantro, mint, jalapeños, and tomatoes; saffron ravioli filled with herbed crabmeat; or yellowfin tuna carpaccio with ginger-lime mayonnaise. Follow with seared Atlantic salmon and olives and sun-dried tomatoes; pan-roasted yellowtail snapper atop balsamic-glazed artichokes with foie gras and truffle sauce; or crispy Chinese spiced red snapper with cèpes, aged Port and Jerez sherry vinegar reduction. Desserts are devastating, including an unusual thyme-and-mint sorbet and a feathery heaven of chocolate mille-feuille layered with chocolate cream. Complementing its seafood menu, the restaurant boasts a well-chosen wine list—concentrating on white burgundies—in a range of prices. ♦ French/Seafood ♦ M-F lunch and dinner; Sa dinner. Reservations required. 155 W 51st St (between Sixth and Seventh Aves). 489.1515

49 Palio ★★$$$$ Named for a horse-racing festival in the Italian town of Siena, this place is worth a visit if only to see the stunning interior designed by **Skidmore, Owings & Merrill.** The lovely table appointments are by Vignelli Associates, and a wraparound Sandro Chia mural dominates the ground-floor bar, where the Bellinis (an apéritif of peach nectar and champagne) are a delight. The second-floor dining room delivers luxury in every detail—from the crystal to each perfect rose. The menu contains such treats as risotto with seafood, ravioli stuffed with duck and foie gras, and fillet of beef with a Barola sauce, but overall, the food doesn't live up to the grandeur of the surroundings. ♦ Italian ♦ M-F lunch and dinner; Sa dinner. Reservations required; jacket and tie recommended, even at the bar. 151 W 51st St (between Sixth and Seventh Aves). 245.4850

50 Cité ★★★$$$ Designed to resemble a grand Parisian cafe, this elegant restaurant is filled with artifacts imported from that city: floral-pattern Art Deco grillwork from the original Au Bon Marché department store and intricate crystal chandeliers from an old Parisian cinema. It's a gracious, sophisticated space in which to enjoy simple, top-quality food. Since the arrival of chef David Amorelli, previously of **Solera** and **Park Avenue Cafe,** some dishes have been given a Mediterranean slant, such as the excellent grilled-corn chowder, grilled tuna with caponata and roasted tomatoes, and herb-crusted salmon steak in red-wine sauce. However, for a truly Parisian experience, order the shrimp or lobster cocktail, which comes perched on a mound of shaved ice in a deep silver platter, followed by a fine roast prime rib or filet mignon au poivre. The extensive wine list is expertly employed in a promotion that's become popular all over town: four excellent wines are included with the prix-fixe dinner after 8PM. For more casual tastes, the less expensive, but equally excellent, bistro is right next door. ♦ French ♦ Daily lunch and dinner. Reservations recommended. 120 W 51st St (between Sixth and Seventh Aves). 956.7100

51 Judson Grill ★$$$ The vast airy space here feels like the main dining room of an ocean liner, complete with massive brass chandeliers, mirrored walls, colorful banquettes, and a brass balcony shaped like the deck of a ship. The menu, composed by chef John Villa, is small but creative, although the execution of the dishes is somewhat hit-and-miss. Try the grilled shrimp salad with Tuscan white beans, eggplant caviar, shaved fennel, artichokes, and black olives with tomato and thyme vinaigrettes; lobster spring roll with Thai dipping sauce; pumpkin ravioli with truffle-scented mushrooms; oven-roasted rack of lamb in a parmesan-herb crust; and grilled salmon with orzo-stuffed Napa cabbage. For dessert, try the Judson chocolate sampler or the toasted-pistachio–butterscotch *semifreddo* (a partially frozen whipped concoction) with butterscotch caramel sauce. There's an interesting well-priced wine list, with a good selection of wines available by the glass. There's also a pre-theater prix-fixe dinner. ♦ American ♦ M-F lunch and dinner; Sa dinner. Reservations recommended. 152 W 52nd St (between Sixth and Seventh Aves). 582.5252 &

Ben Benson's
———— STEAK HOUSE ————

52 Ben Benson's Steakhouse ★★$$$$ Housed in a relatively new building, this classic-style New York restaurant serves massive portions of meat—including T-bones, aged sirloins, and triple-cut lamb chops—that few will be able to finish in one sitting. Crabmeat or lobster cocktail are good starters, and of the side dishes, the crispy home fries stand out. If you have any room left for dessert, try the cheesecake or bread pudding with bourbon sauce. The setting for such weighty fare is certainly appropriate—heavy wood tables and chairs, a wood balcony ledge, and beige walls hung with paintings of game birds and fish. ♦ American ♦ M-F lunch and dinner; Sa-Su dinner. Reservations recommended. 123 W 52nd St (between Sixth and Seventh Aves). 581.8888

53 Gallagher's Steak House ★$$$$ Even confirmed carnivores may flinch as they pass the glass-walled meat locker (also visible from the street) filled with raw slabs of beef. But it's been there since the restaurant opened in 1927, and like many other aspects of the place, it hasn't changed a bit. The steaks are big and satisfying, but having to order the vegetables à la carte makes getting a balanced meal a serious investment. ♦ Steak house ♦ Daily lunch and dinner. Reservations recommended. 228 W 52nd St (between Broadway and Eighth Ave). 245.5336

53 Russian Samovar ★$$ Featured on the menu here are the staples and specialties of Slavic cooking: blini with caviar, grilled fish, and lamb. A four-course prix-fixe dinner keeps the regular customers coming back, who in the bargain enjoy the Russian decor and nightly music. Ask about the delicious flavored vodkas, which you can usually see steeping in large jars behind the bar. ♦ Russian ♦ M dinner; Tu-Sa lunch and dinner; Su dinner. Reservations recommended. 256 W 52nd St (between Broadway and Eighth Ave). 757.0168

54 King Crab ★$$ Spacious it's not, but this pretty seafood restaurant is charming, with gaslit lamps and a gracious staff. The daily specials feature whatever the morning trip to the **Fulton Fish Market** has netted. Don't pass up the soft-shell crabs (if available). ♦ Seafood ♦ M-F lunch and dinner; Sa-Su dinner. Reservations recommended. 871 Eighth Ave (at W 52nd St). 765.4393 ♿

54 Bangkok Cuisine ★★$$ One of the more theatrical-looking Thai places in the area, this restaurant provides colorful relief from the dark walls and gleaming dark tables with paintings and residents of the fish tank. The food is excellent, and among the best dishes are the seafood soups spiced with pepper and lemongrass, any of the satays, *mee krob* (crispy noodles tossed with pork, shrimp, and bean sprouts), chicken *masaman* (with coconut milk, peanuts, avocado, and curry), and baked fish smothered with hot spices. It's crowded in the early evening but becomes increasingly peaceful as the evening wears on. ♦ Thai ♦ M-Sa lunch and dinner; Su dinner. Reservations recommended. 885 Eighth Ave (between W 52nd and W 53rd Sts). 581.6370 ♿

55 St. Famous Bread The first part of this shop's odd name is the result of an amusing phone book mistake that turned the initials S.T. (for original owners Steve and Timothy) into the abbreviation for "saint." All in all, it seemed to be a good sign, and the mistaken name was adopted. While the bread may not be holy, it is heavenly—especially the seven grain, raisin honey nut, and sourdough. Focaccia, muffins, tea cakes, brownies, chocolate chip cookies, and sticky buns are also available. ♦ Daily. 796 Ninth Ave (at W 53rd St). 245.6695

When Gallagher's opened in 1927, a columnist praised the steaks but criticized the high cost. It was $1.50 then; it's $29.50 now.

Beef consumption is serious at New York steak houses. Diners go through approximately 2,000 sirloins and 1,500 filet mignons a week at Gallagher's.

56 Mangia e Bevi ★★$ More like a nonstop party than a restaurant, this lively Italian trattoria misses no opportunity for fun. Even the background music is an occasion to make merry—when the tarantella plays, the diners are handed tambourines so they can play along. In between outbursts of music and general bonhomie, guests enjoy well-prepared meals from a changing menu that might include grilled portobello mushrooms followed by *pappardelle* (broad noodles) with cream, tomatoes, and artichoke hearts. Since the second half of the name means "drink," there is, not surprisingly, a predominantly Italian wine list with good choices at all price levels. ♦ Italian ♦ Daily lunch and dinner. Reservations recommended. 800 Ninth Ave (at W 53rd St). 956.3976

56 Julian's Mediterranean Cuisine $ The owners of the lively **Mangia e Bevi** next door (see above) wanted to take a stab at a more sophisticated restaurant with this place. It's a very pretty, candlelit, dark-toned dining room with brick walls and deeply colored floral paintings. But the menu is only a half-step above typical Little Italy fare, offering chicken with rosemary and portobello mushrooms, grilled tuna steak, and grilled seafood on arugula, and the preparations tend to be hit-and-miss. ♦ Italian ♦ Daily lunch and dinner. 802 Ninth Ave (between W 53rd and W 54th Sts). 262.4288

57 Martini's ★★$$ Wolfgang Puck protégé Richard Krause, formerly of **Melrose** and **Silverado,** has set up an open California-style kitchen in this ocher-colored room with a large outdoor terrace. Come here for very good grilled fish, including charred tuna with green mango, tomato, and spring onion sauce, and fabulous desserts—try the sinful lemon tart. Order the namesake drink, a martini, which comes in a designer glass. One caveat: Try to sit as far away from the kitchen as possible—with all that grilling, it tends to get smoky. ♦ American/Mediterranean ♦ Daily lunch and dinner. Reservations recommended. 810 Seventh Ave (at W 53rd St). 767.1717

58 Au Cafe ★$ This is an idea whose time has certainly come: a coffee bar with a variety of sandwiches, salads, soups, pastas, burgers, and pastries. It's an ideal place to relax with your thoughts or a newspaper. Soft background jazz and small marble pedestal tables create an airy, laid-back environment with a spacious palm-lined outdoor seating area far from the street that is delightful in nice weather. ♦ American ♦ Daily breakfast, lunch, and dinner. 1700 Broadway (at W 53rd St). 757.2233

59 Stage Delicatessen $$ The once-great spot for Damon Runyon characters is now in high disrepute among New Yorkers. The pastrami is fair, but like all the rest of the sandwiches, way overpriced. ♦ Deli ♦ Daily breakfast, lunch, dinner, and late-night meals. 834 Seventh Ave (between W 53rd and W 54th Sts). 245.7850

60 Remi ★★$$$ Fresh antipasti, Venetian-style ravioli filled with fresh tuna and crispy ginger in a light tomato sauce, and a selection of grilled meats and fish please both the deal makers from nearby Time-Warner who lunch here, as well as some of the city's esteemed chefs, who reserve tables here on their nights off. The desserts are worth the splurge, especially the *cioccolatissima* (a warm chocolate soufflé cake with a cappuccino parfait) and the zabaglione *sarah venezia* (broiled zabaglione with fruit and vanilla ice cream). For those who like grappa, there are 45 varieties from which to choose. ♦ Italian ♦ M-F lunch and dinner; Sa-Su dinner. Reservations recommended. 145 W 53rd St (between Sixth and Seventh Aves). 581.4242

61 Carnegie Delicatessen ★★$$ Indulge yourself at *the* classic kosher-style deli, a New York legend that became famous for sandwiches named after other New York legends. The menu may seem a bit pricey at first, but wait until you see the size of the sandwiches—massive affairs that inevitably provide enough to share or cart home. Leave room, if you can, for the cheesecake. The downside: Getting people in and out—not providing gracious service or comfort—is the goal here, and after so many years it's become an honored tradition. The deli made a star appearance in Woody Allen's *Broadway Danny Rose.* ♦ Deli ♦ Daily breakfast, lunch, dinner, and late-night meals. No credit cards accepted. 854 Seventh Ave (between W 54th and W 55th Sts). 757.2245

62 Broadway Diner ★$ This upscale, 1950s-style diner, with lots of tables and counter seats, features a wide variety of good daily specials in the salads, steaks, and fresh fish department. ♦ American ♦ Daily breakfast, lunch, dinner, and late-night meals. No credit cards accepted. 1726 Broadway (at W 55th St). 765.0909. Also at: 590 Lexington Ave (at 52nd St). 486.8838 ♿

63 Siam Inn ★$ Spicy, authentic fare is offered in the humdrum dining room of this noisy and fashionable Thai restaurant. Fish and seafood dishes are best. ♦ Thai ♦ M-F lunch and dinner; Sa-Su dinner. 916 Eighth Ave (between W 54th and W 55th Sts). 974.9583

64 Chantal Cafe ★$$ This cozy cafe serves affordable Italian and French dishes in a prett brick-walled room. Try the steak au poivre or the chicken with rosemary. There's also a good prix-fixe dinner. ♦ French/Italian ♦ M-S lunch and dinner. Reservations recommended. 257 W 55th St (between Broadway and Eighth Ave). 246.7076

64 Soup Kitchen ★$ The name says it all. Thi open storefront serves nothing but rich homemade soup in approximately eight varieties—try the black bean and clam-and-corn chowder. ♦ Soup ♦ M-F lunch. No credi cards accepted. 259A W 55th St (between Broadway and Eighth Ave). 757.7730 ♿

65 Christer's ★★★$$$ After garnering rave reviews during his tenure as chef at the nearby **Aquavit,** Swedish-born Christer Larsson opened his own restaurant in 1993. The rustic decor of split logs and plaid-covered banquettes centers around a stone fireplace, and a number of fish paintings grace the walls. The food, American with Scandinavian leanings, highlights fresh fish and seafood; don't miss the gravlax; house-smoked Serrano salmon with black beans, corn, avocado, and tomatillo salsa; or salmo barbecued on an oak board with bacon and tamales. Desserts include a chocolate cake with an almond crust and peach sauce, the apple leaf (apples baked in phyllo dough topped with vanilla ice cream), and a lingonberry compote with chocolate ice cream. For refreshment try the aquavit, a clear-colored liquor flavored with caraway seeds. ♦ American/Scandinavian ♦ M-F lunch and dinner; Sa dinner. Reservations recommended. 145 W 55th St (between Sixt and Seventh Aves). 974.7224

66 Castellano ★★$$$ The peach-colored dining room is a re-creation of Harry's Bar in Venice, but the food is authentic Tuscan cuisine, although a few dishes from other regions make an appearance. Try the green-and-white fettuccine with cream and ham or any of the grilled fish entrées. ♦ Italian ♦ M- lunch and dinner; Sa-Su dinner. Reservation required. 138 W 55th St (between Sixth and Seventh Aves). 664.1975

67 Corrado ★★$$$ A very, very popular neighborhood lunch spot, this modern trattoria with beige walls and wood trim can get pretty loud—the noise level approaches deafening roar. But diners put up with it to get a taste of wild-mushroom risotto and homemade pastas with light and skillfully spiced sauces, including rigatoni *salsicce* (with hot and sweet sausage, tomatoes, peppers, and cream) and *fusilli siciliana* (with tomatoes, eggplant, and mozzarella). The desserts are excellent—especially the flavorful ice creams. Next door is **Corrado Kitchen** (333.7696), a popular take-out place offering more of the same. ♦ Italian ♦ M-F lunch and dinner; Sa-Su dinner. Reservations recommended. 1373 Sixth Ave (between W 55th and W 56th Sts). 333.3133

57 Ellen's Stardust Diner $ The burgers here won't win any culinary awards, but they're delivered to the shake, rattle, and roll of vintage 1950s music. The menu gets as fancy as grilled swordfish, but your best bet is a Velveeta cheeseburger and strawberry malt, topped off with an ice-cream sundae for dessert. Be prepared to wait. ♦ American ♦ Daily breakfast, lunch, dinner, and late-night meals. 1377 Sixth Ave (at W 56th St). 307.7575 & Also at: 1650 Broadway (at W 51st St). 956.5151

58 The Russian Tea Room ★★$$$ Possibly the most festive place in town, this restaurant sports year-round Christmas decorations, samovars, and bright colors trimmed with gleaming brass. This is a good place for celebrity watching and mingling with beautifully dressed people; try to get a table in the front to be near the "power" booths. Begin with blini and caviar and then move on to *karsky shashlik* (grilled marinated loin of lamb with pilaf), chicken kiev, or beef stroganoff. The menu offers lighter fare as well, including grilled fish, which comes with a choice of sauces and side dishes. A cabaret room upstairs features such performers as Julie Wilson, David Staller, Peter Duchin, and Anne Hampton Callaway on Sunday and Monday nights. ♦ Russian ♦ Daily lunch and dinner. Reservations required; jacket and tie recommended. 150 W 57th St (between Sixth and Seventh Aves). 265.0947

PLANET HOLLYWOOD ®

58 Planet Hollywood ★$$ Owned (though not managed) by a trio of celluloid powerhouses (Sylvester Stallone, Bruce Willis, and Arnold Schwarzenegger), this hot eatery is forever loud and packed. It's also fun: The interior, a veritable museum of movie memorabilia, was created by the set designer for the first *Batman* film. The pizza and burger selections are good, but remember to leave room for the apple strudel, made from Arnold's mother's secret recipe. A gift shop next door sells souvenirs that no trendy eater should be without. ♦ American ♦ Daily lunch, dinner, and late-night meals. 140 W 57th St (between Sixth and Seventh Aves). 333.7827

69 Trattoria Dell'Arte ★★$$$ According to the proud management of this colorful restaurant opposite **Carnegie Hall**, the world's largest antipasto bar resides here. Choose from the impressive assortment, which includes sun-dried tomatoes, roasted fennel, fresh mozzarella, various seasonal vegetables, and a separate seafood bar with lobster, shrimp and scallop salad, calamari, and smoked salmon. The casual Italian menu features delicate thin-crust pizzas. Inspiration for the decor is provided by the noses of some 32 famous Italians and Italian-Americans—Joe DiMaggio and Geraldine Ferraro among them. It's a stylish, bustling place—not the place for a quiet dinner. ♦ Italian ♦ Daily lunch and dinner. Reservations required for dinners before and after Carnegie Hall performances. 900 Seventh Ave (between W 56th and W 57th Sts). 245.9800 &

70 Hard Rock Cafe $$ The tail end of a 1958 Cadillac is the marquee of this mecca for young tourists. Inside, check out the guitar-shaped bar and rock memorabilia that includes dozens of gold records, the purple jacket of the rock star who used to be called Prince, and Jimi Hendrix's guitar. The sandwiches and burgers are decent. Requisite **Hard Rock** T-shirts and sweatshirts are for sale in the gift shop next door. ♦ American ♦ Daily lunch, dinner, and late-night meals. 221 W 57th St (between Seventh Ave and Broadway). 459.9320

70 Cafe Europa ★$ Bright and pretty, with dreamy trompe l'oeil ceilings, this cafe is a convenient spot to have a sandwich (made with very fresh ingredients) or such hot dishes as pizza and pasta. The muffins, tarts, and cakes accompanied by full-flavored coffees make great snacks. ♦ Cafe/Takeout ♦ Daily breakfast, lunch, dinner, and late-night meals. 205 W 57th St (at Seventh Ave). 977.4030 &

Proving that celebrities really do like caviar, the Russian Tea Room goes through 2,647 pounds of the fish eggs in a year.

The Russian Tea Room, founded in 1927 by members of the Russian Imperial Ballet who had fled here following the Bolshevik Revolution, serves 39 vodkas from around the world.

71 India Pavilion ★$ With its low-profile decor, this small underrated restaurant is *the* place for flavorful Indian and Pakistani food before or after the theater. Come here for the best chicken *tikka* (marinated in yogurt and cooked dry—a boneless tandoori) and curries in the neighborhood, and save yourself a trip downtown to Little India on East Sixth Street. ♦ Indian ♦ M-F lunch and dinner; Sa-Su dinner. 240 W 56th St (between Broadway and Eighth Ave). 243.8175 &

SYMPHONY CAFE

72 Symphony Cafe ★★★$$$ The grand-sized dining room may be on the dark and dull side, but the food sparkles, thanks to chefs Neil Murphy and Richard Leach, formerly of **One Fifth.** Murphy's entrées are rich, well balanced, and delicious, especially the soy-honey cured duck with gingered plums, strudel-wrapped shrimp with shaved fennel, and chicken grilled with essences of garlic and sage. Be sure to save room for one of Leach's delicious desserts that are architectural wonders. Warm Raspberry Financier looks like something straight out of the Jetson's—you'll smile when you see it, then smile again when you taste it. The chocolate-mousse torte is another must. There are "hotter" restaurants in New York, but not many where you can eat this well. ♦ American ♦ M-Sa lunch and dinner; Su brunch and dinner. Reservations required for pre-theater dinners. 950 Eighth Ave (at W 56th St). 397.9595

73 Urban Grill ★$ A happy mix of Italian and American fare—pastas, hamburgers, and grilled chicken, any of which are fine for a quick lunch or pre-theater bite—are featured here. ♦ American/Italian ♦ M-F lunch and dinner; Sa-Su dinner. 330 W 58th St (between Eighth and Ninth Aves). 586.3300

74 Petrossian ★★★$$$$ Whether in Paris or New York, this restaurant is *the* place to go for caviar. Many varieties of precious roe are offered at this high-class, Art Deco–influenced marble and mink-trimmed room, with ornate gilded statuettes and enlarged etchings of Erté drawings. Sample the sevruga, ossetra, or beluga, foie gras terrine, or the sampling of salmon—marinated, smoked, and spiced. A popular item is the "teaser" plate with an assortment of such delectables as foie gras and green apple in pastry and pressed caviar on small blini with crème fraîche. These appetizers can be made into a meal in and o themselves, but if you can press on to the main course, you most certainly should. Ch Joseph Pace's innovative and delicious dish include roasted lobster with fricassee of winter vegetables, potato puree, and mushroom truffle sauce; and roasted black sea bass with French lentils, fried oysters, a bittersweet meat glaze. Desserts are similar hard to pass up; try the lemon tart with leme custard and caramel, cranberry spice cake with cinnamon ice cream, or the Valrhona chocolate soufflé with Vermont maple ice cream and caramelized bananas. The wine li is excellent and the very best champagnes c be ordered by the glass. There's a sublime prix-fixe brunch and surprisingly affordable prix-fixe lunch and dinner. Take-home delicacies are available in the adjoining reta shop. ♦ Continental ♦ M-F lunch and dinner Sa-Su brunch and dinner. Reservations required; jacket required. 182 W 58th St (at Seventh Ave). 245.2214

75 Les Célébrités ★★★$$$$ Located withi the **Essex House Hotel Nikko,** the setting he exudes wealth and power with ornate gold-leaf columns, dark red banquettes, and glistening black walls dotted with paintings done by celebrity amateurs—James Dean, Elke Sommer, Pierce Brosnan, Phyllis Diller Billy Dee Williams, to name a few. Chef Christian Delouvrier's food is as princely as the setting, piling one deluxe ingredient upo the next—with mostly good results. His signature foie gras burger, between Granny Smith apple rings, is delicious as well as impressive for the sheer amount of foie gras on the plate; lobster medaillons with truffle and artichokes are delicately flavorful, but c be tough. Regulars tend to stick to meat ane poultry dishes; try the roasted rack and sad of lamb, roast squab, or duck with orange-honey glaze and fig puree (if you don't minc sweet sauces). For dessert, the kitchen turn out airy, if not always flavorful, soufflés and luscious banana tart with rum sauce. The w list is epic; and though parts read like a wisł list for serious connoisseurs with very deep pockets, there are also a number of very goo wines at affordable prices. ♦ French ♦ Tu-S dinner. Reservations required; jacket requir 153 W 58th St (between Sixth and Seventh Aves). 247.0300

café

75 Cafe Botanica ★★$$$ Also within the **Essex House Hotel Nikko** (walk though the lobby or enter around the corner on Central Park South), this light, airy room filled with greenery, the soothing sounds of a running fountain, and park views is the alter ego of the darkly opulent **Les Célébrités** (see above). The food here is less intense, and less expensive, but very flavorful and creative. Try the herbed *pappardelle* with Great Northern beans and black truffle oil, grilled calamari with roasted red-pepper *coulis*, wood-grilled Maine lobster with pumpkin risotto, roasted rack of lamb with eggplant gratin, and seared sea scallops over toasted angel-hair pasta. For dessert, there are excellent fruit tarts, mango mousse, and chocolate truffle cake. There are also good prix-fixe lunches and dinners, as well as a spectacular Sunday brunch. ♦ International ♦ M-Sa breakfast, lunch, and dinner; Su brunch and dinner. Reservations recommended. 160 Central Park S (between Sixth and Seventh Aves). 484.5120

76 Fantino ★★$$$ The name means jockey in Italian, and in its previous incarnation this restaurant was the **Jockey Club** of the **Ritz Carlton Hotel.** Gone are the hunter-green walls and paintings of horses. Today the dining room is a soft peach color with chandeliers and delicately lit 19th-century oil paintings. Like the setting, the menu has been completely transformed. Chef Gennaro Villella, formerly of Los Angeles's Rex II Ristorante, favors the use of infused oils, broths, and herbs, and serves the results on striking, specially designed Gianni Versace plates. Try the house-smoked sea bass and eggplant with Tuscan white beans and basil olive oil, ravioli of fresh wild mushrooms flavored with white truffles, and pan-roasted lamb chops covered in an oregano-pecorino crust and Vernaccia wine. ♦ Italian ♦ M-Sa dinner. Reservations recommended; jacket required. 112 Central Park S (between Sixth and Seventh Aves). 664.7700

77 The Jekyll and Hyde Club $ An expansion of the smaller Greenwich Village original, a playfully creepy 19th-century pub/laboratory, this uptown attraction is equal parts restaurant and haunted house. It offers five floors of horror, each with its own theme—mausoleum, laboratory, grand salon, observatory, and library—and each full of things like monsters, ceilings that lower and threaten to crush you, singing skeletons, and mad doctors, of course. The food—burgers, pasta—is not very interesting, but the setting has attracted lines of customers from the moment the doors opened. ♦ American ♦ Daily lunch, dinner, and late-night meals. 1409 Sixth Ave (between 57th and 58th Sts). 541.9517 &. Also at: 91 Seventh Ave S (between Barrow and Grove Sts). 989.7701

78 San Domenico ★★★★$$$$ After captivating the palates of international food critics for 18 years in a suburb of Bologna, Gianluigi Morino transplanted his labor of love to New York in 1988, and began dazzling food critics here. Today, the same standards are maintained under the watchful eye of present owner Tony May. The marble bar, terra-cotta floor imported from Florence, and smooth, ocher-tinted stucco walls applied by artisans from Rome is lovely, although perhaps a little subdued compared to the theatrical settings that have come recently into vogue. All the dazzle you need, however, will arrive in the form of chef Theo Schoenegger's sublime cooking. Diet for a week if you have to or jog all the way home, but don't miss the meltingly rich soft egg yolk–filled ravioli with truffle butter; it's a taste experience that you'll remember for years. Also try the Alaskan prawns with cannellini beans and rosemary; risotto with red beets and squab; handmade penne with chives, caviar, and asparagus tips; fillet of black sea bass in a tomato broth with vegetables; breast of duck with olive sauce and caramelized endive; and the quintessential tiramisù. The sensational and affordable prix-fixe dinner is a great deal for those who don't mind eating early. ♦ Italian ♦ M-F lunch and dinner; Sa-Su dinner. Reservations required; jacket required. 240 Central Park S (between Seventh Ave and Broadway). 265.5959 &

Bests

Isabelle Stevenson
President, American Theatre Wing

Post House: Two people can share steak.

Frankie & Johnny's

Jim McMullen: Large portions, always good service.

Sardi's: *The* place to take out-of-town guests.

Russian Tea Room: Good atmosphere, good people watching.

Citarella Market: Good fish and meat.

Candy lovers have New York to thank for two of their favorites: Tootsie Rolls were the creation of Leo Hirschfield in 1896 as he rolled out chocolates for his daughter Clara, nicknamed Tootsie. In the mid 1930s, Philip Silverstein mixed chocolate, Brazil nuts, cashews, and raisins, and named it Chunky in honor of his somewhat overweight daughter.

Midtown

The commercial nerve center of Manhattan, Midtown hums, from lofty boardrooms down to subterranean mailrooms. The towering office buildings in this area, bordered by the **East River** and **Sixth Avenue**, and **39th** and **59th Streets**, are the workplaces of hundreds of thousands of people. And these hordes pour out of the skyscrapers every day around noon looking for sustenance—executives dash off to power lunches at places like **Christ Cella**, and their assistants grab a salad or sandwich from such spots as **Mangia**.

Adding to this human gridlock are shoppers at the city's most renowned stores. **Fifth Avenue** and **57th Street** has been called the greatest retailing

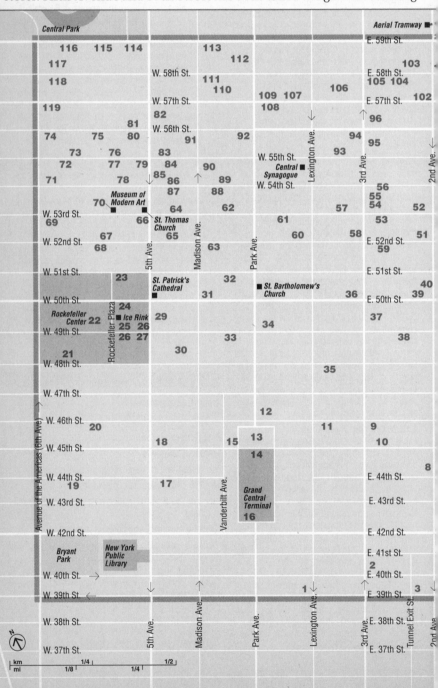

orner in the world—**Tiffany's**, **Van Cleef & Arpels**, **Bergdorf Goodman**, nd **Bulgari** are all within splurging distance. The nearby upscale shops of rump Tower, and such newer additions as the **Warner Brothers** and **Coca-ola** stores, draw customers by the thousands. Closer to **Central Park South** that mecca for kids of all ages, **FAO Schwartz**, while a walk down Fifth venue in the other direction toward **Rockefeller Center** takes you to **Henri endel**, **Mark Cross**, **Cartier**, and **Saks Fifth Avenue** (with its own built-in spite for hungry shoppers). Deluxe treats are offered at **Teuscher hocolates of Switzerland** or **Richart Design et Chocolat**—the onfectionery crème de la crème. Amid all these attractions stand New York's

famous luxury hotels: the **Plaza**, **Peninsula**, **Waldorf-Astoria**, **Ritz-Carlton**, **St. Regis**, **Four Seasons** and **Palace**, with their swanky bars, proper afternoon teas, and sumptuous dining halls.

Not surprisingly, given the high concentration of movers-and-shakers, high-spending shoppers, and affluent tourists, Midtown has the greatest share of New York's most expensive restaurants. Because these prices sometimes more accurately reflect the city's highest per-square-foot rents rather than the quality of the experience, let the diner beware. For those on a limited budget, there are a handful of options. The most reasonable alternative is a snack from the vendors near **Radio City Music Hall**, who offer a variety of street fare, including grilled kebabs, baked potatoes, falafels, honey-roasted nuts, candy by the pound, and gourmet ice creams, in addition to the hot dogs, pretzels, and knishes of yore.

At night, the area is largely deserted, with pockets of activity outside the big-name restaurants—**The Four Seasons**, **Lutèce**, **Vong**, **Monkey Bar**, **La Côte Basque**—and at **Rockefeller Center**. Here, 65 stories high, high-living revelers enjoy dinner, drinks, and dancing at the extremely popular **Rainbow Room**, with its gleaming Art Deco bar and lovely view of Manhattan's twinkling glamour.

Tucked behind the impenetrable wall of skyscrapers are residential areas, including the huge **Tudor City** complex overlooking the **United Nations**; the brownstone neighborhood of **Turtle Bay**, east of **Third Avenue** in the 40s; **Beekman**

Map labels

Queensboro Bridge
(25)
100
99
98
97
E. 56th St.
E. 55th St.
1st Ave.
Sutton Pl.
48
E. 54th St.
E. 53rd St.
46
47
45 44
43
42
Beekman Pl.
Franklin D. Roosevelt Dr.
41
E. 49th St.
E. 48th St.
E. 47th St.
E. 46th St.
East River
E. 45th St.
6
The United Nations
5
Tudor City Pl.
Queens Midtown Tunnel (Toll)
Tunnel Entrance St.
1st Ave.

Place, a tiny enclave of town houses that includes the stretches of **East 49th** through **East 51st Streets** between **First Avenue** and the East River; and **Sutton Place,** an exclusive street above **East 50th Street** that runs along the river. Residents here favor **Billy's, Mayfair,** and the **Metropolitan Cafe** for casual local dining; they pick up fresh fish from **Pisacane Midtown,** and buy cooking implements from **Bridge Kitchenware.**

Apart from the few pocket-size public spaces and parks that provide a bit of respite for visitors and a place for office workers to enjoy lunch al fresco in nice weather, Midtown is not a subtle place. It's where New York puts all its muscle on display, impressive even to New Yorkers who do battle here every day.

1 Stella del Mare ★★$$$ A gracious, old-fashioned seafood restaurant, this place is bustling at lunch but relaxed and romantic at dinner. Have a few samples from the antipasto cart, then try some homemade pasta—linguine with seafood or with clams. Follow with one of the very fresh grilled whole fish, such as Dover sole or snapper; they're boned at the table and served with garlicky olive oil—all that's needed. Regulars never order off the menu, they simply discuss the day's specials with the waiter. ♦ Italian/Seafood ♦ M-F lunch and dinner; Sa dinner. Reservations recommended; jacket required. 346 Lexington Ave (between E 39th and E 40th Sts). 687.4425

2 Docks Oyster Bar and Seafood Grill ★ $$$ A big white-tiled space with a large bar that gets crowded and noisy after work, this midtown branch of the Upper West Side seafood palace lacks personality. But it's a good bet for reliable clam chowder, fried oysters, and fresh grilled fish. ♦ Seafood ♦ M-F lunch and dinner; Sa dinner. Reservations recommended. 633 Third Ave (at E 40th St). 986.8080. Also at: 2427 Broadway (between W 89th and W 90th Sts). 724.5588

3 Phoenix Garden ★$$$ A Chinatown favorite that used to be distinguished by one of the grungiest entrances ever—through a garbage-strewn alleyway—has relocated uptown to a narrow brick-walled dining room a few steps below street level. Although the formerly epic menu has been pared down, such old favorites as the signature salt-and-pepper shrimp, roasted chicken with a crackling skin, and Peking pork chops remain. ♦ Chinese ♦ Daily lunch and dinner. No credit cards accepted. 242 E 40th St (between Second and Third Aves). 983.6666

4 Sichuan Pavilion ★★$$$ The Chinese menu here is one of the most interesting in the city and popular with **United Nations** delegates. During lunch regulars tend to get preferential service, so if you want more evenhanded treatment, come at dinnertime. Chicken with mixed mushrooms, lemon chicken, ginger-and-scallion shrimp, scallops with peppercorn sauce, and crispy fish are all good choices. ♦ Chinese ♦ Daily lunch and dinner. Reservations required for lunch, recommended for dinner. 310 E 44th St (between First and Second Aves). 972.7377

5 Ambassador Grill Restaurant ★$$$ New chef Matthew Mitnitsky is revitalizing this old-fashioned mirrored dining room within the **Park Hyatt Hotel** with dishes such as roasted corn and crab timbale, grilled prawns with mushroom linguine and soy-wasabi dressing, roulade of chicken on parmesan-herb orzo with baby asparagus, Atlantic char over wilted greens in mushroom vinaigrette, and roasted duck with star anise and Szechuan peppercorn sauce. At press time, a new pastry chef was scheduled to come aboard; stay tuned. On Sundays, stop in for the all-you-can-eat/all-the-champagne-you-can-drink brunch buffet, which is deservedly popular. ♦ American ♦ M-Sa lunch and dinner; Su brunch and dinner. Reservations recommended. 1 United Nations Plaza (at E 44th St, between First and Second Aves). 702.5014

6 Delegates' Dining Room ★★$$$ The UN dining room is open to the public for lunch during the week. It offers a very good international luncheon buffet with a choice of 22 dishes, in addition to an à la carte menu that includes asparagus with lemon vinaigrette, lobster salad, barbecued salmon with ginger-honey sauce, loin of venison, and steak with shallot sauce. Try the chocolate terrine or frozen-raspberry soufflé for dessert. A different vegetable is featured monthly, and it's prepared in a new way daily; wines of a specific nation are also offered monthly. The view of the East River is the best of any restaurant in Manhattan. ♦ Continental ♦ M-F lunch. Reservations required; jacket required. UN Conference Building (E 45th St at First Ave) 963.7625

7 Captain's Table ★$$$ Come here for superb fresh fish offered in a variety of preparations—halibut with aioli, grilled red snapper, and breaded shrimp with hot peppers and mozzarella, for example. There's also a separate market section where you can buy fresh fish to take home. ♦ Seafood ♦ M-F lunch and dinner; Sa dinner. Reservations recommended. 860 Second Ave (at E 46th St). 697.9538

8 Palm ★★$$$$ Ranked among the city's best steak houses, this venerable dinning room (opened in 1926) serves huge prime cuts and addictive cottage-fried potatoes. The serious carnivores who come here don't seem to mind the close and chaotic premises, the long wait for a table, or the surly, often rushed service. Caricatures of famous New York journalists are painted on the walls, but you're more likely to recognize faces at the next table. Desserts are basic; try the cheesecake. Across the street is its newer twin (only 20 years old), **Palm Too** (697.5198); it still has sawdust on the floor unlike the original. ♦ Steak house ♦ M-F lunch and dinner; Sa dinner. Reservations required. 837 Second Ave (between E 44th and E 45th Sts). 687.2953

9 Sparks ★★$$$$ As at the other great steak houses, excellent cuts of beef and fresh seafood are cooked to order here. But what makes this place different is the exceptional wine list—the extraordinary selection and fair prices make it a must for oenophiles. Despite all that, this restaurant is probably still best known for the murder of mobster Paul Castellano, who was gunned down out front years ago. ♦ Steak house ♦ M-F lunch and dinner; Sa dinner. Reservations required. 210 E 46th St (between Second and Third Aves). 687.4855

10 Pen & Pencil ★$$$$ A gracious, wood-paneled old-timer, this place served beef downstairs and gin upstairs during Prohibition; and got its name from the artists, journalists, and writers who showed up for both. Today, the restaurant feels a bit stuffy and old-fashioned, but the capable kitchen still turns out adequate meals of steak, rack of lamb, and chicken paillard. ♦ Steak house ♦ M-F lunch and dinner; Sa-Su dinner. 205 E 45th St (between Second and Third Aves). 682.8660

11 Christ Cella ★$$$$ One of the oldest steak houses in New York, for years this place has enjoyed a reputation among visiting sales-people as the best in town—clearly for the food and not the uninspiring decor. When you call for a reservation, ask to sit downstairs; it isn't any more elegant, but it's cozier. There are no printed menus, so feel free to ask the waiter about prices, which are high for both the food and the wine. The lobsters, steaks, and chops are popular with the crowd of power lunchers. ♦ Steak house ♦ M-F lunch and dinner; Sa dinner. Reservations required. 160 E 46th St (between Third and Lexington Aves). 697.2479

an American Restaurant

12 Colors ★$$$ Paintings and gold-net curtains are the only touches of hue in this modern, beige dining room's decor. The menu, however, flies the colors of many nations with its inter-nationally inspired offerings. Before taking over here, new chef Stefano Battistini—a native Italian raised in Switzerland–spent time in the kitchens of **The Four Seasons,** and at Girardet restaurant in France, under noted chef and owner Fredy Girardet. The menu includes such specialties as lobster *tartare* (raw) with tarragon and endive, saffron soup with clams and sea scallops, braised veal shank, baked salmon with a pepper crust, and curried grilled swordfish. Although these dishes tend to sound better than they taste, the cooking could improve as Battistini picks up confidence. The wine list is extensive and features some Swiss varieties, as well as American and French labels. ♦ International ♦ M-F lunch and dinner, Sa dinner. Reservations recommended. 237 Park Ave (entrance on E 46th St). 661.2000

13 Snaps ★★$$ Modern and yellow with brown hanging sculptures and yellow-and-brown drapes, this dining room bustles at lunchtime and is just slightly more subdued at dinner. Like its more sophisticated sibling, **Aquavit** (see below), this place features lots of fish, especially salmon in myriad preparations. Try the blini tart (three levels of blini, smoked salmon, Matjes herring, and salty fish roe); one of the open-faced sandwiches, particularly gravlax with mustard sauce; salmon burger with beet-horseradish crème fraîche; or mesquite-grilled salmon with trout roe and crème fraîche. Non–fish eaters can choose among tasty dishes that include grilled duck breast with lentils, pickled pumpkin, and lingonberry; and *lovbiff* (steak stuffed with mustard, capers, and horseradish). A well-priced prix-fixe dinner is offered throughout the evening. The well-chosen wine list is affordably priced and features selections from France and California. Desserts, however, are not among the restaurant's strengths. ♦ Scandinavian ♦ M-F breakfast, lunch, and dinner; Sa dinner. Reservations recommended. 230 Park Ave (between E 45th and E 46th Sts). 949.7878

TROPICA
Bar and Seafood House

14 Tropica ★★$$$ At lunchtime, it's a capacity crowd with a corresponding noise level in this restaurant in the **MetLife Building**. At night, though, the hubbub recedes and chef Fred Sabo shows off creative seafood preparations to an appreciative audience. Try crab cakes with mustard beurre blanc; barbecued shrimp with an Indo-spice glaze; conch chowder; and grilled red snapper with cashew-basmati rice, avocado, and tropical fruit chutney. ♦ Regional American/Tropical ♦ M-F lunch and dinner. 200 Park Ave (enter on E 45th St), Ground level. 867.6767 &

14 Cucina and Company ★$ A casual feeding station bustling with neighborhood office workers, this rustic place in the **MetLife Building**, with painted tiles on the walls and terra-cotta floors, offers better-than-average sandwiches and such salads as grilled chicken. There's also an affordable prix-fixe dinner for two (served between 5PM and 9PM), featuring such entrées as steak *frites* (with french fries), salmon *en croute* (in a pastry puff), and roulade of beef braised in wine and onions. ♦ American ♦ M-F breakfast, lunch, and dinner. 200 Park Ave (enter on E 45th St), Ground level. 682.2700

CAFÉ CENTRO

14 Cafe Centro ★★$$$ This $5-million brasserie with marble inlay floors, gold-leaf columns, and etched Lalique-style chandeliers is reminiscent of the grand cafes in European train stations. Here in the **MetLife Building,** a quick sprint away from **Grand Central Station,** you can have a meal as simple or as complex as your desire and time frame dictate. Try the roast chicken—perfectly juicy beneath the herb-flavored crispy skin—

cooked to perfection in one of the rotisseries enclosed within the massive stone fireplace near the entrance. Also worth trying are the fish soup, chicken *bisteeya* (a phyllo-dough pie with Moroccan herbs), or any of the steaks. Desserts are hit-and-miss, but the Valrhona chocolate ganache (iced) cake is pretty reliable. There are a few well-chosen, fairly priced wines, but the beer bar offers a whopping 40 selections, 10 of which are on draft. Plus, it's the only place in New York to get an Amberly—a French brew made from whiskey malt instead of the usual barley and hops. At the bar you can order hamburgers, chicken wings, and potato skins—sans reservations. ♦ American/French ♦ M-F lunch and dinner; Sa dinner. Reservations recommended. 200 Park Ave (entrance on 45th St), Ground level. 818.1222 &

15 Takesushi ★★$$$$ The long lines during lunch attest to the fact that this is one of the more popular sushi bars in the city; come after 5:30PM to avoid the crowd. The solicitous staff is more than willing to lead you into the world of raw fish. ♦ Japanese ♦ M-F lunch and dinner; Sa dinner. Reservations required. 71 Vanderbilt Ave (at E 45th St). 867.5120

◇OYSTER BAR & RESTAURANT

16 Oyster Bar and Restaurant ★★$$$ Located in the lower level of **Grand Central Station,** and looking much like what it is—a railroad-station basement with tables—this place offers nicely prepared and absolutely fresh seafood, including, of course, a large variety of oysters. Although the daily menu reflects the fresh catches of the day, you can count on delicious chowder and excellent oysters pan roasted or fried, as well as smoked salmon, rice-battered shrimp, and a selection of clams on the half shell. For a full meal, take a table in the main dining room, but for a quick bite, try the counter bar next to the dining room, or the slightly more sedate bar through the swinging doors. The extensive wine list is exclusively American and given the menu, concentrates, not surprisingly, on whites. There is also a selection of about 80 different wines available by the glass. Due to the tiled, vaulted ceilings, however, the lunch-hour crowd generates megadecibels. ♦ Seafood ♦ M-F lunch and dinner. Reservations recommended. Grand Central Station, Lower level, 42nd St and Park Ave. 490.6650 &

16 Amish Farm The Amish community in Lancaster, Pennsylvania stocks this shop with excellent cheese, sweet butter, baked goods, organic fruit, and preserves and other condiments. ◆ M-Sa. Grand Central Station, Lower level, 42nd St and Park Ave. No phone

16 The Cafe at Grand Central ★$ On the balcony of **Grand Central Station,** this cafe has one of the best views in town, overlooking the grandeur of the main waiting area and the hubbub of commuters. The menu is simple: onion soup, salad niçoise, antipasto salad, chicken potpie, chicken salad, roast beef sandwich with horseradish dressing, apple pie, cheesecake, and chocolate marquis cake. But it's the setting that makes it special. ◆ American ◆ Daily lunch and light dinner. Grand Central Station, 25 Vanderbilt Ave (between E 43rd and E 44th Sts). 883.0009

17 Chikubu ★★★$$$ This plainly decorated restaurant caters to a mostly Japanese clientele and is a good place for the delicate dishes of Kyoto. Specialties include *akabeko-ju* (rice with thin slices of grilled beef and broiled baby flounder) and *omakase* (a tasting menu of seven to eight courses, including appetizers, sushimi, steamed vegetables or fish, tempura, a noodle or rice dish, and dessert). Another alternative, since the menu changes regularly, is to ask the server to recommend seasonal specials. ◆ Japanese ◆ M-F lunch and dinner; Sa dinner. Reservations recommended. 12 E 44th St (between Madison and Fifth Aves). 818.0715

18 Morton's of Chicago ★★★$$$ With all of the wonderful steak houses in New York, especially in this part of town, the sad truth is that this arrival from Chicago tops them all. The extra-thick, extra-aged, extra-tender porterhouse led *New York Magazine* in 1994 to name this the best place for steak, a title shared with Brooklyn's historic **Peter Luger's.** The whalish lobster cooked in butter and sage is as good as the meat. ◆ Steak house ◆ M-F lunch and dinner; Sa-Su dinner. Reservations recommended. 551 Fifth Ave (entrance on E 45th St). 972.3315

19 Restaurant 44 ★★$$$ Philippe Starck's minimalist decor—beige walls, furniture with clean modern lines, a hanging horizontal mirror—is just one of the draws at this dining room in the **Royalton Hotel.** Another is the American nouvelle cuisine created by chef Geoffrey Zakarian. Try the squid salad, salmon *tartare,* preserved duck leg on warm spinach salad, roasted quail with cheese- and mushroom-laced orzo, striped bass with warm fennel, and rare duck breast. Top the meal off with the lemon tart or Valrhona chocolate soufflé. ◆ American ◆ M-F breakfast, lunch, and dinner; Sa-Su brunch and dinner. Reservations required. 44 W 44th St (between Fifth and Sixth Aves). 944.8844

20 Via Brasil ★★$$ Of all the reasonably good Brazilian restaurants squeezed into the block sometimes called "Brazil Row," this is the best place to sample *feijoada,* the national dish.

This hearty, delicious stew of black beans, sausage, beef, bacon, and pork served on rice is perfect on a blustery winter day. During warmer weather, you might want to try one of the lighter grilled meat or poultry dishes, such as *frango ma brasa* (char-broiled breast of chicken); sirloin steak cubed and marinated in garlic, tomatoes, and onions; and a mixed grill of pork, chicken, beef, and Brazilian sausage. Down your meal with a *caipirinha,* the potent national drink made of rumlike *cachaça,* fresh lime juice, sugar, and ice. Diners are regaled with live music all evening, Wednesday through Saturday, and there's no cover charge. ◆ Brazilian ◆ Daily lunch and dinner. Reservations recommended. 34 W 46th St (between Fifth and Sixth Aves). 997.1158

THE RESTAURANT OF INDIA

21 Shaan ★$$ Formerly **Raga,** this plush, comfortable dining room owned by Victor Khubani and Bhushan Arora features the cuisine of Northern India. Try the quail roasted in a tandoori oven; shrimp in cashew, almond, and saffron sauce; tandoori-baked rack of lamb chops with mint curry; and pilaf with peas, raisins, and cashews. Another alternative is to have a little taste of everything at the luncheon buffet. ◆ Indian ◆ Daily lunch and dinner. 57 W 48th St (between Fifth and Sixth Aves). 977.8400

THE RAINBOW ROOM

22 The Rainbow Room ★★$$$$ When this place reopened in 1987 after two years of restoration, *The New York Times* described it as "a room that wants to be filled with people in formal dress and the sounds of Gershwin and Cole Porter." The redesign (architecture by **Hardy Holzman Pfeiffer Associates;** graphic design by Milton Glaser) was supervised by restaurateur Joseph Baum of **The Four Seasons, Windows on the World,** and **Aurora** fame. The results make this place—even without the view—a romantic place for dining and dancing. Start with a Kir Royale (champagne and cassis), which is made at the table, or a glass of champagne. Stick to simple food preparations, such as the cold seafood platter, the trio of caviars on wafers of potato puree, and rack of lamb. It's a stunning place for visitors and New Yorkers alike. The view is at its best from the bar on the south side. There's a $20 cover charge for the **Rainbow Room Orchestra,** which plays Tuesday-Saturday from 7:30 to 1AM, and Sunday from 6 to 11PM. ◆ Continental ◆ Tu-Su dinner. Reservations required; jacket and tie required. 30 Rockefeller Plaza (between 49th and 50th St), 65th floor. 632.5000

22 Rainbow & Stars ★★$$$$ This intimate spot across from the **Rainbow Room** will convince you that indeed life can be a cabaret. Here you can see such top-name performers as Rosemary Clooney, Cybill Shepherd, and Maureen McGovern with nothing less than the northern view of Manhattan as a backdrop. The decor is giddily over-the-top—silver lamé tablecloths dotted with silver stars and a neon rainbow that flashes on and off; and the menu is a veritable museum of classics—lobster bisque, Caesar's salad, and baked alaska, which shouldn't be missed. The cooking can be disappointing, especially when it comes to the more contemporary dishes, so it's best to keep it simple. Try the platter of littleneck oysters and clams, cake of wild mushrooms, tournedos Rossini (a foie gras–topped filet mignon), and herb-roasted rack of lamb. The wine list has some good, affordable selections. ◆ American ◆ Tu-Sa dinner. Reservations required. 30 Rockefeller Plaza (between 49th and 50th St), 65th floor. 632.5000

23 Fashion Cafe $ The newest of the theme-park restaurants, this stylized dining spot is all about fashion. It's fronted by supermodels Claudia Schiffer, Elle Macpherson, and Naomi Campbell, and memorabilia from fashion notables adorn the walls in the same way that the competing **Hard Rock Cafe** displays guitars. Like its competitors, this place is about show—Madonna's jeweled Dolce & Gabbana bustier, towering Vivienne Westwood heels worn by Naomi Campbell, and a Dior suit worn by Sophia Loren—not food. But you can get a decent Cobb salad, burger, or pizza, along with dishes made from the models' own recipes—Elle's shrimp on the barbe', Claudia's New York strip steak, and Naomi's fish and chips. Ignore the fattening, leaden desserts and try the poached pears. ◆ American ◆ Daily lunch and dinner. 51 Rockefeller Plaza (at W 51st St). 765.3131

24 American Festival Cafe ★$$$ The modern wood booths and minimal decor at this eatery are enhanced by the view through the glass wall that overlooks the skating rink, making this an atmospheric, if expensive, place to stop for a lunchtime burger, Cobb salad, or excellent crab cakes. The dinner menu offers a large and very good prime rib, and various

poultry and fish dishes. A good selection of microbrewery beers is featured, but skip dessert. ◆ American ◆ M-F breakfast, lunch, and dinner; Sa-Su brunch and dinner. 20 W 50th St (at Rockefeller Plaza). 246.6699 &

The Sea Grill

25 The SeaGrill ★★★$$$$ Chef Ed Brown, formerly of **Judson Grill** and **Tropica,** was eager to do something creative with seafood and at this handsome restaurant devoted to fresh fish, he has his chance. Don't miss the Baltimore crab cakes served with a stone-ground mustard and scallion sauce, the buttery salmon with a dijon-mustard and roasted-shallot sauce, and grilled Maine lobster with spaghetti vegetables. Such nonfish dishes as guinea hen or steak are available too. Try one of the delectable desserts, including chocolate steamed pudding with Valrhona chocolate sauce and key lime pie. Request a window seat in winter so you can watch the skaters. ◆ Seafood ◆ M-F lunch and dinner; Sa dinner. Reservations required. 19 W 49th St (at Rockefeller Plaza). 246.9201 &

26 Dean & DeLuca Cafe ★$ The latest in **Dean & DeLuca**'s growing chain of Italian gourmet takeouts/restaurants, this airy cafe is a welcome, convenient place to stop for either a full lunch or afternoon tea. The selection of soups, salads, and fresh *panini* (sandwiches on minibaguettes) is innovative and reliably good. ◆ Italian/Takeout ◆ Daily breakfast, lunch, and early dinner. 9 Rockefeller Plaza (at W 49th St). 664.1363 &. Also at: 121 Prince St (between Wooster and Greene Sts). 254.8776; 75 University Pl (at 11th St). 473.1908 &

27 La Réserve ★★★$$$$ Handsome and spacious with peach fabric banquettes, mirrors, and a mural of the sea, this is the right place for a romantic dinner. Since chef Dominique Payraudeau, formerly of **La Terrace,** took over the reins, the classic French food has taken on delicious new dimensions. Try the *cassolette d'escargots niçoises* (casserole of snails with tomatoes and black olives); marinated lamb fillet; saddle of rabbit with wine sauce; and sliced duck breast with cabbage, honey, and balsamic vinegar. The chocolate basket filled with chocolate mousse and raspberries is an absolute must to round off the meal. ◆ French ◆ M-F lunch and dinner; Sa dinner. Reservations required. 4 W 49th St (at Fifth Ave). 247.2993

28 Teuscher Chocolates of Switzerland
Some of the city's best (and most expensive) chocolate bonbons are offered at this fragrant shop. The window displays are stupendous and change with the season. ♦ M-Sa. 620 Fifth Ave (at W 49th St). 246.4416

29 Cafe SFA ★$ Located within the luxurious **Saks Fifth Avenue,** this place is a convenient spot for hungry shoppers. Dark and woody, the elegant room has tables spaced far enough apart to allow for private conversation, and the menu offers a little of everything. Try the roasted half chicken with herbs or any of the huge bowls of salad, such as the tasty Cobb with smoked turkey or Oriental chicken salad. Lucky diners get one of the terrace tables with a view overlooking **St. Patrick's Cathedral.** But getting any table at all may require some patience; the line usually goes out the door—way out—starting at noon. ♦ American ♦ Daily lunch and afternoon tea. Fifth Ave (at E 49th St). 940.4080 &

30 Hatsuhana ★★★$$$ Sushi lovers give this bar top ratings for the freshest sushi, creatively rolled. Sit at a table or the counter, but definitely try to find a spot where you can watch the sushi chef in action. In addition to the raw stuff, good tempura and some skewered grilled dishes are available. A la carte items tend to add up quickly, so if you're on a budget, the prix-fixe lunch menu is a good buy. ♦ Japanese ♦ M-F lunch and dinner; Sa dinner. Reservations recommended. 17 E 48th St (between Madison and Fifth Aves). 355.3345

31 The Hunt Room at the New York Palace Hotel ★★$$$ Newly opened in the luxury hotel formerly owned by Leona and Harry Helmsley, this dining room is strictly Old World in decor—a clubby, dark wood–paneled space, with formal, mannered service. The food, correspondingly, is stately; recommended are such wild game specialties as pheasant, duck, venison, or wild boar, all of which come in rich, complex sauces blending sweet and savory ingredients. Venison medaillons in a juniper currant sauce and angel-hair pasta with rabbit sauce are especially good. Desserts look better than they taste; opt for one of the soufflés, which should be ordered when the main course arrives. ♦ American ♦ Daily breakfast, lunch,

During the course of a year, the Oyster Bar in Grand Central Station sells 1,800,000 raw oysters and 240 gallons of clam chowder. And 2,600 biscuits are consumed daily.

Each year the Rainbow Room serves 206,820 glasses of champagne, or 34,470 bottles.

In the month of December, more than 40,000 skaters twirl around the rink in Rockefeller Center, entertaining diners at The SeaGrill and the American Festival Cafe.

and dinner. Reservations recommended. 455 Madison Ave (at E 50th St). 888.7000

32 Sushisay ★★$$$ The name means fresh sushi and that's exactly what you'll get at this branch of the Tokyo original, complete with white walls and shoji screens. At lunchtime it's filled with Japanese businessmen, so don't count on getting a seat at the sushi bar. ♦ Japanese ♦ M-F lunch and dinner; Sa dinner. Reservations required. 38 E 51st St (between Park and Madison Aves). 755.1780

TSE YANG RESTAURANT

32 Tse Yang ★★$$$ Like the original Tse Yang in Paris, this stateside outpost offers outstanding Beijing cuisine and European-style service in a stunning setting of black mirrors, rich wood paneling, and hammered copper and brass appointments. Try the crab-leg salad, tea-smoked salmon, hot-and-sour soup, orange beef (served cold), and pickled cabbage. For dessert have the caramelized apples for two. There's also an extensive French wine list. ♦ Chinese/French ♦ Daily lunch and dinner. Reservations required; jacket required. 34 E 51st St (between Park and Madison Aves). 688.5447

● DOLCE ●

33 Dolce ★$$$ The lighting in this apricot-colored dining room is so vivid it might well be a stage set. Come here for decent pastas, including chicken, spinach, and artichoke ravioli with tomato-garlic sauce, and penne *bolognese*; simple pizzas; and such fish dishes as pan-seared salmon with lemon-caper crust. ♦ Italian ♦ M-F lunch and dinner; Sa dinner. Reservations recommended. 60 E 49th St (between Park and Madison Aves). 692.9292 &

34 Inagiku Japanese Restaurant ★★$$$$ When Emperor Hirohito stayed at the **Waldorf-Astoria Hotel,** he felt right at home in the hostelry's Japanese restaurant. The menu features sushi, sashimi, tempura, and teriyaki in a setting that would be considered among the nicest and plushest in Tokyo—gold lamé, black lacquer, and rich red velvet. The sushi is top quality—particularly the roe and yellowtail, but if your mood dictates turf over surf, there is also excellent ishiyaki steak, filet mignon seared on a hot stone, and *shabu shabu* (thin slices of beef cooked in a soy broth). ♦ Japanese ♦ M-F lunch and dinner; Sa-Su dinner. Reservations required; jacket required. 111 E 49th St (between Park and Lexington Aves). 355.0440

34 **Peacock Alley** ★★$$$$ The name comes from an old nickname given to the walkway between the **Waldorf** and **Astoria Hotels** (then neighboring on Fifth Avenue). It was used as a shortcut by party-hopping ladies dressed in their finery. Despite the glamourous name, until recently the place had been nothing more than a mediocre dining room for guests of the **Waldorf-Astoria** (merged and rebuilt on Park Avenue in 1931). However, with Gascony-born chef Laurent Manrique in the kitchen, the restaurant has become a destination in its own right. The elegant and subdued room with dark wood paneling, large mirrors, murals depicting peacocks, and a Steinway piano that belonged to the late Cole Porter provides a subtle environment for Manrique's assertively flavored food; don't miss the assortment of foie gras, silky duck ravioli with celery root and aged parmesan sauce, lobster Napoleon with artichokes, stuffed braised river trout with lemon confit and black olives (order it without salt), poached lobster, and the beef combination—hanger steak, oxtail, and black Angus sirloin. For dessert, try the chocolate fondant or citrus tart. The wine list features a wide range of good French and American wines at a variety of price levels. ♦ French ♦ M-F breakfast, lunch, afternoon tea, and dinner; Sa afternoon tea and dinner; Su brunch. Reservations recommended. 301 Park Ave (between E 49th and E 50th Sts). 872.4895

35 **Chiam** ★$$$ This sleek, elegant Chinese restaurant—a black-and-white color scheme with modern high-back black chairs—has a hit-and-miss menu. Mixed dumplings, Mongolian chicken, and crispy orange beef are standouts; others, such as Grand Marnier prawns, tend to be too sweet. The extensive and well-priced wine list is a plus not often found in a Chinese restaurant. ♦ Chinese ♦ M-F lunch and dinner; Sa-Su dim-sum brunch and dinner. Reservations recommended. 160 E 48th St (between Third and Lexington Aves). 371.2323 &

36 **Tatou** $$$ Opulent and slightly decadent-looking, this 1930s opera house sports lamps attached to Mephistophelian heads, a giant chandelier that looks borrowed from the set of *Phantom of the Opera,* statues and paintings of cherubs, and faux-antique windows set against yellow brocade walls. A band performs nightly on the stage where Edith Piaf and Judy Garland once sang. If only the food were as captivating as the setting. After Scott Cohen left for the **Stanhope,** Gadi Weinreich took over in the kitchen; thus far the results are tentative at best and misguided at worst. Stick to simpler dishes—parfait of tuna and salmon *tartare* with Osetra and salmon caviar, tea-smoked chicken salad, linguine with grilled portobello mushrooms, and grilled salmon steak with ginger and soy butter sauce. For dessert, again keep it simple—apple tart, crème brûlée, or the chocolate marquise that's shaped like a piano. ♦ International ♦ M-F lunch and dinner; Sa dinner. Reservations recommended 151 E 50th St (between Third and Lexington Aves). 753.1144

37 **Smith & Wollensky** ★★$$$ Young corporate types favor this meat palace above all others. The decor is dramatic—black lacquered chairs, Chinese-lantern–style lights and gargoyles perched on the sides of the banquettes—and the upstairs dining room has three skylights. The steaks and prime rib are crowd pleasers, and such basic desserts as Austrian strudel don't disappoint either. The restaurant boasts an extraordinary American wine list. ♦ American ♦ M-F lunch and dinner; Sa-Su dinner. Reservations required. 797 Third Ave (at E 49th St). 753.1530

37 **Wollensky's Grill** ★★$$ More casual and less expensive than **Smith & Wollensky** (see above), this place offers many of the same steaks, along with sensational burgers, grilled chicken, lobster, salads, and sandwiches. Dine al fresco when the weather turns warm. The same terrific wines available next door are also served here. ♦ American ♦ Daily lunch, dinner, and late-night meals. Reservations recommended. 205 E 49th St (between Second and Third Aves). 753.0444

38 **Chin Chin** ★★$$$ Chinese cuisine takes an innovative turn in this handsome, sophisticated restaurant with beige walls and recessed lighting. Try the country-style chicken with spinach, crispy sea bass, steamed salmon with black-bean sauce, or sautéed leg of lamb with leeks. ♦ Cantonese ♦ Daily lunch and dinner. 216 E 49th St (between Second and Third Aves). 888.4555

39 **Lutèce** ★★★$$$$ For over thirty years, Andre Soltner's elegant bastion of Alsatian cooking had been tops on every critic's list of special French restaurants, so loyalists were stunned when Soltner sold the restaurant in 1994 to the Ark Corporation and left the following spring. But new chef Eberhard Mueller is committed to retaining some of Soltner's traditions—the restaurant's famous onion tart, beef Wellington, roasted whole duck, rack of lamb, and soufflés, for example—while gently transforming the rest. Seafood will be emphasized on the lighter, seasonal menu—red snapper *tartare* cured in Riesling, crabmeat and potato salad with truffle vinaigrette, and black bass with leek coulis and black squid ink noodles will be among the offerings. Land-based dishes will include grilled pigeon with fresh morels and asparagus, and duck with a pepper crust. Desert selections—sautéed bananas in phyllo dough with banana cashew ice cream with passion fruit sauce and rhubarb pie among them—sound hard to resist. At press time, the wine list was also being updated.♦ French ♦ M, Sa dinner; Tu-F lunch and dinner. Reservations required. 249 E 50th St (between Second and Third Aves). 752.2225

40 Zarela ★★$$ One of the city's top Mexican chefs, Zarela Martinez runs one of the best places for regional Mexican cuisine in the city. The place, decorated with antique Mexican masks, colorful paper cutouts, and very bright fabrics, maintains an ongoing party atmosphere. Don't miss the fresh margaritas and Zarela's famous red snapper hash. Also try the chicken enchiladas with pumpkinseed sauce; roast marinated pork with a salsa of tomato, onion, and chipotle chilies; and grilled smoked salmon with chipotle mayonnaise and cucumber relish. ♦ Mexican ♦ M-F lunch and dinner; Sa-Su dinner. Reservations required. 953 Second Ave (between E 50th and E 51st Sts). 644.6740

41 Zephyr Grill ★$$ Mauve and mahogany, this attractive restaurant is named for the stylish passenger trains of the 1930s—hence the train designs on the etched-glass panels. The menu is basic American fare jazzed up with international influences, and offers a special selection of "heart-healthy" meals. Try the sautéed Maryland crab cakes, artichoke-and-ricotta ravioli, and Fort Bombay shrimp with spicy red curry. Top the meal off with apple-walnut pie. ♦ American/Continental ♦ M-Sa breakfast, lunch, and dinner; Su brunch and dinner. 1 Mitchell Pl (near First Ave and E 49th St). 223.4200

42 Wylie's ★$$ Rib fans don't often agree, so it's not surprising that some call this the best and others call it the worst rib joint in town. The former group must be ahead, because it's always crowded with a satiated-looking crowd of happy habitués. Specialties include juicy beef or pork ribs, or moist barbecued chicken with a side of onion rings, which call out for the restaurant's tasty hallmark dipping sauce. ♦ Barbecue/Ribs ♦ Daily lunch, dinner, and late-night meals. 891 First Ave (between E 50th and E 51st Sts). 751.0700

43 Pisacane Midtown This basic fish store is a favorite with locals and nearby restaurants for the very fresh food from the sea, specifically salmon, swordfish, and tuna steaks sliced to order. Cans of caviar are also on sale, as are a few prepared foods, such as clam chowder and clam sauces, but stick to the fish. ♦ M-Sa. 940 First Ave (between E 51st and E 52nd Sts). 355.1850

44 Le Perigord ★★★$$$ A favorite haunt of UN ambassadors, this formal but cozy French restaurant has been around for about 30 years and may seem, in contrast to newer places, somewhat dated. But the room, with its pink banquettes, is still pretty, and owner George Briguet is a charming host. For his part, chef Antoine Bouterin updates French classics with style. Try the foie gras in apple-and-truffle sauce; chateaubriand; frog's legs; herb-stuffed quail with truffle sauce; lamb chops with eggplant, tomatoes, and olives (a dish from Bouterin's native Provence); and such fish dishes as loup (flown in from Europe). Save room for one of the extraordinary soufflés. ♦ French ♦ M-F lunch and dinner; Sa-Su dinner. Reservations required; jacket and tie required. 405 E 52nd St (at First Ave). 755.6244

45 Billy's ★$$ For over a century, this wood-paneled dining room with its intricate, history-laden mahogany bar and photographs of old New York has been serving plain, reliable food to the neighborhood. Try the roast leg of lamb with mashed potatoes and peas, the juicy prime rib, shepherd's pie, or London broil with mushroom gravy. ♦ American ♦ Daily lunch and dinner. 948 First Ave (at E 52nd St). 355.8920 &

46 Mayfair ★$ Another favorite neighborhood hangout, this dark, clubby place with hunter-green walls and wooden booths offers simple fare—burgers and salads—along with slightly more elaborate entrées, including stuffed, baked cornish hen; herb-roasted chicken; and corned beef and cabbage. ♦ American ♦ Daily lunch and dinner. 964 First Ave (at E 53rd St). 421.6216

47 Metropolitan Cafe ★$$ A huge menu geared to please everyone in the family—kids included—is offered at this large, airy space with exposed-brick walls, light wood, and columns. Try Metro meat loaf, wok-charred ahi, grilled young chicken (whole), roasted Thai curried-chicken salad with peanut dressing, and for lighter appetites, the applewood-smoked chicken sandwich. ♦ American ♦ M-F lunch and dinner; Sa-Su brunch and dinner. 959 First Ave (between E 52nd and E 53rd Sts). 759.5600

47 Parnell's ★$ A comfortable drop-in spot, this is good place for basic American-Irish pub food. There are good soups, sandwiches, salads, such as chicken and Caesar, top-notch chicken potpie, and roast chicken. Don't miss the Irish soda bread. ♦ American/Irish ♦ M-F lunch and dinner; Sa-Su brunch and dinner. 350 E 53rd St (at First Ave). 753.1761

48 Jubilee ★$$ This tiny sliver of a bistro with a charming blue painted storefront and rustic breakfront and tables serves traditional and imaginative French specialties, including fish soup, bouillabaisse, mussels in a curry broth, lamb shank with cumin sauce, ravioli stuffed with duck confit, and a buttery apple tart. There are also dishes that the French don't usually lay claim to, such as beef carpaccio and an Americanized brunch on weekends. ♦ French ♦ M-F lunch and dinner; Sa-Su brunch and dinner. Reservations recommended. 347 E 54th St (between First and Second Aves). 888.3569

49 La Mangeoire ★★$$$ The atmosphere of this warm, rustic Provençal spot is so inviting that it would be worth coming to even if the food were less flavorful. The stucco walls are enlivened with pottery, dried flowers, pots of fresh flowers, and straw hanging from the ceiling. The food, with piquant spices and sunny flavors, includes *pissaladière* (an onion anchovy, and olive tart); penne with tomato, olive puree, and basil sauce; thyme-crusted rabbit; and beef daube with Swiss-chard ravioli. ♦ French ♦ M-F lunch and dinner; Sa-Su dinner. Reservations recommended. 1008 Second Ave (between E 53rd and E 54th Sts). 759.7086

50 Fu's ★★$$$ Decorated in a contemporary style in shades of gray, pink, and burgundy, this is a popular spot for gourmet Chinese food; the kitchen offers a variety of Hunan, Mandarin, Szechuan, and Cantonese specialties Order the Grand Marnier shrimp (it's not on the menu but regulars know to ask for it), lemon chicken, crispy orange beef, or panfried flounder. A faithful and high-powered clientele was cultivated and pampered by former hostess Gloria Chu and they miss her, which is why the restaurant still gets her to come back for special occasions. ♦ Chinese ♦ Daily lunch and dinner. Reservations recommended 972 Second Ave (between E 51st and E 52nd Sts). 517.9670

51 Aria ★★$$ This romantic dining room with marbled walls, subdued lighting, brocade banquettes, and strains of classical music in the background, is a soothing place to enjoy a meal. Should you become too lulled, the zesty food arrives like a wake-up call; try the octopus salad, asparagus with roast-pepper vinaigrette, pumpkin ravioli, yellowfin tuna with sun-dried tomatoes, and herb-crusted free-range chicken. There's also a good early prix-fixe dinner. ♦ American/Italian ♦ M-F lunch and dinner; Sa-Su dinner. Reservations recommended. 253 E 52nd St (at Second Ave). 888.1410

52 Il Nido ★★$$$$ Excellent, if pricey, Italian food is served in this rustic dining room with timber beams and mirrors that are made to look like farmhouse windows. Try *malfatti* (irregularly shaped pasta squares filled with spinach and cheese), linguine *alla amatrician* (in tomato sauce with onions and prosciutto) tortellini with four cheeses, baked red snapper with clams, and braised chicken in a white-wine sauce with mushrooms and tomato. Top the meal off with the delicious apple tart. ♦ Italian ♦ M-F lunch and dinner; Sa dinner. Reservations required; jacket and tie required 251 E 53rd St (between Second and Third Aves). 753.8450

53 Solera ★★$$ Tapas and other Spanish delicacies top the list in this stylishly redesigned town house. The soft lighting and colorful tiling is the ideal stage for chef/owner Dominick Cerrone's food and wine. Specialties include empanadas (meat patties), grilled shrimp with garlic, pheasant and guinea hen terrine with morels, grilled salmon over vegetable purée with stuffed eggplant, roasted duck breast with lemon, and spiced peach and rhubarb compote. ♦ Spanish ♦ M-F lunch and dinner; Sa dinner. Reservations recommended. 216 E 53rd St (between Second and Third Aves). 644.1166

53 Maple Garden Duck House ★$$ Unlike at many places where it's necessary to order Peking duck in advance, here you can satisfy a spontaneous craving for this delectable dish. The duck is carved at tableside, then rolled in a rice pancake with *hoisin* sauce, scallions, and cucumbers. Take a hungry friend along—the portion is a whole duck. ♦ Chinese ♦ Daily lunch and dinner. Reservations required. 236 E 53rd St (between Second and Third Aves). 759.8260

54 Fisher & Levy Caterers Chip Fisher (of **Mr. Chips** Upper East Side ice-cream parlor fame) and Doug Levy are the owners of this decidedly upscale food store that also does a huge catering and delivery business. For breakfast, try the homemade doughnuts and **Petrossian** smoked-salmon platters; for lunch, order a California-style pizza, grilled chicken with grilled vegetables on focaccia, or one of the classiest chef salads around—with filet mignon, Black Forest ham, hickory-smoked turkey, and parmesan dressing. ♦ M-F. 875 Third Ave (at E 53rd St), Concourse level. 832.3880

55 Lipstick Cafe ★★$ In his "spare time," Jean-Georges Vongerichten (of **JoJo** and **Vong**) throws a tasty bone to hungry Midtown workers on a dining budget. Delicious homemade soups, salads, and sandwiches are served to go or stay. The baked goods are a real treat and include toasted-almond brioche, ricotta-cheese danish, and upside-down cranberry cake. ♦ American ♦ M-F breakfast and lunch. 885 Third Ave (at E 54th St). 486.8664 ♿

56 Vong ★★★$$$ Superchef Jean-Georges Vongerichten (of **JoJo** on the East Side and **Lipstick Cafe**) weighs in with his wonderful interpretation of Thai/French cuisine in an elegant Eastern-influenced space designed by architect David Rockwell. The menu reflects the two years Vongerichten spent in Bangkok, and is as healthful as the fare at **JoJo.** Try sautéed duck foie gras with ginger sauce and mango, raw tuna, and vegetables in rice paper with dipping sauce; lobster with Thai herbs; roasted baby chicken marinated with lemongrass and herbs; and black bass with wok-fried cabbage, water chestnuts, and hot chilies. ♦ Thai/French ♦ M-F lunch and dinner; Sa dinner. 200 E 54th St (at Third Ave). 486.9592

Nyborg Nelson

57 Nyborg-Nelson ★★$ The Scandinavian specialties served at this restaurant/takeout shop in the **Citicorp Center** include gravlax, marinated herring, stuffed cabbage, and such sandwiches as Black Forest ham and brie, which the office workers from upstairs often take out. Table service is also available within the bright space, enlivened with hanging plants, mirrors, and a view onto 53rd Street. Popular dishes include Swedish meatballs and beef à la Lindstrom (ground beef with capers and beef served with gravy, dill potatoes, and pickled beets). The homemade Swedish rye bread is a big favorite too. The restaurant has a full bar including aquavit, and although the selection of wines is modest, the beers offered include some you don't see everywhere, such as Pripps Lager (imported from Sweden) and Elephant (imported from Denmark). ♦ Scandinavian ♦ M-Sa lunch and early dinner. 153 E 53rd St (between Third and Lexington Aves), Lobby level. 223.0700

The Brasserie—open round-the-clock since 1959—has only once locked its front door.

Spa cuisine was created at The Four Seasons in 1983 when chef Seppi Renggli, in conjunction with Dr. Myron Winnick of Columbia University's College of Physicians and Surgeons, came up with the concept of delicious, low-calorie, low-fat cuisine. It's still served today at this lavish restaurant.

58 Nippon ★★$$$$ One of the first restaurants to introduce sushi and sashimi to New Yorkers, this gracious place maintains its overall high quality and continues to offer dishes unfamiliar to Western palates—*usuzukuri* (marinated fluke in very thin slices) and *hanazukuri* (marinated raw beef). There are also excellent versions of more familiar dishes, such as *shabu shabu* (beef and vegetables cooked at the table in a hot pot of soy broth) and tempura. ♦ Japanese ♦ M-F lunch and dinner; Sa dinner. Reservations recommended. 155 E 52nd St (between Third and Lexington Aves). 758.0226

59 Bridge Kitchenware Corp. Pros like Craig Claiborne and Julia Child pick up their copper pots, knife sets, and pastry tubes at this exceptional store, which stocks every utensil you could possibly need, no matter how obscure. Kitchen novices are welcome here too; the knowledgeable staff is very patient. ♦ M-Sa. 214 E 52nd St (between Second and Third Aves). 688.4220

60 The Four Seasons ★★★★$$$$ Two dining rooms coexist here at one of New York's hottest eating places. **The Bar Room Grill** is power central at midday, when the top echelon of New York's publishing world gathers to exchange notes and gossip. Featured in this casual space later in the day is the new "Grill at Night," offering one of the city's true fine-dining bargains—an under-$40 three-course meal, including coffee. The **Pool Room** next door, a more formal spot, has been going strong since 1958 and features such dishes as oxtail ravioli with sage, pumpkin bisque with cinnamon, carpaccio of tuna and salmon with ginger, foie gras with figs, sea bass in an herb crust. Be sure to save room for the luscious chocolate velvet cake. Sublime service and innovative continental cuisine are the hallmarks of this institution. ♦ Continental ♦ M-F lunch and dinner; Sa dinner. Reservations required; jacket and tie required. 99 E 52nd St (between Park and Lexington Aves). 754.9494

[handwritten: $190 Sept 30 1995 George & Inn]

61 Brasserie ★$$$ One of the first restaurants to serve New York's round-the-clock needs, this place is still going strong. The menu has changed slightly over the years, but remains basic, hearty French fare—French onion soup, Caesar's salad, snails in garlic-herb butter, crab cakes, vegetable terrine, *choucroute* (sauerkraut cooked with goose fat, onions, juniper berries, and white wine), and duck confit with stewed beans and tomatoes. ♦ American/French ♦ Daily 24 hours. Reservations recommended. 100 E 53rd St (between Lexington and Park Aves). 751.4840

62 Pasqua ★$ In the atrium of the Park Avenue Plaza Building, this cafe is something of an oasis within workaday Midtown, where a pianist serenades lunchtime patrons, and a waterfall gently rushes. In addition to a soothing environment, this place offers dependably good croissants and muffins in the morning, and in the afternoon such sandwiches as roast beef with horseradish sauce and sun-dried cherries. Salads, including a delicious Caesar's and a savory spinach, are enough to satisfy the hungriest eater. The chain's signature coffee is good for a pick-me-up any time. ♦ Cafe ♦ M-F breakfast, lunch, and afternoon snacks. 55 E 53rd St (between Park and Madison Aves). 750.7140 ₺. Also at: Numerous locations throughout the city

63 Fresco ★★$$ This family affair owned by Marion Scotto and her children Anthony Jr., Elaina, and Rosanna (the local newscaster) is an elegant and cheery restaurant. Colors abound, on the ocher walls, in the complex floral displays, bold paintings by SoHo artist and rich flavors in chef Vincent Scotto's (no relation) food. Try spaghettini with clams, garlic, basil, and roasted tomatoes; baked penne with pancetta (Italian unsmoked bacon), parmesan, and cream; ravioli stuffed with duck, portobello mushrooms, and sage; lemon thyme baby rack of lamb; and grilled veal chop. Desserts are irresistible—either the lemon tartlet or cinnamon ice-cream sandwich would make the perfect ending for the meal. ♦ Italian ♦ M-F lunch and dinner; Sa dinner. Reservations recommended. 34 E 52nd St (between Park and Madison Aves). 935.3434 ₺

64 Seryna ★★$$$ Avoid the frenzied crowds at lunch and visit this handsome restaurant for dinner, when it becomes sedate and you can really enjoy the excellent steaks cooked on a hot stone at your table and served with garlic soy and chili sauces. There's also excellent *shabu shabu*, and an array of fresh fish, including poached salmon, stuffed Dover sole, and eel teriyaki. The sushi and sashimi are also very fresh. ♦ Japanese ♦ M-F lunch and dinner; Sa dinner. Reservations recommended. 11 E 53rd St (between Madison and Fifth Aves). 980.9393

LA GRENOUILLE

65 La Grenouille ★★$$$$ The annual budget for flowers here is close to $100,000, and the fresh daily arrangments show it. Mirrors sparkle everywhere, and the lighting is nearly perfect, making the "beautiful people" who frequent this place look even more beautiful (and of course they're the fortunates who get attention from the wait staff). There are wonderful traditional dishes on the menu such as Dover sole, rack of lamb, cheese soufflé, and grilled turbot with beurre blanc, but be prepared to spend big time if you want a good wine to go with them. For predictable, formal elegance, you can't go wrong at this restaurant. ♦ French ♦ Tu-Sa lunch and dinner. Reservations required; jacket and tie required. 3 E 52nd St (at Fifth Ave). 752.1495

66 Top of the Sixes $$$$ Only out-of-towners who don't know any better come here for dinner. But it's a great place for a frozen strawberry daiquiri and a heart-stopping sunset or nighttime view of Midtown in all its illuminated glory—39 floors above it all. ♦ New American ♦ M-Sa lunch and dinner. 666 Fifth Ave (between 52nd and 53rd Sts). 757.6662

67 21 Club ★★$$$$ The iron fence and jockeys out front recall the days when the building housing today's restaurant was a private mansion. Like many of the fine houses that once lined 52nd Street, however, this place harbored a speakeasy during the 1920s. This is the lone survivor, and its cramped and noisy barroom/dining room is as active as ever. Decorated with hanging airplanes, trucks, and other business artifacts, the "club" is strictly for the expense-account crowd. Although traditionalists will want to try the lunch of champions—the "21" burger or chicken hash—the food has gotten more inventive since Michael Lomonaco took over the kitchen in 1989. Innovations include quail salad with truffle oil, crab cakes with horseradish cream, black bean soup, creamy polenta with wild-mushroom pan roast, peppered seared tuna with seared tomatoes, and California squab with truffled risotto. The dessert tasting plate is a fine way to end the meal. The wine list represents a cellar of 40,000 bottles, with excellent choices at all price levels. This was one of Jackie O's favorite lunch spots when she was an editor at Doubleday. ♦ Continental ♦ M-Sa lunch and dinner. Reservations required; jacket and tie required. 21 W 52nd St (between Fifth and Sixth Aves). 582.7200

68 Bombay Palace ★$$ The crisp and light Indian breads, such as the nan stuffed with cashew nuts and dried fruits, are delightful, the curries mild, and the tandoori chicken properly moist and tender at this pleasant, subtly lit Indian restaurant with friendly service. Try the lamb *nilgiri* (in mint and coriander sauce), followed by mango ice cream or Indian rice pudding—subtly flavored with rosewater—for dessert. ♦ Indian

♦ Daily lunch and dinner. 30 W 52nd St (between Fifth and Sixth Aves). 541.7777

68 Cesarina ★$$$ Owned and run by the proprietors of Italy's legendary Villa d'Este Hotel, this airy, elegant restaurant has an efficient and friendly staff eager to make suggestions about the carefully prepared risottos or pastas. The veal cutlet Milanese and osso buco are as delicious as the simple fish specialties that change depending on the market's catch of the day. This is a popular lunch spot for Midtown executives, but it becomes less harried and quieter in the evening—perfect for a pre-theater dinner. ♦ Northern Italian ♦ M-F lunch and dinner. Reservations recommended for lunch. 36 W 52nd St (between Fifth and Sixth Aves). 582.6900

69 China Grill ★★$$$ Although this place is not related to Wolfgang Puck's Santa Monica landmark, Chinois on Main, the cuisine—an amalgam of Asian, French, and California influences—is similar. However, the owners here—Chinois expatriates—can lay claim to the real thing. The modern, airy space is fairly dramatic, with dark gleaming walls and light fixtures that resemble flying saucers hovering overhead. The food is inventive and delicious; try grilled salmon on a bed of Asian greens, grilled rosemary scallops atop beet risotto, Australian lamb with a quinoa salad and mandarin orange sauce, or crispy duck with caramelized black-vinegar sauce. Dishes are served family style, making it fun to share. ♦ Asian ♦ M-F lunch and dinner; Sa-Su dinner. Reservations required. 52 West 53rd St (between Fifth and Sixth Aves). 333.7788 &

70 Sette MoMA ★$$$ Owners of the successful Upper East Side's **Sette Mezzo** and **Vico** opened this restaurant inside the **Museum of Modern Art (MoMA)** in 1993. The dining room is cool and contemporary, fitted with art from the museum's permanent collection, and in nice weather tables are set on the outdoor terrace, which has a lovely view of the sculpture garden. Best bets include the simple grilled vegetable plate, sautéed loin of lamb with juniper berries, or ravioli filled with goat cheese and eggplant. During museum hours, enter through the museum; after 5PM use the entrance on W 54th Street. ♦ Italian ♦ M dinner; Tu, Th-Sa lunch and dinner; W, Su lunch. Reservations recommended. 11 W 53rd St (between Fifth and Sixth Aves). 708.9710 &

71 Ciao Europa ★★$$$ The elaborate floor-to-ceiling murals, depicting a queen receiving her subjects, resemble tapestries hung on palace walls and give this two-level dining room a grand sweep. The food is pretty grand as well, particularly the pastas; try the *malfatti del ghiottone* (moon-shaped pasta filled with ricotta, spinach, and tomato). The homemade mozzarella offered as an antipasto is delicate and sweet and the osso buco is richly flavored and tender enough to cut with a fork. In addition to the Italian fare always offered, each week the menu also features a different continental cuisine, in the spirit of a united Europe, no doubt. ◆ Italian ◆ Daily lunch and dinner. Reservations recommended. 63 W 54th St (between Fifth and Sixth Aves). 247.1200

72 Allegria ★$$ If the weather allows outdoor dining and you stick to the simpler dishes—there are a variety of good pizzas and pastas—you're more than likely to experience "happiness," as this popular Italian restaurant's name translates. Brightly tiled and painted with idyllic Italian countryside scenes and celebrations, this trattoria offers a basic Mediterranean menu: rigatoni with eggplant, pasta with seafood, and a number of chicken dishes that include a grilled version topped with artichokes and fresh tomatoes. ◆ Italian ◆ Daily lunch and dinner. 66 W 55th St (between Fifth and Sixth Aves). 956.7755 &

72 La Côte Basque ★★★★$$$$ Considered by many to be one of the top restaurants in New York, this place was founded by Henri Soule and is now the domain of chef/owner Jean Jacques Rachou, whose classic French cooking is nothing short of masterful. The presentation of lobster terrine (a combination of shellfish, green beans, tomato, shredded carrots, and *celerie rémoulade*—a mustard-flavored mayonnaise-type sauce with shredded celery root) is stunning and sure to please. Also try stuffed quail with a pheasant and wild-mushroom salad, veal medaillons in Madeira sauce, cassoulet, and chocolate mousse cake. The wine list is one of New York's most extensive. The restaurant recently moved here from the other side of Fifth Avenue, and Rachou brought with him a beloved vestige from the ultra-elegant dining room—the *St. Jean de Luz at La Côte Basque* mural. ◆ French ◆ M-F lunch and dinner; Sa dinner. Reservations required; jacket and tie required. 60 W 55 St (between Fifth and Sixth Aves). 688.6525

72 J.P. French Bakery Croissant lovers take note: This shop may have the best croissants in town, as well as a panoply of excellent French breads—from *ficelle* (a thin baguette) to large, round loaves—all baked on the premises. The tarts and cakes are also standouts, including the buttery apple and apricot tarts and the rich chocolate mousse ganache cake. ◆ Daily. 54 W 55th St (between Fifth and Sixth Aves). 765.7575

72 La Bonne Soupe ★$ Soups, omelettes, a variety of chopped beef dishes, and daily provincial French specials such as filet au poivre are good at this popular longstanding bistro. For a retro experience, have a fondue. ◆ French ◆ Daily lunch and dinner. 48 W 55th St (between Fifth and Sixth Aves). 586.7650

73 Tuscany This take-out shop with a few tables in front specializes in light, healthy pastas, salads, and sandwiches. Try angel-hair pasta with fresh tomato and basil sauce; penne with eggplant sauce; grilled chicken with portobello mushrooms on a bed of mesclun; or mozzarella with oven-roasted peppers, tomato, and basil on a baguette with olive oil and balsamic vinegar. ◆ M-F. 61 E 55th St (between Fifth and Sixth Aves). 582.4421 &

73 Giovanni ★$$$ Giovanni Francescotti is the owner and Giovanni Pinato the chef of this restaurant with an imaginative decor. Divided into several separate environments, it includes the **Pavilion Room,** with a painted canopy and trompe l'oeil paintings of gardens; the **Card Room,** with murals of Italian card games, and the **Club Room,** with comfy furniture intended for cigar fanciers. The food is fairly straightforward, a celebration of Italy's northeast regions. Try carpaccio, spinach *tagliolini* (thin noodles) with tomato and basil, or roast rack of lamb with eggplant blini. Finish the meal with amaretto crème brûlée or one of the tarts. ◆ Northern Italian ◆ Daily lunch and dinner. Reservations recommended. 47 W 55th St (between Fifth and Sixth Aves). 262.2828 &

73 La Fondue $ Swiss chocolate and cheese fondues, steaks, seafood, and such pasta dishes as spinach cannelloni are featured here along with chocolate mousse and other familiar desserts. All are served in the warm, casual atmosphere of a European cellar. ◆ Swiss ◆ Daily lunch, dinner, and late-night meals. 43 W 55th St (between Fifth and Sixth Aves). 581.0820 &

73 Menchanko-tei ★$ Japanese businessmen frequent this cozy noodle emporium for hearty soups filled with a variety of ingredients. As authentic a noodle shop as can be found in Midtown, this place is great to duck into for a steamy broth, especially after a winter afternoon visit to the nearby Museum of Modern Art. ◆ Japanese ◆ M lunch, dinner, and late-night meals; Tu-Su breakfast, lunch, dinner, and late-night meals. 39 W 55th St (between Fifth and Sixth Aves). 247.1585 X

73 La Caravelle ★★★$$$$ Opened since 1960, this dining spot is considered one of the city's great French restaurants, although in recent years it hasn't really received the attention it deserves. Thanks to the talent of chef Tadashi Ono, classic French cuisine gets a modern spin here without losing a bit of European finesse. Specialties include "French lasagna" (shrimps and scallops tucked inside thin layers of pasta), crispy duck with cranberries, rack of lamb in a clay crust with wild mushrooms, grilled Dover sole with mustard sauce, medaillons of poached lobster, and for dessert, a pyramid of chocolate. The extensive French wine list includes some great bottles at predictably steep prices. The recently refurbished room, with pink banquettes and murals of Paris, is gracious, subdued, and quiet—even when it's packed. Owners Rita and Andre Jammet also happen to be among the friendliest and most charming hosts in New York. ♦ French ♦ M-F lunch and dinner; Sa dinner. Reservations required; jacket and tie required. 33 W 55th St (between Fifth and Sixth Aves). 586.4252 &

74 Harley Davidson Cafe ★$$ Welcome to Harleywood. First there was the **Hard Rock Cafe,** then **Planet Hollywood,** now this highly hyped newcomer—with a $3-million-plus price tag—has roared into town. Located in the formerly staid American Savings Bank building, the cafe seats up to 300 (in nice weather, 100 more can be accommodated in what is Midtown's largest outdoor seating area). Inside, Harleys dangle from the ceiling in an atmosphere that's somewhere between Mardi Gras and mayhem. The menu features "great American road food," which includes such items as Carolina pulled pork, blackened chicken, burgers, sandwiches, and Mississippi mud pie. ♦ American ♦ Daily lunch, dinner, and late-night meals. 1370 Sixth Ave (at W 56th St). 245.6000 &

75 L'Ermitage ★★$$ Husband and wife Muscovites Andrei and Elena Fedorova opened the first privately owned restaurant in the Russian capital, and then followed up with another venture here in 1994. The cream-colored walls are hung with 19th-century Russian paintings, the lighting is subdued, and the menu reflects both the French and Russian nationals in the kitchen. Don't miss *pelmeni* (nicely spiced Siberian meat dumplings served with just a touch of sour cream), blini with caviar, and marinated lamb. Finish the meal off with a warm fruit tart, particularly if it's plum. ♦ Russian/French ♦ M-F lunch and dinner; Sa dinner. Reservations recommended. 40 West 56th St (between Fifth and Sixth Aves). 581.0777 &

75 Darbar Indian Restaurant ★★★$$$ This is easily one of the best and loveliest Indian dining spots in town. The decor is authentic and beautiful—full of tasteful tapestries and brass appointments; the fabric-covered walls are decorated with copper hangings. Downstairs are several quiet little corner tables, separated by screens that offer complete privacy. The staff is friendly and helpful, and the kitchen thoroughly professional. To start, try the delightful *pakoras* (fried spinach fritters) and move on to *josh vindaloo* (lamb stew cooked with potatoes in a hot curry sauce) or *murgh tikka masala* (chicken in a mild, creamy tomato sauce). ♦ Indian ♦ M-F lunch and dinner; Sa-Su dinner. Reservations recommended. 44 W 56th St (between Fifth and Sixth Aves). 432.7227

76 Caffè del Corso ★$ A simple cafe with white tiles and a painting of an Italian piazza, this is a good place to stop for sandwiches (try the smoked mozzarella, roasted peppers, basil, capers, and olive oil variety), salads (the Mediterranean chicken salad is a winner), poached chicken with herbs and tomatoes in balsamic vinaigrette, and such pastas as rigatoni with grilled eggplant in tomato sauce. ♦ Cafe ♦ M-Sa breakfast, lunch, and early dinner. 19 W 55th St (between Fifth and Sixth Aves). 957.1500

77 Michael's ★★$$ Sleek and airy, this is a popular place with Midtown business types for healthy breakfasts and lunches. The sunny, spare setting is punctuated with an impressive collection of modern art, and the light menu features imaginative California-style cuisine. Michael's signature dish is warm grilled chicken on a bed of goat cheese, grilled peppers, red onions, vine-ripened tomatoes, and baby greens, covered in jalapeño-and-cilantro–seasoned olive oil. Among the other dishes worth trying are seafood risotto, Colorado lamb with a Cabernet and cassis demiglaze, and duck breast with orange slices. A fun dessert is the Heath Bar torte. Service, however, can be snooty and condescending to nonregulars. ♦ American/California ♦ M-F breakfast, lunch, and dinner; Sa dinner. 24 W 55th St (between Fifth and Sixth Aves). 767.0555

77 Lyn's Cafe ★$ A cut above the average (and affordable, to boot), this take-out shop/cafe specializes in soups, salads, sandwiches, and simple sweets. Try a bowl of sweet-potato soup or seafood bisque; five-grain salad with Tuscan white beans, black beans, and red and green lentils; a sandwich of grilled chicken pesto with melted mozzarella or the grilled eggplant, zucchini, and mozzarella on focaccia. ♦ Cafe ♦ M-Sa breakfast and lunch. 12 W 55th St (between Fifth and Sixth Aves). 397.2020

AQUAVIT

78 Aquavit ★★★$$$$ Although Nelson Rockefeller once lived in this town house, he probably wouldn't recognize the eight-story atrium, complete with birch trees and a copper waterfall, that is the main dining room of this lovely, modern restaurant. Since chef Jan Sendel, formerly the sous-chef at **Mesa Grill,** came, the food has been similarly transformed—previously dignified, it now has a definite zest. Try smoked salmon with wasabi crème fraîche and radish sprouts, salmon sashimi with lime and lemon juice and warm sesame oil, foie gras with apples and cabbage, spice-grilled salmon with caraway-scented artichoke broth, rare beef in beer and beef *jus,* and sweet mustard-glazed Arctic char. Be sure to save room for the rich chocolate cake or gingersnap ice-cream sandwich. There's a less elaborate, lower-priced à la carte menu available at the upstairs bar. Don't forget to try the liquor that gives this place its name— a vodkalike spirit often flavored with anise, caraway, fennel, or orange peel—which is typically served neat and very cold. ♦ Scandinavian ♦ M-F lunch and dinner; Sa dinner. Reservations recommended; jacket requested. 13 W 54th St (between Fifth and Sixth Aves). 307.7311

79 Adrienne ★$$$ Like the beautiful **Peninsula Hotel** in which it's located, this dining room is inspired by Belle Epoque style—elaborate mirrors and etched flower-petal lights. The food offered by chef Nicholas Rabalais is French with a mix of other European influences and more than just a pinch of creole flavors from his native Louisiana. Try the crawfish and foie gras with angel-hair vegetables (a thin julienne) and cinnamon-apple compote, pan-seared duck breast with rosemary chambord vinaigrette, and pepper tuna with oyster couscous and papaya-mango ragout. ♦ Continental ♦ M, Su lunch; Tu-Sa lunch and dinner. Reservations required; jacket and tie required. 700 Fifth Ave (at W 55th St). 247.2200

79 Penn-Top Bar and Terrace $ The beautiful view of the Manhattan skyline from this glass-enclosed bar at the top of the hotel can't be beat. There is an adequate buffet-style lunch, which can be eaten on the terrace during the warmer months. ♦ American ♦ M-Sa lunch. 700 Fifth Ave (at W 55th St), 23rd floor. 247.2200

80 Felissimo ★★$ A 1901 landmark town house is the setting for a fourth-floor tearoom in the elegant store of the same name. Providing an oasis of calm in frenzied Midtown, the beige walls, natural wood, and gentle New Age background music here make this an ideal place to linger—even over a long cup of tea. The 27 types of tea, including orange-ginger-mint and mango-Ceylon, are served in Japanese cast-iron pots and go nicely with homemade scones, particularly the spicy ginger heart-shaped variety. There are also pasta dishes, including bowties with chicken, red peppers, and broccoli in a sun-dried tomato–soy vinaigrette, and such sandwiches as Southwestern chicken with cilantro pesto on whole-wheat focaccia or filet mignon with apple-horseradish dressing on organic sourdough. A psychic reads tarot cards during weekday lunches for a small fee. ♦ American ♦ M-Sa breakfast, lunch, and afternoon tea. Reservations recommended. 10 W 56th St (between Fifth and Sixth Aves). 956.4438 ♿

81 Kiiroi Hana ★★$$ With its understated beige decor, this isn't one of the prettiest Japanese restaurants in town, but it does serve absolutely fresh, top-quality sushi at prices that are lower than its Midtown competitors. Good sake and excellent service also distinguish this place. The simple but carefully selected menu offers other dishes besides sushi, including bacon-wrapped filet mignon, *negimaki* (steak wrapped around scallions), salmon teriyaki, and noodle dishes. For an extra treat, sit at the sushi bar and watch the deft assembly behind the counter, but be prepared for a manic lunchtime scene as everyone arrives and scrambles for seats seemingly all at once. ♦ Japanese ♦ M-Sa lunch and dinner; Su dinner. Reservations recommended for dinner. 23 W 56th St (between Fifth and Sixth Aves). 582.7499

82 The Bistro ★$$$ This open bilevel dining room in the **Trump Tower** has marble floors and burgundy banquettes. The menu is mainly Northern Italian fare, but lighter, non-Italian dishes are also offered. Try the *frisée* (curly endive) salad with smoked breast of duck, lobster and avocado salad, gnocchi with meat sauce, spaghetti with shrimp and arugula, osso buco with saffron risotto, and jumbo shrimp in tomato-pesto sauce. Be sure to save room for the flourless chocolate soufflé cake, one of the fruit tarts, or blueberry bread pudding. ♦ Northern Italian ♦ Daily lunch. 725 Fifth Ave (between E 56th and E 57th Sts), Garden level. 832.1555 &

82 **The Cafe** ★$$ Near **Trump Tower**'s signature waterfall, this place features a changing menu of such pasta dishes as linguine with pesto and rigatoni with sweet sausage and tomato, homemade soups, and a variety of salads (try the tuna pasta variety) and sandwiches (smoked turkey is a winner). The same desserts available at **The Bistro** (see above) are also offered here, as both places are served by a common kitchen. ♦ Cafe ♦ Daily breakfast, lunch, and afternoon snacks. 725 Fifth Ave (between E 56th and E 57th Sts), Garden level. 754.4450 &

82 **Tiffany & Co.** Built in 1940, this store is so famous for quality and style that many of its well-designed wares have become classics: the all-purpose wineglass and Wedgewood china, to name just a couple. Given as gifts, these items are further enhanced by the cachet of the telltale light-blue box. In addition to table appointments, the store also offers a selection of jewelry, gems, stationery items, crystals, porcelains, clocks, and watches in all price ranges. Salespeople are friendly and helpful. The windows are worth going out of your way to see—especially at Christmas. ♦ M-Sa. 727 Fifth Ave (between E 56th and E 57th Sts). 755.8000

83 **Richart Design et Chocolat** Rich dark chocolate squares decorated with patterns in mocha and gold are the specialty at this 60-year-old French chocolate company. The designs are so unique—drawn with exquisite tiny details—that it's hard to know if you should eat them or frame them. Such artistry doesn't come cheap—the price per pound just might raise an eyebrow. Luckily for wallet and waistline, you can buy them by the piece. For an unusual taste, try one of the spicy chocolates with clove or bergamot fillings. Assortment packages, which come in

beautiful wood boxes, would make a knockout gift for the discriminating bonbon lover in your life. ♦ M-Sa. 7 E 55th St (between Madison and Fifth Aves). 371.9369 &

84 **Lespinasse** ★★★$$$$ This formal dining room in the **St. Regis** hotel brings forth images of Louis XVI grandeur, with pink satin chairs and gilt-framed oil paintings. As prepared by Gray Kunz, originator of East-West fusion, the food is another story. Each spunky bite is shaded with many different tastes—some brilliant, some less so. Try the sautéed foie gras with lentil salad, risotto with wild mushrooms, steamed black bass scented with kafir and bell pepper, roasted lobster ragout, or seared rack of lamb with eggplant tart. Eastern spices, such as tamarind, make reprise appearances in the desserts; less adventurous types can indulge in the delicious caramelized banana flambé. There is also a four-course vegetarian prix-fixe meal (menu changes seasonally), which includes dessert. The wine list offers a well-chosen selection in a variety of price ranges. The food has been known to be uneven, but if you're fortunate to be here on a good day, the experience will be wonderfully memorable. ♦ Fusion ♦ M-Sa breakfast, lunch, and dinner; Su breakfast. Reservations required; jacket required. 2 E 55th St (between Madison and Fifth Aves). 339.6719

85 **Takashimaya** In this quiet, beige-toned environment, 40 varieties of tea are sold along with a selection of teapots, and Bernachon chocolates which the store imports. ♦ M-Sa. 693 Fifth Ave (between E 54th and E 55th Sts). 350.0100 &

Within Takashimaya:

Tea Box Cafe ★$ This soothing beige cafe in the store's basement is the perfect place for escaping the bustle of Midtown. Try one of the 40 varieties of tea, including apricot, lemongrass, and *hoiji-cha* (a woodsmoked green tea), and a delicate sandwich—shrimp or cucumber on pressed rice, smoked salmon, or chicken with wasabi. As a sublime finish, try the French Bernachon chocolates. The "east-west" afternoon tea features Japanese tea and western sandwiches, cookies, and pastries. ♦ Japanese tearoom ♦ M-Sa lunch and afternoon tea. 693 Fifth Ave (between E 54th and E 55th Sts). 350.0100 &

86 **Bice** ★$$$ Bill Blass, Calvin Klein, and Oleg Cassini frequent this trendy Milanese trattoria, along with scads of European blondes. The long, curved white-marble bar, multilevel

A $1-million refurbishment of the kitchen at Lespinasse to make it more efficient and high-tech was recently undertaken. The space is now so beautiful that diners are invited to tour it between 3 and 3:30PM—as long as they call in advance to arrange it.

seating, bright lighting, and exquisite flower arrangements create a luxurious setting. The food can be a bit uneven, but among the more reliably good main courses are roast rack of veal with new potatoes, baby chicken, and such grilled fish dishes as salmon, swordfish, or sole. Be forewarned: During lunch the noise level is thunderous. ♦ Italian ♦ Daily lunch and dinner. Reservations recommended. 7 E 54th St (between Madison and Fifth Aves). 688.1999

87 San Pietro ★★$$$ Sister restaurant to the Upper East Side's **Sistina,** this place features dishes from Italy's Amalfi Coast. Try the chickpea pasta with pesto, shrimp with peppers and herbs, Black Sea bass braised with fennel and red wine, and monkfish with aioli-pepper marinade. The sunny yellow setting, with jars of olives, sun-dried tomatoes, silver platters stacked with ripening tomatoes, and paintings of outdoor markets, manages to feel simultaneously elegant and homey. ♦ Neapolitan ♦ M-Sa lunch and dinner. Reservations required; jacket and tie required. 18 E 54th St (between Madison and Fifth Aves). 753.9015 ৬

88 Monkey Bar ★★★$$$ This revamped, redesigned bar and restaurant in the **Elysée Hotel,** formerly favored by Tallulah Bankhead and Tennessee Williams, was so popular from day one of its 1994 reopening that people were begging their way past the rope to get in for one drink. The crowds inside the bar are still so thick that it's impossible to see the whimsical monkey murals or red bar stools that architect **David Rockwell** (who also designed **Vong**) contrasted with the plush, drop-dead-glamourous dining room—burgundy suede pillars and velvet banquettes. It's a perfect setting for chef John Schenk's rich, complex food. Try the *brandade* (a salt cod, olive oil, garlic, milk, and cream puree) ravioli; asparagus salad with leeks, beets, and roquefort; followed by roast Amish chicken with a spicy garlic glaze or barbecued squab. Don't miss the lemony mascarpone cheesecake or cappuccino parfait. ♦ American ♦ M-F lunch and dinner; Sa dinner. Reservations required. 60 E 54th St (between Park and Madison Aves). 838.2600

89 Cellini ★★★$$$ After operating this place for 14 years as **Lello,** a very dark restaurant serving Northern Italian food, the restaurant's owners and executive chef Dino Arpaia decided it was time to lighten up and change the name. The decor is now sponged Tuscan

yellow walls, blond wood floors, white damask tablecloths, and Tuscan country ceramics displayed on shelves. The food is more buoyant as well. Try *malfatti con carciofi* (stuffed pasta with thinly sliced baby artichokes and gaeta olives), *dentice al forno* (baked whole red snapper), and *costoletta d'agnello alla griglia* (grilled baby rack of lamb). The well-priced wine menu features Italian and California selections; there's also a "Reserve List" for special occasions. ♦ Italian ♦ M-F lunch and dinner; Sa dinner. Reservations recommended. 65 E 54th St (between Park and Madison Aves). 751.1555

89 Bill's Gay Nineties ★$$ The sirloin steak special at this saloon is named for Diamond Jim Brady, who would be right at home here. A pianist plays in the dining room, where such American fare as salads, roast chicken, and grilled fish are served. ♦ American ♦ M-F lunch and dinner; Sa dinner. 57 E 54th St (between Park and Madison Aves). 355.0243

89 Oceana ★★★$$$$ When Rick Moonen, formerly of **The Water Club,** took charge of this kitchen already known for fine seafood, he proceeded to bring it up another level. Now diners in this pretty pastel room can experience such extraordinary dishes as oven-steamed spaghetti squash with vegetables and tomato *concasse* (reduction), crab cake with chipotle sauce, house-cured salmon gravlax with spicy black-bean cakes and cilantro crème fraîche, and grilled salmon paillard with asparagus in ginger-soy vinaigrette. Finish the meal with the sensational pear *tarte tatin* (an upside-down tart) with spice ice cream, or chocolate lava cake. The wine list is extensive and not unreasonably priced. ♦ Seafood ♦ M-F lunch and dinner; Sa dinner. Reservations required; jacket required. 55 E 54th St (between Park and Madison Aves). 759.5941

90 Morrell & Company, The Wine Emporium A playground for oenophiles, this large, well-organized store carries practically every worthwhile label, including many direct imports. Service is knowledgeable but occasionally impatient. ♦ M-Sa. 535 Madison Ave (between E 54th and E 55th Sts). 688.9370

91 City Bakery ★$ Located in **Sony Plaza,** this uptown offshoot of the well-known Flatiron District bakery has a delicious selection of croissants and pastries, soups, sandwiches, and good salads. For dessert, try a wedge of chocolate cake or one of the fruit tarts. ♦ Cafe ♦ M-F breakfast and lunch. 550 Madison Ave (between E 55th and E 56th Sts). 833.8020 ♿. Also at: 22 E 17th St (between Broadway and Fifth Ave). 366.1414 ♿

otabe

MEANS "TO EAT"

92 Otabe ★★$$$ Spare and elegant, this Japanese restaurant serves authentic traditional dishes, including soba (buckwheat) noodles with fried whitefish and *oshitashi* (steamed spinach, eggplant, broccoli, and shiitake mushrooms), as well as its own artistic renditions—strips of fresh tuna sashimi in ginger-soy broth in varying shades from dark red to pink. Grilled dishes, including such selected ingredients as filet mignon, shrimp, and vegetables, are prepared at the *teppan* (grill) set into the tables. ♦ Japanese ♦ M-F lunch and dinner. 68 E 56th St (between Park and Madison Aves). 223.7575

93 Shun Lee Palace ★★★$$$$ Owner Michael Tong recently collaborated with designer Adam Tihany to renovate this landmark Chinese restaurant. The result includes blue-suede walls with gold-leaf panels, chandeliers of frosted glass, and mahogany cases displaying treasures of past dynasties. The menu was seriously revamped as well, and chefs from Hong Kong and Taiwan were brought in to prepare 200 dishes from five regions. Try the unfortunately named dish *Ants Climb on Tree* (a combination of beef, Chinese broccoli, and cellophane noodles), steamed dumplings, orange beef, or whole poached sea bass with brown-bean sauce. The dessert menu includes such Western favorites as chocolate mousse cake, Asian delicacies, including soy-milk and small-pearl tapioca soup, and such fusion sweets as crepes filled with red-bean paste and topped with ice cream. ♦ Chinese ♦ Daily lunch and dinner. Reservations required. 155 E 55th St (between Third and Lexington Aves). 371.8844. Also at: 43 W 65th St (between Central Park W and Broadway). 595.8895

94 Charlton's ★★$$$$ This stylish steak house with polished wood and maps of old New York is a sophisticated setting in which to enjoy top-notch steaks. Start with the vegetable terrine, eggplant soup, or crab cakes and then head straight for cattle country with a T-bone or a large porterhouse. For a lighter meal, have roasted salmon with a pesto crust. ♦ Steak house ♦ M-F lunch and dinner; Sa dinner. Reservations recommended. 922 Third Ave (between E 55th and E 56th Sts). 688.4646

95 P. J. Clarke's ★$$ There are few better places than this to witness rambunctious young professionals of Midtown getting slowly pickled during cocktail hour. Mysteriously, the hamburgers are famous, although habitués come here looking to meet, not eat meat. ♦ American ♦ Daily lunch, dinner, and late-night meals. 915 Third Ave (at E 55th St). 759.1650

SUTTON
Watering Hole

96 Sutton Watering Hole ★$ Down-home and affordable, this place is a rarity in Midtown. The menu is eclectic; pickings include Cobb and grilled chicken salads, such sandwiches as grilled yellowfin tuna, various pizzas, ribs, roasted loin of pork, and a very satisfying Cajun meat loaf. Save room for the cheesecake. ♦ American ♦ M-F lunch and dinner; Sa-Su brunch and dinner. 209 E 56th St (between Second and Third Aves). 355.6868 ♿

97 Cafe du Pont ★★$$$ This low-key, romantic burgundy-toned cafe has a fashionable mix of well-prepared French and Italian specialties. A la carte offerings include mussels *marinières;* spinach salad with warm goat cheese; risotto with shrimp, scallops, mussels, and diced vegetables with saffron; linguine with fresh salmon and shrimp; cassoulet; and rack of lamb with mustard-herb crust. There's also an excellent, affordably priced early prix-fixe dinner and weekend brunch. ♦ French/Italian ♦ M-F lunch and dinner; Sa-Su brunch and dinner. Reservations recommended. 1038 First Ave (between E 56th and E 57th Sts). 223.1133 ♿

98 Raffaele ★★$$$ Chef/owner Raffaele Esposito (formerly of the Grand Hotel in Rome) presides over this smart and sophisticated restaurant with a black-and-white color scheme and subdued lighting just off Sutton Place. The pastas, such as *capellini* (thin spaghetti) with artichokes, garlic, and baby shrimp in a light tomato sauce, and spaghettini with mixed seafood and spinach puree, are big hits with the neighbors. Baby octopus sautéed with garlic, olive oil, and fresh tomatoes; boneless quail in cognac sauce with raisins, pine nuts, and polenta; and grilled swordfish with fresh mint, carrots, and olive oil are good choices for second courses. ♦ Italian ♦ Daily dinner. Reservations recommended. 1055 First Ave (between E 57th and E 58th Sts). 750.3232 ♿

Rosa Mexicano

■■■■■■■■

98 Rosa Mexicano ★★$$$ When owner Josefina Howard opened this restaurant several years ago, she put a disclaimer on the menu warning diners that they would find a different kind of Mexican food here than what they were used to. Forget about tacos and enchiladas; you won't miss them because in their stead are complex regional dishes—platters of fresh seafood, *carnitas* (barbecued pork), shrimp in mustard-chili vinaigrette, and chicken wrapped in parchment. The guacamole prepared tableside is made to the spiciness you prefer and will, no doubt, set a new high standard for all future guacamoles. The frozen margaritas aren't bad, either. ♦ Mexican ♦ Daily dinner. Reservations recommended. 1063 First Ave (at E 58th St). 753.7407

MARCH
RESTAURANT

99 March ★★★$$$ Tucked away in a fin-de-siècle town house, this romantic restaurant—co-owned by Joseph Salice who oversees the front, and Wayne Nish who is in charge of the kitchen—is fitted with elegant banquettes and tapestries on the walls. The eclectic menu (all dinners are prix-fixe) changes monthly and is always exciting. Appetizers have included ravioli of baby lamb and crayfish with crispy artichokes and rabbit confit with foie gras and white beans. Five-spice salmon with mushrooms and rack of lamb with a sweet mustard and herb crust have been among some of the best entrées. Save room for desserts like crispy pancakes with vanilla ice cream, mango, and berries; Valrhona chocolate cake; and poached pear cake with lemon curd and spiced cranberry sauce. Another plus is the affordable wine list. ♦ American ♦ M-Sa prix-fixe dinner. Reservations recommended. 405 E 58th St (between First Ave and Sutton Pl). 838.9393

100 Il Vigneto ★$ The handsome carved-wood doors of this trattoria lead into a romantic dining room, where the simple, earthy menu features mussels in tomato sauce; baked clams; seafood salad; spinach fusilli with sun-dried red peppers, white beans, and eggplant; ricotta cheesecake; and cappuccino mousse cake. The predominantly Italian wine list is interesting and affordable. ♦ Italian ♦ M-F lunch and dinner; Sa dinner. 1068 First Ave (at E 58th St). 755.6875

100 Eros ★$$ The owners of the Moroccan **Cas La Femme** in SoHo take their evocative desert-fantasy decor uptown with this gold-painted dining room that's an ultraromantic setting with low lights and love-seat banquettes. Try the grilled chicken kebab marinated in lemon and herbs, salmon wrapped in grape leaf, or chicken marinated in lemon and bay leaf. ♦ Nouvelle Greek ♦ Daily lunch and dinner. Reservations recommended. 1076 First Ave (between E 58th and E 59th Sts). 223.2322 ⅃

101 Café Nicholson ★$$$ Dining at this intimate, romantic hideaway with warm, friendly service is a theatrical experience. The fanciful decor, which includes ornate hand-painted 19th-century tiles, is rife with antiques—furniture, paintings, and pottery. The eccentric owner opens the restaurant when he feels like it, so be sure to call in advance. The food is basic—poached salmon roast chicken, and a rice dish that looks suspiciously like Rice-a-Roni. And there's no choice for dessert—the house trademark chocolate soufflé is it. ♦ French/American ♦ Tu-Sa dinner. Reservations required. 323 E 58th St (between First and Second Aves). 355.6769

102 Les Sans Culottes ★$$$ Each meal at this rustic bistro with dark wood beams begins with an overflowing basket of charcuterie. Pace yourself, because most of the food is just as rich. Dinners (all are prix-fixe) begin with such traditional starters as onion soup or escargots. The main course, which changes daily, has been known to include such dishes as baby rack of lamb, shell steak, chicken with tangerine sauce, or duck with sherry sauce. ♦ French ♦ M-Sa lunch and dinner; Su dinner Reservations recommended. 1085 Second Ave (between E 57th and E 58th Sts). 838.6660. Also at: 347 W 46th St (between Eighth and Ninth Aves). 247.4284

103 Felidia ★★$$$$ Owners Felix and Lidia Bastianich preside over their rustic, brick, and Tuscan-tiled namesake, which features such specialties from Lidia's native Istria near Trieste as *stinco di vitello* (roast veal shank sautéed in its own juices). Pastas are especially good, particularly the *pappardelle* (broad noodles) with porcini or gnocchi with tomato sauce. Try the swordfish with balsamic sauce and garlic savoy cabbage, spicy seared shrimp with black beans and polenta, or loin of veal pan sautéed with natural juices and rosemary. The extensive wine list features some of Italy's best, at appropriately high prices. ♦ Italian ♦ M-F lunch and dinner; Sa dinner. Reservations required; jacket required. 243 E 58th St (between Second and Third Aves). 758.1479

104 Bruno ★$$$ This sophisticated Italian restaurant has smooth service and a smart-looking modern dining room, but alas, an inconsistent menu. Among the hits are homemade fettuccine with portobello mushrooms, cognac, and parmesan; grilled veal chop; marinated grilled jumbo shrimp with baby artichoke hearts; and sea bass with leeks and tomatoes. ◆ Italian ◆ M-F lunch and dinner; Sa dinner. Reservations recommended. 240 E 58th St (between Second and Third Aves). 688.4191

05 Anche Vivolo ★$$ A sedate neighborhood restaurant bedecked with floral murals and mirrors, this place specializes in huge portions of traditional Italian food—lasagna; spaghetti with garlic and oil; chicken parmigiana; chicken fiorentina (with lemon, butter, and spinach); and rolled eggplant stuffed with ricotta, parmesan, and mozzarella in tomato sauce. The early prix-fixe and after-9PM specials are very popular for meals either before or after a movie at nearby **Cinema I.**
◆ Italian ◆ M-F lunch and dinner; Sa dinner. Reservations recommended. 222 E 58th St (between Second and Third Aves). 308.0112. Also at: 140 E 74th St (between Lexington and Park Aves). 737.3533

05 Dawat ★★$$$ Actress and cookbook author Madhur Jaffrey is the guiding spirit behind this sophisticated Indian restaurant that's considered one of the best in town. Try *baghari jhinga* (shrimp with garlic, mustard seeds, and curry leaves), Parsi-style salmon steamed in a banana leaf with coriander chutney, and vegetarian stew flavored with tamarind. ◆ Indian ◆ M-F lunch and dinner; Sa dinner. Reservations recommended. 210 E 58th St (between Second and Third Aves). 355.7555

Le Colonial

06 Le Colonial ★★$$ A glamorized Vietnamese bistro with white, black, and brown shutters, potted palms, ceiling fans, and pictures of Indochina during the French colonial years, this place has been packing them in since the day it opened. Choice dishes include spring rolls, ginger-marinated roast duck with tamarind dipping sauce, crispy fried noodles with stir-fried vegetables, beef salad with lemongrass and basil, lemon tart, and crème caramel ice cream. A large after-work crowd convenes in the lovely lounge upstairs. ◆ Vietnamese ◆ Daily lunch and dinner. Reservations required. 149 E 57th St (between Third and Lexington Aves). 752.0808

07 Nonna ★★$ In the kitchen of this casual multilevel cafe in the **Galleria,** David Ruggerio (who also presides over the kitchen of **Le Chantilly,** see below) cooks "from the heart" the Italian specialties he learned from his grandmother. Try the vegetable salads from the antipasto table; *minestra* (a thick soup of pureed fennel); lemon-marinated salmon; fresh linguine with tomato sauce, basil, and herbed ricotta; or fusilli with roasted cremini mushrooms in a red-wine and onion sauce. There's also a take-out shop with a few tables across the way that sells soups, pastas, sandwiches, and pastries at very affordable prices. ◆ Italian ◆ M-Sa lunch and dinner. Reservations recommended. 117 E 57th St (between Lexington and Park Aves). 826.1021

108 Le Chantilly ★★★$$$$ This very formal French restaurant has loosened up quite a bit in recent years. A renovation of the dining room did away with the dark brocade banquettes and a few of the overwhelming murals. The kitchen has been given much the same treatment. Young, creative chef David Ruggerio has infused the predictably classic cuisine with sunny new flavors, as is evident in such dishes as braised salmon in Moroccan spices and pan-seared lamb chop with eggplant tartlet, essence of tomato, and virgin olive oil. Vegetarians take note: There is an imaginative tasting menu with dishes that include crispy mushroom ravioli with a black-bean and arugula salad. Dessert lovers will swoon over Eric Girerd's confections, among them dark chocolate versions of a piano, violin, and bowler hat. The extensive wine list features top-quality red Bordeaux, and is generally expensive. ◆ French ◆ M-Sa lunch and dinner; Su dinner. Reservations recommended; jacket required. 106 E 57th St (between Lexington and Park Aves). 751.2931 &

109 Mitsukoshi ★★★$$$$ Follow the lead of Japanese businessmen and come here for perfect sushi and sashimi in a comfortable setting—dignified beige walls and subdued lighting. The private Tatami rooms—for parties of four to 20—are even more elegant. Try the grilled fish of the day, smoked eel, tempura, and one of the bento boxes during

The famed Round Table of the Algonquin Hotel may have started because of apple pie, not witty conversation. Alexander Woollcott was drawn to the restaurant in 1918 because it served the same type of apple pie that he'd become fond of while serving in World War I. He persuaded friends Heywood Broun and Franklin P. Adams to lunch with him there every Saturday because of it. Soon others joined, and the group was invariably seated in the same corner.

lunch. *Negimaki* (beef rolled around scallions) and *shabu shabu* are also good choices. Dessert is good here too, which cannot be said about very many Japanese restaurants. Try the ginger, green-tea, or red-bean ice cream. ♦ Japanese ♦ M-F lunch and dinner. Reservations recommended. 461 Park Ave (at E 57th St). 935.6444

110 Fifty Seven Fifty Seven ★★$$$$ The restaurant of the **Four Seasons Hotel** has all the glamour of the **I.M. Pei**–designed, Art Deco–style hotel, with marble walls, soaring twenty-two-foot-high ceilings, maple floors with walnut insets, and bronze chandeliers inlaid with onyx. It's a sophisticated setting for the very sophisticated seasonal menus created by executive chef Susan Weaver and supervised in the kitchen by Jeffrey Littlefield. Signature dishes, usually available year-round and well worth trying, include marinated swordfish and asparagus in a vinaigrette of sour cherry, ginger, and citrus and black bass with corn and oyster mushrooms—one of the creative lower-fat and -calorie entrées on the menu. Those willing to splurge shouldn't miss the chocolate crème brûlée or caramelized banana cream pie with peanut ice cream and chocolate sauce. ♦ American ♦ Daily breakfast, lunch, and dinner. Reservations recommended. 57 E 57th St (between Park and Madison Aves). 758.5757 &

COMING OR GOING

111 Coming or Going ★★$$$ This tiny place bustles at lunchtime when professionals from the surrounding office buildings take their regular tables for upscale salads and sandwiches, including seared tuna with avocado and lemon chutney on sourdough. At night, though, it's candlelit and romantic—the lace curtains and antiques give the room a country-inn look. It may also be the only restaurant in the area with its own herb garden; owner Nancy Dziuban grows herbs and tomatoes on the building's roof. Naturally enough, the kitchen emphasizes fresh ingredients in its simple but sophisticated preparations. Try the cremini, shiitake, and portobello mushrooms baked with chevre, gruyère, and parmesan cheeses; yellowfin tuna tartare with seasoned cucumber and black-olive vinaigrette; braised lamb shank; roasted free-range chicken; and warm

apple-and-cranberry cobbler. ♦ American ♦ M-Sa lunch and dinner. Reservations recommended. 38 E 58th (between Park and Madison Aves). 980.5858

112 French Wine Merchant The merchant in question is Maurice Amiel, and he has stocked his store full of carefully chosen French vintages. In some instances, Amiel makes special deals with small vineyard owners, with whom major importers don't bother to do business. This allows him to offer customers some excellent wines that are unavailable elsewhere stateside at very good prices. He also stocks the major names in red and white wines, champagnes, and liqueurs. He and his knowledgable staff are happy to advise you on appropriate selections. ♦ M-Sa. 480 Park Ave (at E 58th St). 935.0533

113 Baccarat The world-famous crystal, Limoges china, plus fine glassware and silver are sold here. ♦ M-Sa. 625 Madison Ave (between E 58th and E 59th Sts). 826.4100

114 Oak Room and Bar ★★$$$ The clubby atmosphere of this room in the **Plaza Hotel** with its massive oak columns practically demands an English accent. The serious and well-prepared food here is composed of such classics as chateaubriand, filet mignon, crabmeat imperial, and chocolate mousse cake. ♦ American ♦ Daily dinner. Reservations recommended. 768 Fifth Ave (at Central Park S), Lobby level. 546.5330 &

114 Gauguin $$$ Formerly the famous **Trader Vic's**, this restaurant in the **Plaza** has been gussied up. In the process, its Tahitian-fantasyland decor has become even more flagrant with the addition of a footbridge through a jungle of bamboo, fake palm trees, Gauguin-esque paintings, and fire-engine red banquettes. The food should have been given half as much attention. It's less than mediocre and even the *pu pu* platters aren't great. For a festive treat, stop in for a very expensive exotic drink and the one flaming dish on the menu, Krakatoa East of Java (a very sweet ice-cream dessert), shaped like a volcano, of course, and situated on a river of dyed-turquoise Curaçao. ♦ Asian ♦ Tu-Su dinner. Reservations required. 768 Fifth Ave (enter at Central Park S), Lower level. 319.0404 &

114 Palm Court ★$$ Since the Trumps's gilding, this hotel lobby lounge looks even more like an opulent Viennese pastry cafe than it did before. The perfect meal to have here is afternoon tea, one of the more lavish experiences around. Pastries and tea are served to the strains of live classical music in a pastel confection of a room. For other meals, the cafe menu includes pastas, sandwiches, and salads. ♦ Cafe ♦ Daily breakfast, lunch, afternoon tea, and dinner. 768 Fifth Ave (at Central Park S), Lobby level. 546.5350

15 Mickey Mantle's ★$$ Sports fans of all ages love this place. They get to watch the day's big game or memorable moments in sports history on huge video screens; they can study the restaurant's collection of uniforms and memorabilia; and if they're lucky, they will meet the man himself, who is often around to greet customers and sign postcards. The basic American fare—gigantic burgers, ribs, hot-fudge sundaes—should please not-too-finicky eaters, but it's a lot better than ballpark franks. ♦ American ♦ Daily lunch and dinner. 42 Central Park S (between Fifth and Sixth Aves). 688.7777

16 Rumpelmayer's $$ A recent renovation stripped down the faded grandeur of this deluxe ice-cream parlor so that it now looks like one of the many overpriced coffee shops of the faux Art Deco variety. But it's still *the* place to go for a fabulously rich hot chocolate. The restaurant of the **San Moritz** hotel, this place also has a full menu of appetizers, entrées, snacks, and desserts, including New Wave Chicken (strips of lemon-pepper chicken served with Caesar's salad), crab cakes with sweet-potato fries and a mixed green salad, the famous Rumpelmayer's club sandwich, and the Banana Royale (with five kinds of ice cream, any number of toppings, whipped cream, and a cherry). ♦ Continental ♦ M-F breakfast, lunch, dinner, and late-night meals; Sa-Su brunch, dinner, and late-night meals. 50 Central Park S (at Sixth Ave). 755.5800

17 The Manhattan Ocean Club ★★★$$$ The excellent seafood here reflects an often overlooked fact—New York is still a port, with easy access to the treasures of the sea. Try appetizers of seared tuna with lattice potatoes and *salsa verde* or baked oysters with morel cream; follow with grilled swordfish with cream of lentil curry, salmon with tandoori spices, and red snapper with rosemary crust. The owner's personal collection of more than a dozen Picasso ceramics is on display. The wine list is extensive, well chosen, and well priced. ♦ Seafood ♦ M-F lunch and dinner; Sa-Su dinner. Reservations recommended; jacket and tie requested. 57 W 58th St (between Fifth and Sixth Aves). 371.7777

118 Jean Lafitte ★★$$$ This cozy Parisian-style neighborhood bistro in the heart of Manhattan is no flash in the pan—it's been around for years, thanks to a reliably good menu and loads of charm. Onion soup is perfect on a wintery day and the authentic *choucroute* come highly recommended. Also try the rack of lamb with roasted garlic, chicken grilled with rosemary, and roast duck with grapes. ♦ French ♦ M-F lunch and dinner; Sa-Su dinner. 68 W 58th St (between Fifth and Sixth Aves). 751.2323

MANGIA

119 Mangia ★★$ A cappuccino and dessert bar just inside the towering glass doors is only one of several good reasons to stop by this restaurant and take-out shop. The most popular item at the upstairs eatery is an antipasto buffet of grilled fish, grilled vegetables, pasta, grains, smoked salmon, portobello mushrooms, and other daily specialties. Also on the menu is a variety of pastas and sandwiches. Downstairs in the back are terrific soups, rolls, antipasti, sandwiches, and pastries to carry out. There's also a deluxe salad bar with many of the same wonderful offerings as the buffet upstairs: roasted vegetables, and bean, grain, and pasta salads. ♦ Italian/Takeout ♦ M-Sa breakfast, lunch, and dinner. Reservations recommended. 50 W 57th St (between Fifth and Sixth Aves). 582.5554. Also at: 16 E 48th St (between Madison and Fifth Aves). 754.0637

Bests

Jennifer and George Lang

Restaurateurs, Café des Artistes, New York; Gundel and Bagolyvár restaurants, Budapest

The mysteries of the universe are revealed little by little, but one even our Nobel prize winners have difficulty solving is: What do restaurateurs like to eat when they go out to other restaurants in New York? Here is a list of our choices, each guaranteed to make you eminently happy.

Bouley: Roasted rack of lamb wrapped in spinach, steamed with lemon thyme.

Les Célébrités: Spit-roasted wood pigeon with foie gras.

Le Cirque: Braised veal shank and marrow with pepper and vinegar sauce.

Manhattan Ocean Club: Crab cakes.

Nobu: Yellowtail *tartare* with caviar.

Felidia: Risotto with seasonal wild mushrooms with white truffle oil.

Palm: Prime aged New York strip with creamed spinach and cottage fries.

km 1/8 1/4
mi 1/16 1/8

N

E. 86th St.
E. 85th St.
E. 84th St.
E. 83rd St.
E. 82nd St.
E. 81st St.

Lexington Ave.
3rd Ave.
2nd Ave.

Metropolitan
Museum
of Art

5th Ave.
Madison Ave.
Park Ave.

E. 80th St.
E. 79th St.
E. 78th St.
E. 77th St.
E. 76th St.

■ Lenox Hill
Hospital

Central
Park

■ Whitney
Museum of
American Art

E. 75th St.
E. 74th St.
E. 73rd St.
E. 72nd St.

61
E. 71st St.
57 56

The Frick
■ Collection

60
E. 70th St.

58
E. 69th St.

59

Hunter
College

E. 68th St.

48 49
50

E. 67th St.

E. 66th St.

51
52

45
E. 65th St.
40 39
38

47
46

44 42 41

The
Zoo

E. 64th St.
43

31
32
34

25 26
27

E. 63rd St.
28
29
30
33

24
23

Lexington Ave.
3rd Ave.
2nd Ave.
1st Ave.

E. 62nd St.

20
11

22 19
12
10

21 18
13
14

Madison Ave.
Park Ave.

16
15
9 8 7

17
E. 60th St.

5th Ave.
1 2
3 4
5

6 Roosevelt Island
Tramway Station ■

E. 59th St.

East Side

Although there are many pockets of wealth throughout the city, when it comes to "old money," this neighborhood—extending from the **East River** to **Fifth Avenue** and from **East 59th** to **East 72nd Streets**—is filled with it. The grand apartment buildings overlooking **Central Park** and the elegant town houses lining the side streets are the very picture of tasteful luxury.

The East Side has been a stomping ground for the prosperous since before the Civil War, when it was a vacation spot for fashionable downtown residents. By the end of the 1700s, mansions in parklike settings lined the shore of the East River up to Harlem. **Boston Post Road**—now **Third Avenue**—made access to the city below Canal Street convenient, but those with more leisure time traveled the river via steamboat. By the late 1860s, these old gracious summer homes were being converted to year-round use, and several years later, when elevated railroads along **Second** and Third Avenues made the area more accessible, a working-class population settled in as well.

Impervious to the demographic changes, the area east of **Central Park** and west of the railroad tracks—running along what is now **Park Avenue**—remained the domain of the wealthy, whose ranks have included the Astors, Fiskes, Havemeyers, Armours, and Tiffanys. Although disfigured by a proliferation of charmless high-rises built during the 1960s, the area still boasts one of the city's most prestigious zip codes. Correspondingly, the shops and restaurants that surround this gilded enclave cater to the most discriminating palates.

Le Cirque, JoJo, Matthew's, Sign of the Dove, or any of the sidewalk cafes on **Madison Avenue** simulate establishments found in Paris, with their customers' panoply of European accents and army of well-dressed

Map labels

Carl Schurz Park

E. 84th St.

York Ave.

East End Ave.

E. 79th St.

Cherokee Pl.

John Jay Park

Franklin D. Roosevelt Dr.

East River

E. 72nd St.

New York Hospital/ Cornell University Medical College

E. 68th St.

Rockefeller University

E. 64th St.

Roosevelt Island

York Ave.

West Promenade

East Promenade

Aerial Tramway

25

Queensboro Bridge

passersby. Try **Grace's** for grocery shopping on a grand scale; stop at **Fletche Morgan Provisions** for small feasts wrapped up to go.

The East Side experience is not entirely upscale, of course; it becomes more democratic as you move farther east, with ethnic restaurants and small markets–especially of German and Eastern European extraction—dotting the streets. Downtown, however, offers a greater variety of ethnic offerings—the attraction here is the good life and its many trappings.

CIPRIANI

1 Harry Cipriani ★★$$$$ If you can't get to Venice to experience the original Harry's Bar, this spin-off comes pretty close. *Bellinis* (made from peach nectar and dry Prosecco wine) are specialties of the house, as are the pastas. Try cannelloni and ravioli with fillings that change daily, tagliatelle with vegetables and smoked chicken, or baked angel hair with ham and béchamel sauce. ♦ Northern Italian ♦ Daily breakfast, lunch, and dinner. Reservations recommended; jacket required. 781 Fifth Ave (at E 59th St). 753.5566

2 Il Toscanaccio ★★★$$$ The name means "naughty Tuscan" and that's the spirit restaurateur Pino Luongo (owner of **Coco Pazzo**, **Le Madri**, and **Mad. 61**) is trying to achieve with this redo of the space formerly occupied by his formal **Amarcord**. This time, the colors are pure sunshine, with beige walls punctuated by orange and yellow Frette table linens and a huge multicolored mural depicting various Italians, such as Sophia Loren and Catherine de' Medici, enjoying an alfresco buffet together. As prepared by Cesare Casella, also chef of **Coco Pazzo**, the food is equally sunny and earthy: Don't miss the antipasto; baby octopus stewed in a spicy tomato sauce: bowtie pasta with spring vegetables, herbs, tomato, and parmigiana; homeade linguine with scallops, clams, mussels, and calamari; the greaseless, succlent *fritto misto* (fried seafood and vegetables); lamb with olives and tomato served in a bread-crust shell; and whatever fish is stewed that day with garlic, tomatoes, herbs, and hot chili peppers. The all-Tuscan wine list has 100 interesting selections. ♦ Tuscan ♦ M-F lunch and dinner; Sa-Su dinner. Reservations recommended. 7 East 59th St (betweeen Madison and Fifth Aves). 935.3535 ᴔ

3 Kaplan's $$ Large, clean, and modern, this delicatessen offers fair prices and better-than-average salads, along with such sandwiches as corned beef and pastrami, soups, and attentive service. ♦ Deli ♦ Daily breakfast, lunch, and dinner. 59 E 59th St (between Park and Madison Aves). 755.5959

4 Caviarteria ★★$$$$ This caviar and champagne bar has an on-site retail store wi a huge variety of fish roe—offered at very good prices because it's the largest caviar importer in the country—pâtés, chocolates, and other delicacies. The helpful staff will graciously answer any questions about the precious stock and arrange for mail-order service. But for more immediate gratification take a seat in the cafe and have a caviar platter, smoked salmon, foie gras, or for a truly rare selection, smoked wild boar. ♦ International/Caviar ♦ M-Sa breakfast and lunch; Su brunch. 502 Park Ave (at E 59th St 759.7410

5 Le Train Bleu ★$$ A re-creation of the dining car on the famous **Orient Express,** thi welcome resting ground in **Bloomingdale's** for worn-out shoppers has a spectacular vie of the Queensboro Bridge and the **Roosevelt Island Tramway.** The food—such as Cajun shrimp and pasta salad, fettuccine with tomatoes and gorgonzola, and grilled chicke over Caesar salad—takes second place. Othe culinary spots in the vast department store include a **Petrossian** boutique (selling caviar smoked salmon, foie gras, bread, and pastries) on the ground floor; **Martine's Chocolates**, specializing in scrumptious hand-dipped Belgian chocolates on the sixth floor; and the **Main Course,** a cornucopia of kitchen gadgets, also on the sixth floor. ♦ Continental ♦ M-F lunch and afternoon tea Sa lunch; Su brunch. Reservations recommended. 1000 Third Ave (at E 59th St), Sixth floor. 705.2100

6 Yellowfingers ★$$ A perfect place to recover after a splurge at **Bloomingdale's,** this spot's open kitchen turns out generous salads, sandwiches (all served on thick focaccia), plentiful burgers, and a hearty entrée called *fa'vecchai* (a pizzalike dough baked with toppings that include grilled mushrooms, braised onions, olives, and eggplant). Owner Joseph Santo's empire als includes **Sign of the Dove, Ecce Panis, Contrapunto, Arizona 206,** and **Arizona Cafe** (see below). ♦ American/Italian ♦ M-Sa breakfast, lunch, and dinner; Su brunch and dinner. 200 E 60th St (at Third Ave). 751.861

Above Yellowfingers:

Contrapunto ★★$$$ This modern glasse in room is great for watching the scene along

Third Avenue. It's also a dependable spot for good pasta, including fresh squares filled with lobster, scallops, fresh fennel, and leeks in a lemon-cream sauce; and delicate angel-hair pasta with littleneck clams. There are also decent desserts, such as a rich chocolate tort, and a good, balanced wine list. ♦ American/Italian ♦ Daily lunch and dinner. 200 E 60th St (at Third Ave). 751.8615

6 Arizona 206 ★★★$$$ Authentically ensconced in lots of adobe, bare wood, and desert flowers, this cavelike place is pleasing to the eyes, but hard on the ears—it gets terribly loud. The crowds are in attendance for chef David Walzog's imaginative Southwestern fare—wild striped bass in a roasted tomatillo broth; barbecued pork tamales with corn and chili sauce; skate salad with corn-mushroom salsa; and grilled rabbit loin with cilantro oil, *habañero* peppers, and a crisp tortilla stuffed with rabbit. Chocoholics will love the Arizona chocolate plate—warm chocolate cake, and chocolate ice cream covered in mint and raspberry cream. ♦ Southwestern ♦ Daily lunch and dinner. Reservations recommended. 206 E 60th St (between Second and Third Aves). 838.0440

6 Arizona Cafe ★★$$ Adjoining **Arizona 206** is this more casual—and less expensive—cafe (although the noise level is about the same). Offered here are such inventive dishes as eggplant tortilla served with feta cheese, tomato salsa, and herb mayonnaise; vegetable pizza with roasted tomato, grilled squash, monterey jack cheese, and jalapeño puree; and shrimp salad with papaya, cucumber, and arugula. Try one of the sensational margaritas or a Mexican brew. ♦ Southwestern ♦ Daily lunch, dinner, and late-night meals. 206 E 60th St (between Second and Third Aves). 838.0440

7 Favia ★$ No frying is allowed and only moderate amounts of oil are used at this casual, health-conscious spot. Specialties include pasta *puttanesca* (with a tomato-based sauce flavored with olives, capers, and anchovies), grilled chicken sandwich with honey mustard (hold the mayo!), and a variety of pizzas made with whole wheat or oat bran. Listed under every item is its calorie, fat, and cholesterol content. ♦ Italian ♦ Daily lunch and dinner. 1140 Second Ave (at E 60th St). 223.9115

8 Serendipity ★$$ The name of this ice-cream parlor and informal restaurant was taken from *The Three Princes of Serendip*, Horace Walpole's retelling of a Persian myth. The over-the-top Victorianesque decorations; fine, simple food–shepherd's pie, barbecued-chicken casserole—and decadent desserts, including the famed frozen hot chocolate, have made this a busy attraction since it opened in 1954. The novelty boutique provides distraction while waiting for a table. ♦ American ♦ Daily lunch, dinner, and late-night meals. 225 E 60th St (between Second and Third Aves). 838.3531

9 Corrado Cafe ★$ This casual outpost of **Corrado** on the West Side features a range of pastas, salads, and sandwiches. Try the tricolored fusilli with smoked mozzarella, sun-dried tomatoes, and basil; Japanese chicken salad in a honey and black-sesame dressing; and apple-smoked turkey and brie on sourdough bread. There are also muffins and croissants for breakfast. ♦ Cafe ♦ Daily breakfast, lunch, and dinner. 1013 Third Ave (between E 60th and E 61st Sts). 753.5100 &

10 Matthew's ★★★$$$ Formerly **Alo Alo**, which closed after an out-of-control taxi rammed through its front window, this immediately successful place has the same talented young chef, Matthew Kenney. Named one of *Food and Wine Magazine*'s chefs of the year in 1994, Kenney now pushes the limits of American cuisine (he formerly specialized in Italian cuisine), creating his own trends. The changing seasonal menu may include such standout dishes as *ahi* (Hawaiian tuna) *tartare* with green-olive *tapenade* (a thick paste made from capers, anchovies, olives, olive oil, and lemon juice); marinated shrimp and yam salad with avocado, lime, and sweet onion; and lemon-glazed lobster with white corn, chanterelles, and asparagus. Rustic yet elegant—white linen, rattan chairs, ceiling fans, and big baskets of fruit—the setting is perfect for the beautiful crowd this fashionable place attracts. The welcoming service, however, keeps it from becoming an intimidating scene. ♦ American ♦ M-Sa lunch and dinner; Su brunch and dinner. 1030 Third Ave (at E 61st St). 838.4343 &

11 Brio ★$$ Thanks to its Italian-style home cooking, this attractive, wood-paneled trattoria is almost always full. The hearty polenta with porcini or aromatic pesto-laden fusilli are two reasons to return again and again. ◆ Italian ◆ Daily lunch, dinner, and late-night meals. Reservations recommended. 786 Lexington Ave (between E 61st and E 62nd Sts). 980.2300

Michelle's Kitchen
French-Belgian Quality Catering

11 Michelle's Kitchen ★$ Popular for snacks of soup, pâté, and salad, this take-out shop and cafe features dishes influenced by French and Belgian cuisine. Try the lobster bisque, rigatoni with sun-dried tomatoes, stuffed fillet of sole, baked salmon with herbs, stuffed cornish hen, or a sandwich of roast beef, watercress, and boursin cheese. Finish with the irresistible lemon mousse or chocolate-crunch cheesecake. ◆ Cafe ◆ M-F breakfast, lunch, and dinner; Sa-Su breakfast and lunch. 792 Lexington Ave (between E 61st and E 62nd Sts). 750.1730 &

12 Il Valletto ★$$$ If the owner, Nanni, is around when you visit, let him order for you. If not, here are some suggestions: *bruschetta* (toast seasoned with garlic and oil), tender baked clams, eggplant *siciliana* (with light ricotta and spinach), and linguine with delicate, tender clams in a light white sauce. For dessert, try the baked pear with zabaglione or fresh fruit salad. ◆ Italian ◆ M-F lunch and dinner; Sa dinner. Reservations required; jacket required. 133 E 61st St (between Lexington and Park Aves). 838.3939

13 Le Pistou ★$$ This "country mouse" cousin of **La Côte Basque** isn't going to dazzle you with new, inventive dishes, but if you're looking for well-prepared, traditional French food, this pleasant white-and-gold room will do the trick. Try *pâté de campagne* (a rough-textured country pâté made several different ways), roast chicken, and profiteroles. An affordable prix-fixe dinner is offered as well. ◆ French ◆ M-Sa lunch and dinner. Reservations recommended. 134 E 61st (between Lexington and Park Aves). 838.7987

14 Gino's ★$$ Bustling and clubby, this place with its wild decor—red wallpaper with zebra stripes—just celebrated its 50th birthday, thanks to a coterie of faithful customers. What keeps them coming back are such dishes as the Gino salad (a massive affair full of lettuce, artichokes, beets, pimento, and anchovies), chicken à la Gino (broiled in olive oil and garlic), chicken Capri (sautéed with olive oil, garlic, and vinegar), and *pasta segreto* (in a tomato-based sauce—the ingredients of which are top secret!). Choose among three excellent desserts—tiramisù, cheesecake, and rum cake—all made daily. ◆ Italian ◆ Daily lunch and dinner. Reservations recommended. No credit cards accepted. 780 Lexington Ave (between E 60th and E 61 Sts). 758.4466

By Bread Alone

As the saying goes, "Bread is the staff of life." And each immigrant group that comes to New York brings along its own style of bread making. Italian, Lebanese, and Eastern European bread bakers fill neighborhood streets with delicious aromas that waft through the night air until the dawn reveals long lines of customers waiting to get the first loaves. Chewy, crusty, and if you time your arrival right, still hot from the oven, bread in New York is a delectable tribute to diversity.

Amy's Bread (672 Ninth Ave, between W 46th and W 47th Sts, 977.3856) Amy Scherber turns out delicious onion and olive twists and rosemary sourdough.

A. Zito & Sons Bakery (259 Bleecker St, between Cornelia and Jones Sts, 929.6139) Stop in for sensational, crusty Italian bread, especially the whole wheat.

Damascus Bakery (195 Atlantic Ave, between Court and Clinton Sts, Brooklyn Heights, 625.7070) This is the place to get your pita bread fresh from the oven.

E.A.T. (1064 Madison Ave, between E 80th and E 81st Sts, 772.0022) The bread from this bakery has infiltrated practically every food store in New York, much to the denizens' general glee.

D & G Bakery (45 Spring St, between Mott and Mulberry Sts, 226.6688) The breads here are crusty and delicious, especially the prosciutto variety.

Ecce Panis (1120 Third Ave, between E 65th and E 66th Sts, 535.2099; 1260 Madison Ave, at E 90th St, 348.0040) The name is pronounced "*ech*-ay *pah*-nis," but however you say it, the bread is glorious—try the sourdough, chocolate loaves, and tomato-olive focaccia.

Orwasher's Bakery (308 E 78th St, between First and Second Aves, 288.6569) Raisin pumpernickel, cinnamon raisin, Hungarian potato bread, and other Old World favorites are here for the tasting.

15 Food Attitude ★$ Baker extraordinaire Pierre Weber turns out buttery fruit tarts, eclairs, chocolate-truffle cakes, and other confectionery delights, making this a perfect place to come during a sweet-tooth attack. If pangs of conscience prevent you from skipping straight to dessert, start with a bowl of soup (tomato-basil or cream of mushroom), chicken gratin, or penne *primavera*. These dishes can be taken out or enjoyed at a table in the back. ♦ Bakery/Cafe ♦ Daily breakfast and lunch. 127 E 60th St (between Lexington and Park Aves). 980.1818

15 Le Veau d'Or ★$$$ Longtime East Siders still flock to this great old bistro for such well-prepared, basic French fare as steak au poivre, baby chicken with tarragon, and chocolate mousse. The service is unpretentious and efficient. ♦ French ♦ M-Sa lunch and dinner. Reservations recommended. 129 E 60th St (between Lexington and Park Aves). 838.8133

LE TAXI

16 Le Taxi ★★$$$ With its etched mirrors and rose-petal light fixtures, this Parisian-style bistro is bustling with fashionable types talking about haute couture and its epicenters. The well-dressed, noisy crowd comes here for very good, classic French food—try lobster bisque, escargots, poached salmon with sorrel mousseline, and *daube provençale* (here, a rich beef stew with red wine) that could take the chill out of New York's coldest eves. For dessert, order whatever seasonal fruit tart comes out of the kitchen that day. ♦ French ♦ M-Sa lunch and dinner. Reservations recommended. 37 E 60th St (between Park and Madison Aves). 832.5500

17 Williams-Sonoma Fans of the upscale cookware catalogue rejoiced when this San Francisco–based company came to New York. This was the first (and main) store; today there are branches throughout the city. Italian ceramic platters, perfect wine glasses, espresso and waffle makers (just a couple of the many kitchen appliances), flavored olive oils, a variety of garlic presses, and any other kitchen or dining accessory is probably available here. ♦ Daily. 20 E 60th St (between Park and Madison Aves). 980.5155. Also at: 1175 Madison Ave (at 86th St). 289.6832; 1309 Second Ave (at 69th St). 288.8408; 110 Seventh Ave (at 17th St). 633.2203

18 Aureole ★★★$$$$ Situated in a town house with plaster reliefs of animals on the walls and baskets of dried flowers for decoration, this is one of the most charming dining rooms in town. Chef Charlie Palmer's complex, architectural food is also among the most admired; lately, though, the presentation

seems to be overshadowing the flavor. Try the terrine of natural foie gras with pressed duck confit, applewood-grilled salmon with basil-braised artichokes, or slow-basted breast of guinea fowl with melted savoy cabbage and a ragout of morels. The desserts are spectacular, particularly the tower of dark-chocolate and praline mousse, warm apple pudding with sour-cream ice cream and honey-spiced apple compote, and caramel mousse with cinnamon-basted fruits. The handmade chocolates, complimentary with dinner, also make a splendid finish. ♦ Continental ♦ M-F lunch and dinner; Sa dinner. Reservations required. 34 E 61st St (between Park and Madison Aves). 319.1660

19 Mme. Romaine de Lyon ★★$$ With more than 500 kinds of omelettes to choose from, it's safe to say that this is New York's ultimate place for the proverbial broken-egg dish. The setting is charming and comfortable, and the staff is friendly. ♦ French ♦ M-Sa lunch and dinner; Su lunch. Reservations recommended. 29 E 61st St (between Park and Madison Aves). 759.5200

20 Sherry Lehman One of the top wine merchants in the country, this place may have the most extensive retail inventory in the world. The store specializes in French, California, and Italian wines, but also stocks German, Spanish, and kosher labels. Catalogues are published five times a year—one each season and an extra issue at Christmas—and the staff offers courteous, expert advice. It's also a handsome store for browsing. ♦ M-Sa. 679 Madison Ave (at E 61st St). 838.7500

20 Georg Jensen/Royal Copenhagen Silver flatware, crystal glassware, and the entire collection of Royal Copenhagen china are available here. ♦ M-Sa. 683 Madison Ave (between E 61st and E 62nd Sts). 759.6457

21 Mad. 61 ★★$$$ Acclaimed restaurateur Pino Luongo (of **Le Madri** and **Coco Pazzo**) opened his latest eatery inside the uptown branch of **Barneys**, a New York shopping shrine. Centered around a marble mosaic pool, the restaurant tempts hungry shoppers with Luongo's trademark rich and rustic Italian cuisine, featuring such dishes as fettuccine with wild mushrooms and truffle oil and loin of rabbit roasted with fennel and pancetta. Surrounding the dining room are a wine bar (the extensive list offers a choice of 160) and an Italian espresso bar, where you can order from a less-expensive, but equally delicious, menu. Of special note are the cheese and charcuterie tasting plates that highlight various national specialities: Spanish, French, English, or Italian. The same fine cheeses are also for sale at the cheese counter. ♦ Italian ♦ Daily breakfast, lunch, and dinner. Reservations required. 10 E 61st St (at Madison Ave). 833.2200 &

22 Le Bistrot de Maxim's ★$$$ An homage to the Belle Epoque original, this downstairs cafe—formerly **L'Omnibus de Maxim's**—specializes in French-Asian fusion cuisine. The menu changes every few weeks and offers a few French staples that bow to tradition: pan-roasted chicken with herbs, endive salad, and filet mignon with a sauce of the day. More imaginative fare includes mushroom and escargot wontons with garlic-herb butter; spicy grilled gulf shrimp with a sauce of tamarind and yellow peppers; and fillet of grilled salmon on a bed of spinach with Chinese black-bean sauce. ◆ Fusion ◆ Tu-Sa lunch and dinner. Reservations required. 21 E 61st St (at Madison Ave). 980.6988

23 Arcadia ★★★$$$$ Chef/owner Anne Rosenzweig made culinary headlines ten years ago as the first woman to storm the hithertofore male bastion of the city's top-rated restaurants. Her cooking remains impressive to this day; signature dishes on the seasonal menu include corn cakes with crème fraîche and caviar, chimney-smoked lobster with tarragon butter, grilled salmon with red grapefruit and rhubarb vinaigrette, and a chocolate bread pudding swimming in a brandy-custard sauce. There are also a host of select—but expensive—wines to accompany your meal. The space is packed with tables, a bit of a challenge for claustrophobic diners, but the enveloping wraparound mural of a countryside scene undergoing seasonal changes is as lovely as the food. ◆ American ◆ M-Sa lunch and dinner. Reservations required; jacket and tie required. 21 E 62nd St (between Madison and Fifth Aves). 223.2900

24 Nello ★★$$$ Visits from such celebrities as Mickey Rourke and Ivana Trump have been documented in the photographs displayed on the wall as you enter. Whether the cuisine or people watching is the greater attraction here is debatable, but on this stretch of Madison Avenue, the latter usually wins. The food, however, is fine and includes *tagliolini* (thin noodles) with smoked salmon, tomatoes, and cream; and red snapper in tomato sauce with capers and olives. ◆ Italian ◆ Daily lunch and dinner. Reservations recommended. 696 Madison Ave (between E 62nd and E 63rd Sts). 980.9099

LE RELAIS

25 Le Relais ★$$$ Models, soap-opera stars, and other beautiful trendies while away evenings here eating such simply prepared French food as poached salmon and steak *frites* (with french fries) when not otherwise occupied with the "view." No surprise: The outdoor cafe is popular during the warmer months. ◆ French ◆ Daily lunch and dinner. Reservations required. 712 Madison Ave (at E 63rd St). 751.5108

26 Le Bilbouquet ★★$$$ This little green-and-blue jewel box of a room is packed with bustling, cheek-kissing crowd at lunch, and only slightly less frenetic at dinner. The food, traditional and well-prepared, includes roast breast of chicken, *blanquette de veau* (veal stew in a thick, white gravy), steak au poivre, and salad niçoise. Service can vary—regular customers receive preferential treatment. ◆ French ◆ Daily lunch and dinner. Reservations required. 25 E 63rd St (between Park and Madison Aves). 751.3036

POST THE HOUSE

27 The Post House ★★★$$$$ Many New York steak houses are strictly for red meat eaters, but this gracious establishment in the intimate **Lowell Hotel** has a softer touch—subdued lighting, peach walls, 18th-century American folk portraits, and models of ship hulls. The menu offers crab cakes and lemon pepper chicken in addition to some of the best beef in the city. The extensive, well-priced wine list is one of New York's best. ◆ American ◆ M-F lunch and dinner; Sa-Su dinner. Reservations required. 28 E 63rd St (between Park and Madison Aves). 935.2888

28 Park Avenue Cafe ★★★$$$ Even when it's packed to the rafters—as it usually is—this whimsical stylish room with blond wood and an American flag mural is a relaxed setting for chef David Burke's creative combinations. Try the tuna and salmon *tartare,* lobster dumplings, crabmeat ravioli in a seafood broth, gazpacho with a smoked-shrimp and jack-cheese quesadilla, baby lamb chops wrapped in pastry, and the trademark swordfish chop. But save room for Dan Budd's desserts. Among the standouts are milk-chocolate crème brûlée, chocolate-caramel cake with caramel ice cream, and Hawaii Vintage (a chocolate and banana tart). The wine list includes excellent French and American choices, but the prices can be a little hard to swallow. ◆ American ◆ M-F lunch and dinner; Sa dinner; Su brunch and dinner. Reservations required. 100 E 63rd St (between Lexington and Park Aves). 644.1900

Circus RESTAURANT

29 Circus ★★$$ Light, inventive interpretations of traditional Brazilian food are offered by chef Valquir Silva in a lighthearted, pretty room with blue and red banquettes and circus paintings. While the Brazilian national dish, *feijoada* (black bean and pork stew), is served here on weekends (just like in the mother country), such dishes as *camarão na moranga* (a delicate stew of shrimp, corn, hearts of palm, and peas cooked inside an acorn squash), *pastel circo* (baked chicken and heart-of-palm pie), and *mariscada* (seafood stew of shrimp, red snapper, clams, and mussels served in a light saffron broth) are offered throughout the week. The samba soundtrack sets the right mood. ♦ Brazilian ♦ Daily lunch and dinner. 808 Lexington Ave (between E 62nd and E 63rd Sts). 223.2566

30 Mulholland Drive Cafe $$ This pastel cafe with a mural of clouds is a pleasant place for such simple fare as chicken potpie, poached salmon, and crab cakes. At night the vibrant singles scene overwhelms the food. Stargazers take note: This place is occasionally frequented by celebrities, co-owner Patrick Swayze among them. ♦ American ♦ M-Sa lunch and dinner; Su brunch and dinner. Reservations recommended. 1059 Third Ave (between E 62nd and E 63rd Sts). 319.7740 &

31 Jackson Hole ★$ Delicious, juicy hamburgers approaching the size of Wyoming are the specialty of this restaurant. Any (or several) of the 12 available toppings can be requested to adorn the seven-ounce burgers; a side order of onion rings or french fries is an integral part of the experience. There's also a large selection of good omelettes. This place is a favorite with kids on weekends, and as could be expected, the noise level increases dramatically. ♦ Hamburgers ♦ Daily lunch, dinner, and late-night meals. 232 E 64th St (between Second and Third Aves). 371.7187. Also at: 521 Third Ave (at 35th St). 679.3264; 1270 Madison Ave (at 91st St). 427.2820 &; 517 Columbus Ave (at 85th St). 362.5177

Tea Time

The Duchess of Bedford is generally credited with starting the English tradition of afternoon tea during the late 18th century. Purportedly a snack to keep her houseguests from becoming peckish in the long hours between a noontime lunch and dinner at eight, the duchess's tea consisted of scones with clotted cream and strawberry jam, delicate crustless sandwiches of smoked salmon, egg, cucumber, or cheese, and an assortment of pastries, accompanied by tea brewed in a pot and poured through silver strainers balanced above each cup. This format is still considered standard.

Recently, afternoon tea has replaced cocktails as a nonalcoholic alternative for getting together with friends or even as a setting for business meetings. Most tearooms host an afternoon affair that does the duchess's memory proud. Here are a few especially accommodating places:

Danal (90 E 10th St, between Third and Fourth Aves, 982.6930) The setting at this cozy place is reminiscent of a rustic inn. Be sure to taste the homemade cakes.

Belissimo (10 W 56th St, between Fifth and Sixth Aves, 956.4438) An oasis amid the madness of Midtown, this fourth-floor tearoom within the store of the same name offers a soothing environment and many types of Asian and Western teas.

Mayfair Baglioni (610 Park Ave, at E 65th St, 288.0800) Tea at this private hotel is a study in European sophistication. It's not unusual to see some famous personalities tucked into the couches.

Palm Court (768 Fifth Ave, at Central Park S, 546.5350) In this grand room at the **Plaza Hotel,** tea is served with pomp and circumstance, just as you

might imagine it in a Viennese palace.

Peacock Alley (301 Park Ave, between E 49th and E 50th Sts, 872.4895) The **Waldorf-Astoria** was the first hotel to devote a room entirely to afternoon tea; years later the service is still formal and elegant.

St. Regis Hotel (2 E 55th St, at Fifth Ave, 753.4500) Teatime in the **Astor Court** takes place in an area between the **King Cole Bar** (with its Maxfield Parrish mural) and the **Lespinasse** restaurant and is served with formality and style.

T (142 Mercer St, at Prince St, 925.3700) Utterly charming, this combination tea salon and tea boutique downstairs from the **SoHo Guggenheim** feels like the quaint Parisian tea room and shop, Mariage Frères.

Tea Box Cafe (693 Fifth Ave, between E 54th and E 55th Sts, 350.0100) Located in the basement of **Takashimaya,** this subdued Asian cafe serves an elegant tea that's equal parts East and West—cucumber sandwiches on pressed rice, Western pastries, and Bernachon chocolates.

Tea and Sympathy (108 Greenwich Ave, between Jane and W 13th Sts, 807.8329) Cozy and often cramped, this place does wonders for conjuring up the feeling of tea at the home of someone's auntie living in the English countryside.

Yaffa Tea Room (19 Harrison St, at Greenwich St, 966.0577) High tea, which features a main course—such as salmon croquettes—along with scones, sandwiches, and desserts, is served every day in this eclectic room decorated with sculptures and wrought-iron lawn furniture.

32 Ideal Cheese Shop This long and narrow 40-year-old gourmet cheese emporium offers hundreds of varieties from all over the world. A knowledgeable staff can help you with your selection. ♦ M-Sa. 1205 Second Ave (between E 63rd and E 64th Sts). 688.7579 &

33 Il Vagabondo ★$$ Robust Italian cooking, mostly Southern style, is one of the draws at this noisy, good-humored neighborhood trattoria. But the main reason to come here is to watch people play boccie at the city's only indoor court (ask for a courtside table). A type of bowling, boccie has been a favorite Italian sport since the days of the Roman Empire. Specialties include homemade gnocchi, tuna steak, a fragrant veal stew, and fillet of sole. ♦ Italian ♦ M-F lunch and dinner; Sa-Su dinner. 351 E 62nd St (between First and Second Aves). 832.9221

34 Manhattan Cafe ★$$$ Come here for traditional steak-house fare in a comfortable, posh setting. There are also decent veal and pasta dishes in all the usual varieties. ♦ American ♦ M-F lunch, dinner, and late-night meals; Sa dinner and late-night meals; Su brunch, dinner, and late-night meals. Reservations recommended. 1161 First Ave (at E 64th St). 888.6556

RONASI RISTORANTE

35 Ronasi ★★$$ With whitewashed walls, hand-painted tiles, and copper pots hanging from the walls, this cheerful trattoria is a relaxing place for good chicken dishes and pasta. Try linguine with clam sauce, chicken *valdostana* (chicken breast stuffed with fontina and proscuitto), or any of the nightly specials. ♦ Italian ♦ M-F lunch and dinner; Sa-Su dinner. 1160 First Ave (between E 63rd and E 64th Sts). 751.0360

36 John's East ★★$ The East Side outpost of the famed **John's Pizzeria** has neither the soul of the Greenwich Village original nor the full bar of the Lincoln Center venue, but it does have the same menu, offering the best pizza in the neighborhood. The pies are thin-crusted, coal oven–baked, and covered with a variety of delicious toppings, including fresh mushrooms and spicy sausage. ♦ Pizza ♦ Daily lunch and dinner. No credit cards accepted. 408 E 64th St (between York and First Aves). 935.2895. Also at: 278 Bleecker St (between Morton St and Seventh Ave S). 243.1680 &; 48 W 65th St (between Central Park W and Columbus Ave). 721.7001

37 Melange This tiny take-out shop is crammed with delicious Mediterranean delicacies—barrels of olives, fresh mozzarella, garlicky salamis, jars of sun-dried tomatoes. The made-to-order sandwiches are a treat: Try country pâté with capers, roasted red peppers, and *cornichons* (small gerkin pickles) on freshly baked French bread; or Toscano salami, *sopressata* (a mild sausage), provolone, and sun-dried tomatoes in herb olive oil on semolina. ♦ Daily. 1188 First Ave (between E 64th and E 65th Sts). 249.3743

38 L'Ardoise ★★$ Those who are tired of quaint-looking bistro furnishings and average fare should visit this little restaurant where the decor is nothing to speak of, but the food is exceptional. The menu changes every three months; specialties include duck confit with pear glaze, filet mignon with roquefort sauce and escargots. ♦ French ♦ M-Sa lunch and dinner; Su brunch and dinner. No credit card accepted. 1207 First Ave (between E 65th and E 66th Sts). 744.4752

39 The Sign of The Dove ★★★$$$$ One of the most romantic settings in the city, this restaurant radiates warmth, with terra-cotta–colored brick archways, Oriental carpets, and lavish flower arrangements. In recent years the quality of the food has risen and equals the beauty of the setting. Chef Andrew D'Amico is one of the most skilled practioners of fusion cooking, taking inspiration from Italy for butternut-squash and parmesan ravioli with butter and sage, Thailand for seared tuna with green chilies and coriander, and Morocco for spiced salmon. Finish the meal with one of the delectable desserts, including chocolate-espresso pudding. The savory bread comes from the restaurant's bakery, **Ecce Panis** (see below). A cafe menu is also available for those who want simpler fare at a lower price. ♦ American ♦ M dinner; Tu-F lunch and dinner; Sa-Su brunch and dinner. Reservations recommended; jacket required. 1110 Third Ave (at E 65th St). 861.8080

39 Ecce Panis True connoisseurs of bread come here for their daily fix of loaves that are crispy outside, chewy and richly flavored inside. A sampling of the day's bounty, which includes sourdough, rye, and whole-wheat currant, sits in a basket on the counter. ♦ Daily. 1120 Third Ave (between E 65th and 66th Sts). 535.2099. Also at: 1260 Madison Ave (at E 90th St). 348.0040

40 Lex ★$$$ A sophisticated hangout for the well heeled, this subdued spot has cream-colored walls dotted with colorful Sonia

Delaunay fashion illustrations, flattering light, and a menu full of upscale comfort food. Try the lobster, crabmeat, avocado and *frisée* (curly endive) salad, wild-mushroom pan roast, roast chicken tarragon, and crab cakes with horseradish-mustard sauce. The desserts tend to be overly sweet, and although the wine list features off-year vintages, there's nothing "off" about the prices. ♦ American ♦ Daily lunch and dinner. Reservations required. 133 E 65th St (between Lexington and Park Aves). 744.2533

41 Toscana ★★$$ Previously located ten blocks south, this sleek, sophisticated Italian cafe with subdued lighting and terra-cotta tiles offers food that's even better than it was before. Tuscan dishes are featured: bean soup, broiled veal chop with thyme, and such homemade pastas as ricotta-stuffed ravioli. ♦ Italian ♦ M-Sa lunch and dinner. Reservations recommended. 843 Lexington Ave (between E 64th and E 65th Sts). 517.2288

41 Hale and Hearty ★$$ Modern and brightly lit, this upscale health-food cafe offers satisfying, if slightly overpriced, fare. Try any of the homemade soups; focaccia with grilled eggplant, goat cheese, and arugula; or braised chicken with leeks and white wine. ♦ American ♦ Daily lunch and dinner. 849 Lexington Ave (between E 64th and E 65th Sts). 517.7600 &

Sel & Poivre

41 Sel et Poivre ★$$ This rustic bistro—with wood beams, terra-cotta tiles, and large salt and pepper shakers on the bar—offers good couscous on Friday and Saturday nights. Otherwise, the reliable traditional French menu includes such dishes as roasted quail with mushrooms in a Madeira sauce, bouillabaisse, and steak *frites*. ♦ French ♦ Daily lunch and dinner. Reservations recommended. 853 Lexington Ave (between E 64th and E 65th Sts). 517.5780 &

FLETCHER MORGAN
Provisions

42 Fletcher Morgan Provisions ★$ Designed by **Peter Sibilia** (the architect who gave Madonna's Miami home the look of rustic Provence), this stylish cafe/take-out shop has ocher walls decorated with trompe l'oeil stencils, copper pots, antique plates, and an antique mantelpiece over the fireplace. The

food, by caterer-to-the-fashion-industry chef Herve Rossano, includes roast chicken with tarragon and tomato, mustard, and vinegar sauce; duck prosciutto with green lentils and walnut oil; lamb *tajine* (a Moroccan stew); and Thai beef salad. For dessert, try the *tarte tatin* (an upside-down apple tart). In good weather, the food can be enjoyed in a back garden, bedecked with flowers, trees, and a flowing fountain. The shelves are stocked with gourmet food gifts. ♦ French ♦ M-Sa breakfast, lunch, and early dinner; Su breakfast and lunch. 864 Lexington Ave (between E 64th and E 65th Sts). 288.6764

42 Ségires à Solanée Classic Provençal appointments: hand-painted wood furniture, iron furniture, faience from Moustiers-Sainte-Marie, and linen place mats and napkins abound in Georgette Buckner's sunny shop. ♦ M-Sa. 866 Lexington Ave (at E 65th St). 439.6109

43 JoJo ★★★$$$ Hailed as a creative genius and forerunner in the movement to replace cream- and butter-based sauces with more healthful infused oils and vegetable juices, chef Jean-Georges Vongerichten (also co-owner of **Vong**) left the formal **Lafayette** in 1991 to open this casual spot simply decorated with ocher walls, plain wood tables and chairs, and a few vivid oil paintings. Not surprisingly, the place has been a hit since the day the sign went up. The limited menu offers Vongerichten's interpretations of bistro fare, including shrimp in carrot juice with Thai lime leaves; chicken roasted with ginger, green olives, and coriander juice; foie gras with quince puree; and for dessert, a spectacular chocolate cake. The wine list spotlights good French wines, some at affordable prices. ♦ French ♦ M-F lunch and dinner; Sa dinner. Reservations recommended. 160 E 64th St (between Third and Lexington Aves). 223.5656

44 Le Regence ★★★★$$$$ Located in the **Hotel Plaza Athénée,** this glittery Louis XIV–style restaurant in a color scheme of aquamarine and shell is bedecked with mirrors, chandeliers, and a ceiling mural of a cloudy sky. The famous French Rostang family are consultants here and the talented Marcel Agnez is chef. Not surprisingly, this place excels in all categories: The service is impeccable and the food top flight. At lunch, choose from an extensive à la carte menu that features lamb chops, veal, and various fruits of the sea. For dinner, consult the à la carte menu or choose between two elaborate prix-fixe meals. Duck-liver salad, Mediterranean seafood soup, and Dover sole are frequently offered. There is also a private dining room available for parties of up to 25. Come on Sundays for a sensational brunch. ♦ French ♦ M-Sa breakfast, lunch, and dinner; Su brunch and dinner. Reservations required;

jacket and tie required. 37 E 64th St (between Park and Madison Aves). 606.4647

45 Ferrier ★$$ If you want to have dinner in relative peace at this dining spot, go early; otherwise it may be difficult to squeeze past the bar, so dense does the scene get. Good bistro cooking is offered in the beige back room: try the coq au vin, roasted salmon in a fennel and champagne sauce, confit of duck marinated and cooked in a red-wine sauce, and roasted monkfish with sautéed spinach. ◆ French ◆ M-F lunch and dinner; Sa-Su brunch and dinner. Reservations recommended. 29 E 65th St (between Park and Madison Aves). 772.9000

NEW YORK

46 Le Cirque ★★★$$$$ The rich and powerful favor this bustling, posh restaurant. Sirio Maccioni, owner and ringmaster, is the city's best host, and customers—titled or not—can expect to get the royal treatment. After a slightly shaky start, in the wake of chef Daniel Boulud's departure to open **Daniel** on the Upper East Side, chef Sylvain Portay is now producing many original dishes along with haute cuisine samplings. The choicest meals are the specials, and although pasta *primavera,* first popularized here, is neither on the menu nor an announced special, it is ordered by patrons in the know. Pastry chef Jacques Torres's spectacular desserts include a towering chocolate mousse cake and the house special crème brûlée. The front banquettes and tables near the bar are "power" seats. The wine list includes a good selection of vintage Bordeaux at surprisingly affordable prices. ◆ French ◆ M-Sa lunch and dinner. Reservations required; jacket and tie required. 58 E 65th St (between Park and Madison Aves). 794.9292

47 Terramare ★$ This exquisite place, with its sponged yellow walls and rustic display cases, offers what any respectable upscale larder should: Beluga and Osetra caviar, quail pâté, Carpegna prosciutto, cured tuna roe from Sicily, foie gras with black truffles, and Sevruga sturgeon. You can also sit at one of the small tables and enjoy a platter of blinis and caviar, smoked Scottish salmon, or carpaccio of smoked swordfish. This is the life. ◆ International ◆ Daily breakfast, lunch, and late-afternoon snacks. 22 E 65th St (between Fifth and Madison Aves). 717.5020

47 Mitchel London Foods A tempting array baked goods—including the best cheesecakes in town, buttery fruit tarts, key lime pie, lemon meringue layer cake, chocolate Grand Marnier mousse cake, and mocha–butter cream layer cake—are offered at this luscious shop. Mitigate the impending sugar shock with seafood salad, white-bean salad with carrots, chicken salad with tarragon, herb-roasted chicken, and such sandwiches as roasted vegetables and mozzarella on a sourdough baguette. ◆ M-Sa 22A E 65th St (between Madison and Fifth Aves). 737.2850

48 Soleil ★★$$ Gone are the dark carpets and Cantonese cuisine of **Fortune Garden,** the former denizen; in their place are bright yellow walls and a decent Italian menu. Start with grilled portobello mushrooms served with arugula and tomato, and move on to any of the pasta dishes, including rigatoni with tomatoes, prosciutto, and basil, or vegetable lasagna. Delicious sandwiches (brie and arugula on Tuscan bread with pesto is a winner) come with a salad and tasty french fries. Try not to fill up on the focaccia with olive oil and rosemary, which is set on the table as a token of good things to come. ◆ Italian ◆ M-Sa lunch and dinner; Su brunch and dinner. Reservations required. 1160 Third Ave (between E 67th and E 68th Sts). 717.1177 &

49 Asia ★$$ Come here for a little bit of all cuisines Asian. The dramatic dining room has inset aquariums lit with blue light and a mural of the Hong Kong skyline. The kitchen offers a truly pan-Asian menu, featuring dishes from nine countries, including dim sum, chicken satay, tiger prawns with Vietnamese basil and chili sauce, and General Tso's chicken. ◆ Asian ◆ Daily lunch and dinner. Reservations recommended. 1155 Third Ave (between E 67th and E 68th Sts). 879.5846 &

50 Le Comptoir ★★$$$ The true French bistro fare here includes endive and roquefort salad, various pâtés, steak au poivre, rack of lamb, and *pommes frites* (french fries). Desserts are simple: Try the chocolate tart and crème brûlée. There's also a good early prix-fixe dinner. The room is quite pretty, with mirrors and deep yellow walls. Watch for a name change. ◆ French ◆ M-F lunch and dinner; Sa dinner; Su brunch and dinner. 227 E 67th St (between Second and Third Aves). 794.4950

51 Mediterraneo ★$$ Convenient to the movie theater across the street, this sunny trattoria is a good bet for such simple, well-prepared pastas as fusilli *Mediterraneo* (with fresh tuna, swordfish, and tomato sauce). In fact anything that comes in a tomato-based sauce here is a favorite. ♦ Italian ♦ Daily lunch and dinner. No credit cards accepted. 1260 Second Ave (at E 66th St). 734.7407

51 Caffe Med ★$ For a coffee and pastry, try this cafe—an outgrowth of **Mediterraneo** (see above), two doors away. This striking deep-blue room decorated with a mural of musical instruments features foccacia sandwiches, carpaccio, salads, homemade gelato, and cakes from Bindi of Milan. ♦ Cafe ♦ Daily lunch and dinner. No credit cards accepted. 1268 Second Ave (between E 66th and E 67th Sts). 744.5370

52 China Fun ★$ With the exception of the tasting menu, which this outpost of the West Side locale doesn't offer, this place is a mirror image. Here, as there, go for the barbecued meats with crisp juicy duck, chicken, and pork; crystal shrimp dumplings; and Mandarin noodle soups, and save yourself the trip to Chinatown. ♦ Chinese ♦ Daily lunch and dinner. 1239 E 65th St (at Second Ave). 752.0810 ᕕ. Also at: 246 Columbus Ave (between W 71st and W 72nd Sts). 580.1516 ᕕ

53 Cafe Evergreen ★★$ Despite its non-Chinese name, this modern, bright place—with a turquoise-and-white color scheme and a center column that looks like a wave—features wonderful dim sum. Favorites include cilantro-shrimp dumplings, lobster rolls, and steamed roast-pork buns. Also try the barbecued meats and *chow fun*. ♦ Chinese ♦ Daily lunch and dinner. 1288 First Ave (at E 69th St). 744.3266

54 The Cream Puff ★$ This old-fashioned, tiny black-and-white pastry shop offers rich mocha tortes, fruit tarts, and black-and-white cakes. These treats can be taken out or served to you at a table, along with a delicious cup of coffee. ♦ Cafe ♦ Daily. 1388 Second Ave (between E 71st and E 72nd Sts). 517.3920

54 Cafe Greco ★$$ Lively and flower-filled, this restaurant offers cuisines that touch upon the Mediterranean's various shores; French, Italian, Spanish, and Moroccan dishes all find their way onto a menu that includes

grilled octopus and penne with black olives, tomatoes, and capers. ♦ Continental ♦ Daily lunch and dinner. 1390 Second Ave (between E 71st and E 72nd Sts). 737.4300

55 Grace's Marketplace It's no coincidence that this gourmet market resembles **Balducci's;** Grace is the daughter of that downtown institution's founding family. Similarly, this place has glorious produce, cheeses, breads, prepared foods, and cakes of the highest quality. But there's also a salad bar here and spectacular fresh pasta in colors seen only on tropical fish. ♦ Daily. 1237 Third Ave (at E 71st St). 737.0600

55 Leonard's The main draw here is the fish—high quality and great selection. The freshest salmon, grouper, stone crab claws, or Maine lobster are offered, along with oak-smoked Irish salmon and homemade clam chowder, in both New England and Manhattan styles. For those who prefer turf to surf, there's a meat counter, too. This neighborhood mainstay has been around since 1910. ♦ Daily. 1241 Third Ave (between E 71st and E 72nd Sts). 744.2600 ᕕ

56 Shelby ★$$ The handsome ocher room with European rattan chairs hosts a stylish neighborhood bar scene; however, many also come for the simple but well-prepared food. Try the seared tuna with Thai stir-fried vegetables, roasted chicken, burgers, and grilled monkfish. ♦ American ♦ M-F lunch and dinner; Sa-Su brunch and dinner. Reservations recommended. 967 Lexington Ave (between E 70th and E 71st Sts). 988.4624

56 Sette Mezzo ★★$$$ A simple whitewashed cafe, this is a local favorite for such pasta dishes as rigatoni with sausage, artichokes, and tomato and ravioli with mixed vegetables and saffron. Note: Service can sometimes

be a bit sloppy—regulars often get better treatment, and the room can get noisy. ♦ Italian ♦ Daily lunch and dinner. Reservations recommended. No credit cards accepted. 969 Lexington Ave (between E 70th and E 71st Sts). 472.0400

56 Le Petit Hulot ★$$$ This pretty dining spot with white walls, blond wood, and a back garden replaced a favorite local bistro, **La Petite Ferme,** in 1994. Like its predecessor, it's a good source for classic well-prepared bistro fare. Try the rack of lamb, cassoulet, *moules marinières* (mussels cooked in herbed white wine), and flourless chocolate cake. ♦ French ♦ M-F lunch and dinner; Sa-Su dinner. Reservations recommended. 973 Lexington Ave (between E 70th and E 71st Sts). 794.9800

57 Patisserie Les Friandises This is not a place for cholesterol watchers—the aromas alone are probably enough to increase LDL counts. But those ready for a splurge should try the buttery croissants and brioche, apple-almond tarte, mocha torte, or chocolate mousse cake; none will disappoint. Coffee is available to go with your sweet, and there are also a couple of tables for quick fixes on the spot. ♦ Daily. 972 Lexington Ave (between E 70th and E 71st Sts). 988.1616 ♿

57 Blanche's Organic Cafe ★$ This spare, gray-and-silver cafe specializes in ultrahealthy, dairy-free vegetarian fare—the fat, calories, and cholesterol counts are all included on the menu for those who want to be sure they're getting a nutritious meal. Try the juice combinations, such as Wake Up (carrot, beet, apple, and ginger); pasta with oven-dried vegetables and grilled sweet-potato salad; and such sandwiches as roasted seasonal vegetables with hummus. ♦ Organic vegetarian ♦ Daily breakfast, lunch, and late-afternoon meals. 972 Lexington Ave (at E 71st St). 717.1923 ♿. Also at: 22 E 44th St (between Madison and Fifth Aves). 599.3445

58 S. Wyler An excellent source of 18th- and 19th-century English sterling silver, Victorian and old Sheffield plates, as well as antique porcelain, this shop is more than a century old. ♦ M-Sa 941 Lexington Ave (at E 69th St). 879.9848

59 The Right Bank ★$$ One of the few casual places in this extremely well-heeled neighborhood, this place offers affordable food with a slight French accent. Try the onion soup, burgers, grilled salmon, or any of the omelettes. There's a pleasant garden for alfresco dining in warmer weather. ♦ Cafe ♦ M-Sa lunch and dinner; Su brunch and dinner. 822 Madison Ave (between E 68th and E 69th Sts). 737.2811

60 The Polo ★★$$$ The atmosphere is clublike—plush brown leather chairs, banquette seating, and dark mahogany walls fitted with equestrian prints and brass sconces. Given the dignified setting, chef Kerry Heffernan's food is appropriately complex; however, some of it works, some doesn't. Try the sautéed foie gras with banyuls vinegar (made with tiny, red, very tart berries); grilled Louisiana shrimp with artichokes, haricots verts, and orange-tarragon vinaigrette; and sautéed Canadian salmon with mustard sauce. Skip the tasteless monkfish and the unpleasantly flavored grilled squab. ♦ American/French ♦ M-Sa breakfast, lunch, and dinner; Su brunch and dinner. Reservations recommended; jacket required. 840 Madison Ave (between E 69th and E 70th Sts). 439.4835 ♿

61 Pierre Deux The French family Demery has spent 300 years creating richly colored paisley and floral fabrics that are quintessentially Provençal, and they sell their best designs—the **Souleiado** line—to this shop. Fabric is offered by the yard or made up into tablecloths, napkins, place mats, and more. ♦ M-Sa. 870 Madison Ave (at E 71st St). 570.9343. Also at: 369 Bleecker St. (at Charles St). 243.7740

Gino's: Distinguished for not having a bad table in the restaurant, and for not having an inedible dish on its menu. A favorite for 50 years, even though it does not accept reservations or credit cards. The waiters never die (same waiters there today were there when I first began going to the place in 1958, although some waiters have been upgraded considerably); three ex-waiters now own the place, having purchased it in the early 1980s from the previous and founding owners—one being Mr. Gino himself, who is still alive, and a regular customer.

Other favorite NY restaurants: **Elaine's,** known for its namesake, Elaine Kaufman, who sits behind the cash register at barside from 8PM until 4AM most nights of the week, greeting regular customers who have been patronizing the place for more than 30 years. I'm one of her oldest customers. I go there because it is the one restaurant a regular can enter without a dinner partner and *find* one there, at one of the tables Elaine ushers you to a spot where you're pleased to be seated. . . with other New Yorkers who are faithful **Elaine's** patrons. It stays open very late and draws an eclectic crowd.

Michael Musto

Columnist, *Village Voice*

Russian Tea Room: Still the place where you can clinch that career-making deal between courses. Caviar- and blini-studded.

Jaffa Cafe: All-night kitsch paradise hangout for the glamorously poor and other **East Village** types. Sensible menu and reasonable prices.

The Big Enchilada: Big, stuffed, juicy, cheap, and they deliver.

Sam's Noodle Shop: The freshest, most diverse Chinese takeout I've encountered. And you won't be hungry an hour later.

Julie Mautner and Monica Velgos

Executive and Associate Editors, *Food Arts Magazine*

Lemongrass Grill on the Upper West Side: Fabulous Thai food, rare for this neighborhood.

Cuisine de Saigon: Very good Vietnamese food.

Kitchen Club: Really cute.

American Renaissance: Fabulous food and setting. And the silver knife rests are great.

Il Padella: Great osso buco.

Cafe St. John: Great food and setting.

Spartina: Hearty homestyle cooking, eclectically ethnic, big portions, great lamb shank.

Louie's Westside Cafe: Great pecan waffles and southwestern eggs. Great brunch overall. And they serve you tea steeped in a teapot instead of in bags.

Thailand Restaurant: Great for groups.

Rona Tison

Executive Vice President, Felissimo

Union Square Greenmarket: This market is a definite must. Union Square transforms into a country market with farmers coming to the city to sell their fresh produce, homemade breads and jams, homespun yarn, plants, etc. Some of the top chefs of New York come to buy at this open market. It's the perfect place to get a taste of the country in the midst of chaotic Manhattan.

Honmura An: For the ultimate experience of "Soba Cuisine." The soba (Japanese noodles) are handmade right on the premises in the glass-enclosed kitchen so one may take note of the technique. The fresh soba is served in various ways–in delicious hot broths, cold with dipping sauce, rolled into sushi-like rolls, and even prepared into a dessert. It's the best outside of Japan.

Restaurant Daniel: For a gastronomic dining experience and impeccable service, **Daniel** is the restaurant of my choice for the city's finest dining. Daniel Boulud's commitment to quality is evident in every dish—from the elegant presentation to the imaginative creations. The ideal setting to splurge on a great bottle of wine and be taken to culinary heaven.

The Oak Room, The Plaza: For a bit of old history, dining in the **Oak Room** at the historical landmark, **The Plaza** hotel, is reminiscent of the grand old days of New York City. The oversized chairs, magnificent wood-paneled interior, and hearty portions are enough to take you back in time. Even the cigar smoking adds a bit of nostalgia.

Murray's Sturgeon: The best place to buy your lox and bagels. **Murray's** carries the finest quality salmon with the orders meticulously sliced to perfection. The shop is small with efficient and personalized service. They will also do a terrific job of shipping orders out of state. It's definitely a neighborhood favorite.

Gary A. Goldberg

Executive Director, Culinary Center of New York, New School for Social Research

Zoë: For New American food in a bustling **SoHo** hot spot.

TriBeCa Grill: A casual celebrity hangout that really does have wonderful food and no attitude.

Bouley: A brilliant chef/owner has created a wonderful evocation of France. Go at lunch for great value and lovely unhurried ambience.

Cascabel: Casually elegant, with superbly flavorful food.

San Domenico: Truly elegant Italian.

Palio: The most beautiful bar in town; some of the best Italian food anywhere.

Petrossian: Elegant "grazing"; have caviar tasting, and champagne.

The Russian Tea Room: A celebrity spot, especially at lunch, with wonderful atmosphere. Supernal blini with caviar, and vodka.

The Tea Box Cafe, Takashimaya: A shopper's oasis of serenity and beauty on Fifth Avenue. Lovely cross-cultural lunches, afternoon teas, and Bernachon chocolates.

Le Chantilly: A favorite French/New American in **Midtown**, with a charming host, elegant roseate decor, and brilliant food. Don't miss dessert.

Arcadia: A celebrated chef and lovely, intimate dining room. Go early for dinner to beat the crowd.

China Grill: Soaring space with soaring New York–Pan-Asian food.

Lespinasse, St. Regis: Some say this formal and elegant spot is the best of the best. Go for very special occasions, and splurge.

March: The perfect elegant town-house restaurant with wonderful food and wines.

Rosa Mexicano: Casually stylish, the owner raises Mexican food to an art.

Upper East Side

The area extending from the **East River** to **Fifth Avenue** and from **East 72nd** to **East 110th Streets** is a region of enormous cultural and culinary variety. It attracts everyone, from art aficionados who take in the world-class **Metropolitan Museum of Art** and the **Solomon R. Guggenheim Museum**, along with the other museums that make up "Museum Mile" along Fifth Avenue, to tourists in search of gourmet food emporia, to locals who lust after the "recycled" breads at the **Vinegar Factory**.

fth, **Madison,** and **Park Avenues** and their quiet side streets are an
xtension of the affluent East Side—well-heeled locals lunch at **Restaurant**
aniel and send servants to pick up filet mignon from **Lobel's Prime Meats.**
he gracious neighborhood of **Carnegie Hill** (between Park and Fifth
venues in the 90s) also boasts a handful of exquisite town-house restaurants.

arther east, the neighborhood becomes less affluent, although there are
ockets of wealth. In **Yorkville** (on and around **First** and **Second Avenues** in
e seventies and eighties), the influence of past German and Hungarian
nmigrants is still strongly felt. This is where to find paprika by the barrelful,
icy Hungarian sausages, or rich mocha pastries. If your mood dictates pasta
ther than goulash, there's an embarrassment of riches in Italian restaurants
n and around **Third Avenue.** If it's a burger you're looking for, choices range
om dimly lit taverns to neon-bright diners. Finally, set amid the many
staurant/bars that host the thriving singles' scene is **Elaine's,** one of New
ork's more famous institutions and a magnet for celebrities.

or a quiet evening at home, numerous take-out shops throughout the area
fer nearly as much variety. There's the rustic **Fatto in Casa,** comprehensive
euman & Bogdonoff,** ethnic **Paprikas Weiss,** and **Lorenzo's and Maria's**
itchen,** where high quality comes at a high price. For top-of-the-line
roduce, there are ever-more stores to choose from: **Porcini Trading**
ompany, Nature's Gifts,** and **Paradise Market** among them. For something
fferent, try one of the simple shops that sell delicious garlicky grilled
icken, on the streets stretching up to **Spanish Harlem** above 110th Street.

he Upper East Side has something for every taste. The bistros will send you
Paris and coffeehouses will transport you to Budapest. You can even find
alian kosher cooking that will make you feel like you're in Rome. There may
more food for sale per square inch in this neighborhood than anywhere
se in town—maybe in the universe. So if you're having trouble finding what
ou're looking for, chances are it's only a block or two away.

1 Zucchini ★$ "Green cuisine" is what this brick- and plant-filled place calls its dishes, featuring organic vegetables and fruits. Vegetarians will find the cooking fairly creative: four-bean chili with roasted peppers, and *paglia e fieno* ("straw and hay"—green and yellow pasta) with "vegimeat" sauce. Poultry and fish dishes are offered as well including black fettuccine with swordfish and grilled cornish hen with peppercorns, rosemary, and plum tomatoes. ♦ Organic ♦ Daily lunch and dinner. 1336 First Ave (between E 71st and E 72nd Sts). 249.0559 &

1 Hi-Life Restaurant & Lounge ★$$ With its oversized wraparound booths in the style of the sophisticated 1950s, this lounge features an interesting menu adapted to appetites of all sizes. Small plates include fried calamari with spicy red sauce, apple and leek potato pancakes, and grilled sesame chicken fingers; big dishes include grilled blackened swordfish and lemon chicken with wild rice and Oriental vegetables. There are also large bowls of pasta; try penne with grilled chicken, peas, sun-dried tomatoes, and broccoli in a light tomato-cream sauce. ♦ American ♦ M-F dinner; Sa-Su brunch and dinner. 1340 First Ave (at E 72nd St). 249.3600 &. Also at: 477 Amsterdam Ave (at W 83rd St). 787.7199

2 Letizia ★$$$ One of many old-fashioned Italian restaurants in the neighborhood, this place features a warmly decorated room with terra-cotta floors and consistently good food. Specialties include *panzotti* (pasta stuffed with porcini) in a cream sauce, veal chops, and red snapper in parchment. ♦ Italian ♦ Daily lunch and dinner. Reservations recommended. 1352 First Ave (between E 72nd and E 73rd Sts). 517.2244

2 Nino's ★$$ This pretty trattoria with apricot-colored walls and Italian rattan chairs is a reliable place for basic Italian fare. Try one of the pastas, such as penne *arrabbiata* (in a hot tomato sauce) and simply prepared meats, including grilled veal chop and cornish hen. ♦ Italian ♦ Daily lunch and dinner. 1354 First Ave (between E 72nd and E 73rd Sts). 988.0002

2 Petaluma ★$$$ Fallen from the fickle graces of the chic and trendy, this eclectic cafe still attracts a decent crowd. Singles flock to the bar, while folks of all shapes and sizes dine in the vast, pastel-colored postmodern space. The food, which includes *spaghetti primavera;* baby chicken in a light mustard sauce; and swordfish with tomatoes, capers, and olives, is fine. And dessert fans shouldn't miss the Belgian chocolate cake. ♦ Italian ♦ Daily lunch and dinner. Reservations required. 1356 First Ave (at E 73rd St). 772.8800

3 Creative Cakes If you want a unique cake for a special occasion, this tiny shop is a good place to come. The talented bakers here are capable of making cakes in the likeness of batmobiles, videogames, cameras, and submarines. Clients include many celebrities—Eddie Murphy, Cheryl Tiegs, and Joan Lunden among them. ♦ Tu-F by appointment; Sa until 11AM. 400 E 74th St (between York and First Aves). 794.9811

4 Campagnola ★$$ This beige, rustic room with a large antipasto table in the center feels very comfortable. The fare is reliable and familiar—gnocchi with pesto, fettuccine *amatriciana* (in a sauce of olive oil, garlic, tomatoes, peppers, onions, and bacon), ravioli with porcini, veal *sorrentino* (cooked in a Marsala sauce with prosciutto and mozzarella), and the like. ♦ Italian ♦ M-F lunch and dinner; Sa-Su dinner. Reservations recommended. 1382 First Ave (between E 73rd and E 74th Sts). 861.1102

CAFE CROCODILE

5 Cafe Crocodile ★★$$ The fresh, earthy foods of the Mediterranean—be they of Greek, French, Italian, or North African origin—are variously featured here on the menu that changes monthly. Owner/chef Andree Abramoff's love of cooking comes through in every dish; Moroccan couscous, seared tuna with ginger, and duck confit are all highly recommended. ♦ Mediterranean ♦ M-Sa dinner. Reservations recommended. 354 E 74th St (between First and Second Aves). 249.6619

6 Corrado Market This uptown outpost of **Corrado** is strictly a take-out shop that carries just about everything edible. Fresh produce, fish, breads, baked goods, international groceries, fresh coffee beans, smoked salmon, caviar, and a range of prepared foods that include basil chicken salad with pine nuts, pasta with sun-dried tomatoes, and hearts-of-palm salad are all here for the buying. ♦ Daily. 1409 Second Ave (between E 73rd and E 74th Sts). 472.9200 &

7 E.J.'s Luncheonette ★$ Like its counterpart on the West Side, this all-American diner serves all-American food—from burgers, salads, and sandwiches to incredibly filling multigrain pancakes and waffles. A local crowd gathers and waits out front in all kinds of weather for brunch. ♦ Diner ♦ M-F breakfast, lunch, and dinner; Sa-Su brunch and dinner. No credit cards accepted. 1271 Third Ave (at E 73rd St). 472.0600. Also at: 447 Amsterdam Ave (between W 81st and W 82nd Sts). 873.3444

8 Lenox Room ★★$$$ Given the pedigree of this suave new cafe—the owners are executive chef Charles Palmer (owner/chef of **Aureole** and **Alva**) and manager Tony Fortuna (formerly of the **Monkey Bar, mad. 61,** and **Lespinasse**)—expectations were high and tables filled from the moment the doors opened. The room is handsome and subdued with beige walls, brown and black banquettes, and huge displays of flowers, and the fare complex and interesting. To start, try a tasting of hors d'oeuvres, such as crispy sweetbreads, green lentil and foie gras terrine and spicy seafood salsa; oysters or chilled lobster from the raw bar; or fennel, beet, and arugula salad. Move on to wild mushroom *agnolotti* (half-moon–shaped filled pasta) with duck confit; roasted lobster and ginger noodles with scallion glaze; angel-hair pasta with shredded veal and fresh morels; or citrus tarragon chicken. Skip dessert—the selection doesn't match the quality of the rest of the menu. The wines are affordable and include a good selection by the glass. ♦ American ♦ M-F dinner; Sa-Su brunch and dinner. Reservations recommended. 1278 Third Ave (between E 73rd and E 74th Sts). 772.0404

9 Word of Mouth If this take-out shop doesn't have what you want, chances are it isn't worth having. The fine array of prepared foods here includes rosemary chicken with artichoke hearts and mushrooms, stuffed pork chops, osso buco, coq au vin, and many pasta dishes—from ravioli in pesto to linguine with sausage in cream. There are myriad pasta, chicken, and vegetable salads perfect for a picnic in the park, and such desserts as gingerbread pudding, chocolate-dusted whiskey cake, and peach upside-down cake. ♦ Daily. 1012 Lexington Ave (between E 72nd and E 73rd Sts). 734.9483 &

Above Word of Mouth:

Cafe Word of Mouth ★$ This tiny cafe is a perfect place to get together with friends for a sandwich of grilled chicken marinated in lime, garlic, cilantro, and cumin; or smoked turkey, saga blue cheese, and apple slices. Afternoon tea and brunch are also popular. There's a reasonably priced prix-fixe dinner, featuring such dishes as chicken potpie and roast pork on a ragout of cabbage and green lentils,

some of which are available downstairs.
♦ American ♦ M lunch; Tu-F lunch and dinner; Sa-Su brunch. 1012 Lexington Ave (between E 72nd and E 73rd Sts). 734.9483

10 Marché Madison It's exactly what you'd expect a grocery store in this gilded neighborhood to be: a repository for only the very best edibles. This popular market features prime meats, a wide array of international cheeses, excellent prepared foods, perfect produce, upscale breads, and top-quality bakery items. ♦ Daily. 931 Madison Ave (at E 74th St). 794.3360 ♿

11 La Maison du Chocolat From the acclaimed Parisian chocolatier Robert Linxe comes a shop for the true connoisseur. And of course, these delicacies that are among the best chocolates in the world don't come cheap. ♦ M-Sa. 25 E 73rd St (between Madison and Fifth Aves). 744.7117

12 Coco Pazzo ★★$$$$ The biggest hit in Pino Luongo's empire (which includes **Mad. 61, Il Toscanaccio,** and **Le Madri**) continues to pack them in, although the type of experience you have might depend upon who you are. Celebrities, including Kate Capshaw (Steven Spielberg's wife), are invariably treated very well; sometimes mere mortals rate the same star treatment, sometimes they don't. Luckily everyone gets to partake of well-prepared, richly flavored food turned out by Tuscan chef Cesare Casella—seafood risotto, grilled calamari, homemade penne with veal and sage, baby chicken with zucchini, onions, and potatoes, and whole roasted red snapper. The desserts, including warm cinnamon-chocolate pudding with caramel sauce and warm apple tart, are impossible to resist. The Italian wine list is fairly esoteric and generally expensive. ♦ Italian ♦ Daily lunch and dinner. Reservations recommended. 23 E 74th St (between Madison and Fifth Aves). 794.0205

13 Boathouse Cafe ★$$$ After a stroll through **Central Park,** stop at this restaurant in the **Loeb Boathouse** and enjoy a meal in one of New York's prettiest settings. Sit on the outdoor terrace in good weather and take in the peaceful view of the lake. The light fare includes perfectly acceptable pasta dishes, grilled chicken, and swordfish. After 7PM, a trolley at 72nd Street and Fifth Avenue will take you right to the restaurant. ♦ Northern Italian ♦ Daily lunch and dinner Mar-Nov. E 74th St (at East Dr). 517.2233

14 Restaurant Daniel ★★★★$$$$ New York's hottest four-star restaurant is the domain of master-chef Daniel Boulud who moved here after an illustrious six-year run at the legendary **Le Cirque.** Boulud has successfully re-created the same celebrated kitchen, much to the delight of the loyal, well-heeled society patrons who followed him to this intimate room with yellow walls, vivid oil paintings, peach fabric chairs, extraordinary floral arrangements, and subdued lighting. The menu changes frequently, but one dish that's fairly standard and definitely worth trying is his signature dish from **Le Cirque**— Black Sea bass in a crispy potato shell with leeks and red-wine sauce. Also sublime are foie gras with quince, Maine Peekytoe crab salad, quail salad, bay scallops with porcini mushrooms, steamed skate in lobster broth, nine-herb ravioli, and smoked-salmon Napoleon. Go ahead and give in to the desserts—particularly the gratin of chocolate and the baked red-wine tart. The wine list is eclectic and moderately priced, with good choices from Italy, California, and France; the sommelier is extremely helpful. The restaurant's popularity is such that getting dinner reservations often requires the patience of Job. To accommodate the demand, the room is packed with tables that are too close together—the only flaw at this very special place. ♦ French ♦ M, Sa dinner; Tu-F lunch and dinner. Reservations required; jacket required. 20 E 76th St (between Madison and Fifth Aves). 288.0033 ♿

15 Sarabeth's at the Whitney ★★$$ This branch of the **Sarabeth's** restaurant family is the perfect place to relax after touring the **Whitney Museum.** Try the lemon linguine with vegetable sauce or choose from a selection of hearty soups and sandwiches. Don't miss one of the famous desserts, including Budapest cake or chocolate mousse cake. ♦ American ♦ Tu-F lunch; Sa-Su brunch. 945 Madison Ave (at E 75th St). 570.3670. Also at: 1295 Madison Ave (between E 92nd and E 93rd Sts). 410.7335; 423 Amsterdam Ave (between W 80th and W 81st Sts). 496.6280

16 Vivolo ★$$ Reasonably priced and therefore crowded, this trattoria features standard, well-prepared dishes that include *capellini primavera;* fettuccine with pesto; chicken with tomatoes and mushrooms; and chicken with lemon, butter, and spinach. For dessert, try the zabaglione and ricotta cheesecake. ♦ Italian ♦ M-Sa lunch and dinner. Reservations required. 140 E 74th St (at Lexington Ave). 737.3533. Also at: 222 E 58th St (between Second and Third Aves). 308.0112

16 Cucina Vivolo ★$ This casual cafe next door to **Vivolo** (see above) specializes in sandwiches—try mozzarella, tomato, and basil on baguette, and grilled chicken on seeded semolina, such simple pastas as penne with tomato and basil, as well as heartier chicken, veal, and fish entrées. The most popular items, however, are the reasonably priced complete take-out dinners, which include breast of chicken with seasonal mushrooms, vegetables, and a salad. ♦ Italian ♦ M-Sa lunch and dinner. 138 E 74th St (between Lexington and Park Aves). 717.4700

17 La Terrine Those searching for the perfect Italian, French, Portuguese, or Hungarian ceramic serving piece come here to find treasures usually discovered only on a trip abroad. Exquisite hand-painted pottery, including faïence from Quimper, France, is in abundance. The bowls, platters, and plates are among the prettiest anywhere. ♦ M-Sa. 1034 Lexington Ave (at E 74th St). 988.3366

18 Fatto in Casa The name means "made at home" and that's how the food tastes in this rustic take-out shop. The dishes are modeled on ones cooked by the owners' mother and grandmother in Sicily, and they're bursting with rich, fresh flavors. The open-kitchen design lets you watch proprietors Dominick and Frank Salvaggi make such tasty delights as *bruschetta* (toasted bread seasoned with oil and garlic); penne with vodka sauce (a light tomato base with onions, *prosciutto di Parma,* vodka, and cream); caponata (eggplant cooked with onions, tomatoes, anchovies, olives, pine nuts, capers, and vinegar); grilled vegetables with portobello mushrooms, grilled zucchini, and peppers flavored with garlic, olive oil, and balsamic vinegar; and grilled chicken breast with sun-dried tomatoes, arugula, and prosciutto. Meat, poultry, Italian grocery items, and freshly made sauces are available as well. ♦ M-Sa. 1047 Lexington Ave (between E 74th and E 75th Sts). 717.6204

BOSCO
RESTAURANT

18 Bosco ★$$ This pretty bilevel trattoria with sponged raspberry walls and dried flowers turns out a variety of successful homemade pastas. Try *capellini* (thin spaghetti) with mushrooms and shrimp, veal *rollatini* (stuffed with ricotta and spinach), and veal chops with shiitake mushrooms in a Barolo wine sauce with risotto. Finish the meal with the delicious pear tart topped with cinnamon gelato. ♦ Italian ♦ Daily lunch and dinner. Reservations recommended. 1049 Lexington Ave (between E 74th and E 75th Sts). 535.8400

18 William Poll A gourmet store for the conservative, well-heeled residents of the neighborhood, this is a place to pick up foie gras, smoked salmon, or tins of champagne biscuits. Assorted hors d'oeuvres, dips, high-quality sandwiches, and soups are also available. ♦ M-Sa. 1051 Lexington Ave (between E 74th and E 75th Sts). 288.0501

19 Mortimer's ★$$$ This unpretentious taver serves simple food. At the bar sit captains of industry, fashionable women, and as gossip columnist Suzy often says about the crowd here, "others too rich and famous to mention." Safe bets from the menu include Caesar salad, steak *frites* (with french fries), and roast chicken. ♦ Continental ♦ Daily lunc and dinner. Reservations required. 1057 Lexington Ave (at E 75th St). 517.6400

20 Bonté The specialties here are extravagantl decorated cakes with exquisite marzipan and spun-sugar work, although there is hardly a pastry or cake that isn't divine. This patisseri also makes croissants and brioches, fruit tarts, and some of the best eclairs in Manhattan. ♦ M-Sa. 1316 Third Ave (betwee E 75th and E 76th Sts). 535.2360

BRIGHTON GRILL

21 Brighton Grill ★★$ The large stuffed fish over the doorway is a less than subtle hint that seafood is the order of the day; octopus paintings on the walls inside provide another clue. Otherwise, this handsome room with wood paneling and ceiling fans serves as a comfortable neighborhood gathering spot. Order the crawfish cakes, grilled lemon-pepper shrimp, monkfish, or for landlubbers, lamb shanks. ♦ American ♦ M-Sa lunch and dinner; Su brunch and dinner. Reservations recommended. 1313 Third Ave (between E 75th and E 76th Sts). 988.6663

21 La Piazzetta di Quisisana ★$$$ Named for a small square in front of Capri's Quisisan hotel, this cozy trattoria—with apricot walls, terra-cotta details, and Italian pottery—features the food of that Italian isle. Try penn with shrimp, red beans, and fresh tomatoes; one of the fresh fish dishes grilled in a wood-burning oven; or roasted baby chicken with rosemary and garlic. ♦ Italian ♦ Daily lunch, dinner, and late-night meals. Reservations recommended. 1319 Third Ave (between E 75th and E 76th Sts). 879.5000

22 Mezzaluna ★$$ This tiny restaurant is quit popular among East Siders for pizzas baked i a wood-burning oven, as well as carpaccio, salads, and pasta specials. Pumpkin *tortello* (large tortellini) is among the favorites. ♦ Italian ♦ Daily lunch, dinner, and late-night meals. 1295 Third Ave (between E 74th and E 75th Sts). 535.9600 ♿

22 Hurricane Island ★★$$ Having lobster in Manhattan usually involves a credit check, but not here. This place has the tasty crustaceans flown in from Maine by pilot friends, which helps keep the prices down. No money was wasted on the decor here, either. Get sweet, steamed lobster, New England clam chowder, grilled salmon, or a pretty decent steak. ♦ Seafood ♦ Daily lunch and dinner. 1303 Third Avenue (between E 74th and E 75th Sts). 717.6600 &

PERSEPOLIS
Restaurant
N.Y.C.

23 Persepolis ★$ Romantically lit, this Persian restaurant is perfect for those nights when you're in the mood for something different. The food is fresh and deeply flavored—try the tabbouleh salad; yogurt mixed with cucumber and mint; charcoal-grilled shish kebab; and a vegetarian stew of spinach, lettuce, kidney beans, parsley, and scallions, served over vegetable rice. ♦ Persian ♦ Daily lunch and dinner. 1423 Second Ave (between E 74th and E 75th Sts). 535.1100

23 Pamir ★$$ The latest ethnic invasion is exotic Afghan cuisine. Try the skewered-meat dishes—lamb and chicken—served with moist rice pilaf and side dishes of yogurt and sautéed eggplant. ♦ Afghan ♦ Tu-Su dinner. Reservations recommended. 1437 Second Ave (between E 74th and E 75th Sts). 734.3791

23 Baraonda ★★$$$ First there was **Mezzaluna** (see above) and now this—owner Enrico Proiotti's latest contribution to the beautiful-people-and-pasta scene. The cheery, fanciful room is fitted with primary-color lanterns, caricatures on the walls, and streamers. Late at night there's even dancing on the tables. Before running completely amok, line your stomach with a good, simple plate of pasta, such as *tagliolini* (thin noodles) with tomato and basil; shrimp risotto; or an entrée—grilled salmon with wild mushroom sauce is a good pick. ♦ Northern Italian ♦ Daily lunch and dinner. Reservations required. 1439 Second Ave (at E 75th St). 288.8555

24 The Red Tulip ★$$ The bright dining room in back of the dimly lit bar is gaily decorated with old, hand-painted pottery, wooden shelves, and cabinets. Booths around the sides of the room provide romantic privacy with high-backed, natural-wood banquettes. All in all, the atmosphere here is pleasant, although the practically nonstop international folk music performed live may not appeal to every taste. The ample portions of rich goulash soup, *crepes hortobagyi* (stuffed with veal and chicken), Hungarian sausage, braised veal shank with vegetables, stuffed cabbage,

and delicate spaetzle are made from fresh ingredients and are full of rich cooked-in flavors. ♦ Hungarian ♦ W-Su dinner. Reservations recommended. 439 E 75th St (between York and First Aves). 734.4893

25 Shabu Tatsu ★★$$ Simple, delicious Japanese barbecue, sukiyaki, and *shabu shabu* (beef and vegetables boiled in a brass pot)—are the specialties of this starkly decorated restaurant. The gimmick is that diners cook it themselves, under their waiter's watchful gaze. ♦ Japanese ♦ Daily dinner. 1414 York Ave (at E 75th St). 472.3322. Also at: 216 E 10th St (between First and Second Aves). 477.2972

26 Voulez Vous ★★$$$ With a glass front, this French bistro looks slicker than most, but the food couldn't be more traditional. Try coq au vin, cassoulet, filet mignon au poivre, or duck confit; and for dessert sample one of the heavenly homemade fruit tarts. There's also an excellent brunch on Sunday offering cheese soufflé, couscous salad, and steak *tartare*. ♦ French ♦ M-Sa lunch and dinner; Su brunch and dinner. Reservations required. 1462 First Ave (at E 76th St). 249.1776

27 Mo's Caribbean Bar and Grille ★$ Loud and vividly colored, this fun spot takes its Caribbean menu fairly seriously. Choose from Cuban black-bean soup, grilled ginger chicken strips with lime vinaigrette, coconut shrimp, Jamaican jerk chicken, and the like. Dishes more often found on the mainland include linguine with rock shrimp, grilled chicken breast, and chicken-fried chicken. Tuesday nights after 9PM get cooking with live reggae. ♦ Caribbean ♦ M-F dinner; Sa-Su brunch and dinner. 1454 Second Ave (at E 76th St). 650.0561

27 Il Monello ★★$$$ Those who like a little razzle-dazzle with their meal will enjoy the way most dishes are given finishing touches in the dining room; otherwise, the food is simple and reliable. Try spaghetti carbonara (with cream, eggs, parmesan, peas, and bacon); breast of chicken with onion, tomato, and basil sauce; and red snapper with a pine-nut crust and balsamic sauce. The in-depth Italian wine list is not only laudable, it's applaudable. ♦ Italian ♦ Daily lunch and dinner. Reservations required. 1460 Second Ave (between E 76th and E 77th Sts). 535.9310 &

27 Zucchero ★$ The pretty yellow dining room with subdued lighting offers an unusually sophisticated setting, given the price range.

The pasta dishes are as good as they are inexpensive—try ravioli in butter and sage or fettuccine with calamari, mussels, and crabmeat in a tomato sauce. ♦ Italian ♦ Daily dinner. No credit cards accepted. 1464 Second Ave (between E 76th and E 77th Sts). 517.2541 &

Jim McMullen

28 Jim McMullen ★$$ At this handsome, modern tavern—an enduring scene for singles and networking—the experience is greater than the sum total of the food. Still, it is possible to get a good meal; try the sesame-crusted salmon with tomato vinaigrette or roasted chicken with a ginger glaze. There are also a number of highly potable wines by the glass. ♦ American ♦ M-Sa lunch and dinner; Su brunch and dinner. Reservations recommended. 1341 Third Ave (between E 76th and E 77th Sts). 861.4700

29 The Velvet Room ★★★$$ Don't be intimidated by the velvet rope out front blocking the entrance; it's just for show. Just walk right up, all are admitted to this funky spot that looks like a bordello decorated by Morticia Addams. There are velvet-covered settees, maroon velvet curtains with gold fringes, and billowing sheets of cheesecloth covering the ceiling. Candles are everywhere, many glued to the spot by their voluminous drippings. The wine and dessert lists are extensive, but you should come for the whole soup-to-nuts experience. Spinach pie topped with tahini and lemon-herb dressing makes a good starter; follow it up with the excellent boneless breast of duck, glazed with mango, orange, and jalapeño chutney, and served with caramelized onions. The dessert menu goes on for a couple of pages, so there should be something for every sweet tooth; but skip the very ordinary crème brûlée. The wine list includes champagne and dessert wines, and although beer is available too, it somehow seems out of place here. ♦ Eclectic ♦ Daily dinner and late-night meals. 209 E 76th St (between Second and Third Aves). 628.6633

coconut grill

30 Coconut Grill ★$ The social scene is usually in high gear at this attractive, deep-yellow and royal-blue spot. The food is quite respectable, particularly such homemade pastas as rigatoni with smoked mozzarella, eggplant, and plum tomatoes; and basil linguine with shrimp, scallops, mussels, and clams in a spicy tomato sauce. There's also good rotisserie chicken with pineapple-ginger soy, tomatillo salsa, or honey-mustard sauce. ♦ American ♦ M-Sa

lunch and dinner; Su brunch and dinner. 1481 Second Ave (at E 77th St). 772.6262

31 Sable's Smoked Fish Kenny Sze, the purveyor of sensational chopped liver, whitefish salad, gefilte fish, stuffed cabbage, and silky smoked salmon, is originally from Hong Kong. But Sze came to this East Side shop by way of **Zabar's**, where he spent 12 years as manager of the smoked fish department. Like at his old training ground across town, the prices here for delectable deli items, and other stock, including olive oil, parmigiano reggiano, and English preserves, are more reasonable than elsewhere. ♦ Daily. 1489 Second Ave (between E 77th and E 78th Sts). 249.6177

32 Caffe Bianco ★$ The pastas, salads, chicken dishes, and such sandwiches as fresh mozzarella and tomato are fine, but desserts like the Valencia orange cake and chocolate truffle cake are sublime. The cappuccinos are pretty terrific too. In summer, the tables spill out onto the sidewalk—just like in Italy. ♦ Italian ♦ M-Th, Su lunch and dinner; F-Sa lunch, dinner, and late-night meals. No credit cards accepted. 1486 Second Ave (between E 77th and E 78th Sts). 988.2655

32 Annie's ★$ A hangout for the young and trendy, this place is decorated with lots of mirrors and modern art. Try the sesame-seared tuna with Japanese slaw (a red and white cabbage mixture with miso vinaigrette), meat loaf with sweet potatoes, or any grilled fish. There are three kinds of chili on the menu, but true aficionados may be disappointed. ♦ Eclectic ♦ Tu-Su dinner. 1491 Second Ave (between E 77th and E 78th Sts). 988.5300

32 Lusardi's ★★$$$ This is one of several informal, clublike uptown trattorie that attract a sleek, affluent crowd. The food here, however, is more reliable than at other places and the service is more attentive. Try calamari with tomato sauce, sun-dried–tomato ravioli, pasta with white truffles (in season), and chicken with artichokes and sausage. ♦ Italian ♦ M-F lunch and dinner; Sa-Su dinner. Reservations recommended. 1494 Second Ave (between E 77th and E 78th Sts). 249.2020

33 Rigo Hungarian Pastry The strudels, cakes, tortes, and other attractions here are legendary. Try the caramel-topped *dobos torte* (rich layers of sponge cake and chocolate buttercream, topped with a hard caramel glaze). ♦ Daily. 318 E 78th St (between First and Second Aves). 988.0052

33 Orwasher's Bakery The hearth ovens Abraham Orwasher built in 1916 are still turning out delicious handmade breads and rolls. The family claims credit for inventing raisin pumpernickel and marble breads, and their versions are still tops. Other breads worth trying are walnut tubes, onion rye, cinnamon raisin, and onion or poppy pockets—large square-shaped rolls that, in fact, have no pocket. ♦ M-Sa. 308 E 78th St (between First and Second Aves). 288.6569

34 Maruzzella ★$$ The wood-burning oven and simple stucco interior here radiate a cheery charm. Start with the heady *ricotta di bufalo* cheese with strips of roasted bell pepper, then move on to the pastas. Chef Giovanni Pinato does wonders with ravioli stuffed with spinach and cheese. Then there are the pizzas—perfect crusts topped with creamy mozzarella and such tasyt add-ons as ham, sausages, and vegetables. ♦ Italian ♦ Daily lunch and dinner. 1479 First Ave (at E 77th St). 988.8877

34 Alla Sera ★$ This small, whitewashed cafe has Italian pottery on the walls and a striking yellow-and-blue painted floor with moon and stars. The kitchen here specializes in such basic, well-prepared pasta dishes as penne with eggplant, ricotta, and tomatoes; and linguine with pesto or white clam sauce. Entrées include sautéed chicken in white wine. The menu won't dazzle, but it won't disappoint either. ♦ Italian ♦ Daily lunch and dinner. 1481 First Ave (at E 77th St). 717.5131

35 Tavola ★★$$$ Whitewashed and rustic, this pretty trattoria with terra-cotta floors, white tiles, and a very appealing central antipasto table features well-prepared Tuscan food. Among the many dishes worth trying are spaghetti in a tomato sauce with seafood, gnocchi with fontina and arugula, fettuccine with artichokes, ravioli filled with ricotta in a butternut-squash sauce with sage, risotto of fresh and smoked salmon in red wine, herb-grilled baby chicken, and braised rabbit in Chianti with mushroom polenta. ♦ Italian ♦ M-Sa dinner; Su brunch and dinner. Reservations recommended. 1481 York Ave (between E 78th and E 79th Sts). 570.9810

36 Agata & Valentina This large gourmet grocery features an equally large counter of prepared foods, including chicken primavera, whole spit-roasted chickens, and baked eggplant, as well as prime meats, fresh fish, smoked fish, smoked mozzarella (among other cheeses), freshly squeezed juices, and a large supply of fresh vegetables and fruits. A quick cappuccino here is a good pick-me-up. ♦ Daily. 1505 First Ave (at E 79th St). 452.0690 ఉ

37 Pranzo The panorama of prepared foods in this pretty, rustic shop is so extraordinary that deciding what to take home can be difficult. Ravioli with wild mushrooms, *farfalle* with roasted tomatoes and eggplant, vegetable

chili, apricot-glazed cornish hens, grilled salmon fillet with gazpacho salsa, and spicy corn salad are all good choices. For dessert, there are several lethal chocolate cakes, cognac-pumpkin cheesecake, and a Key lime tart. There are a couple of tables in the back for those who want to consume their purchases immediately. ♦ Daily. 1500 Second Ave (at E 78th St). 439.7777

38 Tibor Meat Market Cravings for garlicky Hungarian salami can be satisfied at this shop. It's also a good source for pork products, including a pork-and-veal mixture that's good for making meat loaf. ♦ Daily. 1508 Second Ave (between E 78th and E 79th Sts). 744.8292

38 Porcini Trading Co. The name suggests a storeful of the prized Italian mushrooms, but actually the offerings here are pretty diverse. There's a good selection of produce; prepared foods including artichoke salad, *farfalle primavera,* and fusilli with sun-dried tomatoes; and grocery items from the world over. ♦ Daily. 1510 Second Ave (between E 78th and E 79th Sts). 772.3627 ఉ. Also at: 1450 Second Ave (between E 75th and E 76th Sts). 717.4653 ఉ

39 Quatorze Bis ★★$$$ Peter Meltzer and Mark DiGiulio have taken their well-loved Fourteenth Street bistro uptown. Sample the best *choucroute garnie* (sauerkraut with smoky sausages, ham, and pork chops) in town or the excellent sautéed *boudin blanc* (a white veal sausage served with a strong Dijon mustard). Also good are the bouillabaisse, duck confit salad, and cassoulet. The herb-roasted chicken is interesting too. There's an excellent, well-priced French wine list. ♦ French ♦ M-F lunch and dinner; Sa-Su brunch and dinner. Reservations recommended. 323 E 79th St (between First and Second Aves). 535.1414

40 Border Cafe $ Fajitas, nachos, chilis, chicken wings, and of course frozen margaritas are the main draw here. Late in the evening, especially during the weekends, this place becomes a crowded bar scene. ♦ Southwestern ♦ M-F dinner; Sa-Su brunch and dinner. Reservations recommended. 244 E 79th St (between Second and Third Aves). 535.4347

41 Neuman & Bogdonoff The range of delectable foods at this comprehensive gourmet grocery and take-out shop includes pasta salads, stuffed cabbage, vegetable salads, grilled glazed salmon fillets, and grilled cornish hens. There's also a range of grocery items and fresh pasta to take home. Treat yourself to a sweet here; the sour-cream coffee cake and chocolate soufflé cake are terrific to take home or to the rear of the store, where a couple of tables provide a convenient place to eradicate more immediate hunger pangs. ♦ Daily. 1385 Third Ave (between E 78th and E 79th Sts). 861.0303 ♿

42 Luke's Bar & Grill ★$ Popular since the day it opened, this snappy neighborhood spot with white walls and green-and-white tablecloths serves burgers, salads, fish and chips, and marinated chicken breast. There may not be anything fancy about this place, but it's good. ♦ American ♦ M-F lunch and dinner; Sa-Su brunch and dinner. No credit cards accepted. 1394 Third Ave (between E 79th and E 80th Sts). 249.7070

42 Due ★★$$$ This simple, cheerful trattoria with white walls and subdued lighting fills a neighborhood need for well-prepared, no-fuss Italian food in a casual, friendly setting. Try the green gnocchi, linguine with clam sauce, tagliatelle *bolognese,* grilled game hen, or chicken *scarpariello* (chicken sautéed in herbed olive oil and garlic). This place also throws together a great salad. ♦ Northern Italian ♦ Daily lunch and dinner. No credit cards accepted. 1396 Third Ave (between E 79th and E 80th Sts). 772.3331

43 Parma ★$$$ However unlikely it may seem, this plain-looking, wood-paneled room was the first of the now many fashionable uptown trattorias. It's no longer as popular as some of the newer places, but the kitchen has maintained its standards. Pastas and main courses, including linguine with clam sauce, ravioli with ricotta and spinach, osso buco, and veal chops are well prepared, but dessert is not a strong suit. ♦ Italian ♦ Daily dinner. Reservations recommended. 1404 Third Ave (at E 79th St). 535.3520

44 Trois Jean ★★★$$$ The three Jeans of the name refer to owner Jean-Luc Andriot, chef Jean-Louis Dumonet, and the late pastry chef Jean-Marc Burillier (ably succeeded by Bernard Chenivese). Together, they run one of the finest bistros in New York, turning out earthy, delicious food in a candlelit environment with paintings of women on the walls and lace curtains on the windows. It manages to be romantic even with tables pushed very close together, but the most pleasant place to sit is a a table upstairs near the window. Among the many good choices are risotto with wild mushrooms and truffle oil, sautéed sweetbreads and artichokes with cumin served on mixed greens with fried leeks, Hudson Valley foie gras terrine, home-smoked salmon, cassoulet, pan-seared skate with beef broth, chicken roasted with preserved lemons and Moroccan olives, and hanger steak with shallot sauce. Desserts are spectacular: try the warm chocolate cake, *frou-frou au café* (coffee and caramel mousse wrapped in a chocolate ribbon and served with cappuccino sauce), *pyramide au chocolat* (an iced chocolate cake made from three different types of chocolate), and a crème brûlée that sets the standard by which all others should be judged. There's a dessert tasting plate for those who can't bear to choose, and pastries can be taken home for later. The well-chosen and attractively priced wine list offers a good selection of wines by the glass. ♦ French ♦ Daily lunch, afternoon tea, and dinner. Reservations recommended. 154 E 79th St (between Third and Lexington Aves). 988.485▮

45 Rosedale Fish Market Although this 90-year-old store doesn't have the most extensive selection in town, it does offer the freshest. Expect to find top-quality salmon, tuna, red snapper, oysters, and the like, obtained through intense bargaining at **Fulton Fish Market**. ♦ M-Sa. 1129 Lexington Ave (between E 78 and E 79th Sts). 861.4323

46 Mark's ★★$$$$ Chef Erik Maillard, formerly of **Les Célébrités,** is shaking up this formal, plush room in **The Mark Hotel** with his vibrant flavors. The menu changes monthly, as does the selection of vintage wines offered by the glass, but the inventive complexity of Maillard's cooking is constant. Good choices are the Maine Peekytoe crab salad with tangerine-and-lime dressing, fricassee of calamari with braised cabbage and Guinness stout–and–cream sauce, red snapper with black truffles, and sautéed loin of venison with braised cabbage and fricassee of winter vegetables with huckleberry sauce. Simpler fare from the grill includes squab, striped bass, and free-range chicken. The desserts—try the chocolate-pecan passion—are very rich. The prix-fixe lunches and dinners are quite reasonable. ♦ French ♦ M-Sa breakfast, lunch, and dinner; Su brunch and dinner. Reservations recommended. 25 E 77th St (between Madison and Fifth Aves). 879.1864

47 Sant Ambroeus ★★$$$ This Milanese institution is known on both sides of the Atlantic for elegant Italian fare, topped off with the best cappuccino or espresso around. Try the mixed seafood antipasto, risotto with arugula and tomatoes, shrimp with mustard sauce, and grilled salmon. The pastries look terrific and some actually are; stick to simpler confections, such as mocha cake and chocolate mousse. Like the pastries, the divine gelato—try *gianduia* (chocolate and hazelnut) or passion fruit—can be had to go. ♦ Italian ♦ M-Sa lunch and dinner; Su lunch. Reservations recommended. 1000 Madison Ave (between E 77th and E 78th Sts). 570.2211

48 The Restaurant at the Stanhope Hotel ★★★$$$ Since Scott Cohen, formerly of **Tatou**, took over the kitchen of this restaurant in 1994, the quality of the food has soared. The once dour room has been brightened as well. Try the terrine of foie gras with dried cherries, salmon *tartare* with three caviars, honey-mustard–roasted salmon, iron-skillet–roasted baby chicken with cornbread stuffing and sage, and roasted free-range rack of lamb with a mushroom-herb crust. There are also several decadent desserts, including slow-cooked chocolate pudding cake with shaved chocolate and a lemon meringue tartlet. ♦ American ♦ Daily lunch and dinner. Reservations recommended. 995 Fifth Ave (at E 81st St). 288.5800

Parioli Romanissimo

49 Parioli Romanissimo ★★★$$$$ Located in a charming town house, this dining room is sedately decorated with beige walls and beige print fabric window shades and seat cushions. The kitchen turns out some of the most refined Italian cuisine available in New York City. The delicate egg pasta and risotto with porcini (among others) are divine, and the entrées, including baked sea bass with tarragon sauce and baby chicken roasted with black truffles, are impeccable. For dessert, have the tiramisù or zabaglione. The wine list is extensive, well-chosen, and expensive. Because the restaurant is run like a private club for regular patrons, it is often difficult to get a reservation. ♦ Italian ♦ M-Sa dinner. Reservations required; jacket and tie required. 24 E 81st St (between Madison and Fifth Aves). 288.2391

50 E.A.T. ★★$$$ Owned by Eli Zabar (of **Zabar's** fame), this informal eatery makes all its breads with a sourdough starter, including the famous *ficelle* (a super-crusty loaf, 22 inches long with a diameter barely larger than a silver dollar). Popular picks from the menu are linguine with broccoli rabe, the Three-Salad Plate (choose three from a list of 12 salads), lamb sandwich, crab cakes, pot roast, and grilled chicken. For dessert try the chocolate cake or raspberry tart. The prices are high, but so is the quality. Plus, the people watching is pretty good; celebrities occasionally drop in. ♦ American ♦ Daily breakfast, lunch, and dinner. 1064 Madison Ave (between E 80th and E 81st Sts). 772.0022

51 Rosenthal Wine Merchant This store features unique wines, particularly burgundies from California and Europe, as well as a knowledgeable staff to help you choose among them. ♦ M-Sa. 1200 Lexington Ave (between E 81st and E 82nd Sts). 249.6650

52 Girasole ★$$$ A local, conservative crowd of East Siders favors this dependable, noisy Italian restaurant located on the ground floor of a brownstone. Poultry and game dishes—such as chicken sautéed with lemon, and grilled organic cornish hens with peppercorns—are best. ♦ Italian ♦ Daily lunch and dinner. Reservations required. 151 E 82nd St (between Third and Lexington Aves). 772.6690

53 Mambo Grill ★$$ The zesty food at this snappy Venezuelan dining spot includes seviche of scallops, *arepas rellenas* (cornmeal cakes stuffed with roast pork or black beans), sautéed shrimp with tomatoes, and grilled snapper with rice and beans. The atmosphere is made more bustling with live music on Saturday nights. ♦ Venezuelan ♦ M-F dinner; Sa-Su lunch and dinner. Reservations recommended. 174 E 82nd St (between Third and Lexington Aves). 879.5516

53 Le Refuge ★★$$$ Bare wooden tables, kitchen towels for napkins, American stoneware, and etched stemware provide a mood of romantic, rustic elegance. The ever-changing menu is prepared with carefully chosen fresh ingredients, all cooked and seasoned with a sure hand. Fish dishes are particularly delectable, and some consider the bouillabaisse here the best in town. When it's available, don't miss the quail stuffed with morel mousse. ♦ French ♦ M-F lunch and dinner; Sa-Su brunch and dinner. Reservations recommended. 166 E 82nd St (between Third and Lexington Aves). 861.4505

To get the prized spot for his hot dog stand at the south end of the Metropolitan Museum of Art, George Makos got into a bidding war with other concessionaires (including his brother) and wound up offering $288,200 for the privilege, a city record. It was a victory of sorts; now he has to sell 790 hot dogs a day, seven days a week, just to break even.

Cafe Metairie

54 Cafe Metairie ★$$ With rustic wood beams, authentic French country decor, and a fireplace, this bistro can't be beat for charm. The food, however, can be hit-and-miss. Safe choices include a good cassoulet, tender steak au poivre with thin *frites,* a well-spiced rare rack of lamb, and traditional coq au vin. For dessert, there are excellent fruit tarts and crème caramel. ♦ French ♦ M-F lunch and dinner; Sa dinner; Su brunch and dinner. 1442 Third Ave (at E 82nd St). 988.1800

Quattro Gatti
RISTORANTE

55 Quattro Gatti ★★$$ The antipasto table at this trattoria dominates the small room, and its selection includes homemade mozzarella, tomato, and basil, and such marinated goodies as artichokes and peppers. After sampling a few choices, move on to the feathery pastas, including rigatoni with tomato, pancetta, and vodka; *paglia e fieno* with radicchio, basil, and shrimp; and linguine with clams, mussels, shrimp, and calamari. Other specialties include breast of chicken with peppers, prosciutto, and mozzarella; veal chops with porcini sauce; and red snapper with black olives, capers, and tomato sauce. ♦ Italian ♦ Daily lunch and dinner. 205 E 81st St (between Second and Third Aves). 570.1073

56 Ci Vediamo ★★$$ The sophisticated, dimly lit room upstairs caters to an older crowd; downstairs is a younger, rowdier scene. Wherever you decide to sit, try one of the interesting, well-prepared pastas, which include jumbo ravioli filled with lobster in sage and cream sauce. ♦ Italian ♦ M-F lunch and dinner; Sa-Su brunch and dinner. Reservations recommended. 200 E 81st St (between Second and Third Aves). 650.0850

57 Samalita's Tortilla Factory ★$ Within this small, bright, yellow and blue room with Mexican silver lamps, colorful tiles, and wicker chairs, diners are treated to fresh-tasting Mexican and Cal-Mex fare. Try the spicy guacamole; vegetarian burritos with char-grilled corn, red and green peppers, chilies, and broccoli; *carnitas* (grilled chunks of marinated pork); or any of the tacos or tortillas. Wash it all down with a Corona, Pacifico, or Negro Modello. ♦ Mexican ♦ Daily lunch and dinner. 1429 Third Ave (at E 81st St). 737.5070 &

58 Lorenzo and Maria's Kitchen Let the luscious window display tempt you inside. Almost anything you could want for dinner is available here—apricot-glazed cornish hens, *primavera* rice, marinated beet salad, roast stuffed veal, sweet-potato and spinach puree, and flaky apple strudel. The only drawback is the price; it costs dearly to have someone cook this well for you. ♦ M-Sa. 1418 Third Ave (between E 80th and E 81st Sts). 794.1080 &

58 La Folie ★★$$$ With Corinthian columns a high navy-blue ceiling, and French antiques scattered around, this dramatic dining room looks like it would be more at home in SoHo than on the Upper East Side. Perhaps that's one reason for its popularity—it saves locals trip downtown. Now with David Pasternack, former chef of the departed **Privé,** heading th kitchen, the offerings are even more in demand. Among the best entrées are chilled, stuffed artichoke with roasted Maine shrimp, grilled endive, and aged wine vinegar; medaillons of beef with green-peppercorn sauce; and pan-roasted free-range chicken. For dessert, try the *pot de crème*—a chocolate pudding of which dreams are mad• There's also a well-priced, early prix-fixe dinner. ♦ International ♦ M-F dinner; Sa-Su brunch and dinner. Reservations recom- mended. 1422 Third Ave (between E 80th an• E 81st Sts). 744.6327 &

58 Akron Market Owner Robert Shapiro features meats from animals raised in a natural and humane fashion, not only easing the consciences of meat eaters, but resulting in better flavor and texture, and a healthier diet. Angus beef is raised in Texas without antibiotics or hormonal implants; lamb is nourished in California on a diet of clover, rye grass, and alfalfa, which renders the meat unusually tender and lower in cholesterol; pork comes from upstate New York and is lower in fat due to the pigs' organic diet; and chickens are raised in a similar manner to the French *poulet de Bresse.* ♦ M-Sa. 1424 Third Ave (between E 80th and E 81st Sts). 744.1551

59 Tirami Sù ★★$ Whimsically decorated with gold sun and moon masks and mythical figures on the walls, this crowded cafe seems determined to offer its fashionable customers a good time, right down to the food. On the menu are excellent homemade pastas with strong zesty sauces, pizzas with classic and unusual toppings, and authentic Italian desserts served with excellent espresso. Especially good are the *capellini* with shrimp i spicy tomato sauce, risotto with porcini, and carpaccio. ♦ Italian ♦ Daily lunch and dinner. 1410 Third Ave (at E 80th St). 988.9780

60 Istanbul Kebap ★★$ Although there's no decor to speak of in this small Turkish restaurant, the excellent kebabs and rich honey-soaked desserts are so good you won't notice. Also worth trying are the stuffed grape leaves, eggplant dishes, *yogurtlu* kebab (a casserole of chopped lamb, onions, yogurt, paprika, and tomato), and broiled fish, all of which are as authentic as they are cheap. ♦ Turkish ♦ Daily dinner. 303 E 80th St (between First and Second Aves). 517.6880

61 Merenda ★$ This joint venture by the owners of **Lusardi's, Due, Triangolo, Elio's, Petaluma,** and **Luke's Bar and Grill** makes a gallant effort to appeal to all of the people, all of the time. The drawback is that it's hard to do anything particularly well when you're split in so many directions. Among the dishes that do succeed are penne with mozzarella and tomato sauce and the roasted, herbed half chicken. Basically, diners should stick to the American dishes and the simplest ones at that. Dessert lovers will be pleased though, particularly fans of bread pudding. ♦ International ♦ M-F lunch and dinner; Sa-Su brunch and dinner. 1538 Second Ave (at E 80th St). 734.1888

61 Pig Heaven ★$$ The whimsical decor is totally porcine—pigs on the walls, the menus, and just about everything else. Go ahead and pig out on the Cantonese suckling pig and any of the lighter-than-air steamed dumplings. Other recommended dishes include scallion pancakes and lobster with ginger. ♦ Chinese ♦ M-Th, Su lunch and dinner; F-Sa lunch, dinner, and late-night meals. Reservations recommended weekends. 1540 Second Ave (between E 80th and E 81st Sts). 744.4333

61 Cafe Divino ★$ This casual sibling of **Divino Ristorante** (see below) offers *panini* (sandwiches), salads, and a number of good pastas, including tagliatelle with ham and mushrooms, angel hair with tomato and basil, tortellini with ham and peas, and fusilli with julienne of vegetables. The neighboring **Gastronomia Divino** (1542 Second Ave, 861.1533) offers roughly the same menu as well as a take-out department. ♦ Italian ♦ Daily lunch and dinner. 1544 Second Ave (between E 80th and E 81st Sts). 517.9269

61 Divino Ristorante ★$$ Service and pasta are the high points of this unpretentious favorite of Italian expatriates. Specialties include good fettuccine with four cheeses, linguine with baby clams, breaded veal chop Milanese, and shrimp scampi. Top it all off with a wonderful cappuccino. ♦ Italian ♦ Daily dinner. Reservations required. 1556 Second Ave (between E 80th and E 81st Sts). 861.1096

61 Yorkville Packing House Salamis are a big draw here, as are smoked pork chops, homemade sausages, and hams. A large supply of Hungarian grocery items, including fresh fruit preserves and spicy paprika, are offered as well. ♦ M-Sa. 1560 Second Ave (at E 81st St). 628.5147

62 Sistina ★★$$$ Owned by brothers Giuseppe, Gerardo, Antonio, and Cosimo Bruno, this restaurant serves a pleasing mix of Northern and Southern Italian dishes. Try *pappardelle* (broad noodles) in veal sauce with mushrooms and tomatoes, grilled chicken with arugula salad, and sea scallops in a tarragon broth. For dessert, don't miss the almond cake with chocolate and vanilla sauces. As the name suggests, the famous fresco from the Sistine Chapel has been reproduced here as a wall mural. ♦ Italian ♦ Daily dinner. Reservations required. 1555 Second Ave (between E 80th and E 81st Sts). 861.7660

63 Etats-Unis ★★$$$ The Rapp family has no professional culinary training, so the success of the ever-changing, highly personal menu is all the more impressive (based upon sheer natural talent). You never know what you're going to get on any given evening—it could be arugula and beet salad with goat cheese, roasted sea bass with coriander, or grilled veal rib with a tuna and caper sauce. Whatever it is, you'll be in for a taste treat. The gray, subtly lit room is a sophisticated and attractive setting to enjoy these bursts of culinary creativity. ♦ American/Eclectic ♦ M-Sa dinner. Reservations recommended. 242 E 81st St (between Second and Third Aves). 517.8826

64 Gotham City Diner ★$$ Locals pack this stylish black, white, and chrome diner that looks like it popped out of a Dick Tracy comic. The crowd comes for the varied menu of well-prepared food featuring grilled rare-tuna salad niçoise, lamb shank with risotto, paella, and grilled quail. The good basic desserts include brownie à la mode with chocolate sauce and pear crisp. ♦ American ♦ Daily breakfast, lunch, and dinner. 1562 Second Ave (at E 81st St). 570.9334

64 Paprikas Weiss The store is named after its founder, a Hungarian immigrant who sold spices from a pushcart, but paprika is only one among hundreds of imported spices to be found here. Also on the shelves are ingredients from abroad to make Hungarian delights, fresh condiments, and gourmet cooking utensils. Everything sold here is also available by mail; ask for the catalog. ♦ Daily. 1572 Second Ave (between E 81st and E 82nd Sts). 288.6117

65 Le Boeuf à la Mode ★★$$$ Old-fashioned in the best possible sense, this dining spot—handsomely decorated with ornate lighting fixtures, oil paintings, and lace curtains—features some of the most attentive service in town. The signature dish (beef marinated and braised in red wine), escargots, and roast duck with black currants are particularly good. In a city full of bistros, this place is the real thing—even most of the customers are French. ♦ French ♦ Daily lunch and dinner. Reservations recommended. 539 E 81st (between East End and York Aves). 249.1473

66 Sirabella ★★$$ Perpetually packed, this place makes fresh pasta *in casa*. Taste the difference it makes in such standard dishes as linguine with clam sauce. On cold winter nights the rich textured soups are a must, as is the crisp calamari. The osso buco is delectable, and the vegetables—cooked escarole, for example—are redolent of garlic and olive oil. ♦ Italian ♦ Daily lunch and dinner. Reservations recommended. 72 East End Ave (between E 82nd and E 83rd Sts). 988.6557

67 Wilkinson's 1573 Seafood Cafe ★★$$$ The interior of this little gem of a restaurant is relaxed and intimate, with pastel-colored murals adorning the bare-brick walls. Try such creatively prepared seafood dishes as grilled John Dory (a white fish that is also known as St. Peter's fish) with Thai ginger broth, and pan-seared, spice-coated tuna. ♦ Seafood ♦ Daily dinner. Reservations recommended. 1573 York Ave (at E 83rd St). 535.5454

68 Primavera ★$$$$ One of the great watering holes for the older, distinguished smart set, this sedate room has deep-colored wood paneling and upmarket, if not particularly attractive, oil paintings. The food is similarly dignified and usually of good quality. Try the chicken breast with champagne sauce, pasta with truffles, or green and white pasta with peas and ham. ♦ Italian ♦ Daily dinner. Reservations required; jacket and tie required. 1578 First Ave (at E 82nd St). 861.8608

69 Triangolo ★$ This stylish, mustard-colored room with geometric accents on the walls is a popular neighborhood trattoria known for simple, decently prepared dishes. Try

pappardelle with vegetables, black *tagliolini* with seafood, or artichokes with garlic and oil. ♦ Italian ♦ Daily lunch and dinner. No credit cards accepted. 345 E 83rd St (between First and Second Aves). 472.4488

Trastevere

70 Trastevere ★★$$$ Its name refers to an ancient Jewish neighborhood in Rome, but this Italian kitchen didn't become glatt kosher until it was mistakenly listed as such in a local restaurant guide—it turned out there was quite a demand. Dietary laws notwithstanding (all the food served here is glatt kosher), this place features tasty Italian dishes everyone can enjoy. Try carpaccio (without parmesan), *capellini primavera,* polenta with mushrooms, veal *alla Romana* (sautéed with artichokes), chicken with Marsala and mushrooms, and veal chops with tomato salad. ♦ Italian ♦ M-Th, Sa-Su dinner. Reservations required. 309 E 83rd St (between First and Second Aves). 734.6343

Designer Cakes

Should you need an extra-special cake—not merely one with script lettering and a few frosted flowers—talk to one of these artists, who sculpt with cake batter and paint with icing. Ann Warren of **Cupcake Cafe** (522 Ninth Ave, at W 39th St, 465.1530), known for her artistic designs; Lisa Montenegro of **Cakeability** (a home-based operation, 779.1629), who can turn out cakes of all shapes and designs; Margaret Braun (929.1582), who specializes in artistic cakes with pictures; Colette Peters of **Colette's Cakes** (a home-based operation, 366.6530) who once made a triple-tiered cake in the likeness of Madonna for the diva herself; Bill Schultz of **Creative Cakes** (400 E 74th St, between First and York Aves, 794.9811), who makes cakes in all shapes and designs; Gail Watson of **Custom Cakes** (a home-based operation, 967.9167), who constructs fantasy cakes and great wedding cakes; Ron Ben-Israel (627.2418), known for his beautiful party cakes; Mary Cleaver of **The Cleaver Company** (229 W Broadway, at White St, 431.3688), whose cakes come in all shapes, including the Gucci bag done for *Vogue* editor Anna Wintour; and Madeline Lanciani (274.8447), whose specialty is cakes in different shapes and sizes that she can decorate with someone's likeness.

71 Mocca Hungarian ★$ Treat yourself to hearty Hungarian home cooking that will please your purse as well as your palate. The portions are more than generous at prices that are improbably low. As you might expect, the Wiener schnitzel, stuffed cabbage, and strudel are the best picks. ♦ Hungarian ♦ Daily dinner. No credit cards accepted. 1588 Second Ave (between E 82nd and E 83rd Sts). 734.6470 ⅄

72 Enchilada Johnny's ★$ This town doesn't exactly lack enchilada joints, but homesick Texans make a beeline for this place to sink their teeth into fresh-tasting, authentic soft tacos, enchiladas, fried flour-tortilla chimichangas, fajitas, and irresistible chewy pecan pralines. ♦ Tex-Mex ♦ Daily lunch and dinner. No credit cards accepted. 1593 Second Ave (between E 82nd and E 83rd Sts). 570.4002

73 Erminia ★★$$$ The crowning achievements here are the lushly sauced *pappardelle* tossed with artichokes, tomato, sausage, and porcini, and the excellent Tuscan lamb grilled over a wood fire. There are also a number of other roasted dishes, including veal chops. The romantic candlelight atmosphere makes this restaurant a popular place, so be sure to reserve a couple of days in advance. ♦ Italian ♦ M-Sa dinner. Reservations required. 250 E 83rd St (between Second and Third Aves). 879.4284

74 Azzurro ★★$$ In a neighborhood filled with formula Italian trattorias, this casual family-run Sicilian establishment offers delicious homemade pastas. Try the penne with eggplant in tomato sauce, gnocchi with pesto, and ravioli with porcini sauce. There are also such grilled dishes as chicken paillard and sirloin with a black-peppercorn cream sauce. ♦ Italian ♦ Daily dinner. Reservations recommended. 245 E 84th St (between Second and Third Aves). 517.7068

75 Elio's ★★$$$ Wall Streeters and bankers mix with media types and celebs at this trendy neighborhood eatery, a spin-off of the ever-popular **Elaine's**. It's always crowded and noisy, and the food is always good. Order one of the specials, which seem to inspire the kitchen even more than the regular menu does. But the pasta dishes and veal chops are also good picks. ♦ Italian ♦ Daily dinner. Reservations required. 1621 Second Ave (between E 84th and E 85th Sts). 772.2242 ⅄

75 Mustang Grill ★$ With sun-baked apricot walls and steer skulls, the decor here is an homage to the Southwest. The zesty cooking also does the region proud—corn-crab cakes with roasted jalapeño *salsa verde,* pecan-and-honey–crusted chicken, grilled yellowfin tuna with mango–black-bean salsa, and grilled Atlantic salmon with cilantro-tomato broth. ♦ Southwestern ♦ M-F lunch and dinner; Sa-Su brunch and dinner. 1633 Second Ave (at E 85th St). 744.9194

76 Maison Caribe ★★$ This bright Caribbean cafe with vivid yellow walls and murals of ferns is a cheerful foray to the islands, albeit with a slight European spin. Try the octopus salad; chicken empanadas; crab cakes; Cuban chicken stew with onions, peppers, and peas; and chicken curry. ♦ Caribbean ♦ M-Sa dinner. 345 E 85th St (between First and Second Aves).744.1227

76 Paola's ★★$$$ Proprietor and chef Paola Marraccino (who also owns **Maison Caribe** next door) turns out excellent pasta (especially tortellini), hearty soups, good veal and chicken dishes (particularly chicken with sausage), and creamy cheesecake at this delightful Northern Italian restaurant. The atmosphere is romantic and intimate, but the acoustics could be better—when crowded, it's a bit noisy. At press time, the restaurant opened just for dinner, serving lunch only to small parties that booked in advance. However, plans are in the works to open for lunch soon; call for more information. ♦ Italian ♦ Daily dinner. Reservations recommended. 347 E 85th St (between First and Second Aves). 794.1890

77 The Pie ★$ Plastic table coverings and Russian artifacts decorate this dark, snug Russian cafe which turns out very good vegetarian borscht, Russian herring, and blinis and sour cream. But its specialties are, not surprisingly, pies—casseroles of layered blinis, fish, meat, poultry, and vegetables—as well as Siberian *pelmeni* (dumplings stuffed with onions and meat), and salmon poached in white wine. ♦ Russian ♦ Daily lunch and dinner. 340 E 86th St (between First and Second Aves). 517.8717

78 Estia ★★$$$ Here you'll find fresh and always satisfying Greek food in a typical, noisy taverna setting. Every night at about 9PM, the live music starts; by about 10PM, when the instrumentalists are joined by singers, conversation becomes impossible. The Greek antipasto for two, which includes fish roe, eggplant salad, *tzatziki* (yogurt, garlic, and dill), stuffed grape leaves, and pickled octopus, is a good introduction to a hearty meal, as is the fried zucchini, which comes with a wondrous almond-garlic sauce for dipping. The standard specialties, such as moussaka, *pastitsio* (macaroni, chopped meat, and béchamel sauce), and souvlaki are all first-rate, which is why expatriate Greeks flock here. ♦ Greek ♦ Tu-Sa dinner. Reservations required on weekends. 308 E 86th St (between First and Second Aves). 628.9100 ₫

79 Schaller & Weber This incredible store is filled from floor to ceiling with cold cuts. Liverwursts, salamis, bolognas, and other savories are piled on counters, packed into display cases, and hung from the walls and ceilings. ♦ M-Sa. 1654 Second Ave (between E 85th and E 86th Sts). 879.3047

80 Elk Candy Company Moist, chocolate-covered marzipan and other tempting treats, such as almond bark, butter crunch, and chocolate turtles, are for sale in this sweet little hole-in-the-wall. ♦ Daily. 240 E 86th St (between Second and Third Aves). 650.1177

80 Kleine Konditorei ★$$ The wood-paneled and burgundy dining room, fitted with chandeliers and small-shaded table lamps, is reminiscent of the 1950s. Sauerbraten, Wiener schnitzel, roast goose, and *natur schnitzel* (plain, panfried veal cutlet) are the specialties in this old-fashioned restaurant, along with potato pancakes and pastries. This place is definitely not for the calorie conscious. ♦ German ♦ Daily lunch and dinner. 234 E 86th St (between Second and Third Aves). 737.7130 ₫

81 Oven and a Basket Bakery Here are such simple and soul-satisfying treats as rich chocolate cupcakes iced with fudge frosting and good chocolate-chip cookies—in other words, what TV-show moms of the 1950s used to make. ♦ M-Sa. 155 E 84th St (between Third and Lexington Aves). 628.9898

82 Lobel's Prime Meats The sign says it all, "where meat is an art." The Lobels are true experts, and a filet mignon has no equal anywhere else. Of course the same could be said for the prices and of the shop's decor—with the wood paneling, it could almost pass for a den. ♦ M-Sa. 1096 Madison Ave (between E 82nd and E 83rd Sts). 737.1372

82 William Greenberg Jr. Desserts Other bakeries may turn out fancier-looking cakes, but pound for pound, none can match the all-American classics here. Bundt cakes with a slick chocolate icing, pound cakes, brownies, chocolate-chip cookies—all find their richest, most definitive expression here and are utterly delicious. Those who like their pleasures sweetened with guilt can ruminate for a while about the massive amounts of butter and sugar it takes to makes things taste this good. ♦ M-Sa; Su 10AM-4PM. 1100 Madison Ave (between E 82nd and E 83rd Sts). 744.0304. Also at: 518 Third Ave (between E 34th and E 35th Sts). 686.3344

82 Paradise Market Here's the place to buy pearly potatoes, a glistening bunch of spinach, and a handful or two of pert mesclun to accompany that perfect steak from **Lobel** (see above). At this jewel box of a market, every blushing piece of fruit within is spot-fre and buffed to a shine. At these prices, you might think of having them appraised. ♦ M-Sa. 1100 Madison Ave (at E 83rd St). 737.0049. Also at: 1081 Lexington Ave (between E 76th and E 77th Sts). 570.1190

83 Caffe Grazie ★★$ This cheerful yellow caf near the **Metropolitan Museum of Art** serves good sandwiches; a tasty antipasto plate of Genoa salami, provolone, artichoke hearts, olives, prosciutto, and arugula; and such goo simple pastas as linguine *verdura* (with oil, garlic, broccoli, mushrooms, and zucchini). ♦ Italian ♦ Daily lunch and dinner. 26 E 84th St (between Madison and Fifth Aves). 717.4407

84 Demarchelier ★$$ The food here is fine, if not fabulous, and diners can count on well-executed onion soup, leeks vinaigrette, roast chicken, steak *frites,* and *tarte tatin*. But sinc there isn't a great deal of competition on this stretch, crowds seem to pack this simply decorated bistro day and night. ♦ French ♦ Daily lunch and dinner. 50 E 86th (between Park and Madison Aves). 249.6300

85 Schatzie's Prime Meats Owner Tony Schatzie is a fourth-generation butcher. Cou on this tiny shop for prime cuts of beef, veal, and lamb, as well as fresh chicken at prices that are lower than you might expect, given the quality and neighborhood. If you want squab, quail, pheasant, or other game birds, and they're not in stock, Schatzie can have it for you within 24 hours. ♦ M-Sa. 1200 Madison Ave (between E 87th and E 88th Sts 410.1555 ₫

86 Nature's Gifts All of the produce is extraordinarily fresh and beautiful in this market, which also offers a range of gourme items: fresh ravioli and tortellini, cheeses, fresh and dried pasta, barrels of calamata olives, and sun-dried tomatoes. The prices a also reasonable, from the mix-your-own mesclun selection to the usually astronomic blood oranges. ♦ Daily. 1297 Lexington Ave (between E 87th and E 88th Sts). 289.6283. Also at: 320 E 86th St (between First and Second Aves). 734.0298

87 Elaine's $$$ Those whose idea of a good time is watching celebrities eat steamed mussels should be in heaven here. It's a kind club for media celebrities, gossips, and literary types, but they don't necessarily come here for the food, although the spaghetti *bolognese* and grilled veal chops are decent. Try to sit near Elaine—instantly recognizable as the large Earth-mother type with glasses and dark hair; all the action revolves around her. ♦ Italian ♦ Daily lunch, dinner, and late-night meals. Reservations required. 1703 Second Ave (between E 88th and E 89th Sts). 534.8103

88 Twins $$ Seeing double? Don't worry, it's not your eyes, it's the staff, which is comprised completely of identical twins. Actor Tom Berenger obviously thought it was a cute idea because he's one of the owners (and the only one who's not a twin). The food, however, is less well conceived. The mishmash of a menu includes everything from a decent steak au poivre to peanut butter and jelly served on Wonder bread with bananas. Have a quick look, drink, and appetizer, but go elsewhere for dinner. ♦ Eclectic ♦ M-Sa dinner; Su brunch and dinner. Reservations required. 1712 Second Ave (between E 88th and E 89th Sts). 987.1111 &

Sala Thai Restaurant

89 Sala Thai ★★$ The spicy, inventive dishes presented in this popular neighborhood Thai restaurant include salmon with Thai herbs and Bangkok duck (with coconut milk, chilies, and tamarind-curry sauce). The inevitable wait for a table is invariably worth it. ♦ Thai ♦ Daily dinner. Reservations recommended. 1718 Second Ave (between E 89th and E 90th Sts). 410.5557

90 Cafe Andrusha ★$ The decor at this eatery is simple—brick walls, floral tablecloths—but the food, as presented by owner Liana Kirkwood, whose heritage is Russian and Czech, is hearty and satisfying. Try the borscht, beet salad, *pelmeni* with sour cream and dill sauce, roast duck with caraway seeds, blini with caviar, potato pancakes, or *pojarski* (ground veal and chicken patties with mushroom sauce). Finish with a glass of sweet Russian tea. ♦ Russian ♦ M-Sa lunch and dinner; Su brunch and dinner. 1742 Second Ave (between E 90th and E 91st Sts). 360.1128

91 El Pollo ★★$ What this tiny storefront lacks in atmosphere, it more than makes up for with its chicken served with a side order of fried plantains. The crisp chicken gets its distinctive flavor from being marinated in wine, pepper, garlic, oregano, lemon, vinegar, and various spices before being roasted. Wash it all down with an Inca Kola and top it off with an exotic pudding made of raisins,

cinnamon, and quinoa. ♦ Peruvian ♦ Daily lunch and dinner. No credit cards accepted. 1746 First Ave (between E 90th and E 91st Sts). 996.7810

★ THE ★ VINEGAR FACTORY

92 Vinegar Factory Located in an old mustard-and-vinegar factory, this timely brainchild of **E.A.T.**'s owner Eli Zabar recycles unsold prepared foods in a most delicious way. Eli's famous focaccia, wonderful when fresh, is twice as good made into parmesan toast; dried-out loaves of brioche become a scrumptious bread pudding. Foods in their first incarnations are available here as well, at secondhand prices: breads baked fresh daily here are sold at a fraction above wholesale and the cheese prices may be the lowest in town. There's also a full range of fresh produce and homemade pâtés. At press time, there were plans to offer brunch on the balcony above the selling floor. ♦ Daily. 431 E 91st St (between York and First Aves). 987.0885

93 Hanna's If you run out of Parma prosciutto or sun-dried tomatoes in the middle of the night, this is the place to come. It's a 24-hour gourmet store that carries a little of everything—pasta, a selection of cheeses, prepared foods, smoked meats, breads, coffee beans, and a huge produce section. ♦ Daily 24 hours. 1620 Third Ave (at E 91 St). 876.1717

94 Yura and Company ★★$ One of the neighborhood's best cafes, this place has excellent bouillabaisse, braised stuffed chicken breast with wild-mushroom ragout, and osso buco. For dessert, the fruit crisp and devil's food cake are fine choices. Some of this gourmet fare is also available for takeout. Be sure to take a close look at the lighting fixtures; they look like Mexican silver designs, but are actually metal colanders. ♦ American/French ♦ Daily breakfast, lunch, and dinner. 1650 Third Ave (at E 92nd St). 860.8060 &

The "Restless Chef" award goes to David Pasternack, who recently moved from Privé to the Restaurant at the Stanhope Hotel, to a planned—but unrealized—Italian restaurant, to his present stint at La Folie. Should Pasternack be unable to fulfill his duties, the crown would go to Philippe Roussel, who before one full year had elapsed, held court in the kitchens of La Metairie, L'Udo, and Chelsea Bistro, where he remains as of press time.

95 Ecco-Là ★$ Noisy with bright walls painted with clocks, this inexpensive trattoria serves reliable pasta and pizzas to a young neighborhood crowd. Try *taglierini* (narrow, flat noodles) with lobster, calamari, shrimp, clams, and fresh chopped tomatoes, or fusilli with mushrooms, green peas, chicken, sage, and parmesan in a tomato-cream sauce. ♦ Italian ♦ Daily lunch and dinner. No credit cards accepted. 1660 Third Ave (at E 93rd St). 860.5609

96 Barking Dog Luncheonette ★$ More tastefully decorated than the name would suggest, this somewhat upscale diner with ocher walls and wood paneling offers a satisfying menu. Featured are such dishes as leg of lamb with balsamic vinegar and mint sauce, panfried oysters, and good salads and sandwiches. Desserts are lush; try the chocolate–peanut butter pie. This place has no liquor license, so bring your own. ♦ American ♦ Daily breakfast, lunch, and dinner. No credit cards accepted. 1678 Third Ave (at E 94th St). 831.1800

97 Kitchen Arts & Letters Books on low-fat cooking, regional American cooking, cooking with flowers, cooking on boats, along with more traditional cookbooks—approximately 9,000 in all, covering every aspect of food and wine—are displayed in this unique store. There is also an extensive collection of foreign-language books imported from Europe, particularly France. If what you need isn't here—although the stock includes thousands that have since gone out of print—the owners guarantee that they can locate it for you. Paintings and photographs of food, and reproductions of tin biscuit boxes and other culinary memorabilia are on sale as well. ♦ M-Sa; summer hours are irregular, call first. 1435 Lexington Ave (between E 93rd and E 94th Sts). 876.5550

98 La Collina ★$$ Lace curtains and candlelit tables are not the only draws at this small trattoria—it also offers an interesting menu featuring pasta. Try fettuccine with porcini, gnocchi with vegetable-mushroom sauce, and for a main course, chicken with artichokes and sun-dried tomatoes. ♦ Italian ♦ Daily dinner. Reservations recommended. 1402 Lexington Ave (at E 92nd St). 860.1218

Ecce Panis

99 Ecce Panis This uptown branch of the extraordinary bread store is decorated so beautifully with hand-painted wooden cupboards that you'll want to move in or at least spend the weekend. As in the original shop, the crusty sourdough loaves, focaccia, and biscotti (Italian cookies) are sublime. And if you've run out of coffee to serve with them, it's on sale too. ♦ Daily. 1260 Madison Ave (at E 90th St). 348.0040. Also at: 1120 Third Ave (between E 65th and E 66th Sts). 535.2099

100 Canard and Company The sawdust on the floor and the rustic containers displaying the assortment of very good breads give this upscale food shop a cozy feel. There's a large cheese selection, and the excellent baked goods include freshly made pies, chocolate-chip cookies, and coffee cake. In addition, high-quality prepared food is offered—try the guacamole, penne with salmon, and black-bean chili—as are made-to-order sandwiches ♦ Daily. 1292 Madison Ave (at E 92nd St). 722.1046

Table d'Hôte

101 Table d'Hôte ★★$$$ This quaint, intimate restaurant decorated with hand-painted plates on the walls is very romantic if you don't mind sitting in close proximity to neighboring diner The food is uniformly delicious; try the lemon-roasted Amish chicken with hazelnut-herb butter; braised lamb shank with polenta; and seared tuna with sesame and wasabi. There's also a good early prix-fixe dinner and a cafe menu that's offered during the late-afternoon. Wine fanciers shouldn't miss the chance to treat themselves to one of the very good vintages available by the glass. ♦ French ♦ M-lunch and dinner; Sa-Su brunch and dinner. Reservations recommended. 44 E 92nd St (between Park and Madison Aves). 348.8125

102 Busby's ★$$ The white dining room is larg and airy but plainly decorated, a spare settin for the all-American, California-influenced menu that ranges from roasted goat cheese wrapped in roasted eggplant and grilled swordfish with caramelized shallots, to more basic items such as burgers and salads. Because its expansive menu includes something for nearly everyone, it's a good place to take the family. ♦ American ♦ M-Sa lunch and dinner; Su brunch and dinner. Reservations recommended. 45 E 92nd St (at Madison Ave). 360.7373

102 Sarabeth's Kitchen ★★$$ Many a New Yorker has stood on line here for a weekend brunch of gourmet comfort foods: homemad waffles and pancakes crowned with fresh fruit, hot porridge, and warm-from-the-oven muffins (no reservations accepted for brunch On your way out, pick up homemade brownie and cookies for a treat later. ♦ American ♦ M breakfast, lunch, and dinner; Sa-Su brunch and dinner. Reservations recommended for dinner. 1295 Madison Ave (between E 92nd and E 93rd Sts). 410.7335. Also at: 423 Amsterdam Ave (between 80th and 81st Sts) 496.6280; the Whitney Museum, Madison ar 75th St. 570.3670

02 Island ★$$$ You might expect to find this sort of place on the West Side—a room full of young people wolfing down good, if slightly overpriced, pasta and dishes from the grill, including chicken paillard and pepper-roasted tuna. There's also a good hearty braised lamb shank. ♦ Continental ♦ M-F lunch and dinner; Sa-Su brunch and dinner. Reservations recommended. 1305 Madison Ave (between E 92nd and E 93rd Sts). 996.1200 &

02 Patrick Murphy's Market The upper-crust denizens of **Carnegie Hill** need never step into a supermarket as long as this rarified store stocks necessities ranging from French triple crème to Cheerios. High-quality produce, excellent cheeses, smoked hams, smoked salmon, baked goods, breads, a meat counter, and shelves of grocery items from mustards to Vermont maple syrup round out the offerings. ♦ Daily. 1307 Madison Ave (between E 92nd and E 93rd Sts). 831.2696 &

03 Mr. Chips Upper East Sider Chip Fisher, owner of **Lamalle Kitchenware** and **Fisher & Levy** caterers, couldn't help but notice the hordes of young people hanging around his neighborhood. So this savvy businessman dreamed up the idea of an ice-cream parlor—open all year and friendly to in-line skaters (there's a ramp to enter) and teenagers (a phone for conversations out of earshot of parents is available, and local calls are free). The ice cream is pretty good too. Hot dogs, yogurt, and candy are also offered. Enjoy it all at the long counter with stools. ♦ Daily noon-10PM. 27 E 92nd St (between Madison and Fifth Aves). 831.5555 &

04 Vico ★$$$ A handsome white room simply decorated with colored posters is the setting for decent pasta. Specialties include fusilli with meat sauce and cream, *penne puttanesca* (in a tomato sauce with olives, capers, and anchovies), and homemade seafood ravioli with tomato sauce and arugula. Other dishes are also good: carpaccio, fried calamari, and veal paillard with arugula. ♦ Italian ♦ Daily lunch and dinner. Reservations recommended. No credit cards accepted. 1302 Madison Ave (between E 92nd and E 93rd Sts). 876.4160 &

Carnegie Hill Cafe

04 Carnegie Hill Cafe ★★$ The homey menu at this informal cafe with wood accents and blue and white tiles is popular with neighborhood locals. Try roast pork with apricot glaze and breast of chicken with balsamic-vinegar sauce. There's also a good, affordably priced French/California wine list and 30 wines available by the glass. ♦ American ♦ M-F breakfast, lunch, and dinner; Sa-Su brunch and dinner. 1308 Madison Ave (between E 92nd and E 93rd Sts). 534.7522

104 Bistro du Nord ★★$$ This cozy little bistro serves haute versions of dishes you'd expect to find in this kind of place—smoked salmon from **Petrossian** downtown, and baby rack of lamb with ratatouille. Steak *frites* and roasted codfish are among the more basic fare, but the high quality of their preparations renders them special. ♦ French ♦ M-Sa lunch and dinner; Su brunch and dinner. Reservations required. 1312 Madison Ave (at E 93rd St). 289.0997

105 Demi ★$$$ Set in a town house, this romantic dining room—salmon-colored walls, floral oil paintings, red roses—offers a traditional but inventive menu, including grilled duck with a sweet plum sauce; crab cakes with sweet-corn relish; and snapper with braised spinach and roasted-pepper and black-olive vinaigrette. Desserts are uneven, as is the service. ♦ American ♦ M-Sa lunch and dinner; Su brunch and dinner. Reservations recommended. 1316 Madison Ave (at E 93rd St). 534.3475

106 Cadeaux Plus You'd probably have to go to France to see as many hand-painted faïence porcelain plates and platters as in this tiny, exclusive shop. There's a special emphasis on the simple but exquisite Quimper designs. ♦ M-Sa. 1350 Madison Ave (between E 94th and E 95th Sts). 289.5948

10 Saranac ★$ This small American restaurant has the feel of a lodge in the Adirondacks, belying its uptown Manhattan location. The menu offers such dishes as corn chowder, chicken potpie, pan-seared salmon with lemon-brown butter, and Maryland crab cakes, all of which are well prepared. ♦ American ♦ M-F lunch and dinner; Sa-Su brunch and dinner. 1350 Madison Ave (between E 94th and E 95th Sts). 289.9600

Bests

Wendy Wasserstein
Playwright

Orso: After-theater pasta; chance to stare at Bernadette Peters.

The Odeon: Girls in little black dresses for over 20 years.

Cafe Luxembourg: Late-night Upper West Side hip.

Picholine: Where the desserts are high as an elephant's eye.

Mayrose: Julia Robertson and ABT dancers have coffee here in the Flatiron District.

West Side

The thriving performing arts scene of **Lincoln Center** and the nearby offices and television studios of ABC and CBS dominate this neighborhood bounded by **Central Park** and the **Hudson River**, and 59th and 72nd Streets. The area is becoming increasingly residential, however, mostly because of the sky-high apartment complexes that now almost completely overshadow **Lincoln Center**. And along **Central Park West**, grand pre–World War II apartment buildings with spectacular park views personify gracious living. These lofty structures never developed the snobby cachet of their counterparts across the park on the East Side, and for those who choose to live here—with more than a few celebrities among them—that is probably the point.

The food and restaurant scene on the West Side caters to a variety of different needs, ranging from the minimum daily requirements to serious festivity.

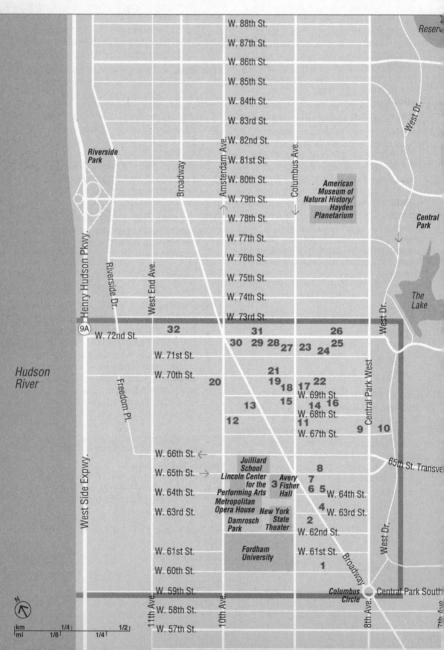

round the streets bordering **Lincoln Center** are myriad restaurants of widely ivergent quality, to accommodate theater- and concertgoers. As a result, any are packed at 7PM, empty at 8:30PM, and then crowded again at 0:30PM. Like the Theater District, this area has long had complacent estaurateurs who think location is everything and charge dearly for it. But he spirit of competition is changing that situation, here as there, with new estaurants making their bids to capture the pre- and post-theater crowds.

ne advantage of the West Side is that where food is concerned, inexpensive nd good are not mutually exclusive: **Harry's Burrito Junction, Café La ortuna,** and **China Fun** are proof of that. And at some of the more ophisticated cafes and **Gabriel's,** which television newspeople have made heir lunch canteen, diners may catch a glimpse of such well-known ersonalities as Barbara Walters, Peter Jennings, Diane Sawyer, or Dan Rather. pecial occasions can be celebrated in high style around here as well: **Tavern n the Green,** just inside **Central Park,** is one of New York's loveliest dining ots, and **Café des Artistes**—the most sophisticated of cafes—makes any eal an event.

addition to the area's well-attended restaurants, there are reminders that cals actually cook and eat at home. The high-end stores selling fine coffee, rime meats, exceptional burgundies, feathery pastries—as well as a specialty op that offers both cheese and antiques—suggest they do so quite well.

verall, this neighborhood has a transitional feel to it—with elements spilling ver from all that surround: Midtown's commercial activity, the Theater istrict's sense of fun, and the Upper West Side's residential character.

---

1 Gabriel's ★★$$$ Come here for arguably the best homemade pasta, risotto, grilled dishes, and desserts in the **Lincoln Center** area. Among the offerings is a good red-wine *pappardelle* (broad noodles) with braised squab, carrots, and rosemary. If you need help deciding what to order, owner Gabriel Aiello is a great source for wine and food recommendations. Don't be surprised to see Dan Rather or Diane Sawyer sitting at the next table. ♦ Northern Italian ♦ M-Sa lunch and dinner. Reservations recommended. 11 W 60th St (between Columbus Ave and Broadway). 956.4600

2 Iridium $$ Modern, amorphic shapes, undulating walls, gilt surfaces, and deep burnished woods create a surrealistic environment that looks to be inspired by Dr. Seuss—inside and out. That's one of the reasons to come here; another is the convenient location across the street from **Lincoln Center.** There's also a Sunday brunch with free jazz featuring a live trio, and a changing roster of jazz musicians who play downstairs nightly from 9:30PM to midnight (the cover charge depends on the act). But the food itself is uneven. Stick to simpler items, such as grilled lemon-pepper salmon or one of the burgers. The shrimp ravioli is good too—if you don't mind sauce made with a pound of butter. The wine list features a range of good, decently priced wines, which can be ordered by the half bottle. ♦ American ♦ M-Sa lunch and dinner; Su jazz brunch and dinner. 44 W 63rd St (at Columbus Ave). 582.2121

2 West 63rd Street Steakhouse ★★$$$ The simple name belies the richness of the experience you're sure to have at this restaurant in the **Empire Hotel.** First, contrary to what the moniker conjures, there's neither sawdust on the floor nor red-and-white checkered tablecloths. Instead, mahogany paneling, elaborately draped windows, handsome table lamps, and Australian aboriginal art appoint this grand environment. The setting is made even more dramatic by the subdued noise level and a jazz pianist playing standard tunes. Although the menu is small, every dish is superb: Shrimp cocktail is succulent and very fresh, and prime cuts of beef—including a 24-ounce T-bone—are enhanced by such excellent sauces as red-wine shallot, herb butter, and Chardonnay-lemon. The french fries are handcut, and the wine list is well chosen and affordable. Desserts, however, are disappointing. ♦ Steak house ♦ M-Sa breakfast and dinner; Su breakfast. Reservations recommended. 44 W 63rd St (between Columbus Ave and Broadway). 246.6363 ♿

PANEVINO
RISTORANTE

3 Panevino ★$$ This is a pleasant place for dinner, a pastry and coffee, or just drinks. During the summer, this cafe in the lobby of **Avery Fisher Hall** spills out onto the plaza. For dinner, try carpaccio, mozzarella with roasted tomatoes, linguine with seafood, rigatoni with eggplant and mozzarella, grilled chicken paillard with balsamic vinegar, and grilled salmon with lentils and herbs. ♦ Italian ♦ M-Sa dinner. Reservations recommended. 132 W 65th St (at Columbus Ave). 874.7000

4 Fiorello's ★$$$ The location across from **Lincoln Center** is only one reason tables continue to fill up here, and fill up they do. Pre-theater, the place is a madhouse, but after 8PM, the wood-paneled room, decorated with burgundy banquettes and Mark Kostabi paintings, is a calm place to sample the antipasto bar, such pastas as lamb *bolognese* and linguine with clams, calamari, and mussels, and main courses that include clay-pot–roasted chicken with rosemary, roasted bass with olives and sun-dried tomatoes, and lamb osso buco. ♦ Italian ♦ M-F lunch and dinner; Sa-Su brunch and dinner. Reservations required. 1900 Broadway (at W 63rd St). 595.5330

5 Picholine ★★★$$$ Having previously held court in the kitchen at the late **Prix Fixe,** Terrance Brennan makes his debut here as chef/proprietor with a homage to the sunny foods of the Mediterranean, especially Provence. Wife Julie designed the room with wallpaper checkered in white and green, the color of the olives that give the restaurant its name. Country touches abound—note the bunches of dried flowers and Italian pottery. From the kitchen come dishes of great imagination and very heady flavor. Don't miss Brennan's signature grilled octopus with fennel, potato, and lemon-pepper vinaigrette; carpaccio of tuna with vegetables *escabèche* (marinated in lemon juice) and *tapenade* aioli (an olive-based mayonnaise); tournedos of salmon with horseradish crust, cucumbers, and salmon caviar; and whole roasted fish (there's a different choice every day). Desserts don't quite live up to the standards set by the main courses, but over time that may change. The 130-bottle wine list concentrates on American and French varieties but also includes Spanish and Italian imports, and has selections in every price range. ♦ Mediterranean ♦ M dinner; Tu-Sa lunch and dinner. 35 W 64th St (between Central Park W and Broadway). 724.8585

5 O'Neals' ★$$$ Fans of the old **O'Neals' Balloon** will be glad to see it has relocated just a block away in the space formerly occupied by the **Ginger Man.** The menu is straightforward and offers predictably decent fare ranging from hamburgers and Chicago-style ribs to tarragon chicken. The dining room is visibly calmer after 8PM, when the crowds empty out to catch the curtain at **Lincoln Center.** ♦ American ♦ Daily lunch, dinner, and late-night meals. 49 W 64th St (between Central Park W and Broadway). 787.4663

5 Lincoln Tavern $$ The menu strains toward ambitious at this casual tavern with wooden booths and checkered red tablecloths

Sports Bars

When there's a big game on, New Yorkers want three things: the biggest TV screen they can find, an ample supply of beer, and eats within easy reach. Sharing the experience with kindred spirits is a definite plus. So throw on jeans, sneakers, a sweatshirt, and baseball cap—worn facing front or back as the mood dictates. Then head down to your favorite sports bar. The atmosphere is generally convivial, especially when the home team is winning, so don't worry if you don't know a free throw from a first down from a face-off from a foul ball—any of the "experts" on hand will fill you in.

The **West Side** seems to be especially fertile soil for these places. Try **Boomer's Sports Club** (349 Amsterdam Ave, between W 76th and W 77th Sts, 362.5400), named after and co-owned by **Jets** quarterback Boomer Esiason. Such basic American food as burgers and steaks is served here to a young and fairly raucous crowd. Nearby is **Lee Mazzilli's Sports Cafe** (208 W 70th St, between Amsterdam and West End Aves, 877.6787). Mazzilli, an outfielder who has shagged balls for both home teams—the **Yankees** and the **Mets,** visits several times a week and often brings along famous friend or two. The atmosphere is fun, and this is a good place to bring the kids: TV screens are everywhere and there is a separate arcade section with video games and even an arcade-style bowling game. The menu ranges from grilled fish to burgers.

When in **Midtown,** try **Mickey Mantle's** (42 Central Park S, between Fifth and Sixth Aves, 688.7777). It is owned by the Yankee great, who has been known to stop in from time to time. The atmosphere is lower-key and more sophisticated than at other sports bars, and there's a great collection of baseball memorabilia—bats, balls, and jerseys. Grilled chicken and steaks are on the menu. In **TriBeCa, The Sporting Club** (99 Hudson St, between Franklin and Leonard Sts, 219.0900) offers up to nine different events beamed in by satellite on screens in every corner of the room—a high-tech sports fanatic's dream. The main event is shown on three 14-foot screens above the bar, and burgers are served.

so stick to simple salads, sandwiches, and sirloin burgers. The braised lamb shank is a safe bet for more substantial fare. ◆ American ◆ Daily lunch and dinner. Reservations recommended. 51 W 64th St (between Central Park W and Broadway). 721-8271

6 The Saloon $$ The service in this cavernous dining room and street cafe is as erratic as the food on the enormous snack and dinner menu; the many offerings include crab cakes, quesadillas, angel-hair pasta with prosciutto, various pizzas, grilled salmon, and escallops of veal. The waiters are fast, if not always efficient; those who can, zoom around on in-line skates. On warm, sunny days, the outdoor tables are great for people watching. **The Saloon Grill** (874.2082) next door serves the same food in a slightly calmer atmosphere. ◆ Continental ◆ M-F lunch and dinner; Sa-Su brunch and dinner. Reservations recommended. 1920 Broadway (at W 64th St). 874.1500 &

7 Sfuzzi ★★$$ Dramatic decor and fun food are served in this lively trattoria. The bar is packed before and after the theater with smart, young trendy types sipping frozen Sfuzzis—a combination of fresh peach nectar, champagne, and peach schnapps—in small, medium, and ridiculously large sizes. You can also sit in the elevated dining area and try one of the inventive pasta, salad, or pizza concoctions. Specialties include veal scallopini with asparagus, parmesan gnocchi, and lemon-sage sauce; salmon with crisp potatoes, green beans, and basil-citrus sauce; and primavera grilled pizza with winter vegetables, low-fat mozzarella, and roasted tomatoes. Stop in during Happy Hour on Monday and Tuesday nights for the complimentary buffet. ◆ Italian ◆ Daily lunch and dinner. Reservations recommended. 58 W 65th St (between Central Park W and Broadway). 873.3700. Also at: 2 World Financial Center (between Liberty and Vesey Sts), Winter Garden Atrium. 385.8080

7 John's West ★★$ The **Lincoln Center** outpost of the famed **John's Pizzeria** has neither the soul nor the lived-in booths of the Greenwich Village original, but this dressed up bilevel pizzeria (with a full bar) does have the best pizza in the neighborhood and a stylish mural of New York City. Pies are thin crusted, coal-oven baked, and covered with such toppings as fresh mushrooms and spicy sausage. ◆ Pizza ◆ Daily lunch and dinner. No credit cards accepted. 48 W 65th St (between Central Park W and Columbus Ave). 721.7001. Also at: 278 Bleecker St (between Morton St and Seventh Ave S). 243.1680 &; 408 E 64th St (between York and First Aves). 935.2895

8 Shun Lee Dynasty ★$$$ Long a favorite of the **Lincoln Center** crowd, the kitchen does many regional Chinese cuisines justice. Try

the steamed dumplings, beggar's chicken (baked in clay), or prawns in black-bean sauce. The vast dining room is dramatic—black banquettes and brightly colored dragon lanterns—though not as fancy as the prices. In the second dining room is the lower-priced **Shun Lee Cafe**, featuring dim sum. ◆ Chinese ◆ Daily lunch and dinner. Reservations required. 43 W 65th St (between Central Park W and Broadway). 595.8895. Also at: 155 E 55th St (between Third and Lexington Aves). 371.8844

9 Café des Artistes ★★★$$$ The West Side's most charming and romantic restaurant is entered through the lobby of the **Hotel des Artistes,** a lavish Elizabethan building that was originally, as the name suggests, intended for artists. Light streams through the leaded-glass windows by day, and the murals of ethereal female nudes, painted in 1934 by Howard Chandler Christy, are an inspiration. Owner George Lang updates the menu and the well-chosen and -priced wine list daily as well as seasonally—his renowned asparagus festival occurs every May and June. But regular dishes you shouldn't miss include the salmon four ways (smoked, poached, gravlax, and *tartare*), duck confit, and rack of lamb with basil crust. Save room for the Great Dessert Plate—it could possibly exceed your sweetest dreams. The famous weekend brunch is a must. ◆ French ◆ M-F lunch and dinner; Sa-Su brunch and dinner. Reservations required; jacket and tie required after 5PM. 1 W 67th St (between Central Park W and Columbus Ave). 877.3500 &

10 Tavern on the Green ★★★$$$$ Designed by Jacob Wrey Mould, the building housing this lovely dining spot was erected in 1870 by Boss Tweed and his corrupt Tammany Hall city government over the strenuous objection of Frederick Law Olmsted, landscape architect and designer of **Central Park.** Originally called the **Sheepfold,** the structure housed the herd of Southdown sheep that grazed in Central Park's **Sheep Meadow** until 1934, when they were exiled to **Prospect Park** in Brooklyn. The **Sheepfold** then became a restaurant, and was completely redesigned in 1976 by **Paul K.Y. Chen** and **Warner LeRoy.** The outdoor garden is a wonderful place to spend a summer evening and is spectacularly lit by twinkling lights in the trees from November through May. But any time of year the **Crystal Room,** dripping with chandeliers, is an unforgettable experience, especially for Sunday brunch. If you're lucky enough to be here when snow is falling outside, you'll never want to go home. But wherever you sit, the food is finally up to the level of the environment, courtesy of May 1995 recruit Patrick Clark, former chef/owner of the restaurant **Metro** and recently executive chef of Washington DC's Hay Adams Hotel. Try the earthy, delicious seared duck foie gras with portobello mushrooms and onions in a plum-wine glaze, the warm house-smoked salmon with mushroom and potato salad in a chive aioli, grilled black angus fillet of beef with wild mushrooms in a red-wine sauce, grilled Port porterhouse with bacon and cabbage mashed potatoes, and the Moroccan-style barbecued salmon on savoy cabbage. Pastry chef Judy Schmitt prepares such luscious constructions as a triple-layer chocolate cake and a napoleon filled with ginger crème brûlée. The wine list is extensive, well-chosen, and reasonably priced. ♦ American ♦ M-F lunch and dinner; Sa-Su brunch and dinner. Reservations required. W 67th St (at Central Park W). 873.3200

11 67 Wine & Spirits The extensive selection of wines and spirits in this store is well known for its diversity, and the prices are fairly gentle. The staff, never known for their helpfulness, recently adopted a new and improved attitude. ♦ M-Sa. 179 Columbus Ave (at W 68th St). 724.6767

11 Vince & Eddie's ★★★$$ Locals pack this rustic-looking, intimate room—especially before a **Lincoln Center** performance—for chef Scott Campbell's earthy but elegantly prepared dishes. The menu changes seasonally, but such dishes as braised lamb shank with Michigan cherry sauce and pan-roasted chicken with spinach and lentils are available all year. Other standouts are the greaseless fried calamari with cilantro-lime sauce and seafood risotto with lobster essence. Vegetable purees, including turnip and pumpkin, may sound humble but are silky and rich and not to be missed. ♦ American ♦ M-Sa lunch and dinner; Su brunch and dinner. Reservations recommended. 70 W 68th St (between Central Park W and Columbus Ave). 721.0068

12 The Good Earth Everything you need to live healthier—all-natural allergy pills, fat- and dairy-free baked goods, organic produce and eggs, and free-range chickens—can be found

at this health-food supermarket. ♦ Daily. 167 Amsterdam Ave (at W 68th St). 496.1616

13 Nevada Meat Market This high-quality butcher shop specializes in game of all varieties—mallard ducks, pheasants, geese, poussins—and all cuts of meat, including the palest veal, baby lamb, and finest shell steak. If by chance the store doesn't have what you want, the staff will order it. ♦ M-Sa. 2012 Broadway (between W 68th and W 69th Sts). 362.0443

14 La Boîte en Bois ★★$$$ A few steps dow and far from the madding crowd on Columbu Avenue, this charming French bistro with a country atmosphere and Provençal menu offers fine fish soup, roast chicken with herb and roast salmon glazed with honey mustard For dessert, there are solid renditions of the classics—crème brûlée, ricotta cheesecake, apple tarts, and chocolate mousse. ♦ French ♦ Daily dinner. Reservations recommended. No credit cards accepted. 75 W 68th St (between Central Park W and Columbus Ave) 874.2705

15 Maya Schaper Cheese & Antiques Exactly as the unusual name suggests, this tiny, brightly lit store features a small but perfect selection of cheeses—domestic varieties as well as British and French imports—along with antique tables, cupboards, and armoires from England and Mexico. Quality breads, including **Eli's** and **Amy's**, are also for sale, as well as platters and other tableware items. ♦ Daily. 106 W 69th St (between Columbus Ave and Broadway). 873.2100 &

16 Santa Fe ★$$ This refurbished town-hous dining room is painted in flattering soft dese tones and fitted with fine Southwestern arts and crafts. All in all, it's a very pleasant place to dine on such Southwestern fare as seviche shrimp in a green tomatillo sauce, and crab cakes in a smoked tomato-and-chile sauce. ♦ Southwestern ♦ Daily lunch and dinner. Reservations recommended. 72 W 69th St (between Central Park W and Columbus Ave) 724.0822

17 World Cafe ★$$ The all-encompassing menu in this beige eatery with ceiling fans spans the globe from East to West. The India spiced yogurt-avocado dip is interesting, as is the grilled tuna in a carrot-ginger glaze. But the most successful item on the menu might well be the humble hamburger, given a

jolt here with chipotle barbecue sauce.
♦ International ♦ M-F lunch and dinner; Sa-Su brunch and dinner. Reservations recommended. 201 Columbus Ave (at W 69th St). 799.8090

18 Rikyu ★$$ Predating the invasion of trendy spots along Columbus Avenue, this popular restaurant is a favorite with locals and the **Lincoln Center** crowd for good traditional dishes and fresh sushi. Another plus: Competition from the neighboring sushi bars keeps the prices reasonable. ♦ Japanese ♦ Daily lunch and dinner. Reservations recommended. 210 Columbus Ave (between W 69th and W 70th Sts). 799.7847

19 Soutine A tiny bake shop with the feel of a French *boulangerie,* this place is a neighborhood favorite. Try the *pain au chocolat* (a chocolate-filled croissant) and bread knots filled with cheddar cheese. ♦ M-Sa; Su until 3PM. 106 W 70th St (between Columbus Ave and Broadway). 496.1450

19 Cafe Mozart $ This replica of a faded grand Viennese coffeehouse—decorated with ornate crystal chandeliers, portraits of the composer, and violins scattered about—features a menu of soups, sandwiches, and salads. The real draw here, however, is the pastry counter. Good bets are the carrot-spice cake, apple strudel, black-and-white espresso cake, mocha-apricot cake, and linzer torte. Wash it down with any of several varieties of coffee. ♦ Coffeehouse ♦ Daily lunch, dinner, and late-night meals. 154 W 70th St (between Columbus Ave and Broadway). 595.9797

CAFE
LUXEMBOURG

20 Cafe Luxembourg ★★$$$ A people watcher's Art Deco brasserie, this cafe is affiliated with TriBeCa's trendy **Odeon.** The zinc-topped bar here draws a stylish, international crowd, and the menu is a mélange of French, Italian, and regional American offerings. Order marinated octopus; lemon risotto with fresh asparagus and parmesan; provençal vegetable tart; roast leg of lamb; duck cassoulet; or striped bass with fresh herbs, garlic, and oil. For dessert, try the

profiteroles with mint-chip ice cream. ♦ French ♦ M-F lunch, dinner, and late-night meals; Sa-Su brunch, dinner, and late-night meals. Reservations recommended. 200 W 70th St (between Amsterdam and West End Aves). 873.7411

20 Lee Mazzilli's Sports Cafe $ The oversized blue **Mets** cap over the door distinguishes this large place from other dining spots in the neighborhood. Inside, it's playtime for children of all ages—TV screens everywhere for watching whatever game is on and a separate arcade section with video games and even a bowling game for younger customers. The food is nothing special, but it won't spoil the fun; the menu features fried chicken fingers, burgers—including a vegetarian variety—blackened Cajun chicken, baby back ribs, prime rib, maple-glazed salmon, and chocolate cake. If you're a stargazer, keep your eyes peeled for the owner, former **Met** Lee Mazzilli, or some of his celebrity friends. ♦ American ♦ Daily lunch and dinner. 208 W 70th St (between Amsterdam and West End Aves). 877.6787

21 Ying ★$$ Pretty flowers and equally attractive food, including unusual salads and such tasty chicken dishes as mango chicken, chicken with spinach and garlic, chicken with sesame sauce, and island chicken (sautéed crispy with orange, litchi, and other fruits), are the draws at this eatery. It may not quite be up to Hong Kong or even Chinatown standards, but it's much better than the average neighborhood joint. ♦ Chinese ♦ Daily lunch and dinner. 117 W 70th St (between Columbus Ave and Broadway). 724.2031

22 The Sensuous Bean It's not the only store that sells coffee beans in the neighborhood, but no other shop concentrates so completely on that product as this little place packed with coffee and tea canisters. Among the 70 kinds of coffee beans are flavored varieties, including coconut and seville orange. The teas, of which there are approximately 30, range from *Lapsang souchong* (a smoked black tea) to strawberry kiwi. Various coffee and tea makers are sold here as well. ♦ Daily. 66 W 70th St (between Central Park W and Columbus Ave). 724.7725 ⑤

23 Harry's Burrito Junction ★$ If **Lincoln Center** tickets have busted your budget or if you happen to be in the market for some great nachos, this is the place. A young crowd that fills the three-level space decorated with memorabilia from the 1960s seems to have a special fondness for the foot-long bay burrito, oozing with black beans and shredded beef. ♦ Mexican ♦ M-F lunch and dinner; Sa-Su brunch and dinner. 241 Columbus Ave (at W 71st St). 580.9494

24 Fishin Eddie ★★$$$ Courtesy of the folks behind **Vince & Eddie's** (see above), this restaurant specializing in seafood is ideal for a pre- or post-**Lincoln Center** meal and a boon for nonsmokers: Smoking is not allowed—at all. Given a stylized log-cabin design by interior decorator Sam Lopata, the room has paneling on the ceiling, barnsiding, antique wood farmhouse tables, and Shaker furniture. The yellow-and-chartreuse color scheme and nautical props, including buoys, however, suggest nothing so much as the inside of a fish tank, an interesting setting for a high-quality fish dinner. Try grilled black bass with thyme pesto, cioppino (a seafood stew in a spicy red broth), grouper sautéed with arugula and tomato sauce, or perfectly steamed lobster. For dessert there's an excellent lemon tart; the chocolate-walnut cake and apple-oat tart are also recommended. ♦ Seafood ♦ Daily dinner. Reservations recommended. 73 W 71st St (between Central Park W and Columbus Ave). 874.3474

24 Café La Fortuna ★$ A mainstay of the neighborhood for years—and one of the late John Lennon's hangouts—this pleasant, unassuming cafe serves excellent Italian coffees and a mouthwatering array of traditional Italian pastries and other sweets. The garden in the back is an ideal respite from summer heat, especially when sipping the cafe's favorite seasonal drink: an unparalleled iced cappuccino laced with homemade chocolate or coffee ice. Sandwiches, antipast and salads are also available. ♦ Cafe ♦ Daily lunch, dinner, and late-night meals. No credit cards accepted. 69 W 71st St (between Centr Park W and Columbus Ave). 724.5846

25 Sidewalkers ★$$ It's not necessary to go all the way to Maryland to find a crab shack when you can step into the lobby of the **Olive Cromwell** building. The decor is plain and the food basic. For those with ambitious appetites, Monday's all-you-can eat "crab bash" is popular, with good reason. The crab cakes have many loyal devotees, and the broiler plate—scallops, fresh fish, shrimp, and a half lobster—is delicious, too. The tremendous international beer list is impressive. ♦ Seafood ♦ Daily dinner. 12 W 72nd St (between Central Park W and Columbus Ave). 799.6070

26 Dallas BBQ $ The barbecued ribs and chicken are well seasoned, tender, and juicy. But the big draw for many of the neighborhood fans of this large, informal, an noisy restaurant is the huge loaf of greasy onion rings. ♦ Barbecue ♦ M-Th, Su lunch and dinner; F-Sa lunch, dinner, and late-nigh meals. 27 W 72nd St (between Central Park W and Columbus Ave). 873.2004. Also at: 1265 Third Ave (at E 73rd St). 772.9393; 21 University Pl (at E Eighth St). 674.4450; 132 Second Ave (at St Mark's Pl). 777.5574

Kitchen Casting

Dining out in a fine restaurant is a little bit like attending the theater. Many people work behind the scenes to produce that dramatic dish the waiter carries so ceremoniously to your table. The Executive Chef, sometimes called the *Chef de Cuisine*, functions as the director, overseeing the entire production. But the task requires that he or she have a whole supporting cast working with him or her. Here's a program note to let you know who's who:

Chef de Cuisine

Sous-Chefs ⚬⚬⚬ Pastry Ch

Chefs de Partie (Heads of stations)
Cold appetizers *(garde-manger)*
Fish *(poissonier)*
Hot appetizers
Meats *(rotisseur)*
Pastry
Sauces *(saucier)*
Side dishes, soups *(entremetier)*

Commis de Cuisine (Assistants to Chefs de Partie)

Prep cooks

27 China Fun ★$ A twin of the East Side restaurant of the same name, this place is definitely a cut above what you generally find outside of Chinatown. Don't miss the platter of barbecued meats with crispy, juicy duck, chicken, and pork; crystal shrimp dumplings; and Mandarin noodle soups. The tasting menu is a great deal, allowing you to try a variety of dim sum, roast meats, and an entrée for a reasonable price. ♦ Chinese ♦ Daily lunch and dinner. 246 Columbus Ave (between W 71st and W 72nd Sts). 580.1516 &. Also at: 1239 E 65th St (at Second Ave). 752.0810 &

28 Fine & Schapiro ★$$ This long-established classic kosher delicatessen makes one nostalgic for the days before cholesterol counts. There's a salt-free corner on the menu, but if you need to consult it, you're probably in the wrong place. ♦ Jewish deli ♦ Daily lunch and dinner. 138 W 72nd St (between Columbus Ave and Broadway). 877.2874

29 Acker-Merrall-Condit Experts on Burgundy, these established liquor merchants boast a reputation for good service. The store is nicely designed too. ♦ M-Sa. 160 W 72nd St (between Columbus Ave and Broadway). 787.1700 &

30 Gray's Papaya $ Nowhere else does a dollar get so much. A cast of characters frequents this super-cheap round-the-clock hot dog stand that brags its tube steaks are "tastier than filet mignon" and its papaya drink is "a definite aid to digestion." Unless you're made of cast iron, your digestion will need all the help it can get. The fruit ade is definitely worth a stop here. ♦ Hot dogs ♦ Daily 24 hours. 2090 Broadway (at W 72nd St). 799.0243

31 Eclair $$ Open since 1939, this venerable cafe is the last remnant of the time when West 72nd Street was known as Little Vienna. The restaurant is not what it used to be, but the traditional midafternoon *kaffee und kuchen* (coffee and cake) is wonderful—try the *schwarzwälder kirschtorte* (a flat, dense Viennese torte with a chocolate or raspberry filling) or linzer torte. There is also a scattershot menu to choose from, featuring substantial specialities such as Wiener schnitzel, sauerbraten, and yankee pot roast, along with lighter fare—broiled fish dishes, vegetarian plates, and sandwiches. ♦ Cafe ♦ Daily breakfast, lunch, and dinner. 141 W 72nd St (between Columbus Ave and Broadway). 873.7700

32 Giacomo Co-owners Mike Calderone and Joe Aguilera named this shop as a tribute to Calderone's late dog, reputedly a gourmet. The selection of smoked fish, breads, cheeses, Italian salamis and hams, such prepared foods as penne with eggplant and three beans *provençale*, and pastries makes this place something of a mini-**Balducci's**. It's not surprising—the owners learned the trade

at that downtown food emporium. ♦ Daily. 269 W 72nd St (between Broadway and West End Ave). 799.6828 &

Bests

Morton L. Janklow
Literary Agent, Janklow & Nesbit Associates

Le Cirque: Because every visitor should experience a great international restaurant. Try the black sea bass in a potato shell with red-wine sauce—extraordinary!

Restaurant Daniel: The newest example of a great young French chef preparing food for the 1990s with style and élan. Try the nine-herb ravioli—a cloud in the mouth.

The Four Seasons Grill: Where simplicity and elegance are raised to an art form under the benevolent eyes of Tom Margittai and Paul Kovi and their protégés, Alex and Julian. The tuna *tartare* is the best in New York.

San Pietro: A family-run, warm, and gracious Northern Italian restaurant featuring haute cuisine and warm smiles. No one makes fresh pasta in greater variety and combinations than Gerardo and his brothers, and the porcini mushrooms send you back to the hills of Tuscany. The same family owns **Sistina,** which is just as good if you're uptown.

Mortimer's: There is something unique about Glenn Birnbaum's creation of a simple and stylish American restaurant featuring crab cakes and all the things you always wanted but your mother never made for you.

21 Club: Nothing more need be said than that in its newest incarnation, the restaurant has returned to its former elegance and glory. If you want to know what life was like in the good old days in New York, and if you want to have service and food in the greatest American tradition, this is your place.

Café des Artistes: George Lang, the last of the Hungarian restaurant impresarios, serves up in this gloriously beautiful series of rooms on the **West Side,** convenient to **Lincoln Center,** some of the truly great dishes of Europe in an atmosphere reminiscent of a Vienna cafe.

Tavern on the Green: I confess to a certain prejudice because this glorious institution is owned by my brother-in-law, Warner LeRoy, but it is truly one of the great landmark restaurants of the United States. The setting in **Central Park** is glorious and the food has a wide variety and all of it is excellent. Kids and families and celebrants of all kinds love "Tavern" and can always retreat to hear the best jazz in New York in the **Chestnut Room** when they have finished dinner. These are views to be found nowhere else in the world.

Elaine's: What more need be said? No trip to New York should end without one late dinner here to meet the La Pasionaria of the writer's profession and to see a "Who's Who" of the arts.

Elio's: The greatest of all the wonderful Italian restaurants with wonderful Tuscan food and outstanding service. Saltimbocca is a joy here, as is the roasted bass.

W. 113th St.   65

W. 112th St.

W. 111th St.
64   63
Cathedral Pkwy.
W. 109th St.   62
61
W. 108th St.
60   Broadway
W. 107th St.

W. 106th St.
59
W. 105th St.
58
W. 104th St.

W. 103rd St.

W. 102nd St.

W. 101st St.

W. 100th St.

W. 99th St.
57   56
W. 98th St.

W. 97th St.

Riverside Dr.
Riverside Park
Amsterdam Ave.

W. 96th St.
West End Ave.
Broadway
Amsterdam Ave.
W. 95th St.

54 55

W. 94th St.

W. 93rd St.

W. 92nd St.

W. 91st St.
53

Riverside Park
52
51   50
49   48

West End Ave.
Riverside Dr.
45

44
42 43   39
41
40   38
37

27

26   24
25   20
       19
       18

16 15

W. 90th St.
W. 89th St.
W. 88th St.   47
W. 87th St.
46
W. 86th St.

W. 85th St.
W. 84th St.   34
35
W. 83rd St.   33
36   31 32
W. 82nd St.
28   30
W. 81st St.   29
23   22
W. 80th St.

W. 79th St.   17

W. 78th St.   14

W. 77th St.
7   12 13
11

W. 76th St.
5   6   8
W. 75th St.
4   2   3   9   10
W. 74th St.
1
W. 73rd St.

Hudson River

Henry Hudson Pkwy.
9A

Columbus Ave.
Central Park West

American Museum of Natural History/ Hayden Planetarium
21

Central Park

West Dr.

The Lak

9A
Inwood Hill Park
77
10th Ave.
I-87
Fordham Rd.

9
W. 207th St.
76
Dyckman St.

Broadway
St. Nicholas Ave.
Harlem River Dr.
Major Deegan Expwy.
University Ave.
Jerome Ave.
Grand Concourse Blvd.
Webster Ave.

Riverside Dr.
9
W. 181st St.
Highbridge Park

1   95
Melrose Ave.

9A
W. 158th St.
75
W. 155th St.
74
W. 145th St.

Harlem River
Harlem River Dr.
E. 161st St.
E. 149th St.
E. 138th S
87

Willis Ave.

Broadway
Amsterdam Ave.
St. Nicholas Pl.
St. Nicholas Ave.
W. 138th St.
W. 135th St.
72
73   W. 125th St.
5th Ave.
3rd Ave.
2nd Ave.
1st Ave.
67
68
66   E. 110th St.

M.L.K. Jr. Blvd.
F. Douglas Blvd. (8th Ave.)
A. C. Powell Jr. Blvd. (7th Ave.)
Lenox Ave.
Park Ave.
W. 115th St.

71
70
69

Henry Hudson Pkwy.
Cathedral Pkwy.
Central Park

Hudson River

km mi   1/4   1/8   1/4   1/2

km mi   1/2
N

Upper West Side/ Harlem/Heights

The northernmost section of Manhattan covers an extensive area, from **West 72nd Street** all the way up to Inwood—near **225th Street**—where the **Hudson** and **Harlem Rivers** join. Within this district are a number of neighborhoods that not only span a large physical distance, but a spectrum of lifestyles as well.

The Upper West Side (bordered by **Central Park**, the Hudson River, West 72th Street, and **110th Street**) has become one of the city's most preferred places to live. As such, it's full of professionals with enough disposable income to support a thriving food and restaurant scene. Famous for its quality food stores, the neighborhood boasts **Citarella** for fresh fish, **Fairway** for high-end produce, and **Zabar's** for everything else, including the best Nova Scotia lox with which to crown Sunday morning bagels from **H&H**. New cafes are continually popping up on **Columbus Avenue**, a trendy stretch that seems to reinvent itself every few years, and **Amsterdam Avenue,** which now rivals Columbus for smart new bistros and stores set amid a sprinkling of breakfast joints that are packed on the weekends.

Farther north, in the 90s, **Broadway** becomes a dividing line, with renovated brownstones and chic boîtes to the west and massive housing projects and dusty bodegas to the east. Around **Columbia University** (West 110th to **West 125th Streets**), the Upper West Side becomes more solidly gentrified, with quaint bistros and top-of-the-line food stores to satisfy the appetites of students and professors.

Above **125th Street** (also called **Martin Luther King Jr. Boulevard**) is Harlem, which takes its name from the 1658 Dutch settlement of **Nieuw Haarlem**. During the 1920s and 1930s, the neighborhood experienced its famous renaissance—a flourishing of the arts, including jazz at the **Sugar Cane** and **Cotton Clubs**, where everybody who was anybody would come to hear Count Basie, Duke Ellington, and other legendary musicians play. Today the neighborhood's biggest attraction is food—chicken or ribs at **Copeland's** or brunch at **Sylvia's**. East of **Fifth Avenue**, Harlem becomes **Spanish Harlem**, but the area's large Latino population refers to it as *El Barrio* (the neighborhood). Here **Patsy**'s serves some of the best pizza in town and the indoor **La Marqueta** boasts stalls full of Caribbean and Latin American favorites—yucca, papaya, suckling pig, and eel.

Washington Heights encompasses the area from **Trinity Cemetery** at **154th Street** to **Dyckman Street**; Inwood continues thereafter to the top of the island. Once predominantly German-Jewish and Irish, the northernmost part of Manhattan is now populated by a variety of groups—African-Americans, Hispanics, Greeks, Armenians, and Russians among them. People of all ethnic and economic stripes live together here, and the shops and restaurants reflecting their individual tastes form a fascinating mosaic throughout the neighborhoods.

1 Vinnie's Pizza ★$ At this neighborhood favorite, the thin-crusted pizza is loaded with cheese and super-fresh toppings. The parlor itself wouldn't win any design awards, so get your pie to go. ♦ Pizza ♦ Daily lunch and dinner. 285 Amsterdam Ave (between W 73rd and W 74th Sts). 874.4382

2 Josie's ★★$ Owned in part by Rob Morrow (formerly the doctor on the television show *Northern Exposure*), this place offers food that is appropriately health conscious: The grains and produce are organic, the water is filtered, and all dishes are dairy-free. But healthy doesn't mean boring here—the nightly crowds attest to that. The creative cuisine features such dishes as ginger-grilled calamari with pineapple–red pepper salsa and sweet-potato ravioli with Gulf shrimp, sweet corn, and roasted peppers in white-wine and leek sauce. Avoid any pasta in red sauce, which inexplicably tastes like it came from a jar. There are a couple of unrepentantly sinful desserts, including lemon-ribbon ice-cream pie and banana crunch (a pastry shell filled with vanilla ice cream, bananas, and butterscotch sauce). ♦ American ♦ Daily dinner. Reservations required. 300 Amsterdam Ave (at W 74th St). 769.1212 ᕕ

3 Freddie and Pepper's Gourmet Pizza
★$ This popular no-frills pizza place makes a good tomato base for its myriad toppings. Try the unusual seafood smorgasbord pie. ♦ Pizza ♦ Daily lunch and dinner. No credit cards accepted. 303 Amsterdam Ave (between W 74th and W 75th Sts). 799.2378

3 Shark Bar ★$ Within a swanky setting— dark, split-level, candlelit—is a beautiful and well-dressed crowd, including more than a few models and music industry types. Among the inventive appetizers that shouldn't be missed is the soul roll (pastry filled with vegetables, chicken, and rice). Otherwise, skip the Cajun side of the menu and stick to classic soul food dishes—barbecued ribs, fried chicken, collard greens, black-eyed peas, macaroni and cheese, yams, and sweet-potato pie. ♦ Soul food/Cajun ♦ M-Tu dinner; W-F lunch and dinner; Sa-Su brunch and dinner. Reservations recommended. 307 Amsterdam Ave (between W 74th and W 75th Sts). 874.8500

4 Fairway Residents swear by this all-purpose market which offers produce, excellent cheeses, charcuterie, coffee, chocolates, baked goods, breads, prepared foods, and smoked fish. Avoiding the crowds here is something of a local sport; the prevailing current strategy seems to entail arriving early in the morning or after 8PM. The staff can be a little flippant or distracted, but that may come from being surrounded all day long by shoppers who engage in near-guerrilla warfare. ♦ Daily. 2127 Broadway (between W 74th and W 75th Sts). 595.1888 ᕕ

4 Citarella This retail fish store and raw seafood bar is ideal for a quick stand-up snack before a show at the **Beacon Theatre.** The elaborate fish-sculpture displays take the art of window-dressing to new heights. Not in the mood for fish? Then try the prime cuts of meat, homemade pasta, and appetizers. ♦ Daily. 2135 Broadway (at W 75th St). 874.0383

5 Ernie's $$ Recently reopened after a long renovation, this barnlike restaurant now has a fresh, airy look with its light-wood floor, white walls, and spotlights. The menu is basically the same, though shorter, and such favorites as angel-hair pasta with lobster, Caesar salad, grilled chicken, and "death by chocolate" were retained as they were. Other dishes, including ravioli filled with lobster, shrimp, and crab and tossed in a sauce of spinach and leeks; penne with grilled chicken, artichokes, and rosemary; and lamb medaillons marinated in red wine, were improved. But this place has always been more about chatting with friends than about food. ♦ Italian ♦ M-Th lunch and dinner; F lunch, dinner, and late-night meals; Sa brunch, dinner, and late-night meals; Su brunch and dinner. Reservations recommended. 2150 Broadway (at W 75th St). 496.1588

6 Benny's ★$ Stop in here to pick up an inexpensive lunch to eat in nearby **Central Park.** Lemon chicken with snow peas, ricotta chicken, sautéed spinach with lemon and garlic, cauliflower with carrot and tahini sauce, tabbouleh, couscous with vegetables, and spinach pie are among the offerings. Choose three items for a combination plate or buy them by the pound. There's also a small sit-down area. ♦ Lebanese/Takeout ♦ Daily lunch and dinner. No credit cards accepted. 321 Amsterdam Ave (between W 75th and W 76th Sts). 874.3032. Also at: 102 E 25th St (at Park Ave S). 674.4337

7 Boomer's Sports Club $ Named after Jets quarterback Boomer Esiason, this sports bar is a casual meeting place and a good spot to watch a game. The food is simple: burgers, steaks, grilled chicken, salads, and it's sufficient for staving off distracting hunger pangs during the action. ♦ American ♦ Daily lunch and dinner. 349 Amsterdam Ave (between W 76th and W 77th Sts). 362.5400

8 Mughlai $$ For Indian food that never errs on the too-spicy side, this is the place. The tandoori here is best, and the mango chutney served with the curry is quite good. Desserts are uninspired, except for the highly recommended rice pudding with rosewater. ♦ Indian ♦ M-F dinner; Sa-Su brunch and dinner. Reservations recommended. 320 Columbus Ave (at W 75th St). 724.6363

9 Jerry's ★$$ SoHo cool came uptown with the opening of this chic diner, a clone of the original place downtown, with black Formica tables, red banquettes, and mirrored walls. The food here is simpler though, and includes a good roasted brook trout, juicy roast chicken, grilled rib steak, and "Mom's" pot roast with horseradish mashed potatoes. As befits such honest, down-to-earth food, there are simple but rich desserts; don't miss the ice-cream sandwich made with brownies and the lemon tart. ♦ American ♦ M-F lunch and dinner; Sa-Su brunch and dinner. Reservations recommended. 302 Columbus Ave (between W 74th and W 75th Sts). 501.7500. Also at: 101 Prince St (between Mercer and Greene Sts). 966.9464

9 Pappardella $$ Even though the food is only average, this is a popular destination for pasta and *secondi* (second, or main, dishes) with a Tuscan accent. Try a thin-crusted pizza with a glass of Chianti, ravioli with mushrooms, or *bistecca fiorentina* (grilled T-bone steak marinated in olive oil, rosemary, and a touch of garlic, served with sautéed vegetables), and relish the escape from the bustle of Columbus Avenue. ♦ Italian ♦ Daily lunch and dinner. Reservations recommended. 316 Columbus Ave (at W 75th St). 595.7996

10 Nancy's Wines for Food Whatever fears you may have about selecting the right wine will be allayed by the service here. While browsing, check out the posted tips suggesting which wines to serve with fried foods, Chinese food, various preparations of meats, etc. If you need help, just ask; the friendly staff is only too happy to offer recommendations that complement your menu. There's also a good variety, including hard-to-find white wines, Italian reds, and California Zinfandels. ♦ M-Sa. 313 Columbus Ave (between W 74th and W 75th Sts). 877.4040

11 Caffe Popolo ★$ This tiny place with a few marble tables is a good spot to drop into for *panini* (sandwiches), cakes, pizzas, and simple pastas with a variety of sauces, including a garlicky fresh tomato and eggplant variety, and a marinara with sweet sausage and wild mushrooms. ♦ Italian ♦ M-F lunch and dinner; Sa-Su brunch and dinner. 351 Columbus Ave (between W 76th and W 77th Sts). 362.1777

12 Isabella ★$$ Well liked for its simple, pleasant decor and inviting sidewalk cafe, this place offers such homemade pasta as cheese-and-herb ravioli in tomato sauce, and grilled dishes, including veal chops and chicken, all of which are good. The kitchen makes a conscious effort to keep fat content down—lower-fat ice creams come in such sinfully good flavors as cookies and cream, chocolate, and coffee. ♦ Italian ♦ M-F lunch and dinner; Sa-Su brunch and dinner. 359 Columbus Ave (at W 77th St). 724.2100

13 Scaletta ★★$$$ A large dinner menu, fast and efficient service, and excellent pasta and antipasto (especially the prosciutto) are highlights of this lovely Northern Italian restaurant. The walls of the spacious, comfortable dining room are painted in pale salmon, peach, blue, and green to look like Venetian stucco. The large 25-foot bar is marble topped and behind it are numerous wine racks. Try the specials of the day, which might include risotto with wild mushrooms, and veal *sorrentino* (sautéed with eggplant and mozzarella). Desserts are of the rich Italian variety, and the espresso is good too. ♦ Northern Italian ♦ Daily dinner. 50 W 77th St (between Central Park W and Columbus Ave). 769.9191

MUSEUM ♦ CAFE

14 Museum Cafe $$ Its location just across the street from the **American Museum of Natural History** and the **Hayden Planetarium** makes this place is a convenient stop. Another plus is that the restaurant stays open all night on Thanksgiving Eve, when the **Macy's** Thanksgiving Day Parade floats are inflated out front. Best bets here are the Grecian chicken salad or one of the gargantuan bowls of pasta. The interior is a dull, restful pink with wood trim; it's better to sit at a table in the enclosed sidewalk cafe. ♦ American ♦ M-F lunch and dinner; Sa-Su brunch and dinner. 366 Columbus Ave (at W 77th St). 799.0150

15 Brothers Barbecue ★$ Larger and more elaborate (it has chandeliers) than the Greenwich Village original, this uptown barbecue shack adds good boiled blue crabs to the familiar roster of respectable rib and chicken dishes. ♦ Barbecue ♦ M-Sa lunch, dinner, and late-night meals; Su brunch, dinner, and late-night meals. 2182 Broadway (at W 77th St). 873.7364. Also at: 228 W Houston St (at Varick St). 727.2775

16 La Caridad $ Expect a fairly long wait at this popular and inexpensive Cuban/Chinese beanery where such standards as roast pork and shredded beef are the standouts. ♦ Cuban/Chinese ♦ Daily lunch and dinner. No credit cards accepted. 2199 Broadway (at W 78th St). 874.2780

17 Phoebe's ★$ A cozy place with exposed-brick and terra-cotta–colored walls, it has a great bar area, dominated in winter by a roaring fireplace surrounded by couches. The menu offers food that's basic and satisfying—New England clam chowder, charred tuna with sesame noodles, chicken potpie, and roasted chicken with terrific garlic mashed potatoes. For dessert get the fruit cobbler. ♦ American ♦ M-Sa lunch and dinner;

Su brunch and dinner. Reservations recommended. 380 Columbus Ave (at W 78th St). 724.5145

17 Mackinac Grill ★$$ With its brick-red walls and old-fashioned chandeliers, this looks like the dining room of a grand Midwestern hotel. The fish paintings, however, are harbingers of good dishes to come, such as rainbow trout stuffed with crabmeat and grilled swordfish filled with shrimp and herbs. There's also a very creative brunch, featuring omelettes with salmon caviar or Smithfield ham, as well as banana-pecan pancakes with banana compote and honey-maple syrup. ♦ American ♦ M-F dinner; Sa-Su brunch and dinner. Reservations recommended for dinner Friday-Sunday and Sunday brunch. 384 Columbus Ave (between W 78th and W 79th Sts). 799.1750

18 Eastern Seafood Company ★$ The decor at this simple seafood house consists of brown vinyl booths and green-and-white checkered tablecloths. The food isn't fancy either, but when it tastes this good, it doesn't have to be. Get the littleneck clams on the half shell, steamed mussels, grilled swordfish with sweet-apple salsa, or seared tuna steak in a red-wine sauce. There's also an adjoining retail market for fresh fish. ♦ Seafood ♦ M-Sa lunch and dinner; Su brunch and dinner. 212 W 79th St (between Amsterdam Ave and Broadway). 595.5007

18 Two Two Two ★★★★$$$$ This skylit town-house restaurant is *the* place to go on the Upper West Side for a special occasion—the detailed oak paneling, classic oil paintings, and ornate crystal chandelier set the tone for the exquisite and sometimes very rich food prepared by chef Frank Dalla Riva. Don't miss the foie gras sandwich (seared duck foie gras on a crisp potato pancake with currant-and-cassis *jus*); foie gras ravioli in a balsamic-Madeira sauce; fresh white and black truffles served on homemade gnocchi simmered in gorgonzola, white truffle butter, cream sauce, and wild mushrooms; poached lobster with avocado, Japanese pickled ginger, and mustard sauce; pan-seared scallops with sweet corn risotto and infused coriander broth; herb-roasted chicken served on potato puree with wild mushrooms and a sherry-vinegar sauce; and rack of lamb with white beans,

tomatoes, and greens. For those with room left for dessert, try the excellent maple crème brûlée or fresh fruit sorbets. There are two wine lists, one American and one French, both full of exceptional (and expensive) selections. ♦ Continental ♦ Daily dinner. Reservations recommended. 222 W 79th St (between Amsterdam Ave and Broadway). 799.0400 &

19 Chaz & Wilsons Grill ★$$ The bar scene at this renovated cafe, formerly known just as **Wilsons,** is popular on weekends with singles, but the wood-paneled dining room also has its fans who come for cedar-planked grilled salmon, smoked brisket, and pasta. Free live music is played nightly except Friday and Saturday (there's a cover charge on Sunday). ♦ American ♦ Daily dinner and late-night meals. 201 W 79th St (between Amsterdam Ave and Broadway). 769.0100

20 Baci $$ Zippy but uneven Sicilian fare is served in this upbeat, handsome candlelit dining room. Pasta dishes are the best bets here, particularly the gnocchi with pesto and rigatoni with cauliflower, raisins, pine nuts, and tomato sauce. ♦ Italian ♦ Daily lunch and dinner. No credit cards accepted. 412 Amsterdam Ave (between W 79th and W 80th Sts). 496.1550

21 Garden Cafe $ Tucked away on the lower level of the **American Museum of Natural History,** this tiny cafe surrounded by greenery is a good place to rest your feet while munching on a hamburger or a salad. ♦ Cafe ♦ M-Th lunch; F lunch and early dinner; Sa brunch and early dinner; Su brunch. Central Park West (at 79th St). 769.5865

22 Pizzeria Uno $ The deep-dish, Chicago-style pizza at this chain outpost is a decent pie. This place also happens to be one of the very few near the **American Museum of Natural History** that is appropriate for children—the express lunch is ready in five minutes. ♦ Pizza ♦ Daily lunch, dinner, and late-night meals. 432 Columbus Ave (at W 81st St). 595.4700. Also at: South Street Seaport. 791.7999; 391 Sixth Ave (between Waverly Pl and W 8th St). 242.5230

23 Sarabeth's Kitchen ★★$$ One of the better—and busier—brunch spots in the neighborhood, this place serves pancakes and waffles with fresh fruit that are simply delicious. In winter, Sarabeth's hot porridge is something of a miracle cure. If you don't feel like waiting on line for weekend brunch, try

---

Lots and lots of lox: Proving that the lines are long for a reason, Zabar's sells 3,000 pounds of smoked salmon a week.

any meal during the week. Don't miss the lemon linguine with a rich, spicy vegetarian sauce of tomato, eggplant, onion, pepper, olives, and basil. For dessert, try the Budapest cake (a buttery cinnamon bundt cake). ♦ American ♦ M-F breakfast, lunch, and dinner; Sa-Su brunch and dinner. Reservations accepted for dinner only. 423 Amsterdam Ave (between W 80th and W 81st Sts). 496.6280. Also at: 1295 Madison Ave (between E 92nd and E 93rd Sts). 410.7355; the Whitney Museum, 945 Madison Ave (at E 75th St). 570.3670

23 **Luzia** ★$ Portuguese chef Luzia Pinhao's tiny shop—filled with pottery bowls and terra-cotta pots—is mostly for takeout, but there are a few pretty blue-and-white tiled tables for instant consumption of her flavorful, hearty food. Try cornbread, string beans with tomato, fish stew, and *caldo verde* (a potato broth with bits of kale). ♦ Portuguese ♦ Daily. 429 Amsterdam Ave (between W 80th and W 81st Sts). 595.2000 ♿

23 **Monsoon** ★$ More like a breath of fresh air than a natural disaster, this brightly decorated Vietnamese restaurant—lacquered bamboo baskets, black-and-white photos of Vietnam, and bamboo hats hanging on the yellow walls—has been mobbed since the day it opened. As a result, the service and food can be inconsistent; when the line is out the door, the service is rushed and the kitchen shows the strain. Lunch tends to be calmer and more reliable. Try the shredded green papaya and grilled beef salad, grilled lemongrass chicken on skewers, coconut curry shrimp noodle soup, steamed salmon with ginger, coriander and black-bean sauce, any of the noodle dishes, and the rich banana pudding. ♦ Vietnamese ♦ Daily lunch and dinner. 435 Amsterdam Ave (at W 81st St). 580.8686 ♿

24 **Café Con Leche** ★$ This small, sunny yellow-and-blue room is a friendly spot for a strong, sweet coffee or a Cuban roast pork sandwich at the counter. For something more substantial, have a seat at one of the few tables and dig into paella, shredded beef, or pork stew. ♦ Cuban ♦ Daily lunch and dinner. 424 Amsterdam Ave (between W 80th and W 81st Sts). 595.7000 ♿

24 **Amsterdam's Bar and Rotisserie** ★$$ The bar crowd is noisy and young, but the roast chicken with french fries and the generous salads are definitely above average. Take a table in the back, keep it simple, and skip dessert. ♦ American ♦ M dinner; Tu-Su lunch and dinner. 428 Amsterdam Ave (between W 80th and W 81st Sts). 874.1377. Also at: 454 Broadway (at Grand St). 925.6166

25 **H&H Bagels West** It turns out 60,000 bagels a day, some of which are shipped as far as London! Count on getting one fresh from the oven around the clock. This also happens to be one of the last Manhattan bastions of the "baker's dozen" (buy 12, get 13). While you're at it, check out the section of kosher and nonkosher deli products. ♦ Daily 24 hours. 2239 Broadway (at W 80th St). 595.8003, 800/692.2435 ♿. Also at: 639 W 46th St (at 12th Ave). 261.8000 ♿

26 **Zabar's** This food bazaar is like no other in the world. Evolved from a small Jewish deli, it's now a giant grocery and housewares store. Cookware and appliances, and packaged, prepared, and fresh foods from all over the world are yours for the buying. On weekends, a long line forms for the Western Nova Salmon (if you're lucky, the counter help will pass you a slice to nosh on). If shopping in the crowded, narrow aisles of this store induces an attack of claustrophobia, the reward is unrivaled quality at prices that beat the competition. ♦ Daily. 2245 Broadway (at W 80th St). 787.2000 ♿

Adjacent to Zabar's:

Zabar's Cafe ★$ Cappuccino as good as any that can be found on the West Side is served in the neighborhood's most undistinguished interior. Try a warm knish or pastry with your coffee for a superlative afternoon delight. An espresso may be just the restorative you need after a shopping trip to **Zabar's**. ♦ Cafe/Takeout ♦ Daily. 787.2000

27 **Teachers Too** $ Originally an annex of the now defunct **Teachers**, this restaurant patronized by locals features a pub menu with such dishes as blackened catfish and chicken *moutard* (in a mustard sauce). ♦ American ♦ M-Th, Su lunch and dinner; F-Sa lunch, dinner, and late-night meals. 2271 Broadway (between W 81st and W 82nd Sts). 362.4900 ♿

27 **Barnes & Noble Cafe** $ One of the singles bars of the 1990s (*New York Magazine* recently listed this particular place as one of "Fifteen Ways to Meet Your Lover"), this cafe offers decent espresso, fairly good muffins and cakes, and a sedate, literary atmosphere. The people who come here, however, are probably more interested in finding a good man or woman than a good book. ♦ Daily. 2289 Broadway (at W 82nd St). 362.8835. Also at: 4 Astor Pl (between Broadway and Lafayette St). 420.1332; 675 Sixth Ave (between 21st and 22nd Sts). 727.1227; Citicorp Center, 160 E 54th St (between Third and Lexington Aves). 750.8033

Louie's WESTSIDE CAFÉ

28 **Louie's Westside Cafe** ★$$ Grand yet casual, this cafe with peach walls, subdued lighting, and French rattan chairs offers a

basic but well-prepared American menu, with something for everyone. Try the crab cakes, spinach linguine with turkey *bolognese,* herb-roasted chicken, hanger steak, lamb chops with Tuscan white-bean stew, or pasta *primavera.* For dessert, have the mocha torte, chocolate velvet cake, or carrot cake. Brunch may be the best meal to have here; try the pecan waffles or Southwestern style eggs. ♦ American ♦ M-F breakfast, lunch, and dinner; Sa-Su brunch and dinner. Reservations recommended. 441 Amsterdam Ave (at W 81st St). 877.1900 &

28 E.J.'s Luncheonette ★$ A stylish version of a Middle American diner, with tile floors and blue vinyl booths, this is a friendly neighborhood spot for tempting sandwiches and salads. Especially good are the breakfast dishes, including thick almond-crusted French toast and massive platters of buttermilk pancakes. ♦ Diner ♦ Daily breakfast, lunch, and dinner. No credit cards accepted. 447 Amsterdam Ave (between W 81st and W 82nd Sts). 873.3444. Also at: 1271 Third Ave (at E 73rd St). 472.0600

Silk Road Palace

28 Silk Road Palace ★$ The name of this small restaurant is a tad overstated (the place is most unpalatial), but the crowd forever outside waiting for a table is proof enough that the management is on to something with its combination of good, reasonably priced Chinese food and friendly service. ♦ Hunan/Szechuan ♦ M-Th, Su lunch and dinner; F-Sa lunch, dinner, and late-night meals. 447B Amsterdam Ave (between W 81st and W 82nd Sts). 580.6294

29 Main Street ★$$ A great spot for Sunday dinner with a group, this large, plainly decorated place serves huge portions of such basic, good food as meat loaf, a whole roast chicken, and ribs. ♦ American ♦ M-F dinner; Sa-Su brunch and dinner. Reservations recommended for six or more. 446 Columbus Ave (between W 81st and W 82nd Sts). 873.5025 &

30 Rain ★★$$ Jeffrey Kadish and Steven Scher, owners of nearby **Main Street,** took over the space formerly occupied by **Dish.** They turned it into a Pan-Asian cafe that's been packed since day one. The space is airy, brick-walled, and filled with rattan couches and plants; the food is creative and sensationally flavored. Excellent choices include the zesty charred beef salad with lemongrass, basil, and chilies in a lime vinaigrette; pad thai, the traditional Thai noodle dish, here done with maximum flavor and minimum oil; crispy chicken with green curry and coconut milk; whole fish with a rich, slightly sweet three-flavor sauce; and cracked lobster and shrimp with Thai eggplant and sweet yellow curry. Pass up the ginger crème brûlée for one of the simple fruit desserts, such as bananas in coconut milk. ♦ Pan-Asian ♦ Daily dinner. Reservations recommended. 100 W 82nd St (between Columbus and Amsterdam Aves). 501.0776

31 Columbus Bakery ★★$ This pretty bakery/cafe with beige, stenciled walls occupies the space that used to house the French restaurant **Poiret.** Come in to pick up some of the delicious breads and cakes that are for sale, or have a seat and let the sweet smells tantalize you while you decide what to order. In the morning it's a great spot for a coffee and *pain au chocolat* (a chocolate-filled croissant). Lunchtime offerings include high-quality salads—smoked mozzarella with roasted tomatoes, or tuna with capers, olive oil, and lemon, for example—as well as heartier dishes, such as roast chicken or beef fillet with horseradish sauce. Save room for dessert, especially the rich chocolate cake or blood-orange tart. ♦ Bakery/Cafe ♦ Daily breakfast, lunch, and early dinner. No credit cards accepted. 474 Columbus Ave (between W 82nd and W 83rd Sts). 724.6880 &

32 Fujiyama Mama ★$$ Not your ordinary Japanese restaurant, this place has loud rock music and waitresses dressed in traditional kimonos. The menu has some interesting offerings, especially the *yakitori* (broiled dishes), but gives dishes strange, incomprehensible names: Chicken teriyaki, for some reason, is called "Chicken the Chicken" and sirloin with vegetables in a curry sauce is "Agony and Ecstasy." ♦ Japanese ♦ Daily dinner. Reservations recommended. 467 Columbus Ave (between W 82nd and W 83rd Sts). 769.1144

33 Isola ★$$ The apricot and yellow walls, covered with wave and fish stencils, evoke an

Italian island feeling. Good picks from the menu include delicious thin-crusted pizzas; pasta with sardines, pine nuts, fennel, and raisins; spaghetti in a puree of black olives; and a salad of oranges, olives, and fennel. The food is vibrant, and unfortunately, so is the noise level. ♦ Italian ♦ Daily lunch and dinner. 485 Columbus Ave (between W 83rd and W 84th Sts). 362.7400 &

LE SELECT

34 Le Select ★$$ The West Side isn't exactly bistroland, so this place owned by the Demarchelier family, who also are responsible for the East Side's **Demarchelier**, is extremely popular. Well-dressed locals who pack the attractive exposed-brick and white-walled room raise a nightly din as they enjoy pâté, onion soup, duck confit, and rack of lamb. The wine list features good French wines at affordable prices. The desserts leave something to be desired. ♦ French ♦ Daily lunch and dinner. Reservations recommended. 507 Columbus Ave (between W 84th and W 85th Sts). 875.1993 &

35 Good Enough to Eat ★★$$ Breakfast or a weekend brunch are the best bets at this tiny Vermont-style outpost. But be prepared to wait in line for pecan-flecked waffles, cinnamon-swirl French toast, or the lumber-jack breakfast—it's as big as it sounds. Lunch and dinner are prepared with a homey, if less inventive, touch. Popular picks include a turkey dinner with gravy, stuffing, and cranberry sauce, meat loaf, and turkey club sandwich. All breads, soups, and desserts are homemade, and pasta and pizza specials change daily. ♦ American ♦ M-F breakfast, lunch, and dinner; Sa-Su brunch and dinner. Reservations recommended for dinner. 483 Amsterdam Ave (between W 83rd and W 84th Sts). 496.0163

36 Avventura Gorgeous hand-painted pottery imported from all over the world, particularly Italy, is on display at this handsome store. The one-of-a-kind platters, bowls, and plates are absolute knockouts. ♦ M-Th, Su; F until sunset. 463 Amsterdam Ave (between W 82nd and W 83rd Sts). 769.2510

36 Hi-Life Restaurant & Lounge ★$$ The quilted metallic walls and Formica dining tables give this place a 1950s feel with 1990s style. The menu offers an interesting selection that caters to appetites of all sizes. Small plates include fried calamari with spicy red sauce, apple and leek potato pancakes, and grilled sesame chicken fingers. Entrées featured are lemon chicken with wild rice and Oriental vegetables and grilled blackened swordfish. If pasta is your thing, try a hearty bowl of penne with grilled chicken, peas, sun-dried tomatoes and broccoli in a light tomato cream sauce. ♦ American ♦ Daily brunch and dinner. 477 Amsterdam Ave (at W 83rd St). 787.7199. Also at: 1340 First Ave (at E 72nd St). 249.3600 &

37 Gelateria Richard This small ice-cream store offers 24 or so sophisticated flavors of exceptional Italian gelato such as zuppa inglese (English trifle), chocolate hazelnut, and marsala. There are a few tables to accommodate those who want to consume their purchase on the spot. ♦ Tu-Su. 464 Amsterdam Ave (between W 82nd and W 83rd Sts). 875.1877 &

38 Cafe Lalo ★$ This dessert-only cafe with brick walls and a wooden floor has long French-style windows that open onto the street. During the day, it's quite pleasant to linger over a cappuccino and such desserts as cappuccino tart, Snicker's Bar cheesecake, lemon mousse cake, chocolate Vienna torte, and assorted fruit pies. At night, it tends to get crowded and loud. ♦ Cafe ♦ Daily until 2AM weeknights, 4AM weekends. 201 W 83rd St (at Amsterdam Ave). 496.6031

39 Harriet's Kitchen Excellent chicken soup and straightforward family fare—roast chicken with green beans and carrots, fudge layer cake—are available from this unpretentious take-out shop that opens its doors in late afternoon, just when hard-working parents and professionals decide they're not in the mood to cook. ♦ M-Sa 4:30-11PM; Su 4:30-10PM. 502 Amsterdam Ave (between W 84th and W 85th Sts). 721.0045

40 Ollie's Noodle Shop ★$ Cold sesame noodles; scallion pancakes; vegetable, pork, or shrimp dumplings are all favorites at this bargain-priced Chinese restaurant. ♦ Chinese ♦ Daily lunch, dinner, and late-night meals. 2315 Broadway (at W 84th St). 362.3712 & Also at: 2957 Broadway (at 116th St). 932.3300; 200 W 44th St (between Broadway and Eighth Ave). 921.5988

41 Edgar's Cafe ★$ This beautiful cafe with beige stone walls and apricot-colored frescoes was designed to resemble a palazzo ruin. Presiding over it all is a painting of the eponymous Edgar—Edgar Allan Poe. Come here for good salads, particularly carpaccio, and the smoked turkey and blue cheese combination. Save room for the spectacular desserts, among them oreo cheesecake, mocha mousse cake, lemon tart, cognac-pumpkin cheesecake, and an impressive assortment of fruit pies. ♦ Cafe ♦ Daily lunch, dinner, and late-night meals. No credit cards accepted. 255 W 84th St (between Broadway and West End Ave). 496.6126

42 Eden Rock ★$ The room is not much to look at, but for a fast meal of good, freshly prepared Lebanese food, this is a local favorite. Try *kafta* kebab (a spiced ground-lamb dish), rotisseried chicken *shawarma* (roasted on a spit), and *baba ganooj*. ♦ Lebanese ♦ Daily lunch and dinner. No credit cards accepted. 2325 Broadway (between W 84th and W 85th Sts). 873.1361

43 Patzo $ The pizza at this two-level Italian restaurant has a thin, well-baked crust, and the list of toppings offered will make you dizzy. Good pasta is also available. It's crowded on the weekends but peaceful at lunchtime during the week. ♦ Italian ♦ Daily lunch and dinner. 2330 Broadway (at W 85th St). 496.9240 &

44 Williams Bar-B-Que Well before the current rotisserie craze took the city by storm, this place was serving birds to appreciative locals. Side dishes include egg barley with onions and chicken fat—food a Jewish grandmother would love. ♦ Daily. 2350 Broadway (between W 85th and W 86th Sts). 877.5384 &

45 La Mirabelle ★$$$ A fresh, inviting decor, efficient service, and food that is a notch above the ordinary keep this French bistro busy. Good choices are escargots, soft-shell crabs cooked with lots of garlic and tomatoes, a pink, spicy rack of lamb, and the best steak *frites* (with french fries) on the West Side. Go elsewhere to satisfy your sweet tooth. ♦ French ♦ Daily dinner. Reservations recommended. 333 W 86th St (between West End Ave and Riverside Dr). 496.0458

46 Barney Greengrass (The Sturgeon King) ★★$ Supplying the West Side with appetizing since 1908, this place, run by Barney's son Moe and grandson Gary, is folksier than **Zabar's**, though not as complete. On one side is a smoked fish counter with perfect smoked salmon, sturgeon, pickled herring, and chopped liver. On the other is an earthy dining room with brown vinyl seats, fluorescent lighting that makes everyone look like they need to be hospitalized, and, inscrutably, a mural of New Orleans. The wait can be long, but the smoked fish platters and scrambled eggs with Nova Scotia salmon and onions couldn't be better. Autographed pictures of occasional guests Alec Baldwin and Dustin Hoffman hang on the walls as testimonials to the excellence of the fare here. ♦ Deli ♦ Tu-Su breakfast and lunch. No credit cards accepted. 541 Amsterdam Ave (between W 86th and W 87th Sts). 724.4707

46 Popover Café ★$$ A cozy spot with white brick walls and paisley banquettes, this place has teddy bears scattered around the room for company. Breakfast is a popular meal here— the neighborhood piles in for freshly made popovers served with strawberry butter, raspberry jam, or apple butter; omelettes; and scrambled eggs with smoked salmon, cream cheese, and chives. There are also good salads and sandwiches at lunchtime, and at dinner, more serious food is offered, including grilled prime rib, blackened swordfish, and duck breast with raspberry sauce. ♦ American ♦ M-F breakfast, lunch, and dinner; Sa-Su brunch and dinner. 551 Amsterdam Ave (at W 87th St). 595.8555 &

47 Grossinger's Uptown Bake Shop An old-fashioned kosher bakery, this place sells such traditional Jewish baked goods as coffee cake, cheesecake, chocolate layer cookies, danish, and the kind of buttercream-frosted birthday cakes you had as a kid. ♦ M-Th, Su; F until sundown. 570 Columbus Ave (at W 88th St). 874.6996

48 Ozu ★$ This simple earthy room with exposed-brick walls and wood furniture serves good salmon teriyaki, and such macrobiotic fare as soba (buckwheat) noodle dishes; salads; a variety of grains, steamed vegetables and seaweeds; and soups that include miso, pea, and carrot ginger. ♦ Japanese ♦ M-F lunch and dinner; Sa-Su brunch and dinner. 566 Amsterdam Ave (between W 87th and W 88th Sts). 787.8316 &

48 Pandit ★$ Save yourself the trek down to the East Village's Little India and have a memorable meal here in this cozy brick-walled room. Try any of the curries, chicken *saag* (cooked with spinach in a spicy sauce), or chicken *biryani* (curried and served on a mound of fragrant rice). ♦ Indian ♦ Daily dinner. 566 Amsterdam Ave (between W 87th and W 88th Sts). 724.1217

48 Les Routiers ★$$ This quaint French bistro with wood beams and baskets of dried flowers has a fairly classic menu that features such items as onion soup; *boeuf bourguignon;* braised lamb shank with tomato, lentils, and Provençal herbs; roast duck with raspberry and green-peppercorn sauce; lemon tart; and chocolate mousse. The wine list is well chosen and reasonably priced. Selecting a bottle is easy here: Numbers corresponding to appropriate wine selections follow each entrée on the menu. ♦ French ♦ Daily dinner. 568 Amsterdam Ave (between W 87th and W 88th Sts). 874.2742

48 Mo' Better ★$ A sophisticated soul food restaurant with subdued lighting, banquettes, and a billiard corner, this place offers good traditional, earthy fare, such as barbecued ribs, blackened salmon, panfried catfish, candied yams, and black-eyed peas. Also on the menu are corn-and-shrimp bisque and grilled chicken. Live music (mostly jazz and blues) is featured without cover charge Wednesday through Saturday nights. ♦ American ♦ Tu-Su dinner. 570 Amsterdam Ave (between W 87th and W 88th Sts). 580.7755

49 Boulevard $ The wide-ranging menu at this big, comfortable place with a nice outdoor cafe includes so-so barbecue brisket, ribs, roast chicken, burgers, burritos, and angel-hair pasta *primavera*. The Monday dinner special, all-you-can-eat chicken and ribs, is a deal. ♦ American ♦ M-Th lunch and dinner; F lunch, dinner, and late-night meals; Sa-Su brunch, dinner, and late-night meals. 2398 Broadway (at W 88th St). 874.7400 &

50 The Armadillo $ The Tex-Mex food here isn't the best around, but it's not the worst, either. And if you're in the mood for a lively scene, this is the place. Have the chili, or for something slightly more ambitious, try the pork loin with apple salsa or grilled Gulf shrimp with orange and green-onion salsa. ♦ Tex-Mex ♦ M-F dinner and late-night meals; Sa-Su brunch, dinner, and late-night meals. 2420 Broadway (at W 89th St). 496.1066

51 Whole Foods This uptown outpost of the SoHo original has the same full selection of vitamins, grains, organic vegetables, kosher chicken and turkeys, cosmetics, and healthy-living books. The only thing missing is fresh fish, which is available only at the downtown store. ♦ Daily. 2421 Broadway (at W 89th St). 874.4000 &. Also at: 117 Prince St (between Greene and Wooster Sts). 982.1000

52 Jake's Fish Market Named after co-owner Mark Conley's young son, this sparkling market has a cornucopia of the freshest fish. The long bar at the front has a great selection of seafood—snapper, tiny scallops, tuna, salmon, clams, and mussels. The back counter is heaped with luscious prepared foods—grilled swordfish, seared tuna, seafood salad, and grilled shrimp. Weekends feature a complete dinner—soup, salad, fish, side dishes, and dessert—perfect for when you're too tired to cook. ♦ Daily. 2425 Broadway (between W 89th and W 90th Sts). 580.5253 &

52 Docks Oyster Bar and Seafood Grill ★★$$ Fresh seafood is featured in this lively black-and-white–tiled neighborhood haunt. The catch of the day varies, but fried oysters coated in cornmeal are a sure bet anytime, and the french-fried yams are an inspiration. Also worth trying are the crab cakes, grilled snapper, and fried calamari. Dessert specials include mud cake and Key lime pie. Stop in on Sunday or Monday night for a full New England clambake. ♦ Seafood ♦ M-F lunch and dinner; Sa-Su brunch and dinner. Reservations recommended. 2427 Broadway (between W 89th and W 90th Sts). 724.5588. Also at: 633 Third Ave (at E 40th St). 986.8080

52 Murray's Sturgeon For more than a half-century, the ultimate Jewish appetizing store has continued to live up to its reputation for high-quality sturgeon, herring, lox, whitefish, and all other smoked fish items. The store also carries caviar, coffee beans, and dried fruit. ♦ Daily. 2429 Broadway (between W 89th and W 90th Sts). 724.2650

53 Mana ★$ Good and good for you, the delicious food here contains no sugar, dairy products, or chemical preservatives; grains and produce are organic; and the water is filtered. The menu features such Japanese dishes as fish teriyaki, *yakisoba* (stir-fried vegetables served on soba noodles), and fish and shrimp tempuras. Other dishes include such vegetable-protein inventions as tofu-skin roll, seitan stroganoff, and seitan with spaghetti and beet sauce accompanied by vegetables. Even desserts—baked apple with granola, for example—are pretty noble.

♦ Japanese/Health food ♦ Daily lunch and dinner. 2444 Broadway (between W 90th and W 91st Sts). 787.1110 ♿

53 Carmine's $$ Come hungry and bring at least one friend to share the huge portions; all meals are meant for two or more. The dishes are basic Southern Italian fare—chicken parmigiana, rigatoni with broccoli, and linguine with calamari. There's also a take-out shop next door. ♦ Italian ♦ Dinner. 2450 Broadway (between W 90th and W 91st Sts). 362.2200. Also at: 200 W 44th St (between Broadway and Eighth Ave). 221.3800

54 Key West Diner $ The salmon-and-turquoise decor is straight out of the sunshine state, just as the name suggests. Nevertheless, this place is just a basic New York coffee shop with decent burgers, sandwiches, salads, omelettes, bagels, and challah French toast. ♦ Diner ♦ Daily breakfast, lunch, dinner, and late-night meals. 2532 Broadway (between W 94th and W 95th Sts). 932.0068

54 Lemongrass Grill ★★$ An Upper West Side outpost of the Brooklyn original, this place serves the same spicy and delicious food Park Slopers so enjoy. Try the *gai tom kha* (chicken soup with lime juice and red pepper), fish cakes with scallions and kaffir lime leaves, lemongrass pork chops, and *pla jean* (seared fillet of salmon with herbs). ♦ Thai ♦ Daily lunch and dinner. 2534 Broadway (between W 94th and W 95th Sts). 666.0888. Also at: 61A Seventh Ave (between Lincoln Pl and Berkeley St), Brooklyn. 718/399.7100

55 Mimi's Macaroni ★$ A crisply decorated room, with royal-blue walls and white ceiling fans, this is a comfortable and reasonably priced place for a bowl of pasta or a sandwich. It's also child-friendly—a special kids' menu is available. Try the calamari and shrimp in an olive-oil–lemon marinade, linguine with grilled shrimp and whole roasted garlic, rigatoni *bolognese,* and spaghetti with veal and pork meatballs. Desserts are the usual offerings served in Italian restaurants—tiramisù,

cheesecake, and *tartuffo* (scoops of chocolate and vanilla ice cream covered in chocolate and frozen). ♦ Italian ♦ M-Sa lunch and dinner; Su brunch and dinner. 718 Amsterdam Ave (at W 95th St). 866.6311 ♿

56 H. Oppenheimer Meats For about 50 years, Harry Oppenheimer has been serving the neighborhood and those who make a special trip just to come here to get top-quality meat and game. One of the few butchers left that cuts all meat to order, he'll tell you everything you need to know about your purchase, including how to cook it. ♦ M-Sa 2606 Broadway (between W 98th and W 99th Sts). 662.0246

57 Health Nuts Hypoallergenic vitamins, natural breads, and organic goods—grains, nuts, herbs, and honey—are sold here. ♦ Daily. 2611 Broadway (at W 99th St). 678.0054. Also at: Numerous locations throughout the city

58 Positively 104th Street Cafe ★$ Simple and cozy, this cafe offers a range of fare. Try one of the well-prepared salads—spinach with goat cheese and sun-dried tomatoes, an Cobb—or such sandwiches as roast beef with homemade coleslaw. More ambitious entrées include turkey meat loaf and fillet of salmon with caper, tomato, basil, and balsamic-vinaigrette sauce. For dessert, the calorie-conscious can indulge in angel-food cake with raspberry puree; those ready to splurge have their pick of the daily selection of pies or the chocolate cake. ♦ American ♦ Daily breakfast, lunch, and dinner. 2725 Broadway (between W 104th and W 105th Sts). 316.0372

58 Au Petit Beurre $ Signs of student-inspired, whole-earth consciousness abound in this pleasant, airy resting spot. The eclectic Middle Eastern, French, and Mediterranean menu includes a variety of kebab dishes, good tabbouleh, and such French dishes as chicken cooked slowly in Port. Sandwiches and burgers are also available. Decent cappuccino, muffins, and cakes are very popular with the neighborhood clientele. ♦ Eclectic ♦ Daily breakfast, lunch, and dinner. 2737 Broadway (at W 105th St). 663.7010

59 Metisse ★★★$ Since the day it opened in the space of the former **Santerello,** this cozy bistro has been wowing the neighborhood. But that shouldn't be surprising considering the pedigrees of its principals: Owner Claude Waryniak learned the ropes working with

---

Main Street restaurant, known for family-style dinners, goes through 1,600 chickens a week.

When a New Yorker says, "Let's grab a slice," the pie in question is none other than the ubiquitous pizza pie.

The farthest a New York pizza has traveled is to Japan by Federal Express. The recipient was a former diplomat who had been based in New York and couldn't live without his favorite pie. The pizzas were baked especially for traveling: three-quarters through with tin foil underneath; when the pie arrived in Japan, the nostalgic dignitary finished the cooking.

Jean-Georges Vongerichten at **Lafayette** and **JoJo**; chef J.D. Cadona was sous-chef at **Palio**. Simple, perfect French food is the result of their efforts; try sautéed sweetbreads with whole-grain mustard, potato and goat-cheese terrine with arugula juice, salmon with creamy mushroom polenta, and the ultimate steak *frites*. Desserts are also exceptional, particularly crème brûlée and a warm chocolate *gâteau* (cake) with vanilla ice cream. The wine list is small but well chosen and affordable, with a few Alsatian wines representing the native land of the owner. ♦ French ♦ M-Sa lunch and dinner. Reservations recommended. 239 W 105th St (between Amsterdam Ave and Broadway). 666.8825

60 107 West ★$$ A mostly young, upscale crowd keeps this three-room establishment bustling. The overall tone is Cajun, but the menu throws a few Mexican and pasta specialties into the mix. Try grilled chicken and shrimp, fried chicken, jambalaya, mesquite-smoked chicken, vegetable lasagna, rigatoni with chicken and arugula, crab cakes, or blackened catfish. The wine list offers decent selections at affordable prices. ♦ American ♦ Daily dinner. 2787 Broadway (between W 107th and W 108th Sts). 864.1555

60 Indian Cafe ★$ A bright glassed-in restaurant with comfy banquettes and a pink color scheme, this place turns out well-prepared standard Indian fare. Try the Bombay Beach Snack (an appetizer of chickpeas, noodles, peanuts, diced onions, and tomatoes), lamb *muglai* (simmered in creamy curry sauce with almonds), and any of the tandoori dishes. ♦ Indian ♦ Daily lunch and dinner. Reservations recommended on weekends. 2791 Broadway (between W 107th and W 108th Sts). 749.9200 &

60 Fish $ The owners of the **Indian Cafe** (see above) branched out and opened this cute seafood cafe. It's very popular with the locals, mainly because the room itself is attractively decorated—sea blue with fish motifs—and because there are no other good fish houses in the neighborhood. The best bets here are simply grilled fish, such as snapper, or the sizzling whole catfish with ginger and cornmeal pudding. ♦ Seafood ♦ M-F lunch and dinner; Sa-Su brunch and dinner. Reservations recommended. 2799 Broadway (at W 108th St). 864.5000 &

61 La Rosita ★$ This noisy, always crowded Cuban spot is not much to look at, but the cab drivers, locals, and **Columbia** students who pile in here don't come for the decor. They turn up for great strong coffee, a glass of fresh mango juice, and Cuban breakfasts— eggs with yellow rice and black beans. For lunch or dinner, there's chicken or shrimp in soupy rice, chicken with garlic, roast pork, and cinnamon-laced rice pudding. ♦ Cuban

♦ Daily breakfast, lunch, dinner, and late-night meals. No credit cards accepted. 2809 Broadway (between W 108th and W 109th Sts). 663.7804

62 Cafe St. John ★$ Located on a deserted stretch of Amsterdam Avenue in the shadow of the imposing **St. John the Divine** cathedral, this pretty bistro with a wood bar, black-and-white tiles, and lace curtains serves good French food that lures customers east from the **Columbia University** area. Try juicy roast chicken saturated with garlic; steak *frites;* and mussels in garlic, butter, and white wine. Save room for the fruit tart of the day. ♦ French ♦ M-F lunch and dinner; Sa-Su dinner. Reservations recommended. 1018 Amsterdam Ave (at W 110th St). 932.8420

63 V&T Pizzeria ★$ Its fans maintain that this place has the best pizza on the Upper West Side—hefty, thick-crusted, with fresh tomato sauce, whole-milk mozzarella, and flavorful toppings, such as sausage. The pies can be a bit oily, but they satisfy in a way that designer pizzas never could. ♦ Pizza ♦ Daily lunch and dinner. No credit cards accepted. 1024 Amsterdam Ave (between W 110th and W 111th Sts). 663.1708

64 Columbia Hot Bagels Some people swear by **H&H** bagels, but others rave about the chewy texture and rich flavors of the ones that are sold here. Sample the salt, onion, or cinnamon-raisin bagels and see if they're not up there with the best you've ever had. ♦ Daily 24 hours. 2836 Broadway (between W 110th and W 111th Sts). 222.3200

65 Symposium $ Greek specialties such as moussaka, spinach pie, and *exohiko* (lamb, feta cheese, artichoke hearts, and peas wrapped in phyllo dough) are featured at this popular and comfortable spot. During spring and summer, the garden is available for dining. ♦ Greek ♦ Daily lunch and dinner. 544 W 113th St (between Amsterdam Ave and Broadway). 865.1011

66 La Marqueta First established in 1936 by Mayor La Guardia, this is the oldest public market still in operation. When it first began, the market catered to the Jews, Irish, Italians, and Puerto Ricans living here. As the neighborhood's ethnic character has changed, so have the products; today it exclusively offers Caribbean and Latin staples. Yuccas, papayas, *batatas* (a tubular root vegetable), suckling pig, octopus, eel, and a variety of herbs are all for sale. There isn't much of a scene during the week, but on Saturdays, despite the decline in active stalls over the years, it's vibrant with colors and life. ♦ Daily Park Ave between 110th and 116th Sts

67 Patsy's Pizzeria ★$ It's worth making the trip uptown for some of the best pizza in the city. Connoisseurs will appreciate the thin crust and perfect balance of ingredients. ♦ Pizza ♦ Daily lunch, dinner, and late-night meals. No credit cards accepted. 2287 First Ave (between E 117th and E 118th Sts). 534.9783. Also at: 509 Third Ave (between E 34th and E 35th Sts). 689.7500

Cooking by the Book

If you want to cook something fabulous for dinner but the only thing you know how to make is a reservation, don't despair. The talent, training, and experience of the city's foremost chefs can be yours for less than the price of an entrée with any of the following books written by the experts:

Bobby Flay's Bold American Food by the chef of **The Mesa Grill** and **Bolo** (Warner Books, 1994)

Cooking Provence by **Le Perigord**'s Antoine Bouterin with Joan Schwartz, (Macmillan, 1994)

Cooking with Daniel Boulud by the owner/chef of restaurant **Daniel,** (Random House, 1993)

Cooking with David Burke by the **Park Avenue Cafe** chef and Carmel Berman Reingold (Knopf, 1994)

Food From My Heart by **Zarela**'s own Zarela Martinez (Macmillan, 1992)

La Cucina di Lidia by **Felidia**'s Lidia Bastianich and Jay Jacobs (Doubleday, 1990)

The Russian Tea Room: A Tasting by Faith Stewart-Gordon with Starla Smith (Clarkson Potter, 1993)

The Tribeca Cookbook by Mary Cleaver, Joy Simmen Hamburger, and Mimi Shanley Taft (Ten Speed Press, 1994), which includes recipes from several noted restaurants in the area, including **Arqua, Barocco, Tribeca Grill,** and **Montrachet.**

The Union Square Cookbook by owner Danny Meyer and Michael Romano, (HarperCollins, 1994)

Venetian Taste by **Remi**'s owner/chef Adam D. Tihany and Francesco Antonucci with Florence Fabricant (Abbeville Press, 1994)

For a taste of what a day in the life of the restaurant world is like, try: *Flash in the Pan, The Life and Death of an American Restaurant (The Falls)* by David Blum (Simon & Schuster, 1992) and *Lutèce, a Day in the Life of America's Greatest Restaurant* by Irene Daria (Random House, 1993).

68 Rao's ★★$$$$ The limousines parked outside give the impression that this is one of the most exclusive Italian restaurants in Manhattan, and despite the location, it is. Even with a hard-to-come-by reservation in hand, you could be shut out by Sinatra and his entourage at this eight-table establishment. But the risk is worth it because this unassuming little bistro, run by the Rao family, serves such first-rate Southern Italian specialties as baked clams, linguine with sausage, and veal chops. ♦ Italian ♦ M-Sa dinner. Reservations required. No credit cards accepted. 455 E 114th St (at Pleasant Ave). 534.9625

69 The Terrace ★★$$$$ The sparkling wraparound views of the glittering George Washington Bridge to the northwest and skyscrapers to the south are made even more romantic by the reflection of tabletop candles in the windows and harp music wafting in from the bar area. If only the food were as completely wonderful as the ambience. Chef Ossama Mikhail is at his best when he sticks to classic French dishes—*feuilletée* (puff pastry) of seafood with lobster sauce and herb-crusted rack of lamb—but is less successful when he goes out on a creative limb with seared calamari stuffed with Norwegian salmon and cracked-wheat salad with curry and truffle oil or loin of venison and grilled foie gras sausage with barley and sun-dried apricot *jus*. The wine list is very well-chosen but you won't be able to touch a bottle for under $45. ♦ Continental ♦ Tu-F lunch and dinner; Sa dinner. Reservations recommended 400 W 119th St (at Morningside Dr). 666.9490

70 The Bread Shop ★$ The whole-grain breads baked here are dense without being heavy and are seriously delicious. So are the flaky buttermilk biscuits and herb-onion rolls. Take them home or enjoy them in the small six-table cafe in the back. Homebaked pizza, two soups of the day, and a couple of daily specials that range from chicken curry to lasagna are prepared by the multicultural staff. ♦ Bakery/Cafe ♦ Daily breakfast, lunch, and dinner. 3139 Broadway (at W 123rd St). 666.4343

71 The Cotton Club ★$$ The legendary Harlem nightclub (at this location since 1978) is becoming almost as well known for its food as its entertainment. The earthy Southern fare is served in a white-walled dining room with white leather banquettes. Try the ribs or fried chicken, and don't forget the greens and ham hocks. For dessert have a piece of cheesecake or the light chocolate cake. The original home of the weekend gospel brunch (seatings at noon and 2:30PM), it offers a prix-fixe buffet, with offerings ranging from scrambled eggs and grits to meat loaf and rice pilaf.

♦ Southern ♦ W-F dinner; Sa-Su brunch and dinner. Reservations recommended. 656 W 125 St (between Broadway and Riverside Dr). 633.7980

72 Sylvia's ★★$$ The most renowned soul-food restaurant in Harlem and perhaps in New York City has expanded into a second dining room, and during the warmer months, into an open patio next door. Southern-fried and smothered chicken are standouts, as are the dumplings, candied sweets (yams), greens, and desserts—especially the cinnamony sweet-potato pie. The atmosphere is homey and relaxed; there's a snow-scene mural on the wall and one of the most comprehensive jukeboxes in town. ♦ Southern ♦ M-Sa breakfast, lunch, and dinner; Su gospel brunch and dinner. 328 Lenox Ave (between W 126th and W 127th Sts). 996.0660

73 Jamaican Hot Pot ★★$ Owned by Yvonne Richards and Gary Walters, this place turns out fabulous Jamaican specialties—fried chicken, oxtail stew, garlic shrimp, jerk chicken, curried goat, and pepper steak, to name just a few. Understandably, locals love this place. ♦ Jamaican ♦ Daily lunch, dinner, and late-night meals. 2260 Adam Clayton Powell Jr. Blvd (at W 133rd St). 491.5270

74 Copeland's ★$$ Although the dining room is gussied up with linens and fresh flowers, the food here couldn't be any earthier; try the oxtails, corn fritters, Louisiana gumbo, and barbecued jumbo shrimp. Come on a Friday or Saturday night and be treated to live jazz; the first set starts at 7:30PM (no cover charge). ♦ Southern/Continental ♦ Tu-Sa dinner; Su brunch and dinner. Reservations recommended. 547 W 145th St (between Amsterdam Ave and Broadway). 234.2356

75 Wilson's Bakery & Restaurant ★★$$ The menu changes daily, but no matter what's listed, you'll be assured of a satisfying meal any day of the week at this Harlem institution. When they're available, don't miss the chicken and dumplings, barbecued ribs, fried chicken, smothered steak, ham hocks, and meat loaf. Save room for dessert, particularly the peach cobbler, coconut cake, and sweet-potato pie, which come from the excellent bakery adjoining the restaurant. ♦ Bakery/Southern ♦ Daily breakfast, lunch, and dinner. 1980 Amsterdam Ave (at W 158th St). 923.9821 &

76 International Gourmet and Gift Center China, cutlery, crystal, appliances, food, and cosmetics imported mainly from Germany can be found in this well-stocked store—one of the last outposts of Washington Heights's erstwhile German-Jewish community. ♦ M-Th, Su; F until 2PM. 4797 Broadway (between Dyckman and Academy Sts). 569.2611

77 Carrot Top Pastries ★$ Owner Renee Allen Mancino bakes the single best carrot cake in New York, as well as delicious pecan, sweet-potato, and pumpkin pies. Special orders can be requested. Devoted customers of her two cafes include such celebrities as Stevie Wonder and Richard Pryor. This branch, near **Columbia-Presbyterian Medical Center,** has a small seating area and offers a light cafe menu. The other location, farther downtown, is much bigger and also serves pasta dishes, and chicken, eggplant, and meatball parmigiana, in addition to the lighter offerings available here. ♦ Cafe ♦ M-Sa; Su until 4PM. 5025 Broadway (at W 214th St). 569.1532. Also at: 3931 Broadway (at W 164th St). 927.4800

Bests

Serena Lightner
Head Concierge, Paramount Hotel

Three of Cups: Personally I could go on and on about why this is my favorite restaurant but I will try to keep it simple. I love the brick-oven pizza, the super cozy atmosphere and hearty pastas. The owners Santo, Lenny, and Anthony are very entertaining and will keep you laughing all night. They have a groovy downstairs lounge where I always seem to run into someone I know.

Blue Ribbon: One of my favorites because the food is excellent, fresh seafood that's reasonably priced, and happens to be one of the few restaurants that serves cheese fondue. You can always count on a fun, lively atmosphere and they serve until 4AM. They don't take reservations, but it's worth the wait!

Corner Bistro: Best burgers!

Danal: A little, charming, unknown bistro that feels like eating in someone's cozy living room. It's nice to get away from the "scene" sometimes, and this is the perfect place to escape. They have a seasonal menu that is limited but always fresh and satisfying. High tea is served Friday and Saturday at 4PM.

Universal Grill: Wildest, craziest party every night. Jack the owner guarantees a "fabulous" time.

Union Square Greenmarket: Fresh flowers, fresh fruit, fresh produce, homebaked goods, candles, and delicious pretzels.

Gourmet Garage: Sell to the public, starting at 12 noon everyday. Super fresh gourmet food. The kind of place you wished you lived next door to.

Boroughs

Area code 718 unless otherwise noted.

The psychological distance between Manhattan and its surrounding boroughs is far greater than the physical span, which can often be bridged in minutes. Manhattanites allude to **Brooklyn, Queens, the Bronx,** and **Staten Island** as the "outer" boroughs, while borough residents refer to Manhattan as "the city," as they have probably since the days when these areas were outlying agrarian tracts. Today borough dwellers take a great deal of pride in their home territories. After all, the boroughs are home to the **Brooklyn Academy of Music (BAM), Brooklyn Museum, Brooklyn** and **New York Botanic Gardens, The International Wildlife Conservation Park,** (formerly the **Bronx Zoo**), **Shea** and **Yankee Stadiums,** and numerous other cultural and educational places, not to mention the many colorful ethnic enclaves generously sprinkled throughout the four areas.

Waves of immigration, past and present, continue to support a panoply of restaurants and shops so diverse and interesting as to reverse the migration—Manhattanites cross the borders into Brooklyn, Queens, and the Bronx. These forays have their culinary rewards—the best hummus with fresh pita bread; blinis and a seemingly never-ending supply of vodka; fresh, hand-cut pasta; spicy, shredded jellyfish; and the most authentic Jamaican beef patties in town are just a few of the treats in store. If you've come to the boroughs for an eating adventure, you've come to the right place.

Brooklyn

With over 300 years of history and more than 75 square miles of land, Brooklyn had long been a city in its own right (the US's fourth-largest) until it was annexed by the City of New York in 1898. Brooklyn-born newspaper reporter and author Pete Hamill still refers to this act as the "great mistake." By turns a suburban step up the ladder for immigrant groups, an oceanfront resort, shipping capital, cultural mecca, teeming slum, and front-runner of an urban

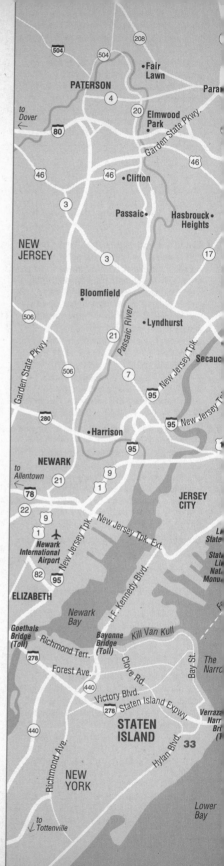

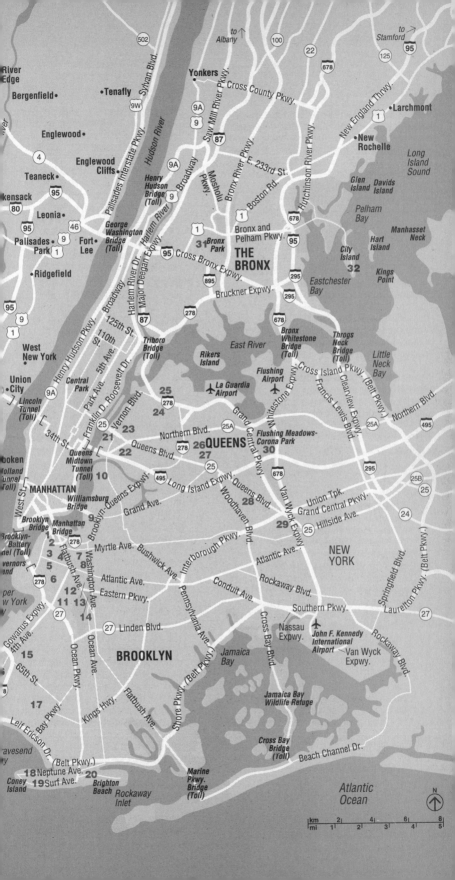

renaissance, Brooklyn is as multifaceted as it is multiracial. It has all the earmarks of a major metropolis.

Brooklyn's mystique is built on vaudeville jokes, an inimitable accent, urban conflict, and a host of famous natives—Henry Miller, George Gershwin, Woody Allen, Mel Brooks, Barbra Streisand, Beverly Sills, and Spike Lee among them. Easily as famous as any individuals, however, are the neighborhoods. Affluent **Brooklyn Heights** has some of the borough's oldest buildings, including that cultural icon, the **Brooklyn Bridge,** and a thriving Middle Eastern development along **Atlantic Avenue. Coney Island** is renowned for its famous amusement park, boardwalk, and beach; and nearby **Brighton Beach**—dubbed "Little Odessa by the Sea," bustles with a growing population of Russian immigrants. Other ethnic colonies include the Italian enclave of **Bensonhurst** and the overlapping areas of **Williamsburg** and **Greenpoint,** where the respective Hispanic and Polish communities have absorbed many of the artists who were priced out of Manhattan by skyrocketing rents. Finally, there's **Park Slope,** an integrated, family-oriented community close to **Prospect Park.** What distinguishes these neighborhoods is their unique sense of history, linking them to times and places other than New York in the 1990s. If Brooklyn once was an autonomous city, today it's nearer to a conglomerate of many, each with its own distinct culinary treats.

The River Café

1 River Café ★★★$$$$ The backdrop of this lovely dining spot—the towering, glittering Manhattan skyline seen from the foot of the Brooklyn Bridge—is unequaled. Huge bouquets of flowers and a dressed-to-the-nines crowd offer other visual distractions on this handsome, anchored barge, but only until the food arrives. Chef Rick Laakkonen turns out such vibrant, exciting dishes as salmon and tuna *tartare* with wasabi, ragout of grilled octopus and Manila clams, sautéed yellowfin tuna with fennel and hundred-year-old balsamic vinegar, grilled cumin and black-pepper–rubbed squab, and charred saddle of venison. And don't miss dessert. Pastry chef Christophe Rey's Valrhona marquise (a chocolate mousse layer cake), shaped like the Brooklyn Bridge, will put a smile on your face—and a few pounds around your middle. Save the diet for tomorrow; it's worth it. The wine list features the most extensive selection of California labels you'll find this side of the Golden Gate Bridge. ♦ American ♦ M-F lunch and dinner; Sa-Su brunch and dinner. Reservations required; jacket required. 1 Water St (on the East River under the Brooklyn Bridge), Brooklyn Heights. 522.5200

1 Patsy's Pizza ★★$ Patsy Grimaldi learned the art of pizza making from his late uncle (also named Patsy), owner of the famed **Patsy's** pizzeria in East Harlem. Fans of the pizza here feel that it has surpassed even Uncle Patsy's. The fresh dough is charred in a brick oven and the mozzarella is made fresh, as is the tomato sauce; such toppings as mushrooms, roasted peppers, and sausage are all top-quality. This may be as close to pizza heaven as you can get. It's also Sinatra heaven, with that most famous of the Grimaldi family friends heavily represented on the jukebox and in photos all over the walls. ♦ Pizza ♦ M, W-Su lunch and dinner. No credit cards accepted. 19 Old Fulton St (between Water and Front Sts), Brooklyn Heights. 858.4300 ♿

2 Henry's End ★$$ This cozy—and often loud—neighborhood bistro is known for its wild-game festival, which runs annually from September through January, when the adventurous can dig into such dishes as elk chops, venison, and alligator stew. All year, though, the menu showcases simple, well-prepared dishes including raspberry duck, blackened salmon, and lemon chicken. The exclusively American wine list has received awards from *Wine Spectator Magazine* every year since 1987. ♦ Continental ♦ Daily dinner. Reservations required for three or more. 44 Henry St (at Cranberry St), Brooklyn Heights. 834.1776

3 Montague Street Saloon ★$ A friendly, casual atmosphere fills this local hangout. The basic pub fare is good, and the quaint outdoor cafe is open during the warmer months. Try fried calamari, steamed mussels, Cajun catfish, steak Delmonico, grilled steak topped with fried onions, chicken piccata, and tomato-basil chicken. Finish the meal with mud cake, Key lime pie, or peanut butter pie. ♦ American ♦ Daily lunch, dinner, and late-night meals. 122 Montague St (between Henry and Hicks Sts), Brooklyn Heights. 522.6770

4 Gage & Tollner ★★★$$$ The menu, famous for its length, promises "to serve the nostalgic atmosphere that serves to bring back fond recollections." Around for about a century (making it the oldest restaurant in New York), this place truly delivers on that promise. Part of the enjoyment is the grand setting, a handsome 19th-century stage of gaslit chandeliers, arched mirrors, dark-wood paneling, and well-worn mahogany tables. Another factor is the old-fashioned, gracious service. But the fondest memories you come away with may well be of the food. Although famed chef Edna Lewis, whom the management lured back from South Carolina, has retired, she still checks in from time to time, and her signature specialties, now cooked by the very able Betty Deepe, are still on the menu. Try Charleston she-crab soup, shrimp-and-crab gumbo, crab cakes, clam bellies (the main section of steamer clams) coated in cornmeal and broiled, broiled mustard catfish, and Cajun shrimp-and-monkfish scampi. Be sure to save room for one of the delicious desserts, including bourbon pecan pie, apple-cranberry pie, and vanilla ice cream with raspberry sauce served on hazelnut meringue. The wine list spotlights an extensive, affordable selection of American wines, with several choices available by the glass. At press time there were rumors that the restaurant had been sold and the space and menu were to be overhauled. ♦ Seafood ♦ M-F lunch and dinner; Sa dinner; Su brunch and dinner. Reservations recommended. 372 Fulton St (between Jay St and Boerum Pl), Downtown. 875.5181

5 Tripoli ★$$ Atlantic Avenue is the city's center for Middle Eastern cuisine, and among the numerous small restaurants, this bilevel place is probably the best and most authentic. Sit downstairs in a dusky room fitted with chandeliers, rugs, touches of brass, and a dome-shaped ceiling. Upstairs is outfitted and decorated like a sea voyage—there's a ceiling mural of the sky, wall paintings of the ocean and pirate vessels, and even a balcony made from part of a ship. Regardless of where you sit, order any of the decent Lebanese fare, including falafel, hummus, lamb kebabs, stuffed grape leaves, lamb stew, and one of the heavily honeyed desserts. There's live music and entertainment Saturday nights. ♦ Middle Eastern ♦ Daily lunch and dinner. Reservations required Friday and Saturday nights. 156 Atlantic Ave (at Clinton St), Brooklyn Heights. 596.5800

Junior's runs through 7,500 pounds of cream cheese a week to turn out their estimable cheesecakes.

New York can't claim to be the birthplace of the hot dog but it can get credit for the name. As the story goes, Harry Stevens, a concessionaire at New York's Polo Grounds, was hawking frankfurters and called out "Get your dachshund sausages while they're hot!" Hearst sports cartoonist Tad Dorgan was in the stands and the next day he published a cartoon featuring talking dachshunds. But since he couldn't spell dachshunds, he called them hot dogs, a name that persists to this day. The sausages were briefly banned when rumors flew they were made with dog meat, and the Coney Island Chamber of Commerce forbade the use of the term. After the rumors were disproved, however, the prohibition was lifted.

5 Moroccan Star ★$ With its yellow walls and minimal decoration—a few Middle Eastern scenes and pictures of Morocco—this narrow dining spot is a suitably low-key setting for good, earthy Moroccan food. Try the shish kebab, beef kebab, Moroccan chicken (chunks of white meat cooked with onions, peppers, and spices), and the moist, delicious couscous with lamb, *merguez* (sausage), chicken, or just vegetables. Bring your own alcoholic beverages. ♦ Moroccan ♦ Daily lunch and dinner. Reservations recommended on weekends. 205 Atlantic Ave (between Court and Clinton Sts), Brooklyn Heights. 643.0800

5 Sahadi Importing Company Even though the shop was renovated to complement the surrounding gentrification of the neighborhood, this store continues to carry the same wide assortment of fine products, and their exotic, spicy aromas permeate the air. The high-quality olives, olive oil, pine nuts, dried fruits, grains, pasta, coffee, herbs, and spices are as wonderful as ever. There are also good prepared Middle Eastern foods, including tabbouleh, stuffed grape leaves, *baba ganooj*, and hummus. ♦ M-Sa. 187 Atlantic Ave (between Court and Clinton Sts), Brooklyn Heights. 624.4550

5 Damascus Bakery Pita bread stacked in plastic bags on a grocery shelf will never taste the same after you sample these breads fresh from the oven. Top-quality meat pies and pastries are also offered. ♦ Daily. 195 Atlantic Ave (between Court and Clinton Sts), Brooklyn Heights. 625.7070

5 The Oriental Pastry and Grocery Company Locals generally come to this all-purpose Middle Eastern store for the delicious lamb sausages, although bins of grains, dried fruits, olives, spices, candies, and coffees also abound. Don't miss the counter full of honeyed pastry treats and spinach pies. ♦ Daily. 170 Atlantic Ave (between Court and Clinton Sts), Boerum Hill. 875.7687

6 Casa Rosa ★$$ Good—and inexpensive—home-style cooking is this unpretentious trattoria's trademark. Have pork chops with broccoli rabe; *zuppa di pesce a la Rosa* (fish soup); clams, shrimp, and calamari in a light tomato sauce; or lobster *fra diavolo* (half lobster with mussels, clams, and shrimp on a bed of linguine). Be forewarned: The service can be extremely slow. ♦ Italian ♦ Tu-F lunch and dinner; Sa-Su dinner. Reservations recommended. 384 Court St (at Carroll St), Carroll Gardens. 625.8874 ♿

7 Junior's ★$ Some say the cheesecake here is the best in New York, and it just may be. The rest of the food is standard deli/diner fare, such as pastrami sandwiches and roast chicken, distinguished only by the large size of the portions. Weekend evenings, however, the place jumps, and the cars are double- and triple-parked out front. ◆ Deli ◆ Daily breakfast, lunch, dinner, and late-night meals. 386 Flatbush Ave (at DeKalb Ave), Downtown. 852.5257

8 New City Cafe ★★$ Between them, owners Raoul Richardson and Rebecca Scanlon have quite a pedigree: she has worked with noted chefs Brendan Walsh of **Arizona 206** and Edna Lewis of **Gage & Tollner;** he's logged time at **Gage & Tollner,** the **River Café, Park Avenue Cafe,** and **Aureole.** Now they have their own place at this location convenient to the **Brooklyn Academy of Music.** The intimate restaurant designed by Richardson's father is filled with fresh flowers. Seasonal additions include a blazing fireplace in winter, and a lush garden in summer. The hearty, well-prepared fare matches the setting: Try the earthy black- bean soup, pan-roasted shrimp with *achiote* (a mix of Mexican spices) broth, grilled duck breast with corn pudding, and cornmeal- crusted catfish. Top the meal off with a warm fruit cobbler. ◆ American ◆ Tu-Su dinner. Reservations recommended. 246 DeKalb Ave (at Vanderbilt Ave), Fort Greene. 622.5607

9 Stacy's ★★★$ Like most of the newer residents of the Williamsburg section, Stacy Pearl is an artist, drawn to this neighborhood by the large loft spaces and lower rents. When they need to take a break, many of her fellow artists generally can be found in this oldtime diner (works by the local talent are displayed on the walls), enjoying Pearl's creative dishes and affordable prices. Try the pink hummus made with kidney beans; coriander strudel stuffed with eggs, onions, and mushrooms; roast pork loin filled with prunes and glazed with apricots, mustard, and ginger; and Moroccan vegetable stew with carrots, tomatoes, chickpeas, and cumin. But the breakfasts are the real draw here: You won't be able to get enough of the challah French toast with homemade strawberry syrup or potato pancakes with parsnips, sweet potatoes, and white potatoes, served with homemade apple sauce. Coffee lovers will be more than content with the brew served here and everyone will be thrilled with the professional wait staff. ◆ Eclectic ◆ M-F breakfast, lunch, and dinner; Sa-Su brunch and dinner. No credit cards accepted. 85 Broadway (at Berry St), Williamsburg. 486.8004

9 Peter Luger ★★★$$$ One of the oldest and still one of the better, more colorful steak houses in the city, this place is great for one thing only: well-charred porterhouse steak made from prime, aged Iowa corn-fed beef. These hefty heifer parts, for two or more, are always cooked perfectly to order and come presliced unless you request otherwise. Potato side dishes are all serviceable, but skip

the other vegetables. For dessert, try cheesecake or ice cream. ◆ Steak house ◆ Daily lunch and dinner. Reservations required. No credit cards accepted. 178 Broadway (at Driggs Ave), Williamsburg. 387.7400

10 The Garden This huge (5,000 square feet) gourmet emporium with a fountain in the center caused quite a stir when it opened in 1994 among Greenpoint's more traditional Polish food shops. Here, prepared foods come in all ethnic casts, but the Polish fare is given a nontraditional spin—stuffed cabbage, for instance, is made with ground chicken, not beef, and the fresh tomato sauce is served on the side. Otherwise, the offerings are more akin to the store that this place likes to compare itself to—**Dean & DeLuca.** Roasted portobello mushrooms, stuffed baked fish, homemade fruit butters and chutneys, and freshly baked breads and pastries are all in abundance. Other delectables include organic fruits and vegetables, homemade ice cream, and cappuccino and espresso. ◆ Daily. 921 Manhattan Ave (at 10th St), Greenpoint. 389.6448 &

10 W. Nassau Meat Market The locals line up at this small shop to buy what some consider to be the best kielbasa in the neighborhood, as well as other dried and freshly made sausages. There's also a variety of smoked hams—including an excellent Black Forest—for sale. ◆ M-Sa. 915 Manhattan Ave (between Greenpoint Ave and 10th St), Greenpoint. 389.6149

10 Steve's Meat Market Those who want to comparison shop for kielbasa may want to come here—this place claims (and many agree) to sell the best version of that garlicky sausage in the neighborhood. The pierogi are also a good reason to stop in at this friendly store where the staff greets regulars by name. ◆ M-Sa. 104 Nassau St (between Leonard and Ecford Sts), Greenpoint. 383.1780

11 Two Little Red Hens For many years, this bakery was the domain of Faith Drobbin. In 1994 she sold the shop to Mary Louise Clemens and Christina Winkler, who brought their wholesale baking business from Manhattan to this new location. Patrons are pleased they can still purchase porterhouse delectables made from Drobbin's original recipes, including the popular sour-cream chocolate cake and coconut angel-food cake, along with the new owners' specialties—genoise cake, hazelnut sponge, fruit pies and tarts, decorated birthday cakes, and fabulous gingerbread. ♦ Tu-Su. 1112 Eighth Ave (at 11th St), Park Slope. 499.8108

11 Aunt Sonia's ★★$$ Perfect following a late-afternoon stroll through **Prospect Park** or a visit to the **Brooklyn Museum**, this small, crowded restaurant has an eclectic menu that changes with the season—and the chef's mood. The food is dependably decent and sometimes extraordinary. Try the organic chicken couscous with vegetables, herb-crisped salmon with mussels and scallops in a bouillabaisse sauce, or filet mignon au poivre with eggplant mashed potatoes. Top it off with a Valrhona chocolate–pecan pie, coconut basmati rice pudding, or maple crème brûlée. The service is uneven, but good humored. ♦ Eclectic ♦ M-F dinner; Sa-Su brunch and dinner. 1123 Eighth Ave (at 12th St), Park Slope. 965.9526 &

12 The New Prospect At Home If you'd rather take out than eat in at the nearby **New Prospect Café** (see below), stop here and pick up a salad or muffin in one of the first of such places to pop up in this upscale neighborhood. ♦ Daily. 52 Seventh Ave (between Lincoln and St. John's Pls), Park Slope. 230.89003

12 Ozzie's ★$ Park Slope's only espresso bar is a perfect place to enjoy a luscious *latte* or marvelous mochaccino. For edibles, there are bagels, muffins, croissants, sandwiches, and a variety of pastries and cookies. Any time of the day and into the night, this joint is jumping. ♦ Cafe ♦ M-Sa until midnight; Su until 11PM. 57 Seventh Ave (at Lincoln Pl), Park Slope. 398.6695. Also at: 136 Montague St (between Clinton and Henry Sts), Brooklyn Heights. 852.1553

12 Santa Fe Grill ★$ At this popular spot for the young after-work crowd, the bar offers a variety of fancy concoctions and thirst-quenching margaritas. The serene South-western setting, rich in New Mexican artifacts, is lovely; the noise level, however, makes for a less-than-peaceful mood. The food is quite respectable for this far north—try the vegetable quesadilla, any of the burritos and enchiladas (including a spinach and cheese variety), or one of the decent burgers. ♦ Tex-Mex ♦ Daily dinner. 62 Seventh Ave (at Lincoln Pl), Park Slope. 718/636.0279

12 Lemongrass Grill ★★$$ Unusual Thai fare is offered at this small, always packed, dining spot. (A pleasant alternative is to eat alfresco in the back in the warmer weather.) But it's worth the wait to indulge in such delicacies as steamed vegetable dumplings with a basil dipping sauce, house salad topped with a delicious spicy peanut sauce, tofu sheets stuffed with shiitake mushrooms over spinach, or any one of the curry dishes. Down it all with a Singha beer. ♦ Thai ♦ Daily lunch and dinner. 61A Seventh Ave (between Lincoln Pl and Berkeley St), Park Slope. 399.7100. Also at: 2534 Broadway (between W 94th and W 95th Sts), Upper West Side. 212/666.0888

12 Leaf & Bean Approximately 50 types of coffee beans and 20 types of loose tea are offered here, along with other gourmet items, including truffle candies, fancy jams, and white cocoa. There's also a large supply of kitchen accessories—wine glasses, cookie jars, place mats, Italian ceramic plates, candles, cloth napkins, and of course, a variety of coffeemakers and teapots. ♦ Daily. 83 Seventh Ave (between Union and Berkeley Sts), Park Slope. 638.5791

12 Cucina ★★★$$ This warm inviting place has a stylish decor—maple tables and Art Deco chairs, dried flowers, a vibrant mural, and a colorful antipasto table featuring platters of marinated vegetables, grilled shiitake mushrooms, various tarts including an onion and olive variety, eggplant and roasted pepper terrine, grilled marinated shrimp with white beans and escarole, and *soppressata* (a mild sausage). Pasta dishes and entrées are also earthy and alluring: try linguine *nostra* (with clams, mussels, shrimp, lobster, and calamari); *fusilli puttanesca* (with capers, olives, diced tomatoes, garlic, and olive oil); fillet of red snapper; grilled cornish hen; and osso buco served with *pappardelle* (broad noodles). Save room for the chocolate tasting plate or richly fruity sorbets. Reasonably priced wines from Italy, France, and California are available. ♦ Italian ♦ Daily dinner. No credit cards accepted. 256 Fifth Ave (between Carroll St and Garfield Pl), Park Slope. 230.0711 &

the NEW PR★SPECT

13 The New Prospect Café ★★$$ The spicy corn-and-shrimp chowder is not to be missed in this place that's always crowded with folks being served tasty meals at very good prices. Other dishes to try include black-bean soup, New Prospect Salad (a mélange of lettuce, mushrooms, radishes, tomatoes, sprouts, and cheese), linguine with shrimp and arugula, cheese enchiladas, roasted free-range chicken with rosemary and great lumpy mashed potatoes, or any of the tasty sandwiches. There's also a daily vegetarian entrée. Don't leave without having dessert; specialties include chocolate mousse cake and cheesecake. The wine list features mainly California selections. ♦ American ♦ M dinner; Tu-F lunch and dinner; Sa-Su brunch and dinner. 393 Flatbush Ave (between Plaza St and Sterling Pl), Prospect Heights. 638.2148

14 Cafe at Brooklyn Museum ★$ Rest your tired feet after viewing the museum's exhibits in this bright, cheery room decorated with prints on the walls and fresh flowers on the tables. The small gourmet sandwich menu includes roasted eggplant with mozzarella, tomato, and basil on focaccia, Black Forest ham and brie with honey mustard on a baguette, vegetable tuna on a croissant, and grilled chicken with pesto sauce. There's also a salad bar, a daily roasted-vegetable platter, couscous with sun-dried tomatoes, apple-pear watercress salad, lemon-chicken salad, and pasta *primavera*. For dessert try raspberry cheesecake or carrot cake. ♦ Cafe ♦ W-Su breakfast, lunch, and afternoon snacks. No credit cards accepted. 200 Eastern Pkwy (at Washington Ave), Prospect Heights. 638.5000 &

14 Terrace Cafe, Brooklyn Botanic Garden ★$ From April through October, this cafe is outdoors on a patio; during the winter, it's located inside the glassed-in, plant-filled conservatory. The menu throughout the year is simple, with such homemade offerings as chicken and potato-leek soups; a variety of sandwiches, including chicken salad, ham and brie, and tomato and mozzarella; hamburgers; fruit platters; and chicken potpie. ♦ Cafe ♦ Tu-Su breakfast and lunch. 1000 Washington Ave (between Empire Blvd and Eastern Pkwy), Prospect Heights. 622.4433

15 Ocean Palace Seafood Restaurant ★$ Located on a stretch of Eighth Avenue that has become Brooklyn's "Chinatown," this place is the largest in the area and somewhat dressier than the average store-front joint. As the name implies, seafood is what to order here; on the way in you can greet your dinner swimming around in the tanks. Trout and sea bass dishes are fresh and subtly flavored, and the sesame jumbo shrimp is good (despite a slightly sweet coating). Both the regular menu and chef's specials include meat and vegetarian dishes; be sure not to miss the vegetable dumplings, which come in a cellophane-noodle wrapper. In addition to the regular offerings, vegetables come in Hong Kong–style varieties (miniature bok choy, snow pea leaves) to satisfy the demands of the new immigrant group. There are also a number of steamed dishes for the health conscious or those on restricted diets. Plan are afoot to open a second location on Avenue U at East 15th Street; call for more information. ♦ Chinese ♦ Daily lunch and dinner. 5421-5423 Eighth Ave (at 55th St), Sunset Park. 871.8080 &

16 Areo ★$$ Solid Italian fare is served in this restaurant. The impressively titled Ram's Feast—veal and filet mignon with mushroom and fried zucchini—will satisfy nearly every gourmand; other dishes to try include veal paillard, chicken with portobello mushrooms in a champagne cream sauce, chicken with pancetta and balsamic vinegar, and lobster in a tomato or lemon white sauce. There's also good cheesecake and tiramisù. ♦ Italian ♦ Tu-Sa lunch and dinner; Su dinner. Reservations recommended. 8424 Third Ave (at 85th St), Bay Ridge. 238.0079

17 18th Avenue Bakery The aroma of fresh baked bread will draw you in like a magnet. Baked in brick ovens, the loaves taste as good as they smell—try the crusty semolina and the lard bread made with flavorful pieces of prosciutto. ♦ Daily. 6016 18th Ave (between 60th and 61st Sts), Bensonhurst. 256.2441

TRUNZO BROS., INC.

17 Trunzo Bros. Founded 20 years ago by brothers Pasquale and Francesco Trunzo, this store began primarily as a meat market. Now the locals flock here not just for meat, but for focaccia baked right in the store, prosciutto bread, antipasto, pasta dishes, chicken parmigiana, sausage and peppers, bottles of imported Italian olive oil, cans of San Marzano tomatoes, boxes of dried pasta, fresh mozzarella, and provolone. ♦ Daily. 6802 18th Ave (at 68th St), Bensonhurst. 331.2111

17 Piccolo Mondello Pescheria The fish glistens in this neighborhood fish market, particularly the baby octopus, mussels, scallops, and red snapper. ♦ M-Sa. 6824 18t

Ave (at Bay Ridge Ave), Bensonhurst. 236.3930

17 18th Avenue Fruit Market This enormous warehouse-style store is packed with stands piled high with tomatoes, grapefruit, asparagus, cabbages, green beans, peaches, all kinds of apples, along with every other fruit and vegetable you can imagine. The large volume of sales keeps prices low. ♦ Daily. 1767 Bay Ridge Ave (at 18th Ave), Bensonhurst. No phone

17 Alba Italian Pastry Shoppe Owner Anna Alba's parents opened this neighborhood favorite in 1932, and it's *the* place in Brooklyn to come for wedding cakes, particularly for the masterpiece decorated with giant chocolate-dipped strawberries. But you don't have to be betrothed to love this place; stop in for cannoli, cookies, Italian cheesecake, handmade marzipan fruit, *zeppole,* panettone, and traditional Easter and Christmas pastries. The shop is in the *Guinness Book of Records* for producing the largest cannoli in the world (seven feet) and has fans all across the country, including Alaska and Hawaii. In summer, have one of the real fruit ices—watch out for the seeds. ♦ Daily. 7001 18th Ave (at 70th St), Bensonhurst. 232.2122

17 Villabate Pasticceria & Bakery This old-fashioned bakery produces excellent breads, including semolina, and such rich pastries as cannoli, irises (round brioche-style buns filled with ricotta cheese and chocolate chips), and lobster tails (puff pastries filled with cream).♦ Daily. 1771 18th Ave (between 71st and 72nd Sts), Bensonhurst. 331.8430

18 Totonno's ★★$ The decor—old vinyl booths, fluorescent lights—may not impress, but on the few days a week that it's open, this pizzeria packs them in, as it has since 1924. There isn't pizza like this anywhere else. The homemade dough forms a very thin and delicious crust, the high-quality mozzarella is the freshest there is, and the homemade tomato sauce is bursting with flavor. For pizza this good, toppings are superfluous, and in fact, Totonno doesn't offer any. ♦ Pizza ♦ Th-Su lunch and dinner. No credit cards accepted. 1524 Neptune Ave (between W 15th and W 16th Sts), Coney Island. 372.8606

19 Nathan's Famous ★$ Indeed, this is probably the most famous and elaborate hot dog stand in the world, having served spicy hot franks and fabulously greasy, crinkle-cut fried potatoes for nearly a century. There are locations all over Manhattan as well, but this was the first. ♦ American ♦ Surf Ave (at Stillwell Ave), Coney Island. 946.2202. Also at: Numerous locations throughout the city

19 Rasputin ★★$$ Designed as a glitzy fantasy nightclub, this is a fun place to come on Friday and Saturday nights when the floor show is on—the acts, like the menu, are a smorgasbord of international offerings. On weeknights, there's live music to accompany the always large and interesting dinners. Don't miss the traditional blini with salmon caviar, chicken Kiev, sturgeon shish kebab, and the platter of smoked fish; those who want to venture into other cuisines should try penne with sausage and lobster salad with fennel. Whatever you order, however, should be accompanied by the requisite iced vodka. ♦ Russian/International ♦ Daily dinner. Reservations required. 2670 Coney Island Ave (at Ave X), Coney Island. 332.8111

20 Mrs. Stahl's Knishes Since the 1930s, when Mrs. Stahl made knishes in her kitchen and sold them on the Coney Island boardwalk, these wonders have attracted a legion of fans. There are now 22 delicious varieties, including potato, sweet potato, apple, mixed vegetable, and cherry cheese. ♦ Daily. 1001 Brighton Beach Ave (at Coney Island Ave), Brighton Beach. 648.0210

20 M&I International Considered the **Zabar's** of Brighton Beach, both for its extensive merchandise and constant crowds, this shop sells sausages and other meats, along with cheeses. Prepared foods include such salads as herring and cucumber, stuffed cabbage, beef stroganoff, and veal with mushrooms. There are also good bakery products—try the apple strudel. ♦ Daily. 249 Brighton Beach Ave (between Second and Third Sts), Brighton Beach. 615.1011

NATIONAL
Restaurant and Catering

20 National Restaurant ★★$$$ Yet another colorful Russian restaurant in the area dubbed "Little Odessa by the Sea." Film buffs will recall it as the location where Soviet defector Robin Williams sang and danced with his compatriots in *Moscow on the Hudson.* Known for its boisterous good times and late-night bonhomie, this restaurant is the place to come with friends for the rivers of vodka that will have you singing tunes from the motherland with the live band before you know it. The set dinners are huge, featuring a parade of cold appetizers, such as herring with potatoes or beet salad, and five main courses, including shish kebab or roast chicken. Truth be told, however, the food here is not the high point of the experience. ♦ Russian ♦ Daily dinner and late-night meals. 273 Brighton Beach Ave (between Second and Third Sts), Brighton Beach. 646.1225

20 **White Acacia** This place is so authentic that the signs will be perfectly unintelligible unless you know Russian. But if you ask, the salespeople will explain what's on display. The extensive stock includes excellent herring, Siberian *pelmeni* (meat dumplings usually served with a sour-cream sauce), stuffed cabbage, vegetable salads, sausages, and pickles. ♦ Daily. 281 Brighton Beach Ave (between Second and Third Sts), Brighton Beach. 648.2525

PRIMORSKI
Restaurant

20 **Primorski** ★★$$ Owner Buba Khotovili was a boxer back in Russia who had always wanted to be a cook. So upon reaching the land of opportunity, that's what he set out to do. The dishes he serves are made from his mother's recipes. Now, he has a whole menu full of traditional foods from what was formerly known as Soviet Georgia. Try the flaky blintzes, roasted eggplant caviar, or stuffed cabbage. ♦ Russian ♦ Daily lunch and dinner. 282 Brighton Beach Ave (between Second and Third Sts), Brighton Beach. 891.3111

20 **Odessa** ★★$$$ Make a night of it with the decked-out Eastern European regulars indulging in vodka on ice and an endless parade of "appetizers" (here indistinguishable from the entrées). Try the herring, eggplant caviar, baked salmon, or any of the many other dishes that will come your way. There's dancing and live music nightly. All in all, this is an extraordinary experience. ♦ Russian ♦ Daily lunch and dinner. Reservations required. 1113 Brighton Beach Ave (between 13th and 14th Sts), Brighton Beach. 332.3223

Queens

Sprawling Queens has always been a conglomeration of towns, villages, model communities, and real estate developments. Suburban in spirit and design, it has grown far too dense to be anything but urban in essence. And it has, of late, become the type of immigrant staging ground that Manhattan, Brooklyn, and the Bronx used to be (next to Athens, the Queens neighborhood of **Astoria** has the world's largest Greek community). Another "Little India" has sprouted in **Jackson Heights**, side by side with "Little Colombia," and **Flushing** has become another Chinatown. As a result, there are wonderful ethnic restaurants and shops in Queens well worth seeking out.

21 **Water's Edge** ★★$$$ Surrounded by glass walls on three sides, the tables in this swank riverside restaurant all have spectacular west-looking views of Midtown and Lower Manhattan. In the kitchen, however, chef Carlo Zuccarello looks to the East for his culinary inspiration. Don't miss the Oriental crab and lobster dumplings with enoki mushrooms and pea shoots in carrot lobster broth, spinach fettuccine with artichokes, escargots, and parsley in a Pernod lemon sauce, black bass with arugula vinaigrette, and red snapper in *tapenade* (a thick paste of anchovies, capers, olives, olive oil, and lemon juice) crust. Manhattanites need not fret about transportation to and from Queens—the restaurant runs a ferry from East 34th Street every hour between 6 and 11PM, Tuesday through Saturday (except during January and February, when it runs only Thursday through Saturday). ♦ Seafood ♦ M-F lunch and dinner; Sa dinner. Reservations required; jacket and tie required. 44th Dr (at the East River), Long Island City. 482.0033

Manducatis

22 **Manducatis** ★★$$ Family atmosphere and a cozy fireplace give this place an authentic trattoria feeling. Chef Ida's fine, straightforward touch with fresh ingredients brings people from all over town to this out-of-the-way spot. One of the best dishes on the menu is *pappardelle* with garlic and white beans, but most regulars don't even look at the menu. They simply ask Vincenzo what looks good that day. ♦ Italian ♦ M-F lunch and dinner; Sa-Su dinner. Reservations recommended. 13-27 Jackson Ave (at 47th Ave), Long Island City. 729.4602

23 **Pearson's Stick to Your Ribs** ★$ The decor is nothing to write home about, but many claim that this place has the best barbecue in town (although others complain that the ribs are too greasy). The Texas-style ribs, chopped chicken, beef ribs, chopped beef, and smoked brisket are succulent and spicy; the crunchy onion rings and sharp coleslaw go well on the side. ♦ Barbecue ♦ M-Sa lunch and dinner. No credit cards accepted. 5-16 51st Ave (between Vernon Blvd and Fifth St), Long Island City. 937.3030 Also at: 433 Amsterdam Ave (between W 80th and W 81st Sts), Upper West Side. 212/501.7897

ROUMELI TAVERNA

24 **Roumeli Taverna** ★$$ A favorite among the abundant supply of Greek eateries in Queens, this place, named after a Greek

mountain range, also happens to be a shade fancier than most of the others, decorated with exposed-brick walls and a fountain. But it's the high-quality, authentic food and background bouzouki music that draws in locals and visitors alike. Start with such traditional appetizers as stuffed grape leaves, hummus, and grilled octopus, and then move on to roast suckling pig, charcoal-grilled baby lamb, moussaka, or broiled snapper. ♦ Greek ♦ Daily lunch and dinner. 33-04 Broadway (between 33rd and 34th Sts), Astoria. 278.7533

24 Vergina ★★$ This place has to be seen to be believed—decorated with stars and painted stone slabs, it's like being inside the ruin of a Greek temple looking out at the night. But it has more than just a unique atmosphere; this dining spot offers very fresh, flavorful food. Start with char-broiled octopus or panfried calamari, followed by rotisseried chicken, chicken baked in puff pastry, or baked baby lamb. ♦ Greek ♦ Daily lunch and dinner. Reservations recommended. 32-11 Broadway (between 32nd and 33rd Sts), Astoria. 274.6611 ⅙

24 Karyatis ★★$$ Every politician running for office, from the local to the presidential, seems to pass through these doors—note the collection of photos decorating the entryway. Inside you'll find peach walls, exposed brick, and a pianist/singer warbling pop standards. The food is creative and well prepared; try the charcoal octopus, calamari filled with rice and herbs, *arni psito* (roast leg of lamb), zucchini stuffed with rice and meat, or *sinagrida plaki* (red snapper baked with onions, garlic, tomatoes and herbs). ♦ Greek ♦ Daily lunch and dinner. Reservations recommended. 35-03 Broadway (between 35th and 36th Sts), Astoria. 204.0666

25 Elias Corner ★★$ This simple taverna recently moved across the street to a bigger, glassed-in space—with guitars and stuffed

fish on the walls—and the crowds obligingly followed. Pick dinner from among the day's catches on the ice-laden counter and have it grilled over charcoal. While you wait, try one of the traditional and richly flavored appetizers, such as *taramasalata* (a creamy mixture of carp roe, lemon juice, milk-soaked breadcrumbs, olive oil, and seasonings) served with crackers or stuffed grape leaves. If in doubt, ask owner Elias Sidiroglou for advice; he's always in the dining room shmoozing with customers. ♦ Greek/Seafood ♦ Daily dinner. No credit cards accepted. 24-02 31st St (at 24th Ave), Astoria. 932.1510

25 Hunter of the Sea The selection at this tiny but sophisticated fish market includes many crustaceans flown in from Europe and not usually available here, such as marida or smelts, red mullet, and tiny scorpina (a deeply flavored fish usually used in soups). There are also the usual suspects—snapper, tuna, salmon, and swordfish. ♦ M-Sa. 22-78 31st St (at 23rd Ave), Astoria. 726.6390 ⅙

25 Titan Foods The place for olives and feta cheese, this shop stocks about 12 varieties of olives, including kalamata and alphonso, as well as eight types of feta from different parts of the country. The staff obligingly offers a taste to help you decide which to buy. Scan the aisles for fruit preserves, olive oils, canned grape leaves, rice, beans, coffee, crackers, and any other grocery item you might need. ♦ Daily. 25-56 31st St (at 28th Ave), Astoria. 626.7771 ⅙

26 Delhi Palace ★$$ Recently remodeled, this is Queens's most elegant "Little India" dining choice, with crisp white tablecloths, fresh flowers, attentive service, and quiet background music. In addition to selections from the menu, choose from the extensive buffet which appears at both lunch and dinner. Don't miss the chicken with creamy cashew sauce or tandoori shrimp with *masala* (a mild creamy) sauce. ♦ Indian ♦ Daily lunch and dinner. 37-33 74th St (between Roosevelt and 37th Aves), Jackson Heights. 507.0666

26 Jackson Diner ★$ Much like a North Indian *dhaba* (truck stop—the connotations are better there), this no-frills Indian restaurant is good for cuisine made from owner Gian Saini's family recipes. Local Indian families pack the place for tandoori chicken, *murg lajwab* (chicken simmered with tomatoes, ginger, chili, herbs, and spices), *kadai ghost*

(lamb with spinach, tomatoes, ginger, and cumin seeds), and *paneer palak* (puree of spinach with spices and homemade cheese). There are a few Southern Indian dishes, including *dosas* (crepes), and plenty of choices for vegetarians. There's no liquor license, but the mango *lassi* (a sweet yogurt drink) is a big hit, especially with kids. ♦ Indian ♦ No credit cards accepted. 37-03 74th St (between Roosevelt and 37th Aves), Jackson Heights. 672.1232

26 La Pequeña Colombia ★$ In the section of Jackson Heights known as "Little Colombia," this brightly lit cafe is a favorite. Try the octopus salad, tamale of cornmeal and vegetables with a chicken leg wrapped inside, and *cazuela mixta* (a seafood casserole with shrimp, squid, and assorted fish). There are also such great fruit drinks as passionfruit and soursop, and entertaining place mats—take the quiz on American presidents while you wait for the food to arrive. ♦ Colombian ♦ Daily breakfast, lunch, and dinner. 83-27 Roosevelt Ave (at 84th St), Jackson Heights. 478.6528

26 Plaza Garibaldi ★$ The tacos and tostadas at this popular, noisy *taqueria* are bursting with flavor, and the *tortas* (layered sandwiches) are also top-notch. Give the roast pork a try, and top the meal off with a very respectable flan. ♦ Mexican ♦ Daily lunch and dinner. No credit cards accepted. 89-12 Roosevelt Ave (at 90th St), Jackson Heights. 478.3194

27 Jaiya Thai Oriental Restaurant ★★$$ The extensive, original menu at this Thai eatery includes more than 300 choices. Try the excellent spicy chicken and coconut soup; spicy shredded jellyfish; pork with very hot chili peppers and onions; pad thai; naked shrimp (rare shrimp with lime, lemongrass, and chili); and pork with string beans, red chili, and basil. The level of spiciness is indicated by the number of stars—two-star dishes should require a doctor's note. ♦ Thai ♦ Daily lunch and dinner. Reservations recommended for dinner Friday-Sunday. 81-11 Broadway (between 81st and 82nd Sts), Elmhurst. 651.1330. Also at: 396 Third Ave (at E 28th St), Murray Hill. 212/889.1330

28 London Lennie's $$ As befits the name of this place, prints of palace guards grace the dining room wall; otherwise this is a basic wood-paneled, nautically decorated fish house. Try the chowder, panfried oysters, big pots of steamers, Maryland crab cakes, and fried soft-shell crabs. There's also an extensive wine list. ♦ Seafood ♦ M-F lunch and dinner; Sa-Su dinner. 63-88 Woodhaven Blvd (between 63rd Dr and Fleet Ct), Forest Hills. 894.8084

29 Pastrami King ★$ New Yorkers old enough to remember like to reminisce about a time when every neighborhood had delis as good as this one. This place smokes its own pastrami and corned beef, and luckily, these delicacies can be shipped worldwide. Needless to say, pastrami and corned beef sandwiches are the items to order. ♦ Deli ♦ Daily breakfast, lunch, and dinner. 124-24 Queens Blvd (at 82nd Ave), Kew Gardens. 263.1717

30 Penang ★★$ The colorful murals on the walls and vibrant batiks on the waiters give this long-popular place plenty of atmosphere, and the food is good too. Try the *roti canai* (flat bread dipped into a chicken and meat stock filled with chunks of chicken and potato); egg noodles in meat broth with baby corn, black mushrooms, and sesame oil; and steamed crabs with scallion and ginger. ♦ Malaysian ♦ Daily lunch and dinner. No credit cards accepted. 38-04 Prince St (near 37th Ave and Main St), Flushing. 321.2078. Also at: 109 Spring St (between Greene and Mercer Sts), Soho. 212/274.8883

30 Jade Palace ★★$ This modern dining room with fish tanks—displaying what's on the menu—gets absolutely mobbed at night, but regulars patiently wait for what many feel is the best Chinese seafood in the area. Try shark fin soup; steamed, live shrimp; and any of the evening's specials—often striped or sea bass, eel, shrimp, or crab. The dim sum selection is also a standout. If your mood dictates meat instead of fish, you'll have plenty to choose from, as well—lamb a hot pot is a winner. ♦ Cantonese/Seafood ♦ Daily lunch and dinner. 136-14 38th St (between Main and Union Sts), Flushing. 353.3366 &

30 Dragon Village ★★$ Tony Yee (formerly the chef at **Shun Lee Palace** and **Shun Lee West**) and family opened this stylish place in 1994. Decorated in pastels, it wouldn't look out of place in Miami's fashionable South Beach district. The food, though, tastes straight out of Shanghai. Don't miss the Shanghai braised honey pork served on a bed of spinach, smoked duck, Beijing duck, steamed carp with ginger scallion oil and soy sauce, and on weekends, the traditional Shanghai breakfast with hot soybean milk, fried dough and scallions, sweet bean paste, and turnip pastries. ◆ Shanghai ◆ M-F lunch and dinner; Sa-Su breakfast, lunch, and dinner. Reservations recommended on weekends. 135-20 40th Rd (at Main St), Flushing. 762.1717 ⑆

30 **Shin Jung** ★★$ On a stretch packed with Korean barbecue places, this dining spot stands out both for its decor—fancier than most with ornate chandeliers—and the array of unusual dishes it features. The basic fare, though, is barbecue, so don't miss the delicious marinated and sliced rib steak, short ribs, and squid marinated in a garlic and pepper sauce. Also try the fish roe soup; tofu in hot pepper, scallion, and garlic sauce; egg, scallion, and seafood pancake with a garlic-soy dipping sauce; rice flour pancake with oysters; pork dumplings in broth; or goat meat and vegetables in a spicy broth. ◆ Korean ◆ Daily lunch and dinner. 136-33 37th Ave (between Main and Union Sts), Flushing. 460.5026 ⑆

he Bronx

e only county of New York that is part of the mainland, the Bronx was once a bustling hive ere struggling immigrants built grand onuments to their own success. But over the ars, this borough suffered more than any other om the general decline experienced throughout w York City, and remains somewhat beyond the le of the gentrification that has changed the face Brooklyn. Today, it's a mélange of devastated ements, suburban riverfront mansions, seaside ttages, massive housing projects, and faded ulevards of grand Art Deco apartment towers. On culinary level, the only sections that lure visitors e City Island and the longstanding Italian velopment in **Fordham**, along **Arthur Avenue**. th its pungent grocery stores, and large, isterous restaurants emphasizing the familiar d-sauce Southern Italian food, Arthur Avenue els like a larger, less touristy Mulberry Street rth.

31 **Arthur Avenue Retail Market** This covered market is packed with stalls selling everything from high-quality Tuscan virgin olive oil to wheels of parmigiano reggiano, fresh eggs, thinly sliced veal, baby eggplant, and zucchini. For the best cheese, stop by **Mike & Sons'** stall. ◆ M-Sa. 2344 Arthur Ave (between E 187th and E 189th Sts), Fordham. 367.5686

31 **Frank Randazzo's Sons Fish Market** Piled high with clams and oysters, crabs, squid, eels, snapper, and swordfish, this tiny store offers fish that's as fresh as can be. ◆ M-Sa. 2327 Arthur Ave (at E 187th St), Fordham. 367.4139

31 **Calabria Pork Store** Choose, if you can, among the 500 kinds of sausage dangling from the ceiling; all are delicious, either hot or sweet, many studded with peppercorns or garlic. ◆ M-Sa. 2338 Arthur Ave (at E 187th St), Fordham. 367.5145

31 **Borgatti's Ravioli and Noodle Company** The delicious fresh pasta here is handmade and handcut into flat strips, and comes in such different flavors as carrot, spinach, and tomato. ◆ M-Sa; Su until 1PM. 632 E 187th St (between Belmont and Hughes Aves), Fordham. 367.3799

31 **Terranova Bakery** The homemade breads here are dense and crusty and come in all shapes and sizes, from huge loaves to pizza bread to bread sticks. Don't miss the olive or lard bread, which is studded with prosciutto. ◆ Daily. 691 E 187th St (at Fordham Rd), Fordham. 733.3827

31 **Dominick's** ★★$ Don't let the lines outside dissuade you from eating at this noisy and chaotic restaurant. Once inside, you'll be greeted with terrific home-style Southern Italian fare and a solicitous staff. The platters of spaghetti with garlic and oil, or spicy *puttanesca* sauce, and such main courses as osso buco come in giant servings that are guaranteed to lead to overeating because it all tastes so good. ◆ Italian ◆ M, W-Sa lunch and dinner; Su dinner. No credit cards accepted. 2335 Arthur Ave (between E 187th St and Crescent Ave), Fordham. 733.2807

31 **Mario's** ★$$$ Made famous by the movie, *The Godfather,* this place has been a local favorite since its founding in 1919. It's a bit fancier than others in the neighborhood, with its pink banquettes, mural of Italy, and valet parking. But what locals line up for are delicious preparations of fresh fish, including seafood antipasto of mussels, octopus, squid, and shrimp, and lobster served in a spicy tomato sauce. ◆ Italian ◆ Tu-Su lunch and dinner. 2342 Arthur Ave (between E 187th St and Crescent Ave), Fordham. 584.1188

31 **Tony & Roberto's** ★$$$ This simple trattoria is the bastion of Salerno-born chef/owner Roberto Paciullo. Pasta is the specialty here, particularly *farfalle* (bowties with artichokes and portobello mushrooms) and *agnolotti* (half-moon shaped ravioli) filled with seafood; also recommended are shrimp and cannellini beans in a balsamic vinegar sauce, and baby lamb chops with tomato. Be prepared to wait on line. ◆ Italian ◆ Tu-F, Su lunch and dinner; Sa dinner. 632 Crescent Ave (at E 186th St), Fordham. 733.9503

New York Cooking Schools

As you might expect in a city filled with ethnic and health-conscious dining spots, there are a number of cooking schools specializing in a wide range of cuisines. For a quick afternoon refresher, check **Macy's** ads in the paper for information about the popular "De Gustibus" program (151 W 34th Street, between Broadway and Seventh Ave, Eighth floor, 439.1714) held in the store's demonstration kitchen. The course, which runs seasonally—March through June and September through November—has featured such chefs as David Bouley, Alfred Portale, Andre Soltner, and Claude Troisgros. For a longer commitment, bring your apron along to one of the following.

A La Bonne Cocotte (23 Eighth Ave, between W 12th and Jane Sts, 675.7736) Learn to cook French cuisine from the famed cookbook author and teacher Lydie Marshall, who studied at Les Trois Gourmandes in Paris with Simone Beck and Louisette Bertholle—although she claims to have learned all the basics from her mother and aunt back in her native France. Classes are offered in a series of five in the spring and fall. Students do *all* of the cooking and feast upon their accomplishments. Marshall also offers classes at the Marshall château in Provence, France, in June and September.

Anna Teresa Callen Italian Cooking School (59 West 12th Street, between Fifth and Sixth Aves, 929.5640) Well-respected cookbook author and teacher Anna Teresa Callen offers the five-class series, "Regional Cooking of Italy," as well as pasta and holiday dinner workshops, which can last from one to three sessions. Enrollment is limited to six per class, and the school is closed during the summer.

China Institute in America (125 E 65th St, between Lexington and Park Aves), 744.8181) Learn Classic Chinese as well as vegetarian and kosher Chinese cooking from instructors Dorothy Lee, Eileen Yin-fei Lo, and Millie Chan at this school. A variety of regional styles—Hunan, Cantonese, and Szechuan—are also covered. Held year-round, classes vary from season to season and can range from one-day workshops in dumpling making to six-session courses on dim sum.

The French Culinary Institute (462 Broadway, at Grand St, 219.8890) Aspiring professionals come here to learn classic French techniques. The complete six-month program (nine months part-time) includes intruction in wines and wine service, the history of classic and regional French cuisine, menu development, restaurant organization, beverage service, budgeting, and pricing. Students participate in preparation of food at the institute's restaurant, **L'Ecole.**

Julie Sahni's School of Indian Cooking (101 Clark St, at Henry St, Brooklyn Heights, 718/625.3958) Unique, intensive weekend programs (limited to three students) teach classic and regional Indian cuisine. Students shop for Indian ingredients, learn to use spices and herbs to make sauces, master traditional bread-making techniques, and try their hand at vegetable, grain, and seafood dishes. Sahni organizes a group trip to India twice a year.

La Cuisine Sans Peur (216 W 89th St, between Amsterdam Ave and Broadway, 362.0638) The school's name translates as "Cooking Without Fear," making this a good place for novices. Although classic French cuisine is taught here, the emphasis is on the regional specialities of Alsace and Provence. Classes are small in size—generally three or four students—and flexibly scheduled.

The Natural Gourmet (48 W 21st St, between Fifth and Sixth Aves, 645.5170) Reasonably priced five-course dinners offered on Friday evenings (reservations required) are a persuasive demonstration of how luscious healthy vegetarian cuisine can be. Once you're hooked, you can sign up for such courses as "Vegetarian Cooking Techniques" and "Principles of Balance." Some classes are three-hour single sessions, others are part of a series, and a few weekend workshops are offered as well.

New School Culinary Arts Department (100 Greenwich Ave, at W 12th St, 255.4141) Take classes or work toward a Master's degree at the **New School for Social Research;** the comprehensive program offers over 150 courses, representing a wide range of culinary experiences and cuisines. Single-session programs—"Behind the Scenes at the Great Restaurants of New York," conducted by famous chefs—and Saturday workshops on food-business–related topics are also available.

New York Cake & Baking Distributor (56 W 22nd St, between Fifth and Sixth Aves, 675.2253) Serious amateurs and professional pastry chefs come here for advanced courses that teach blown-sugar techniques, the art of making gum-paste flowers, and how to work with chocolate. A recently added baking series includes courses on cake bases, petit fours, tarts, and hotel and restaurant desserts. Classes are offered year-round; some last a few hours, others a few weeks.

New York Restaurant School (75 Varick St, at Canal St, 226.5500) Four 7-12 month programs are offered here—culinary arts, restaurant management, pastry arts, and culinary skills—and certificates are awarded upon successful completion. A variety of cuisines are featured, including Cajun, Creole, Southern, Northern Italian, French, Asian, to name just a few. Classes are held 24 hours a day.

Peter Kump's Schools (307 E 92nd St, between First and Second Aves, 410.4601) Kump offers two schools: **Peter Kump's New York Cooking School,** a half-year vocational program that culminates in a culinary arts or pastry and baking arts diploma, and **Peter Kump's School of Culinary Arts,** which include courses and weekend workshops on such subjects as "Sweet and Savory Baking of the Mediterranean," and "Great Spa Cooking." There are satellite locations on Long Island, in Westchester, New Jersey, and the Washington DC area, and at press time, a second Manhattan location was scheduled to open at 50 West 23rd Street.

31 Calandra Salted braids and unsalted balls of very fresh mozzarella made on the premises are sold here. A wide selection of cheeses from Europe as well as South America is also available. ◆ M-Sa. 2314 Arthur Ave (at E 183rd St). 365.7572

32 Lobster Box ★★$$$ The Masucchia family turned this small white 1812 house into a restaurant more than 50 years ago. Over the years this popular spot has grown and now serves up to 2,000 pounds of fresh lobster a week. Pick from almost two dozen variations on the lobster theme—beginning with the simple steamed-and-split (lobsters here are never boiled), or any of the fresh seafood, and watch the fleet of local boats glide by. ◆ Lobster/Seafood ◆ Daily lunch and dinner Apr-Oct. 34 City Island Ave (near Rochelle St), City Island. 885.1952

Staten Island

Geographically distant from and unconnected by subway to the rest of New York City, Staten Island is spiritually and physically closer to New Jersey, only a narrow stretch of water away. In fact, Staten Island's political ties to New York City are a historical accident: The island was ceded to Manhattan as a prize in a sailing contest sponsored by the Duke of York in 1687. Previously accessible only by ferry from Manhattan or car from New Jersey, Staten Island became connected to Brooklyn in 1964, when the **Verrazano-Narrows Bridge** opened. Ever since, Brooklynites longing for more suburban pastures have been migrating over the bridge, slowly but surely creating a politically critical mass. In 1993, residents of the "forgotten borough" voted two to one in favor of secession from New York City, but at press time, the plan hadn't been approved yet. Still, in their own minds, residents of this borough have already left the city far behind.

33 Aesop's Tables ★$$ Emblematic of how Staten Island sees itself—closer at heart to the country than the city, this rustic restaurant has country-garden wicker furniture, lots of dried flowers, and a patio for al fresco dining. The eclectic food can be a little uneven, but most dishes are interesting and deeply flavored; try the smoked mozzarella with portobello mushrooms, jerk chicken and beef, pork chops with a chili crust, and grilled catfish over greens. ◆ Eclectic ◆ Tu-Sa dinner. No credit cards accepted. 1233 Bay St (at Hylan Blvd), Rosebank. 720.2005

Guests

Robert T. Buck
Director, The Brooklyn Museum

Though Brooklyn is called the "Borough of Churches," it might more aptly be named the "Borough of Culinary Delights" because of its wide range of restaurants and gastronomic shopping. Among my favorites are:

La Cucina in **Park Slope** offers some of the most superb Italian cusine to be found anywhere—especially its excellent pasta dishes.

New Prospect Café, close to the **Brooklyn Museum** on Flatbush Avenue in Park Slope, has become one of the museum staff's off-site favorites. Its eclectic menu features so-called California cuisine and what is possibly the best chocolate cake on the planet.

The River Café, on the waterfront close to the **Brooklyn Bridge,** is a favorite for its unparalleled view of the Manhattan skyline and superlative cuisine that combine to make dining there always a very special occasion.

The Brooklyn Museum Café (of course I'm somewhat prejudiced) is another rave, for its reasonably priced salad bar, sandwiches, and swell desserts.

Ocean Palace in Brooklyn's Chinatown is among the best of the many great Chinese restaurants in the borough.

New City Café, lodged in a town house setting with a charming garden, offers a refined menu in a warm and friendly setting. The restaurant is located conveniently near the **Brooklyn Academy of Music, Pratt Institute,** and the **Brooklyn Museum.**

And, of course, those venerable Brooklyn institutions, **Gage & Tollner, Junior's,** and **Peter Luger's** steak house, should not be overlooked.

The first beer brewed in America was made by Governor Wilhelm Kieft in 1640; he built a private brewery on his estate in Staten Island.

The beginnings of seltzer go back to 1809 when a man named Joseph Hawkins got a patent for the machinery to carbonate water. In the 1830s carbonated water hit the market in a big way; forty years later fruit syrups and ice cream were available, paving the way for the creation of the soda fountain. By 1891, in the wake of the temperance movement, there were more soda fountains in New York than bars.

Index

A

Abby Restaurant and Bar ★$$ 102
Accessibility for the disabled 5
Acker-Merrall-Condit 193
Acme Bar & Grill ★$$ 81
Acropolis $ 122
A C.T. Secret Recipe 99
Adoré, The ★★$ 74
Adrienne ★$$$ 146
Aesop's Tables ★$$ 221
Agata & Valentina 175
Aggie's ★$ 56
Aja ★★★$$$ 97
Akron Market 178
Alba Italian Pastry Shoppe 215
A.L. Bazzini Company 35
Alison on Dominick Street
    ★★★$$$ 42
Alla Sera ★$ 175
Allegria ★$$ 144
Alleva Dairy 27
Alley's End ★★$ 107
Alva ★★$$$ 97
Ambassador Grill Restaurant
    ★$$$ 132
American Festival Cafe ★$$$
    136
American Place, An ★★$$$ 102
American Renaissance ★★$$$
    38
Amici Miei ★$$$ 49
Amish Farm 134
Amsterdam's Bar and Rotisserie
    ★$$ 199
Amy's Bread 118
An American Place ★★$$$ 102
Anche Vivolo ★$$ 151
Andalousia ★$ 60
Andrusha, Cafe 183
Angelica Kitchen ★$ 89
Angelo's of Mulberry Street ★$$
    27
Anglers & Writers ★$ 62
Annie's ★$ 174
Aphrodisia 60
Aquavit ★★★$$$$ 146
Arcadia ★★★$$$$ 160
Areo ★$$ 214
Aria ★★$$ 140
Arizona Cafe ★★$$ 157
Arizona 206 ★★★$$$ 157
Armadillo, The $ 203
Arqua ★★$$$ 37
Artepasta ★$ 68
Arthur Avenue Retail Market 219
Artistes, Café des 189
Arturo's Pizzeria ★$ 50
Asia ★$$ 164
Asti $$$ 74

Astor Wines and Spirits 81
Au Bon Coin ★$ 57
Au Cafe ★$ 125
Au Mandarin ★$$ 15
Aunt Sonia's ★★$$ 213
Au Petit Beurre $ 204
Aureole ★★★$$$$ 159
Aux Delices des Bois 35
Avanti ★★$$$ 122
Avventura 201
A. Zito & Sons Bakery 60
Azzurro ★★$$ 181

B

Baby Jake's ★$ 78
Baccarat 152
Baci $$ 198
Bagel, The ★$ 61
Balducci's 72
Bali Burma ★$ 117
Baluchi's ★★$ 43
B & H Dairy and Vegetarian
    Cuisine Restaurant ★$ 83
Bangkok Cuisine ★★$$ 125
Baraonda ★★$$$ 173
Barbetta ★★$$$ 118
Barking Dog Luncheonette ★$
    184
Barnes & Noble Cafe $ 199
Barney Greengrass (The
    Sturgeon King) ★★$ 202
Barocco ★★$$$ 37
Barocco Food to Go 70
Barolo ★★$$$ 46
Bar Pitti ★$ 58
Bar Six ★★$ 71
Basset Coffee & Tea Co. ★$ 34
Bayamo ★$$ 81
Becco ★$$ 118
Bell Caffè $ 42
Ben Benson's Steakhouse
    ★★$$$$ 124
Bendix Diner ★$ 109
Benito I and Benito II ★$ 27
Benny's Burritos ★$ 70
Benny's (Gramercy Park) $ 98
Benny's (Upper West Side) ★$
    196
Be Our Guest 51
Ben's Cheese Shop 31
Berrys ★$$ 44
Bespeckled Trout 62
Beulah, Cafe 94
Bianca Pasta 58
Bianco, Caffe 174
Bice ★$$$ 147
Big Apple Meat Market 115
Big Cup $ 109
Big Enchilada, The (Greenwich
    Village) ★$ 74

Big Enchilada, The (Murray Hill
    ★$ 100
Bill's Gay Nineties ★$$ 148
Billy's ★$$ 139
Biricchino ★★$$ 111
Bistro du Nord ★★$$ 185
Bistro, The ★$$$ 146
Black Hound 88
Black Sheep, The ★★$$$ 67
Blanche's Organic Cafe ★$ 166
Bleecker Street Pastry Shop ★$
    59
Blu ★★$$ 110
Blue Ribbon ★★$$$ 43
Boathouse Cafe ★$$$ 171
Boca Chica ★$ 78
Bo Ky Restaurant ★$ 24
Bolo ★★$$$ 97
Bombay Palace ★$$ 143
Bondì, Caffe 96
Bonsignour 69
Bonté 172
Book-Friends Cafe $ 93
Boom ★$$$ 46
Boomer's Sports Club $ 196
Border Cafe $ 175
Borgatti's Ravioli and Noodle
    Company 219
Borgia, Caffè 57
Boroughs 208 (chapter and map)
Bosco ★$$ 172
Botanica, Cafe 128
Boulevard $ 203
Bouley ★★★★$$$$ 34
Bowery Bar ★$$ 80
Boxers $ 61
Bradley's ★$$ 75
Brasserie ★$$$ 142
Bread Shop, The ★$ 206
Bridge Cafe ★★$$ 12
Bridge Kitchenware Corp. 142
Bright Food Shop ★★$ 109
Brighton Grill ★★$ 172
Brio ★$$ 157
Briscola ★★$$$ 81
Broadway Diner ★$ 126
Broadway Grill ★$$$ 122
Broadway Panhandler 41
Bronx, The 208 (chapter and
    map), 219
Brooklyn 208 (chapter and map)
Brooklyn Museum, Cafe at 214
Brothers Barbecue ★$ 197
Brother's Bar-B-Q ★$ 56
Brunch Bunch, The 44
Brunetta's ★★$ 89
Bruno ★$$$ 150
Bruno The King of Ravioli 117
Bruxelles, Cafe de 70
Bryan-Brown, Adrian 52 (bests

Smith's ★$$$ 122
ubby's ★$ 36
uck, Robert T. 221 (bests)
urgundy Wine Company 67
usby's ★$$ 184
uses 248 (map)
v Bread Alone 158

abana Carioca ★★$$ 120
adeaux Plus 185
afe Andrusha ★$ 183
afe at Brooklyn Museum ★$ 214
afe at Grand Central, The ★$ 135
afe Beulah ★★$$ 94
afe Botanica ★★$$$ 128
afe Centro ★★$$$ 134
afé Con Leche ★$ 199
afe Crocodile ★★$$ 170
afe de Bruxelles ★$$ 70
afé des Artistes ★★★$$$ 189
afé Des Sports ★$ 123
afe Divino ★$ 179
afe du Pont ★★$$$ 149
afe Español $$ 59
afe Europa ★$ 127
afe Evergreen ★★$ 165
afe Fledermaus $ 12
afe Gitane ★$ 29
afe Greco ★$ 165
afe Journal ★$ 102
afé La Fortuna ★$ 192
afe Lalo ★$ 201
afe Le Gamin ★$ 52
afe L'Etoile $ 113
afe Loup ★★$$ 70
afe Luxembourg ★★$$$ 191
afe Metairie ★$$ 178
afe Mogador ★$$ 84
afe Mona Lisa ★$ 62
afe Mozart $ 191
afé Nicholson ★$$$ 150
afe Orlin $ 85
afe Picasso ★$ 66
afe Riazor ★$ 106
afe Risque $$ 68
afe SFA ★$ 137
afe St. John ★$ 205
afe-Tabac ★$$ 85
afe, The ★$$ 147
afe Un Deux Trois ★$$ 120
afe Word of Mouth ★$ 170
affe Bianco ★$ 174
affe Bondì ★★$$$ 96
affè Borgia ★$ 57
affé Cefalú ★$ 66
affè Dante ★$ 57
affè del Corso ★$ 145

Caffè della Pace ★$ 83
Caffe Grazie ★★$ 182
Caffè Lucca $ 58
Caffè Lure ★★$ 57
Caffe Med ★$ 165
Caffè Napoli ★$ 25
Caffè Pane e Cioccolato ★$ 75
Caffe Popolo ★$ 197
Caffè Reggio ★$ 57
Caffè Roma ★★$ 28
Caffè Vivaldi ★$ 62
Cajun ★$$ 106
Cake Bar & Cafe, The ★★$ 74
Calabria Pork Store 219
Calandra 221
Cal's ★★$$ 96
Campagna ★★$$$ 95
Campagnola ★$$ 170
Can ★$$ 50
Canard and Company 184
Canton ★★$$ 20
Capsouto Frères ★★$$$ 39
Captain's Ketch, The ★$$$ 12
Captain's Table ★$$$ 133
Caravan of Dreams ★$ 79
Caribe ★$ 67
Carmine's (Theater District) $$ 119
Carmine's (Upper West Side) $$ 204
Carnegie Delicatessen ★★$$ 126
Carnegie Hill Cafe ★★$ 185
Carrot Top Pastries ★$ 207
Carter, Sylvia 15 (bests)
Casa di Pré ★$$ 68
Casa La Femme ★$$ 48
Casani's ★$$ 78
Casa Rosa ★$$ 211
Cascabel ★★★$$$ 28
Castellano ★★$$$ 126
Catherine St Meat Market 19
Caviarteria ★★$$$$ 156
"Cawffee" Breaks 65
Ceci-Cela 29
Cedar Tavern $ 75
Cefalú, Caffé 66
Cellar Grill $ 113
Cellar in the Sky 13
Cellar, The 113
Cellini ★★★$$$ 148
Cent' Anni ★$$$ 58
Central Fish 114
Centro, Cafe 134
Century 21 12
Century Cafe ★★$$ 120
Cesarina ★$$$ 143
Cesar Pelli & Associates 14
Chantal Cafe ★$$ 126
Chantale's Cajun Kitchen ★$ 114

Chanterelle ★★★★$$$$ 35
Charlton's ★★$$$$ 149
Chaz & Wilsons Grill ★$$ 198
Chelsea 104 (chapter and map)
Chelsea Bistro and Bar ★★$$ 110
Chelsea Cafe ★★$ 110
Chelsea Trattoria ★$$ 106
Chen, Paul K.Y. 189
Chez Bernard ★$ 40
Chez Brigitte ★$ 68
Chez Jacqueline ★★$$ 57
Chez Josephine ★★$$$ 115
Chez Laurence Patisserie ★$ 103
Chez Ma Tante Cafe ★$$ 65
Chez Michallet ★$$$ 63
Chez Napoléon ★★$$$ 123
Chiam ★$$$ 138
Chikubu ★★$$$ 135
Child's Play 121
China Fun (East Side) ★$ 165
China Fun (West Side) ★$ 193
China Grill ★★$$$ 143
Chinatown 16 (chapter and map)
Chinatown Ice Cream Factory 24
Chin Chin ★★$$$ 138
Choshi ★★$$ 94
Christ Cella ★$$$$ 133
Christer's ★★★$$$ 126
Chumleys $$ 63
Chutney Mary ★★$$ 95
Ciao Europa ★★$$$ 144
Circus ★★$$ 161
Citarella 196
Cité ★★★$$$ 124
City Bakery (Midtown) ★$ 148
City Bakery, The (Union Square) ★★$ 92
City Crab ★$$ 94
Ci Vediamo (East Village) ★$ 79
Ci Vediamo (Upper East Side) ★★$$ 178
Claire ★$$ 108
Cleaver Company, The 37
Cloisters Cafe $ 85
Coconut Grill ★$ 174
Coco Pazzo ★★$$$$ 171
Coffee Shop ★$ 92
Cola's ★★$ 107
Col Legno ★★$ 85
Colors ★$$$ 133
Columbia Hot Bagels 205
Columbus Bakery ★★$ 200
Coming or Going ★★$$$ 152
Commodities 36
Con Leche, Café 199
Connecticut Muffin Co. 30
Contrapunto ★★$$$ 156
Cooking by the Book 206
Copeland's ★$$ 207

Cornelia Street Café, The ★$ 61
Corner Bistro $ 68
Corrado ★★$$$ 126
Corrado Cafe ★$ 157
Corrado Market 170
Corso, Caffè del 145
Cotton Club, The ★$$ 206
Cottonwood Cafe $$ 67
Country Cafe ★★$ 42
Cowgirl Hall of Fame ★$ 64
Cream Puff, The ★$ 165
Creative Cakes 170
Crocodile, Cafe 170
C.T. ★★★★$$$ 98
C3 ★★$ 72
C.T. Secret Recipe, A 99
Cub Cafe ★$ 50
Cub Room ★$$$ 50
Cucina ★★★$$ 213
Cucina and Company ★$ 134
Cucina Della Fontana $ 66
Cucina di Pesce ★$ 80
Cucina Stagionale $ 62
Cucina Vivolo ★$ 172
Cuisine de Saigon ★$ 71
Cupcake Cafe 114
Cupping Room Cafe, The ★$$ 41

D

Dallas BBQ (East Village) $ 83
Dallas BBQ (Greenwich Village) $ 73
Dallas BBQ (West Side) $ 192
Dama ★$ 59
Damascus Bakery 211
Danal ★★$ 82
D & G Bakery 29
Da Nico ★$ 27
Daniel, Restaurant 171
Daniel's Market 50
Dante, Caffè 57
Darbar Indian Restaurant ★★★$$$ 145
Da Silvano ★$$ 58
Da Umberto ★★$$$ 105
Dawat ★★$$$ 151
Day-O $ 70
Dean & DeLuca 47
Dean & DeLuca Cafe (Midtown) ★$ 136
Dean & DeLuca Cafe (SoHo) ★$ 48
de Bruxelles, Cafe 70
del Corso, Caffè 145
Delegates' Dining Room ★★$$$ 132
Delhi Palace ★$$ 217
della Pace, Caffè 83
Demarchelier ★$$ 182
Demi ★$$$ 185

DeRobertis Pastry Shop 88
des Artistes, Café 189
Des Sports, Café 123
Designer Cakes 180
DiLuca Dairy and Deli 113
Dim Sum and Then Some 22
DiPalo Dairy 27
Disabled travelers, accessibility 5
Dish of Salt $$$ 121
Diva ★$ 40
Divino, Cafe 179
Divino Ristorante ★$$ 179
Dix et Sept ★$$ 66
Docks Oyster Bar and Seafood Grill (Midtown) ★$$$ 132
Docks Oyster Bar and Seafood Grill (Upper West Side) ★★$$ 203
Dojo ★$ 83
Dojo West ★$ 75
Dolce ★$$$ 137
Dolci On Park Caffè ★$$ 103
Dominick's ★★$ 219
Donald Sacks ★★$$ 15
Dragon Village ★★$ 218
Drinking 6
D. Sokolin 102
Duane Park Cafe ★★$$$ 34
Due ★★$$$ 176
du Pont, Cafe 149

E

Ear Inn, The $ 42
East Corner Wontoṅ ★$ 20
Eastern Seafood Company ★$ 198
East Side 154 (chapter and map)
East Village 76 (chapter and map)
East Village Cheese Store 83
E.A.T. ★★$$$ 177
Ecce Panis (East Side) 162
Ecce Panis (Upper East Side) 184
Ecco $$$ 15
Ecco-Là ★$ 184
Eclair $$ 193
Economy Candy Company 31
Eden Rock ★$ 202
Edgar's Cafe ★$ 201
Eighteenth and Eighth ★$ 107
18th Avenue Bakery 214
18th Avenue Fruit Market 215
Eileen's Special Cheesecake 29
E.J.'s Luncheonette (Upper East Side) ★$ 170
E.J.'s Luncheonette (Upper West Side) ★$ 200
Elaine's $$$ 182
El Charro Español (Greenwich Village) ★$$ 72

El Charro Español (Murray Hill) ★$$ 103
El Cid ★★$ 106
El Faro ★$$ 69
Elias Corner ★★$ 217
Elio's ★★$$$ 181
Elk Candy Company 182
Ellen's Cafe and Bake Shop ★$ 15
Ellen's Stardust Diner $ 127
El Parador ★★$$$ 102
El Pollo ★★$ 183
El Rincon de España ★$$ 56
El Sombrero $ 31
El Teddy's ★$$$ 37
Emery Roth & Sons 13
Empire Coffee and Tea 115
Empire Diner ★$ 109
Enchilada Johnny's ★$ 181
Ennio & Michael ★★$$$ 56
Erminia ★★$$$ 181
Ernie's $$ 196
Eros ★$$ 150
E. Rossi & Co. 27
Español, Cafe 59
Essex Street Pickles 30
Estia ★★$$$ 181
Etats-Unis ★★$$$ 179
Etoile, Cafe L' 113
Europa, Cafe 127
Evergreen, Cafe 165

F

Fabulous Food Festivals 6
Faicco's 60
Fairway 196
Family Noodle Restaurant ★$ 1
Famous Ray's Pizza $ 71
Fanelli Cafe $ 48
Fantino ★★$$$ 129
Fashion Cafe $ 136
Fatto in Casa 172
Favia ★$ 157
Felidia ★★$$$$ 150
Felissimo ★★$ 146
Felix ★$$$ 39
Ferrara ★ 27
Ferrier ★$$ 164
Ferruci's Gourmet 88
Fifty Seven Fifty Seven ★★$$$ 152
Film Center Cafe ★$ 117
Fine & Schapiro ★$$ 193
Fiorello's ★$$$ 188
First ★★$$ 79
First Taste ★★★$$ 21
Fish $ 205
Fisher & Levy 141
Fishin Eddie ★★$$$ 192
Fishs Eddy 67

lamingo East ★$$ **89**
lavors **93**
ledermaus, Cafe **12**
letcher Morgan Provisions ★$ **163**
lorence Meat Market **61**
lorent, Restaurant **69**
lowers ★★$$$ **92**
ollonico ★★$$$ **97**
ood Attitude ★$ **159**
ood Bar ★$ **107**
ood phone **6**
ood tours **6**
ord, Eileen O. **111** (bests)
or Lovers Only **49**
4 Southwest $ **116**
orzano Italian Imports Inc. **25**
our Seasons, The ★★★★$$$$ **142**
rankie and Johnnie's ★$$$ **120**
ranklin Station ★$ **37**
rank Randazzo's Sons Fish Market **219**
ank's ★★$$$ **107**
aunces Tavern Restaurant ★$$$ **10**
eddie and Pepper's Gourmet Pizza ★$ **196**
ench Roast ★$ **71**
ench Wine Merchant **152**
esco ★★$$ **142**
esco Tortilla Grill ★$ **98**
iend of a Farmer ★$$ **94**
ontiere ★★$$$ **52**
jjiyama Mama ★$$ **200**
ilton Fish Market **11**
ilton Market **12**
ilton Street Cafe $$ **12**
's ★★$$$ **140**

abriel's ★★$$$ **187**
age & Tollner ★★★$$$ **210**
allagher's Steak House ★$$$$ **124**
amin, Cafe Le **52**
ansevoort Market **70**
arden Cafe $ **198**
arden, The **212**
ascogne ★★$$ **107**
uguin $$$ **152**
elateria Richard **201**
m Spa Smoke Shop **83**
eorg Jensen/Royal Copenhagen **159**
ertel's Bake Shop **30**
acomo **193**
anni's ★$$ **12**
gino ★$$ **32**
llen, William **53** (bests)

Gino's ★$$ **158**
Giovanni ★$$$ **144**
Giovanni Esposito & Sons Meat Shop **114**
Girasole ★$$$$ **177**
Gitane, Cafe **29**
Global 33 ★$ **80**
Goldberg, Gary A. **167** (bests)
Goldberg, Howard **89** (bests)
Golden Unicorn ★★★$$ **20**
Good & Plenty to Go **116**
Good Earth, The **190**
Good Enough to Eat ★★$$ **201**
Goods on Greenmarkets, The **19**
Gotham Bar and Grill ★★★$$$$ **74**
Gotham City Diner ★$$ **179**
Gourmet Garage **41**
Grace's Marketplace **165**
Gramercy Park **90** (chapter and map)
Gramercy Tavern ★★$$$ **95**
Gran Caffè Degli Artisti ★$ **72**
Grand Central, The Cafe at **135**
Grand Ticino ★★$$ **56**
Grange Hall, The ★$ **62**
Gray's Papaya $ **193**
Grazie, Caffe **182**
Great Jones Cafe $ **80**
Great Shanghai ★★$ **20**
Greco, Cafe **165**
Greenhouse Cafe ★$$ **14**
Greenwich Cafe ★$ **67**
Greenwich Village **54** (chapter and map)
Grossinger's Uptown Bake Shop **202**
Grotta Azzurra ★$$ **28**
Grove ★★$ **63**
Grove Street Cafe ★$$ **63**
Guido's ★$$ **114**
Gus' Place ★$$ **63**

H

Hale and Hearty ★$$ **163**
Hamburger Harry's ★$ **120**
H&H Bagels West **199**
Hanna's **183**
Harbour Lights $$$ **11**
Hard Rock Cafe $$ **127**
Hardy Holzman Pfeiffer Associates **135**
Harlem **194** (chapter and map)
Harley Davidson Cafe ★$$ **145**
Harriet's Kitchen **201**
Harry Cipriani ★★$$$$ **156**
Harry's Burrito Junction ★$ **191**
Hatsuhana ★★★$$$ **137**
Hat, The $ **31**
Haveli ★$ **80**

Health Nuts **204**
Hee Seung Fung (HSF) ★$$ **21**
Heights **194** (chapter and map)
Henry's End ★$$ **210**
Hero Boy ★$ **114**
Hi-Life Restaurant & Lounge (Upper East Side) ★$$ **169**
Hi-Life Restaurant & Lounge (Upper West Side) ★$$ **201**
Home ★★$$ **60**
Honmura An ★★★$$$ **48**
H. Oppenheimer Meats **204**
Hors d'Oeuvrerie at Windows on the World, The **13**
Hour Glass Tavern $ **118**
Hours **6**
House of Vegetarian ★$ **24**
Hudson River Club ★★★★$$$$ **14**
Hunan Garden ★★$ **18**
Hunter of the Sea **217**
Hunt Room at the New York Palace Hotel, The ★★$$$ **137**
Hurricane Island ★★$$ **173**

I

Ideal Cheese Shop **162**
Idone, Christopher **53** (bests)
Il Cantinori ★★$$$ **75**
Il Cortile ★$$$ **25**
Il Monello ★★$$$ **173**
Il Mulino ★★★$$$ **56**
Il Nido ★★$$$$ **140**
Il Ponte Vecchio ★$$ **56**
Il Toscanaccio ★★★$$$ **156**
Il Vagabondo ★$$ **162**
Il Valletto ★$$$ **158**
Il Vigneto ★$ **150**
Inagiku Japanese Restaurant ★★$$$$ **137**
Indian Cafe ★$ **205**
India Pavilion ★$ **128**
Indochine ★★$$ **81**
In Padella ★$ **85**
Integral Yoga Foods **70**
International Gourmet and Gift Center **207**
International Groceries & Meat Market **114**
Iridium $$ **187**
Isabella ★$$ **197**
Island ★$$$ **185**
Iso ★$$ **88**
Isola ★$$ **200**
Istanbul Kebap ★★$ **179**
Italian Food Center **27**
I Tre Merli ★$$$ **49**
I Trulli ★★★$$$ **99**

J

Jackson Diner ★$ 217
Jackson Hole ★$ 161
Jade Palace ★★$ 218
Jaiya Thai Oriental Restaurant (Murray Hill) ★★$$ 100
Jaiya Thai Oriental Restaurant (Queens) ★★$$ 218
Jake's Fish Market 203
Jamaican Hot Pot ★★$ 207
James Beard House ★★★★$$$$ 71
Jane Street Seafood Cafe ★$$ 69
Janklow, Morton L. 193 (bests)
Japonica ★★★$$ 74
Jean Claude ★$ 50
Jean Lafitte ★★$$$ 153
Jefferson Market 71
Jekyll and Hyde $ 61
Jekyll and Hyde Club, The $ 129
Jerry's (SoHo) ★$$ 48
Jerry's (Upper West Side) ★$$ 196
Jezebel ★★$$$ 117
Jim McMullen ★$$ 174
Jing Fong ★★$$ 21
Joe Allen $$ 118
Joe Babbington's Joint ★$ 109
Joe's Dairy 51
Johnney's Fish Grill ★★$$ 15
John's East ★★$ 162
John's of Twelfth Street ★$$ 89
John's Pizzeria ★★$ 62
John's West ★★$ 189
JoJo ★★★$$$ 163
Josie's ★★$ 195
Jour et Nuit ★★$$$ 39
Journal, Cafe 102
J.P. French Bakery 144
Jubilee ★$$ 140
Judson Grill ★$$$ 124
Jules ★★$$ 84
Julian's Mediterranean Cuisine $ 125
Junior's ★$ 211

K

Kadouri Import Corp. 30
Kaffeehaus ★$ 106
Kalustyan's 100
Kamil, Seth 31 (bests)
Kam Kuo Food Corp. 18
Kam Man Food Products, Inc. 24
Kaplan's $$ 156
Karyatis ★★$$ 217
Katz's Delicatessen ★$ 31
Kelley and Ping ★★$ 48
Kenn's Broome Street Bar $ 41
Key West Diner $ 204
Khyber Pass ★$ 83

Kiev ★$ 83
Kiiroi Hana ★★$$ 146
King Crab ★$$ 125
Kin Khao ★★$$ 46
Kitchen Arts & Letters 184
Kitchen Casting 192
Kitchen Club ★★$$ 29
Kitchen Market 109
Kleine Konditorei ★$$ 182
Knickerbocker Bar & Grill ★$$ 73
Kossar's Bialystoker 30
Koyote Kate's $$ 122
Kump, Peter 75 (bests)
Kurowycky 84
Kwanzaa ★★$$ 28

L

La Barca ★$$$ 10
La Bohème ★$$ 58
La Boîte en Bois ★★$$$ 190
La Bonne Soupe ★$ 144
La Boulangère ★$ 95
L'Acajou ★$$$ 96
La Caravelle ★★★$$$$ 145
La Caridad $ 197
La Collina ★$$ 184
La Colombe d'Or ★★★$$$ 98
La Côte Basque ★★★★$$$$ 144
La Focaccia ★$$ 68
La Folie ★★$$$ 178
La Fondue $ 144
La Fortuna, Café 192
La Grenouille ★★$$$$ 142
La Jumelle ★$ 40
La Linea ★$ 78
Lalo, Cafe 201
La Lunchonette ★$$ 107
La Madama Cafe and Bakery ★$ 109
La Maison du Chocolat 171
Lamalle Kitchenware 97
La Mangeoire ★★$$$ 140
La Marqueta 205
La Mela ★$ 28
La Metairie ★★$$$ 66
La Mirabelle ★$$$ 202
Landmark Tavern ★$$ 117
Lang, Jennifer and George 153 (bests)
La Pequeña Colombia ★$ 218
La Piazzetta di Quisisana ★$$$ 172
L'Ardoise ★★$ 162
La Réserve ★★★$$$$ 136
La Ripaille ★★$$ 69
La Rosita ★$ 205
La Taza de Oro ★$ 106
La Terrine 172

La Tour D'Or ★$$$ 12
Lattanzi ★$$$ 118
L'Auberge du Midi ★★$$ 68
Leaf & Bean 213
Le Bernardin ★★★★$$$$ 123
Le Bilbouquet ★★$$$ 160
Le Bistrot de Maxim's ★$$$ 160
Le Boeuf à la Mode ★★$$$ 180
Le Cafe ★$$ 105
Le Chantilly ★★★$$$$ 151
Le Cirque ★★★$$$$ 164
L'Ecole ★★$$ 40
Le Colonial ★★$$ 151
Le Comptoir ★★$$$ 164
Lee Mazzilli's Sports Cafe $ 191
Le Figaro Café $ 57
Le Gamin, Cafe 52
Le Madeleine ★$$$ 116
Le Madri ★★★$$$ 108
Le Max ★$$ 119
Lemongrass Grill (Brooklyn) ★★$$ 213
Lemongrass Grill (Upper West Side) ★★$ 204
Lenox Room ★★$$$ 170
Leonard's 165
Le Pactole ★★$$$ 14
Le Perigord ★★★$$$ 139
Le Pescadou ★★$$ 52
Le Petit Hulot ★$$$ 166
Le Pistou ★$$ 158
Le Poème Restaurant Tea Room and Bakery ★★$ 30
Le Refuge ★★$$$ 177
Le Regence ★★★★$$$$ 163
Le Relais ★$$$ 160
L'Ermitage ★★$$ 145
LeRoy, Warner 189
Les Célébrités ★★★$$$$ 128
Les Deux Gamins ★$ 63
Le Select ★$$ 201
Les Halles ★★$$ 101
Lespinasse ★★★$$$$ 147
Les Pyrénées ★$$$ 123
Les Routiers ★$$ 203
Les Sans Culottes ★$$$ 150
Les Sans Culottes West ★$$$ 118
Le Streghe ★$$ 40
Le Taxi ★★$$$ 159
Letizia ★$$$ 169
L'Etoile, Cafe 113
Le Train Bleu ★$$ 156
Let Them Eat Cake ★$ 42
Le Veau d'Or ★$$$ 159
Lex ★$$$ 162
Liberty Cafe $$ 11
Life Cafe ★$ 88
Lightner, Serena 207 (bests)
Li-Lac Chocolates 64

mbo ★$ **79**
ncoln Tavern $$ **188**
n's Sister Associates Corp. **21**
on's Head ★$$ **64**
pstick Cafe ★★$ **141**
ttle Cafe $ **66**
ttle Italy **16** (chapter and map)
ttle Pie Company **116**
ve Bait $$ **97**
bel's Prime Meats **182**
bster Box ★★$$$ **221**
, Eileen Yin-Fei **7** (bests)
la ★$$$ **96**
mbardi's ★★$ **29**
ndon Lennie's $$ **218**
ng Shine Restaurant ★★$ **20**
renzo and Maria's Kitchen **178**
tfi's Moroccan ★$ **118**
uie's Westside Cafe ★$$ **199**
uisiana Community Bar and
    Grill ★$$ **78**
up, Cafe **70**
wer East Side **16** (chapter and
    map)
wer Manhattan **8** (chapter and
    map)
x Around the Clock $ **96**
cca, Caffè **58**
cky Cheng's ★$ **78**
cky Strike $$ **40**
dlow Street Cafe, The ★$ **31**
Jdo ★$$ **81**
ke's Bar & Grill ★$ **176**
ma ★★$$$ **109**
na ★$$ **25**
ng Fong Bakery **24**
re, Caffè **57**
sardi's ★★$$$ **174**
tèce ★★★$$$$ **138**
xembourg, Cafe **191**
zia ★$ **199**
n's Cafe ★$ **146**

cKenzie, Patricia **53** (bests)
ckinac Grill ★$$ **198**
cmed Spuntino ★$ **82**
d. 61 ★★$$$ **159**
gris, Roberto **43**
in Street ★$$ **200**
ison Caribe ★★$ **181**
laysia & Indonesia ★★$ **20**
mbo Grill ★$$ **177**
na ★$ **203**
ndarin Court ★★$ **24**
l International **215**
nducatis ★★$$ **216**
nganaro Foods **113**
ngia ★★$ **153**
ngia e Bevi ★★$ **125**

Manhattan Bistro ★$ **46**
Manhattan Brewing Co. $$ **41**
Manhattan Cafe ★$$$ **162**
Manhattan Chili Company, The
    ★$ **119**
Manhattan Fruitier **101**
Manhattan Ocean Club, The
    ★★★$$$ **153**
Man Ray ★$$ **108**
Map Key **5**
Maple Garden Duck House ★$$
    141
Mappamondo Restaurant ★$ **69**
March ★★★$$$ **150**
Marché Madison **171**
Marchi's ★$$$ **102**
Marion's Continental Restaurant
    and Lounge ★$$ **80**
Mario's ★$$$ **219**
Markham Cafe, The ★★$ **73**
Markham, The ★★★$$$ **73**
Mark's ★★$$$$ **176**
Marlowe ★$$ **118**
Marquet Patisserie ★$ **74**
Martini's ★★$$ **125**
Maruzzella ★$$ **175**
Marylou's ★★$$$ **73**
Marys ★$ **59**
Match ★$$ **47**
Matthew's ★★★$$$ **157**
Mautner, Julie **167** (bests)
Mavalli Palace ★$ **101**
Maya Schaper Cheese &
    Antiques **190**
Mayfair ★$ **140**
Mayrose ★$ **95**
Mazer Store Equipment Co. **30**
McDonald's $ **12**
McNulty's Tea and Coffee
    Company **64**
Meals on Reels: Take One **82**
Med, Caffe **165**
Mediterraneo ★$$ **165**
Mekka ★★$ **78**
Melampo Imported Foods **43**
Melange **162**
Melanie's Natural ★$ **72**
Menchanko-tei ★$ **144**
Merenda ★$ **179**
Meriken ★$$ **108**
Mesa Grill ★★$$$ **92**
Metairie, Cafe **178**
Metisse ★★★$ **204**
Metropolitan Cafe ★$$ **140**
Mezzaluna ★$$ **172**
Mezzanine, The ★$$$ **120**
Mezzogiorno ★★$$$ **43**
Michael's ★★$$ **145**
Michael's and Sons Meat Market
    114

Michelle's Kitchen ★$ **158**
Mickey Mantle's ★$$ **153**
Mi Cocina ★★$ **69**
Midtown **130** (chapter and map)
Mika ★★$$ **41**
Mike's American Bar and Grill
    ★$ **117**
Milady ★$ **50**
Mimi's Macaroni ★$ **204**
Minetta Tavern ★$$ **57**
Minoru Yamasaki & Associates **13**
Miracle Grill ★★$$ **83**
Mitali ★★$$ **80**
Mitchel London Foods **164**
Mitsukoshi ★★★$$$$ **151**
Miyacaki, Stomu **50**
Mme. Romaine de Lyon ★★$$
    159
Mo' Better ★$ **203**
Mocca Hungarian ★$ **181**
Mogador, Cafe **84**
Mona Lisa, Cafe **62**
Monck's Corner **117**
Monkey Bar ★★★$$$ **148**
Monsoon ★$ **199**
Montague Street Saloon ★$ **210**
Montrachet ★★★$$$ **37**
Moondance Diner ★$ **39**
Morgan Cafe ★$ **103**
Moroccan Star ★$ **211**
Morrell & Company, The Wine
    Emporium **148**
Mortimer's ★$$$ **172**
Morton's of Chicago ★★★$$$
    135
Mo's Caribbean Bar and Grille
    ★$ **173**
Mott Street General Store **18**
Mould, Jacob Wrey **189**
Moustache ★$ **62**
Mozart, Cafe **191**
Mr. Chips **185**
Mrs. Stahl's Knishes **215**
Mughlai $$ **196**
Mulholland Drive Cafe $$ **161**
Murray Hill **90** (chapter and map)
Murray's Cheese Store (Chelsea)
    108
Murray's Cheese Store
    (Greenwich Village) **60**
Murray's Sturgeon **203**
Museum Cafe $$ **197**
Mustang Grill ★$ **181**
Musto, Michael **167** (bests)
Myers of Keswick **69**

N

ñ ★$ **41**
Nadine's ★$$ **69**
Nam Wah Tea Parlor ★$ **21**

Nancy's Wines for Food **197**
Napoli, Caffè **25**
Nathan's Famous ★$ **215**
National Restaurant ★★$$$ **215**
Nature's Gifts **182**
Negril Island Spice (Chelsea) ★★$ **110**
Negril Island Spice (Theater District) ★★$ **116**
Nello ★★$$$ **160**
Neuman & Bogdonoff **175**
Nevada Meat Market **190**
New Chao Chow ★$ **25**
New City Cafe ★★$ **212**
New Hong Kong City ★★$ **20**
New Prospect At Home, The **213**
New Prospect Café, The ★★$$ **214**
News Bar ★$ **93**
New World Grill ★$ **122**
New York area map **2** (map)
New York buses **248** (map)
New York Cooking Schools **220**
New York subways **246** (map)
Nha Trang ★★$ **24**
Nice Restaurant ★★★$ **20**
Nicholson, Café **150**
Nick & Eddie ★★$$ **43**
Nicola Paone ★★$$$ **102**
9 Jones Street ★★$$ **61**
Nino's ★$$ **169**
Ninth Avenue Cheese Market **114**
Nippon ★★$$$$ **142**
Nobu ★★★$$$$ **36**
Noho Star ★$ **78**
Nonna ★★$ **151**
Nosmo King ★★$$$ **39**
Novità ★★$$ **98**
Nyborg-Nelson ★★$ **141**
N.Y. Cake and Baking Distributor, The **96**
N.Y. Noodletown ★$ **21**

O

Oak Room and Bar ★★$$$ **152**
Oceana ★★★$$$$ **148**
Ocean Palace Seafood Restaurant ★$ **214**
Odeon, The ★$$ **35**
Odessa ★★$$$ **216**
Old Devil Moon ★★$ **88**
Old Homestead ★★$$$$ **106**
Old Town Bar ★$ **93**
Ollie's Noodle Shop ★$ **201**
Olmstead, Pat **7** (bests)
Omen ★★$$ **43**
Once Upon a Tart ★$ **50**
O'Neals' ★$$$ **188**
One City Cafe ★$ **106**

One If By Land, Two If By Sea ★★$$$$ **61**
One on One **78**
107 West ★$$ **205**
Orbit ★$ **59**
Oriental Garden Seafood ★★$$ **21**
Oriental Pastry and Grocery Company, The **211**
Oriental Pearl ★$ **25**
Orientation **4** (chapter)
Orlin, Cafe **85**
Orologio ★$ **88**
Orso ★$$$ **118**
Orwasher's Bakery **174**
Osteria al Doge ★★$$ **119**
Otabe ★★$$$ **149**
Ottomanelli's Meat Market **62**
Oven and a Basket Bakery **182**
Oyster Bar and Restaurant ★★$$$ **134**
Ozu ★$ **202**
Ozzie's ★$ **213**

P

Pace, Caffè della **83**
Palermo Bakery **89**
Palio ★★$$$$ **124**
Palm ★★$$$$ **133**
Palm Court ★$$ **152**
Pamir ★$$ **173**
Pandit ★$ **202**
Pane e Cioccolato, Caffè **75**
Panevino ★$$ **187**
Paola's ★★$$$ **181**
Pappardella $$ **197**
Paprikas Weiss **179**
Paradise Market **182**
Parioli Romanissimo ★★★$$$$ **177**
Paris Commune ★$$ **67**
Park Avalon ★$ **93**
Park Avenue Cafe ★★★$$$ **160**
Park Bistro ★★$$$ **101**
Parma ★$$$ **176**
Parnell's ★$ **140**
Pasqua ★$ **142**
Passage to India ★$ **80**
Passport ★$ **84**
Pasta Place **88**
Pastrami King ★$ **218**
Patio Restaurant $ **113**
Patisserie Claude **61**
Patisserie J. Lanciani ★$ **66**
Patisserie Les Friandises **166**
Patria ★★$$$ **94**
Patrick Murphy's Market **185**
Patsy's Pizza ★★$ **210**
Patsy's Pizzeria ★$ **206**
Patzo $ **202**

Peacock Alley ★★$$$$ **138**
Peacock Caffè $ **72**
Pearson's Stick to Your Ribs ★$ **216**
Pedro Paramo ★★$ **89**
Pei, I.M. **152**
Peking Duck House ★★$ **18**
Pen & Pencil ★$$$$ **133**
Penang ★★$ (Queens) **218**
Penang ★★$$ (SoHo) **46**
Penn-Top Bar and Terrace $ **148**
Per Bacco ★$ **99**
Periyali ★★$$$ **96**
Persepolis ★$ **173**
Peruvian Restaurant ★$ **122**
Petaluma ★$$$ **169**
Peter Luger ★★★$$$ **212**
Pete's Tavern ★$$ **94**
Petrossian ★★★$$$$ **128**
Pho Bâng Restaurant ★$ **19**
Phoebe's ★$ **197**
Phoenix Garden ★$$$ **132**
Picasso, Cafe **66**
Piccolo Angolo ★$ **69**
Piccolo Mondello Pescheria **214**
Picholine ★★★$$$ **188**
Pick of the Pasta **26**
Piemonte Ravioli Company **27**
Pier 17 **11**
Pierogi and Deli **84**
Pierre au Tunnel ★★$$$ **120**
Pierre Deux **166**
Pie, The ★$ **181**
Pigalle ★★$$ **101**
Pig Heaven ★$$ **179**
Pink Pony Cafe $ **31**
Pink Teacup ★$ **63**
Pipeline ★$$ **14**
Pisacane Midtown **139**
Pisces ★★$$ **79**
Pizza—What's Old is What's New **38**
Pizzeria Uno $ **198**
P. J. Clarke's ★$$ **149**
Planet Hollywood ★$$ **127**
Platypus **46**
Plaza Garibaldi ★$ **218**
Po ★★★$ **60**
Polo, The ★★$$$ **166**
Pong Sri ★$$ **122**
Popolo, Caffe **197**
Popover Café ★$$ **202**
Porcini Trading Co. **175**
Porto Rico **57**
Poseidon Greek Bakery **116**
Positively 104th Street Cafe ★$ **204**
Post House, The ★★★$$$$ **160**
Pot Belly Stove Cafe $ **64**
Pranzo **175**

Pravinie Gourmet Ice Cream **57**
Primavera ★★$$$ **180**
Primorski ★★$$ **216**
Prince Street Bar & Restaurant ★$ **48**
Provence ★★★$$ **52**
Puglia Restuarant $ **25**
Pure Mädderlake **40**

Q

Quatorze Bis ★★$$$ **175**
Quattro Gatti ★★$$ **178**
Queens **208** (chapter and map), **216**

R

Rachel's ★★$ **116**
Rafaella Restaurant ★$$ **66**
Raffaele ★★$$$ **149**
Raffetto's **56**
Rain ★★$$ **200**
Rainbow & Stars ★★$$$$ **136**
Rainbow Room, The ★★$$$$ **135**
Rangoon Cafe ★$ **84**
Rao's ★★$$$$ **206**
Raoul's ★★$$$ **50**
Rasputin ★★$$ **215**
ratings of restaurants **6**
Ratner's ★$$ **30**
Ravioli Store, The **42**
Raw Deal, The **86**
Reality Bake Shop **72**
Red Tulip, The ★$$ **173**
Reggio, Caffè **57**
Remi ★★$$$ **126**
René Pujol ★★$$ **123**
reservations **6**
Restaurant at the Stanhope Hotel, The ★★★$$$ **177**
Restaurant at Windows on the World, The **13**
Restaurant Daniel ★★★★$$$$ **171**
Restaurant Florent ★★$$ **69**
Restaurant 44 ★★$$$ **135**
Revolution ★$ **116**
Razor, Cafe **106**
Rice and Beans ★$ **123**
Richart Design et Chocolat **147**
Right Bank, The ★$$ **166**
Rigo Hungarian Pastry **174**
Rikyu ★$$ **191**
Risque, Cafe **68**
Ristorante Taormina ★$$ **27**
River Café ★★★$$$$ **210**
Riverrun Cafe ★$$ **36**
Riviera Cafe $$ **64**
Road to Mandalay ★★$$ **28**
Rocco Pastry Shop & Cafe ★$ **59**

Rockwell, David **141**, **148**
Roettele A.G. ★$$ **83**
Rolf's Restaurant ★$$ **98**
Roma, Caffè **28**
Ronasi ★★$$ **162**
Rooms with a View **13**
Rosa Mexicano ★★$$$ **150**
Rose Cafe ★★$$ **73**
Rosedale Fish Market **176**
Rosemarie's ★★$$$ **34**
Rosenthal Wine Merchant **177**
Rossini's $$$ **103**
Roumeli Taverna ★$$ **216**
Royal Siam ★★$ **110**
Rubyfruit Bar & Grill ★$ **64**
Rumbul's Pastry Shop ★$ **63**
Rumpelmayer's $$ **153**
Russ & Daughters **31**
Russian Samovar ★$$ **125**
Russian Tea Room, The ★★$$$ **127**
Russo's Mozzarella & Pasta Corp. **88**

S

Sable's Smoked Fish **174**
Sahadi Importing Company **211**
Sahara East ★$ **89**
Saigon House Restaurant ★★$ **24**
Salaam Bombay ★★$ **32**
Salam ★$ **71**
Sal Anthony's $$ **93**
Sal Anthony's S.P.Q.R $$ **25**
Sala Thai ★★$ **183**
Saloon, The $$ **189**
Salumeria Biellese **111**
Samalita's Tortilla Factory ★$ **178**
Sammy's Famous Roumanian Jewish Steakhouse ★★$$$ **30**
Sam's ★$ **120**
Sam's Noodle Shop ★$ **100**
San Domenico ★★★★$$$$ **129**
San Pietro ★★$$$ **148**
Santa Fe ★$$ **190**
Santa Fe Grill ★$ **213**
Sant Ambroeus ★★$$$ **177**
Sapporo ★$ **122**
Sarabeth's at the Whitney ★★$$ **171**
Sarabeth's Kitchen (Upper East Side) ★★$$ **184**
Sarabeth's Kitchen (Upper West Side) ★★$$ **198**
Saranac ★$ **185**
Sardi's ★$$$ **119**
Savoy ★★$$$ **47**
Sazerac House ★★$$ **64**

Scaletta ★★$$$ **197**
Schaller & Weber **182**
Schapiro's House of Kosher and Sacramental Wines **31**
Schatzie's Prime Meats **182**
Sea Breeze Fish Market **115**
SeaGrill, The ★★★$$$$ **136**
2nd Avenue Deli ★$$ **88**
Ségires à Solanée **163**
Sel et Poivre ★$$ **163**
Sensuous Bean, The **191**
Sequoia $$ **11**
Serendipity ★$$ **157**
Seryna ★★$$$ **142**
Sette Mezzo ★★$$$ **165**
Sette MoMA ★$$$ **143**
7A $ **83**
Sevilla ★$$ **66**
SFA, Cafe **137**
Sfuzzi (Lower Manhattan) ★$$ **15**
Sfuzzi (West Side) ★★$$ **189**
Sgarlato's Cafe $$$ **11**
Shaan ★$$ **135**
Shabu Tatsu ★★$$ **173**
Shark Bar ★$ **196**
Shelby ★$$ **165**
Sherry Lehman **159**
Shin Jung ★★$ **219**
Shun Lee Dynasty ★$$$ **189**
Shun Lee Palace ★★★$$$$ **149**
Siam Inn ★$ **126**
Sibilia, Peter **163**
Sichuan Pavilion ★★$$$ **132**
Sidewalkers ★$$ **192**
Sign of The Dove, The ★★★$$$$ **162**
Silk ★★$$ **100**
Silk Road Palace ★$ **200**
Silver Palace ★★$$ **21**
Simon, Lisa **103** (bests)
Singer, Lou **111** (bests)
Sirabella ★★$$ **180**
Sistina ★★$$$ **179**
67 Wine & Spirits **190**
Skidmore, Owings & Merrill **124**
Sloppy Louie's ★$$$ **10**
Smith & Wollensky ★★$$$ **138**
Smoking **6**
Snaps ★★$$ **133**
SoHo **32** (chapter)
SoHo **33** (map)
SoHo Kitchen and Bar ★$ **46**
SoHo Wine & Spirits **49**
Soleil ★★$$ **164**
Solera ★★$$ **141**
Sonia Rose ★★$$$ **100**
Souen Downtown ★$ **52**
Soup Kitchen ★$ **126**
South Street Seaport **11**

Index

Soutine **191**
Spanier & Dennis **37**
Sparks ★★$$$$ **133**
Spartina ★$$ **35**
Sporting Club, The $$ **36**
Sports Bars **188**
Sports, Café Des **123**
Spring Street Natural ★$ **47**
Stacy's ★★★$ **212**
Stage Delicatessen $$ **126**
Stanhope Hotel, The Restaurant at the **177**
Staten Island **208** (chapter and map), **221**
Steak Frites ★$$ **92**
Stella del Mare ★★$$$ **132**
Stevenson, Isabelle **129** (bests)
Steve's Meat Market **212**
St. Famous Bread **125**
Stiles Farmers Market **115**
St. John, Cafe **205**
St. Maggie's Cafe ★$$ **10**
Strand Bookstore **89**
Streit's Matzoth Company **31**
Subways **246** (map)
Sullivan, Chris **41**
Sullivan Street Bakery **42**
Sun Lin Garden ★$ **24**
Sunrise Kitchen Supplies **20**
Sushisay ★★$$$ **137**
Sutton Watering Hole ★$ **149**
Sweet Life, The **30**
S. Wyler **166**
Sylvia's ★★$$ **207**
Symphony Cafe ★★★$$$ **128**
Symposium $ **205**

T

T ★$$ **47**
Tabac, Cafe- **85**
Table d'Hôte ★★$$$ **184**
Tai Hong Lau ★$ **24**
Takahachi ★★$ **79**
Takashimaya **147**
Takesushi ★★$$$$ **134**
Talese, Gay **166** (bests)
Taliesin ★$$$ **13**
Tall Ships Bar & Grill ★$$ **14**
Tammany Hall ★★$$ **100**
Tanti Baci Caffè ★★$ **66**
Taormina, Ristorante **27**
Taquería de México ★$ **68**
Tartine ★★$ **67**
Tasca Porto ★★$ **42**
Tatou $$$ **138**
Tavern on the Green ★★★$$$$ **189**
Tavola ★★$$$ **175**
Taylor's (Chelsea) **108**
Taylor's (Greenwich Village) **64**

Tea and Sympathy ★$ **70**
Tea Box Cafe ★$ **147**
Teachers Too $ **199**
Tea Time **161**
Tempo ★★$$$ **101**
Tennessee Mountain ★$$ **46**
10 Pell Street ★★★$ **21**
Teresa's ★$ **79**
Terrace Cafe, Brooklyn Botanic Garden ★$ **214**
Terrace, The ★★$$$$ **206**
Terramare ★$ **164**
Terranova Bakery **219**
Teuscher Chocolates of Switzerland **137**
Thai House Cafe ★$ **39**
Thailand Restaurant ★★$$ **24**
The Adoré ★★$ **74**
The Armadillo $ **203**
Theater District **112** (chapter and map)
The Bagel ★$ **61**
The Big Enchilada (Greenwich Village) ★$ **74**
The Big Enchilada (Murray Hill) ★$ **100**
The Bistro ★$$$ **146**
The Black Sheep ★★$$$ **67**
The Bread Shop ★$ **206**
The Bronx **208** (chapter and map), **219**
The Brunch Bunch **44**
The Cafe ★$$ **147**
The Cafe at Grand Central ★$ **135**
The Cake Bar & Cafe ★★$ **74**
The Captain's Ketch ★$$$ **12**
The Cellar **113**
The City Bakery (Union Square) ★★$ **92**
The Cleaver Company **37**
The Cornelia Street Café ★$ **61**
The Cotton Club ★$$ **206**
The Cream Puff ★$ **165**
The Cupping Room Cafe ★$$ **41**
The Ear Inn $ **42**
The Four Seasons ★★★★$$$$ **142**
The Garden **212**
The Good Earth **190**
The Goods on Greenmarkets **19**
The Grange Hall ★$ **62**
The Hat $ **31**
The Hors d'Oeuvrerie at Windows on the World **13**
The Hunt Room at the New York Palace Hotel ★★$$$ **137**
The Jekyll and Hyde Club $ **129**
The Ludlow Street Cafe ★$ **31**

The Manhattan Chili Company ★$ **119**
The Manhattan Ocean Club ★★★$$$ **153**
The Markham ★★★$$$ **73**
The Markham Cafe ★★$ **73**
The Mezzanine ★$$$ **120**
The New Prospect At Home **213**
The New Prospect Café ★★$$ **214**
The N.Y. Cake & Baking Distributor **96**
The Odeon ★$$ **35**
The Oriental Pastry and Grocery Company **211**
The Pie ★$ **181**
The Polo ★★$$$ **166**
The Post House ★★★$$$$ **160**
The Rainbow Room ★★$$$$ **135**
The Ravioli Store **42**
The Raw Deal **86**
The Red Tulip ★$$ **173**
The Restaurant at the Stanhope Hotel ★★★$$$ **177**
The Restaurant at Windows on the World **13**
The Right Bank ★$$ **166**
The Russian Tea Room ★★$$$ **127**
The Saloon $$ **189**
The SeaGrill ★★★$$$$ **136**
The Sensuous Bean **191**
The Sign of The Dove ★★★$$$$ **162**
The Sporting Club $$ **36**
The Sweet Life **30**
The Terrace ★★$$$$ **206**
The Velvet Room ★★★$$ **174**
The Viceroy ★$$ **108**
The Vodka Bar and Cafe ★$ **38**
The Water Club ★★★$$$ **102**
Thompson, Ben **11**
Thompson, Jane **11**
3 Degrees North $$ **43**
Three of Cups ★$ **79**
Tibor Meat Market **175**
Tiffany & Co. **147**
Time Cafe ★$$ **81**
Tipping **6**
Tirami Sù ★★$ **178**
Tison, Rona **167** (bests)
Titan Foods **217**
Toast ★★$$ **81**
Todaro Brothers **102**
Tony & Roberto's ★$$$ **219**
Top of the Sixes $$$$ **143**
Tortilla Flats $ **69**
Toscana ★★$$ **163**
Totonno's ★★$ **215**

oukie's ★$ **56**
out Va Bien ★$$ **123**
rastevere ★★$$$ **180**
rattoria Dell'Arte ★★$$$ **127**
rattoria Pesce Pasta ★★$$ **60**
rattoria Spaghetto ★$ **58**
riangolo ★$ **180**
riBeCa **32** (chapter)
riBeCa **33** (map)
ribeca Grill ★★$$$ **36**
rio French Bakery **113**
riple 8 Palace Restaurant ★$$ **20**
riplet's Roumanian Restaurant ★$$$ **39**
ripoli ★$$ **211**
rois Jean ★★★$$$ **176**
rompe l'Oeil ★$$ **59**
ropica ★★$$$ **134**
runzo Bros. **214**
se Yang ★★$$$ **137**
urett, Wayne **93**
urkish Cuisine ★★$ **116**
uscany **144**
utta Pasta Ristorante ★$ **58**
4-Hour New York **111**
0 Mott Street ★★$ **18**
1 Club ★★$$$$ **143**
wins $$ **183**
wo Boots ★$ **78**
wo Eleven ★$$ **37**
wo Little Red Hens **212**
wo Two Two ★★★★$$$$ **198**

J

krainian ★$ **85**
makatta ★$ **52**
mberto's Clam House $$ **25**
ncle Nick's ★$ **123**
n Deux Trois, Cafe **120**
nion Square **90** (chapter and map)
nion Square Cafe ★★★★$$$ **92**
nion Square Greenmarket **91**
nion Square Wines & Spirits **92**
niversal Grill ★$ **59**
pper East Side **168** (chapter and map)
pper West Side **194** (chapter and map)
rban Grill ★$ **128**

&T Pizzeria ★$ **205**
egetarian Paradise 2 ★$ **57**
egetarian's World **114**
elgos, Monica **167** (bests)

Velvet Room, The ★★★$$ **174**
Veniero's Pasticceria & Cafe ★$ **88**
Verbena ★★★$$$ **94**
Vergina ★★$ **217**
Vernon's Jerk Paradise ★$ **110**
Veselka ★$ **85**
Vesuvio's Bakery **50**
Via Brasil ★★$$ **135**
Viceroy, The ★$$ **108**
Vico ★$$$ **185**
Vietnam ★★★$ **21**
Villabate Pasticceria & Bakery **215**
Village Atelier ★$$$ **62**
Vince & Eddie's ★★★$$ **190**
Vincent's Clam Bar ★$ **25**
Vinegar Factory **183**
Vinnie's Pizza ★$ **195**
Virgil's ★$$ **119**
Vivaldi, Caffè **62**
Vivolo ★$$ **171**
Vodka Bar and Cafe, The ★$ **38**
Vong ★★★$$$ **141**
Voulez Vous ★★$$$ **173**
Vucciria ★★$ **44**

W

Walkers $ **37**
Washington Heights **194** (chapter and map)
Washington Market ★$ **34**
Wasserstein, Wendy **185** (bests)
Water Club, The ★★★$$$ **102**
Water's Edge ★★$$$ **216**
Waverly Inn, Ye **68**
West Bank Cafe ★$$ **115**
West Side **186** (chapter and map)
West 63rd Street Steakhouse ★★$$$ **187**
Wheelchair accessibility **5**
Where's the Beef? **115**
White Acacia **216**
White Horse Tavern $ **67**
White, Kevin **34**
Whole Foods (SoHo) **48**
Whole Foods (Upper West Side) **203**
Wilkinson's 1573 Seafood Cafe ★★$$$ **180**
William Greenberg Jr. Desserts **182**
William Poll **172**
Williams Bar-B-Que **202**
Williams-Sonoma **159**
Wilson's Bakery & Restaurant ★★$$ **207**
W. Nassau Meat Market **212**

Wolfman-Gold & Good Company **46**
Wollensky's Grill ★★$$ **138**
Wolsk's **30**
Wong Kee ★$ **25**
Wonton Garden ★$ **25**
Woo Chon ★$$ **103**
Woody's ★$ **66**
Word of Mouth **170**
Word of Mouth, Cafe **170**
World Cafe ★$$ **190**
World Financial Center (WFC) **14**
World Trade Center (WTC) **13**
World Yacht Cruises ★$$$$ **115**
W.S.W. Market **20**
Wylie's ★$$ **139**

Y

Yaffa Cafe ★$ **84**
Yaffa Tea Room ★$ **35**
Yellowfingers ★$$ **156**
Ye Waverly Inn $$ **68**
Ying ★$$ **191**
Yonah Schimmel ★$ **31**
Yorkville Packing House **179**
Yura and Company ★★$ **183**

Z

Zabar's **199**
Zabar's Cafe ★$ **199**
Zarela ★★$$ **139**
Zen Palate (Theater District) ★★★$ **117**
Zen Palate (Union Square) ★★★$$ **91**
Zephyr Grill ★$$ **139**
Zigolini's Cafe ★$ **10**
Zinno ★$$ **71**
Zitella ★$ **84**
Zito & Sons Bakery, A. **60**
Zoë ★★$$$ **47**
Zucchero ★$ **173**
Zucchini ★$ **169**
Zuni ★★$ **116**
Zut! ★$$$ **34**

Restaurants by Star Ratings

Only restaurants with star ratings are listed below and at right. All restaurants are listed alphabetically in the main (preceding) index. Always call in advance to ensure a restaurant has not closed, changed its hours, or booked its tables for a private party. The restaurant price ratings are based on the average cost of an entrée for one person, excluding tax and tip.

★★★★ An Extraordinary
      Experience
★★★ Excellent
★★ Very Good
★ Good

$$$$ Big Bucks ($30 and up)
$$$ Expensive ($20–$30)
$$ Reasonable ($15–$20)
$ The Price Is Right (less than $15)

★★★★

Bouley $$$$ **34**
Chanterelle $$$$ **35**
C.T. $$$ **98**
Hudson River Club $$$$ **14**
James Beard House $$$$ **71**
La Côte Basque $$$$ **144**
Le Bernardin $$$$ **123**
Le Regence $$$$ **163**
Restaurant Daniel $$$$ **171**
San Domenico $$$$ **129**
The Four Seasons $$$$ **142**
Two Two Two $$$$ **198**
Union Square Cafe $$$ **92**

★★★

Aja $$$ **97**
Alison on Dominick Street $$$ **42**
Aquavit $$$$ **146**
Arcadia $$$$ **160**
Arizona 206 $$$ **157**
Aureole $$$$ **159**
Café des Artistes $$$ **189**
Cascabel $$$ **28**
Cellini $$$ **148**
Chikubu $$$ **135**
Christer's $$$ **126**
Cité $$$ **124**
Cucina $$ **213**
Darbar Indian Restaurant $$$ **145**
First Taste $$ **21**
Gage & Tollner $$$ **210**
Golden Unicorn $$ **20**
Gotham Bar and Grill $$$$ **74**
Hatsuhana $$$ **137**
Honmura An $$$ **48**
Il Mulino $$$ **56**
Il Toscanaccio $$$ **156**
I Trulli $$$ **99**
Japonica $$ **74**
JoJo $$$ **163**
La Caravelle $$$$ **145**
La Colombe d'Or $$$ **98**
La Réserve $$$$ **136**
Le Chantilly $$$$ **151**

Le Cirque $$$$ **164**
Le Madri $$$ **108**
Le Perigord $$$ **139**
Les Célébrités $$$$ **128**
Lespinasse $$$$ **147**
Luma $$$ **109**
Lutèce $$$$ **138**
March $$$ **150**
Matthew's $$$ **157**
Metisse $ **204**
Mitsukoshi $$$$ **151**
Monkey Bar $$$ **148**
Montrachet $$$ **37**
Morton's of Chicago $$$ **135**
Nice Restaurant $ **20**
Nobu $$$$ **36**
Oceana $$$$ **148**
Parioli Romanissimo $$$$ **177**
Park Avenue Cafe $$$ **160**
Peter Luger $$$ **212**
Petrossian $$$$ **128**
Picholine $$$ **188**
Po $ **60**
Provence $$ **52**
River Café $$$$ **210**
Shun Lee Palace $$$$ **149**
Stacy's $ **212**
Symphony Cafe $$$ **128**
Tavern on the Green $$$$ **189**
10 Pell Street $ **21**
The Manhattan Ocean Club $$$ **153**
The Markham $$$ **73**
The Post House $$$$ **160**
The Restaurant at the Stanhope Hotel $$$ **177**
The SeaGrill $$$$ **136**
The Sign of The Dove $$$$ **162**
The Velvet Room $$ **174**
The Water Club $$$ **102**
Trois Jean $$$ **176**
Verbena $$$ **94**
Vietnam $ **21**
Vince & Eddie's $$ **190**
Vong $$$ **141**
Zen Palate (Theater District) $$ **117**
Zen Palate (Union Square) $$ **91**

★★

Alley's End $ **107**
Alva $$$ **97**
American Renaissance $$$ **38**
An American Place $$$ **102**
Aria $$ **140**
Arizona Cafe $$ **157**
Arqua $$$ **37**
Aunt Sonia's $$ **213**
Avanti $$$ **122**
Azzurro $$ **181**

Baluchi's $ **43**
Bangkok Cuisine $$ **125**
Baraonda $$$ **173**
Barbetta $$$ **118**
Barney Greengrass (The Sturgeon King) $ **202**
Barocco $$$ **37**
Barolo $$$ **46**
Bar Six $ **71**
Ben Benson's Steakhouse $$$$ **124**
Biricchino $$ **111**
Bistro du Nord $$ **185**
Blu $$ **110**
Blue Ribbon $$$ **43**
Bolo $$$ **97**
Bridge Cafe $$ **12**
Bright Food Shop $ **109**
Brighton Grill $ **172**
Briscola $$$ **81**
Brunetta's $ **89**
Cabana Carioca $$ **120**
Cafe Beulah $$ **94**
Cafe Botanica $$$ **128**
Cafe Centro $$$ **134**
Cafe Crocodile $$ **170**
Cafe du Pont $$$ **149**
Cafe Evergreen $ **165**
Cafe Loup $$ **70**
Cafe Luxembourg $$$ **191**
Caffe Bondì $$$ **96**
Caffe Grazie $ **182**
Caffè Lure $ **57**
Caffè Roma $ **28**
Cal's $$ **96**
Campagna $$$ **95**
Canton $$ **20**
Capsouto Frères $$$ **39**
Carnegie Delicatessen $$ **126**
Carnegie Hill Cafe $ **185**
Castellano $$$ **126**
Caviarteria $$$$ **156**
Century Cafe $$ **120**
Charlton's $$$$ **149**
Chelsea Bistro and Bar $$ **110**
Chelsea Cafe $ **110**
Chez Jacqueline $$ **57**
Chez Josephine $$$ **115**
Chez Napoléon $$$ **123**
China Grill $$$ **143**
Chin Chin $$$ **138**
Choshi $$ **94**
Chutney Mary $$ **95**
Ciao Europa $$$ **144**
Circus $$ **161**
Ci Vediamo (Upper East Side) $$ **178**
Coco Pazzo $$$$ **171**
Cola's $ **107**
Col Legno $ **85**

olumbus Bakery $ **200**
oming or Going $$$ **152**
ontrapunto $$$ **156**
orrado $$$ **126**
ountry Cafe $ **42**
3 $ **72**
anal $ **82**
a Umberto $$$ **105**
awat $$$ **151**
elegates' Dining Room $$$ **132**
ocks Oyster Bar and Seafood
    Grill (Upper West Side) $$ **203**
ominick's $ **219**
onald Sacks $$ **15**
ragon Village $ **218**
uane Park Cafe $$$ **34**
ue $$$ **176**
A.T. $$$ **177**
Cid $ **106**
ias Corner $ **217**
io's $$$ **181**
Parador $$$ **102**
Pollo $ **183**
nnio & Michael $$$ **56**
minia $$$ **181**
stia $$$ **181**
ats-Unis $$$ **179**
ntino $$$ **129**
lidia $$$$ **150**
lissimo $ **146**
fty Seven Fifty Seven $$$$ **152**
rst $$ **79**
shin Eddie $$$ **192**
owers $$$ **92**
llonico $$$ **97**
ank's $$$ **107**
esco $$ **142**
ontiere $$$ **52**
's $$$ **140**
abriel's $$$ **187**
ascogne $$ **107**
ood Enough to Eat $$ **201**
amercy Tavern $$$ **95**
rand Ticino $$ **56**
eat Shanghai $ **20**
ove $ **63**
rry Cipriani $$$$ **156**
me $$ **60**
nan Garden $ **18**
rricane Island $$ **173**
antinori $$$ **75**
Monello $$$ **173**
Nido $$$$ **140**
agiku Japanese Restaurant
    $$$$ **137**
dochine $$ **81**
anbul Kebap $ **179**
de Palace $ **218**
iya Thai Oriental Restaurant
    (Murray Hill) $$ **100**

Jaiya Thai Oriental Restaurant
    (Queens) $$ **218**
Jamaican Hot Pot $ **207**
Jean Lafitte $$$ **153**
Jezebel $$$ **117**
Jing Fong $$ **21**
Johnney's Fish Grill $$ **15**
John's East $ **162**
John's Pizzeria $ **62**
John's West $ **189**
Josie's $ **195**
Jour et Nuit $$$ **39**
Jules $$ **84**
Karyatis $$ **217**
Kelley and Ping $ **48**
Kiiroi Hana $$ **146**
Kitchen Club $$ **29**
Kwanzaa $$ **28**
La Boîte en Bois $$$ **190**
La Folie $$$ **178**
La Grenouille $$$$ **142**
La Mangeoire $$$ **140**
La Metairie $$$ **66**
L'Ardoise $ **162**
La Ripaille $$ **69**
L'Auberge du Midi $$ **68**
Le Bilbouquet $$$ **160**
Le Boeuf à la Mode $$$ **180**
L'Ecole $$ **40**
Le Colonial $$ **151**
Le Comptoir $$$ **164**
Lemongrass Grill (Upper West
    Side) $ **204**
Lemongrass Grill (Brooklyn) $$
    213
Lenox Room $$$ **170**
Le Pactole $$$ **14**
Le Poème Restaurant Tea Room
    and Bakery $ **30**
Le Refuge $$$ **177**
L'Ermitage $$ **145**
Les Halles $$ **101**
Le Taxi $$$ **159**
Lipstick Cafe $ **141**
Lobster Box $$$ **221**
Lombardi's $ **29**
Long Shine Restaurant $ **20**
Lusardi's $$$ **174**
Mad. 61 $$$ **159**
Maison Caribe $ **181**
Malaysia & Indonesia $ **20**
Mandarin Court $ **24**
Manducatis $$ **216**
Mangia $ **153**
Mangia e Bevi $ **125**
Mark's $$$$ **176**
Martini's $$ **125**
Marylou's $$$ **73**
Mekka $ **78**
Mesa Grill $$$ **92**

Mezzogiorno $$$ **43**
Michael's $$ **145**
Mi Cocina $ **69**
Mika $$ **41**
Miracle Grill $$ **83**
Mitali $$ **80**
Mme. Romaine de Lyon $$ **159**
National Restaurant $$$ **215**
Negril Island Spice (Chelsea) $
    110
Negril Island Spice (Theater
    District) $ **116**
Nello $$$ **160**
New City Cafe $ **212**
New Hong Kong City $ **20**
Nha Trang $ **24**
Nick & Eddie $$ **43**
9 Jones Street $$ **61**
Nippon $$$$ **142**
Nonna $ **151**
Nosmo King $$$ **39**
Novità $$ **98**
Nyborg-Nelson $ **141**
Oak Room and Bar $$$ **152**
Odessa $$$ **216**
Old Devil Moon $ **88**
Old Homestead $$$$ **106**
Omen $$ **43**
One If By Land, Two If By Sea
    $$$$ **61**
Oriental Garden Seafood $$ **21**
Osteria al Doge $$ **119**
Otabe $$$ **149**
Oyster Bar and Restaurant $$$
    134
Palio $$$$ **124**
Palm $$$$ **133**
Paola's $$$ **181**
Park Bistro $$$ **101**
Patria $$$ **94**
Patsy's Pizza $ **210**
Peacock Alley $$$$ **138**
Pedro Paramo $ **89**
Peking Duck House $ **18**
Penang (Queens) $ **218**
Penang (SoHo) $$ **46**
Periyali $$$ **96**
Pierre au Tunnel $$$ **120**
Pigalle $$ **101**
Pisces $$ **79**
Primorski $$ **216**
Quatorze Bis $$$ **175**
Quattro Gatti $$ **178**
Rachel's $ **116**
Raffaele $$$ **149**
Rain $$ **200**
Rainbow & Stars $$$$ **136**
Rao's $$$$ **206**
Raoul's $$$ **50**
Rasputin $$ **215**

Remi $$$ **126**
René Pujol $$ **123**
Restaurant Florent $$ **69**
Restaurant 44 $$$ **135**
Road to Mandalay $$ **28**
Ronasi $$ **162**
Rosa Mexicano $$$ **150**
Rose Cafe $$ **73**
Rosemarie's $$$ **34**
Royal Siam $ **110**
Saigon House Restaurant $ **24**
Salaam Bombay $ **32**
Sala Thai $ **183**
Sammy's Famous Roumanian Jewish Steakhouse $$$ **30**
San Pietro $$$ **148**
Sant Ambroeus $$$ **177**
Sarabeth's at the Whitney $$ **171**
Sarabeth's Kitchen (Upper East Side) $$ **184**
Sarabeth's Kitchen (Upper West Side) $$ **198**
Savoy $$$ **47**
Sazerac House $$ **64**
Scaletta $$$ **197**
Seryna $$$ **142**
Sette Mezzo $$$ **165**
Sfuzzi (West Side) $$ **189**
Shabu Tatsu $$ **173**
Shin Jung $ **219**
Sichuan Pavilion $$$ **132**
Silk $$ **100**
Silver Palace $$ **21**
Sirabella $$ **180**
Sistina $$$ **179**
Smith & Wollensky $$$ **138**
Snaps $$ **133**
Soleil $$ **164**
Solera $$ **141**
Sonia Rose $$$ **100**
Sparks $$$$ **133**
Stella del Mare $$$ **132**
Sushisay $$$ **137**
Sylvia's $$ **207**
Table d'Hôte $$$ **184**
Takahachi $ **79**
Takesushi $$$$ **134**
Tammany Hall $$ **100**
Tanti Baci Caffè $ **66**
Tartine $ **67**
Tasca Porto $ **42**
Tavola $$$ **175**
Tempo $$$ **101**
Thailand Restaurant $$ **24**
The Adoré $ **74**
The Black Sheep $$$ **67**
The Cake Bar & Cafe $ **74**
The City Bakery (Union Square) $ **92**

The Hunt Room at the New York Palace Hotel $$$ **137**
The Markham Cafe $ **73**
The New Prospect Café $$ **214**
The Polo $$$ **166**
The Rainbow Room $$$$ **135**
The Russian Tea Room $$$ **127**
The Terrace $$$$ **206**
Tirami Sù $ **178**
Toast $$ **81**
Toscana $$ **163**
Totonno's $ **215**
Trastevere $$$ **180**
Trattoria Dell'Arte $$$ **127**
Trattoria Pesce Pasta $$ **60**
Tribeca Grill $$$ **36**
Tropica $$$ **134**
Tse Yang $$$ **137**
Turkish Cuisine $ **116**
20 Mott Street $ **18**
21 Club $$$$ **143**
Vergina $ **217**
Via Brasil $$ **135**
Voulez Vous $$$ **173**
Vucciria $ **44**
Water's Edge $$$ **216**
West 63rd Street Steakhouse $$$ **187**
Wilkinson's 1573 Seafood Cafe $$$ **180**
Wilson's Bakery & Restaurant $$ **207**
Wollensky's Grill $$ **138**
Yura and Company $ **183**
Zarela $ **139**
Zoë $$$ **47**
Zuni $ **116**

★

Abby Restaurant and Bar $$ **102**
Acme Bar & Grill $$ **81**
Adrienne $$$ **146**
Aesop's Tables $$ **221**
Aggie's $ **56**
Alla Sera $ **175**
Allegria $$ **144**
Ambassador Grill Restaurant $$$ **132**
American Festival Cafe $$$ **136**
Amici Miei $$$ **49**
Amsterdam's Bar and Rotisserie $$ **199**
Anche Vivolo $$ **151**
Andalousia $ **60**
Angelica Kitchen $ **89**
Angelo's of Mulberry Street $$ **27**
Anglers & Writers $ **62**
Annie's $ **174**
Areo $$ **214**
Artepasta $ **68**

Arturo's Pizzeria $ **50**
Asia $$ **164**
Au Bon Coin $ **57**
Au Cafe $ **125**
Au Mandarin $$ **15**
Baby Jake's $ **78**
Bali Burma $ **117**
B & H Dairy and Vegetarian Cuisine Restaurant $ **83**
Barking Dog Luncheonette $ **18**
Bar Pitti $ **58**
Basset Coffee & Tea Co. $ **34**
Bayamo $$ **81**
Becco $$ **118**
Bendix Diner $ **109**
Benito I and Benito II $ **27**
Benny's Burritos $ **70**
Benny's (Upper West Side) $ **19**
Berrys $$ **44**
Bice $$$ **147**
Bill's Gay Nineties $$ **148**
Billy's $$ **139**
Blanche's Organic Cafe $ **166**
Bleecker Street Pastry Shop $ **5**
Boathouse Cafe $$$ **171**
Boca Chica $ **78**
Bo Ky Restaurant $ **24**
Bombay Palace $$ **143**
Boom $$$ **46**
Bosco $$ **172**
Bowery Bar $$ **80**
Bradley's $$ **75**
Brasserie $$$ **142**
Brio $$ **157**
Broadway Diner $ **126**
Broadway Grill $$$ **122**
Brothers Barbecue $ **197**
Brother's Bar-B-Q $ **56**
Bruno $$$ **150**
B. Smith's $$$ **122**
Bubby's $ **36**
Busby's $$ **184**
Cafe Andrusha $ **183**
Cafe at Brooklyn Museum $ **21**
Café Con Leche $ **199**
Cafe de Bruxelles $$ **70**
Café Des Sports $ **123**
Cafe Divino $ **179**
Cafe Europa $ **127**
Cafe Gitane $ **29**
Cafe Greco $$ **165**
Cafe Journal $ **102**
Café La Fortuna $ **192**
Cafe Lalo $ **201**
Cafe Le Gamin $ **52**
Cafe Metairie $$ **178**
Cafe Mogador $$ **84**
Cafe Mona Lisa $ **62**
Café Nicholson $$$ **150**
Cafe Picasso $ **66**

Cafe Riazor $ **106**
Cafe SFA $ **137**
Cafe St. John $ **205**
Cafe-Tabac $$ **85**
Cafe Un Deux Trois $$ **120**
Cafe Word of Mouth $ **170**
Caffe Bianco $ **174**
Caffè Borgia $ **57**
Caffé Cefalú $ **66**
Caffè Dante $ **57**
Caffè del Corso $ **145**
Caffè della Pace $ **83**
Caffe Med $ **165**
Caffè Napoli $ **25**
Caffè Pane e Cioccolato $ **75**
Caffè Popolo $ **197**
Caffè Reggio $ **57**
Caffè Vivaldi $ **62**
Cajun $$ **106**
Campagnola $$ **170**
Can $$ **50**
Captain's Table $$$ **133**
Caravan of Dreams $ **79**
Caribe $ **67**
Carrot Top Pastries $ **207**
Casa di Pré $$ **68**
Casa La Femme $$ **48**
Casani's $$ **78**
Casa Rosa $$ **211**
Cent' Anni $$$ **58**
Cesarina $$$ **143**
Chantal Cafe $$ **126**
Chantale's Cajun Kitchen $ **114**
Chaz & Wilsons Grill $$ **198**
Chelsea Trattoria $$ **106**
Chez Bernard $ **40**
Chez Brigitte $ **68**
Chez Laurence Patisserie $ **103**
Chez Ma Tante Cafe $$ **65**
Chez Michallet $$$ **63**
Chiam $$$ **138**
China Fun (East Side) $ **165**
China Fun (West Side) $ **193**
Christ Cella $$$$ **133**
City Bakery (Midtown) $ **148**
City Crab $$ **94**
Ci Vediamo (East Village) $ **79**
Claire $$ **108**
Coconut Grill $ **174**
Coffee Shop $ **92**
Colors $$$ **133**
Copeland's $$ **207**
Corrado Cafe $ **157**
Cowgirl Hall of Fame $ **64**
Cub Cafe $ **50**
Cub Room $$$ **50**
Cucina and Company $ **134**
Cucina di Pesce $ **80**
Cucina Vivolo $ **172**
Cuisine de Saigon $ **71**

Dama $ **59**
Da Nico $ **27**
Da Silvano $$ **58**
Dean & DeLuca Cafe $ (Midtown) **136**
Dean & DeLuca Cafe $ (SoHo) **48**
Delhi Palace $$ **217**
Demarchelier $$ **182**
Demi $$$ **185**
Diva $ **40**
Divino Ristorante $$ **179**
Dix et Sept $$ **66**
Docks Oyster Bar and Seafood Grill (Midtown) $$$ **132**
Dojo $ **83**
Dojo West $ **75**
Dolce $$$ **137**
Dolci On Park Caffè $$ **103**
East Corner Wonton $ **20**
Eastern Seafood Company $ **198**
Ecco-Là $ **184**
Eden Rock $ **202**
Edgar's Cafe $ **201**
Eighteenth and Eighth $ **107**
E.J.'s Luncheonette (Upper East Side) $ **170**
E.J.'s Luncheonette (Upper West Side) $ **200**
El Charro Español (Greenwich Village) $$ **72**
El Charro Español (Murray Hill) $$ **103**
El Faro $$ **69**
Ellen's Cafe and Bake Shop $ **15**
El Rincon de España $$ **56**
El Teddy's $$ **37**
Empire Diner $ **109**
Enchilada Johnny's $ **181**
Eros $$ **150**
Family Noodle Restaurant $ **19**
Favia $ **157**
Felix $$$ **39**
Ferrier $$ **164**
Film Center Cafe $ **117**
Fine & Schapiro $$ **193**
Fiorello's $$$ **188**
Flamingo East $$ **89**
Fletcher Morgan Provisions $ **163**
Food Attitude $ **159**
Food Bar $ **107**
Frankie and Johnnie's $$$ **120**
Franklin Station $ **37**
Fraunces Tavern Restaurant $$$ **10**
Freddie and Pepper's Gourmet Pizza $ **196**
French Roast $ **71**
Fresco Tortilla Grill $ **98**
Friend of a Farmer $$ **94**
Fujiyama Mama $$ **200**

Gallagher's Steak House $$$$ **124**
Gianni's $$ **12**
Gigino $$ **32**
Gino's $$ **158**
Giovanni $$$ **144**
Girasole $$$ **177**
Global 33 $ **80**
Gotham City Diner $$ **179**
Gran Caffè Degli Artisti $ **72**
Greenhouse Cafe $$ **14**
Greenwich Cafe $ **67**
Grotta Azzurra $$ **28**
Grove Street Cafe $$ **63**
Guido's $$ **114**
Gus' Place $$ **63**
Hale and Hearty $$ **163**
Hamburger Harry's $ **120**
Harley Davidson Cafe $$ **145**
Harry's Burrito Junction $ **191**
Haveli $ **80**
Hee Seung Fung (HSF) $$ **21**
Henry's End $$ **210**
Hero Boy $ **114**
Hi-Life Restaurant & Lounge (Upper East Side) $$ **169**
Hi-Life Restaurant & Lounge (Upper West Side) $$ **201**
House of Vegetarian $ **24**
Il Cortile $$$ **25**
Il Ponte Vecchio $$ **56**
Il Vagabondo $$ **162**
Il Valletto $$$ **158**
Il Vigneto $$ **150**
Indian Cafe $ **205**
India Pavilion $ **128**
In Padella $ **85**
Isabella $$ **197**
Island $$$ **185**
Iso $$ **88**
Isola $$ **200**
I Tre Merli $$$ **49**
Jackson Diner $ **217**
Jackson Hole $ **161**
Jane Street Seafood Cafe $$ **69**
Jean Claude $ **50**
Jerry's $$ (SoHo) **48**
Jerry's $$ (Upper West Side) **196**
Jim McMullen $$ **174**
Joe Babbington's Joint $ **109**
John's of Twelfth Street $$ **89**
Jubilee $$ **140**
Judson Grill $$$ **124**
Junior's $ **211**
Kaffeehaus $ **106**
Katz's Delicatessen $ **31**
Khyber Pass $ **83**
Kiev $ **83**
King Crab $$ **125**
Kin Khao $$ **46**
Kleine Konditorei $$ **182**

Knickerbocker Bar & Grill $$ **73**
La Barca $$$ **10**
La Bohème $$ **58**
La Bonne Soupe $ **144**
La Boulangère $ **95**
L'Acajou $$$ **96**
La Collina $$ **184**
La Focaccia $$ **68**
La Jumelle $ **40**
La Linea $ **78**
La Lunchonette $$ **107**
La Madama Cafe and Bakery $
   109
La Mela $ **28**
La Mirabelle $$$ **202**
Landmark Tavern $$ **117**
La Pequeña Colombia $ **218**
La Piazzetta di Quisisana $$$ **172**
La Rosita $ **205**
La Taza de Oro $ **106**
La Tour D'Or $$$ **12**
Lattanzi $$$ **118**
Le Bistrot de Maxim's $$$ **160**
Le Cafe $$ **105**
Le Madeleine $$$ **116**
Le Max $$ **119**
Le Pescadou $$$ **52**
Le Petit Hulot $$$ **166**
Le Pistou $$ **158**
Le Relais $$$ **160**
Les Deux Gamins $ **63**
Le Select $$ **201**
Les Pyrénées $$$ **123**
Les Routiers $$ **203**
Les Sans Culottes $$$ **150**
Les Sans Culottes West $$$ **118**
Le Streghe $$ **40**
Letizia $$$ **169**
Le Train Bleu $$ **156**
Let Them Eat Cake $ **42**
Le Veau d'Or $$$ **159**
Lex $$$ **162**
Life Cafe $ **88**
Limbo $ **79**
Lion's Head $$ **64**
Lola $$$ **96**
Lotfi's Moroccan $ **118**
Louie's Westside Cafe $$ **199**
Louisiana Community Bar and
   Grill $$ **78**
Lucky Cheng's $ **78**
L'Udo $$ **81**
Luke's Bar & Grill $ **176**
Luna $$ **25**
Luzia $ **199**
Lyn's Cafe $ **146**
Mackinac Grill $$ **198**
Macmed Spuntino $ **82**
Main Street $$ **200**
Mambo Grill $$ **177**

Mana $ **203**
Manhattan Bistro $ **46**
Manhattan Cafe $$$ **162**
Man Ray $$ **108**
Maple Garden Duck House $$ **141**
Mappamondo Restaurant $ **69**
Marchi's $$$ **102**
Marion's Continental Restaurant
   and Lounge $$ **80**
Mario's $$$ **219**
Marlowe $$ **118**
Marquet Patisserie $ **74**
Maruzzella $$ **175**
Marys $ **59**
Match $$ **47**
Mavalli Palace $ **101**
Mayfair $ **140**
Mayrose $ **95**
Mediterraneo $$ **165**
Melanie's Natural $ **72**
Menchanko-tei $ **144**
Merenda $ **179**
Meriken $$ **108**
Metropolitan Cafe $$ **140**
Mezzaluna $$ **172**
Michelle's Kitchen $ **158**
Mickey Mantle's $$ **153**
Mike's American Bar and Grill $
   117
Milady $ **50**
Mimi's Macaroni $ **204**
Minetta Tavern $$ **57**
Mo' Better $ **203**
Mocca Hungarian $ **181**
Monsoon $ **199**
Montague Street Saloon $ **210**
Moondance Diner $ **39**
Morgan Cafe $ **103**
Moroccan Star $ **211**
Mortimer's $$$ **172**
Mo's Caribbean Bar and Grille $
   173
Moustache $ **62**
Mustang Grill $ **181**
ñ $ **41**
Nadine's $$ **69**
Nam Wah Tea Parlor $ **21**
Nathan's Famous $ **215**
New Chao Chow $ **25**
News Bar $ **93**
New World Grill $ **122**
Nicola Paone $$$ **102**
Nino's $$ **169**
Noho Star $ **78**
N.Y. Noodletown $ **21**
Ocean Palace Seafood
   Restaurant $ **214**
Old Town Bar $ **93**
Ollie's Noodle Shop $ **201**
Once Upon a Tart $ **50**

O'Neals' $$$ **188**
One City Cafe $ **106**
107 West $$ **205**
Orbit $ **59**
Oriental Pearl $ **25**
Orologio $ **88**
Orso $$$ **118**
Ozu $ **202**
Ozzie's $ **213**
Palm Court $$ **152**
Pamir $$ **173**
Pandit $ **202**
Panevino $$ **187**
Paris Commune $$ **67**
Park Avalon $ **93**
Parma $$$ **176**
Parnell's $ **140**
Pasqua $ **142**
Passage to India $ **80**
Passport $ **84**
Pastrami King $ **218**
Patisserie J. Lanciani $ **66**
Patsy's Pizzeria $ **206**
Pearson's Stick to Your Ribs $
   216
Pen & Pencil $$$$ **133**
Per Bacco $ **99**
Persepolis $ **173**
Peruvian Restaurant $ **122**
Petaluma $$$ **169**
Pete's Tavern $$ **94**
Pho Bâng Restaurant $ **19**
Phoebe's $ **197**
Phoenix Garden $$$ **132**
Piccolo Angolo $ **69**
Pig Heaven $$ **179**
Pink Teacup $ **63**
Pipeline $$ **14**
P. J. Clarke's $$ **149**
Planet Hollywood $$ **127**
Plaza Garibaldi $ **218**
Pong Sri $$ **122**
Popover Café $$ **202**
Positively 104th Street Cafe $ **204**
Primavera $$$$ **180**
Prince Street Bar & Restaurant $
   48
Rafaella Restaurant $$ **66**
Rangoon Cafe $ **84**
Ratner's $$ **30**
Revolution $ **116**
Rice and Beans $ **123**
Rikyu $$ **191**
Ristorante Taormina $$ **27**
Riverrun Cafe $$ **36**
Rocco Pastry Shop & Cafe $ **59**
Roettele A.G. $$ **83**
Rolf's Restaurant $$ **98**
Roumeli Taverna $$ **216**
Rubyfruit Bar & Grill $ **64**

umbul's Pastry Shop $ 63
ussian Samovar $$ 125
ahara East $ 89
alam $ 71
amalita's Tortilla Factory $ 178
am's $ 120
am's Noodle Shop $ 100
anta Fe $$ 190
anta Fe Grill $ 213
apporo $ 122
aranac $ 185
ardi's $$$ 119
nd Avenue Deli $$ 88
el et Poivre $$ 163
erendipity $$ 157
ette MoMA $$$ 143
evilla $$ 66
fuzzi (Lower Manhattan) $$ 15
haan $$ 135
hark Bar $ 196
helby $$ 165
hun Lee Dynasty $$$ 189
am Inn $ 126
idewalkers $$ 192
ilk Road Palace $ 200
loppy Louie's $$$ 10
oHo Kitchen and Bar $ 46
ouen Downtown $ 52
oup Kitchen $ 126
partina $$ 35
pring Street Natural $ 47
teak Frites $$ 92
t. Maggie's Cafe $$ 10
un Lin Garden $ 24
utton Watering Hole $ 149
  $$ 47
ai Hong Lau $ 24
aliesin $$$ 13
all Ships Bar & Grill $$ 14
aquería de México $ 68
ea and Sympathy $ 70
ea Box Cafe $ 147
ennessee Mountain $$ 46
eresa's $ 79
errace Cafe, Brooklyn Botanic
  Garden $ 214
erramare $ 164
hai House Cafe $ 39
he Bagel $ 61
he Big Enchilada (Greenwich
  Village) $ 74
he Big Enchilada (Murray Hill) $
  100
he Bistro $$$ 146
he Bread Shop $ 206
he Cafe $$ 147
he Cafe at Grand Central $ 135
he Captain's Ketch $$$ 12
he Cornelia Street Café $ 61
he Cotton Club $$ 206

The Cream Puff $ 165
The Cupping Room Cafe $$ 41
The Grange Hall $ 62
The Ludlow Street Cafe $ 31
The Manhattan Chili Company $
  119
The Mezzanine $$$ 120
The Odeon $$ 35
The Pie $ 181
The Red Tulip $$ 173
The Right Bank $$ 166
The Viceroy $$ 108
The Vodka Bar and Cafe $ 38
Three of Cups $ 79
Time Cafe $$ 81
Tony & Roberto's $$$ 219
Toukie's $ 56
Tout Va Bien $$ 123
Trattoria Spaghetto $ 58
Triangolo $ 180
Triple 8 Palace Restaurant $$ 20
Triplet's Roumanian Restaurant
  $$$ 39
Tripoli $$ 211
Trompe l'Oeil $$ 59
Tutta Pasta Ristorante $ 58
Two Boots $ 78
Two Eleven $$ 37
Ukrainian $ 85
Umakatta $ 52
Uncle Nick's $ 123
Universal Grill $ 59
Urban Grill $ 128
V&T Pizzeria $ 205
Vegetarian Paradise 2 $ 57
Veniero's Pasticceria & Cafe $$ 88
Vernon's Jerk Paradise $ 110
Veselka $ 85
Vico $$$ 185
Village Atelier $$$ 62
Vincent's Clam Bar $ 25
Vinnie's Pizza $ 195
Virgil's $$ 119
Vivolo $$ 171
Washington Market $ 34
West Bank Cafe $$ 115
Wong Kee $ 25
Wonton Garden $ 25
Woo Chon $$ 103
Woody's $ 66
World Cafe $$ 190
World Yacht Cruises $$$$ 115
Wylie's $$ 139
Yaffa Cafe $ 84
Yaffa Tea Room $ 35
Yellowfingers $$ 156
Ying $$ 191
Yonah Schimmel $ 31
Zabar's Cafe $ 199
Zephyr Grill $$ 139

Zinno $$ 71
Zitella $ 84
Zucchero $ 173
Zucchini $ 169
Zut! $$$ 34

Restaurants by Description

The following index lists restaurants by the type of food served. All restaurants are listed alphabetically in the main index (above) and restaurants with stars are listed in the ratings index (also above).

Afghan

Khyber Pass 83
Pamir 173

African, North

Moroccan
Andalousia 60
Cafe Mogador 84
Lotfi's Moroccan 118
Moroccan Star 211

Tunisian
Le Poème Restaurant Tea Room
  and Bakery 30

American

Aggie's 56
Alley's End 107
Alva 97
Ambassador Grill Restaurant 132
American Festival Cafe 136
American Renaissance 38
Amsterdam's Bar and Rotisserie
  199
An American Place 102
Anglers & Writers 62
Arcadia 160
Aria 140
Au Cafe 125
Baby Jake's 78
Barking Dog Luncheonette 184
Ben Benson's Steakhouse 124
Bill's Gay Nineties 148
Billy's 139
Book-Friends Cafe 93
Boomer's Sports Club 196
Boulevard 203
Bowery Bar 80
Boxers 61
Bradley's 75
Brasserie 142
Brighton Grill 172
Broadway Diner 126

Index

Broadway Grill 122
Bubby's 36
Busby's 184
Cafe Centro 134
Cafe Risque 68
Cafe SFA 137
Cafe-Tabac 85
Cafe Word of Mouth 170
Cal's 96
Carnegie Hill Cafe 185
Cedar Tavern 75
Chaz & Wilsons Grill 198
Christer's 126
Chumleys 63
City Bakery (Midtown) 148
Cloisters Cafe 85
Coconut Grill 174
Coming or Going 152
Contrapunto 156
Corner Bistro 68
C3 72
Cub Room 50
Cucina and Company 134
Dallas BBQ (East Village) 83
Dallas BBQ (Greenwich Village) 73
Dallas BBQ (West Side) 192
Danal 82
Demi 185
Donald Sacks 15
E.A.T. 177
Eighteenth and Eighth 107
Ellen's Cafe and Bake Shop 15
Ellen's Stardust Diner 127
Empire Diner 109
Etats-Unis 179
Fanelli Cafe 48
Fashion Cafe 136
Felissimo 146
Fifty Seven Fifty Seven 152
Film Center Cafe 117
Frank's 107
Fraunces Tavern Restaurant 10
Friend of a Farmer 94
Good Enough to Eat 201
Gotham Bar and Grill 74
Gotham City Diner 179
Gramercy Tavern 95
Great Jones Cafe 80
Greenhouse Cafe 14
Grove 63
Hale and Hearty 163
Hamburger Harry's 120
Hard Rock Cafe 127
Harley Davidson Cafe 145
Hi-Life Restaurant & Lounge
    (Upper East Side) 169
Hi-Life Restaurant & Lounge
    (Upper West Side) 201
Home 60
Hour Glass Tavern 118

Hudson River Club 14
Iridium 187
Jekyll and Hyde 61
Jerry's (SoHo) 48
Jerry's (Upper West Side) 196
Jim McMullen 174
Joe Allen 118
Joe Babbington's Joint 109
Josie's 195
Judson Grill 124
Kaffeehaus 106
Kenn's Broome Street Bar 41
Knickerbocker Bar & Grill 73
Landmark Tavern 117
Lee Mazzilli's Sports Cafe 191
Lenox Room 170
Lex 162
Liberty Cafe 11
Lincoln Tavern 188
Lion's Head 64
Lipstick Cafe 141
Louie's Westside Cafe 199
Luke's Bar & Grill 176
Luma 109
Mackinac Grill 198
Main Street 200
Manhattan Cafe 162
March 150
Martini's 125
Marys 59
Matthew's 157
Mayfair 140
Melanie's Natural 72
Metropolitan Cafe 140
Michael's 145
Mickey Mantle's 153
Mike's American Bar and Grill
    117
Milady 50
Mo' Better 203
Monkey Bar 148
Montague Street Saloon 210
Moondance Diner 39
Mulholland Drive Cafe 161
Museum Cafe 197
Nathan's Famous 215
New City Cafe 212
Nick & Eddie 43
9 Jones Street 61
Nosmo King 39
Oak Room and Bar 152
Old Devil Moon 88
Old Homestead 106
Old Town Bar 93
O'Neals' 188
107 West 205
Orbit 59
Park Avalon 93
Park Avenue Cafe 160
Parnell's 140

Patio Restaurant 113
Penn-Top Bar and Terrace 146
Pete's Tavern 94
Phoebe's 197
Pipeline 14
P.J. Clarke's 149
Planet Hollywood 127
Popover Café 202
Positively 104th Street Cafe 204
Pot Belly Stove Cafe 64
Rachel's 116
Rainbow & Stars 136
Restaurant 44 135
River Café 210
Riviera Cafe 64
Rose Cafe 73
Rubyfruit Bar & Grill 64
Sam's 120
Sarabeth's at the Whitney 171
Sarabeth's Kitchen (Upper East
    Side) 184
Sarabeth's Kitchen (Upper West
    Side) 198
Saranac 185
Serendipity 157
7A 83
Shelby 165
Smith & Wollensky 138
SoHo Kitchen and Bar 46
Spring Street Natural 47
St. Maggie's Cafe 10
Sutton Watering Hole 149
Symphony Cafe 128
T 47
Taliesin 12
Tall Ships Bar & Grill 14
Tavern on the Green 189
Teachers Too 199
Tennessee Mountain 46
The Bagel 61
The Cafe at Grand Central 135
The City Bakery (Union Square)
    92
The Ear Inn 42
The Grange Hall 62
The Hunt Room at the New York
    Palace Hotel 137
The Jekyll and Hyde Club 129
The Markham 73
The Markham Cafe 73
The Mezzanine 120
The New Prospect Café 214
The Odeon 35
The Polo 166
The Post House 160
The Restaurant at the Stanhope
    Hotel 177
The Sign of The Dove 162
The Sporting Club 36
The Viceroy 108

The Water Club **102**
Time Cafe **81**
Top of the Sixes **143**
Tribeca Grill **36**
Trompe l'Oeil **59**
Tropica **134**
Union Square Cafe **92**
Universal Grill **59**
Urban Grill **128**
Verbena **94**
Village Atelier **62**
Vince & Eddie's **190**
Walkers **37**
West Bank Cafe **115**
White Horse Tavern **67**
Wollensky's Grill **138**
Yellowfingers **156**
Ye Waverly Inn **68**
Yura and Company **183**
Zephyr Grill **139**
Zigolini's Cafe **10**
Zoë **47**

Asian

Asia **164**
Bright Food Shop **109**
China Grill **143**
Gauguin **152**
Kelley and Ping **48**
Lucky Cheng's **78**
Rain **200**
Zen Palate (Theater District) **117**
Zen Palate (Union Square) **91**

Burmese

Bali Burma **117**
Rangoon Cafe **84**
Road to Mandalay **28**

Chinese

Au Mandarin **14**
Bayamo **81**
Cafe Evergreen **165**
Canton **20**
Chiam **138**
China Fun (East Side) **165**
China Fun (West Side) **193**
Chin Chin **138**
Dish of Salt **121**
Dragon Village **218**
East Corner Wonton **20**
Family Noodle Restaurant **19**
First Taste **21**
Fu's **140**
Golden Unicorn **20**
Great Shanghai **20**
Hee Seung Fung (HSF) **21**
House of Vegetarian **24**
Hunan Garden **18**
Jade Palace **218**
Jing Fong **21**

La Caridad **197**
Long Shine Restaurant **20**
Mandarin Court **24**
Maple Garden Duck House **141**
Nam Wah Tea Parlor **21**
New Chao Chow **25**
New Hong Kong City **20**
Nice Restaurant **20**
N.Y. Noodletown **21**
Ocean Palace Seafood
    Restaurant **214**
Ollie's Noodle Shop **201**
Oriental Garden Seafood **21**
Oriental Pearl **25**
Peking Duck House **18**
Phoenix Garden **132**
Pig Heaven **179**
Sam's Noodle Shop **100**
Shun Lee Dynasty **189**
Shun Lee Palace **149**
Sichuan Pavilion **132**
Silver Palace **21**
Sun Lin Garden **24**
Tai Hong Lau **24**
10 Pell Street **21**
The Silk Road Palace **200**
Triple 8 Palace Restaurant **20**
Tse Yang **137**
20 Mott Street **18**
Vegetarian Paradise 2 **57**
Wong Kee **25**
Wonton Garden **25**
Ying **191**

Indonesian

Bali Burma **117**
Malaysia & Indonesia **20**

Japanese

Chikubu **135**
Choshi **94**
Dojo **83**
Dojo West **75**
Fujiyama Mama **200**
Hatsuhana **137**
Honmura An **48**
Inagiku Japanese Restaurant **137**
Iso **88**
Japonica **74**
Jour et Nuit **39**
Kiiroi Hana **146**
Kitchen Club **29**
Mana **203**
Menchanko-tei **144**
Meriken **108**
Mika **41**
Mitsukoshi **151**
Nippon **142**
Nobu **36**
Omen **43**
Otabe **149**
Ozu **202**

Rikyu **191**
Sapporo **122**
Seryna **142**
Shabu Tatsu **173**
Sushisay **137**
Takahachi **79**
Takesushi **134**
Tea Box Cafe **147**
Umakatta **52**

Korean

Shin Jung **219**
Woo Chon **103**

Malaysian

Franklin Station **37**
Malaysia & Indonesia **20**
Penang (Queens) **218**
Penang (Soho) **46**
3 Degrees North **43**

Thai

Bangkok Cuisine **125**
Jaiya Thai Oriental Restaurant
    (Murray Hill) **100**
Jaiya Thai Oriental Restaurant
    (Queens) **218**
Kin Khao **46**
Lemongrass Grill (Upper West
    Side) **204**
Lemongrass Grill (Brooklyn) **213**
Pong Sri **122**
Road to Mandalay **28**
Royal Siam **110**
Sala Thai **183**
Siam Inn **126**
Thai House Cafe **39**
Thailand Restaurant **24**
Vong **141**

Vietnamese

Bo Ky Restaurant **24**
Can **50**
Cuisine de Saigon **71**
Indochine **81**
Le Colonial **151**
Monsoon **199**
Nha Trang **24**
Pho Bâng Restaurant **19**
Saigon House Restaurant **24**
Vietnam **21**

Austrian

Kaffeehaus **106**

Bakery

Cafe Journal **102**
Caffè Roma **28**
Chez Laurence Patisserie **103**
Columbus Bakery **200**
Ferrara **27**
Food Attitude **159**

Index

La Boulangère **95**
Let Them Eat Cake **42**
Marquet Patisserie **74**
Rumbul's Pastry Shop **63**
Tartine **67**
The Bread Shop **206**
The Cake Bar & Cafe **74**
Veniero's Pasticceria & Cafe **88**
Wilson's Bakery & Restaurant **207**

Barbecue

Brothers Barbecue **197**
Brother's Bar-B-Q **56**
Dallas BBQ (East Village) **83**
Dallas BBQ (Greenwich Village) **73**
Dallas BBQ (West Side) **192**
Pearson's Stick to Your Ribs **216**
Virgil's **119**
Wylie's **139**

Belgian

Cafe de Bruxelles **70**

Bistro

Bar Six **71**
Cafe Le Gamin **52**
Caffè Lure **57**
French Roast **71**
Le Figaro Café **57**
Mika **41**
Paris Commune **67**
Rose Cafe **73**
Steak Frites **92**
Tartine **67**
The Cornelia Street Café **61**

Cafe

Basset Coffee & Tea Co **34**
Bell Caffè **42**
Big Cup **109**
Bleecker Street Pastry Shop **59**
Cafe at Brooklyn Museum **214**
Cafe Europa **127**
Cafe Fledermaus **12**
Cafe Gitane **29**
Cafe Journal **102**
Café La Fortuna **192**
Cafe Lalo **201**
Cafe L'Etoile **113**
Cafe Mona Lisa **62**
Cafe Mozart **191**
Cafe Orlin **85**
Cafe Picasso **66**
Caffè Borgia **57**
Caffè Dante **57**
Caffè del Corso **145**
Caffè della Pace **83**

Caffè Lucca **58**
Caffe Med **165**
Caffè Napoli **25**
Caffè Pane e Cioccolato **75**
Caffè Reggio **57**
Caffè Roma **28**
Caffè Vivaldi **62**
Carrot Top Pastries **207**
Cellar Grill **113**
Chez Bernard **40**
Chez Laurence Patisserie **103**
City Bakery (Midtown) **148**
Columbus Bakery **200**
Corrado Cafe **157**
Cub Cafe **50**
Dean & DeLuca Cafe (Midtown) **136**
Dean & DeLuca Cafe (SoHo) **48**
Eclair **193**
Edgar's Cafe **201**
Ferrara **27**
Food Attitude **159**
Garden Cafe **198**
Gran Caffè Degli Artisti **72**
La Boulangère **95**
La Linea **78**
Le Cafe **105**
Le Figaro Café **57**
Let Them Eat Cake **42**
Life Cafe **88**
Limbo **78**
Lyn's Cafe **146**
Macmed Spuntino **82**
Marquet Patisserie **74**
Michelle's Kitchen **158**
Morgan Cafe **103**
News Bar **93**
Once Upon a Tart **50**
Ozzie's **213**
Palm Court **152**
Pasqua **142**
Patisserie J. Lanciani **66**
Peacock Caffè **72**
Rocco Pastry Shop & Cafe **59**
Rumbul's Pastry Shop **63**
Tea Box Cafe **147**
Terrace Cafe, Brooklyn Botanic Garden **214**
The Adoré **74**
The Bread Shop **206**
The Cafe **147**
The Cake Bar & Cafe **74**
The City Bakery (Union Square) **92**
The Cornelia Street Café **61**
The Cream Puff **165**
The Right Bank **166**
Veniero's Pasticceria & Cafe **88**
Washington Market **34**
Zabar's Cafe **199**

Cajun/Creole

Baby Jake's **78**
Cajun **106**
Chantale's Cajun Kitchen **114**
Great Jones Cafe **80**
Louisiana Community Bar and Grill **78**
Sazerac House **64**
Shark Bar **196**
The Ludlow Street Cafe **31**
Two Boots **78**

Caribbean/Tropical

Day-O **70**
La Madama Cafe and Bakery **109**
Lola **96**
Maison Caribe **181**
Mo's Caribbean Bar and Grille **173**
Tropica **134**

Cuban

Bayamo **81**
Café Con Leche **199**
La Caridad **197**
La Rosita **205**
La Taza de Oro **106**

Jamaican

Jamaican Hot Pot **207**
Negril Island Spice (Chelsea) **11**
Negril Island Spice (Theater District) **116**
Vernon's Jerk Paradise **110**

West Indian

Caribe **67**

Continental

Adrienne **146**
Aureole **159**
Berrys **44**
Cafe Greco **165**
Cellar in the Sky **13**
Copeland's **207**
Delegates' Dining Room **132**
Duane Park Cafe **34**
Grove Street Cafe **63**
Henry's End **210**
Island **185**
Kitchen Club **29**
Le Train Bleu **156**
Marion's Continental Restaurant and Lounge **80**
Mortimer's **172**
One If By Land, Two If By Sea **61**
Petrossian **128**
Restaurant Florent **69**
Riverrun Cafe **36**
Rumpelmayer's **153**
Sardi's **119**

avoy **47**
e Cupping Room Cafe **41**
he Four Seasons **142**
e Rainbow Room **135**
e Saloon **189**
he Terrace **206**
l Club **143**
wo Two Two **198**
'orld Yacht Cruises **115**
ephyr Grill **139**

eli
arney Greengrass (The
   Sturgeon King) **202**
arnegie Delicatessen **126**
ne & Schapiro **193**
nior's **211**
aplan's **156**
atz's Delicatessen **31**
ox Around the Clock **96**
astrami King **218**
age Delicatessen **126**
e Bagel **61**

iner
endix Diner **109**
J.'s Luncheonette (Upper East
   Side) **170**
J.'s Luncheonette (Upper West
   Side) **200**
ey West Diner **204**
ayrose **95**

astern European
atner's **30**
ammy's Famous Roumanian
   Jewish Steakhouse **30**
iplet's Roumanian Restaurant **39**
anah Schimmel **31**

ungarian
occa Hungarian **181**
e Red Tulip **173**

olish
eresa's **79**

ussian
afe Andrusha **183**
ev **83**
Ermitage **145**
ational Restaurant **215**
dessa **216**
imorski **216**
asputin **215**
ussian Samovar **125**
e Pie **181**
e Russian Tea Room **127**

kranian
krainian **85**
eselka **85**

Eclectic
Aesop's Tables **221**
Annie's **174**
Aunt Sonia's **213**
Au Petit Beurre **204**
Blue Ribbon **43**
Boom **46**
Casa La Femme **48**
Coffee Shop **92**
Etats-Unis **179**
First **79**
Flowers **92**
Food Bar **107**
James Beard House **71**
Le Max **119**
Nadine's **69**
Noho Star **78**
One City Cafe **106**
Prince Street Bar & Restaurant **48**
Revolution **116**
Spartina **35**
Stacy's **212**
The Velvet Room **174**
Twins **183**
Two Eleven **37**
Woody's **66**
Yaffa Cafe **84**
Yaffa Tea Room **35**

English
Tea and Sympathy **70**

French
Alison on Dominick Street **42**
Au Bon Coin **57**
Bistro du Nord **185**
Bouley **34**
Brasserie **142**
Cafe Centro **134**
Cafe de Bruxelles **70**
Café des Artistes **189**
Café Des Sports **123**
Cafe du Pont **149**
Cafe Loup **70**
Cafe Luxembourg **191**
Cafe Metairie **178**
Café Nicholson **150**
Cafe St. John **205**
Cafe Un Deux Trois **120**
Can **50**
Capsouto Frères **39**
Casani's **78**
Chantal Cafe **126**
Chanterelle **35**
Chelsea Bistro and Bar **110**
Chez Bernard **40**
Chez Brigitte **68**
Chez Jacqueline **57**
Chez Josephine **115**

Chez Ma Tante Cafe **65**
Chez Michallet **63**
Chez Napoléon **123**
Cité **124**
Country Cafe **42**
C.T. **98**
Demarchelier **182**
Dix et Sept **66**
Felix **39**
Ferrier **164**
Fletcher Morgan Provisions **163**
Franklin Station **37**
Frontiere **52**
Gascogne **107**
Indochine **81**
Jean Claude **50**
Jean Lafitte **153**
JoJo **163**
Jour et Nuit **39**
Jubilee **140**
Jules **84**
La Bohème **58**
La Boîte en Bois **190**
La Bonne Soupe **144**
L'Acajou **96**
La Caravelle **145**
La Colombe d'Or **98**
La Côte Basque **144**
La Grenouille **142**
La Jumelle **40**
La Lunchonette **107**
La Mangeoire **140**
La Metairie **66**
La Mirabelle **202**
L'Ardoise **162**
La Réserve **136**
La Ripaille **69**
La Tour D'Or **12**
L'Auberge du Midi **68**
Le Bernardin **123**
Le Bilbouquet **160**
Le Boeuf à la Mode **180**
Le Chantilly **151**
Le Cirque **164**
L'Ecole **40**
Le Comptoir **164**
Le Madeleine **116**
Le Pactole **14**
Le Perigord **139**
Le Pescadou **52**
Le Petit Hulot **166**
Le Pistou **158**
Le Poème Restaurant Tea Room
   and Bakery **30**
Le Refuge **177**
Le Regence **163**
Le Relais **160**
L'Ermitage **145**
Les Célébrités **128**
Les Deux Gamins **63**

Le Select **201**
Les Halles **101**
Les Pyrénées **123**
Les Routiers **203**
Les Sans Culottes **150**
Les Sans Culottes West **118**
Le Taxi **159**
Le Veau d'Or **159**
Lucky Strike **40**
L'Udo **81**
Lutèce **138**
Manhattan Bistro **46**
Mark's **176**
Metisse **204**
Mme. Romaine de Lyon **159**
Montrachet **37**
Park Bistro **101**
Peacock Alley **138**
Pierre au Tunnel **120**
Pigalle **101**
Provence **52**
Quatorze Bis **175**
Raoul's **50**
René Pujol **123**
Restaurant Daniel **171**
Sel et Poivre **163**
Sonia Rose **100**
Table d'Hôte **184**
The Black Sheep **67**
The Odeon **35**
The Polo **166**
Tout Va Bien **123**
Trois Jean **176**
Tse Yang **137**
Vong **141**
Voulez Vous **173**
Yura and Company **183**
Zut! **34**

Fusion
Aja **97**
Blu **110**
Le Bistrot de Maxim's **160**
Lespinasse **147**
Marlowe **118**
Match **47**
New World Grill **122**
9 Jones Street **61**
Silk **100**
Toast **81**

German
Kleine Konditorei **182**
Roettele A.G. **83**
Rolf's Restaurant **98**

Greek
Acropolis **122**
Elias Corner **217**
Eros **150**
Estia **181**
Gus' Place **63**
Karyatis **217**
Periyali **96**
Roumeli Taverna **216**
Symposium **205**
Uncle Nick's **123**
Vergina **217**

Health Food
Dojo **83**
Dojo West **75**
Mana **203**

Organic
Angelica Kitchen **89**
Blanche's Organic Cafe **166**
Chutney Mary **95**
Zucchini **169**

Vegetarian
Angelica Kitchen **89**
B & H Dairy and Vegetarian
  Cuisine Restaurant **83**
Blanche's Organic Cafe **166**
Caravan of Dreams **79**
House of Vegetarian **24**
Mavalli Palace **101**
Souen Downtown **52**
Vegetarian Paradise 2 **57**
Zen Palate (Theater District) **117**
Zen Palate (Union Square) **91**

Indian
Baluchi's **43**
Bombay Palace **143**
Chutney Mary **95**
Darbar Indian Restaurant **145**
Dawat **151**
Delhi Palace **217**
Haveli **80**
Indian Cafe **205**
India Pavilion **128**
Jackson Diner **217**
Mavalli Palace **101**
Mitali **80**
Mughlai **196**
Pandit **202**
Passage to India **80**
Salaam Bombay **32**
Shaan **135**

International
Abby Restaurant and Bar **102**
Bridge Cafe **12**
B. Smith's **122**
Cafe Botanica **128**
Caviarteria **156**
Century Cafe **120**
Colors **133**

Flamingo East **89**
Global 33 **80**
La Folie **178**
Little Cafe **66**
Manhattan Brewing Co. **41**
Man Ray **108**
Merenda **179**
Rasputin **215**
Tatou **138**
Terramare **164**
The Hors d'Oeuvrerie at
  Windows on the World **13**
The Restaurant at Windows on
  the World **13**
The Vodka Bar and Cafe **38**
World Cafe **190**

Irish
Parnell's **140**

Italian
Alla Sera **175**
Allegria **144**
Amici Miei **49**
Anche Vivolo **151**
Angelo's of Mulberry Street **27**
Areo **214**
Aria **140**
Arqua **37**
Artepasta **68**
Asti **74**
Avanti **122**
Azzurro **181**
Baci **198**
Baraonda **173**
Barbetta **118**
Barocco **37**
Barolo **46**
Bar Pitti **58**
Becco **118**
Benito I and Benito II **27**
Bice **147**
Biricchino **112**
Boathouse Cafe **171**
Bosco **172**
Brio **157**
Briscola **81**
Brunetta's **89**
Bruno **150**
Cafe Divino **179**
Cafe du Pont **149**
Caffe Bianco **174**
Caffe Bondì **96**
Caffé Cefalú **66**
Caffe Grazie **182**
Caffe Popolo **197**
Campagna **95**
Campagnola **170**
Carmine's (Theater District) **119**
Carmine's (Upper West Side) **20**

Casa di Pré 68
Casa Rosa 211
Castellano 126
Cellini 148
Cent' Anni 58
Cesarina 143
Chantal Cafe 126
Chelsea Cafe 110
Chelsea Trattoria 106
Ciao Europa 144
Ci Vediamo (East Village) 79
Ci Vediamo (Upper East Side) 178
Coco Pazzo 171
Cola's 107
Col Legno 85
Contrapunto 156
Corrado 126
Cucina 213
Cucina Della Fontana 66
Cucina di Pesce 80
Cucina Stagionale 62
Cucina Vivolo 172
Da Nico 27
Da Silvano 58
Da Umberto 105
Dean & DeLuca Cafe (Midtown) 136
Dean & DeLuca Cafe (SoHo) 48
Diva 40
Divino Ristorante 179
Dolce 137
Dolci On Park Caffè 103
Dominick's 219
Due 176
Ecco 15
Ecco-Là 184
Elaine's 182
Elio's 181
Ennio & Michael 56
Erminia 181
Ernie's 196
Fantino 129
Favia 157
Felidia 150
Fiorello's 188
Follonico 97
44 Southwest 116
Fresco 142
Frontiere 52
Gabriel's 187
Gianni's 12
Gigino 32
Gino's 158
Giovanni 144
Girasole 177
Grand Ticino 56
Grotta Azzurra 28
Guido's 114
Harry Cipriani 156
Hero Boy 114

Il Cantinori 75
Il Cortile 25
Il Monello 173
Il Mulino 56
Il Nido 140
Il Ponte Vecchio 56
Il Toscanaccio 156
Il Vagabondo 162
Il Valletto 158
Il Vigneto 150
In Padella 85
Isabella 197
Isola 200
I Tre Merli 49
I Trulli 99
John's of Twelfth Street 89
John's Pizzeria 62
Julian's Mediterranean Cuisine 125
La Barca 10
La Collina 184
La Focaccia 68
La Mela 28
La Piazzetta di Quisisana 172
Lattanzi 118
Le Madri 108
Le Streghe 40
Letizia 169
Lola 96
L'Udo 81
Luna 25
Lusardi's 174
Mad. 61 159
Manducatis 216
Mangia 153
Mangia e Bevi 125
Mappamondo Restaurant 69
Marchi's 102
Mario's 219
Maruzzella 175
Mediterraneo 165
Mezzaluna 172
Mezzogiorno 43
Mimi's Macaroni 204
Minetta Tavern 57
Nello 160
Nicola Paone 102
Nino's 169
Nonna 151
Novità 98
Orologio 88
Orso 118
Osteria al Doge 119
Palio 124
Panevino 187
Paola's 181
Pappardella 197
Parioli Romanissimo 177
Parma 176
Patzo 202

Per Bacco 99
Petaluma 169
Pete's Tavern 94
Piccolo Angolo 69
Po 60
Primavera 180
Puglia Restaurant 25
Quattro Gatti 178
Rafaella Restaurant 66
Raffaele 149
Rao's 206
Remi 126
Ristorante Taormina 27
Ronasi 162
Rosemarie's 34
Rossini's 103
Sal Anthony's 93
Sal Anthony's S.P.Q.R. 25
San Domenico 129
San Pietro 148
Sant Ambroeus 177
Scaletta 197
Sette Mezzo 165
Sette MoMA 143
Sfuzzi (Lower Manhattan) 15
Sfuzzi (West Side) 189
Sgarlato's Cafe 11
Sirabella 180
Sistina 179
Soleil 164
Stella del Mare 132
Tammany Hall 100
Tanti Baci Caffè 66
Tavola 175
Tempo 101
The Bistro 146
Three of Cups 79
Tirami Sù 178
Tony & Roberto's 219
Toscana 163
Trastevere 180
Trattoria Dell'Arte 127
Trattoria Pesce Pasta 60
Trattoria Spaghetto 58
Triangolo 180
Tutta Pasta Ristorante 58
Two Boots 78
Urban Grill 128
Vico 185
Vivolo 171
Vucciria 44
Yellowfingers 156
Zigolini's Cafe 10
Zinno 71
Zitella 84
Zucchero 173

Jewish

Fine & Schapiro 193
Ratner's 30

Sammy's Famous Roumanian
Jewish Steakhouse **30**
2nd Avenue Deli **88**
Triplet's Roumanian Restaurant **39**
Yonah Schimmel **31**

Lebanese

Benny's (Gramercy Park) **98**
Benny's (Upper West Side) **196**
Eden Rock **202**

Mediterranean

Cafe Crocodile **170**
Cascabel **28**
Greenwich Cafe **67**
Gus' Place **63**
Martini's **125**
Picholine **188**

Mexican

Bright Food Shop **109**
El Parador **102**
El Teddy's **37**
Fresco Tortilla **Grill 98**
Harry's Burrito Junction **191**
Mi Cocina **69**
Mike's American Bar and Grill **117**
Passport **84**
Pedro Paramo **89**
Plaza Garibaldi **218**
Rosa Mexicano **150**
Samalita's Tortilla Factory **178**
Taquería de México **68**
The Hat/El Sombrero **31**
Zarela **139**
Zuni **116**

Middle Eastern

Cafe Mogador **84**
Moustache **62**
Sahara East **89**
Salam **71**
Tripoli **211**

Miscellaneous

Cellar Grill **113**
McDonald's **12**
Jackson Hole **161**
Gray's Papaya **193**
Pink Pony Cafe **31**
Soup Kitchen **126**

Persian

Persepolis **173**

Pizza

Arturo's Pizzeria **50**
Famous Ray's Pizza **71**

Freddie and Pepper's Gourmet
Pizza **196**
John's East **162**
John's Pizzeria **62**
John's West **189**
Lombardi's **29**
Patsy's Pizza **210**
Patsy's Pizzeria **206**
Pizzeria Uno **198**
Totonno's **215**
V&T Pizzeria **205**
Vinnie's Pizza **195**

Portuguese

Luzia **199**

Scandinavian

Aquavit **146**
Christer's **126**
Nyborg-Nelson **141**
Snaps **133**

Seafood

Captain's Table **133**
Caviarteria **156**
City Crab **94**
Claire **108**
Dama **59**
Docks Oyster Bar and Seafood
Grill (Midtown) **132**
Docks Oyster Bar and Seafood
Grill (Upper West Side) **203**
Eastern Seafood Company **198**
Elias Corner **217**
Fish **205**
Fishin Eddie **192**
Fulton Street Cafe **12**
Gage & Tollner **211**
Harbour Lights **11**
Hurricane Island **173**
Jade Palace **218**
Jane Street Seafood Cafe **69**
Johnney's Fish Grill **15**
King Crab **125**
La Barca **10**
Le Bernardin **123**
Liberty Cafe **11**
Lobster Box **221**
London Lennie's **218**
Marylou's **73**
Oceana **148**
Oriental Garden Seafood **21**
Oyster Bar and Restaurant **134**
Pisces **79**
Sequoia **11**
Sgarlato's Cafe **11**
Sidewalkers **192**
Sloppy Louie's **10**
Stella del Mare **132**

The Captain's Ketch **12**
The Manhattan Ocean Club **153**
The SeaGrill **136**
Umberto's Clam House **25**
Vincent's Clam Bar **25**
Water's Edge **216**
Wilkinson's 1573 Seafood Cafe
180

South American

Boca Chica **78**

Brazilian

Cabana Carioca **120**
Circus **161**
C.T. **98**
Rice and Beans **123**
Via Brasil **135**

Colombian

La Pequeña Colombia **218**

Peruvian

El Pollo **183**
Peruvian Restaurant **122**

Venezuelan

Mambo Grill **177**

Southern

Acme Bar & Grill **81**
Cafe Beulah **94**
Copeland's **207**
Cottonwood Cafe **67**
Cowgirl Hall of Fame **64**
Day-O **70**
Live Bait **97**
Mekka **78**
Pink Teacup **63**
Sylvia's **207**
The Cotton Club **206**
Toukie's **56**
Wilson's Bakery & Restaurant
207

Soul Food

Jezebel **117**
Kwanzaa **28**
Shark Bar **196**

Southwestern

Arizona Cafe **157**
Arizona 206 **157**
Border Cafe **175**
Mesa Grill **92**
Miracle Grill **83**
Mustang Grill **181**
Santa Fe **190**

Spanish

Bolo **97**
Cafe Español **59**

fe Riazor **106**
Charro Español (Greenwich Village) **72**
Charro Español (Murray Hill) **103**
Cid **106**
Faro **69**
Rincon de España **56**
41
tria **94**
sca Porto **42**
villa **66**
lera **141**

teak House

arlton's **149**
rist Cella **133**
ankie and Johnnie's **120**
llagher's Steak House **124**
orton's of Chicago **135**
lm **133**
n & Pencil **133**
ter Luger **212**
arks **133**
est 63rd Street Steakhouse **187**

wiss

Fondue **144**
ettele A.G. **83**

akeout

nny's (Gramercy Park) **98**
nny's (Upper West Side) **196**
fe Europa **127**
an & DeLuca Cafe (Midtown) **136**
an & DeLuca Cafe (SoHo) **48**
angia **153**
bar's Cafe **199**

ex-Mex

nny's Burritos **70**
chilada Johnny's **181**
yote Kate's **122**
nta Fe Grill **213**
e Armadillo **203**
e Big Enchilada (Greenwich Village) **74**
e Big Enchilada (Murray Hill) **100**
e Manhattan Chili Company **119**
rtilla Flats **69**

urkish

anbul Kebap **179**
rkish Cuisine **116**

Features

A C.T. Secret Recipe **99**
Be Our Guest **51**
By Bread Alone **158**
"Cawffee" Breaks **65**
Child's Play **121**
Cooking by the Book **206**
Designer Cakes **180**
Dim Sum and Then Some **22**
Fabulous Food Festivals **6**
For Lovers Only **49**
Kitchen Casting **192**
Meals on Reels: Take One **82**
New York Cooking Schools **220**
Pick of the Pasta **26**
Pizza—What's Old is What's New **38**
Rooms with a View **13**
Sports Bars **188**
Tea Time **161**
The Brunch Bunch **44**
The Goods on Greenmarkets **19**
The Raw Deal **86**
24-Hour New York **111**
Where's the Beef? **115**

Bests

Bryan-Brown, Adrian (Broadway Press Agent, Boneau/Bryan-Brown) **52**
Buck, Robert T. (Director, The Brooklyn Museum) **221**
Carter, Sylvia (Restaurant Critic, New York Newsday) **15**
Ford, Eileen O. (Ford Models, Inc.) **111**
Gillen, William (Publisher, The NY Food Letter) **53**
Goldberg, Gary A. (Executive Director, Culinary Center of New York, New School for Social Research) **167**
Goldberg, Howard (President, Adventure on a Shoestring) **89**
Idone, Christopher (Food Consultant and Cookbook Author) **53**
Janklow, Morton L. (Literary Agent, Janklow & Nesbit Associates) **193**
Kamil, Seth (Director, Big Onion Walking Tours) **31**
Kump, Peter (President, The James Beard Foundation) **75**
Lang, Jennifer and George (Restaurateurs, Café des Artistes, New York; Gundel and Bagolyvár restaurants, Budapest) **153**

Lightner, Serena (Head Concierge, Paramount Hotel) **207**
Lo, Eileen Yin-Fei (Cookbook Author; Writer; Teacher, China Institute in America) **7**
MacKenzie, Patricia (Publisher, The NY Food Letter) **53**
Mautner, Julie (Executive Editor, Food Arts Magazine) **167**
Musto, Michael (Columnist, Village Voice) **167**
Olmstead, Pat (Owner, Urban Explorations) **7**
Simon, Lisa (Supervising Producer/Director, "Sesame Street") **103**
Singer, Lou (Food Tour Guide) **111**
Stevenson, Isabelle (President, American Theatre Wing) **129**
Talese, Gay (Author) **166**
Tison, Rona (Executive Vice President, Felissimo) **167**
Velgos, Monica (Associate Editor, Food Arts Magazine) **167**
Wasserstein, Wendy (Playwright) **185**

Maps

Boroughs **208**
Buses **248**
Chelsea **104**
Chinatown **16**
East Side **154**
East Village **76**
Gramercy Park **90**
Greenwich Village **54**
Harlem **194**
Heights **194**
Little Italy **16**
Lower East Side **16**
Lower Manhattan **8**
Map Key **5**
Midtown **130**
Murray Hill **90**
New York area map **2**
New York buses **248**
New York subways **246**
SoHo **33**
Subways **246**
Theater District **112**
TriBeCa **33**
Union Square **90**
Upper East Side **168**
Upper West Side **194**
Washington Heights **194**
West Side **186**

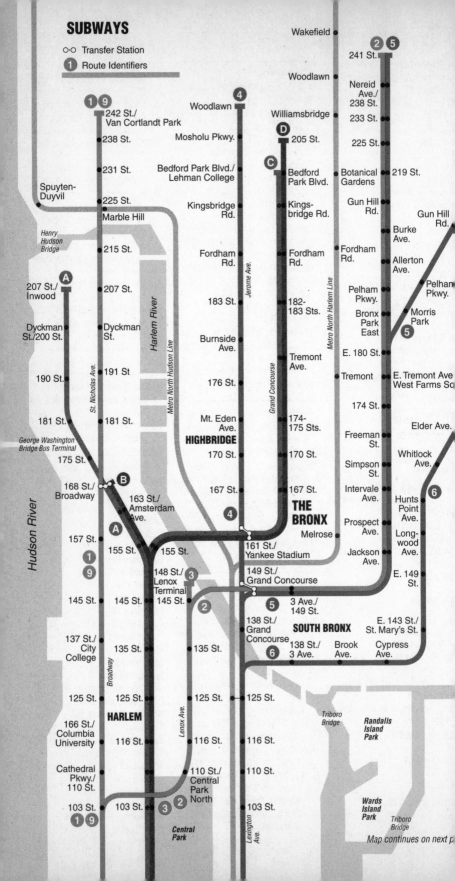

SUBWAYS

○—○ Transfer Station
① Route Identifiers

Wakefield

241 St. ② ⑤

Woodlawn

Nereid Ave./ 238 St.

Williamsbridge

233 St.

D **205 St.**

225 St.

① ⑨ **242 St./ Van Cortlandt Park**

4 **Woodlawn**

Botanical Gardens

219 St.

238 St.

Mosholu Pkwy.

C **Bedford Park Blvd.**

Gun Hill Rd.

231 St.

Bedford Park Blvd./ Lehman College

Bedford Park Blvd.

Burke Ave.

Gun Hill Rd.

Spuyten-Duyvil

225 St.

Kingsbridge Rd.

Kings-bridge Rd.

Allerton Ave.

Marble Hill

Pelham Pkwy.

Henry Hudson Bridge

215 St.

Fordham Rd.

Fordham Rd.

Fordham Rd.

Bronx Park East

Morris Park

A

207 St.

183 St.

182-183 Sts.

Pelham Pkwy.

⑤

207 St./ Inwood

Dyckman St.

Burnside Ave.

Tremont Ave.

E. 180 St.

Dyckman St./200 St.

191 St

176 St.

Tremont

E. Tremont Ave/ West Farms Sq

190 St.

174 St.

Elder Ave.

181 St.

181 St.

Mt. Eden Ave.

174-175 Sts.

Freeman St.

Whitlock Ave.

George Washington Bridge Bus Terminal

175 St.

HIGHBRIDGE

170 St.

170 St.

Simpson St.

B

168 St./ Broadway

167 St.

167 St.

Intervale Ave.

Hunts Point Ave.

⑥

163 St./ Amsterdam Ave.

THE BRONX

Prospect Ave.

Long-wood Ave.

A

4

Melrose

157 St.

155 St.

155 St.

161 St./ Yankee Stadium

Jackson Ave.

E. 149 St.

①

⑨

148 St./ Lenox Terminal

149 St./ Grand Concourse

145 St.

145 St.

③

145 St.

⑤ **3 Ave./ 149 St.**

②

138 St./ Grand Concourse

SOUTH BRONX

E. 143 St./ St. Mary's St.

137 St./ City College

135 St.

135 St.

⑥ **138 St./ 3 Ave.**

Brook Ave.

Cypress Ave.

125 St.

125 St.

125 St.

125 St.

Triboro Bridge

Randalls Island Park

166 St./ Columbia University

HARLEM

116 St.

116 St.

116 St.

Cathedral Pkwy./ 110 St.

110 St./ Central Park North

110 St.

103 St.

103 St.

③ ②

103 St.

Wards Island Park

Triboro Bridge

① ⑨

Central Park

Map continues on next p

Map continued from previous page

Wards Island Park

Triboro Bridge

N Ditmars Blvd./ Astoria

96 St. **2** **A** **B**
3 **C** **D**

96 St.

4 **6**
5

30 Ave./ Grand Ave.

Astoria Blvd./ Hoyt Ave.

86 St. **A** **B**
C **D**

Central Park

86 St.

LONG ISLAND CITY

Steinway St.

79 St.

81 St./ Amer. Museum of Nat.Hist.

Broadway

36 Ave./ Washington Ave.

36 St.

72 St. 72 St.

77 St.

Roosevelt Island

39 Ave./ Beebe Ave.

66 St./ Lincoln Center

68 St./ Hunter College

21 St./ Queensbridge

Queens Plaza

59 St./ Columbus Circle

B **Q**
Lexington Ave.

7 Ave. **B**

Metro North

5 Ave.

2 Ave.

Aerial Tram

B **Q**

33 St./ Rawson St.

57 St.

59 St.

N **R** Queensboro Plaza

47-50 Sts./ Rockefeller Center

5 Ave.

51 St.

Lexington Ave./ 3 Ave.

F **E** **QUEENS**

22 St./ Ely Ave.

50 St.

49 St.

S

42 St. Grand Central

21 St./ Van Alst

45 Rd./Court House Square

42 St.

5 Ave.

Hunters Point Ave.

42 St./ Times Square

42 St.

7

Vernon Blvd./ Jackson Ave.

G

34 St.

Long Island RR

Long Island RR

34 St./ Penn Station

33 St.

Long Island City Station

23 St.

28 St.

23 St.

18 St.

Greenpoint Ave.

GREENPOINT

14 St./ 8 Ave.

L

14 St./ Union Square

Nassau Ave.

L Lorimer St.

Christopher St.

6 Ave.

3 Ave. 1 Ave.

Bedford Ave.

Metropolitan Ave./Grand St.

Christopher St./ Sheridan Square

14 St.
9 St.

8 St./ NYU

Astor Pl.

MANHATTAN

West 4 St./ Washington Square

Bleecker St. Broadway/ Lafayette St.

2 Ave.

F

BROOKLYN

Houston St.

A
C
E

Prince St.
Spring St.

Delancey St./ Essex St.

1

Bowery

2

3

J
M
Z

Grand St.

East Broadway

9

Canal St.

B **D** **Q**

Franklin St.

City Hall

Brooklyn Bridge/ City Hall

Chambers St.

Park Pl.

Chambers St.

York St.

Brooklyn Bridge

World Trade Center

Broadway/ Nassau St.

A **C**

High St./ Brooklyn Bridge

Cortlandt St.

E

Fulton St.

Wall St.

Jay St./ Borough Hall

Lawrence St./ Metro Tech

Clark St.

Hoyt St./ Schermerhorn St.

Broad St. **2** **3**

Court St.

DeKalb Ave.

Rector St.

N

R

Nevins St.

Atlantic Ave.

South Ferry

Whitehall St./ South Ferry Bowling Green

4 **5**

Borough Hall

1 **9**

Bergen St.

G

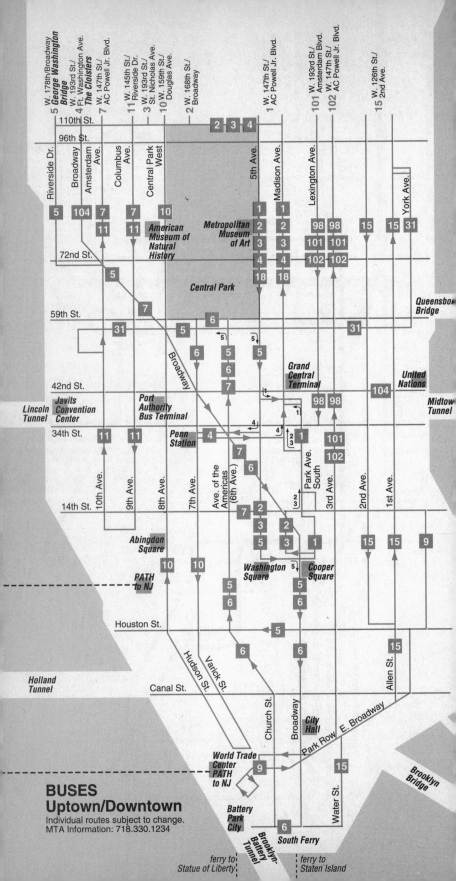

BUSES
Uptown/Downtown
Individual routes subject to change.
MTA Information: 718.330.1234

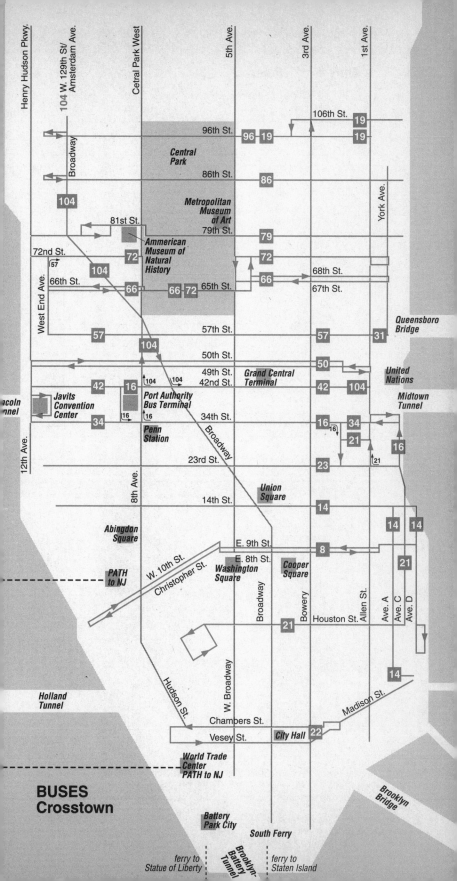

BUSES
Crosstown

Page	Entry #	Notes

age	Entry #	Notes

Page	Entry #	Notes

Credits

Writer and Researcher
Laurie Werner

Researchers
Leslie Brenner
Sarah Poole

ACCESS®PRESS

Editorial Director
Lois Spritzer

Managing Editor
Laura L. Brengelman

Senior Editors
Mary Callahan
Beth Schlau

Editor
Jill Kadetsky

Associate Editors
Patricia Canole
Gene Gold
Susan McClung

Map Coordinator
Marcy Pritchard

Editorial Assistant
Susan Cutter Snyder

Contributing Editor
Tina Posner

Senior Art Director
C. Linda Dingler

Designer
Elizabeth Paige Streit

Map Designer
Patricia Keelin

Associate Director
of Production
Dianne Pinkowitz

Manager,
Electronic Publishing
John R. Day

Special Thanks
Karine Bakoum
Beverly Barbour
Fern Berman
Gayle Conran
Geralyn Delaney
Jim Devine
Lisa Donoughe

Fiona Dorst
Allen Evans
Lynn Fredericks
Andrew Friedman
Daniel Fuchs
Elizabeth Hlinko
Phyllis Isaacson, James
    Beard Foundation
Bobbie Leigh
Alice Marshall
Sari Marvel
A. McConnell
Kate Merlino
Kenny Morris
Bob Nicolades
E.P
Tom Passavant
Pam Schecter
Philip Schlau
Kitty Shields
Sara Widness
Jeanne Willensky

ACCESS® Guides

Order by phone, toll-free: 1-800-331-3761

Travel: Promo # R00111

Name _____ Phone _____

Address _____

City _____ State _____ Zip _____

Please send me the following ACCESS® Guides:

☐ **BARCELONA** ACCESS® $17.00
0-06-277000-4

☐ **BOSTON** ACCESS® $18.50
0-06-277143-4

☐ **BUDGET EUROPE** ACCESS® $18.00
0-06-277120-5

☐ **CAPE COD** ACCESS® $18.00
0-06-277123-X

☐ **CARIBBEAN** ACCESS® $18.50
0-06-277128-0

☐ **CHICAGO** ACCESS® $18.50
0-06-277144-2

☐ **FLORENCE/VENICE/MILAN** ACCESS® $18.50
0-06-277081-0

☐ **HAWAII** ACCESS® $18.50
0-06-277142-6

☐ **LAS VEGAS** ACCESS® $18.50
0-06-277177-9

☐ **LONDON** ACCESS® $18.50
0-06-277129-9

☐ **LOS ANGELES** ACCESS® $18.00
0-06-277131-0

☐ **MEXICO** ACCESS® $18.00
0-06-277127-2

☐ **MIAMI & SOUTH FLORIDA** ACCESS® $18.50
0-06-277178-7

☐ **MONTREAL & QUEBEC** ACCESS® $18.00
0-06-277079-9

☐ **NEW ORLEANS** ACCESS® $18.50
0-06-277176-0

☐ **NEW YORK CITY** ACCESS® $18.00
0-06-277124-8

☐ **NEW YORK CITY RESTAURANT** ACCESS®
$12.00
0-06-277130-2

☐ **ORLANDO & CENTRAL FLORIDA** ACCESS®
$18.50
0-06-277175-2

☐ **PARIS** ACCESS® $18.00
0-06-277132-9

☐ **PHILADELPHIA** ACCESS® $18.00
0-06-277065-9

☐ **ROME** ACCESS® $18.50
0-06-277150-7

☐ **SAN FRANCISCO** ACCESS® $18.00
0-06-277121-3

☐ **SAN FRANCISCO RESTAURANT** ACCESS®
$12.00
0-06-277126-4

☐ **SANTA FE/TAOS/ALBUQUERQUE** ACCESS®
$18.00
0-06-277148-5

☐ **SEATTLE** ACCESS® $18.00
0-06-277149-3

☐ **SKI COUNTRY** ACCESS®
Eastern United States $18.00
0-06-277125-6

☐ **SKI COUNTRY** ACCESS®
Western United States $18.50
0-06-277174-4

☐ **WASHINGTON DC** ACCESS® $18.00
0-06-277077-2

☐ **WINE COUNTRY** ACCESS®
France $18.50
0-06-277151-5

☐ **WINE COUNTRY** ACCESS®
Northern California $18.00
0-06-277122-1

Prices subject to change without notice.

Total for **ACCESS®** Guides:	$
Please add applicable sales tax:	
Add $4.00 for first book S&H, $1.00 per additional book:	
Total payment:	$

☐ Check or Money Order enclosed. Offer valid in the United States only.
Please make payable to HarperCollins*Publishers*.

☐ Charge my credit card   ☐ American Express   ☐ Visa   ☐ MasterCard

Card no. _____ Exp. date _____

Signature _____

Send orders to: HarperCollins*Publishers*
P.O. Box 588
Dunmore, PA 18512-0588

No Reservations Required!

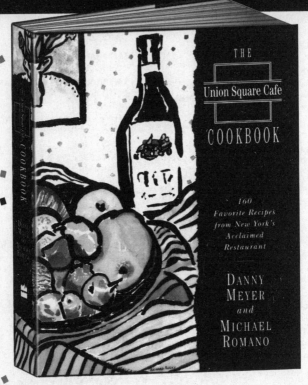

■ Your trip to New York City should surely include a visit to the restaurant *Food & Wine* rated one of America's 25 best. But if you can't get in (and especially if you do) you'll be happy to know you can still take home 160 unique recipes from Danny Meyer's and Michael Romano's famed Union Square Cafe.

"The next best thing to having dinner at the marvelous Union Square Cafe is to know how to prepare the imaginative but simple dishes they create. You will find this book a joy."
—Lee Bailey